PENGUIN BOOKS

A HISTORY OF CIVILIZATIONS

Fernand Braudel was born in 1902 in Luméville, north-western Lorraine, France. The son of a teacher, he took his degree in history at the Sorbonne in 1923. He spent much of the war as a prisoner in Germany, where he wrote most of his Mediterranean thesis. In 1949 it was published as *The Mediterranean and the Mediterranean World in the Age of Philip II*, and it remains one of this century's seminal works. In 1984 he was elected to the Académie Française. Fernand Braudel died in Paris in 1985.

FERNAND BRAUDEL

A HISTORY OF
CIVILIZATIONS

TRANSLATED BY RICHARD MAYNE

PENGUIN BOOKS

PENGUIN BOOKS

Published by the Penguin Group

Penguin Group (USA) Inc., 375 Hudson Street, New York, New York 10014, U.S.A.

Penguin Books Ltd, 80 Strand, London WC2R 0RL, England

Penguin Books Australia Ltd, 250 Camberwell Road, Camberwell, Victoria 3124, Australia

Penguin Books Canada Ltd, 10 Alcorn Avenue, Toronto, Ontario, Canada M4V 3B2

Penguin Books India (P) Ltd, 11 Community Centre, Panchsheel Park, New Delhi – 110 017, India

Penguin Group (NZ), cnr Airborne and Rosedale Roads, Albany, Auckland 1310, New Zealand

Penguin Books (South Africa) (Pty) Ltd, 24 Sturdee Avenue,
Rosebank, Johannesburg 2196, South Africa

Penguin Books Ltd, Registered Offices: 80 Strand, London WC2R 0RL, England

First published in the United States of America by Allen Lane The Penguin Press, an imprint of
Viking Penguin, a division of Penguin Books USA Inc., 1993
Published in Penguin Books 1995

20

Copyright © Les Editions Arthaud, Paris, 1987
Translation copyright © Richard Mayne, 1993
All rights reserved

This work was first published in France in the collected works of S. Baille, F. Braudel, R. Philippe,
Le Monde actuel, histoire et civilisations, librairie Eugène Belin 1963
First published in France as *Grammaire de Civilisations*, Les Editions Arthaud 1987

THE LIBRARY OF CONGRESS HAS CATALOGUED THE HARDCOVER AS FOLLOWS:
Braudel, Fernand.
[Grammaire des civilisations. English]
A history of civilizations/Fernand Braudel; translated by Richard Mayne.
p. cm.
Includes index.
ISBN 0–713–99022–8 (hc.)
ISBN 0 14 01.2489 6 (pbk.)
1. Civilization—History. I. Title.
CB78.B73 1993
909—dc20   93–30639

Printed in the United States of America
Set in Lasercomp Bembo

Contents

List of Maps

———

Translator's Introduction

BY RICHARD MAYNE

===

Anyone new to the work of the late Fernand Braudel may need not one Introduction but four: first, to the man himself; then to the *Annales* group of French historians he represented and helped to lead; thirdly, to the present book; and finally to its translation.

I

'For us he is a prince,' wrote Georges Duby of the Collège de France in 1967, when Fernand Braudel was sixty-five. Like many a fairy-tale hero, he had been born in a village – Luméville, in the Meuse province of north-western Lorraine.

Here were the same rows of large adjoining houses (containing barn and stable as well as living quarters) with their backs turned on the gardens behind, but their massive barn doors opening directly, at the front, on to the broad streets, *les rues à usoirs*, cluttered on both sides with carts, harrows, ploughs, dungheaps. The houses were roofed with the curved tiles known as 'Roman' tiles, although it is not thought today that this Lorraine tradition has anything to do with Rome . . .

I confess that during my travels, which tend to create illusions, I have dreamed of a Europe starting on the banks of the Somme, the Meuse or the Rhine and stretching away to Siberia and distant Asia. Such thoughts came to mind because, from the Rhine to Poland, I kept coming across the same rural architecture as in the Lorraine countryside of my boyhood: the same clustered villages, the same open farming, the same cornfields, the same triennial rotation, the same images . . .

No doubt if one were to be spirited back into a French farmhouse of, say, the 1920s, one would have plenty of cause for complaint. Working the land was hard, and there was no end to it, despite a deceptive freedom. One had a choice, yes, but only between equally backbreaking kinds of work. Nevertheless, people did not complain to each other, whether about the lack of running water (it had to be fetched from the well or the village pump), or about the poor light at night (no electricity), the drab clothes, only occasionally renewed, or the lack of conveniences and distractions to be found in the towns. Everyone had enough to eat, thanks to the kitchen garden, to the fields, which now included potatoes as a crop, thanks to preserved fruits and vegetables, butcher meat on Sundays and the family pig, which was usually killed and eaten at home. But can I count as a reliable source my own childhood memories?

Like Alsace, Lorraine has suffered over the centuries from invasion and annexation. Perhaps on account of its frontier position, it has been a home of French patriotism. Joan of Arc came from Domrémy-la-Pucelle, Maurice Barrès from Charmes-sur-Moselle; Verdun was its major battlefield; the double-barred Cross of Lorraine was the emblem of General Charles de Gaulle. 'I love France,' wrote Fernand Braudel, 'with the same demanding and complicated passion as did Jules Michelet; without distinguishing between its good points and its bad, between what I like and what I find harder to accept.' But France was not his only love. 'I have loved the Mediterranean with passion,' he wrote elsewhere, 'no doubt because I am a northerner like so many others in whose footsteps I have followed. I have joyfully dedicated long years of study to it – much more than all my youth.'

The son of a teacher, as a student he went to the Lycée Voltaire in Paris, near the Père Lachaise cemetery, and then to the Sorbonne, where he took his degree in history in 1923. His first teaching post took him south, across the Mediterranean to Constantine in Algeria. For a young man, the experience was rewarding.

I have been fortunate enough to find myself all my life on the side of tolerance. I am comfortable with it. But I cannot claim any personal credit on that account. I only really discovered the Jewish question for instance in Algeria, in 1923, when I was already over twenty years old. For the next ten years, still in Algeria, I was living in a Muslim country where I learnt to understand and respect Arabs and Berbers.

Was it there that he also began to consult local archives? He was later able to say, of those from the former Government General building in Algiers – 'a rather odd collection of Spanish documents' – 'I have read the entire collection.'

Braudel returned to Paris in 1932, to teach at the Lycée Condorcet in the rue du Havre near the boulevard Haussman, and then at the Lycée Henri IV in the Latin Quarter behind the Panthéon. But after three years he was off again – this time to the other side of the world.

In 1934, a new university was founded in Brazil, the state-supported Universidade de São Paulo, incorporating the historic Faculdade de Direito or Faculty of Law as well as other existing institutions. And in 1935 Fernand Braudel joined the new venture for a three-year stint in its Faculty of Arts.

This too was a heady experience. 'Living in Brazil,' wrote Braudel, 'I met black people in an atmosphere that reminded me of *Gone with the Wind*.'

Before 1939, when Latin America was still semi-colonial, only a few actors seemed to occupy the small stage of political life and culture, at the same time as they dominated the peaceful world of business. Charming, likeable, and cultivated, they owned hundreds, thousands of acres, as well as the richest of libraries. Some of them were veritable Renaissance princes, just the type to captivate a journalist, traveller or intellectual from Europe. On the eve of the Second World War, however, they already gave the impression of being a social anachronism. They bore immense responsibilities – one in charge of almost all British capital in Brazil, another the representative of something like the Dearborn Chemical Society, another running public finance, governing a State or trying to become President of the Republic, and yet another a General risen from the ranks. But they all seemed to rule, as it were, from the inner sanctum of their thoughts and their libraries, as if in an unreal universe. They believed in the virtues of culture, civilization, and reason.

They seemed to belong to the liberal and aristocratic mode of nineteenth-century Europe, in an atmosphere of benevolent despotism, or perhaps enlightened paternalism.

And at the same time, outside their charmed and firmly closed circle, there were new men, industrialists and immigrants who had made their fortune. They were beginning to achieve astonishing economic success; and only their children would acquire a certain polish.

As well as observing Brazilian society, Fernand Braudel had by this time been working for some years on the research for his massive thesis on the Mediterranean. Already in 1932 he had visited Palermo – only to find that 'the Archivio di Stato and the Archivio Comunale had closed their doors, and I was only able to spend a few days in the former and view the outside of the huge registers of the latter'. He made up for this disappointment in 'the rich Biblioteca Comunale'; but like all research workers he had to face other setbacks, including a ban on photographing documents in the invaluable Ragusa Archives, where he worked in 1935. This, he noted, 'made my research a hundred times more difficult'.

Far worse difficulties lay ahead. In 1938, Braudel returned to Paris and became a member of the prestigious postgraduate Ecole Pratique des Hautes Etudes. Working again in the Latin Quarter, he was once more well placed to use the French Archives Nationales, the Bibliothèque Nationale, and the document collections in the Ministry of Foreign Affairs. Research further afield posed problems. 'I could do no more than take cognizance, from a distance, of the German, Austrian, and Polish archives. My intention was to supplement the many published works available by taking samples from documents in the archives.' But, as he put it, 'circumstances' prevented this. War broke out in 1939, and in 1940 France fell. Fernand Braudel was serving as a lieutenant on the Rhine frontier and became a prisoner of war.

Is there any Frenchman after all who has not asked himself questions about his country, whether at the present time or in particular during the tragic hours through which our destiny has repeatedly taken us as it has run its course? Such catastrophes are like great rents in the canvas of history, or like those gaping holes in the clouds glimpsed from an aeroplane, plunging shafts of light at the bottom of which we see the earth below. Yawning disasters, gaping chasms, plunging tunnels of gloomy light – there is no shortage of these in our history. To go no further back than the nineteenth century, we have had the fateful dates 1815, 1871, 1914. And then there was 1940, when the knell tolled for us a second time at Sedan: when the drama of Dunkirk was played out in the indescribable disorder of defeat. It is true that in time even these monstrous wounds heal, fade, are forgotten – according to the iron law of all collective life: a nation is not an individual or a 'person'.

I have lived through some of these disasters. Like many other people, I was brought face to face with these questions in that summer of 1940 – which by an irony of fate was gloriously hot, radiant with sunshine, flowers and *joie de vivre*. We the defeated, trudging the unjust road towards a suddenly-imposed captivity, represented the lost France, dust blown by the wind from a heap of sand. The real France, the France held in reserve, *la France profonde*, remained behind us. It would survive, it did survive.

So did Fernand Braudel – and so did his fighting spirit. He spent the next five years as a prisoner at Lübeck in Germany, until the end of the war. But in captivity, astonishingly, he wrote most of his Mediterranean thesis – partly, he said, as a 'direct existential response to the tragic times I was passing through'.

All those occurrences which poured in upon us from the radio and the newspapers of our enemies, or even the news from London which our clandestine receivers gave us – I had to outdistance, reject, deny them. Down with occurrences, especially the vexing ones! I had to believe that history, destiny, was written at a much more profound level.

When the war was over and Fernand Braudel returned to France, he put the whole thesis into shape, and successfully defended it before the examiners in 1947. Two years later, it was published as *La Méditerranée et le monde méditerranéen à l'époque de Philippe II* – and it made his name. By the time of his death in

1985, he had been elected to the Académie Française; but he was also famous among historians and general readers far beyond the frontiers of France, and he held honorary degrees from universities all over the world.

Well into his eighties, he wrote and published steadily. In 1963 came *Grammaire des civilisations*, the original of the present book, part of *Le Monde actuel: Histoire et civilisations*, whose other two parts were by Suzanne Baille and Robert Philippe. In 1966 came a thoroughly revised and enlarged edition of *La Méditerranée* (translated by Siân Reynolds as *The Mediterranean and the Mediterranean World in the age of Philip II*, 1972 and 1973). In 1967, Braudel published *Civilisation matérielle et capitalisme* (translated by Miriam Kochan as *Capitalism and Material Life, 1400–1800*, 1973). He followed this in 1969 with a collection of articles, *Ecrits sur l'histoire* (translated by Sarah Matthews as *On History*, 1980). Next, in 1979, came the three-volume *Civilisation matérielle, économie et capitalisme, XVe–XVIIIe siècle* (translated by Siân Reynolds as *The Structures of Everyday Life*, 1981, *The Wheels of Commerce*, 1982, and *The Perspective of the World*, 1984). Fernand Braudel's last large-scale work was *L'Identité de la France*.

I have come rather late in the day [he wrote] to my home ground, though with a pleasure I will not deny: for the historian can really be on an equal footing only with the history of his own country; he understands almost instinctively its twists and turns, its complexities, its originalities and its weaknesses. Never can he enjoy the same advantages, however great his learning, when he pitches camp elsewhere. So I have saved my white bread until last; there is some left for my old age.

There was more than enough. Fernand Braudel the perfectionist was still working on the book when he died. It was seen through the press by his widow Mme Paule Braudel, and published in 1986 (English translation by Siân Reynolds as *The Identity of France*, two volumes, 1988 and 1990). The year 1987, finally, saw the second French edition of *Grammaire des civilisations*, the last of Fernand Braudel's books to be translated into English.

II

As an historian, then, Fernand Braudel was not without honour, even in his own country. As a prophet, pioneering a new kind of history, he found a less ready response. In the last public lecture he gave, at Chateauvallon on 20 October 1985, he said: 'People I like tell me not to be "unreasonable, as usual". Do you think I've heeded their advice?' His listeners appreciated the irony, for what made him seem unreasonable to some traditional historians was the breadth of his approach to the past.

Despite the fact that his thesis on the Mediterranean had been accepted by the examiners,

without drum and trumpet and with a thousand nice-sounding words in my ear, I . . . was excluded from the Sorbonne in 1947. When I defended my thesis that year, one of the judges suavely said to me: 'You are a geographer, let me be the historian.' I was named indeed to the Collège de France in 1949, but the Collège is and always has been marginal to the University. In the same year I was designated to chair the history section of the national programme of teacher certification (*président du jury d'agrégation d'histoire*) but only by the individual will of Gustave Monod, Director General of Secondary Education, who in an effort to reform this venerable system of competition was eager to turn the house upside-down. I was not remiss in my duties but, in 1954, I was ousted, and the Sorbonne took the operation back into its own hands. If, in those years, Lucien Febvre and I were included in the commissions of scientific research, to which we were elected by the *entire group* of French historians, we were a minority in them: heading the list came the right-thinking persons, and one year, indeed, I was blackballed by the electors.

Braudel could have said, with Racine's Phèdre, *'Mon mal vient de plus loin.'* The dispute with the Sorbonne dated back at least as far as 1929, when Lucien Febvre and Marc Bloch had founded in Strasbourg the *Annales d'histoire économique et sociale.* Although its first editorial committee included two Sorbonne professors, neither was an orthodox historian: one, Albert Demangeon, was Professor of Human Geography, and the other, Henri Hauser, was Professor of Economic History. Of the rest, one was an archivist at the French Foreign Ministry, one a professor of sociology at Strasbourg, one a professor of Roman history there, one a professor of political economy at the Faculty of Law in Paris, one a professor at the Paris School of Political Science, one a Deputy Governor of the Bank of France, and the last the Belgian expert on economic history, Henri Pirenne.

As its title implied, the *Annales* sought to broaden the scope of historiography, introducing economic and social concerns alongside politics and diplomacy. 'Nothing could be better,' wrote Bloch and Febvre in their first Introduction, 'than for each person, concentrating on a legitimate specialization, laboriously cultivating his own back yard, nevertheless to force himself to follow his neighbour's work. But the walls are so high that, very often, they hide the view . . . It is against these deep schisms that we intend to raise our standards.'

'It is certain,' wrote Fernand Braudel, looking back,

that they were conscious of labouring towards an absolutely new and even revolutionary history. Their means were relatively simple. History was for them one human science among others. Without even standing on tiptoe, the historian could glimpse the fields and gardens of the neighbouring disciplines. Was it so complicated, then, so extraordinary, to set out to see what was happening there, to plead in favour of a community of the human sciences, despite the walls that separated them from one another, and to regard them as necessary auxiliaries of history? To think that the historian might be able to render service for service? An exchange of services: such was and such is still, I believe, the last and profoundest motto of the *Annales*, its only rallying cry.

Today, when historians have revealed so many more facets of the past, and cross-fertilized historical disciplines once firmly divided into constitutional, political, diplomatic, military, economic, social, and cultural studies, such a slogan may seem superfluous.

But in 1929 the cry was new, and the programme it called for seemed aberrant or ludicrous to traditional historians, perhaps too ambitious even for the partisans of the new current of thought . . .

The task of the two Strasbourg professors was crystal clear: to go out among the other disciplines, return with the booty, and set forth again on the quest of discovery, demolishing obstructing walls at each occasion. To pounce on their opponents, moreover, seemed the best defence.

In Strasbourg, those opponents were nicknamed '*les Sorbonnistes*'.

That name, as Professor Gertrude Himmelfarb has pointed out, 'lost some of its sting when the *Annales* moved from Strasbourg to Paris'. But although Lucien Febvre joined the Collège de France and Marc Bloch was appointed to a chair at the Sorbonne, neither had escaped what Braudel called 'the Sorbonne's wary surliness'. Bloch had been defeated as a candidate for the Fifth Section of the Ecole Pratique des Hautes Etudes in an election that Braudel denounced as 'shameful', and he had been 'side-stepped' by the Collège de France. He won his Sorbonne professorship only because, as Braudel put it, 'there simply was no other candidate sufficiently qualified to seek to succeed Henri Hauser in the chair of economic history, the only chair of economic history in the French university system'.

In that same year, 1937, Braudel joined the editorial committee of the *Annales*. He described it, nostalgically, as

a small group that could be contained with ease – despite the advent of the 'new men', Henri Brunschwig, Ernest Labrousse, Jacques Soustelle, and myself – in Lucien Febvre's combined salon and office in the rue du Val-de-Grâce, known to us intimately as 'le Val'.

Marc Bloch did not survive what Braudel called 'the heinous gash of the Second World War': as a member of the French Resistance he was shot by the Nazis in 1944. But the *Annales* continued. It had already gone through two changes of name, being known for a time as the *Annales d'histoire sociale* and for a time at the *Mélanges d'histoire sociale*; and in 1946 it adopted a still more ambitious title

– *Annales: Economies, Sociétés, Civilisations.* By now, Braudel had become one of its leading lights, and from 1956 to 1968 he was virtually its editor.

It was certainly a new period [he wrote]. But the second *Annales* generation added nothing essential to the lot of ideas put into circulation by the first. None of us newcomers, Charles Morazé, Georges Friedmann, and I, contributed any really new idea or concept to the existing arsenal of theory . . . It is a fact that a whole new generation of historians chose their 'thesis subjects', that is, their line of future work and endeavour, within the framework of *Annales* thought. I therefore envisage that period as one of translation into practice, as a time of confrontation of the *Annales* model with the huge reality of history, through a blossoming of admirable works all related to one another, although dispersed across time and space.

Scholars associated with the *Annales* at the time included some cited in the present book – not only historians such as Henri-Irénée Marrou, Alphonse Dupront, Joseph Chappey, and Lucien Goldmann, but also the structuralist Roger Bastide and the anthropologist and sociologist Marcel Mauss. As Gertrude Himmelfarb said of the *Annalistes*, 'under the editorship of Fernand Braudel their journal became the most influential historical organ in France, possibly in the world. It has also proved to be remarkably innovative. Going well beyond the more traditional forms of economic and social history, it now derives both its subjects and its methods from anthropology, sociology, demography, psychology, even semiotics and linguistics.' 'It aims similarly,' as the American anatomist of the *Annales* Traian Stoianovich has said, 'at the "demasculinization of history" and at the development of a history of women, of youth, of childhood, of oral cultures, of voluntary associations, of non-Western civilizations, of nonconsensual cultures.'

In practice, Fernand Braudel and the *Annales* cast their net wider still. In their quest for 'total history' they included geography, climatology, physics, biology, religion, mythology, navigation, and much else, not forgetting literature and the cinema. In *La Méditerranée*, for example, Braudel referred not only to the Sardinian novelist Grazia Deledda's *La via del male* (1986) and *Il Dio dei viventi* (1922) and to books by Gabriel Audisio, Jean Giono, Carlo Levi, André Chamson, and even Lawrence Durrell, but also to Vittorio De Seta's 1961 film *Banditi a Orgosolo*.

The authority of the *Annales* scholars had been greatly strengthened after the Second World War by the addition to the Ecole Pratique des Hautes Etudes of a Sixth Section. This, in the words of Traian Stoianovich, 'was conceived as a graduate but non-degree-granting centre at which scholars associated with the *Annales* journal and other distinguished or promising scholars would train advanced students and carry on discourse with them in the methods and problems of social and economic history, of economics, and of the behavioural or communications sciences. Set up under the Section almost from the start were a new Centre de Recherches Historiques under Braudel and a Centre de Recherches Economiques under Charles Morazé.'

Allowed to be born [as Braudel added] only because the Ecole des Hautes Etudes, like the Collège de France, did not have the right to grant university degrees, the Sixth Section developed, slowly and with difficulty, as a marginal institution equipped only for the purpose of research. That it knew how to turn this restriction into its strengh, into the basis of its autonomy, and into the very motor of its expansion, is another matter. In any case, the more successful it became the more opposition and hostility it met from the traditional University – along with, it is true, examples of exceptional friendship.

In 1963, a new Maison des Sciences de l'Homme was established, initially scattered, but gathered together in 1970 in a single steel-and-glass building with Braudel as President Administrator.

This institution at its inception [wrote Braudel] was the last refuge to which we resorted only after the University had blocked our plan for an experimental faculty of economic and social sciences. Yes, we were heretics until almost 1968, ever more numerous and stronger perhaps but compelled, willy-nilly, to fight ceaselessly for each concession.

The troubles of May and June 1968 changed everything ... By an irony of fate, this was for me the Establishment period. After collapsing at one blow in 1968, the citadel of the Sorbonne was divided into a dozen different institutions of higher learning. From the reforms that followed, a new life began to take hold, and more than one innovation was meritorious. As a conclusion to these reforms, the Sixth Section in 1975 lost its numerical rank and honoured name, to become the Ecole des Hautes Etudes en Sciences Sociales, with degree-granting rights.

So the *Annales* group, as Braudel suggested, had in a sense become the Establishment. As such, they in turn faced criticism, not only from those they had once challenged. 'The lay reader,' wrote Professor Arthur Marwick, 'will find *Annales* a rather forbidding journal: like any other learned journal, it does not try to fulfil the necessary historical role of communication with the wider audience, society as a whole ... In *Annales* discourse statistical tables abound, their precise significance not always being made very clear (save that, allegedly, they demonstrate a solid structural base); flow charts and diagrams, too, sometimes seem designed more to impress than to illuminate; visual sources are sometimes reproduced as if they spoke for themselves (which, of course, they never do).'

More serious were three further points that Marwick stressed: 'a hostility to, and neglect of, political history; a concentration on medieval and early modern history, with a general avoidance of industrial and contemporary societies; and an attempt, not always completely comprehensible to the uninitiated, to annex stucturalism to history.'

Few of Marwick's mild reproaches applied to Fernand Braudel. But in the last paragraph of the second edition of *La Méditerranée*, written on 26 June 1965, he confessed:

I am by temperament a 'structuralist', little tempted by the event, or even by the short-term conjuncture which is after all merely a grouping of events in the same area.

Earlier, he had called events 'crests of foam that the tides of history carry on their strong backs'. And the last words of his unfinished *L'Identité de la France* were:

Men do not make history, rather it is history above all that makes men and thereby absolves them from blame.

It was Braudel's apparent detachment from more immediate human concerns that led Professor Geoffrey Elton to write in 1967 that *La Méditerranée* 'offers some splendid understanding of the circumstances which contributed to the shaping of policy and action; the only things missing are policy and action. There is a clear and admirable sense of life, but how those lives passed through history is much less clear.'

It was a criticism with which Braudel was already familiar. He had already distanced himself from the 'over-simple theories' and 'sweeping explanations' of Arnold Toynbee and Oswald Spengler. He was equally dismissive of any historian who too slavishly adopted Marxist social models, which had been 'congealed in their simplicity and given the value of law'. But he was aware that his own view of '*la longue durée*', the long term, might be called 'Olympian'.

The question is frequently put to me, both by historians and philosophers, if we view history from such a distance, what becomes of man, his role in history, his freedom of action?

Gertrude Himmelfarb put the question very pertinently, pointing out that in 1940, when Braudel was a prisoner of war, exclaiming, 'Down with occurrences', and working on his long-term history, 'Europe was being convulsed by the passions of a single man.'

Yet, in his own way, Braudel had already acknowledged what might be called 'the Hitlerian paradox'. In *La Méditerranée* he had written:

That is not to say that this brilliant surface is of no value to the historian, nor that historical reconstruction cannot perfectly well take this micro-history as its starting-point ... To put it another way, history is the keyboard on which these individual notes are sounded ... I would conclude with the paradox that the true man of action is he who can measure most nearly the constraints upon him, who chooses to remain within them and even to take advantage of the weight of the inevitable, exerting his own pressure in the same direction. All efforts against the prevailing tide of history – which is not always obvious – are doomed to failure.

Indeed, as Traian Stoianovich put it: 'Braudel may be a structuralist by temperament, as he claims, but his structuralism is that of a poet, painter, theatrical director, or music conductor . . . In the work of such an historian, even geographic entities such as the sea may be "raised to the rank of historical personages" (as Lucien Febvre remarked). For this historian, the world is theatre . . . In the final analysis, however, the director must return to the actors, without whom there would be no theatre.'

Braudel was familiar with the technical problems that this caused. In 1963 he had asked:

Is it possible somehow to convey simultaneously both that conspicuous history which holds our attention by its continual and dramatic changes – and that other, submerged history, almost silent and always discreet, virtually unsuspected either by its observers or its participants, which is little touched by the obstinate erosion of time?

He found an answer by measuring time on three scales or levels: the quasi-immobile time of structures and traditions (*la longue durée*); the intermediate scale of 'conjunctures', rarely longer than a few generations; and the rapid time-scale of events. Each was represented in one of the three parts of *La Mediterranée*, as he explained:

The first part is devoted to a history whose passage is almost imperceptible, that of man in his relationship to the environment, a history in which all change is slow, a history of constant repetition, ever-recurring cycles . . .

On a different level from the first there can be distinguished another history, this time with slow but perceptible rhythms. If the expression had not been diverted from its full meaning, one could call it *social history*, the history of groups and groupings . . .

Lastly, the third part gives a hearing to traditional history – history, one might say, on the scale not of man, but of individual men, what Paul Lacombe and François Simiand called '*l'histoire événementielle*', that is, the history of events . . . It is the most exciting of all, the richest in human interest, and also the most dangerous. We must learn to distrust this history with its still burning passions, as it was felt, described, and lived by contemporaries whose lives were as short and as short-sighted as ours.

III

As may be seen later in the present book, Fernand Braudel was by no means short-sighted, whether looking to the future or to the past. But he had long perceived the need to shift focus at will, from one scale or type of history to another. As long ago as September 1936, he had set out some of his essential ideas in a lecture to the São Paulo Institute of Education.

Its subject was 'The Teaching of History', and it began by asking how to turn the 'educational story' into a 'tale of adventure'. The secret, said Braudel, was simplicity – not

simplicity that distorts the truth, produces a void, and is another name for mediocrity, but simplicity that is clarity, the light of intelligence. Find the key to a civilization: Greece, a civilization of the Aegean, from Thrace to Crete – and not a Balkan peninsula. Egypt, a civilization that tamed the Nile.

His model, he said, was Henri Pirenne, 'the foremost French-language historian today'. To be understood, avoid abstract terms. To hold the attention, 'let history have its dramatic interest'. Teaching history meant above all knowing how to narrate it.

Moving from research to teaching history is like moving from one watercourse to another . . . Take care that your teaching is not guided by your preferences as a research worker. I insist on that. It would be a dereliction of duty to talk to students only about firms, cheques, and the price of wheat. Historiography has slowly gone through various phases. It has been the chronicle of princes, the history of battles, or the mirror of political events; today, thanks to the efforts of bold pioneers, it is diving into the economic and social realities of the past. These stages are like the treads of a stairway leading to the truth. Do not omit any of them in the presence of students.

These principles came to mind some twenty years later, when Fernand Braudel found himself in the thick of the French secondary-school reforms that indirectly gave rise to the present book. History teaching was one of their targets. Since 1945, it had been divided chronologically along the students' career in the lycée, beginning with Mesopotamia and Ancient Egypt and ending, in the top two classes, with so-called 'contemporary history': 1789–1851 in the last class but one (*première*), 1851–1939 in the final (*terminale*) class. From 19 July 1957, the syllabus was pushed back one year, so that 1789–1851 was taught in the last class but two (*seconde*) and 1851–1945 in *première*, while *terminale* was devoted to studying 'the main contemporary civilizations'. These were divided into six 'worlds': Western, Soviet, Muslim, Far Eastern, South-East Asian, and Black African.

This reform was largely the work of Gaston Berger, then Director of Higher Education, who also initiated what later became the Maison des Sciences de l'Homme. But the breadth of the new subject – to include gleanings from 'neighbouring social sciences: geography, demography, economics, sociology, anthropology, psychology' – clearly showed the influence of the *Annales* and of Fernand Braudel. Not unexpectedly, it aroused considerable resistance. Two years later, in 1959, the geographical specification was modified: 'the civilizations of the contemporary world' now included only five regions, since the Far East and South-East Asia were amalgamated into 'the Indian and Pacific Oceans', while a final section was added to cover 'the major problems of today'. More significantly, the period 1914–45 was brought back into the first term of the *terminale* class.

It was a setback, but not a defeat. The new syllabus was close enough to Braudel's ideas to spur him to write the present book –

partly, perhaps, to forestall any further backtracking. The *Annaliste* Maurice Aymard was right to call it 'a fighting book'. Originally published as the central and most controversial part of a collective work with Suzanne Baille and Robert Philippe, *Le Monde actuel: Histoire et civilisations*, it was aimed primarily to support the new history being taught in *terminale*. As Braudel wrote in 'By Way of Preface' below,

It seems to me essential that at the age of eighteen, on the brink of preparing for whatever career, our young people should be initiated into the problems of society today, the great cultural conflicts in the world, and the multiplicity of its civilisations.

Unfortunately, despite his victory at university level, Braudel eventually lost the battle of the secondary schools. Already in 1964, Maurice Aymard, newly appointed to a provincial lycée North of Paris, found to his surprise that the teachers' council had decided that Braudel's book was 'too hard for the students'. In 1965, moreover, the Ministry of Education further truncated the 'civilizations' syllabus. As Maurice Aymard put it, 'In the midst of decolonization, at the very moment when the newly independent States were gamely trying to write their own history, a decree dated 10 August 1965 purely and simply eliminated "the African world".'

In 1970, Braudel's book was discreetly withdrawn from sale; and soon afterwards the secondary school syllabus was altered again, freeing the top forms from an innovation that had disturbed too many old habits, and restoring old-fashioned narrative 'contemporary history', 1914–45. The syllabus now taught 'new history' to the junior classes and traditional history to the seniors. It was the reverse of what Braudel had proposed. As he told his audience at Chateauvallon in 1985,

I find it appalling, abominable, that students should be questioned in the baccalauréat about the period from 1945 to 1985 as is done today. I'm sure that if I were an examiner I should fail any historian at the bac-calauréat! And if I were examining myself, I'd fail myself too!

But the present book is more than just a weapon from a battle that Fernand Braudel lost. Written between the first and second editions of *La Méditerranée* and before the first volume of *Civilisation matérielle*, it forms a solid part of his *oeuvre*, his work as a whole. During the 1960s, it was translated into Spanish for university students and into Italian as a pocket book, regularly reprinted. In 1987 it was reissued in France, shorn of its pedagogic apparatus but with a Preface reproduced from an article by Fernand Braudel in the *Corriere della Sera* in 1983. That second French edition is the version translated here.

IV

Translating Fernand Braudel into English is a task that compels respect and requires ingenuity. Professor J. H. Plumb has accused Braudel's translators of destroying the original's distinctive sparkle; and Braudel himself admitted that

It is no small task to adapt my not uncomplicated style to the vigorous rhythms of the English language.

I agree. The quotations from Braudel in this Introduction I have left in their respective translators' versions, without attempting embellishments of my own. The book itself I have treated more freely, in two respects.

Madame Paule Braudel has been kind enough to say 'Your translation is free, like all good translations', and to call it 'rapid and lively, as befits a work of this sort'. I am very grateful for the compliment, as I am for Mme Braudel's meticulous assistance throughout the task. Any errors or infelicities that remain are my own, save for possible misprints; and I should be glad to correct them in any future edition.

There is a second sense in which this is a 'free' translation. Had Fernand Braudel lived to see this book republished, he would surely have wanted to rewrite it. In his Preface to the English edition of *La Méditerranée* he declared:

I would not have wanted to reissue the book without thoroughly revising it.

For ten years, he was asked to 'adapt' the present book for a wider public; and although he never refused to do so, he always postponed the task. But, as Mme Braudel has said, 'it is unusual to translate in 1993 a book that is a reflection on the world of 1962'. For this reason, mainly by changing tenses, I have very hesitantly adjusted the text − a form of gentle *remuage*, as in the maturing of champagne. I hope that this delicate operation has merely, as it were, helped shift the sediment towards the cork for easy extraction. I am encouraged to think that Fernand Braudel would not have objected too strongly: he himself added some pages to the book − mainly on Sino-Soviet relations − for the Italian translation.

What struck me, continually, while working on the text, was how little updating it really needed − and how prescient Fernand Braudel was. I happened to be completing the chapter on the Soviet Union and its centrifugal tendencies just when the plot against Mikhail Gorbachev was hatching. It was as if Braudel were looking on. Not to say 'I told you so', for that was never his manner; but reminding one reader, at least, in those dangerous moments, how *la longue durée*, in the hands of a master, can help explain the most dramatic convulsions in the past, the present, and the future.

By Way of Preface

One word from François Mitterrand, in a speech on 16 September 1982, was enough to revive the debate about history teaching. It was no doubt only waiting to flare up again.

It is an old debate, but one which is always popular and leaves nobody unmoved. It interests the public, more than ever devoted to history, and the politicians, obliged to keep up to date; it interests the press and, above all, the teachers of history. It is an old debate, and promises no surprises; yet its scope is continually broadening. It offers shelter to every conceivable cause. They all take cover at the sound of gunfire, like well-trained troops.

In principle, the debate concerns only the curricula of the primary schools (about which, strangely, very little is said) and those of the secondary schools (which are mentioned more often than they are studied). It concerns also the disaster – or so-called disaster – of these schools as measured by our children's allegedly scandalous results. But could these results have been perfect? Have they ever been? In 1930 or thereabouts, an historical review was pleased to print a large collection of schoolchildren's howlers. And yet, at that time, orthodox teaching relied on the sacrosanct Malet-Isaac textbook, which so many polemicists praise today.

Finally, critics attack the various ways in which history itself has developed. For some, traditional history, faithful to narrative and indeed a slave to it, overloads the memory, weighing it down needlessly with dates, with the names of heroes and with the lives and deeds of notabilities. For others, 'the new history', seeking to be 'scientific', dealing with the long term and neglecting events, is supposedly responsible for catastrophic didactic failures, involving at the very least unpardonable ignorance of chronology. This dispute between Ancients and Moderns has done a great deal of harm. In a discussion which is about teaching, not scientific theory, it conceals problems and failings instead of shedding light on them.

Is the problem really so complex? You have before you, in the secondary school, first children and then adults. At some point, necessarily, their teaching has to change, in history as in other subjects. The question is how the things to be taught should be spread over the successive – and very different – school years. At the beginning, the pupils are children: at the end, they are adults. What suits the former will not suit the latter. The curriculum must be divided; and this requires an over-all plan, a choice of priorities and needs, and a guiding intelligence.

For children, I have always recommended simple narrative, pictures, television series and films – in other words, traditional history improved, adapted to include the media with which children are familiar. I speak from experience. Like all the academics of my generation, I was for a long time a *lycée* teacher; and, as well as the top forms assigned to me, I always asked to take also the most junior class, with children aged ten to twelve. They make a delightful, spontaneously spellbound audience, to whom one could show history unfolding as if with a magic lantern. The main problem is to help them, in the process, to discover a sense of perspective, of the reality of past time, its direction and significance, and the successive landmarks which first gave it a recognizable shape. I am appalled if a pupil of average ability does not know where Louis XIV comes in relation to Napoleon, or Dante in relation to Machiavelli. A feeling for chronology, gradually acquired, should help to dispel confusion. But plain narrative should also open out quite naturally into spectacular scenes, landscapes and panoramas. We are in specific places – Venice, Bordeaux, London. And as pupils come to understand time, they need to learn vocabulary, so as to be precise about words, ideas and things. Plus some key concepts: a society, a State, an economy, a civilization. All of which should be done as simply as possible.

Require familiarity with essential dates; show when prominent, important, or even hateful people lived. Put them in their context.

And now we have crossed the dividing-line: we face young people, freer perhaps than we were at their age, yet less happy; rebellious, when in fact it is society, the world and life today that are changing around them – the real source of their movements, their constraints and their outbursts. They may be less intellectual, less bookish, than we were when we finished our apprenticeship, but they are just as intelligent, and certainly more inquisitive. What account of history are we to give them?

The absurd curricula enforced in France inflict on the next-to-top form 'The world from 1914 to 1939', and then on the top form 'The world since 1939'. Twice the vast world is to be studied; but a world of politics, wars, institutions and conflicts – a prodigious mass of dates and events. I defy any historian, even those with photographic memories, to guarantee to pass an examination on this mass of often trivial facts, one after another without rhyme or reason. I have before me the latest textbook on *The Present Day* – the best of the bunch, I am told. It seems to me useful and well produced, but disappointing. It contains not a word of any value on capitalism, on economic crises, on the world's population, on civilizations outside Europe, or on the underlying causes of conflicts rather than just the conflicts themselves.

Why this scandalous state of affairs? Because of an absurd decision taken by the French Ministry of Education. Personally, as I have always said, I should have introduced 'the new history' only in the *very top form*. The new history deliberately draws upon a number of the social sciences which study and explain the contemporary world and seek to make sense of its confusion. And it seems to me essential that at the age of eighteen, on the brink of preparing for whatever career, our young people should be initiated into the problems of society and the economy today, the great cultural conflicts in the world, and the multiplicity of its civilizations. To take a simple illustration, they should be enabled to read a serious daily newspaper and understand what they read.

But no: the new history has been placed or planted in the junior forms, where it has clearly played havoc. What else could have been expected?

In fact, the two kinds of history have both been misplaced, one in the lower forms of the *lycée*, the other at the top, with mutually damaging results. The ensuing confusion has been compounded by the liberties that teachers have taken since 1968: with the best will in the world, they have stressed one part of the curriculum to the detriment of another. Owing to such haphazard choices by a succession of teachers, some pupils have gone through their whole school careers without hearing about one or another important period in history. This hardly helps them to follow the thread of chronology.

Unhappily, the history taught to our children has suffered the same fate as their mathematics or their grammar. Why teach in bits and pieces a subject which is a *whole*? Especially to ten-year-olds who will never master elementary calculus or will very rarely, and only much later, tackle higher mathematics. The study of linguistics has ravaged grammar like a wild boar's snout burrowing through a potato field. It has cloaked it in pedantic, complicated, incomprehensible language which is also quite inappropriate. The result? Grammar and spelling have never been so badly neglected. But anomalies like these should not be blamed on linguistics, higher mathematics or the new history. They do what they have to do, without worrying about what can or cannot be taught at various ages. The blame lies, in fact, with the intellectual ambitions of those who draw up school curricula. They want to go too far. I am delighted that they are ambitious for themselves. But for those in their charge they should try to be simple, even – and especially – when this is difficult.

I wonder how much this debate can interest a non-French reader. Yet, if one really considers it, what is at stake is of immense importance, and cannot be ignored. Who can deny the violence that has stemmed from history? Of course, historians have no business fabricating dubious national myths – or even pursuing only humanism, which I myself prefer. But history is a vital element in national self-awareness. And without such self-awareness there can be no original culture, no genuine civilization, in France or anywhere else.

Introduction:
History and the Present Day

These preliminary pages seek to explain what the new history curriculum requires of students in the senior forms. Logically, they had to figure here, at the beginning of the book; but for teaching purposes they belong elsewhere. Ideally, in fact, they should be read towards the end of the second term, when the first part of the course has been completed and serious study of the great civilizations is about to begin. By that time, students will already be more familiar with philosophical terminology and debate. There is a case, however, for tackling the subject, at least initially, here and now.

The new history curriculum for the senior forms poses difficult problems. It amounts to a survey of the contemporary world in all its confusion and complexity, but made intelligible in various ways by an historical approach which may involve any of the kindred social sciences – geography, demography, economics, sociology, anthropology, psychology, etc.

It would be pretentious to profess to explain the present-day world. All one can hope is to understand it better by a variety of means. Your curriculum offers three such methods.

First, the present can partly be understood by reference to the immediate past. In this brief look backwards, history has an easy task. The first part of your course, therefore, covers the dramatic and often brutal days and years that the world has experienced since the outbreak of the First World War in August 1914, and continuing to the present time. These upheavals have shaken and shaped the twentieth century, and in countless ways they affect our lives still.

By themselves, however, the events of yesterday cannot fully explain the world of today. In fact, in varying degrees, the present is the outcome of other experiences much longer ago. It is the fruit of past centuries, and even of 'the whole historical evolution of humanity until now'. That the present involves so vast a stretch of the past should by no means seem absurd — although all of us naturally tend to think of the world around us only in the context of our own brief existence, and to see its history as a speeded-up film in which everything happens pell-mell: wars, battles, summit meetings, political crises, *coups d'état*, revolutions, economic upsets, ideas, intellectual and artistic fashions, and so on.

Clearly, however, the life of human beings involves many other phenomena which cannot figure in this film of events: the space they inhabit, the social structures that confine them and determine their existence, the ethical rules they consciously or unconsciously obey, their religious and philosophical beliefs, and the civilization to which they belong. These phenomena are much longer-lived than we are; and in our own lifetime we are unlikely to see them totally transformed.

For an analogy, consider our physical environment. It certainly changes: mountains, rivers, glaciers and coastlines gradually shift. But so slow is this process that none of us can perceive it with the naked eye, unless by comparison with the distant past, or with the help of scientific studies and measurements which go beyond mere subjective observation. The lives of countries and civilizations, and the psychological or spiritual attitudes of peoples, are not so seemingly immutable; yet generation succeeds generation without really radical change. Which by no means lessens — far from it — the importance of these deep, underlying forces that invade our lives and indeed shape the world.

The recent and the more or less distant past thus combine in the amalgam of the present. Recent history races towards us at high speed: earlier history accompanies us at a slower, stealthier pace.

This early history — long-distance history — forms the second part of the course. To study the great civilizations as an explanatory background to the present means stepping aside from the headlong rush of history since 1914. It invites us to reflect on history with a slower pulse-rate, history in the longer term. Civilizations are extraordinary creatures, whose longevity passes all understanding. Fabulously ancient, they live on in each of us; and they will still live on after we have passed away.

Recent and remote history, then, are the first two keys to understanding the present. Finally, the course provides a third. This involves identifying the major problems in the world today. Problems of every kind – political, social, economic, cultural, technical, scientific. In a word, what is required goes beyond the double historical approach already outlined: it means looking at the world around us to distinguish the essential from the peripheral.

Normally, historians work and reflect on the past; and if the available documentation does not always enable them to grasp it completely, at least they know in advance, when studying the eighteenth century for instance, what the Enlightenment led to. This in itself greatly enhances their knowledge and understanding. They know the last line of the play. When it comes to the present day, with all its different potential dénouements, deciding which are the really major problems essentially means imagining the last line of the play – discerning, among all the possible outcomes, those which are most likely to occur. The task is difficult, hazardous, and indispensable.

Condorcet, the eighteenth-century *encyclopédiste* whose best known work was his *Sketch for an Historical Tableau of the Progress of the Human Spirit*, thought such a task legitimate. Serious historians today also defend forecasting – with some courage, given its risks. In 1951, a world-famous economist, Colin Clark, used the statistics then available to predict the probable scale of the future economy. In 1960, Jean Fourastié calmly discussed *The Civilization of 1980*, which in his view determined – or should have determined – the policy to be followed at the time he wrote. A very precarious 'science', which the philosopher Gaston Berger has called 'prospective', claims to specialize in forecasting the near future – the 'futurible', to use a frightful word beloved of certain economists. The 'futurible' is what now can legitimately be described in the future tense – that thin wisp of tomorrow which can be guessed at and very nearly grasped.

Such proceedings are sometimes mocked. But although they may be only half-successful, they at least offer an escape route from the confusion of the present day, looking ahead to identify the biggest problems and try to make some sense of them. The world of today is a world in evolution.

The accompanying map shows the probable distribution of the world's population in the year 2000. It contains food for thought. It should make clear among other things that no planners – and planning means the attentive and 'prospective' study of today's major problems – can do their job properly without such a map (and many other documents) in their mind's eye. It certainly corroborates the remark by Félix Houphouët-Boigny, President of the Ivory Coast Republic, that planning must take different forms in Asia and in Black Africa, because poverty in Asia must cope with over-population, whereas in Black Africa under-population is the challenge.

History, a house of many mansions

It may seem surprising that history should be open to such diversions and speculations – that it should seek, in a word, to be a science of the present, and of a present which is ambiguous, at that. Is it not going astray? Is it not, like the wolf in the fable, putting on false clothing stolen from other social sciences? We shall return to this question at the beginning of Part II. By then, the problem should have been clarified, for it is a problem relating to time itself, and the nature of time will have been broached in the course of studying philosophy.

The obvious multiplicity of the explanations that history provides, the gaps between different points of view, and even their mutual contradictions, together form a *dialectic* which is specific to history, and based on the different varieties of time which it

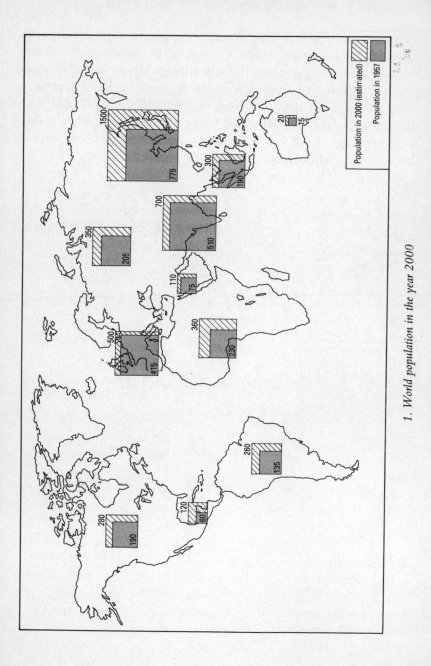

Population in 2000 (estimated) Population in 1957

1. *World population in the year 2000*

describes: rapid for events, slower for periods, slower still, even sluggish, for civilizations. For any particular study one can choose a particular variety of time. But any attempt at a *global* explanation – like the history of civilizations – needs a more eclectic approach. One must consult many different snapshots of the past, each with its own exposure time, then fuse times and images together, rather as the colours of the solar spectrum, focused together, combine at last into pure white light.

I. A History of Civilizations

1. Changing Vocabulary

It would be pleasant to be able to define the word 'civilization' simply and precisely, as one defines a straight line, a triangle or a chemical element.

The vocabulary of the social sciences, unfortunately, scarcely permits decisive definitions. Not that everything is uncertain or in flux: but most expressions, far from being fixed for ever, vary from one author to another, and continually evolve before our eyes. 'Words,' says Claude Lévi-Strauss, 'are instruments that people are free to adapt to any use, provided they make clear their intentions.' In the social sciences, in fact, as in philosophy, there are wide and frequent variations in the meaning of the simplest words, according to the thought that uses and informs them.

The word 'civilization' – a neologism – emerged late, and unobtrusively, in eighteenth-century France. It was formed from 'civilized' and 'to civilize', which had long existed and were in general use in the sixteenth century. In about 1732, 'civilization' was still only a term in jurisprudence: it denoted an act of justice or a judgement which turned a criminal trial into civil proceedings. Its modern meaning, 'the process of becoming civilized', appeared later, in 1752, from the pen of the French statesman and economist Anne Robert Jacques Turgot, who was then preparing a universal history, although he did not publish it himself. The official début of the word in print occurred in 1756, in a work entitled *A Treatise on Population* by Victor Riqueti, Marquis of Mirabeau, the father of the celebrated revolutionary Honoré, Count Mirabeau.

He referred to 'the scope of civilization' and even 'the luxury of a false civilization'.

Oddly enough, Voltaire omitted the useful word 'civilization' from his *Essay on the Customs and Spirit of Nations* (1756), although as the Dutch historian Johan Huizinga remarked, 'he is just the man to have conceived the notion . . . and first outlined a general history of civilization'.

In its new sense, civilization meant broadly the opposite of barbarism. On one side were the civilized peoples: on the other, primitive savages or barbarians. Even the 'noble savage' dear to Jean-Jacques Rousseau and his disciples in the eighteenth century was not regarded as *civilized*. Without a doubt, the French at the end of the reign of Louis XV were pleased to see in this new word the image of their own society – which at a distance may still appeal to us even today. At all events, the word appeared because it was needed. Until then, *poli* (polite), *policé* (organized), *civil* and *civilizé* had no corresponding nouns. The word *police* rather connoted social order – which distanced it somewhat from the adjective *polite*, defined in Furetière's 1690 *Universal Dictionary* as follows: 'Used figuratively in ethics to mean civilized. To civilize: to polish the manners, make civil and sociable . . . Nothing is more apt to civilize a young man than the conversation of ladies.'

From France, the word 'civilization' rapidly spread through Europe. The word 'culture' went with it. By 1772 and probably earlier, the word 'civilization' had reached England and replaced 'civility', despite the latter's long history. *Zivilisation* took root in Germany without difficulty, alongside the older word *Bildung*. In Holland, on the other hand, it met opposition from *beschaving*, a noun based on the verb *beschaven*, to refine, ennoble or civilize, although the word *civilisatie* did later appear. 'Civilization' encountered similar resistance South of the Alps, where Italian already had, and soon used in the sense of 'civilization', the fine old word *civiltà*, found in Dante. Deeply entrenched, *civiltà* prevented the intrusion of the new word, but not the explosive arguments that came with it. In 1835, Romagnosi tried in vain to launch the word *incivilmento*, which in his mind signified 'civiliz-ing' as much as 'civilization' *per se*.

In its travels round Europe, the new word 'civilization' was accompanied by an old word, 'culture'. Cicero had used its Latin equivalent, as in '*Cultura animi philosophia est*' – 'Philosophy is the cultivation of the soul.' It was now rejuvenated, and took on more or less the same sense as civilization. For a long time, indeed, the words were synonyms. At the University of Berlin in 1830, for instance, Hegel used them interchangeably. But at length the need to distinguish between them began to be felt.

Civilization, in fact, has at least a double meaning. It denotes both moral and material values. Thus Karl Marx distinguished between the *infrastructure* (material) and the *superstructure* (spiritual) – the latter, in his view, depending heavily on the former. Charles Seignobos remarked: 'Civilization is a matter of roads, ports, and quays' – a flippant way of saying that it was not all culture. 'It is all that humanity has achieved,' declared Marcel Mauss; while for the historian Eugène Cavignac it was 'a minimum of science, art, order and virtue'.

So civilization has at least two levels. Hence the temptation felt by many authors to separate the two words, culture and civiliz-ation, one assuming the dignity of spiritual concerns, the other the triviality of material affairs. The difficulty is that no two people agree on how the distinction is to be drawn: it varies from country to country, and within one country from period to period, and from one author to another.

In Germany, after some confusion, the distinction finally gave culture (*Kultur*) a certain precedence, consciously devaluing civiliza-tion. For the sociologists A. Tönnies (1922) and Alfred Weber (1935), civilization was no more than a mass of practical, technical knowledge, a series of ways of dealing with nature. Culture, by contrast, was a set of normative principles, values and ideals – in a word, the spirit.

This explains a remark by the German historian Wilhelm Momm-sen which at first sight strikes a Frenchman as strange: 'It is humanity's duty today [1851] to see that civilization does not destroy culture, nor technology the human being.' The first part of the sentence sounds bizarre to French ears because for us the word 'civilization' takes precedence, as it does in Britain and the United States, whereas in Poland and Russia culture is more highly prized, as it is in Germany (and through German influence). In France, the word 'culture' retains its power only when it denotes what Henri Marrou has called 'any personal form of the life of the spirit'. We speak of Paul Valéry's culture, not his civilization, because the latter word more usually refers to the values of the group.

There remains one further complication, greater than all the rest. Since the year 1874, when E. B. Taylor published *Primitive Culture*, British and American anthropologists have tended more and more to use the word 'culture' to describe the primitive societies they studied, as against the word 'civilization', which in English is normally applied to modern societies. Almost all anthropologists have followed suit, speaking of primitive cultures as compared with the civilizations that more developed societies have evolved. We shall make frequent use of this distinction in the course of the present work.

Fortunately, the useful adjective 'cultural', invented in Germany in about 1850, suffers from none of these complications. It applies, in fact, to the *whole* of the content of a civilization or a culture. One can say, for example, that a civilization (or a culture) is the sum total of its cultural assets, that its geographical area is its cultural domain, that its history is cultural history, and that what one civilization transmits to another is a cultural legacy or a case of cultural borrowing, whether material or intellectual. Perhaps, indeed, the word 'cultural' is *too* convenient: it has been called barbaric or ill-formed. But until a replacement is found, it remains indispensable. No other, at present, fits the bill.

In about 1819 the word 'civilization', hitherto singular, began to be used in the plural. From then onwards, it 'tended to assume a new *and quite different* meaning: i.e., the characteristics common to the collective life of a period or a group'. Thus one might speak of the civilization of fifth-century Athens or French civilization in the century of Louis XIV. This distinction between singular and plural, properly considered, raises a further substantial complication.

In the twentieth century, in fact, the plural of the word predominates, and is closest to our personal experience. Museums transport us in time, plunging us more or less completely into past civilizations. Actual travelling is more instructive still. To cross the Channel or the Rhine, to go south to the Mediterranean: these are clear and memorable experiences, all of which underline the plural nature of civilizations. Each, undeniably, is distinct.

If we were asked, now, to define civilization in the singular, we should certainly be more hesitant. The use of the plural signifies, in fact, the gradual decline of a concept – the typically eighteenth-century notion that there was such a thing as civilization, coupled with faith in progress and confined to a few privileged peoples or groups, humanity's 'élite'. The twentieth century, happily, has abandoned a certain number of such value-judgements, and would be hard put to it to decide – and on what criteria – which civilization was the best.

This being so, civilization in the singular has lost some of its cachet. It no longer represents the supreme moral and intellectual value that it seemed to embody in the eighteenth century. Today, for example, we more naturally tend to call some abominable misdeed 'a crime against *humanity*' rather than against *civilization*, although both mean much the same thing. We feel somewhat uneasy about using the word *civilization* in its old sense, connoting human excellence or superiority.

In the singular, indeed, civilization now surely denotes something which all civilizations share, however unequally: the common heritage of humanity. Fire, writing, mathematics, the cultivation of plants and the domestication of animals – these are no longer confined to any particular origin: they have become the collective attributes of civilization in the singular.

This spread of cultural assets which are common to all humanity has become phenomenal in the modern world. Industrial technology, invented in the West, is exported everywhere and eagerly adopted. Will it unify the world by making everywhere look alike – the same ferro-concrete, steel and glass buildings, the same airports, the same railways with their stations and loudspeakers, the same vast cities that gradually engulf so much of the population? 'We have reached a phase,' wrote Raymond Aron, 'where we are discovering both the limited validity of the concept of civilization and the need to transcend that concept . . . The phase of civilizations is coming to an end, and for good or ill humanity is embarking on a new phase' – that of a *single* civilization which could become universal.

Nevertheless, the 'industrial civilization' exported by the West is only one feature of its civilization as a whole. By accepting it, the world is not taking on Western civilization lock, stock and barrel: far from it. The history of civilizations, in fact, is the history of continual mutual borrowings over many centuries, despite which each civilization has kept its own original character. It must be admitted, however, that now is the first time when one decisive aspect of a particular civilization has been adopted willingly by all the civilizations in the world, and the first time when the speed of modern communications has so much assisted its rapid and effective distribution. That simply means that what we call 'industrial civilization' is in the process of joining the collective civilization of the world. All civilizations have been, are being, or will be shaken by its impact.

Still, even supposing that all the world's civilizations sooner or later adopt similar technology, and thereby partly similar ways of life, we shall nevertheless for a long time yet face what are really very different civilizations. For a long time yet, the word civilization will continue to be used in both singular and plural. On this point, the historian is not afraid to be categorical.

2. The Study of Civilization
Involves All the Social Sciences

To define the idea of civilization requires the combined efforts of all the social sciences. They include history; but in this chapter it will play only a minor role.

Here, it is the other social sciences that in turn will be called in aid: geography, sociology, economics and collective psychology. This means four excursions into very contrasting fields. But, despite initial appearances, the results will be seen to tally.

Civilizations as geographical areas

Civilizations, vast or otherwise, can always be located on a map. An essential part of their character depends on the constraints or advantages of their geographical situation.

This, of course, will have been affected for centuries or even millennia by human effort. Every landscape bears the traces of this continuous and cumulative labour, generation after generation contributing to the whole. So doing, humanity itself has been transformed by what the French historian Jules Michelet called 'the decisive shaping of self by self', or (as Karl Marx put it) 'the production of people by people'.

To discuss civilization is to discuss space, land and its contours, climate, vegetation, animal species and natural or other advantages. It is also to discuss what humanity has made of these basic conditions:

agriculture, stock-breeding, food, shelter, clothing, communications, industry and so on.

The stage on which humanity's endless dramas are played out partly determines their story-line and explains their nature. The cast will alter, but the set remains broadly the same.

For the expert on India, Hermann Goetz, there are two essential Indias. One is humid, with heavy rainfall, lakes, marshes, forests and jungles, aquatic plants and flowers – the land of people with dark skins. It contrasts with the dryer India of the Indo-Gangetic plain, plus the Deccan plateau – the home of lighter-skinned people, many of them warlike. India as a whole, in Goetz's view, is a debate and a tug-of-war between these two contrasting areas and peoples.

The natural and man-made environment, of course, cannot predetermine everything. It is not all-powerful. But it greatly affects the inherent or acquired advantages of any given situation.

To take inherent advantages, every civilization is born of immediate opportunities, rapidly exploited. Thus in the dawn of time, river civilizations flourished in the old world: Chinese civilization along the Yellow River; pre-Indian along the Indus; Sumerian, Babylonian and Assyrian on the Euphrates and the Tigris; Egyptian on the Nile. A similar group of vigorous civilizations developed in Northern Europe, around the Baltic and the North Sea – not to mention the Atlantic Ocean itself. Much of the West and its dependencies today, in fact, are grouped around that ocean, rather as the Roman world of former times was grouped around the Mediterranean.

These classic instances reveal above all the prime importance of communications. No civilization can survive without mobility: all are enriched by trade and the stimulating impact of strangers. Islam, for instance, is inconceivable without the movement of its caravans across the 'dry seas' of its deserts and steppes, without its expeditions in the Mediterranean and across the Indian Ocean as far as Malacca and China.

Mentioning these achievements has already led us beyond the

natural and immediate advantages which supposedly gave rise to civilizations. To overcome the hostility of the desert or the sudden squalls of the Mediterranean, to exploit the steady winds of the Indian Ocean, or to dam a river – all that needed human effort, to enjoy advantages, or rather to create them.

But why were some people capable of such achievements, but not others, in some places but not others, for generations on end?

Arnold Toynbee offered a tempting theory. All human achievement, he thought, involved challenge and response. Nature had to present itself as a difficulty to be overcome. If human beings took up the challenge, their response would lay the foundations of civilization.

But if this theory were carried to the limit, would it imply that the greater the challenge from Nature, the stronger humanity's response? It seems doubtful. In the twentieth century, civilized men and women have taken up the forbidding challenge of the deserts, the polar regions and the equator. Yet, despite the material interests involved, such as gold or oil, they have not yet settled and multiplied in those areas and founded true civilizations there. A challenge, yes, and also a response: but civilization does not always follow – at least until improved technology makes the response more adequate.

Every civilization, then, is based on an area with more or less fixed limits. Each has its own geography with its own opportunities and constraints, some virtually permanent and quite different from one civilization to another. The result? A variegated world, whose maps can indicate which areas have houses built of wood, and which of clay, bamboo, paper, bricks or stone; which areas use wool or cotton or silk for textiles; which areas grow various food crops – rice, maize, wheat, etc. The challenge varies: so does the response.

Western or European civilization is based on wheat and bread – and largely white bread – with all the constraints that this implies. Wheat is a demanding crop. It requires field use to be rotated annually, or fields to be left fallow every one or two years. Equally, the flooded rice-fields of the Far East, gradually spreading into low-lying areas, impose their own constraints on land use and local customs.

Responses to natural challenges thus continually free humanity from its environment and at the same time subject it to the resultant solutions. We exchange one form of determinism for another.

A cultural zone, as defined by anthropologists, is an area within which one group of cultural characteristics is dominant. In the case of primitive peoples, these may include not only their language but also their food crops, their marriage ceremonies, their religious beliefs, their pottery, their feathered arrows, their weaving techniques and so on. Defined by anthropologists on the basis of precise details, these zones are generally small.

Some cultural zones, however, cover much larger areas, united by characteristics common to the group and differentiating them from other large communities. Marcel Mauss claims that the primitive cultures surrounding the vast Pacific Ocean, despite the obvious differences and immense distances between them, are all part of a single human or rather cultural whole.

Naturally enough, following the example of the anthropologists, geographers and historians have taken to discussing cultural zones – this time with reference to advanced and complex civilizations. They identify areas which in turn can be subdivided into a series of districts. Such subdivision, as we shall see, applies essentially to large civilizations: these regularly resolve themselves into smaller units.

Western civilization, so-called, is at once the 'American civilization' of the United States, and the civilizations of Latin America, Russia and of course Europe. Europe itself contains a number of civilizations – Polish, German, Italian, English, French, etc. Not to mention the fact that these national civilizations are made up of 'civilizations' that are smaller still: Scotland, Ireland, Catalonia, Sicily, the Basque country and so on. Nor should we forget that these divisions, these multi-coloured mosaics, embody more or less permanent characteristics.

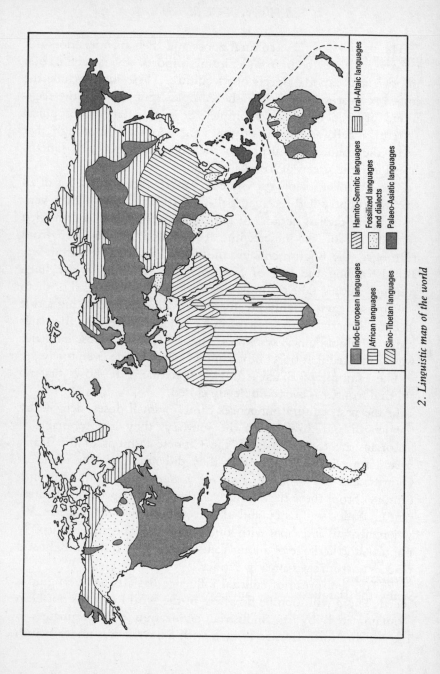

2. *Linguistic map of the world*

Indo-European languages

African languages

Sino-Tibetan languages

Hamito-Semitic languages

Fossilized languages and dialects

Palaeo-Asiatic languages

Ural-Altaic languages

The stability of these cultural zones and their frontiers does not however isolate them from cultural imports. Every civilization imports and exports aspects of its culture. These may include the lost-wax process for casting, the compass, gunpowder, the technique for tempering steel, a complete or fragmentary philosophical system, a cult, a religion or the song about Marlborough that went the rounds of Europe in the eighteenth century: Goethe heard it in the streets of Verona in 1786.

The Brazilian sociologist Gilberto Freyre once made a list of all that his country had received pell-mell from Europe – then very distant – in the last decades of the eighteenth century and the first five or six of the nineteenth. It included brown beer from Hamburg, the English cottage, the steam engine (a steamship was already plying the *baia* of San Salvador in 1819), white linen summer clothes, false teeth, gas lighting and – ahead of all of them – secret societies, notably Freemasonry, which played so big a role in Latin America at the time of independence. A few decades later came the philosophical system of Auguste Comte, whose influence was so marked that traces of it can be detected there even today.

The example of Brazil is one among many. It shows that no cultural frontier is ever completely closed.

In the past, cultural influences came in small doses, delayed by the length and slowness of the journeys they had to make. If historians are to be believed, the Chinese fashions of the T'ang period travelled so slowly that they did not reach the island of Cyprus and the brilliant court of Lusignan until the fifteenth century. From there they spread, at the quicker speed of Mediterranean trade, to France and the eccentric court of Charles VI, where hennins and shoes with long pointed toes became immensely popular, the heritage of a long vanished world – much as light still reaches us from stars already extinct.

Today, the spread of cultural influence has attained vertiginous speed. There will soon be nowhere in the world that has not been 'contaminated' by the industrial civilization that originated in Europe. In North Borneo (which with Sarawak was under British rule until 1963), a few loudspeakers used to relay radio programmes from Communist China and Indonesia. Their listeners understood nothing of what the broadcasts were saying, but the rhythms they heard very soon affected their traditional music and dancing. How much greater is the influence of the cinema, especially from Europe and America, on the tastes and even the customs of countries on the far side of the world.

No example, however, could be more telling than an experience described by the American anthropologist Margaret Mead. In her youth she had studied a Pacific island people whose life she had shared for several months. The war brought them into unexpected contact with the outside world. After the war, Margaret Mead returned and wrote a book in which she movingly described what had happened, with photographs showing many of the same people as they had been and as they were, totally transformed.

Such, again, is the dialogue between civilization and civilizations of which we shall hear so much in this book. Will the ever faster spread of cultural influence remove the frontiers between civilizations that were once so firm in world history? Many people fear – and some rejoice – that they will. Yet, however avid civilizations are to acquire the material adjuncts of 'modern' life, they are not prepared to take on everything indiscriminately. It even happens, as we shall see, that they stubbornly reject outside influence. This is why, now as in the past, they are still able to safeguard characteristics that everything seems to threaten with extinction.

Civilizations as societies

There can be no civilizations without the societies that support them and inspire their tensions and their progress. Hence the first inevitable question: was it necessary to invent the word 'civilization' and encourage its academic use, if it remains merely a synonym for 'society'? Arnold Toynbee continually used the word 'society' in place of 'civilization'. And Marcel Mauss believed that 'the idea of civilization is certainly less clear than that of society, which it presupposes'.

Society and civilization are inseparable: the two ideas refer to the same reality. Or, as Claude Lévi-Strauss put it, 'they do not represent different objects, but two complementary views of a single object, which can perfectly well be described by either term according to one's point of view.'

The idea of 'society' implies a wealth of content. In this it closely resembles that of civilization, with which it is so often linked. The Western civilization in which we live, for example, depends on the 'industrial society' which is its driving force. It would be easy to characterize Western civilization simply by describing that society and its component parts, its tensions, its moral and intellectual values, its ideals, its habits, its tastes, etc. – in other words by describing the people who embody it and who will pass it on.

If a society stirs and changes, the civilization based on it stirs and changes too. This point is made in a fine book by Lucien Goldmann, *The Hidden God* (*Le Dieu caché*, 1955), which deals with the France of Louis XIV. Every civilization, Goldmann explains, draws its essential insights from the 'view of the world' it adopts. And in every case this view of the world is coloured, if not determined, by social tensions. Civilization simply reflects them like a mirror.

The age of Jansenism, Racine, Pascal, the abbé de Saint-Cyran and the abbé Barcos, whose fascinating letters Goldmann has rediscovered, was as *The Hidden God* shows an impassioned moment in the history of France; and the tragic view of the world that prevailed then had originated with the parliamentary upper middle classes, disillusioned by the monarchy with which they were at odds. The tragedy of their fate, their awareness of it, and their intellectual ascendancy all combined to imbue the period with their own dominant mood.

In a quite different spirit, Claude Lévi-Strauss also identifies civilizations with societies when he argues the difference between primitive and modern societies — or, as most anthropologists put it, between cultures and civilizations. Cultures in this sense are societies

which produce little disorder — what doctors call 'entropy' — and tend to remain indefinitely as they originally were: which is why they look to us like societies that lack both history and progress. Whereas our societies (those that correspond to modern civilizations) ... are powered by a difference of electrical pressure, as it were, expressed in various forms of social hierarchy ... Such societies have managed to establish within them a social imbalance which they use to produce both much greater order — we have societies that work like machines — and much greater disorder, much less entropy, in relations between people.

For Lévi-Strauss, then, primitive cultures are the fruit of egalitarian societies, where relations between groups are settled once and for all and remain constant, whereas civilizations are based on hierarchical societies with wide gaps between groups and hence shifting tensions, social conflicts, political struggles, and continual evolution.

The most obvious external sign of these differences between 'cultures' and 'civilizations' is undoubtedly the presence or absence of towns. Towns proliferate in civilizations: in cultures they remain embryonic. There are of course intermediate stages and degrees. What is Black Africa but a group of traditional societies — of cultures — embarked on the difficult and sometimes cruel process of fostering civilization and modern urban development? African cities, taking their models from abroad in a style now international, remain islands amid the stagnation of the countryside. They prefigure the society and the civilization to come.

The most brilliant societies and civilizations, however, presuppose within their own borders cultures and societies of a more elementary kind. Take, for example, the interplay of town and country, never to be underestimated. In no society have all regions and all parts of the population developed equally. Under-development is common in mountain areas or patches of poverty

off the beaten track of modern communications – genuinely primitive societies, true 'cultures' in the midst of a civilization.

The West's first success was certainly the conquest of its
countryside – its peasant 'cultures' – by the towns. In the Islamic
world, the duality remains more visible than in the West. Islamic
towns were quicker to arise – were more precociously urban, so to
speak – than in Europe, while the countryside remained more
primitive, with vast areas of nomadic life. In the Far East, that
contrast is still the general rule: its 'cultures' remain very isolated,
living by themselves and on their own resources. Between the most
brilliant cities lie tracts of countryside whose way of life is almost
self-sufficient, at subsistence level, and sometimes actually barbaric.

Given the close relationship between civilization and society,
there is a case for adopting the sociological mode when looking at
the long history of civilizations. As historians, however, we should
not simply confuse societies with civilizations. We shall explain in
the next chapter what we believe the difference to be: in terms of
the time-scale, civilization implies and embraces much longer
periods than any given social phenomenon. It changes far less
rapidly than the societies it supports or involves. But this is not yet
the moment to go fully into that question. One thing at a time.

Civilizations as economies

Every society, every civilization, depends on economic, technological, biological and demographic circumstances. Material and
biological conditions always help determine the destiny of
civilizations. A rise or a fall in the population, health or illness,
economic or technological growth or decline – all these deeply
affect the cultural as well as the social structure. Political economy
in the broadest sense is the study of all these massive problems.

For a long time, people were humanity's only major implement
or form of energy – the sole resource for building a civilization by
sheer brawn and brain. In principle and in fact, therefore, an

increase in the population has always helped the growth of civilization – as in Europe in the thirteenth, sixteenth, eighteenth, nineteenth and twentieth centuries.

Just as regularly, however, when the population grows faster than the economy, what was once an advantage becomes a drawback. Such was the case, undoubtedly, by the end of the sixteenth century, as it is today in most underdeveloped countries. The results in the past were famines, a fall in real earnings, popular uprisings and grim periods of slump: until epidemics and starvation together brutally thinned out the too-serried ranks of human beings. After such biological disasters (like that in Europe in the second half of the fourteenth century, with the Black Death and the epidemics that followed it), the survivors briefly had an easier time and expansion began again, at increasing speed – until the next setback.

Only industrialization, at the end of the eighteenth century and the beginning of the nineteenth, seemed to have broken this vicious circle and made even surplus people valuable again, able to work and live. As the history of Europe showed, the growing value and cost of human labour, and the need to economize on employees, encouraged the development of machines. Classical antiquity, intelligent as it was, had no machines to match its intelligence. It never really tried to acquire them. Its failing was that it possessed slaves. Imperial China, flourishing long before the eighteenth century, very intelligent and technically skilful, nevertheless suffered also: it had too many people. They cost very little, and performed almost all the tasks required by an economy virtually lacking animal power. As a result, although China enjoyed a long lead in matters scientific, it never crossed the threshold of modern science and technology. That privilege, that honour, that profit it left to Europe.

Economic life never ceases to fluctuate, at intervals sometimes long and sometimes short. Good times and bad times succeed each other; and societies and civilizations feel their effects, especially when the upturn or downturn is prolonged. The pessimism and disquiet that were widespread in the late fifteenth century – what

Johan Huizinga called *The Waning of the Middle Ages* – reflected a marked recession in the economy of the West. European Romanticism, likewise, coincided with a long economic recession between 1817 and 1852. The expansion in the mid-eighteenth century (from 1733 onwards) saw some setbacks (for instance on the eve of the French Revolution); but in general at that time economic growth placed the intellectual development of the Enlightenment in a context of material well-being, active trade, expanding industry, and growing population.

Whether in boom or slump, economic activity almost always produces a surplus. The expenditure, or squandering, of such surpluses has been one of the indispensable conditions for luxury in civilizations and for certain forms of art. When today we admire architecture, sculpture or portraits we are also contemplating, not always consciously, the calm pride of a city, the vainglorious folly of a prince or the wealth of a *nouveau-riche* merchant banker. In Europe from the sixteenth century onwards (and probably earlier), the ultimate phase of civilization wears the emblem of capitalism and wealth.

So civilization reflects a redistribution of wealth. Civilizations acquire different characteristics, first at the top and then among the mass of the people, according to their way of redistributing wealth, and according to the social and economic machinery which takes from the circulation of wealth whatever is destined for luxury, art or culture. In the seventeenth century, during the very hard times of Louis XIV's reign, there were very few patrons except at Court. Literary and artistic life was confined to this small circle. In the lavish, easy-going economic climate of the eighteenth century, aristocracy and bourgeoisie joined with royalty in spreading culture, science and philosophy.

But luxury, at that time, was still the privilege of a social minority. The civilization underlying it, that of modest workaday life, had very little share in it. And the ground floor of a civilization is often its crucial level. What is freedom – what is an individual's culture – without enough to live on? From this point of view the much-maligned nineteenth century, that boring century of the *nouveaux riches* and the 'triumphant bourgeoisie', was the harbinger (if not yet the exemplar) of a new destiny for civilizations and for the human personality. While the population rapidly increased, more and more of its members were able to enjoy a certain collective civilization. No doubt the social cost of this transformation – unconscious, admittedly – was very heavy. But its advantages were great. The development of education, access to culture, admission to the universities, social progress – these were the achievements of the nineteenth century, already rich, and full of significance for the future.

The great problem for tomorrow, as for today, is to create a mass civilization of high quality. To do so is very costly. It is unthinkable without large surpluses devoted to the service of society, and without the leisure that mechanization will no doubt soon be able to offer us. In the industrialized countries, such a future can be envisaged not too far ahead. The problem is more complex in the world as a whole. For, just as economic growth has made civilization more accessible to some social classes than to others, it has similarly differentiated various countries in the world. Much of the world's population is what one essayist has called 'the foreign proletariat', better known as the Third World – an enormous mass of people, many of whom have yet to earn a bare living before they can enjoy the benefits of their own countries' civilization, which to them is often a closed book. Unless humanity makes the effort to redress these vast inequalities, they could bring civilizations – and civilization – to an end.

Civilizations as ways of thought

After geography, sociology and economics, we must finally turn to psychology. With this difference: that, as a science, collective psychology is less self-confident and less rich in results than the other social sciences so far considered. It has also rarely ventured along the paths of history.

Collective psychology, awareness, mentality or mental equipment? It is impossible to choose among them. Such uncertainties about vocabulary show what a youthful science collective psychology still is. 'Psychology' is the expression preferred by Alphonse Dupront, a great specialist in this field. 'Awareness' refers only to a phase of development, generally the final phase. 'Mentality' is obviously more convenient. Lucien Febvre, in his excellent *Rabelais*, prefers to speak of 'mental equipment'. But the words matter little: they are not the problem. In every period, a certain view of the world, a collective mentality, dominates the whole mass of society. Dictating a society's attitudes, guiding its choices, confirming its prejudices and directing its actions, this is very much a fact of civilization. Far more than the accidents or the historical and social circumstances of a period, it derives from the distant past, from ancient beliefs, fears and anxieties which are almost unconscious – an immense contamination whose germs are lost to memory but transmitted from generation to generation. A society's reactions to the events of the day, to the pressure upon it, to the decisions it must face, are less a matter of logic or even self-interest than the response to an unexpressed and often inexpressible compulsion arising from the collective unconscious.

These basic values, these psychological structures, are assuredly the features that civilizations can least easily communicate one to another. They are what isolate and differentiate them most sharply. And such habits of mind survive the passage of time. They change little, and change slowly, after a long incubation which itself is largely unconscious too.

Here religion is the strongest feature of civilizations, at the heart of both their present and their past. And in the first place, of course, in civilizations outside Europe. In India, for instance, all actions derive their form and their justification from the religious life, not from reasoning. The Greeks were astonished by this, to judge from an anecdote reported by Eusebius, Bishop of Caesarea (265–340): 'Aristoxenus the musician tells the following story about the Indians. One of them met Socrates in Athens and asked him to describe his philosophy. "It is the study of human reality," replied Socrates. At which the Indian burst out laughing. "How can a man study human reality," he asked, "when he knows nothing of divine reality?"'

Siniti Kunar Chatterji, a contemporary Hindu philosopher, gives the following well-known illustration of humanity's inability to fathom the immense mystery and unity of the supernatural. 'We are like blind people who, feeling this or that part of an elephant's body, are severally convinced that one of them is touching a pillar, another a snake, a third something hard, the fourth a wall and another a brush with a flexible handle – according to whether they are in contact with a leg, the trunk, a tusk, the body or the tail.'

By comparison with this deep religious humility, the West seems forgetful of its Christian sources. But, rather than stress the break that rationalism has supposedly made between religion and culture, it is more to the point to consider the coexistence of laicism, science and religion and the serene or stormy dialogue in which, despite appearances, they have always been engaged. Christianity is an essential reality in Western life: it even marks atheists, whether they know it or not. Ethical rules, attitudes to life and death, the concept of work, the value of effort, the role of women and children – these may seem to have nothing to do with Christian feeling: yet all derive from it nevertheless.

Since the development of Greek thought, however, the tendency of Western civilization has been towards rationalism and hence away from the religious life. That is its distinguishing characteristic, and something to which we shall return. With very few exceptions (certain Chinese sophists, and certain Arab philosophers in the twelfth century), no such marked turning away from religion is to be found in the history of the world outside the West. Almost all civilizations are pervaded or submerged by religion, by the supernatural, and by magic: they have always been steeped in it, and they draw from it the most powerful motives in their particular psychology. This is a phenomenon we shall have many opportunities to observe.

3. The Continuity of Civilizations

The time has come for history to join this complex debate. It may add further complexity: but its use of a time-scale and its capacity to explain matters should make sense of the subject. In fact, no existing civilization can be truly understood without some knowledge of the paths it has followed, the values it has inherited, and the experiences it has undergone. A civilization always involves a past, lived and still alive.

The history of a civilization, then, is a search among ancient data for those still valid today. It is not a question of telling us all there is to be known about Greek civilization or the Middle Ages in China – but only what of former times is still relevant today, in Western Europe or in modern China: everything in which there is a short-circuit between past and present, often across many centuries' gap.

Periods within civilizations

But let us begin at the beginning. Every civilization, both yesterday and today, is immediately manifest in something easily grasped: a play, an exhibition of paintings, a successful book, a philosophy, a fashion in dress, a scientific discovery, a technological advance – all of them apparently independent of one another. (At first sight, there is no link between the philosophy of Maurice Merleau-Ponty and a late painting by Picasso.)

These manifestations of a civilization, it may be noted, are always short-lived. How then can they help us to map out a past which is also present, when they seem so often to replace and destroy each other, rather than show any sort of continuity?

These spectacles are in fact subject to relentless change. The programme is continually altered: no one wants it to run for too long. This can be seen by the way in which literary, artistic and philosophical periods succeed one another. It can be said, borrowing a phrase from the economists, that there are cycles in cultural affairs as there are in economics – more or less protracted or precipitate fluctuations which in most cases violently counter those that went before. From one period to another, everything changes or seems to change, rather as stage lighting, without striking the set or changing the actors' make-up, can show them in new colours and project them into a different world. Of these periods, the Renaissance is the finest example. It had its own themes, its own colours and preferences, even its own mannerisms. It was marked by intellectual fervour, love of beauty, and free, tolerant debates in which wit was another sign of enjoyment. It was also marked by the discovery or rediscovery of the works of classical antiquity, a pursuit in which all of civilized Europe enthusiastically joined.

Similarly, there was a Romantic era (roughly from 1800 to 1850, but with both earlier and later manifestations); it coloured people's minds and feelings over a long, troubled, difficult period, in the joyless aftermath of the French Revolution and the Empire, which coincided with an economic recession throughout Europe, between 1817 and 1852. We should certainly not claim that the recession alone explained – still less, created – Romantic *Angst*: there are not only economic cycles, but also cycles in sensibility, in the arts of living and thinking, which are more or less independent of external events ... Every generation, at all events, likes to contradict its predecessor; and its successor will do the same and more. So there is likely to be a perpetual swing of the pendulum between classicism and romanticism (or baroque, as Eugenio d'Ors called it), between cool intelligence and warm, troubled emotion – often in striking contrast.

The resultant pattern, therefore, is a constant alternation of mood. A civilization, like an economy, has its own rhythms. Its history is episodic, easy to divide into sections or periods, each virtually distinct. We refer quite happily to 'the century of Louis XIV' or to 'the Enlightenment': we even, in French, speak of 'classic civilization' in the seventeenth century, or 'the civilization of the eighteenth century'. To call such short periods civilizations, according to the philosophically minded economist Joseph Chappey, is 'diabolical': it seems to him to contradict the very idea of civilization, which (as we shall see) involves continuity. But for the moment let us leave this contradiction aside. Unity and diversity, after all, always coexist uneasily. We have to take them as they come.

'Turning-points', events, heroes: all help to clarify the special role of exceptional events and people in the history of civilizations.

Every episode, when studied closely, dissolves into a series of actions, gestures and characters. Civilizations, in the last analysis, are made up of people, and hence of their behaviour, their achievements, their enthusiasms, their commitment to various causes, and also their sudden changes. But the historian has to select: among all these actions, achievements and biographies, certain events or people stand out and mark a 'turning-point', a new phase. The more important the change, the more clearly significant its harbingers.

One example of a crucial event was the discovery of universal gravitation by Sir Isaac Newton in 1687. Significant events include the first performance of *Le Cid* in 1638 or of *Hernani* in 1830. People stand out likewise, in so far as their work marks an epoch or sums up an historical episode. This is the case with Joachim du Bellay (1522–60) and his *Defence and Illustration of the French Language*; with Gottfried Wilhelm Leibniz (1646–1716) and his infinitesimal calculus; or with Denis Papin (1647–1714) and his invention of the steam-engine.

But the names that really dominate the history of civilizations are those which survive a number of episodes, as a ship may ride out a series of storms. A few rare spirits mark the limits of vast periods, summing up in themselves a number of generations: Dante (1265–1321) at the end of the 'Latin' Middle Ages; Goethe (1749–1832) at the end of Europe's first 'modern' period; Newton on the threshold of classical physics; or Albert Einstein (1879–1955), herald of today's sub-atomic physics with all its enormous significance for the world.

The founders of great philosophies also belong in this exceptional category: Socrates or Plato, Confucius, Descartes or Karl Marx – each dominates more than one century. In their way, they are founders of civilizations, scarcely less important than those outstanding founders of the world's abiding religions, Buddha, Christ and Muhammad.

In fact, the measure of an event's or a person's importance in the hurly-burly of history is the time they take to be forgotten. Only those that endure and are identified with an enduring reality really count in the history of civilization. Thus may be discerned, through the screen of familiar historical events, the emerging outlines of the more continuous reality which we must now seek to discover.

Underlying structures

Looking at historical periods has produced only transient pictures: projected on the backcloth of civilizations, they appear and then vanish again. If we look for the permanent features behind these changing images, we shall find other, simpler realities which present a quite new interest. Some last for only a few seasons; others endure for several centuries; others still persist so long as to seem immutable. The appearance, of course, is illusory; for, slowly and imperceptibly, they too change and decay. Such are the realities referred to in the previous chapter: the ceaseless constraints imposed by geography, by social hierarchy, by collective psychology and by economic need – all profound forces, barely recognized at first, especially by contemporaries, to whom they always seem perfectly natural, to be taken wholly for granted if they are thought about at all. These realities are what we now call 'structures'.

Even historians may not notice them at first: their habitual chronological narratives are often too busy to see the wood for the trees. To perceive and trace underlying structures one has to cover, in spendthrift fashion, immense stretches of time. The movements on the surface discussed a moment ago, the events and the people, fade from the picture when we contemplate these vast phenomena, permanent or semi-permanent, conscious and subconscious at the same time. These are the 'foundations', the underlying *structures* of civilizations: religious beliefs, for instance, or a timeless peasantry, or attitudes to death, work, pleasure and family life.

These realities, these structures, are generally ancient and long-lived, and always distinctive and original. They it is that give civilizations their essential outline and characteristic quality. And civilizations hardly ever exchange them: they regard them as irreplaceable values. For the majority of people, of course, these enduring traits, these inherited choices, these reasons for rejecting other civilizations, are generally unconscious. To see them clearly one has to withdraw, mentally at least, from the civilization of which one is a part.

Take as a simple example, with very deep roots: the role of women in the twentieth century in a society like ours in Europe. Its peculiarities may not strike us – so 'natural' do they seem – until we make a comparison with, say, the role of Muslim women or, at the other extreme, that of women in the United States. To understand why these differences arose, we should have to go far back into the past, at least as far as the twelfth century, the age of 'courtly love', and begin to trace the Western conception of love and of the couple. We should then have to consider a series of factors: Christianity, women's access to schools and universities, European ideas about the education of children, economic conditions, the standard of living, women's work outside the home and so on.

The role of women is always a structural element in any civilization – a test: it is a long-lived reality, resistant to external pressure, and hard to change overnight. A civilization generally refuses to accept a cultural innovation that calls in question one of its own structural elements. Such refusals or unspoken enmities are relatively rare: but they always point to the heart of a civilization.

Civilizations continually borrow from their neighbours, even if they 'reinterpret' and assimilate what they have adopted. At first sight, indeed, every civilization looks rather like a railway goods yard, constantly receiving and dispatching miscellaneous deliveries.

Yet a civilization may stubbornly reject a particular import from outside. Marcel Mauss has remarked that every civilization worthy of the name has refused or rejected something. Every time, the refusal is the culmination of a long period of hesitation and experiment. Long meditated and slowly reached, the decision is always crucially important.

The classical instance is the Turkish capture of Constantinople in 1453. A modern Turkish historian claims that the city gave itself up, that it was conquered from within, before the Turkish attack. Although an exaggeration, this thesis is not unfounded. In fact, the Orthodox Church (or Byzantine civilization) preferred to submit to the Turks rather than unite with the Latins who were its only possible saviours. This was not a 'decision', taken hastily on the spot under the pressure of events. It was rather the natural outcome of a long process, as long in fact as the decadence of Byzantium, which day after day made the Greeks more and more reluctant to draw closer to the Latins across the great divide of their theological disputes.

Greco-Latin union would have been possible. The Emperor Michael Palaeologus had accepted it at the Council of Lyon in 1274. The Emperor John V, in 1369, had professed the Catholic faith in Rome. In 1439, the joint Council of Florence had once more shown that union was attainable. The most eminent Greek theologians, John Beccos, Demetrios Lydones and John Bessarion, had all written in favour of union, with a talent which their opponents could not equal. Yet, between the Turks and the Latins, the Greeks preferred the Turks. 'Because it was jealous of its independence, the Byzantine Church appealed to the enemy and surrendered to him the Empire and Christendom.' Already in 1385 the Patriarch of Constantinople had written to Pope Urban VI that the Turks offered to the Greek Church 'full liberty of action' – and that was the decisive phrase. Fernand Grenard, from whom these points are taken, added: 'The enslavement of Constantinople by Muhammad II was the triumph of the separatist Patriarch.' The West, for its part, was well aware of how much the Eastern Church disliked it. 'These schismatics,' wrote Petrarch, 'feared and hated us with all their guts.'

Another refusal which was slow to take shape was the closing of Italy and the Iberian Peninsula to the Protestant Reformation. In France, there was more hesitation: for nearly a hundred years the country was a battleground between two different forms of belief.

A further refusal, and one which was not wholly political (or unanimous), was that which so long divided the industrialized West, including North America, from the totalitarian Marxist Socialism of Eastern Europe. The Germanic and Anglo-Saxon countries said No categorically: France and Italy – and even the Iberian Peninsula – gave a more mixed and equivocal response. This, very probably, was a clash between civilizations.

One might add that, if Western Europe had taken to Communism, it would have done so in its own way, adapting it as it is currently adapting capitalism, very differently from the USA.

Just as a civilization may welcome or refuse elements from another civilization, so it may accept or reject survivals from its own past. It does so slowly, and almost always unconsciously or partly so. In this way, it gradually transforms itself. Little by little, it sifts the mass of data and attitudes offered by the remote or recent past, stressing one or setting aside another; and as a result of its choices it assumes a shape which is never wholly new but never quite the same as before.

These internal rejections may be firm or hesitant, lasting or short-lived. Only the lasting rejections are essential in the areas which are gradually being explored by psychological history, and which may be as large as a country or a civilization. Examples of such exploration include: two pioneering studies of life and death in the fifteenth and sixteenth centuries, by Alberto Tenenti; an examination of *The Idea of Happiness in Eighteenth-century France*, by R. Mauzi; and a fascinating, fascinated book by Michel Foucault on *The History of Madness in the Classical Age*, 1961. These three cases are instances of a civilization working over its own heritage – something rarely brought fully to light. The process is so slow that contemporaries never notice it. Each time, the rejection – and the occasional acceptance of alternatives – takes centuries, with prohibitions, obstacles and healing processes which are often difficult and imperfect and always very prolonged.

This is what Michel Foucault, in his own peculiar terminology, calls 'dividing oneself off' – that is, in the case of a civilization, expelling from its frontiers and from its inner life any value that it spurns. 'One might,' writes Foucault,

trace the history of the *limits*, of those obscure actions, necessarily forgotten as soon as they are performed, whereby a civilization casts aside something it regards as alien. Throughout its history, this moat which it digs around itself, this no man's land by which it preserves its isolation, is just as characteristic as its positive values. For it receives and maintains its values as continuous features of its history; but in the area which we have chosen to discuss it makes its essential choice – the *selection* [our emphasis] – which gives it its positive nature – the essential substance of which it is made.

This text deserves close attention. A civilization attains its true persona by rejecting what troubles it in the obscurity of that no man's land which may already be foreign territory. Its history is the centuries-long distillation of a collective personality, caught like any individual between its clear, conscious objective and its obscure, unconscious fate, whose influence on aims and motives is often unobserved. Clearly, such essays in retrospective psychology have been affected by the discoveries of psychoanalysis.

Michel Foucault's book studies a particular case: the distinction between reason and madness, between the sane and the mad, which was unknown in the Middle Ages, when the Fool, like any unfortunate, was more or less mysteriously held to be an emissary from God. But the mentally deranged were imprisoned, at first harshly and brutally, in the seventeenth century with its passion for social order. It regarded them as mere jetsam, to be banished from the world like delinquents or the incorrigibly idle. Then, in the nineteenth century, they were treated more fairly, even kindly, because they were recognized as ill. Yet, although attitudes changed, the central problem remained. From the classical age until today, the West has distanced itself from madness, banning its language and banishing its victims. Thus the triumph of reason has been accompanied, under the surface, by a long, silent turbulence, the almost unconscious, almost unknown counterpart to the public victory of rationalism and of classical science.

One could of course give other examples. Alberto Tenenti's book patiently traces the way in which the West distanced itself from the Christian idea of death as envisaged in the Middle Ages – a simple transition from exile on earth to real life beyond the grave. In the fifteenth century, death became 'human' – humanity's supreme ordeal, the horror of decomposing flesh. But in this new conception of death people found a new conception of life, prized anew for its own intrinsic worth. Anxiety about death abated in the following century, the sixteenth, which – at least at the beginning – was marked by *joie de vivre*.

So far, the argument has presupposed peaceful relations between civilizations, each free to make its own choice. But violence has often been the rule. Always tragic, it has often proved ultimately pointless. Successes like the Romanization of Gaul and of much of Western Europe can be explained only by the length of time the process took – and, despite what is often alleged – by the primitive level from which Rome's vassals began, by their admiration for their conquerors, and in fact by their acquiescence in their own fate. But such successes were rare: they are the exceptions that prove the rule.

When contact was violent, in fact, failure was more frequent than success. 'Colonialism' may have triumphed in the past: but today it is an obvious fiasco. And colonialism, typically, is the submergence of one civilization by another. The conquered always submit to the stronger; but their submission is merely provisional when civilizations clash.

Long periods of enforced coexistence may include concessions or agreements and important, often fruitful, cultural exchange. But the process always has its limits.

The finest example of cultural interpenetration in a climate of violence is described in Roger Bastide's outstanding book on *African Religions in Brazil* (1960). This tells the tragic story of black slaves torn from their roots in Africa and flung into the patriarchal Christian society of colonial Brazil. They reacted against it; but at the same time they adopted Christianity. A number of runaway black slaves founded independent republics – *quilombos*: that of Palmeiras, north-east of Bahia, was not conquered without a full-scale war. Although stripped of everything, blacks such as these reinstated old African religious practices and magic dances. In their *candomblés* or *macumbas* they fused African and Christian rites in a synthesis which is still alive today, and even making further headway. It is an amazing example. The vanquished surrendered – but preserved themselves too.

History and civilization

Looking back over civilizations' resistance or acquiescence in the face of change, their permanence and their slow transformation, we can perhaps offer one last definition, which may restore their unique and particular essence: that is, their long historical continuity. Civilization is in fact the longest story of all. This is a truth which the historian may at first not realize. It will emerge in the course of successive observations, rather in the same way that the view of a landscape broadens as the path ascends.

History operates in tenses, on scales and in units which frequently vary: day by day, year by year, decade by decade, or in whole centuries. Every time, the unit of measurement modifies the view. It is the contrasts between the realities observed on different time-scales that make possible history's dialectic.

For the sake of simplicity, let us say that the historian works on at least three planes.

One, which we may call A, is that of traditional history, habitual narrative, hurrying from one event to the next like a chronicler of old or a reporter today. A thousand pictures are seized on the wing, making a multi-coloured story as full of incident as an unending serial. No sooner read than forgotten, however, this kind of history too often leaves us unsatisfied, unable to judge or to understand.

A second plane – B – is that of episodes, each taken as a whole: Romanticism, the French Revolution, the Industrial Revolution, World War II. The time-scale here may be ten, twenty or fifty years. And facts are grouped, interpreted and explained in accordance with these phenomena, whether they be called periods, phases, episodes or cycles. They can be regarded as events of long duration, stripped of superfluous detail.

A third plane – C – transcends these events: it considers only phenomena that can be measured over a century or more. At this level, the movement of history is slow and covers vast reaches of time: to cross it requires seven-league boots. On this scale, the French Revolution is no more than a moment, however essential, in the long history of the revolutionary, liberal and violent destiny of the West. Voltaire, likewise, is only a stage in the evolution of free thought.

In this final perspective – sociologists, who have their own imagery, might say 'on this last deep level' – civilizations can be seen as distinct from the accidents and vicissitudes that mark their development: they reveal their longevity, their permanent features, their structures – their almost abstract but yet essential diagrammatic form.

A civilization, then, is neither a given economy nor a given society, but something which can persist through a series of economies or societies, barely susceptible to gradual change. A civilization can be approached, therefore, only in the long term, taking hold of a constantly unwinding thread – something that a group of people have conserved and passed on as their most precious heritage from generation to generation, throughout and despite the storms and tumults of history.

This being so, we should hesitate before agreeing with the great Spanish historian Rafaël Altamira (1951) or with François Guizot (1855) that the history of civilizations is 'all of history'. No doubt it is: but only if seen in a particular way, using the largest time-scale that is compatible with human and historical concerns. Not, to borrow the well-known comparison made by Bernard de Fontenelle, the history of roses, however beautiful, but that of the gardener, whom the roses must think immortal. From the point of view of societies, economies and the countless incidents of short-term history, civilizations must seem immortal too.

This long-term history, history-at-a-distance – blue-water cruising on the high seas of time, rather than prudent coastal navigation never losing sight of land – this way of proceeding, call it what you will, has both advantages and drawbacks. Its advantages are that it forces one to think, to explain matters in unaccustomed terms, and to use historical explanation as a key to one's own time. Its drawbacks or dangers are that it can lapse into the facile generalizations of a philosophy of history more imaginary than researched or proved.

Historians are surely right to mistrust over-enthusiastic explorers like Oswald Spengler or Arnold Toynbee. Any history which is pressed to the point of general theory requires constant returns to practical reality – figures, maps, precise chronology and verification.

Rather than any theory of civilizations, therefore, we must study real instances if we wish to understand what civilization is. All the rules and definitions that we have outlined so far will be clarified and simplified by the examples that follow.

II. CIVILIZATIONS OUTSIDE EUROPE

PART I: ISLAM AND THE MUSLIM WORLD

4. History

Civilizations take ages to be born, to settle, and to grow.

It is true to say that Islam arose with Muhammad in a few short years: but the statement is also misleading and hard to understand. Christianity, likewise, was born with Christ, yet also in a sense predated Him. Without Christ or Muhammad, there would have been neither Christianity nor Islam: but each of these new religions seized upon the body of a civilization already in place, in each case breathing a soul into it. Each was able to draw upon a rich inheritance – a past, a living present, and – already – a future.

Islam as a successor civilization: the Near East in new form

As Christianity inherited from the Roman Empire of which it was a prolongation, so Islam instantly took hold of the Near East, perhaps the world's oldest crossroads of civilized humanity. The consequence was immense. Muslim civilization made its own a series of ancient geopolitical obligations, urban patterns, institutions, habits, rituals and age-old approaches to faith and to life itself.

Faith: even in its religion Islam is linked with Judaism and Christianity, with the family of Abraham, and with the Old Testament and its rigorous monotheism. For Islam, Jerusalem is a holy city, and Jesus is the greatest prophet before Muhammad, who alone surpasses Him.

Life: Islam has perpetuated, down to the present day, forms of behaviour thousands of years old. In the *Arabian Nights* stories, to salute the sovereign is 'to kiss the earth between one's hands'. This was a practice current at the court of King Chosroes I of Persia (AD 531–79) and no doubt earlier still. In the sixteenth and seventeenth centuries and later, European ambassadors at Istanbul, Isphahan and Delhi tried to avoid it because they thought it humiliating for themselves and, still more, for the princes they represented. Long before, Herodotus was indignant at Egyptian manners which he found disgusting. 'In the open street, as a salutation, they half-prostrate themselves to one another; they behave like dogs, lowering their hands to their knees.' This greeting is still practised today. Nor are these the only instances. Turkish baths or hammams are in fact a survival of ancient Roman baths, which the Arab conquests brought to Persia and elsewhere. The hand of Fatima, the Muslim equivalent of 'our medals and scapularies', already adorned Carthaginian gravestones. And Emile Félix Gautier, who reports these facts, does not hesitate to recognize traditional Muslim costume in the dress of the Babylonians, as described by Herodotus more than twenty-four centuries ago. 'The Babylonians,' wrote Herodotus, 'wear first of all a linen tunic which hangs down as far as their feet.' In Algeria, Gautier comments, this would be called a *gandura*. 'Above it they wear another tunic made of wool [a jellaba]; over that, a little white cloak [a small white burnous]; and on their heads a conical cap' – a fez or tarboosh.

It is hard to know where to draw the line when inquiring what in the Islamic countries is truly Muslim and what is not. The couscous of North Africa has even been said to be of Roman or Punic origin. And the characteristically Muslim low-built house with a patio, so frequently seen in Egypt and the Maghreb, is certainly pre-Islamic: it resembles both the porticoed Greek house and 'the African house from the earliest centuries of our era'.

These are details, but their message is clear: Muslim civilization, like Western civilization, is derivative – a civilization of the second degree, to use the terminology of Alfred Weber. It was not built on a *tabula rasa*, but on the lava of that fluid, lively and motley civilization which preceded it in the Near East.

So it was not with the preaching of Muhammad, or the first decade of dazzling Muslim conquests (632–42), that the biography of Islam began. Its real origins lie deep in the immemorial history of the Near East.

The history of the Near East

United by the Assyrians, the Near East was further welded together, for many years, by the conquests of the Persian kings Cyrus the Great, Cambyses and Darius (521–485 BC). Two centuries later, the immense structure built by the Achaemenides dynasty fell to the onslaught of the Greeks and Macedonians under Alexander the Great (336–23 BC). Their victory was even more rapid than that of the Arabs ten centuries later.

Those ten centuries, broadly speaking, were an extraordinary 'colonial' period, during which the Greeks dominated an immense ill-defined area between the Mediterranean and the Indian Ocean. As colonists, they founded cities and great ports like Antioch and Alexandria, and formed vast States – the Syria of the Seleucids and the Macedonia of the Ptolemys. Although moving among their subjects, they did not mix with them: they never lived in the countryside, which remained foreign territory. In fact, the tiny Greco-Macedonian people colonized this vast tract of Asia as Europeans later colonized Africa, imposing their language and administration and imparting some of their dynamism.

The Roman conquest also extended to Asia Minor, Syria and Egypt, continuing this colonial era. Behind the Roman façade Greek civilization lived on; and it regained its dominance when the Roman Empire fell in the fifth century and Byzantium – Greek civilization again – took its place. E. F. Gautier, living in Algeria not so long ago, was obsessed by this immense colonial adventure which history one day swept aside, leaving barely a vestige behind.

As a colony, the Near East disliked its masters. From 256 BC onwards, the vast State of the Parthian Arsacidae dynasty, then that of the Persian Sassanids (from AD 224), established themselves across Iran from the edge of the Indus to the fragile frontiers of Syria. Rome and Byzantium fought exhausting wars against this powerful, organized and bellicose neighbour – seignorial, bureaucratic, with large cavalry forces and links in the Far East with India, Mongolia and China. The bows used by the Persian knights, whose arrows could pierce Roman breastplates, were probably of Mongol origin. Inspired by 'the superior religion of Zoroaster', Persia vigorously resisted 'the intruder – hellenism'. Yet this political hostility did not prevent its welcoming, on occasion, cultural influence from the West. Greek philosophers banished by Justinian took refuge in the great capital of Ctesiphon on the Tigris; and it was through Iran that Christian heretics persecuted by Byzantium reached China, where they later enjoyed singular success.

In the troubled Near East, converted to Christianity, a prey to continual and violent religious strife, and struggling against the presence of the Greeks, the first Arab conquerors (634–42) found immediate accomplices. Syria in 634 and Egypt in 639 welcomed the new arrivals. More unexpectedly, Persia rapidly succumbed in 642. The old Empire, exhausted by its long struggle with Rome and Byzantium, defended itself ineffectively – despite its horses and elephants – or failed to defend itself at all, against the cruel raids of the Arab warriors on their camels. The Near East surrendered, abandoning itself to the invaders. The Arabs found it harder to conquer North Africa, between the middle of the seventh and the beginning of the eighth centuries; but thereafter they overran Spain very rapidly in 711.

Altogether, except for the mountains of Asia Minor, which were defended and saved by Byzantium, the Arab conquerors very quickly seized the whole of the Near East, and then pushed well beyond it towards the West.

Was the speed of their success (a) the result of surprise, favouring an attack that no one expected? (b) the natural outcome of fast, destructive raids which isolated the towns and forced them to surrender one by one? or (c) the culmination of slow changes in the Near East, which was in the process of what today would be called 'decolonization'?

All three hypotheses are no doubt valid. Yet, in the history of civilizations, such short-term explanations are not enough. Neither connivance nor lassitude on the part of the vanquished can account for so lasting a defeat. Would it not make more sense to suppose that there was some deep and ancient religious and moral affinity between the conquerors and the conquered, the result of lengthy coexistence? The new religion preached by Muhammad, in fact, was forged at the heart of the Near East, in accordance with its fundamental spiritual vocation.

Islam, in the springtime of its expansion, simply revived that ancient oriental civilization which had long been so powerful – at the very least the 'second pillar' of the edifice of which the first was Arabia itself. As a civilization, it was solidly based in extremely wealthy areas, alongside which Arabia then seemed very poor.

It was the destiny of Islam to relaunch that civilization in a different orbit, and to carry it to undreamed-of heights.

Muhammad, the Koran and Islam

The immediate origins of Islam confront us at once with a man, a book and a religion.

Muhammad's decisive achievements took place between about 610 or 612 and the date of his death in 632. Arabia at that time was fragmented by rival tribes and confederations, and wide open to foreign influence and to the colonizing efforts of Persia, of Christian Ethiopia, of Syria and of Byzantine Egypt. Without Muhammad, it would never have achieved unity and, thus strengthened, sent its marauders towards the broad frontiers in the North.

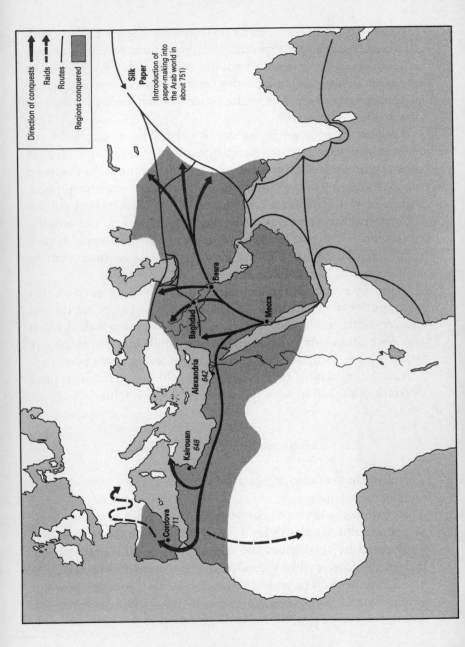

Direction of conquests
Raids
Routes
Regions conquered

Silk
Paper
(Introduction of paper-making into the Arab world in about 751)

Basra

Mecca

Baghdad

Alexandria
642

Kairouan
648

Cordova
711

3. *Arab conquests*

Neither Byzantium nor the Parthians, rivals for so many centuries, had had the least fear or intimation that a serious enemy might emerge from among such impoverished neighbours. True, they staged violent raids; but the raiders came and went. There seemed no cause for alarm, especially in the frontier areas – often a no man's land – which the Persians and Greeks quarrelled over, on the edge of the 'fertile crescent'.

With the success of Muhammad, everything changed. Scholarly research has freed his biography from some of its later embellishments; but the picture which appears once the gilt is removed is all the more attractive and moving. Born in about 570, Muhammad endured many hardships in the first forty years of his life. He emerged from obscurity only in his fortieth year, between 610 and 612. 'One night in the last ten days of Ramadan, in a cave in Mount Hira,' not far from Mecca, while he was sleeping, 'the Uncreated Word was infused into the finite world, and the Book came down into the heart of the Prophet.' In a dream, a mysterious being showed him 'a roll of fabric covered with signs, and commanded him to read it. "I cannot read," said Muhammad. "Read, read," said the Angel, wrapping the fabric round Muhammad's neck. "What am I to read?" "Read, in the name of your Lord who created man."... "The chosen one came to himself, aware that a book had come down into his heart."' (E. Dermenghem) A small detail: the word translated here as 'read' can also mean 'preach': so it remains uncertain whether or not the Prophet could read and write.

The sacred story is well known. How Muhammad, after hearing the words of the Archangel Gabriel (his mysterious visitor) considered himself an emissary of God, the last and greatest of the prophets in the biblical tradition. How, to begin with, his only supporter was his wife Khadija, while his relations, rich merchants from Mecca, were almost immediately hostile; how at that time he was full of uncertainty and on the edge of despair, madness and suicide. There is no need to retrace step by step Muhammad's 'pilgrimage' as glimpsed through the accounts of contemporaries, through the *hadits* or sayings of the Prophet, and through the *suras* or chapters of the Koran, the posthumous collection of Muhammad's revelations. The essential point is to realize the beauty, the explosive force and the 'pure music' of this 'inimitable' text (a proof of its divine origin), and of Muhammad's preaching (often preceded by trances in which he remained unconscious for a long time). The poetry is extraordinary and powerfully rhythmic: even in translation it retains much of its force. Pre-Islamic Arabia was in that sense Homeric: poetry opened its ears and its hearts.

For years, the Prophet preached only to a small group of the faithful – some relatives, some unfortunates, some of the very poor. Alongside the merchants enriched by the caravan trade between Egypt, Syria and the Gulf, Mecca also had its labourers, artisans and slaves. One such was Bilal, the black slave whose freedom was bought by Abu Bakr, the friend and future father-in-law of the Prophet. Bilal became the first Islamic *muezzin*, whose duty was to call Muslims to prayer.

The rich, for their part, were soon alarmed by Muhammad's teachings, which at first had amused and then begun to annoy them. Under threat, some of Muhammad's disciples took refuge in Christian Ethiopia, while some sixty others fled to the oasis of Yatrib, north of Mecca. Muhammad joined them there. Yatrib became Medina, the City of the Prophet, and his flight or *hegira* marked the starting-point of the Islamic calendar (16 July 622). A minute detail may be noted in passing: Medina seems to have acquired its name before the actual *hegira*.

At that time, three-quarters of its inhabitants were peasants, with two rival Arab tribes and a number of Jews, most of whom were merchants. Muhammad's policy *vis-à-vis* the Jews, originally friendly, grew defiant and finally hostile. Islamic prayers, previously offered in the direction of Jerusalem, were now turned towards Mecca. All this took place against a background of continual strife: in order to live, the fugitive Muslims raided their neighbours and plundered the long Mecca caravan routes. Ten years fighting at last enabled the Prophet to return in triumph to

Mecca, having shown singular decisiveness, prudence and patience in the face of appalling difficulties.

A revealed religion, gradually formed from the chapters of the future Koran, and from the words and deeds of the Prophet, Islam (submission to God) is a faith of exemplary simplicity. Its 'five pillars' are: the proclamation of a single God, Allah, with Muhammad as His emissary – that is the *chahada*; prayer five times a day; fasting during the twenty-nine or thirty days of Ramadan; alms for the poor; and pilgrimage to Mecca. The *jihad* or holy war was not one of these fundamental rules, but it became highly important later.

Islam's religious symbolism presents no mysteries, although a number of points in it are controversial, opening the way to various complicated interpretations of its mysticism. From this point of view, Islamic theology resembles Christianity: both involve potentially difficult spiritual paths.

As regards prayer, the Prophet was inspired by Christian and Jewish practices. In respect of pilgrimage, however, he remained faithful to Arab and Meccan traditions. He preserved, in fact, the customs of earlier, interlinked pilgrimages – to the Kaaba in Mecca and to Mt Arafat near the city, perhaps an ancient spring feast and an ancient autumn festival, the former analogous to the Feast of the Tabernacles in the Old Testament. These age-old rites, whose deepest meaning was in any case lost in the mists of time, were transposed into a new form. 'Muhammad annexed the old institution, justifying it *a posteriori* by means of a cultural legend. He claimed that Abraham, with his son Ishmael, the ancestor of the Arabs, had in his day organized the cult of the Holy Kaaba and its attendant pilgrimages. Thus Islam acquired priority over Judaism, founded by Moses, and over Christianity, identified with Jesus.' Is it adequate to explain the invocation of Abraham as political calculation, the mere desire to assert the priority of Islam? Do religions not have their own religious logic, their own truths? This is what Youakim Moubarac argues in *Abraham in the Koran* (1958). And for Louis Massignon, 'Islam reveres in Abraham the first of the Muslims – which is true, *theologically true*.'

The essential point is to realize how much religious beliefs and practices matter in the life of Muslims, imposing their own strict discipline. Everything, including the law, derives from the Koran. Religious practice remains far more alive in Islam today than in the Christian countries. 'For 1360 years,' wrote Louis Massignon in 1955, '150,000 people from every country have made an annual pilgrimage to Arafat.' There are as many such pilgrims from a typical village in Egypt as there are Easter church-goers in a typical village in France. The advantage is clearly with Islam. But does this necessarily imply more intense faith? Christianity has had to undergo internal ordeals, often due to the civilization it brings with it. Most of these Islam has so far been spared. Is that not because it is still based, for the most part, in ancient, archaic societies where religious rites continue unchanged, like other forms of social behaviour, and like the rest of life itself?

Arabia: the problem of a barely urbanized culture

What precise role did the huge Arabian Peninsula play in the success of Muhammad and the expansion of Islam? The answer is by no means simple.

Towns were of prime importance in Islam: Muhammad lived and worked in the urban world of Mecca, in the margin of an Arabia that remained primitive. Mecca's prosperity at that time was still recent, born of its caravan links with distant, foreign cities, and confined to large-scale trade and the emerging capitalism of the Meccan merchants. It was in Syrian towns, no doubt, rather than in Arabia itself, that Muhammad first encountered Jewish and Christian circles in the days before his revelation, when he was still a convoy courier. At all events, his commandments presuppose an urban background: the call of the *muezzin*, collective prayers on Fridays, the veil for women, the dignity required of the faithful and their *imams* or prayer leaders – all these imply witnesses, crowds and the press of an urban throng.

'These strict and prudish ideals were those of the austere Hejaz merchants. There too Islam sought the decorum of the cities rather than the disorder of the fields.' (X. de Planhol) It is against this background that some of the Prophet's *hadits* must be understood. 'What I fear for my people is milk in which the devil lurks between the froth and the cream. They will eagerly drink it and return to the desert, *leaving the centres of communal prayer.*' (Our emphasis.) Another remark attributed to the Prophet concerns his seeing a ploughshare: 'That never enters the house of the faithful but it brings with it degradation.' In a word, as the Koran itself declares: 'The Arabs of the desert are the most hardened in their impurity and hypocrisy.' The centres of faith, in those early days of Islam, were therefore in the towns, in a way that recalls the beginnings of the Christian church in the West. At that time, the infidel was the pagan, the *paganus* – the peasant. True, the Arabian bedouin were unusual 'peasants'. It was still possible to encounter them, at the beginning of the twentieth century, living as they always had. It may still be possible, sometimes, in the heart of Arabia today.

An expert on Islam, Robert Montagne (1893–1954) wrote a very fine book on this *Civilization of the Desert* – a civilization which any ethnographer would undoubtedly call a culture.

It had virtually no towns, in fact; and those it had were very primitive indeed. Yatrib, at the time of the *hegira*, was not even a match for Thebes, in Boeotia, at the time of Epaminondas. Around these 'towns', in valleys with a minimum of water, there were a few settled peasants, serfs bound to the soil, but in very small numbers. The majority of Arabs were nomads, 'like swarms of bees', forming very small social groups – patriarchal families, sub-clans, clans, tribes and confederations of tribes. These labels, invented by those studying Arabian society, are based purely on number: a clan implies 100 to 300 tents, and a tribe – the biggest unit with any cohesion – means 3,000 people. On that scale it was possible to maintain, or at least to believe in, the blood relationship, which was the only link the Bedouin recognized. The tribe was the great fighting unit, comprising brothers, cousins and clients. The confederation, on the other hand, was only a fragile union whose members were scattered over vast distances.

The very hard life lived by the bedouin in the deserts and semi-deserts of Arabia was made possibly only by camel-breeding. Frugal and resistant to thirst, camels made possible long journeys from one pasture to the next. On plundering raids or *rezzous*, they carried fodder, leathern water-bottles and grain. The horses, spared until the last moment, were used in the final attacking charge.

Nomadic daily life followed the vanishing grass. With their pack-camels and their white racing she-camels, the bedouin travelled as much as a thousand kilometres from North to South and vice versa. In the North, on the edge of the fertile crescent between Syria and Mesopotamia, nomadic habits were weakened by contact with settled peasants. As well as camels, sheep were bred; and their travelling range was very limited. Once the Bedouin became sheep-farmers, they were no more than *chaouya* or shepherds – only one step above the despised lowest category, the breeders of oxen or buffaloes, firmly tied to one place.

In central and southern Arabia, camel-breeding nomads remained untainted, retaining their claims to nobility. These aristocratic tribes were continually at war: the stronger drove out the weak. The desert, teeming with more people than it could support, thereby shed its surplus population, most of which moved Westwards: Sinai and the narrow ribbon of the Nile were no barriers on the way to the Sahara and the Maghreb.

There were both geographical and historical reasons for this exodus towards the West. Geographically, the Northern deserts were cold and inhospitable after the heat of the South. The Arabs failed to conquer Asia Minor in the seventh century because their camels could not withstand the sharp cold of what are now the Anatolian plains, where the Bactrian camel was more at home. The Sahara, however, is in effect the prolongation of the Arabian Desert beyond the Red Sea. Historically, the deserts in the North and in central Asia were already occupied by nomads of their own, with two-humped camels, horses, and mounted warriors, as mobile as they were fierce. Here there were no empty spaces for easy occupation by newcomers.

Not without hesitation, bedouin Arabia supplied Islam with an exceptional fighting force. The nomads were not converted overnight: they remained combative and unpredictable. Even in Spain, at the time of the Ommayad caliphs, old quarrels between parties from Yemen and from Qais flared up again, thousands of miles from their place of origin.

When the Prophet died, moreover, the nomads who had supposedly accepted his authority rose up against Islam. The fight was long and bitter; and Muhammad's successor, caliph Omar (634–44) found no better solution to these infernal disputes than to send horsemen and cameleers on the *jihad* or holy war – thereby removing them from Arabia and transcending the quarrels between the tribes.

Thus the bedouin accomplished Islam's first conquests. They traversed huge distances, these small groups – miniature nations – with their desert convoys, their goatskin or camelskin tents, their habits and customs, their pride and their deep concern to remain pastoral people and avoid the ignoble, stifling life of settled peasants. They rained down like hailstones on those vast Western spaces which Islam was to conquer. Wherever they went, they brought their language, their folklore, their faults and their virtues. One of their greatest virtues was their passionate belief in hospitality, a shining characteristic of all Islam.

One example is the long odyssey of the Beni Hilal tribe. Having left the South of the Hejaz in the seventh century, they were in a bad way in upper Egypt in about 978, but descended on North Africa in the mid-eleventh century like a swarm of locusts. In the twelfth century, they were crushed by the Berbers at the battle of Setif in 1151, and they dispersed throughout the Maghreb. Their epic still survives in folklore today – 'from the desert of Transjordania to Biskra and Port-Etienne' in Mauritania.

Islam, soon to become so fine a civilization, owed almost all its successive victories to the power of belligerent 'cultures', primitive Arab peoples whom each time it rapidly assimilated and 'civilized'. For a century, the Arab tribes gave Islam the first of these victories. Then the rough mountain peoples of North Africa, the Berbers, helped it to conquer Spain and organize Fatimid Egypt. Finally, it used the Turko-Mongols, central Asian nomads, on and almost within its borders, whom it was able to convert. From the tenth century onwards, Turkish mercenaries formed the bulk of the armies serving the caliphs of Baghdad. They were first-rate soldiers and archers, and extraordinary horsemen.

Jahiz, the great Arab writer of the ninth century, was a little condescending towards these rough people, whom he portrayed in unforgettable terms. But once again, history repeated itself. The poor became rich, the nomads became citizens, and both set out to show that it is sometimes but a small step from servant to sovereign. Mercenaries one day, masters the next, the Seljuk Turks and then the Ottoman Turks became the new princes of Islam. 'The great lord' or 'the Grand Turk' – that was the title the West accorded to the Ottoman leader, once the capture of Constantinople in 1453 had fully confirmed Turkish power.

Perhaps it has been the destiny of Islam to attract and use the primitive peoples who surround or cross its territory, but then to fall prey to their violent power. Ultimately, order is restored and wounds are healed. The successful primitive warrior is tamed by the all-powerful urban life of Islam.

5. Geography

While the areas covered by Islam are interlinked, they vary considerably, especially in outlying regions. Islam's history, in fact, has never been untroubled. In a broader context, however, these variations have their limits. Seen in its entirety, Islam is an immense and stable system, if with different facets that need to be explained.

Islam's lands and seas

Maps tell the essential story. They show the regions held and then abandoned by Islam, each time in the face of foreign, rival civilizations: against the West in Sicily, the Iberian Peninsula, Languedoc, Southern Italy and the Western Mediterranean; against Eastern Europe and Orthodox Christianity in Crete and the Balkan Peninsula; against the Hindu world in the Indo-Gangetic Plain and in North and Central Deccan.

The areas that are still Islamic today – as they have been since the beginning, or at least for a very long time – remain immense. Not always very wealthy, they stretch from Morocco and the Atlantic Sahara as far as China and the Indian Archipelago – 'from Dakar to Jakarta', to quote the subtitle of a recent book.

In this survey we should not forget the broad high seas, once more or less thoroughly exploited, but now largely deserted by the Muslim States, except for limited coastal navigation. The sea belongs to those who sail it, and today there is almost no Muslim shipping left. It was very different in the past, in the Mediterranean, the Red Sea, the Persian Gulf, the Caspian and above all in the Indian Ocean. Arab sailing dhows, their planks secured with palm-fibre ropes and no nails, used the monsoon cycle to pursue active and large-scale trade. By the ninth century they had reached Canton. In 1498, Vasco da Gama pursued and pillaged them. But neither Portugal nor, later, Holland was able to exclude them from low-cost trade in the Indian Ocean. Only at the end of the nineteenth century were they outclassed by steamships.

So the Arabs' maritime epic was long-lived. Islam owed its ancient glory not only to its horsemen but also to its seamen. Their symbol was Sindbad the Sailor. Although Sindbad described odysseys amid the marvels, miracles and catastrophes encountered in the India Ocean, it was surely in the Mediterranean that Islam's fate as a world sea-power was decided. There, the Muslims first conquered, then fought desperately, and finally were defeated.

Islam's important conquests included not only Syria, Egypt, Persia, North Africa and Spain, but also almost the whole Mediterranean. Its victory would have been permanent if, having taken Crete in 825, it had remained there. But in 961 Byzantium recaptured that vital outpost, and held on to Rhodes and Cyprus – all commanding the sea routes that led to the Aegean.

In the East, then, Islam suffered a setback. Byzantium continued to dominate the Aegean and its countless islands, as well as, on either side of the Balkan Peninsula, both the vast Black Sea and the Adriatic, that doorway to Italy which the Venetians used to make their first, modest fortune as shippers of wood, salt and wheat for the wealthy Byzantines.

The Western Mediterranean, on the other hand, succumbed to the sea power of Egypt, North Africa and Spain – all by now flying the green flag of Islam. In 825 the Andalusians conquered Crete; between 827 and 902 the Tunisians settled in Sicily, which flourished prodigiously under their rule. It became the vital heart of the 'Saracen' Mediterranean, with Palermo its finest city, on the edge of the Conca d'Oro, that great hill-girt plain which irrigation now turned into a Garden of Eden.

The Muslims also reached various places in Corsica and Sardinia, and briefly in Provence; they threatened and insulted Rome, and landed unopposed at the mouth of the Tiber. They also occupied in force the Balearic Islands, a key port of call for Western Mediterranean trade, making possible direct rather than coastal voyages between Sicily and Spain.

So the Western Mediterranean, that highway of wealth, was dominated by Islam. This breathed life and prosperity into seaports like Palermo, Alexandria (hitherto a coastal outpost of the great metropolis of Cairo) and Tunis (ten miles from the sea, as if prudently keeping its distance). Other cities grew or recovered: Bejaia (Bougie) with its nearby forests, essential for shipbuilding; Algiers and Oran, both then still modest; the lively Spanish port of Almeria; and, on the navigable part of the Guadalquivir River, flowing into the Atlantic, the flourishing city of Seville.

Islam's ascendancy lasted more than a hundred years. True, it was soon a prey to Christian piracy: the rich always tempt pillage by the poor. And in and around the tenth century, in contrast to what later became familiar, the rich were Muslims and the pirates were Christians. Amalfi, Pisa and Genoa were all hornets' nests. The situation grew dramatic with the Norman conquest of Sicily. No less than the pirate vessels, the Normans' fast ships ran down the Muslim dhows. The occupation of Sicily, in fact, was the first breach in the 'heathen' domination of the sea.

There followed a slow strangulation, a gradual constriction whose ill-effects were soon felt throughout the 'Muslim lake'. In about 1080, at the time of the Cid Campeador, and just before the arrival of the Almoravids (who came from Sudan and North Africa in 1085 to help the Muslims in Spain), an Arab poet from Sicily hesitated to accept an invitation to Spain, despite the fifty gold dinars which he was offered by Motamid, the King of Toledo. 'Do not be surprised,' he wrote, 'to see how my hair has turned white with grief; save your surprise for the fact that my eyes' pupils are still black! The sea belongs to the Christians, and our ships sail there only at enormous risk. All that the Arabs now hold is the land.' The tables had indeed been turned.

The Crusades, which soon followed (1095–1270), enabled the Italian city–states' fleets to reconquer their home waters – as well as those held by the Byzantines. The great historical episodes (the capture of Jerusalem in 1099, the foundation of the States of the Holy Land, the Latin capture of Constantinople in 1204 after the extraordinary diversion of the Fourth Crusade) should not be allowed to disguise another major event: the conquest of the Mediterranean's maritime trade routes. When in 1291, with the fall of St John of Acre, Christianity lost its last important outpost in Asia, it nevertheless retained uncontested supremacy throughout the Mediterranean.

Islam did not react until two or three centuries later. Then, the Ottoman Turks did their best to recover naval supremacy. Their victory at Préveza in 1538 seemed to promise them domination of the Mediterranean; but their crushing defeat at the Battle of Lepanto in 1571 very soon halted their resurgence, which in any case had been purely military. Against the teeming fleets of Venice, Genoa and Florence, the Turks had been able to muster only a limited number of merchant ships, most of them Greek, and plying only between Istanbul, the Black Sea and Egypt. Later, of course, came the incessant activity of the Muslim corsairs, and the exceptional ascendancy of Algiers. Even so, Islam never again acquired a merchant fleet.

Thus, in the Mediterranean, triumphs and disasters followed one another. In the Indian Ocean, life was more peaceful – until the appearance of the Portuguese there in 1498, after they had rounded the Cape of Good Hope. From then onwards, Islam's flank was turned.

The essayist Essad Bey rightly remarked: 'Islam is the desert.' But that desert or group of deserts is surrounded on the one hand by two navigable stretches of salt water, the Mediterranean and the Indian Ocean, and on the other by three land masses fairly densely populated – the Far East, Europe and Black Africa. Above all, Islam is an 'intermediary continent' linking these vast regions.

Clearly, between the Atlantic and Northern China or the Siberian forests there are different kinds of desert: the hot deserts of the South, the home of the Arabian dromedary, are very unlike the cold deserts of the North, whose camels are the true, two-humped variety. The dividing line between them runs roughly from the Caspian to the mouth of the Indus.

Every desert, of course, has somewhere its river bank or seashore, its 'sahels' with settled peasants, its steppes and its oases where the hoe and the swing-plough can prepare the ground for crops. There are even, in these ancient civilized countries, idyllic river oases like the fertile valleys of the Nile, the Tigris, the Euphrates, the Indus, the Amou Daria and the Syr Daria, with exceptionally rich soil – though often tilled so long as to be exhausted. Given the climate, these places are vulnerable, and far too easily affected by the least human error or natural misfortune. An invasion, a long war, torrential rain or over-population – with any of these, vast farming areas are likely to be literally lost: the desert will engulf and bury towns and countryside alike.

The fate of Islam, therefore, rests on precarious foundations. Its overcrowded towns swollen by commerce, its sparse agricultural areas and its intense civilization all face constant difficulties. A present-day demographic map shows this clearly. Islam consists of a few densely populated regions, separated by vast stretches of empty space. Despite ingenious irrigation plans, despite the success of dry farming, despite the tenacity of patient, hard-working peasants, and despite the use of wonderfully well-suited trees like olives and date-palms, Islam has never enjoyed stable sufficiency, still less abundance. Any abundance has always been temporary, the fruit of a passing fashion for some luxury item, or the privilege of some especially fortunate town.

Such – at first sight paradoxically – was the case with Mecca, enormously enriched by the influx of pilgrims. There, miraculously, everything seemed possible. In 1326 Ibn Batûta, the greatest of all Arab travellers, sang the praises of Mecca's affluence: the 'delicious flavours' of its 'rich viands', the excellence of its fruits, grapes, figs, peaches, dates 'the like of which is found nowhere else in the world', and its incomparable melons. He concluded: 'Altogether, every kind of merchandise from every country can be found gathered in this town.' Elsewhere, all too often, hunger was a daily companion. 'I can enclose my hunger in the recesses of my belly,' wrote one Arab poet, 'just as an expert spinner can twist her fingers and tighten the threads in her hand.' And it was one of the Prophet's followers who said of him: 'He left this life without once having satisfied his hunger for barley bread.'

The results can easily be seen. One was the prevalence of nomadic, pastoral life, as in Arabia. With variations, this was the pattern throughout the deserts where Islam was obliged to live. The constraints were rigorous. The bedouin have often been portrayed, unsparingly, as savages, despite their noble pedigree. If they failed to understand the settled peasants, the latter returned the compliment. One Islamic expert, Jacques Berque, has tried to redress the balance: 'These bedouin, so often decried, how magnificent they are!' Yes, they were splendid specimens of the human animal. For Islam, they were allies whom it was hard to tame and lead. And yet they were useful allies. Without them, Islam would have been lost.

Condemned as they were to an austere and frugal existence, they had little chance of what today would be called 'social progress', especially since it would have required them to adopt a settled life – as indeed so many Muslim States have done today, and on a gigantic scale. For good or ill, the Ottoman Empire followed this course as early as the sixteenth century, settling its colonies of nomadic *yourouks* in both Asian and European Turkey. This closed and resolutely nomadic culture had its own inevitable logic. In the terminology of Arnold Toynbee, it was a prisoner of its own 'response'.

As a civilization that lacked manpower, Islam was obliged in the past to recruit it where it could. This shortage of people was

The most vigorous of these nomads overran Iran and threatened Baghdad. The map on p. 86 shows the magnitude of the Mongol incursion in the thirteenth century.

For centuries, nevertheless, Islam alone sent Sudanese gold and black slaves to the Mediterranean, and silk, pepper, spices and pearls to Europe from the Far East. In Asia and Africa, it controlled trade with the Levant. Only from Alexandria, Aleppo, Beirut or Syrian Tripoli did Italian merchants take over.

Islam was therefore above all a civilization based on movement and transit. This meant long sea voyages and multiple caravan routes – between the Indian Ocean and the Mediterranean, from the Black Sea to China and India, and from the Dark Continent to North Africa.

Despite the presence of elephants in the East and of horses and donkeys everywhere, these caravans consisted mainly of camels. A pack-camel could carry a load of some six hundredweight or 300 kilograms. Since a caravan might consist of five or six thousand camels, its total capacity equalled that of a very large merchant sailing-ship.

A caravan travelled like an army, with a leader, a general staff, strict rules, compulsory staging-posts, and routine precautions against marauding nomads – with whom it was prudent to come to terms. At fixed intervals along the way, equivalent to a day's march except in the heart of the desert, there were huge buildings, the caravanserais or khans, where both people and animals could find partial lodging. These in effect were stations on the caravan line. Every European traveller described their gigantic halls and tolerable comfort. Some, like the notable khans of Aleppo, still survive today.

This caravan system could not be coordinated with maritime trade except by means of an extensive semi-capitalist organization. Islam had its merchants, some of them Muslim, some not. Chance has preserved letters from the Jewish merchants in Cairo at the time of the First Crusade (1095–9). They show knowledge of every method of credit and payment, and every form of trade association (disproving the too facile belief that these were invented later by the Italians). They also bear witness to trade over long distances. Coral travelled from North Africa to India; slaves were bought in Ethiopia; iron was brought back from India at the same time as pepper and spices. All that implied large-scale movement of money, merchandise and people.

There is nothing surprising, therefore, in the extent of the Arabs' travels, although they seemed fabulous at the time. Islam itself, which was always in movement, which lived by movement, led the way. Ibn Batûta, a Moroccan born in Tangier in 1304, travelled 'round the world' between 1325 and 1349, going to Egypt, Arabia, the Lower Volga, Afghanistan, India and China. In 1352, he went to Black Africa and the banks of the Niger, where he complained that the Sudanese, although Muslim, showed too little respect for 'the Whites'. In the gold town of Sijilmassa, he was surprised to meet a compatriot from Ceuta, the brother of a certain Al-Buchri, whom he had known in China. Islam at that time abounded in wanderers of this kind, who were unfailingly welcomed, from the Atlantic to the Pacific, by Muslim hospitality, comparable to that of the Russians.

Such travels would have been unthinkable without powerful towns. These naturally flourished in Islam, and were the motors which made possible the circulation of people, money and goods. Everything passed through them: merchandise, pack-animals, people and rare acquisitions. Of these last, on their way to Europe, an incomplete list might include: exotic plants (sugar cane, cotton), silkworms, paper, a compass, Indian (so-called Arabic) numerals, perhaps gunpowder, and – as well as a certain very famous medicine – the germs of terrible epidemic illnesses from China and India, the homes of cholera and the plague.

Broadly speaking, all these towns looked alike. Their streets were narrow and generally sloping, so as to be washed automatically by the rain. A *hadit* of the Prophet's prescribed that streets should be seven cubits wide, or between ten and thirteen feet, permitting two laden asses to pass each other. But this was often impossible: houses encroached on the street despite the letter of the law, and very often had an overhanging upper floor, like medieval houses in the West. This was partly because Islam forbade multi-storey houses (except in Cairo and in Mecca and its port of Jedda): building too high was held to be a mark of reprehensible pride on the owner's part.

Given the anarchic absence of municipal administration, any serious population pressure in a town led to a proliferation of these low houses, each invading vacant space, crowding its neighbours, and creating a higgledy-piggledy effect.

A French traveller by the name of Thévenot, in 1657, was astonished to note that 'there is not a single fine street in Cairo, but a multiplicity of little twisted alleys, making it obvious that all the houses were built without any kind of plan, taking up whatever space they chose and oblivious of whether they blocked the passageway or not.' Another Frenchman, Volney, a century later in 1782, described these same narrow streets.

Since they are not paved, the masses of people, camels, asses and dogs which crowd into them kick up a disagreeable dust. Frequently, people throw water in front of their doors, and the dust gives way to mud and malodorous fumes. Contrary to normal custom in the East, the houses are two or three storeys tall, topped by a paved or loamed terrace. Most of them are built of mud or badly fired brick; the rest are made from soft stone from the nearby Mt Moqattam. All of them look like prisons, because they have no windows on to the street.

A similar picture was painted of Istanbul in the nineteenth century: 'Not only carriages but even horses can hardly pass each other. The Street of the Divan, at that time the broadest in the city, was no wider than 2.5 or 3 metres at certain points.' True as a general observation. However, eleventh-century Cairo had some houses of seven to twelve storeys; and ninth-century Samarra had a grand straight avenue several kilometres long and 50 to 100 metres wide. These, perhaps, were exceptions that proved the rule.

Narrow as it was, the street in any Muslim country was always very lively – a permanent meeting place for people who enjoyed open-air display. It was 'the essential artery, the rendezvous for story-tellers, signers, snake-charmers, mountebanks, healers, charlatans, barbers and all those professionals who are so suspect in the eyes of Islam's moralists and canon lawyers. Add to that the children and their often violent games.' And as well as the streets, the terraces were inter-communicating, although they were reserved for the women.

Such teeming disorder, however, never excluded an overall plan – especially since this was based on the very structure of the town and the life of its inhabitants. At its centre was the Great Mosque for the weekly sermon. 'To it and from it everything flows, as if it were a heart' (Jacques Berque). Nearby was the bazaar, i.e. the merchants' quarter with its streets of shops (the souk) and its caravanserais or warehouses, as well as the public baths which were established and maintained despite frequent condemnations. Artisans were grouped concentrically, starting from the Great Mosque: first, the makers and sellers of perfumes and incense, then the shops selling fabrics and rugs, the jewellers and food stores, and finally the humblest trades – curriers, cobblers, blacksmiths, potters, saddlers, dyers. Their shops marked the edges of the town.

In principle, each of these trades had its location fixed for all time. Similarly, the *maghzen* or Prince's quarter was in principle located on the outskirts of the city, well away from riots or popular revolts. Next to it, and under its protection, was the *mellah* or Jewish quarter. The mosaic was completed by a very great variety of residential districts, divided by race and religion: there were forty-five in Antioch alone. 'The town was a cluster of different quarters, all living in fear of massacre.' So Western colonists nowhere began racial segregation – although they nowhere suppressed it.

This rigidity in spite of apparent disorder was increased by the fact that towns were often confined within walls with grandiose gateways, and surrounded by huge cemeteries on which it was difficult to build. Present-day traffic problems have necessitated change – sometimes beyond all proportion. In a frenzy of street widening, Istanbul recently became an incredible building-site, with houses cut in two so that the doors of rooms open on to nothing, with a new main thoroughfare, its lateral tributaries suspended 'like glacial valleys', and with forests of pipework high in the air as a result of hasty excavation.

Broadly speaking, Muslim towns had neither the political liberties nor the sense of architectural order that Western cities strove for once they were sufficiently developed. But they did have all the elements of genuine town life: a conformist bourgeoisie, plus a mass of poorer people, indigent artisans and pickpockets, all living more or less off crumbs from rich men's tables. They enjoyed sophisticated pleasures, less constrained than elsewhere, which seemed to purists appallingly perverse. They were also bastions of education, with their schools attached to the mosques, their *medersas*, and their universities. Finally, they were a constant pole of attraction for people from the surrounding countryside, whom they tamed and domesticated as towns have always done since the very beginning. 'No one in the world has more need of punishment, for they are thieves, wastrels and felons,' wrote a citizen of Seville, thinking no doubt of the endless quarrels which broke out at the gates or even in the market-place with people from the country, come to sell animals, meat, hides, rancid butter, dwarf palm-trees, 'green grass' or chick-peas. He need not have worried: nine times out of ten, townspeople's vigilance or cunning won the day. Any robber was robbed in his turn, and without mercy, for town-dwellers in Islam, even more than in the West, had a very firm grip on the highly primitive peasantry outside the gates. Thus Damascus controlled the peasants near the Ghouta and the mountain people of Jebel ed Druze; Algiers controlled the corsairs and the peasants of the Fahs, the Mitija and the Kabyle Mountains. Similarly, the silk-wearing bourgeoisie of Granada contrasted with the poor, cotton-clad peasants from the mountains nearby.

Once again, however, these are the characteristics of all towns,

Muslim and Western alike. What distinguished the Muslim towns, essentially, were their early growth and their exceptional size.

The importance of towns in Islam is not surprising: they were of the essence of its civilization. Towns, roads, ships, caravans and pilgrimages were all part of a single whole, all, as Louis Massignon has aptly said, elements of *movement*, all 'lines of force' in Muslim life.

6. The Greatness and Decline of Islam

Islam's splendid apogee was between the eighth and the twelfth centuries AD. Everyone agrees about that. But when did its decadence begin? Its decisive decline is often said to have dated from the thirteenth century. That, however, confuses two very different things: the end of an ascendancy and the end of a civilization.

In the thirteenth century, Islam clearly lost its position of leadership. But its really dangerous decline hardly began until the eighteenth century, which in the long life of civilizations is a very short time ago. It shared the fate of many nations that are now called 'under-developed' because they missed the Industrial Revolution – the first revolution whereby the world could advance at the dizzy speed of machines. This failure did not kill Islam as a civilization. All that happened was that Europe gained two centuries of rapid material progress, leaving Islam behind.

No Muslim civilization before the eighth or ninth century

Islam became a political entity in the few years it took the Arabs to conquer an empire. But Islamic civilization was born of the union between that empire and the ancient civilizations whose territory it touched. This took a long time and many generations. To begin with, the conquering Arabs scarcely sought to convert their new subjects: quite the reverse. They contented themselves with exploiting the rich civilizations they had vanquished: Persia, Syria, Egypt, Africa (Roman Africa, which the Arabs called Ifriqya, broadly present-day Tunisia) and Spain (or Andalusia, el-Andalous). Any Christians who tried to convert to Islam were whipped. Since only non-Muslims paid taxes, why should the conquerors allow their revenue to be thus reduced? 'The population of the occupied countries maintained their own way of life without being molested, but . . . were treated like superior cattle, to be taken care of because they paid most of the taxes' (Gaston Wiet).

Such was the situation under the first four successors of Muhammad, the 'well directed caliphs' (632–60). (The word caliph or *kalifa* can be rendered as 'successor', 'lieutenant', or 'deputy ruler', as the translator prefers.) It continued under the Omayyad caliphs (660–750) who established their capital in Damascus. During these years of continual warfare, religious questions were seldom if ever brought to the fore. The struggle with Byzantium, for example, was political rather than religious.

What was more, the administration of the occupied territories remained in the hands of the 'natives', and documents continued to be written either in Greek or in Pahlavi (Sassanian Persian). Art and architecture, too, remained hellenistic in inspiration, even when it came to building mosques. Their central courts, colonnades, arcades and cupolas followed the Byzantine model. Only the minaret, designed for the muezzin's call to prayer, was truly Islamic, although it too resembled the Christian bell-tower. In this first phase of conquest, the Arabs created an Empire and a State, but not yet a civilization.

Only towards the middle of the eighth century did decisive changes come about – a vast political, social and eventually intellectual upheaval, when the caliphate passed to the Abbasid dynasty, and their black flag replaced the white flag of the Omayyads.

Then it was that the Muslim world turned back towards the East and withdrew a little from the Mediterranean, which had previously absorbed so much of its attention. Under the new caliphs the capital of Islam in effect shifted from Damascus to Baghdad, causing great discontent among those who saw their influence thus diminished, as well as among client or conquered peoples. It was the end of the reign of the 'thoroughbred' Arabs, which had lasted at most for a century – three or four brilliant generations – during which their higher caste of warriors had sunk into the delights of wealth and luxury, otherwise known as civilization, which Ibn Khaldun, an Arab nobleman from Andalusia, later described as 'evil personified'.

Then, quite naturally, the old civilized countries reasserted their supremacy, at a time of rapidly growing material prosperity on every side. In about 820 the caliph's annual revenue was perhaps five times that of the Byzantine Empire. Huge fortunes were made under a capitalist trading system, well ahead of its time, that extended as far as China and India, the Persian Gulf, Ethiopia, the Red Sea, Ifriqya and Andalusia.

'Capitalist' is not too anachronistic a word. From one end of Islam's world connections to the other, speculators unstintingly gambled on trade. One Arab author, Hariri, had a merchant declare: 'I want to send Persian saffron to China, where I hear that it fetches a high price, and then ship Chinese porcelain to Greece, Greek brocade to India, Indian iron to Aleppo, Aleppo glass to the Yemen and Yemeni striped material to Persia . . .' In Basra, settlements between merchants were made by what we should now call a clearing system.

Trade meant towns. Enormous cities were built as its headquarters. They included not only Baghdad, which from 762 until its brutal destruction by the Mongols in 1258 was a real 'city of light', the largest and richest capital in the Old World, but also – not far away on the Tigris – huge Samarra, as well as the great port of Basra, Cairo, Damascus, Tunis (a reincarnation of Carthage) and Cordoba.

Starting from the words of the Koran and of traditional poetry, all these cities made or virtually remade so-called 'classical' Arabic – a learned, artificial, literary language which became the idiom common to all Islamic countries, as Latin was to their Christian counterparts. By contrast with it, the forms of Arabic spoken in the different countries, and even Arabian Arabic itself, came more and more to seem like dialects. Classical Arabic was not only a language: it was also a literature, a philosophy, a fervent universal faith and a civilization, evolving in Baghdad and from there spreading far and wide.

The result, even before the Abbasids, was a serious crisis in the recruitment of public officials. In 700, the Omayyad caliph Abd'-el-Malik summoned the future monk Joannes Damascenus (655–749), who was then his adviser, and told him that he had decided henceforth to ban the Greek language from all public administrative documents. 'This,' wrote the Arab historian Baladhori, 'greatly displeased Sargoun [i.e. Sergius, Joannes Damascenus's other name], and when he left the Caliph he was very sad. Meeting some Greek officials, he told them: "You had better seek another profession to earn your living: your present employment has been withdrawn by God."'

It was the end of a long *modus vivendi* by which Christians and Muslims had lived in mutual tolerance. A completely new era was beginning.

Linguistic unity in the Arab world, in fact, had created an essential tool for intellectual exchanges, for business, for government and for administration. The Jewish merchants' letters mentioned earlier were written in Arabic, although using the Hebrew alphabet. Culture gained immense advantage from this linguistic asset. The son of the famous Haroun al-Rashid, Mâmûn (813–33), had large numbers of foreign and especially Greek works translated into Arabic. Knowledge of them spread all the more rapidly in so far as Islam very soon began using paper, which was so much cheaper than parchment. In Cordoba the Caliph El-Hakam II (961–76) was said to have a library of 400,000 manuscripts, with forty-four volumes of catalogues. Even if these figures are exaggerated, it is worth noting that the library of Charles V of France ('Charles the Wise', son of 'John the Good') contained only 900.

These crucial centuries saw the internal transformation of Islam. The religion of Muhammad was complicated by Byzantine-style exegesis, and supplemented by a form of mysticism that many specialists see as a resurgence of neo-Platonism. Even the driving-force of the Shi'ite schism seems to have come in part from depths outside the scope of early Arabic Islam. The Shi'ites venerated the pious Caliph Ali, assassinated by the Omayyds, and they opposed the Sunni Muslims who represented the majority and the mainstream of Islam. One of their places of pilgrimage, Karbala in Iraq, still attracts thousands of the faithful. 'Ali seemed like a second Christ, and his mother Fatima like a second Virgin Mary. The death of Ali and his sons was recounted like a Passion' (E. F. Gautier).

Even at the heart of its religion, therefore, Islam renewed itself by borrowing from ancient Eastern and Mediterranean civilizations, now rejuvenated and recruited for a common spiritual and temporal task with the help of a common language. Arabia had been only an episode. From one point of view, indeed, Muslim civilization began only when multitudes of non-Arabic peoples were converted to Islam, and when Islamic schools spread throughout the '*Umma*' or community of the faithful, from the Atlantic to the Pamirs. Once again, old wine was poured into new bottles.

The golden age of Islam: eighth to twelfth centuries

For four or five centuries, Islam was the most brilliant civilization in the Old World. That golden age lasted, broadly speaking, from the reign of Mâmûn, the creator of the House of Science in Baghdad (at once a library, a translation centre and an astronomical observatory), to the death of Averroës, the last of the great Muslim philosophers, which took place at Marrakesh in 1198, when he was just over seventy-two years old. But the history of the arts and of ideas is not the only key to the time of Islam's greatness.

Léon Gautier, an historian of Muslim philosophy, has pointed out that those periods when Islamic thought most flourished were

times of peace and general prosperity, when good fortune afforded the protection of an enlightened and all-powerful caliph. Such, in the East, in the eighth and ninth centuries, were the Abbasid caliphs who, from Al-Mansur to El-Mutawakkil, unceasingly encouraged for nearly a century the spread of Greek science and philosophy in the Muslim world, thanks to a vast effort of translation made by Nestorian Christians . . . Such also, in the West in the twelfth century, were the Almohad caliphs, who had the habit of holding long, speculative talks alone with their favourite doctor or philosopher. Other favourable periods were those when, on the contrary, the decadence of the Empire enabled bold thinkers to choose from among competing minor potentates a benevolent patron such as Sayf al-Dawla, Emir of Aleppo in the first half of the ninth century and protector of the philosopher Al-Farabi.

Léon Gautier, clearly, sees the problem in terms of political history. For him, civilization depends on princes and 'enlightened despots'. Yet the rapid decline of the Baghdad caliphate after a series of misfortunes, which led to unprecedented political fragmentation, by no means hindered the development of philosophy. On the contrary, it made possible a degree of intellectual freedom, if only by enabling a scholar to flee from one State or one princely protector to another nearby. This was a regular feature of Renaissance Italy and of seventeenth- and eighteenth-century Europe. Islam often enjoyed the same opportunity.

But intellectual advantages are never enough by themselves. Important material advantages both sustain and explain them.

By about AD 750, Islam had largely attained its greatest geographical extent. Further expansion was blocked by counter-attacks from outside. Constantinople, besieged in 718, was saved by the courage of the Emperor Leo III, the Isaurian, and by Greek fire; Gaul and the West were saved by Charles Martel's victory at the Battle of Tours or Poitiers in 732 or 733, and by the simultaneous uprising in the Maghreb. The result was some slight degree of stability on the frontiers of Islam, while within it, throughout the Empire, a vast economic system took root, grew and bore fruit.

This growth involved the establishment of a market economy, a money economy and a progressive 'commercialization' of agricultural goods, not all of which were consumed on the spot, the surpluses being sold in the towns and adding to their general prosperity. The date trade mobilized every year more than 100,000 pack-camels. Market halls in the towns acquired names like the 'melon house'. Melons from Merv in Transoxiana were particularly prized. In dried form they were shipped westwards in large quantities and over long distances; as fresh fruit they were sent to Baghdad by special relay stages, in leather containers packed with ice. The cultivation of sugar-cane, likewise, became an industry. Also to be noted when considering foodstuffs was the development of flour-milling. There were water-mills near Baghdad, for instance, and windmills by 947 at Seistan, while at Basra the flow of the Tigris was used to turn the wheels of floating mills.

This enterprising economy explains the development of numerous industries – iron, wood and textiles (linen, silk, cotton and wool) – as well as the enormous spread of cotton-fields in the East. Carpets from Bokhara, Armenia and Persia were already famous. Basra imported vast quantities of kermes and indigo to dye textiles red and blue. Indian indigo, which came via Kabul, was reputed to be finer than that from Upper Egypt.

All this activity had countless repercussions. The money economy shook the foundations of a society composed mainly of lords and peasants. The rich became richer, and arrogant; the poor became poorer still. The growth of irrigation techniques increased the demand for peasant slaves; and Islam's wealth enabled it to pay five or six times as much for them as any of its competitors. Social tension was the inevitable result.

Islamic prosperity was not the only factor: but it explained a great deal. In particular, it helped to foster a revolutionary climate and an uninterrupted series of urban and agrarian disturbances, often linked with nationalist movements like those that broke out in Iran. Literature from the period too easily suggests modern expressions and concepts: nationalism, capitalism, the class struggle. Take a pamphlet by Al-Ifriki, written in about the year 1000. 'No, assuredly I shall not pray to God, so long as I remain poor. Leave praying to the Sheik, the commander of armies, with his cellars full to bursting. Why should I pray? Am I powerful? Do I have a palace, horses, fine clothes, or a golden belt? To pray would be sheer hypocrisy when I don't even own the meanest plot of land.'

Since all things are interconnected, the Islamic heresies that proliferated during these hectic centuries all had, like Europe's medieval heresies, social and political roots. A dissident group appears, develops and takes different shapes under encouragement or persecution. The history of Muslim thought is intimately linked with that of such volatile cabals.

One historian, A. Mez, has used the ambiguous word 'Renaissance' to describe Islam's golden age. This suggests that its brilliance can be compared only with that of the astonishing Italian Renaissance. The comparison has in any case the advantage of stressing the fact that intellectual and material wealth were both involved in Islamic civilization, as they were in fifteenth-century Italy. Both, in fact, were based on urban societies enjoying the benefits of trade and riches. Both were the product of small, brilliant circles of exceptional people who drew deeply on the ancient civilization which they revered and revived, and who lived centuries ahead of their contemporaries. Both, however, were under external threat from barbarians more or less thinly disguised.

For Italy at the end of the fifteenth century, the barbarians were the mountain-dwellers of the Swiss cantons, the Germans to the north of the Brenner Pass, the French, the soft-shod Spaniards or the Turks (who captured Otranto in 1480). For the Islam of Avicenna or Averroës, the barbarians were the Seljuk Turks, the Berbers, the Saharan nomads or the Western Crusaders. Frequently barbarians were sought after, invited – as happened later in Italy. From the earliest days of the Baghdad Caliphate, as we have seen, there was a demand for Turkish slaves and mercenaries. These slaves were offered to buyers by their own parents, 'to secure their future'. In Spain for a very long time a few gold coins were enough to buy off Christian invaders from the North and send them back home. Then, one fine day, the battle became serious. The King of Seville, Al-Mutamid, now had to protect himself from the Christian barbarians by asking for help from other barbarians, the Almoravids of North Africa.

Paradoxical as it may seem, Islamic civilization as a whole, between 813 and 1198, was both one and many, universal and regionally diverse. First, its unity. Everywhere Islam built mosques and *medersas* whose decoration was deliberately and uniformly 'abstract'. All took the same form: a central courtyard, arcades, a basin for ritual washing, a *mihrab* or niche to show the direction for prayer, a *minbar* or pulpit in the pillared nave, and a minaret. All used the same architectural repertoire: columns with capitals, different-shaped arches (splayed, Moorish, trefoiled, multilobular, ogival, stalactitic), ribbed cupolas, mosaics, ceramics and finally the evocative calligraphic art of the arabesques.

Everywhere, likewise, Islam produced poetry on the same principles and with the same favourite phrases. It celebrated God ('the flawless rose is God'), nature, love, bravery, noble blood, the horse, the camel ('as massive as a mountain . . . Its beaten track forms a girdle round the earth'), knowledge, the forbidden pleasures of wine, and flowers of every kind. The whole Islamic world also shared the same folktales, originally from India, which we know today as *The Arabian Nights*, collected in writing in the fourteenth century after long gestation by word of mouth.

Everywhere Islamic philosophy (*falsafa*) took over that of Aristotle and the Peripatetics: it made immense efforts to place God in a cosmos which, following the Greeks, it regarded as eternal and hence excluding any notion of the Creation.

Everywhere there were the same techniques, industries, industrial objects and furniture, as can be seen from excavations like those of Madînat al-Sahra, near Cordoba. Everywhere, too, there were the same fashions, copying the tastes of Baghdad. Spain was the final destination of such cultural imports from the East, and their gradual impact can be traced across the country: the growing fashion for masquerading under surnames borrowed from famous Eastern poets, the general adoption of the burnous after the arrival of the Almoravids, the vogue for certain literary themes or certain medical prescriptions and so on.

Everywhere from Persia to Andalusia wandering entertainers performed. They came mostly from Egypt; but there were also girl dancers and singers, trained in Medina or Baghdad, and wearing yellow in the East and red in the West. All the poets spoke of them. Everywhere, finally, Muslims played chess and the very popular *kurâg*, using wooden carved figures of barded horses. It was an absorbing game: 'The Captain of Al-Mutamid, Ibn Martin, was surprised in his dwelling at Cordoba by a detachment of enemy soldiers while he was playing *kurâg*.'

Two further examples show the cohesion of Islam. One is that of a vizier, the regent of Khorassan in Persia at the beginning of the tenth century, 'sending missions to all countries to ask for copies of the customs of all the Courts and all the ministeries, in the Greek empire, in Turkestan, in China, in Iraq, in Syria, in Egypt, in Zenjan, Zabol and Kabul . . . He studied them carefully and selected those he judged best' to enforce on the court and administration of Bokhara. The other example, more strictly within the limits of the Muslim world, is that of Hakam II, the Caliph of Cordoba, who bought books written in Persia, Syria and elsewhere as soon as they appeared, and 'sent a thousand dinars in pure gold to Abulfaraj al-Isfahani to obtain the first copy of his famous anthology' (Renan).

But this cultural unity did not destroy clear and lively regional characteristics. In the tenth century when the Muslim empire split, each region recovered something of its independence, with room to breathe and reaffirm its own particular character, which it had always jealously preserved despite its borrowings from and contributions to Islam as a whole. A new geographical pattern began to take shape.

Muslim Spain, responding and adapting to successive outside influences, gradually acquired its own Spanish character – one of its many incarnations in the course of history.

Iran asserted its individuality still more strongly and vigorously. With the Baghdad Caliphate it recovered its energy and its own style. Baghdad was an Iranian city. The Abbasid period saw the great success of enamelled terracotta, whose homeland was Persia, and of another of its treasures, pottery with a metallic glaze. Persia's *iwâns* or huge porches recalled the palaces of Chosroës. The Arabic language remained dominant, but Persian – written in Arabic script – became a second great literary language, and spread very far afield, especially towards India (and, much later, throughout the Ottoman Empire). Half demotic, it had the advantage of reaching a broad public; and it also gained from the almost complete eclipse of Greek. At the end of the tenth century the poet Fidawsi wrote *The Book of the Kings* in praise of the ancient Iranians. From the eleventh century onwards Persian was increasingly used for books on popular science.

Persia was certainly a national civilization with its own power-fully individual character – but from now on *within* the vast civilization of Islam. The great exhibition of Iranian art in Paris in 1961 was illuminating in this respect. It showed how profoundly the pre-Islamic and Islamic periods differed, yet revealed continuity between them nevertheless.

This polarity between universality and regionalism existed throughout Islam. Extreme cases were Muslim India, Muslim Indonesia and Black Africa, deeply penetrated by Islam but still overwhelmingly itself.

In India the interaction of two civilizations gave rise to genuinely Indo-Islamic art, whose apogee came in the twelfth and especially the thirteenth century. In Delhi, in particular, amazing examples of it still remain. Their strangeness is explained by their eclecticism. For example the great mosque in the city, which dates from 1193, was designed by Muslims and then built by Indian masons and sculptors, who mixed Indian-style floral scrolls with Arab calligraphic decoration. In this fashion a whole new art evolved, sometimes predominantly Muslim, sometimes mainly Hindu, according to the time and the place. Eventually, by the eighteenth century each strain had so much affected the other that it became impossible to tell them apart.

At its higher levels the golden age of Muslim civilization was both an immense scientific success and an exceptional revival of ancient philosophy. These were not its only triumphs; literature was another: but they eclipse the rest.

Science and philosophy

First, science: it was here that the Saracens (as they were sometimes called at that time) made the most original contributions. These, in brief, were nothing less than trigonometry and algebra (with its significantly Arab name). In trigonometry the Muslims invented the sine and the tangent. The Greeks had measured an angle only from the chord of the arc it subtended: the sine was half the chord. The Chosranian (the adopted name of Mohammed Ibn-Musa) published in 820 an algebraic treatise which went as far as quadratic equations: translated into Latin in the sixteenth century, it became a primer for the West. Later, Muslim mathematicians resolved biquadratic equations.

Equally distinguished were Islam's mathematical geographers, its astronomical observatories and instruments (in particular, the astrolabe) and its excellent if still imperfect measurements of latitude and longitude, correcting the flagrant errors made by Ptolemy. The Muslims also deserve high marks for optics, for chemistry (the distillation of alcohol, the manufacture of elixirs and of sulphuric acid) and for pharmacy. More than half the remedies and healing aids used by the West came from Islam, including senna, rhubarb, tamarind, nux vomica, kermes, camphor, syrups, juleps, plasters, pomades, unguents and distilled water. Muslim medical skill was incontestable. The Egyptian Ibn al-Nafis – although his findings remained unused – discovered the pulmonary circulation of the blood three centuries before Michael Servetus and long before the later discoveries of William Harvey.

In the field of philosophy, what took place was rediscovery – a return, essentially, to the themes of peripatetic philosophy. The scope of this rediscovery, however, was not limited to copying and handing on, valuable as that undoubtedly was. It also involved continuing, elucidating and creating. The philosophy of Aristotle, transplanted into the Muslim world, inevitably looked like a dangerous explanation of the world and of humanity, confronting as it did a revealed religion, Islam, which was also a general explanation of the world, and an extremely rigorous one. But Aristotle obsessed and conquered all the *falasifat* (i.e. practitioners of *falsafa*, or Greek philosophy). There, again, A. Mez's comparison with the Renaissance makes sense: there was indeed such a thing as Muslim humanism, valuable and varied, which can only be summarized here.

It involved a long succession of thinkers at different times and places. Of these, five names stand out: Al-Kindi, Al-Farabi, Avicenna, Al-Gazali and Averroës. Avicenna and Averroës are the best-known, and the latter was the more important, owing to the immense repercussions of what was called Averroism in medieval Europe.

Al-Kindi (we know only the date of his death in 873) was born in Mesopotamia, where his father was Governor in Kûffah. Because of his birthplace, he was known as 'the philosopher of the Arabs'. Al-Farabi, born in 870, was of Turkish origin. He lived in Aleppo and died in 950 in Damascus, where he had gone with his patron Sayf al-Dawla when the city was captured. He was known as 'the second Master' – the first being Aristotle. Avicenna (properly, Ibn-Sina) was born at Afshena, near Bokhara, in 980; he died at Hamadan in 1037. Al-Gazali, born in Tūs in Persia, died there in 1111; towards the end of his life he became something of an anti-philosopher, a passionate spokesman for traditional religion. Averroës, whose real name was Ibn-Rushd, was born at Cordoba in 1126 and died at Marrakesh on 10 November 1198.

These dates and place-names show that Muslim humanism was widespread and long-lived throughout Islam – all the more so in that each of these leading figures was surrounded by colleagues, students and devoted readers.

The list also shows that the last major Muslim philosopher flourished in Spain – the last, but not the greatest, although it was he who acquainted the West with Arab philosophy and with Aristotle himself.

In this long perspective, the real question is that which Louis Gardet has put very forcefully (and, incidentally, answered in the negative): was there a truly Muslim philosophy? Which means: was there a single philosophical tradition, running from Al-Kindi to Averroës? Was such philosophy a function of the atmosphere of Islam? Was it original? As is often the case, the cautious countryman's answer 'Yes and no' is not only prudent here, but indispensable.

Yes, there was one philosophical tradition. Trapped between Greek thought on one side and the revealed truth of the Koran on the other, it was tossed to and fro between them. It owed to Greece, and to Islam's scientific bent, its clear but not exclusive rationalism. All the philosophers in question were what we should call scientists, concerned with astronomy, chemistry, mathematics and – always – medicine. Medicine it was that often won them the favour of princes and enabled them to earn a living. Avicenna wrote a medical *Canon*, or encyclopaedia. Averroës did likewise; and in Europe Muslim medecine was for a long time the *nec plus ultra*, even as late as the comedies of Molière.

Greek influence gave Muslim philosophy internal cohesion. 'The author of this book is Aristotle,' wrote Averroës in his preface to the *Physics*. 'He was the son of Nicomachus and the wisest of the Greeks. He founded and completed logic, physics and metaphysics. I say that he founded them, because none of the works written on these subjects before him is worth discussing ... None of those who have followed him until now, that is, over some 1,500 years, has been able to add anything to his works, or find in them any significant error.' As admirers of Aristotle the Arab philosophers were forced into an interminable debate between prophetic revelation, that of the Koran, and a human philosophical explanation, that of the Greeks. The agonizing dispute between revelation and explanation required mutual concessions by both reason and faith.

Faith, revealed through Muhammad, had imparted to humanity a divine message. Could the thinker, unaided, discover the truth of the world and set his own reason in judgement over the value of dogma? In the face of this dilemma all our philosophers revealed great, perhaps excessive, dialectical skill. Avicenna, says Maxim Rodinson, 'was not a genius for nothing: he found a solution.' His solution, which was not his alone, ran roughly as follows: the prophets had revealed higher truths 'in the form of fables, symbols, allegories and images or metaphors'. Theirs was a language for the mass of the people, aimed at keeping them happy. The philosopher, by contrast, has the right to go far beyond such language. He insists on very great freedom to choose, even when there is stark and utter contradiction between the rival approaches.

For example the philosophers normally believed like the Greeks that the world was eternal. But if it had always existed, how could it have been created at a certain time, as revelation maintained? Pushing his logic to the limit, Al-Farabi declared that God could not know particular objects or beings, but only concepts or 'universals' – whereas the God of the Koran, like God in the Old Testament, 'knows all that is on land or in the sea. No leaf falls without His knowledge. No seed in the darkness of the earth, no green shoot nor dried twig exists that has not been recorded and written.' There were other contradictions. Al-Farabi did not believe in the immortality of the soul. Avicenna did: but he did not believe in the resurrection of the body, affirmed by the Koran. After death, he thought, the soul returned to its own universe, that of disembodied beings. Logically therefore there could be no individual reward or punishment, no paradise and no Hell. God, disembodied beings and souls are the ideal world, in face of which matter is incorruptible and eternal – because 'movement did not precede stillness, nor stillness movement . . . All movement is caused by previous movement . . . God has no reason to be new.'

These quotations, borrowed from Ernest Renan, may arouse curiosity, but they fall short of satisfying it. Close attention and hard work would be needed to follow the dubious logic of such explanations.

Those philosophers who since Renan have taken an interest in these now distant dilemmas have not found it easy to resolve them. Their interpretations depend on their own cast of mind, rationalist or idealist – or, which amounts to the same thing, their preference for one philosopher or another. Al-Kindi sailed on religious waters that raised no storms; Avicenna was undeniably idealistic; Averroës was a philosopher for the end of the world. Al-Gazali, the defender of the faith, made his own the stubborn dogma of early Muslim theologians: he sought to ignore or even to destroy peripatetic philosophy, for his own thought led him into very different, mystical paths. He renounced the world to take up the white woollen mantle or *sûf* worn by the sufi, adherents of mystical faith rather than rational theology. They were known as 'God's fools'.

Averroës, the Cordoba physician, became the faithful editor of and commentator on the works of Aristotle. The advantage of his work was that it gave both the full Arabic translation of the Greek text and a dissertation on it, consisting of remarks and digressions. The text and commentary were translated from Arabic into Latin in Toledo, and thereby reached Europe, where they sparked off the great philosophical revolution of the thirteenth century. So Muslim philosophy, despite what is sometimes said, did not die an immediate death under the powerful, desperate blows of Al-Gazali. In the end, however, it did die, together with Muslim science, before the end of the twelfth century. Then it was that the West took up the torch.

Stagnation or decadence: twelfth to eighteenth centuries

In the twelfth century, after quite extraordinary triumphs, 'Saracen' civilization was suddenly checked. Even in Spain scientific, philosophical and material progress barely continued after the last decades of the century. The suddenness of this change poses a number of questions.

Was it caused, as used to be argued, by the passionate and all too effective onslaughts made by Al-Gazali against philosophy and free thought? No one can take that theory very seriously. Al-Gazali was a product of his time – a symptom as much as a cause. Besides, philosophy had always had its detractors from its earliest days, as can be seen from the countless times when books were ordered to be burned – a proceeding unthinkable unless there was violent public hostility. Equally, many philosophers were publicly disgraced and condemned to exile – at least until circumstances changed; and there were also times when the *fiq*, the Koranic science of law, reigned supreme and reduced any philosopher to silence. What is more, after Al-Gazali philosophy flourished once again, and not only with Averroës.

Was it the fault of the 'Barbarians'? This is what a recent historian, S. D. Gothein, has suggested. They had been the military saviours of Islam against the threats from Asia and the West. Had they also sapped it from within?

In Spain, these dangerous rescuers had been, first, the Almoravids or Barbarians from the Sudan and the Sahara, then the Almohads from North Africa. In the Near East, Islam's saviours had been the Seljuk Turks, nomads from the cold steppes of Central Asia, or slaves from the countries of the Caucasus. In S. D. Gothein's view, decadence began 'when power was taken over by barbarian soldier slaves in almost all of the Muslim States' and 'the unity of the Mediterranean world was broken'. Unity had been the making of Islam, but it meant nothing to 'these barbarian peoples who in no way shared Mediterranean traditions'.

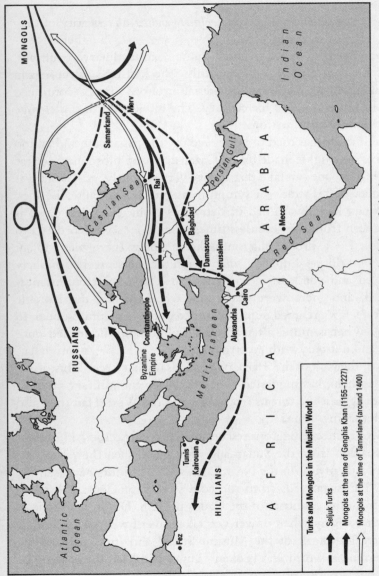

4. *Did the Mongols hasten the decline of Islam?*

Genghis Khan (the 'universal king' 1155–1227) imposed his domination on the Mongol tribes (1205–8). He then conquered Northern China. Next, he turned Westwards and reached the Caucasus via the 'Ural–Caspian gateway'. In his wake, the Mongols descended on Europe and Asia: in 1241 they reached Poland and Hungary, and in 1258 they took Baghdad. Tamerlane (1336–1406) relaunched the conquest: in 1398 he took Delhi, in India; in 1401 he destroyed Baghdad.

Turks and Mongols in the Muslim World

Seljuk Turks

Mongols at the time of Genghis Khan (1155–1227)

Mongols at the time of Tamerlane (around 1400)

MONGOLS

RUSSIANS

HILALIANS

Samarkand
Merv
Rai
Baghdad
Damascus
Jerusalem
Alexandria
Cairo
Mecca
Tunis
Kairouan
Fez

Constantinople
Byzantine Empire

Caspian Sea

Persian Gulf

Red Sea

Indian Ocean

Mediterranean

Atlantic Ocean

ARABIA

AFRICA

One might retort that these barbarians, in the West as in the East, were not much more barbaric than the great majority of the Arabs who had made the first conquests; and that, like them, they were more or less rapidly civilized by contact with the ancient Islamic countries. The Almohad Caliphs were the protectors of Averroës. In traditional accounts of the Crusades Saladin, the great Kurdish Sultan and opponent of Richard the Lion-Heart, is a rather noble figure, at least in the eyes of Christian barbarians. Finally thanks to Egypt Islam re-established its autonomy by crushing the Mongols at Ain Jalut in Syria on 3 September 1260, and by seizing Acre, the last Christian outpost in the Holy Land, in 1291.

Was the problem rather, the loss of the Mediterranean? As the eleventh century drew to a close, Europe began its reconquest of that inland sea, and Islam began to lose the benefits of it. The historian Henri Pirenne believed that in the eighth and ninth centuries the Muslim conquest of the Mediterranean had deprived the West of free movement there, and forced it back upon itself. Now Pirenne's thesis worked the other way round. The Mediterranean began to be closed to Islam, which found itself permanently handicapped, unable to expand and ill-equipped for its ordinary daily life.

It seems strange that E. F. Gautier, who in 1930 was the first to stress this sudden setback to Saracen civilization, did not seek to apply to it Henri Pirenne's theory, which at that time was widely discussed. In the present state of our knowledge, it is probably the best explanation for Islam's abrupt reverse.

Islamic civilization survived this rebuff. It may not have matched its past achievements, but it continued nevertheless. In 1922, when Paul Valéry declared 'Civilizations, we know you to be mortal,' he was surely exaggerating. The seasons of history cause the flowers and the fruit to fall, but the tree remains. At the very least, it is much harder to kill.

After the twelfth century, Islam undoubtedly saw some very

dark days. From the West it suffered the long ordeal of the Crusades (1095–1270), from which it emerged half-victorious with the recapture of Acre in 1291. But although it recovered the land, it lost control of the sea. From Asia it was half-submerged by long, cruel and savage Mongol invasions between 1202 and 1405: Turkestan, Iran and Asia Minor never fully recovered from their destructive onslaught. The capture of Baghdad in 1258 was the symbol of these misfortunes. Islam recovered from its wounds, but only partially.

At the same time, during these dark centuries – the thirteenth, fourteenth and fifteenth – Islam's particular hardships were worsened by economic difficulties on a world scale. From China to India and Europe, the Old World as a whole endured a protracted crisis. Everything and everyone suffered, and for centuries on end. In Europe, the crisis seems to have come later (from 1350 or 1357 onwards) and to have been of shorter duration (it ended between 1450 and 1510): but it was none the less real. Its most obvious manifestation was the so-called Hundred Years' War, from 1337 to 1453, accompanied by a long series of other foreign, civil and social conflicts, and by desolation and poverty. When assessing Islam's misfortunes, therefore, one has to distinguish between what were world phenomena and what was specifically Muslim.

At all events, it was in a climate of general gloom and pessimism that Ibn-Khaldun, the last great Muslim philosopher, wrote his magisterial works. An historian (and, as we should say now, a sociologist) of Andalusian origin, he was born in Tunisia in 1332. He led a busy and eventful life as a diplomat and statesman in Granada, Tlemcen, Bejaia, Fez and Syria; he died a *cadi* or judge in Cairo in 1406, a year after Tamerlane, to whom he had been sent as ambassador.

Ibn-Khaldun's major work was the *Kitab Al-Ibar* or *Book of Examples*, a vast compilation dealing in an original way with the history of the Berbers. Its Introduction alone is a masterpiece, the first systematic treatise on the methodology and sociology of

Muslim history; it was translated into French in the nineteenth century under the title of *Prolégomènes*, and into English in 1958 as *The Muqaddimah: an Introduction to History*.

With the return of better times and a recovery in the world economy, broadly in the sixteenth century, Islam once more profited from its intermediary position between East and West. The greatness of Turkey lasted until 'the so-called tulip period' in the eighteenth century. In Istanbul the 'tulip period' was when unmistakable real or stylized representations of the flower appeared constantly on pottery and in miniatures or embroidery. The tulip period is a fitting title for an age that lacked neither strength nor grace. Politically this recovery was marked by the rapid and brilliant victories of the Ottoman Turks, which began well before their conquest of Constantinople in 1453. That resounding success, moreover, was followed by others. By the sixteenth century they had made Turkey one of the great powers in the Mediterranean.

The new masters of Byzantium and of the Arabian holy places soon more or less restructured the whole of Islam. After 1517 the Ottoman Sultan, the Grand Turk, became the Caliph of all the faithful. The only areas outside Turkish control were distant Turkestan, Morocco beyond the 'Regency' of Algiers, and Shi'ite Persia, which became more nationalist than ever with the growth of the Sefavi dynasty. Mongol and Turkish Muslim mercenaries, led by Zehir-Eddin Muhammad Baber (1495–1530), a distant descendant of Tamerlane, seized the Empire of Delhi, and in 1526 founded the Empire of which Baber was the first Great Mogul. It soon dominated most of India.

In the same year, 1526, the Turks defeated Christian Hungary at the Battle of Mohacs. It was clear that Islam was enjoying a general renaissance under Turkish and Sunni influence, which everywhere entailed total victory for Muslim orthodoxy and traditional religion. Power reasserted itself; independent thinking was curbed; an iron regime was imposed.

In the Balkans and the Near East Turkish domination coincided with visible material prosperity, rapid population growth and the

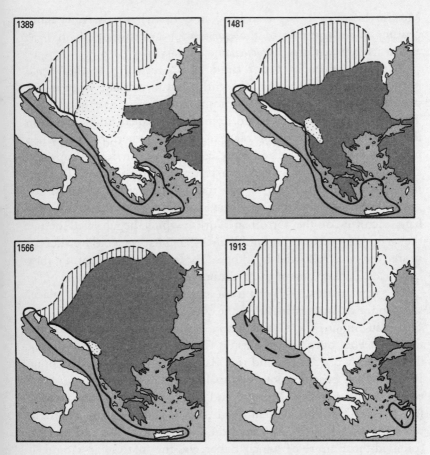

5. The destiny of the Ottoman Empire

In grey, Ottoman possessions. The dotted areas show Serbia. Vertical lines show Hungary. Surrounded by a thick black line, Venetian and (after 1913) Italian possessions.

establishment of flourishing towns. In 1453 Constantinople had had barely 80,000 inhabitants. In the sixteenth century, when it had become Istanbul, there were 700,000 spread among the city itself, the Greek quarter of Pera beyond the Golden Horn and Scutari (Üsküdar) on the Asian side of the Bosphorus. This capital, which like all great cities combined great luxury and appalling poverty, provided the much envied model of a civilization that under the Ottomans spread its influence far and wide, exporting for instance the pattern of its huge mosques, including the Süleymaniye, built for Süleyman the Magnificent.

Turkey's real greatness, denied for a long time in the West, is now gradually re-emerging through research by historians. The superlative Turkish archives, at last classified and catalogued, are being opened to scholars: they reveal, one by one, the workings of a multifarious, painstaking, advanced and authoritarian bureaucracy which was able to compile a detailed census, devise a coherent administrative policy, amass huge reserves of gold and silver, and systematically colonize the Balkans, the bastion of the Empire against Europe, by settling nomads there. It also imposed forced labour, and maintained an astonishing, rigorously trained army. It all seems curiously modern.

This great machine ran down eventually, but not before the end of the seventeenth century. Its last great tremor was the siege of Vienna in 1687. Thereafter, was the Turkish Empire stifled by its lack of maritime outlets? Morocco stood between it and the open space of the Atlantic; the Red Sea gave it inadequate access to the Indian Ocean; and in the Persian Gulf it faced the violent opposition of the Persians and, still more, of new arrivals from Europe with their superior fleets and their powerful commercial backers.

Or did the Turkish Empire die because it failed to adapt well and quickly to new technology?

Or, again, and more obviously still, because in the eighteenth and above all in the nineteenth century it faced the powerful rivalry of modern Russia? The victories of the Austrian cavalry during Prince Eugene's campaigns (especially from 1716 to 1718) had endangered only the edges of Turkey in Europe. With Russian intervention a young colossus had arrived to challenge a moribund or at least a tired one.

Even so, the Turkish Empire was not at first the 'sick man of Europe' that the great powers' diplomacy maltreated so shamelessly in the nineteenth century. Turkish Islam remained for a long time powerful, brilliant and formidable. So did Sefavi Persia, admired in the seventeenth century by the observant French traveller Tavernier. So did the Great Mogul, who at the beginning of the eighteenth century almost seized the whole of Deccan in the South, despite close surveillance by the British and the French.

Beware, therefore, of hasty judgements about the early decadence of Islam, which tend to anticipate history.

7. The Revival of Islam Today

Islam relapsed into that inferno or purgatory of living humanity that we euphemistically call the Third World. Relapsed, because it had previously enjoyed what was undoubtedly a better relative position.

This decline, definite if more or less belated, led in the nineteenth century to humiliation, suffering and bitterness, followed by general foreign domination. The facts are well known. Only Turkey escaped that fate – hence its brilliant and brutal reaction, on the brink of disaster, under Mustapha Kemal Pasha (1920–38). This indeed served as a model for later national reactions and triumphs. Today, the liberation of Islam is very nearly complete. But it is one thing to secure independence, and quite another to keep pace with the rest of the world and look clearly towards the future. That is much more difficult.

The end of colonialism and the birth of new nationalist movements

Nothing is easier than to retrace today the chronology of colonization and then of 'decolonization' in Islam's various regions. One by one (except for the ex-Soviet Muslim Republics) they have all attained full political independence.

Soviet colonialism? Habitually, under this heading, only British, French, Belgian, German or Dutch colonies are mentioned. They certainly make up a great part of the whole. But there has also been Russian and then Soviet colonialism, of which less is usually said. To all appearances, it kept a grip on at least 30 million Muslims – more than the entire population of the Maghreb today.

Is the word colonialism appropriate here? In the years that followed the Russian Revolution of 1917, there were certainly efforts to emancipate and decentralize the Soviet Union. Concessions were made to local autonomy, and immense material progress was achieved. 'Today, all the Muslim nations of the USSR, above all in Turkestan and the Caucasus, have their own scientific, administrative, and political managerial classes, their intelligentsia. They have closed the gap between themselves and the Tartars, and no longer need to seek help from the intellectuals in Kazan' – the old, once exclusive centre of Muslim culture in Russia.

In the process, however, the natural solidarity among the various Muslim Republics has been weakened, and the idea of a vast 'Turanian' State has passed into limbo. In the Soviet federal system, culture was 'national in its form, but proletarian and socialist in its content'. The results were clearly secularization, to the detriment of Islam's religious values, and nationalism, now practically limited to the horizons of the region, with no reference to the *Umma* of fellow-Muslims, and normally making only short-term demands for 'the reform of the institutions' or 'a bigger role for administrators from the minority nationalities'.

In other words, the Muslim problems of the USSR were for the moment unrelated to the ordinary demands of Islam as expressed, vociferously, on the international stage. The Muslim Soviet Republics enjoyed a degree of independence, but were tightly bound within the USSR, with a common foreign policy, and wholly dependent on the Union for defence, finance, education and rail transport.

All this was a long way from the experience and the visions of Sultan Galiev, who from 1917 to 1923 was a senior Communist official, but then an anti-revolutionary agitator until he was sentenced to death in 1929. As a Muslim, he had dreamed of uniting all the Muslims in the Soviet Union into a single State, and using it, like a long probe pointing Eastwards, to inject the Revolution and its ideology into the heart of Asia – a continent he thought ripe for political upheaval, whereas industrial working-class Europe seemed to him no more than an 'extinct revolutionary furnace'. Would Islam have been able to set Asia alight? In centre-stage today, one would-be political heir of divided Islam is Pan-Arabism, which in public international disputes is only too ready to take over. The purely Arab world is the ambitious heart and crossroads of Islam. It is easy, therefore, to mistake the Middle East (and its North African outposts) for the whole of Islam, and to see no more than this or that region, this or that well-known figure. This happens all the time in the daily news. Clearly, the part should not be confused with the whole.

But the essential, insistent characteristic of Islam today is precisely its internal division, the insidious fragmentation of its identity and its lands. In some places, this is the result of relentless political pressures; in others, it is due to geography, which has placed Islam under the exclusive influence of other civilizations or economic systems.

In the Indian Archipelago, the 80 million Muslims who live alongside or intermingle with deep Hindu and animist traditions, and in a very individual economic structure, are in a sense already half lost. In the Indian subcontinent, Pakistan consists of two enormous areas separated by the teeming breadth of India, whose very numbers make it somewhat of a threat. In China, the 10 million Muslims are a group apart, very definitely 'lost'. In Black Africa, victorious Islam itself fell part-victim to, and was partly deformed by, various powerful animistic cults.

The Islamic faith of such peoples often serves them as an argument for nationalism and a means of resistance. But for Islam as a whole, all those countries which no longer look towards Mecca as strictly as before, which no longer flock on pilgrimages or fully subscribe to the political ideal of an effective and united Pan-Islam – these countries are undoubtedly lost or very likely to be lost. Distance, politics and the growth of atheism and secularism all play their part. Since 1917, only a few hundred Soviet pilgrims have made their way to Mecca.

Is Islam at present 'at the Garibaldi stage'? In the heart of the Muslim countries, in the Near East, Pan-Islam is coming into conflict with sharp and vehement local nationalism. The dissolution of the United Arab Republic of Egypt and Syria in September 1961 was a striking example. Pakistan, Afghanistan, Iran, Turkey, Lebanon, Syria, Iraq, Jordan, Saudi Arabia, Tunisia, Morocco, Mauritania and Yemen are all of them attached to their particular prerogatives, and often more or less openly hostile to each other, even if they sometimes achieve momentary solidarity against the outside world and its threats.

Such vehement nationalism, which drives people – and especially young people and students – to violent and dramatic gestures, too often seems out of date, in the unsympathetic eyes of Westerners. We have too many good reasons for regretting our own past nationalist excesses, for which Europe paid so dearly, not to look on new explosions of nationalism, when Europe is uniting, with a certain lack of enthusiasm and, indeed, rather unfairly, all the more so when the nationalists are attacking the West.

Unfairly? Here, very justly expressed, are the feelings of one Afghan intellectual, Najm oud-Din Bammat, writing in 1959:

Islam today has to go through a number of revolutions at once: a religious revolution like the Reformation; an intellectual and moral revolution like the eighteenth-century Enlightenment; an economic and social revolution like the European Industrial Revolution of the nineteenth century; and, in the age of the two great Eastern and Western blocs or systems, a number of small nationalist revolutions of its own. At a time when pacts are being forged on a world scale, the Muslim countries are still waiting and searching for their Garibaldis.

There is no question – far from it – of casting aspersions on the shining reputation of Garibaldi. But the wars of national unity that were so necessary in the past were followed in Europe by Armageddon.

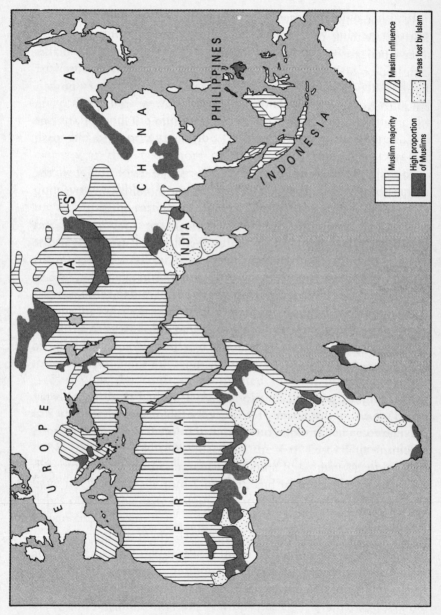

6. *Muslims in the world today*

(This sketch does not indicate Islam's almost total domination of India in ancient times.)

Is nationalism likely to profit Islam any more than it profited Europe? May it not lead Muslim States into an impasse, in an interdependent world economy where such fragmentation makes little sense? Still more, does it not engender dangerous conflicts? Every independent country, so long as it has some military power, tends to interpret Pan-Islam or Pan-Arabism in its own way, in the sole light of its own interests and ambitions. This, as everyone knows, is how Pakistan, Iraq and Egypt have behaved in the past; and the lists are open to all comers.

Nationalism, however, can also be a necessary stage in the struggle for independence – a form of anti-colonialism, rejecting foreign domination, and backing liberation by strength.

It should be no surprise that all forms of Arab nationalism converge in hostility to their old enemy Israel. Established in the aftermath of World War II, the State of Israel seemed to them the work of the West at its worst. Israel's admirable technological triumphs, backed by capital from all over the world, its demonstrations of strength against Egypt in 1948 and at the time of Suez in 1956, when its tiny army overran the vast Sinai Peninsula – these and other achievements arouse envy, fear and animosity, adding to ancient scores. Jacques Berque has written with some justice:

Arabs and Jews are both, if I may say so, peoples of God. Two peoples of God at once – that is really too much for diplomats and generals! The inevitable conflict arises precisely from the fact that the two sides are cousins, both descendants of Abraham, both ennobled by a belief in one God . . . In the face of the West they have followed different paths. The Jews, in the diaspora, have adapted their ways to the insistent technology of the Gentiles, but maintained all the more their community ideal. The Arabs, remaining in their own lands, have been invaded and divided, but have had the privilege or the misfortune to stay more or less what they were. Hence the present inequality of resources on either side, and the difference in both words and deeds. The most lucid Arab essayists have meditated bitterly on what they call the 'disaster' of 1948. Like Taine or Renan after 1870, they have advised their compatriots to take the necessary steps to avoid any return to adventures of that sort.

Nationalism has a role to play in the near future: all Muslim countries will have to adopt and apply strict austerity plans. They will need, in fact, plans for solidarity and social discipline; and nationalism will help all these young countries to deal with the serious economic difficulties they face. It will make it easier to accept essential innovations which clash with very ancient social, religious and family structures – age-old ancestral habits, perpetuated in Islam's traditionalism, and only too likely to spark off violent reactions.

For, at all costs, Islam has to modernize and adopt in large measure the technology of the West, on which the world now so much depends. The future hangs on the acceptance or rejection of this world civilization. Powerful traditions call for its refusal; but nationalist pride may incite people to accept what they would instinctively reject.

Islam has often been denied the flexibility needed for so drastic a change. So much so, that numerous observers claim that, owing to its 'impermeable', 'intransigent' heart, spirit and civilization, Islam will find all its efforts to modernize effectively blocked. Is this true?

In fact, Islam has already accepted some aspects of the modern world by which it feels besieged, and it could accept more. It was not without hesitation and conflict that Christianity did so in the past; yet in the end its integrity survived the process of adaptation. To regard Islam as an exceptionally intransigent religion, totally lacking flexibility, is to forget how many heresies it has nurtured. They alone bear witness to uneasiness and possible stress. The Koran itself, moreover, offers to reformers the ever-open door of the *ijtihad*. 'The Prophet,' wrote Pierre Rondot, 'is deemed to have foreseen cases where the Koran or the *sounna* (tradition) give no guidance: in which instances he recommended reasoning by analogy or *qiyas*; and if that could not be done, then one should submit all possible precedents to one's judgement and vision or *ray*. This personal effort of interpretation, the *ijtihad*, played a considerable role in the future development of Muslim thought. In our day, the reform movement explicitly intends to reopen that door.' Every religion, indeed, has its emergency exits. Islam may delay or oppose changes; but it can also be influenced and outflanked.

Economists, at grips with daily reality, continually protest against ready-made, stereotyped explanations based on the supposedly unchangeable 'facts' of Muslim life. The real difficulty, they say, is much more mundane: it is simply the scale of the transformation to be made. Islam has dropped two centuries behind the West – and the centuries in question are those which changed Europe much more than during the whole of the past between classical antiquity and the eighteenth century. How could Islam make up so much leeway in a short time? It would mean taking hold of its archaic societies and reshaping them – but with a farming system still poor and precarious, and with industries which are isolated within an economy incapable of reaching and enriching the inert mass of a rapidly growing population. Furthermore, like all societies, Islam has its plutocrats, few in number but all the more powerful for that. Beliefs and traditions often serve as pretexts whereby the privileged defend their own interests, keeping in being some societies that are truly 'medieval' as in Yemen, feudal as in Iran, or archaic as in Saudi Arabia – despite, or perhaps even because of, its oil.

These difficulties severely tested the work of the reformers: brilliant and brutal on the part of Mustapha Kemal in Turkey; accompanied by violent rhetoric from Kassem in Syria; marked by stubbornness in the case of Nasser in Egypt; or wise and capable on the part of Bourguiba in Tunisia. Whatever their nature or their style, they mostly faced similar obstacles. All their reforms had to overcome various supposed taboos inherent in Muslim civilization; and the supreme, unmistakeable test was the emancipation of women, first beginning to be proclaimed, then – more slowly – on the way to being achieved. The end of polygamy, the limitation of husbands' right to repudiate their wives unilaterally, the abolition of the veil and the admission of women to universities, employment and the vote: all these are or will be of the utmost importance.

Moves towards them prove that reform is not a lost cause, but that it needs champions and decisive battles. The struggle will be many-sided. The most serious danger would be to be tempted away from it by the attractions, the convenience or the imperatives of political situations inflamed on any excuse or none at all.

The ideal tactic would be to take only one step at a time, and each time choose the essential step. But politics is not a Cartesian theorem. Economic progress alone requires from Islam – as from everyone – a concentrated, perhaps exclusive political effort. And in the practical world this may well mean tackling problems as they arise, whether they be old or new.

Thus all these States, proud of their independence, have demanding and passionate political ambitions to be met and diverted from blind alleys. They have susceptibilities which need careful handling: Islam has as many as Europe, which is not notably thick-skinned. Islam also has its young people, its impatient students, who rather resemble the French *polytechniciens* in the 'July Revolution' of 1830. It has its soldiers, as apt for uprisings and *coups d'état* as those in Latin America before 1939. It has its power-hungry political parties, and its politicians pursuing the mirage of their own image and carried away by the sheer violence of their speeches. They have to raise their voices to be heard above the clamour of the world.

Clearly, foreign interests are present: France in North Africa, Britain in Kuwait and the sparsely populated Southern part of Arabia; the United States everywhere, calmly supplying credits and advice; the USSR, sparing or prodigal according to circumstances, and always vigilant in this vast, contested no man's land. Everywhere, finally, social revolution lies in wait, showing its colours and sharpening its demands.

History is on its side. In Turkey, where the military *coup d'état* of 27 May 1960 led many to hope for social reforms which have been long in coming. In Iran, where a first revolution came from above, at once conservative and modern-minded, made some progress despite the hostility of young people, fundamentalists, partisans of the former Minister Dr Mossadeq, and the Iranian Communist Party, the *Toudeh*. In Jordan, where a courageous king stands up to dangers on every side. In Lebanon, which in happier and wiser times sought to be the Switzerland of the Near East. In Iraq, where change was more verbal than real, but where the Kurdish problem remains a deep running sore. In Egypt, where after the secession of Syria from the United Arab Republic the country embarked on a form of social Communism whose partial success may well prove infectious. One might complete the picture by adding the uneasiness of Pakistan, disquieted by India, which now seems more bellicose than had been thought, and has its eyes on Kashmir; the ambitions of Indonesia, which has been encouraged by India's success against Goa to want to establish a protectorate over Irian, or Dutch Guinea; and the uncertainties in all of North Africa, which is waiting to see what course to follow after the denouement of the Algerian tragedy.

All these worries weigh on the policies of the Islamic States, exposing them to unexpected explosions of violence which greatly harm both them and their neighbours. Who can evaluate how much the Bizerta affair of 1961 cost France (which is rich) and Tunisia (which is poor)? In that crisis, was Bizerta the real issue, or was it mutually wounded pride? France was bitter because she thought she had done a great deal for Islam (which was obviously true); Islam was bitter because it believed that the independence it had been given was not complete. Indeed, no country is truly independent if its economy is such as to consign it at once to the Third World.

Yet the former mother countries are only partly responsible for this continued state of economic dependence. It results also from other specific causes, including Islam's past, its dearth of natural resources and its immoderate birth-rate. All these are serious handicaps; but they can be remedied.

Muslim States in the modern world

Growth is always hard-won: Islam faces the same dilemma as the rest of the Third World: to be integrated into the world economy, it must as soon as possible complete its own Industrial Revolution. The task is simple to describe: but it will be costly, requiring hard work whose results will not be immediate or very quickly affect the standard of living. The Muslim countries' time as colonies by no means prepared them for this responsibility; and that is certainly the colonial powers' most serious failing.

True, the colonists made an important contribution to the places they ruled. Very backward countries, where life had not changed for centuries, were suddenly brought into contact with highly developed civilizations. They gained something from that: modern medicine and hygiene, which greatly reduced the death-rate; more or less effective education, depending on circumstances (and here the French colonies were better than most); many material investments, in ports, roads and railways; modern agricultural arrangements, often with irrigation dams; and in some cases a sensible approach to industrialization.

That, some may say, is a lot. Yes and no. On the one hand, the colonists' contribution partially destroyed old structures; on the other, it replaced them very imperfectly. What was set up was not designed for a national economy, but for an economy linked with the mother country, dependent upon it and upon the life of the world. Hence the very uneven levels of development from one sector to another, and the need for newly independent States to reform the structure of their economies so as to meet all their national requirements. This difficulty adds one more to the many others they face, arising from the nature of their civilization and the poor quality of most of their land.

To tackle these tasks, the Muslim countries need help as well as self-help. They have to adapt to the changing policy of the privileged world – of which they are well aware and at which they are adept. They lack neither intelligence nor political skill. Still more, however, they have to adapt themselves and grapple with the real world. This squaring of the circle is the hardest of their tasks.

There is no single, simple solution. Not even that offered by oil, which seems so great a benefactor. Petroleum is an undoubted asset, and its benefits have raised the standard of living in all the oil-producing countries. Nature, as we know, has accorded it generously to the Near East. Nevertheless, the major international oil companies, which alone could afford the huge costs of prospecting and extracting, remained for a long time the chief beneficiaries of oil: they took possession of it at source in exchange for royalties; they refined it; they distributed it. Early attempts to retain it at source, as Iran briefly did in 1951 and Iraq proposed in 1961, were effectively thwarted: oil was valuable only when it was sold. Today, ownership patterns have changed; but at present there is no shortage of oil in the world, and with other forms of energy, including nuclear energy, on the horizon, Islam's virtual monopoly of fuel supplies may not last for ever.

Incidentally, foreign exploitation was not the only evil involved. In the Muslim countries, oil royalties enriched a privileged class. The money was not distributed fairly, but too often financed artificial luxury on the part of a particular caste. Nor did this luxury stimulate local production: it was wasted on foreign imports which could never become productive at home. Saudi Arabia used much of its oil revenue to build new cities, new roads, new railways and new airports. That was obviously progress. But much of it also went into the unbridled and anachronistic opulence of the royal family and the main tribal chiefs. Such a spectacle pleased neither the young, excited by the revolution in Egypt, nor the middle classes, eager to play their part in public affairs.

To some observers, Middle Eastern oil looks very like the silver of South America in the sixteenth century, which passed through Spain without stimulating the economy there, and went on to enrich still further the flourishing economies of the rest of Europe.

In any case, oil is and will remain the starting-point of endless conflicts in the Near East. One early example was that between General Kassem of Iraq and the eight major international oil companies whose representative on the spot was the IPC or Irak Petroleum Co. Talks went on for three years before being suspended. Fields within the concessions that were not being exploited were withdrawn from company control. Reconciliation no doubt remained possible by making concessions to Iraq, including a better than fifty-fifty division of profits. There was also the possibility of bringing in more accommodating newcomers as oil prospectors, from Japan and Italy, notably to explore under-sea resources in the Persian Gulf. But even so the oil-producing countries do not hold all the aces, and they still risk future setbacks.

All the Muslim States have set to work and achieved great things, including general growth in production. But the growth of the population continually undermines their efforts. Everything is progressing, yet everything has to be begun afresh.

The demographer Alfred Sauvy pointed this out in an article on the Near East in *Le Monde* (7 August 1956) which has lost none of its force. 'The Arab world,' he wrote (and he could have written 'the Muslim world as a whole'),

is a demographic volcano. At fifty per thousand, or six to seven children per family, the birth-rate is one of the highest in the world. Far from falling, it has actually gained from the decline of polygamy, as well as from better hygiene. And while the birth-rate reaches new heights, the death-rate is falling rapidly, owing to fewer epidemics, famines or inter-tribal wars. The present mortality rate is not precisely known, but it is certainly tending downwards, towards twenty per thousand. There is nothing exceptional in a population growth of 2.5 to 3 per cent a year. This is the case in Algeria, in Tunis and probably in Egypt. Such a rate of growth, which doubles the population in a single generation, is far in excess of that which flooded Europe in its heyday (1 to 1.5 per cent a year), and it lacks the safety-valve of emigration and colonization. The Muslim world combines the death-rate of Europe in 1880 with a birth-rate such as Europe attained only in the most flourishing periods of the Middle Ages. It is an explosive mixture.

Sauvy added, presciently: 'It would be näive to think that these countries, which have rapidly growing populations and needs, and which between them have the oil, the pipelines and the Suez Canal, will resign themselves to watching so much wealth flow across and out of their territory without demanding an important share of it for themselves.'

The result of so rapid an increase in the population of the Muslim countries is to prevent any rise in the standard of living, despite the growth of production. This is a frequent phenomenon in the Third World. Everywhere, however, positive steps have been taken to deal with it. As a result, unemployment has decreased. In Tunisia, to take only one example, 200,000 or 300,000 unemployed were found jobs without outside help or very large-scale investments: they set to work making roads, terracing farmland against erosion, building houses, or simply planting trees. One economist calculated that between 1952 and 1958 agricultural production in the Near East increased roughly as much as that in the world as a whole. Every branch of industry has made similar progress. In Egypt, the index of manufacturing industries, based on 100 in 1953, rose as follows over the same period: 1951, 95; 1952, 98; 1953, 100; 1954, 107; 1955, 117; 1956, 125; 1957, 132; 1958, 143. In Pakistan, industrial production rose from 100 in 1952 to 128 in 1954 and 215 in 1958.

So there was progress, a general increase in the national revenue and hence, it would seem, a greater chance to devote more to investment and encourage growth. So far so good: but against that ran the rising tide of population. The number of people increased still faster than the quantity of goods to be shared among them, and the income per head fell – as in every quotient whose denominator (in this case, the population) grows faster than the numerator. The more a swimmer battles against an overwhelming tide, however much progress he makes through the water, the more he is driven back over the ground. Islam, where everything is advancing, nevertheless has to watch its standard of living receding, or barely staying the same.

It should be added, however, that these calculations of income per head are only estimates. The figures for population are themselves often uncertain, with a margin of error which may be as much as 20 per cent. The national income, too, is hard to calculate exactly in the frequent absence of reliable national statistics. Equally, it is far from easy to evaluate precisely the output of scattered and primitive artisans, or of a rural economy with vast areas of subsistence farming where the peasants live on what they produce. All our figures, therefore, are no more than approximate indications. But that is already enough.

Given the growth of the population, the mere fact of maintaining the standard of living per head is a proof that the economy is vigorous and able to cope with this massive biological threat. The Muslim countries as a whole bear witness to this vigour; and if some are losing ground, their loss is small. Their people consume on average less than 2,600 calories a day (the lower limit in rich countries), but in general they are above subsistence level and everywhere (except in parts of Africa) outside the world's pitiless famine zones. They are below the line dividing wealth and poverty, but above the line dividing poverty from destitution. This, at least, is something gained.

Between these two dividing-lines, different countries occupy different positions. In terms of national revenue per head of population, measured in US dollars in the 1960s, they ranked in ascending order as follows: Libya 36; Afghanistan 50; Nigeria 64; Pakistan 66; Indonesia 88; Jordan 100; Syria 110; Iran 115; Egypt 122; Tunisia 132; Iraq 142; Morocco 159; Algeria 210; Turkey 219; Lebanon 247. The figures are modest indeed by comparison with Europe (more than 1,000) and the United States (2,200). They look substantial only when compared with those for Black Africa and elsewhere.

It may be noted that some of the best figures in the above list

are those for countries once or still associated with France –
Lebanon, Syria, Morocco, Algeria and Tunisia. French colonization as such can hardly claim credit for that, although at one time
it had its merits, essentially because it trained a range of intellectuals
and managers and bridged the gap, more effectively than
elsewhere, between different peoples and different civilizations.

Lebanon owed its relative prosperity to the spread of its trade,
its capitalism and its culture throughout Islam, Black Africa and
Latin America, as well as to its dual religious heritage, Christian
and Muslim. Algeria benefited from French and international
investments (in agriculture, dams, roads, schools, medical services,
Saharan oil) and from labour migration to France – none of them
interrupted by the long Algerian War which began in 1954.

In the struggle for development, every economy has certain
advantages or trump cards. Iraq, Iran, Saudi Arabia, and Algeria
have oil; Egypt has the fertile Nile Valley, the Suez Canal, high
quality cotton and a flourishing textile industry; Turkey and
Morocco have industrial development, very often intelligently
devised; Indonesia has rubber, oil and tin mines; Pakistan has vast
resources of wheat and jute.

These assets are invaluable: but the task remains difficult and risky.

The problems to be solved are intricate. At once economic and
social, they are so closely interrelated that it seems impossible to
tackle them one by one. Taken together, they demand a formidable
plan of campaign.

This involves, in fact:

- *Above all, better farming*. This means doing violence to archaic
  property laws, attacking the multiple problems of irrigation,
  and stopping the erosion and devastation of arable land. In a
  word, agrarian policy and technology.
- *Establishing industrial firms* (State-owned or private, in heavy
  industry or light), and if possible integrating them into the
  country's economy as a whole. They need to be based on the
  economy's global structure and to contribute to its general
  growth.

- *Solving the problem of investments* – a burning question because it involves foreign aid (which may be private international capital, brought in via Swiss banks, or Governmental assistance from the Soviet Union, the United States, France, or the European Community).
- *Creating a market.* Here, there are two problems. First, a market presupposes a certain standard of living (which is what all these measures are intended to attain); and secondly, any effective market needs to be far bigger than on a merely national scale. Hence various plans, launched with more enthusiasm than success, for a Pan-Arab market, a Maghreb market or an African market. The dreams are sensible: what is hard is to make them come true.
- *Educating and training the workforce,* all the more necessary in that automation, otherwise feasible in industries starting from scratch, would not solve the urgent, crucial problem of unemployment and surplus labour.
- *Training managers and others*: engineers, teachers and administrators. Teaching and technical training are on the agenda, and they are long-term tasks. Only great eagerness to learn, on the part of the people, will make it possible to overcome immense difficulties here.

Altogether, enormous investments are needed, and in some cases they will not pay for a very long term. As J. Berque puts it: 'Generations of people will be sacrificed to the future. Only a few have the sad privilege of realizing this. Certain young Syrian–Lebanese poets, trying to grasp this phenomenon, have invoked the myth of Thannus, the Eastern God destined for a painful death but also for rebirth. This is how they account for their people's permanent fear and present bitterness.'

A choice has to be made: in the face of such stark problems, such urgent and difficult solutions, and such huge unavoidable sacrifices, the leaders of the various States very naturally hesitate over what strategy to adopt. The world proposes at least two; and the choice to be made determines and transcends the whole future of Islam.

The options, broadly speaking, are as follows: either to maintain Western-style capitalism, half interventionist and half *laissez-faire*, with a degree of political liberalism; or to follow the Communist experiments – Soviet, Yugoslav or Chinese. Put more simply still, it means either retaining Government and society as they are, with whatever improvements are possible; or overthrowing the whole structure with a view to building afresh on a different basis. These alternatives are not, unfortunately, purely intellectual or even purely practical. They are affected by a myriad other factors, both foreign and domestic.

Everywhere, or almost everywhere, a middle class is emerging, composed partly of intellectuals, many of them young. They still resent the deep disappointment that has followed attempts to imitate the West. In politics, for example, all the Muslim States except Afghanistan and Yemen have Parliaments: but what advantage has this been to the emerging middle class? Disillusioned, and impatient for a role in public affairs, its members

turn to Communism, which they see as a means of one day taking control. Bureaucracy, and the Soviet ideal of planning, seem to promise guarantees of stability and ways of solving almost impossible economic problems. The young Muslim intelligentsia is tempted by the modern, scientific air of Marxist dialectic. Admittedly, this is only a reaction against the medieval constraints that still paralyse Islamic thinking; but it is all the more dangerous in that those who promote it have already looked in vain in the liberal, democratic thought of the West for ways into a modern, rational philosophy. Henceforward, Marxism seems to them the only possible solution (A. Benigsen).

The West is too inclined to see in the Islamic States' past dealings with the USSR only moves to obtain machines, arms and credits at low cost. There is much more to it than that. Communist experiments still fascinate young people in the Islamic countries. The West often relies on nothing but retrograde aristocracies in a *papier-mâché* theatrical decor. Here, as elsewhere, it lacks a truly global policy. The answer is not, in fact, to convince Islam that the Western model is better in itself or preferable to some other. Nor is it even to offer, more or less generously, a gold-mine of credits. Instead, it is to give developing countries an effective model of planning which suits their needs and gives them the hope and the prospect of a better future.

Muslim civilization in the twentieth century

Is Muslim civilization itself endangered by this deep crisis? The question arises in several forms.

Is there still, amid the immense fragmentation of nationalities and political rivalries, anything like a united Muslim civilization?

If so, is it not threatened by what Jacques Berque has called 'the adoption of universal fashions in technology and behaviour'? Can it, in other words, survive the impact of industrial civilization, now becoming universal, but in fact the creation of the West?

And would this risk not be all the greater if Islam were to choose as its path to modernity a Marxist creed which could destroy the religion that is so important in binding it together?

Is there still a Muslim civilization? The political divisions within Islam seem to have put paid to Pan-Islamic dreams for a long time to come. But, as in the past, Pan-Islamism is still a fact and a facet of Muslim civilization. That civilization is still unmistakably visible in daily life. From one end of Islam to the other, there are similar beliefs, morals, habits, family relationships, tastes, leisure pursuits, games, behaviour and even cooking. A European, whisked from one town to another in the Muslim countries of the Mediterranean, would be far more struck by their resemblances than by their differences. In Pakistan and the Indian Archipelago, the differences are greater, and greater still in Muslim Black Africa: there, in fact, Islamic civilization encounters its rivals, often no less powerful, and sometimes more so.

In Black Africa, Muslims are linked by little more than religion – if that. Preaching (for Egypt has launched a missionary campaign in the name of Pan-Arabism) is often done in French, in countries where that language is spoken. This implies that cultural links are more or less non-existent, or at least fragile and indirect. Nor is it certain that the religious link really works among the African masses, who in fact are transforming – *Africanizing* – Islam as freely as they do Christianity. In short, the strength of Pan-Islamism in Black Africa, when it exists at all, is political and social at most. It is not a facet of civilization as such.

Pakistan, meanwhile, is part of a civilization which has rightly been called Indo-Muslim. Its language, Urdu, mixes words of Iranian or Arabic origin with others derived from Sanskrit. It is written from right to left, like Arabic, but is otherwise quite different.

One of the surest proofs that countries are truly part of the unity of Muslim civilization remains that of language. The twentieth century has preserved 'literary' Arabic, which was always the cement of Islam: it is the common written language, used in newspapers and books. The national languages are purely oral.

And there is a further link. Islam's economic and social problems are almost all essentially identical, in so far as they arise from the clash between an archaic and traditional Muslim civilization, still largely unchanged, and a modern civilization which challenges it everywhere. In some places the problem has scarcely yet appeared; in others it is already acute: but everywhere the solutions required are very likely to be similar. This is only logical, since the starting-points are the same. Those countries that have made most headway in their reforming efforts are simply the precursors of the others.

Here again, however, 'Islam in exile' – in Black Africa, the Indian Archipelago and subcontinent, and China – differs from the rest because its future is linked with that of other civilizations.

A further question: will Islam cast off its old traditional civilization, like a worn-out garment, as it draws closer to industrialization and modern technology?

This question is not specific to Islam. What it really means is: will modern civilization, with computers, artificial intelligence, automation and nuclear technology, make the world uniform, for good or ill, and destroy individual civilizations?

Mechanization, with all that it involves, is certainly able to distort, destroy and reconstruct many aspects of a civilization. But not all. In itself, mechanization is not a civilization. To suggest that it is would be to claim that Europe today was born entirely anew at the time of the Industrial Revolution. That was certainly a brutal shock: but European civilization long predates it. The nations of Europe, indeed, make it very doubtful whether mechanization could unite or homogenize the planet. Moulded already by a single civilization, that of the Christian and humanist West; caught up almost simultaneously, more than a century ago, in the same adventure of industrialization; sharing the same technology, the same science, similar institutions and all the social consequences of mechanization — these nations should surely have lost, long ago, those strong individual quirks which still enable us to speak of French civilization, or German, or English, or Mediterranean. Yet a Frenchman has only to cross the Channel, an Englishman to set foot on the Continent, or a German to enter Italy, and each of them can see at once that industrialization does not mean standardization. And if technology cannot destroy regional differences, how could it annihilate the great civilizations, founded on such powerfully different and individual religions, philosophies and human and moral values?

Would matters be different if the Muslim world embraced technology together with Marxism, whose tenets are so much opposed to the traditional spiritual values of Islam? This more precise question is frequently asked; and to answer it is neither easy nor indeed completely possible. Yet part of the answer may be suggested by what has been said already.

To be plain: Marxism is not in itself a substitute civilization. It is a social movement, a purposive form of humanism, a rationalization of human affairs. If one day it were adopted by Islam, it would lead to coexistence and sharing, as in the Soviet Union Marxism coexisted with Russian civilization, or in China with Chinese. And while it has greatly affected both these civilizations, it has not extinguished either. Nor is that part of its programme.

Y. Moubarac is undoubtedly right when he argues that in such a situation, 'Islam would find it harder to resist the grip of Marxism than Christianity has, because Muslims still make no distinction between spiritual and temporal affairs. For this reason, the spiritual is in greater danger of being submerged in the technological materialism of a Communist Muslim society.' Why is Moubarac right? Because *before* the Industrial Revolution, everywhere or almost everywhere, Christianity had had to absorb the impact of secular scientific rationalism. It had taken its time to adapt, and it had counter-reacted; but it had kept its balance and given up only what it could spare. This initiation, which had armoured it against rationalism, had armoured it against technology and Marxism too.

For Islam, in which religion determines every action in life, technology (Marxist or otherwise) is a wall of fire that has to be leapt through at a single bound, rejecting a civilization grown too old and finding fresh stimulus in the new world beyond the flames. Islam's choice will depend upon itself and upon the rest of the world, swinging like a pendulum first one way and then the other, East and West. Like the Third World as a whole, Islam seems likely to have to follow not its own inclination, but rather the bloc that has the greater weight.

PART II: AFRICA

The perfection of holiness sought by the Taoists was mystic union with the eternal *tao*: it was 'to efface oneself alive in this original and sovereign presence which envelopes everything without itself ever being enveloped' – in the 'formlessness which engenders all forms, in the *tao* which possesses eternal life.' To do so was at the same time to 'achieve unity'.

'In a mystic experience,' a sage master announces, 'one must listen not only by a certain and secret way... Listen not with the ear, but with the Heart [which] for the Chinese means the Spirit; listen not with the heart but with the Breath ... It is the Breath which, when empty, attains reality. Union with the *tao* can be reached only by Emptiness; this Emptiness is the fasting of the Heart.'

The sage was an achiever: by long years of meditation and purification, by renunciation, he could achieve what an adept has to achieve in a few days. After three days, he could detach himself from the outside world; after seven days, from the things around him; after nine days, from his own existence. Then ... he attained clear insight and saw what was Unique. Having seen what was Unique, he could reach the state in which there was neither present nor past, and finally that in which there was neither life nor death.

These ... again into company with all the great mystical experiences, whether Christian, Hindu or Buddhist.

But the perfection sought by the Taoists was not only the salvation of the soul: it was also physical immortality, thanks to a series of means for long life, purifying and unburdening the body. These involved countless practices: breathing exercise, to help the free circulation of the breath and the blood, and avoid obstruction; regulation of clothing; careful dieting, to avoid ordinary foodstuffs (especially cereals) and replace them with vegetable or mineral nutrients; finally, alchemy. This last included the gold vessel which immortalized food, liquid gold (gold liquor) and above all cinnabar (red mercuric sulphide) when it had nine times been transforming into mercury and back again so as to make 'the red pill of immortality'.

8. The Past

Black Africa (which is really composed of many Black Africas) is almost entirely surrounded, by two deserts and two oceans: the huge Sahara in the North and the Kalahari in the South; the Atlantic on the West and the Indian Ocean on the East. These are serious barriers, especially since most of Africa's ocean outlets are poor: there are no good ports, and the rivers are not easily navigable owing to rapids, waterfalls and the silting up of estuaries.

Still, the barriers can be crossed. Very early on, the Indian Ocean was used by sailing boats taking advantage of the monsoons. European explorers conquered the Atlantic in the fifteenth century. The Kalahari only partly closes the way to the South; and the Sahara was crossed as early as classical antiquity. When the dromedary arrived from North Africa in the first centuries of the Christian era, traffic across the Sahara increased tenfold, with salt and then textiles coming Southwards, and black slaves and gold dust going North.

Altogether, however, Black Africa made only slow and imperfect contact with the outside world. Yet it would be wrong to suppose that its doors and windows remained closed and barred for centuries. Nature is powerful, but not omnipotent: history too often influences events.

★

Geography

That geography does not determine everything can be seen immediately by looking at the frontiers or marginal zones of Black Africa, which itself occupies only part of the continent as a whole.

In the North, North-East and East, the Sahara characteristically limits Black Africa, whether or not it forms an impenetrable barrier.

Black Africa, as a European Community committee puts it, is 'Africa South of the Sahara'. From the Mediterranean coast as far as the Sudanese Sahel, the population is white; and this 'White Africa' also includes Ethiopia, which undoubtedly has white ethnic strains within a mixed population very different from true Black Africans. Other factors, too, make Ethiopia a world apart: its very individual civilization, its Christian religion (from AD 350 onwards), its mixed agriculture, based on stockbreeding and arable farming, growing wheat and vines. In the past it successfully resisted not only the attacks of Islam, which had managed to encircle it, but also the efforts of European powers to cut it off from the Indian Ocean and the Red Sea.

Prehistorians and ethnographers even believe that in the earliest times Ethiopia was a secondary source of both arable farming and animal husbandry, which had originated in India. Without its intermediary role, multitudes of black peasants working the soil with the hoe might never have discovered the unexpected advantages of stockbreeding.

In fact, Ethiopia can be seen as the heart of a vast area of East Africa, stretching North as far as the sixth Nile falls, East as far as the Somali Deserts, and South as far as Kenya, if not beyond. This is an intermediary Africa, neither black nor white but both at once, possessing like White Africa a written language (and hence a history): a civilization linked to the great centres in the North and undeniably involved in the crucial interplay of Asia, the Mediterranean and Europe. It may be noted, finally, that the Sahara is continued to the East of Ethiopia in Eritrea and the Somali lands – a long, dry, desolate area which marks a further boundary of Black Africa.

To the South, the accidents of history halted, and will continue to halt, the natural expansion of Black Africa. In the seventeenth century, wanting to establish a port of call on the sea passage to India, the Dutch settled in the Southern tip of the continent, in an area then virtually empty. In 1815, the British seized this strategic stronghold; and soon the Dutch colonists, the Boers or farmers, moved North and occupied the grassy plains of the veld, where they set up prosperous stock-breeding farms.

So a White Africa was gradually established in the South of the continent as well as in the North. It flourished on the wealth of its gold and diamond mines and its industries. To withstand what it saw as a rising black tide (10 million blacks, 3 million whites and 1.5 million coloured), South Africa steeled itself within a defiant racist policy (apartheid or segregation) which in 1960 led it to break with the Commonwealth. Was that a mere episode, or a definite break? It could not by itself arrest the progress of history: nor will it.

A final exception, again due to historical reasons, is the island of Madagascar, which must also be regarded as outside Black Africa. Its population consists of two elements: black Bantu from the nearby mainland, and Malaysian tribes which came in several waves from the East. Many inhabitants of Madagascar are of mixed descent, but the Western part of the island is mainly Bantu and the Eastern mainly Malaysian. According to still incomplete research, mixed inheritance predominates, with the African strain about twice as strong as the Malaysian.

Despite this ethnic diversity, Madagascar enjoys great cultural unity; and here the dominant strain is Malaysian. The language is Indonesian; so, undoubtedly, are the craft and farming techniques: 'land-clearing by fire, long-handled spades, flooded rice-fields, taro

growing, yams, bananas, dog-breeding, black pigs, poultry . . .
sperm-whaling, turtle-fishing, outrigger canoes, hunting with
spears, blow-pipes and slings, weaving of baskets and rush mats (of
which most of their furnishings consist) . . .' Madagascar's Eastern
immigrants probably came via the North rather than straight
across the India Ocean. The proof, slender but sufficient, is that
the Mascarene Islands of Mauritius, Réunion and Rodriguez were
uninhabited until the seventeenth century, whereas they would
have been natural and even necessary ports of call for anyone
sailing from the Indian Archipelago to Madagascar direct.

In other words, the history and civilization of the Indian Ocean
long dominated Madagascar, separating it from the mainland.
Today, however, proximity is linking Africa more and more with
the young Malagasy Republic.

In understanding Black Africa, geography is more important than
history. The geographical context is not all that matters, but it is
the most significant. Climate accounts for the alternation of vast
areas of grass and trees which inevitably involve different ways of
life.

In the West, equatorial rainwater collects, forming an immense
mass of virgin forests, akin to those of the Amazon and Indonesia,
on roughly the same latitudes. These forests act as 'sponges, soaked
with water; they are thick with giant trees and tangled underbrush,
dark and silent. They resist – or have resisted – attempts to clear
them; they are not propitious for human settlement or even for
travel, except by river; life there is precarious and isolated, based
on fishing and hunting.' Typically, such forests are the refuge of
the remaining African pygmies, survivors of the negrillos who
were probably Africa's earliest inhabitants.

The forest is more widespread to the North of the Equator than
to the South: it borders the Gulf of Guinea on its Northern side,
from Liberia to Cameroon. The gap in it shown on the map,
mainly wooded savanna and palm plantations, is the Southern part

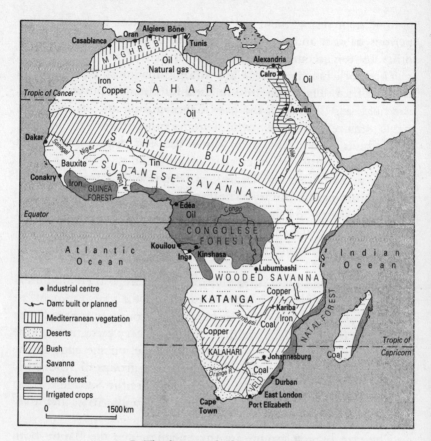

7. The diversity of Africa: geography

of Benin. To the East, the equatorial forest ends at the Congo
Basin, on the edge of the East African uplands.

Around the rain forest, in roughly concentric rings, there are
tropical forests which become drier and drier the further away
they are, then wooded savanna with tall grass, clumps of trees, and
spinneys along the watercourses, then bare savanna, and finally the
steppes.

In human terms, there are two distinct areas, both subject to periods of rain and drought: one is stock-breeding country, the other not (on account of the tsetse fly).

The stock-breeding areas are among the most flourishing in Black Africa. The cattle are not used for draught purposes, since the fields are tilled with the hoe. Crops include millet, sorghum, yams, maize and rice; while for export there are cotton, groundnuts, cocoa, and palm oil – this last one of the richest resources, especially in Nigeria.

The great distinction, clearly, is between the areas with and without animal husbandry. The former, in the North and East – the outer zone – are the richest, the best balanced, and for a long time have been the most open to the outside world. They have also been an important focus for much of Africa's history.

Superimposed on these rural divisions there are also ethnic differences. Black Africans – who must never for one moment be thought of as belonging to a single ethnic group – can broadly be divided into four. There are the pygmies, a very primitive residue of the past, with a barely articulate language; on the edge of the Kalahari Desert there are small and ancient groups of Khoi-khoi or Hottentots and Saan or Bushmen; there are the Sudanese, from Dakar to Ethiopia; and from Ethiopia to South Africa there are the Bantu.

The two biggest groups are the Sudanese and the Bantu, both of them linguistic and cultural entities in their own right. The Bantu, who probably originated in the area of the Great Lakes, have maintained greater cohesion than the Sudanese. But both groups include many profoundly different peoples, owing partly to the accidents of history and partly to regional variations. In the case of the Sudanese, there has also been interbreeding with Islamic and Semitic peoples, given the immigration of Moors and Muhammadanized Berber Peuls, who had begun as herdsmen and become more and more settled. A detailed ethnic map of Africa defies any rationale not based on solid practical experience: it reveals endless conflicts, movements and migrations, some pressing forward, others retreating. Hence the mixtures and tensions that are found all over Black Africa; in both the remote and the recent past, successive waves of people either overlapped or fought with each other. There is still not complete stability. It would be fascinating to know of all these migrations, their dates, their direction and their speed. To a diligent research worker, that would not be impossible: it is rare for 'the inhabitants of a village not to know from which village the founders of their community came'.

The tensions were most acute, perhaps, in the area between the twelfth and fifteenth parallels of latitude, populated by the Sudanese. The most typical example is that of the refugee peoples known as palaeo-negritic (implying, as is quite likely, that they are the oldest ethnic group except for the pygmies). They were primitive hunter–gatherers and peasants assiduously fertilizing mountain terrain which was often very poor. By dint of very intense cultivation, they managed to sustain some fifty people in a square kilometre or so; and they usually occupied strongholds which were easy to defend. The same is true of the Dogons, the most northerly of these deeply entrenched people, as it is of all the so-called 'naked tribes' of Africa – 'the Coniagis and Bassaris of Guinea, the Bobos and Lobis of the Ivory Coast, the Nankasas of modern Ghana, the Kabrei and Sombas of Togo and Benin, and the Fabis and Angus of Nigeria'. These are all small ethnic groups, mere specks on the map.

Among the large groups, mention should be made of the Toucouleurs, the Mandingues, the Bambarras, the Hausas, the Yoruba and the Ibo – the last two of which are the two main groups in Nigeria, the richest and most densely populated country in Black Africa.

Each of these peoples has its own beliefs, its own way of life, its own social structure, and its own culture, no two of which are identical. This diversity is what makes Africa so immensely interesting. Experiences differ so markedly from one place to another that it is difficult to imagine a common future for all those concerned.

'The areas in which native Africans have taken refuge from external authority are often quite close to the most highly developed capitals.'

Variations in skin colour, which range from the deepest black of the Sudanese to the light, almost yellow pigmentation of the Hottentots and the pygmies, are only the anthropological, physiological counterparts of a much more essential diversity of societies and cultures.

The African continent suffers, and has suffered in the past, from many privations and serious general weaknesses. It would be impossible to list them all or to describe how at different times they have been better or worse. We have seen that Black Africa has had few outlets to the rest of the world – a serious handicap, because all progress in civilization is made easier by mutual contact and influence. This relative isolation explains the important gaps which were scarcely filled, if at all, before the arrival of the Europeans and the establishment of their colonies. The wheel, for example, was unknown: so were the plough and the use of pack-animals: so was writing except in Ethiopia (which is not really part of Black Africa) and the countries of the Sudan and the East coast (where writing came from Islam, which they very soon adopted).

These examples show that, very often, external influence filtered only very slowly, drop by drop, into the vast African continent South of the Sahara.

The same is true of the often discussed but still unsolved problem of how much Ancient Egypt influenced Black African societies. Glass beads have been found in Gabon, a statuette of Osiris has been discovered at Malonga in South-East Zaïre, and another South of the Zambesi. This is flimsy evidence, but it suggests the possibility of limited relationships, especially in the broad domain of art and its techniques, such as casting by the lost-wax process.

It has to be admitted, however, that exotic plants – certain kinds of rice from the Far East, maize, sugar cane and cassava – came to Africa rather late in the day. They were probably unknown there in ancient times.

There were other weaknesses. One was the shallowness of the red lateritic soil (contrasting with the bright red of rarer deposits, which were deeper and more friable); another was the climatic limit on the number of days when the land could be worked; a third was the regular shortage of meat in most people's diet.

In most African tribes, meat was eaten only at great feasts. The goats and sheep which Kikuyu farmers in Kenya fed on rough pasture around their fields were reserved for sacrifices and public ceremonies. The Kikuyu's nomadic neighbours, the pastoral Masai, lived off the produce of their flocks, but the animals were too valuable to be killed. Meat, seen as a source of strength and virility, was scarce everywhere, and was the subject of longings crudely expressed in this pygmy hunting chant:

> In the forest where no one else goes,
> Hunter, lift up your heart: glide, run and leap.
> Meat is before you, great joyous meat –
> Meat which strides like a hill,
> Meat which rejoices the heart,
> Meat which will roast on your hearth,
> Meat which your teeth will bite,
> Fine red meat, and steaming blood to drink.

Even so, the disadvantages should not be overstressed. First, Black Africa made progress in ancient times that was no less rapid than in prehistoric Europe. There were also artistic triumphs, and not only in the fine Benin bronzes of the eleventh to fifteenth centuries, or the equally fine textiles made from various vegetable fibres. Last but not least, Africa was an early pioneer in metallurgy – as early as 3000 BC in the case of iron. It is absurd – and untrue – to claim that Black Africans were introduced to iron only after the Portuguese reached Cape Bojador on the coast of the Western Sahara in AD 1434. Iron weapons were known very early on. Metalworking was perfected in what is now Zimbabwe as early as the Middle Ages. Tin-working was probably practised in Upper Nigeria 2,000 years ago. Finally – a significant detail – it has often been remarked that in Black African societies the blacksmiths form a separate, powerful and much respected caste. This is certainly the product of very ancient traditions.

The dark past

The long past of Black Africa is little known, as is that of all peoples lacking a written language. Its history has come down to us only through oral traditions, archaeological research and the accounts of occasional outside observers.

Three sets of facts, however, emerge from this dark past: the growth of cities, kingdoms and empires, all of mixed civilization and mixed blood; trade in black slaves, a very ancient practice, which reached diabolical proportions in the sixteenth century, when opening up the American continent proved too great a task for Europe alone; finally, the brutal irruption of the European powers, which in the Final Act of the Berlin Conference in 1885 completed the partitioning, with the aid of a map, of what theoretically remained 'unclaimed' in the huge African continent, still only half explored by Europeans but henceforth totally colonized.

In Black Africa, history favoured the development of higher political and cultural arrangements only where there were, on the one hand, the combined resources of tillage and animal husbandry and, on the other, contacts with the outside world – either along the edge of the Sahara or on the shores of the Indian Ocean. It was there that ancient empires and flourishing ancient cities were to be found.

Here there developed a special Africa whose past is relatively well-known, with societies and cultures organized into States, as against an elusive Africa which left far less trace on history. Referring to some natives on the Atlantic coast of the Sahara, a fifteenth-century Portuguese explorer remarked scornfully: 'They do not even have kings.' So there was one Africa with kings – whose history is not wholly unknown – and another without them, lost in oblivion.

Black Africa, then, developed along two of its outer margins, in which it was in contact with Islam. That contact was not always peaceful and agreeable. It often involved colonization – although it was through colonization that Black Africa was able to breathe the air of the outside world.

The first glimmerings appeared on Africa's Eastern coast. Centuries before the Christian era, it had been in contact with Arabia and the Indian subcontinent. But it was only with the first Muslim expansion, in the seventh century, that very firm links were formed between Arabia and Persia on the one hand and East Africa on the other. From 648 onwards, a series of market towns sprang up: Mogadishu, Sofala, Malindi, Mombasa, Brava and Zanzibar – this last founded in 739 by Arabs from the South of the Peninsula, while Kilwa was founded in the tenth century by the Shirazi, from Shiraz in Persia.

These towns were busy and prosperous on account of the trade in slaves, ivory and gold. Gold was found in large quantities up-country from Sofala, as witness Arab geographers like Masudi (916) and Ibn al Wardi (975). The goldfields and mines seem to have been in Matabeleland, between the Zambesi and the Limpopo, as well as – although some deny it – in what is now the Transvaal. The gold was found in both dust and nuggets. All this trade was linked – thanks to the monsoon – with India, which exported iron and cotton goods.

Mainly African, these towns had only a small minority of Arab or Persian colonists: they also had closer links with India than with Arabia. Their apogee was in the fifteenth century, but at that time their economy was still based on barter, not money, at least as regards trade with the African interior. The latter profited from it nevertheless. Far away as it was, it had political structures like the Kingdom of Monomotapa in what is now Zimbabwe (Monene Motapa signified 'Lord of the Mines'). Admittedly, we know less about the kingdom than its fame might suggest: it is said to have been destroyed in the seventeenth century by the Mambo or sovereign of the Rowzi.

It used to be thought that after Vasco da Gama's voyage in 1498, the establishment of the Portuguese in the Indian Ocean dealt a mortal blow to the trading towns of the Southern African coast. Today, this view is no longer held. Their hybrid civilization – half-African, half-Arab – continued to spread through the interior, although the coastal towns made no attempt to conquer it. The coastal ruins in Kenya and Tanzania, which used to be thought medieval, seem in fact to date from the seventeenth, eighteenth and even the nineteenth centuries. All, incidentally, used blue-and-white Chinese porcelain.

The Empires on the bend of the Niger bring us to another busy and fruitful contact with Islam. As we have said, trade links with the edge of the Sahara increased at the beginning of the Christian era, with the arrival of the dromedary in North Africa and on the desert trails. The growth of trade (in gold and slaves) and the increase in the number of caravans led White (chamito-Semitic) Africa into the land of the Blacks (which the Arabs called the *Bled es Sudan*).

The first of these Niger empires, Ghana, seems to have been established around AD 800 (and so was contemporary with Charlemagne). Its capital, also called Ghana and proverbial for its wealth, was at Kumbi Saleh, 340 kilometres North of Bamako in present-day Mali, on the edge of the Sahara. It may have been built by white men from the North; in any case, it soon belonged to Black people of the Soninke tribe, a branch of the Mande people, who in turn were part of the Mandingos. Attacked by the Muslims, the capital was captured and destroyed in 1077.

But because the trade in gold continued (from the goldfields of Senegal, the Benue River and the Upper Niger), another Empire soon came into being slightly to the East, benefiting the Mandingos and owing allegiance to Islam. This was the Mali Empire, which spread throughout the whole bend of the Niger. Under the reign of Kankan Musa (1307–37), who went on pilgrimage to Mecca, a number of merchants and educated people reached the banks of the Niger. Timbuktu then became an influential capital, regularly frequented by the nomadic Touaregs. Later, they seized the town and contributed to the downfall of the Empire.

A further Eastward thrust then brought prosperity to the Songhay Empire, with its capitals in Gao and Timbuktu. The Empire benefited from its links with Cyrenaica and from the exploits of Sonni Ali (1464–92), who was no doubt the strongest of all these builders of Empires. He himself was not a very orthodox Muslim, but his successor's defeat by the usurper Muhammad Askia marked the definitive victory of Islam in the new Empire.

By now, however, the glorious heyday of the Nigerian Empires was over. The Atlantic sea-route discovered by the Portuguese became the new channel for Black African gold; and although this did not kill the Saharan trade it greatly weakened it. During this general decline, a Moroccan expedition led by Spanish renegades conquered Timbuktu and destroyed the Songhay Empire in 1591. This success earned the Sultan of Morocco, Moulay Ahmed, the titles of El Mansur (the victorious) and El Dehbi (the golden). Yet the expedition was a complete disappointment for its organizers, who had hoped to conquer a fabulous El Dorado. The Sultan retained only formal and distant sway over these impoverished countries, where from 1612 to 1750 there were no fewer than 120 pashas, pawns in the hands of the Moorish garrisons which elected and, if necessary, dismissed them.

In the eighteenth century, in fact, power in the countries of the Niger was shared between the nomads and the Bambarras of Segu and Kaarta. The age of the great Empires was past. The prosperous trans-Saharan trade alone had established and maintained their brilliant and precocious supremacy. They died with it.

These great States, therefore, should not be regarded as typical: they were the exception rather than the rule. Few other States in Black Africa attained such proportions. Thus Benin, already outstanding in the eleventh century and enjoying a degree of artistic perfection in the fifteenth, was of very limited size. Essentially, it was a clearing, none too well organized, in the dense

mass of equatorial rain forest between the waters of the Gulf of
Guinea and the inland tablelands. It was in Yoruba country,
between the Niger Delta and present-day Lagos, in a region very
early built up.

Its reputation outstripped its size. It enjoyed the equivocal
advantage of fairly early contact, via the Northern trade routes,
with Cairo's artists and wealthy customers, and later with the
Portuguese. These links gave it the further benefit of becoming an
astonishing artistic centre for sculptors in ivory and workers in
bronze. Its amazing, prodigious success was not the work of its
princes. According to one Africanist, Paul Mercier, Benin owed
far more to the high density of its Yoruba population, its urban
structure, and its climatic good fortune. Being close to the Gulf of
Guinea, it had two rainy seasons (at the sun's two zeniths) and
therefore two harvests a year instead of one.

The major phenomenon of the fifteenth century, and still more of the
sixteenth, was the development of the trade in Black slaves. Despite
official bans, this continued until about 1865 in the North Atlantic
and probably still later in the South Atlantic, while it persisted
into the twentieth century along the Red Sea routes leading to the
East.

Black slave-trading was not a diabolical invention from Europe.
It was Islam, in very early contact with Black Africa, through the
countries between Niger and Dar-Fur and via its markets in East
Africa, which first practised the Black slave trade on a large scale.
Its reasons were the same, incidentally, as those which led Europe
to follow suit: it lacked manpower for many laborious tasks. But
trade in slaves has been a universal phenomenon, affecting all
primitive societies. And although Islam was then a slave society
par excellence, neither slavery nor the slave trade was its invention.

The Black slave trade has left behind very many documents (for
example in the commercial archives of both Europe and the New
World), from which one can glean statistics and series of prices.

This bookkeeping history, unpleasant in itself, is not the whole of the story: but it gives a necessary sense of scale.

In the sixteenth century, annual shipments of Black slaves to America amounted to between 1,000 and 2,000; in the eighteenth, they were between 10,000 and 20,000; and the biggest total, some 50,000, was reached in the nineteenth century just before the trade was banned. These figures are approximate, as are global estimates of the number of Black Africans transported to the New World. The most convincing are those published by P. Rinchon: about 14 million – which is more than Moreau de Jonnès thought in 1842 (12 million), but fewer than the estimate made by the demographer Carl Saunders, who perhaps went too far in approaching the 20 million mark. Saunders's figures would presuppose an average of sixty thousand slaves a year for the three and a half centuries between 1500 and 1850 – a number which seems not to tally very well with even the transport that was available.

We also have to distinguish between departures from Africa and arrivals in the New World. There were considerable losses, owing partly to the circumstances of capture and partly to the very severe conditions on the voyage. So the damage done by the European slave trade alone no doubt greatly exceeds what the above figures would suggest. The slave trade caused huge human losses to Black Africa.

These were all the more catastrophic in so far as the slave trade with Islam continued too, and even increased at the end of the eighteenth century. Caravans arriving in Cairo from Dar-Fur could bring 18,000 to 20,000 slaves in one trip. In 1830, the Sultan of Zanzibar claimed dues on 37,000 slaves a year; in 1872, 10,000 to 20,000 slaves a year left Suakin for Arabia. At first sight, the Islamic slave trade seems to have affected far more people than the European slave trade, which was limited by the length of the voyage, the smallness of the ships and the abolition of the trade itself, proclaimed several times in the nineteenth century – which proves that trading continued despite its prohibition, although against the difficulties that all smuggling has to meet.

V. L. Cameron, in 1877, reckoned that the annual outflow to Islam, via the North and the East, was some 500,000 people, and he concluded: 'Africa is bleeding from every pore.' This enormous figure can be accepted only with reservations; but the traffic was certainly very extensive and the demographic loss for Africa was appalling.

The question then arises: how far did the Black population compensate for this catastrophic deficit by increasing the birth-rate? In about AD 1500 the population of Africa was between 25 and 35 million, White Africans included. This, of course, is an historical estimate. By 1850, it was at least 100 million. So, despite the great depredations of the slave trade, there was demographic growth. It was a growing population that made possible the terrible trade in slaves. This may explain how the trade continued so long – but as a hypothesis only.

It has to be recognized, frankly, that the European slave trade stopped at the very moment when America no longer urgently needed it. European emigration to the New World took the place of the Black slave trade, in the first half of the nineteenth century towards the United States, in the second towards South America. One may add, in Europe's defence, that there had always been reactions of pity and indignation *vis-à-vis* Black slavery. Nor were these purely formal, for they culminated, eventually, in William Wilberforce's great movement, in Britain, for the liberation of the blacks and the abolition of slavery.

Without claiming that one branch of the slave trade (towards America) was more humane – or less inhumane – than the other (towards Islam), one might further point out a fact which is important for the present time: i.e. that there are still African communities in the New World. Powerful ethnic groups have developed and survived in both North and South America, whereas no such exiled African communities are still to be found in Asia or the lands of Islam.

This is not the place to condemn, still less to praise, the European colonization of Africa, but simply to note that colonization, like almost all culture-contact between civilizations, had both positive and negative cultural impact.

Colonization was ugly: it involved both atrocities and absurdities, such as the purchase of vast territories for a few rolls of cloth or a little alcohol. One is not defending such things by admitting that the shock of colonization was often decisive and even at length beneficial for the social, economic and cultural development of the colonized Black peoples themselves. For Europe, after the final act of the Congress of Berlin in 1885, the colonization of Africa was the last great overseas adventure. And if this tardy takeover was short-lived (lasting less than a century), it took place rapidly, and at a time when Europe and the world economy were in full expansion.

It was a developed and demanding industrial society, with modern means of action and communication, which met and invaded Black Africa. And Africa itself was receptive, more flexible than ethnographers even recently believed: it was able to seize the objects and practices offered by the West, and reinterpret them, giving them new meaning, and matching them whenever possible to the needs of its traditional culture.

Even in South Africa, where the Bantu world was subjected to cultural uprooting (entering another civilization) that was all the more rapid in that industrialization and urbanization were more intense there than elsewhere, educated Africans, living in Western style, nevertheless held to the traditions inherited from their past, if only as regards marriage, the family and the roles of brothers and of eldest or youngest sons. To take one example, the dowry for the bride's father is today paid in cash, but reckoned in heads of cattle in accordance with former custom.

Referring to colonialism's positive impact, we were not thinking of purely material benefits such as roads, railways, ports and dams, or those systems for exploiting the soil or the subsoil which the

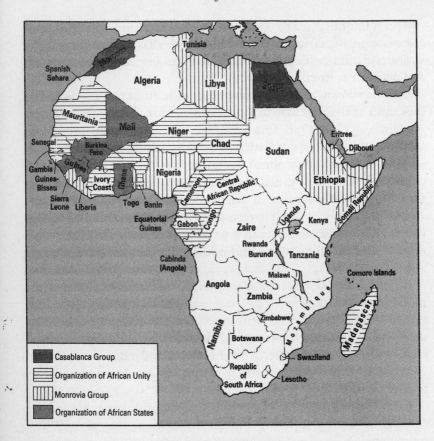

8. Africa's internal diversity

Over and above national diversity there are fragile links between groups of States.

colonists established, very much for their own ends. This legacy, important as it sometimes seems, would be of little use and short lifespan if those who received it had not also acquired, in the painful ordeal of colonization, the ability to use it rationally today. Education and a certain level of technology, of hygiene, of medicine and of public administration: these were the greatest benefits left by the colonists, and some measure of compensation

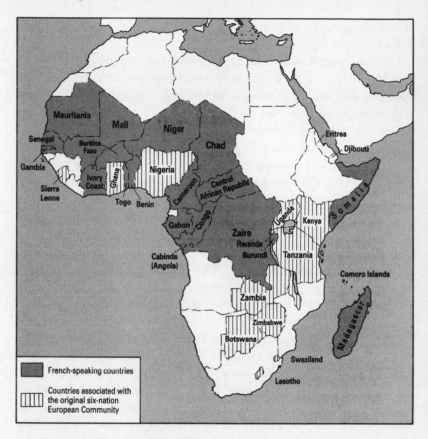

9. Africa and the West

Alongside French-speaking Africa, there is English-speaking Africa, slightly more scattered. Economic ties reflect these cultural links.

for the destruction which contact with Europe brought to old tribal, family and social customs, on which all of Africa's organization and culture were based. It will never be possible to gauge the full results of such novelties as employment for wages, a money economy, writing and individual ownership of land. Each was undoubtedly a blow to the former social regime. Yet these blows were surely a necessary part of the evolution taking place today.

On the other hand, colonization had the real disadvantage of dividing Africa into a series of territories – French, English, German, Belgian, and Portuguese – whose fragmentation has been perpetuated today in too large a cluster of independent States, which are sometimes said to have 'Balkanized' Africa.

Some of these divisions are artificial, and some are geographical. Very few have any cultural basis. But are they irreparably harmful? They may well seriously hinder the fulfilment of some visions of a united Africa, or at least of an African common market. But it is not certain whether Africa is ready, as yet, for political or even cultural unity. It is not only the old colonial administrative frontiers that divide the continent: there is also ethnic, religious and even linguistic diversity. The main weakness of today's national divisions is their failure to correspond to cultural frontiers. But could they have been expected to do so, more than a hundred years ago?

A still more serious reproach is that colonization, when giving Black Africans the useful tool of a modern international language, actually played a bad trick on them by giving them at least two: French and English. It is to be feared that everything a language brings with it, shaping and colouring education and habits of thought, will tend to thwart Africa's efforts for unity by dividing it into two camps, English-speaking and French-speaking. It seems unlikely that one will swamp the other – for example that the numerical advantage of English-speaking Africa will overcome French-speaking Africa, which is culturally stronger and which has enjoyed for far longer an effective educational system producing the political and administrative infrastructure which is the best guarantee of success.

None the less, it is regrettable for the future of African unity that this important division should have been added to all those which history and geography have already too lavishly conferred.

9. Black Africa: Today and Tomorrow

For a study of civilizations, Black Africa is a very rich source. Most of it, in recent years, has achieved independence. 'Negritude' or the search for indigenous roots, which has been called 'a form of humanism in the making', has begun to articulate specifically African values and possibilities. Africans are eagerly seeking their own history, which has to be pieced together and almost invented. All this gives Black Africa one great advantage: it is a cultural world in full and rapid evolution. To the outside observer it offers every conceivable pattern of life, from the most archaic to the most modern and urban. It also embodies every stage of culture-contact.

The awakening of Africa

All African experts seem to agree on one point: they have every confidence in Africans' immense adaptability, their great powers of assimilation and their exemplary patience. All these will be needed if they are to travel alone, and increasingly alone, the very long road that will lead them from a still rudimentary economy to a fully developed one, from a still tempting traditional life to the hard necessities of change, from a still partly tribal society to the national discipline required for modernization and industrialization. Everything has to be created – even the right mentality.

We should not forget that Black Africa is facing this long-drawn-out challenge with little organization, limited resources, and a great variety of attitudes in different regions and among different peoples.

To begin with, much of the continent is still underpopulated, lacking the superabundance of manpower which both handicaps and helps most under-developed countries. In the league table of development, Black Africa comes last. This will no doubt make possible the most spectacular progress: but it also implies the longest distance to go.

In the bedrock of its ancient cultures, Africa is not really one entity. Its traditional civilization, which already embodied many different beliefs and attitudes, acquired new religious elements from outside. It was affected above all by Islam, with its social and intellectual prestige and its admittedly mediocre Koranic schools. Islam, in fact, made great concessions to primitive religions, which it transcended but did not exclude. The second great outside influence was that of Christianity, which generally developed where trade was most intense. It too superimposed itself on a whole series of ancient beliefs and customs.

One must add to these differences a number of economic contrasts, notably the huge gulf between areas open to trade and those closed to it, or between town and country.

Such is the rather incongruous whole which is rapidly being transformed to meet a future that black statesmen and intellectuals seem to contemplate with both courage and common sense.

This transformation is undoubtedly essential; and it does not depend solely on the policies and attitudes of the newly independent African countries *vis-à-vis* the rest of the world or the problems of Africa itself – including its possible unity or its passionate disputes, as exemplified in the Conferences of Casablanca (January 1961), Monrovia (May 1961) and Lagos (February 1962).

Admittedly, policy is important: but it is only a means to an end. It changes, and can be deflected by the least puff of wind. Above all, it alone cannot fully control the enormous change of which it is a part.

Steeped as it is in primitive religion and culture, the weight of past tradition slows down the general impetus and complicates, or at least delays, the changes that need to be made.

Most of the people in Black Africa (especially in the rural areas which make up the vast majority of the continent) still owe allegiance to primitive cultures and religions which form the basis of their whole society. Traditional religion takes different forms according to regions and ethnic groups. Everywhere, however, it is animistic, in the sense of believing that all natural beings are inhabited by spirits which survive their death, and that spirits also inhabit objects (fetishism). Another common and almost universal feature is ancestor-worship. Legendary chiefs or heroes, revered at first as ancestors, are eventually assimilated into the ranks of the higher gods, often headed by the Great God of Heaven, of the Earth or of the Creation. The spirits of African ancestors or gods not only show themselves to the living, but may also return to take possession of them. This is the significance of a number of sacred dances, like those in Benin in which the gods Vodun or Orishas 'descend upon the head' of certain performers, who go into a trance as soon as the god inhabits them.

In all these cults, 'prayers and invocations are said, gifts of food and palm oil are offered, and animals are sacrificed' on the altars of gods or ancestors, who are thereby 'fed'. In return, they are expected to help and protect the living.

This religious organization is the guarantor of Africa's social organization, invariably based on the notion of kinship and the patriarchal family, in accordance with strict hierarchy which gives the patriarch absolute authority over the whole community of the family or clan (that authority normally being inherited through the male line from father to son, and more rarely through the female line).

In those societies which were formerly under the influence of the great African Empires, the social hierarchy gives certain families aristocratic superiority over the others; there are also 'castes' based on the artisan professions. Each of them has gods and ancestors whose respective power closely corresponds to that of the social groups themselves.

So strong is the link between religion and society that in the towns, where this social order is dislocated by modern life (and especially by education), either Christianity or Islam, according to circumstances, has tended very largely to replace animism, which remains the religion of the rural areas. Every town and every region affected by education, by modernization or by industry and organized labour, has therefore to grapple with the difficult problems of culture-contact.

One example is the survey made in 1958 in Porto Novo, in Benin (formerly Dahomey), by the sociologist Claude Tardits. Obviously, it cannot be valid for the whole of Africa. But it gives an idea of the problem. Porto Novo, which is Benin's capital, is an old city with awkward access to the sea and therefore somewhat superseded by the port of Cotonou. Despite this relative decline, Porto Novo remains lively, in a country which is better educated and more intellectual than its neighbours. Benin, as Emmanuel Mounier said, 'is the Latin Quarter of Black Africa'.

This does not mean that education forever guarantees the future of those known locally as '*évolués*' – those who have gone to school and, as the saying goes, 'seen the light'. (In 1954, 43,419 children, or 15 per cent of those of school age, actually attended school. For Africa, this was a record figure, but its importance should not be exaggerated.) There are high-grade and low-grade *évolués*. At the top of the social pyramid, in a population of perhaps just over 1.5 million people, only 100,000 of them city-dwellers, the genuine élite of truly cultivated people would number at the most 1,000 – three times the number of the former white colony, which was only 300 strong. And how hard it is to train even this tiny minority!

In Porto Novo itself the chief obstacle, naturally, is the inertia of a traditional society which is already diverse and divided – into at least three groups. One consists of the Gun, the descendants of Benin peasants now settled in the town. A second is the Yoruba, merchants from neighbouring Nigeria. A third is made up of 'Brazilians', Africans who have returned from Brazil, often Christians, but sometimes Islamic converts who have had astonishing adventures. Each of these groups has its own insignia, its own susceptibilities, its own ways of resisting change. Each, too, has its clans; and it is according to clan that houses are grouped, that marriages were and often still are arranged, and that religious rules and practices are maintained. On the value of religion as a social cement, a missionary at Porto Novo had this to say: 'On fetishism I will make only one remark, but it may have some value as coming from a missionary: it is a fine institution which is on the wane.' He added: 'I do not say that it is a fine religion.'

Women were the first to revolt against family tradition, so as to be able to make (as one in two of them now do) the marriage of their choice. But emancipation has still to contend with a polygamous and deeply conservative past, as witness this confession by a Benin woman: 'When my husband took other wives, he gave me the money because I was his first, and I distributed it to the others. It was I who chose my husband's other two wives, whom he took some years after we were married. My fellow-wives kneel to me and perform the services I ask of them.' Another added:

I kneel to my father-in-law, to my mother-in-law, and to the uncles and aunts and elder brothers and sisters of my husband. I do not kneel to the younger brothers and sisters, but I owe them respect. I serve all my husband's family: I run errands, I do the housework, I draw water for everyone, I go to market, I grind the pimento. When I prepare a meal, I from time to time offer a little of the food I have cooked to an aunt, an uncle or a brother of my husband's, or to my mother-in-law or my father-in-law.

Imagine, therefore, an *évolué* in the midst of such a clan, and in a city still more than half rustic. He will be torn between his new cultural habits, sometimes acquired abroad, and these rituals which have not necessarily lost all hold on him – between affection for his family and the impossibility of obeying all its laws.

What dislocates everything is the urban environment – work, school, even the sight of street life, in contrast with rural surroundings, where everything remains stubbornly unchanged. A certain dressmaker, an *évoluée*, learned her trade with the nuns in Cotonou, then married a civil servant. She was happy in her workshop and with her clients. 'After we had been married for a year my husband, who is a clerk in the administration, was sent to the North. There I had nothing to do, because the women either dress in leaves or go naked.' Finally, the husband was moved back. 'For the last year I have lived in Porto Novo ... My husband has bought me another sewing-machine.'

In line with this example one has only to think of the elegant women of the cities, or the Dakar models draped in sumptuous white. A vision of the future, like the bold modernity of the city: less poetic no doubt than the old colonial houses of Gorée on the island opposite Dakar, but more in the spirit of the times.

Town and country here are engaged in the age-old dialogue between advanced civilizations and primitive cultures. But in Africa the towns are only a minority. And the speed of African development will finally depend on their relative strength or weakness.

Although quickly established, Africa's independent governments have shown in practice unexpected stability. Since this is a general phenomenon it calls for a general explanation, interesting as individual instances may be. In fact, in the face of these governments, the governed have shown unlimited patience, much greater for instance than the deference of Louis XIV's subjects *vis-à-vis* their *Roi Soleil*. To rule, in Black Africa, necessarily means to reign. Surprising as it may seem, the exercise of power there rejuvenates and reinvigorates rather than wearying the ruler. The President of Liberia, Mr Tubman, in office since 1944, was still there in 1962, and was re-elected in 1963: an impressive record. There seems to be something about power here which shields it from European instability: perhaps it has an almost royal tinge.

At all events, on the base of the statue of the Osagyefo ('Victori-ous in All') of Ghana, President Kwame Nkrumah, the following inscription is carved: 'Seek ye first the kingdom of politics, and all these things shall be added unto you.' It corresponds to the terser French maxim: 'Politics first.'

So power has to be seized and retained. Since it cannot be divided and can barely be supervised, the opposition has no role. To show itself, indeed, would be fatal. Ghana, Sierra Leone and Guinea have shown this plainly enough. Already there are young intellectuals, at odds with their countries' dictatorial governments, who travel through Europe or find places in American universities: some of them are dismissed ambassadors who think it wise not to return home. Hence the remark by the Prime Minister of Senegal: 'Ghanocracy does not interest us' – a proof that Africa is far from uniform, even on the political plane.

We should recognize, however, that African rulers need a great deal of wisdom to resist very tangible temptations. If Europeans are not to be unfair in judging governments and one-party States which seem to them outlandish, they have to realize how small, in Africa, is the governing class. The rulers of Black Africa are always surrounded by the same exiguous élite, far fewer in number than those who in the past served René of Anjou or Philip the Fair. Liberia, for example, is run by some 2 per cent of its popula-tion, Afro-Americans of whom not all are even probably full-time employees. The mass of the population remains inert, alienated from the official apparatus of the State, or what the French call '*le pays légal*'. This does not mean that the small élites are undivided: there are endless disagreements within them, and sudden energetic action by the authorities is not without justification.

At the same time, if governing poses few political problems, its administrative problems are immense. If people are to be commit-ted to modernization, they must be convinced and recruited. In tackling this difficult task, some governments have been trapped in their own demagogic schemes.

Effective administration needs people, managers, unswerving

devotion and discipline; building from scratch needs capital and carefully calculated investment. Above all, reason must reign supreme – which is the rarest of all situations, in every country in the world.

In Guinea-Bissau, the first of France's former possessions in Africa to choose freedom and independence when they were offered by the Government of General de Gaulle in 1958, President Sékou Touré's Socialist Government produced a three-year plan. In itself, it was not wrong-headed or mistaken: but it had been drawn up on the basis of economic criteria and statistical series – whereas traditional society is always a further element of the problem that should be taken into account. 'One after another, various State enterprises in charge of importing foreign produce collapsed: Alimag, which specialized in food; Libraport, for paper and books; Ematec, for technical supplies; Pharmaguinée, for pharmaceuticals; and all their sister firms.' Their failure was not due only to internal (and external) scandals: it was also the result of miscalculation – creating organizations which took no account of Guinea's human element. These presupposed not only honest and well-educated people, but an administrative hierarchy, managers, and a system of checks. All nationalized industries require very competent and ubiquitous managers. Here, they have to be trained.

Economic and social issues at stake

The future of the Black African States is still uncertain: it is being decided on the chessboards of Africa and the world – with vigour, and with some illusions.

Some of the players have short-term and perhaps ill-judged designs on the territory of their immediate neighbours. Africa's artificial frontiers are no justification for this: but they sometimes serve as a pretext.

Morocco has in the past laid claim to the whole of Mauritania, to the Rio de Oro, to Ifni and to part of the Algerian Sahara. Guinea-Bissau has cast envious eyes on densely populated Sierra Leone. Ghana — whose name deliberately recalls the great Empire of the past — has historical arguments for seeking to annexe Togo and the Ivory Coast. Mali — whose name is equally significant — dreams of 'federating' with Burkina Faso and Niger, and helping itself to part of the Algerian Sahara. Broader if more abstruse ambitions have included the gathering of African States into two groups, as at the time of the two rival Conferences in 1961. The Casablanca group — the extremists — comprised Morocco, Ghana, the United Arab Republic as it then was (Egypt and Syria), Guinea, the provisional Government of Algeria, and Mali. The Monrovia group — the sensible moderates — consisted of Tunisia, Libya, Mauritania, Senegal, Sierra Leone, Liberia, the Ivory Coast, Upper Volta (now Burkina Faso), Nigeria, Niger, Chad, Cameroon, the Central African Republic, Gabon, Congo Brazzaville (now Congo), Ethiopia, Somalia and Madagascar.

Even at the time, such classification looked impermanent, if only because the independence of Algeria was shortly to introduce an unpredictable new element. Much has changed since then; and the future remains undecided — including the future of African unity or the quest for it. This was the subject of the third Conference at that time, held in Lagos in February 1962, and badly prepared by the Nigerian Government. It failed: the 'Brazzaville Twelve' faced opposition from the Casablanca group, for whom the failure to invite the provisional government of Algeria provided a good pretext for intransigence.

These and subsequent manoeuvres were inevitably complex. Everyone is in principle committed to an Africa entirely free: but freedom can mean many different things. President Nkrumah wanted the last of European occupation to come to an end by 31 December 1962; but at the same time he sought to secure from this 'strong man' policy a position of leadership which the other States were not eager to grant him. This was also what held up the proposed union between Ghana and Guinea.

Even a generation later, it remains very hard to see which if any country or group of countries is likely to emerge above the others and impose unity on all of them. Leadership is as much a matter of wisdom as of brute force, and more a matter of real power than of political strength.

In size of population – which implies so much in a continent short of people – English-speaking Africa certainly predominates, owing both to a high general density and to the towns of Ghana, Sierra Leone and Nigeria. Progress is in the towns: those of Nigeria are the largest in Black Africa. In 1963, Lagos had more than 300,000 inhabitants and Ibadan more than 500,000; by 1980, Lagos had more than 4 million, and Ibadan about 1 million.

French-speaking Black Africa, at first with the exception of Guinea, quickly became associated with the European Community; English-speaking Black Africa followed suit when the Community was enlarged to include Britain.

Despite its relative demographic weakness, French-speaking Black Africa also enjoys the advantage of a well-educated middle class. Geographers add that one city in French-speaking Africa, because of its position and its power, is of world status. That is Dakar, which commands both the South Atlantic and the trans-African air route. All this of course may either change as world communications change, or in fact be confirmed.

What is really at stake, surely, is development – an evolution in terms of power, numbers, and economic progress. Except for the oil-works of Senegal and the aluminium factories of Guinea, Africa's backward economy supplies raw minerals and foodstuffs, and buys industrial products. Its future will necessarily depend on both suppliers and purchasers. In normal conditions of reciprocal trade, the possibilities for development and for annual investment remain meagre, and their growth is slow. In trying to improve matters, one is liable to turn to a credit policy, which opens the way to immediate dependence, whether one likes it or not. If the USSR supplied the rails for the Conakry–Kankan railway, which had to be maintained and repaired, this raised the question of which technicians would do the job, and what role there was for the railwaymen and their trade unions. If Senegal or Benin undertook to set up an important university faculty, they would no doubt do so on an almost totally non-fee-paying basis, along the lines they had inherited from France. But for this they would need both teachers and credits from France, as they have needed technicians and secondary-school teachers too. One thing leads to another.

So Black Africa cannot avoid seeking aid from the two great industrial blocs, and indeed from the third, China, which offers its services in a missionary spirit, but always with a large human contingent owing to its own abundance of people.

Without accepting one or other of these solutions, or all of them at once, Black Africa has no hope of completing important public works or carrying out economic plans. It is not enough even to make sacrifices as remarkable as those agreed to in Nigeria on 19 December 1961, the anniversary of its independence. These included: reduced salaries for members of the Government, no more official cars, no more paid overtime and an increase in taxes. There still remained a need for machine tools. Mali, likewise, after its break with Senegal, was saved only by the lorries supplied by the German Federal Republic to give it an outlet to Kankan, the Conakry railway and the ocean beyond.

Equally, all the machinery in the world would be useless without the skilled manpower to use it. This vital problem depends on prior conscious effort on the part of the African countries themselves.

In Guinea, under the Communist-inspired regime of Sékou Touré, a Swiss journalist reported on a conversation with some Czechoslovak technicians. 'Look,' said one of them:

the French had an advantage over us. They could give orders. Yesterday, my car's battery went flat. That was all; but at the official garage no one would listen to me, and the black mechanic immediately fiddled with the carburettor. They have a mania for getting at the most delicate parts of the engine. The result is that since then I have to walk everywhere, and it may last quite a while. A Frenchman would have blown his top. We're not allowed to. But in this heat and humidity it would have been justified and might have done some good. Africa! I really can't understand why France and Britain ever put this millstone round their necks. My contract runs for a year, and I shall be glad to get away. I shan't have trained anyone: it's quite impossible.

The moral of this small psychodrama is very simple. Education works only if the recipients really want it.

A more hopeful augury is the testimony of a young French teacher who came to the Ivory Coast in October 1961. He was delighted to find what a thirst for knowledge, what spontaneous hard work and what intelligence his second- and third-form pupils showed. They at least knew that they were Africa's future.

Art and literature

What evidence do art and literature provide about this changing world, straddled between today and tomorrow? All observers have to admit that the native African art which the West so greatly admired – masks, bronzes, ivories, wood carvings – is declining and dying before our eyes. It is already dead. Is that because, as is often said – and with some justice – the social and above all the religious framework which had always nurtured such art is itself collapsing under the violent and repeated onslaughts of urban industrial civilization?

At all events, it is undeniable that the Africa we once knew is growing ever more distant, with its songs, its dances, its artistic vision, its religions, its intoned or chanted legends, its conception of time past, of the universe, of people, of plants, of animals and of gods – a whole traditional civilization which, as we know from the example of the West itself, will be swept away if its present deterioration gathers speed.

Yet Europe has conserved more than a little of its traditional past, which it continues to cherish, sometimes unawares. What will Africa retain of its own civilization?

African art takes us back to a vanished civilization, far older than that of the present day. Young Black African literature is different. It is highly Westernized, if only because it uses European languages: there are few literary experiments in African languages, which are oral and have only lately and with difficulty been transcribed. This new literature, moreover, deals with the far end of black evolution – with what the situation is likely to be when the majority of Africans have 'seen the light'. These sturdy, lively stories in fact reflect African reality as seen by the *évolués*, and they cast extraordinary light on those aspects of it which are the most original and the least compatible with the values of other civilizations.

Take for example the *Nouveaux Contes d'Amadou Koumba*, by the already well-known West African writer Birago Diop. Their subject-matter may be the past: but their form, the linear fashion in which they are enclosed in a balanced narrative obeying literary rules, goes well beyond what Jean Duvignaud has called 'the lost paradise' of folk-tales. Their Western style alone denotes a literature 'uprooted from the communities of which it continues to dream'. There is a parallel here with the first Latin writers in Gaul. Wherever new Black literature has arisen (in Africa or in the New World, and in whichever Western language – French, English, Spanish, or Portuguese) – with Langston Hughes, Richard Wright, Aimé Césaire, Senghor (former President of Senegal), Diop, Fanou, Glissant, Ferdinand Oyono, Diolé or Camara Laye – wherever it may be, there should be no talk of betrayal, but rather of passionate attachment across the inevitable gap created by changing times.

'They have modified the very structure of their beings,' as Jean Duvignaud so aptly remarks, 'in so far as a language is a living thing and a way of life. In the process, something has died for ever – the immediacy of mythology.' That is no doubt true. But the change of language is not the only dislocation that has affected these writers. It is a complete metamorphosis, as described in *L'Enfant noir* by Camara Laye, the autobiography of a young villager, a son 'of the great family of blacksmiths', who goes to study in Paris. His mother looks on, helpless, every time he leaves.

Yes, she had had to watch this process, this mechanism that had led from the village school in Kouroussa to Conakry and from there to France; and all this time, while she had struggled, she had had to see the mechanism in motion: first this wheel, then that, then a third, and then others, many others that no one else may have seen. And what could have been done to prevent the wheels turning? One could only watch them, watch the workings of destiny: my destiny was to go!

Yes, a new civilization is emerging, as best it may, fragile or firm, from the age-old flux of a traditional living civilization which still nourishes its peoples. That is the important point. Africa is leaving behind it a civilization many centuries old; but it will not thereby lose *its* civilization. Transformed and divided as it may be, it will remain itself, deeply marked by a psychology, by tastes, by memories, and by everything that gives a land its character. Senghor has even spoken of an African 'physiology' which dictates a certain 'emotive attitude' to the world, so that 'the magic world is more real to the Black African than the visible world' – a path to knowledge, in fact. Those Black writers who appear most Westernized in their work are also those who insist most strongly on the particular psychological insight of their people.

This is confirmed by a further passage from *L'Enfant noir*, which describes the extraordinary, almost magical gifts of its hero's mother.

These wonders – and they really were prodigious – seem to me today like fabulous features of the far distant past. Yet that past was recent – only yesterday. Still, the world is moving and changing, and mine is changing more rapidly, perhaps, than any other: so much so that we seem no longer to be what we were, that we *are* no longer what we were, and that we were already not quite ourselves when these wonders took place before our eyes. Yes, the world is moving and changing: it is moving and changing so much that my own totem – I have my own totem, too – is unknown to me.

Can the break with the past be more vividly described? But the author adds:

I hesitate a little about saying what these powers of my mother's were, and I do not even want to describe all of them: I know that my account will arouse scepticism. Myself, when I remember them, I am uncertain how to take them. They seem incredible; they are incredible! But all I need is to remember what I have seen, what my eyes have seen ... I have seen these incredible things; I see them in my mind's eye as I saw them then. Are there not things everywhere which are not explained? With us, there are countless things that are not explained, and my mother lived in intimacy with them.

'Things that are not explained': they are perhaps the secret that every civilization makes its own.

PART III: THE FAR EAST

10. An Introduction to the Far East

Our intention is to consider *exclusively* the common, convergent characteristics of the Far East, with the successive aid of geography and history, and then to look at the very distant origin of its civilizations, which are still flourishing today. This last is the most important characteristic of all.

What geography shows

Simply to see the Far East in all its immensity is already to go halfway towards understanding its strange destiny and civilizations. For this first contact, travellers, journalists and geographers are the best guides. Provided, that is, that they do not explain everything in authoritarian fashion on the basis of some absolute geographical determinism, which is no more appropriate in Asia than it is in Europe, or in any country long worked upon by history and patient human effort.

The Far East is broadly speaking a tropical and sub-tropical world. It includes the 'furnace' of India, its forests and jungles; Southern China, hot and rainy; and the Indian Archipelago with its giant forests and rapidly growing plants (a metre a day in the case of certain lianas in the Botanical Gardens of Buitenzorg, in Java).

But India itself is also the Indus, the middle Ganges, central Deccan and its dry climate, sheltered by the Western Ghats – in other words arid and semi-arid areas. China, likewise, is also

Northern China, the immense open plains of loess and recent alluvial deposits, with very hard winters, as well as wooded Manchuria and the frozen deserts of the far North.

The whole of Northern China, with Peking, the imperial capital, on its South-Eastern edge, suffers from biting cold. In the winter there, peasants sleep on their stoves. A proverb runs: 'Let everyone sweep the snow from in front of his own door and pay no heed to the white frost on his neighbours' roof-tiles.' 'In winter, when it freezes,' declared a cultivated man in the eighteenth century, 'if poor relations and friends come to our door, we first boil up a big bowl of rice to give them, and we add a small saucer of pickled ginger. This is the best way to warm up old people and comfort those in need. We cook thick soups which we drink with the bowl held in both hands and our necks hunched into our shoulders: on frosty or snowy mornings, when one takes this meal, all of one's body feels warm.'

Sometimes, these cold snaps and sudden snows move down towards the tropical South. In 1189, it snowed at Hangchow, the capital of the Southern Sung dynasty, not far from the Yangtze-Kiang. 'The stalks of the bamboos snapped with a strange sound.'

At first sight, then, geography bears witness to the diversity rather than the unity of these many-faceted countries. But perhaps it is misleading to see things in these terms. The geography of South-East Asia is certainly very varied: but it is not geography which unites the area, but rather a fairly homogeneous *material* civilization which is dominant almost everywhere alongside geographical, physical and human factors. This civilization is too ancient, too deeply rooted in the distant past, and 'the product of too much individual and collective psychology to be regarded as simply a function of local physical conditions' (P. Gourou). It has an autonomous existence as a semi-independent force and an influence on its own.

All reports show that this civilization is everywhere frankly the same, and almost entirely vegetarian. This has been repeatedly affirmed by all Western travellers, in the past as in the present, as soon as they set foot in Asia.

A Spanish visitor in 1609 reported that the only meat eaten by the Japanese was game. A German doctor in about 1690 declared they knew nothing of milk and butter. They fed on *gokost*, 'the five products of the earth' (as in China, the figure 5 is sacred in Japan). These products were: rice, 'white as snow'; sake, liquor made from rice; barley, intended in principle for cattle, but used to make flour and cakes (the ears of barley in the fields, said this same doctor, were of an 'admirable red'); finally, white peas not unlike butter beans. To which were added millet, vegetables and fish, but always very, very little meat.

Twenty years earlier, in India, a French doctor watched the huge crowd of the procession which accompanied the Great Mogul Aurangzeb on his journey from Delhi to Kashmir. He was astonished by the sobriety of the soldiers, 'whose food was very simple . . . Of all these horsemen, not a tenth, not even a twentieth eat meat on the march. They are happy so long as they have their *kicheris*, a mixture of rice and other vegetables, over which they pour browned butter.'

The inhabitants of Atchin on the island of Sumatra were no more demanding. 'Their only food is rice,' said a traveller in 1620. 'The rich add a little fish and some greenstuffs. One has to be a great lord in Sumatra to have a roast or boiled chicken . . . They say that if there were 2,000 Christians on the island they would soon exhaust its stock of beef and poultry.'

China lived on the same diet. 'If the Chinese ate as much meat as we in Spain do,' wrote Father de las Cortes in 1626, 'there would not be nearly enough grazing for it.' Even the rich were content with little. 'To give themselves an appetite they garnish their meals with small pieces of pork or chicken or other meat' – what we might call titbits. A British traveller in the eighteenth century made the same point. Even in Peking, supplied with animals from Tartary, 'the people eat only very little meat, which they mix with vegetables to give it some taste. Milk, butter, and cheese . . . are little known to the Chinese.' Not that they disliked meat: far from it. If an animal – a cow, a camel, a sheep or an ass –

died from an accident or a disease, it was eaten at once. 'These people do not know the difference between clean and unclean meat,' the British traveller concluded in some disgust. In China, they ate snakes, frogs, rats, dogs, bats and so on.

These observations are confirmed by innumerable passages of Chinese literature itself, which is admirably precise about matters of daily life. A character in one novel, a spoiled young widow, 'one day wants duck, the next day fish and at other times fresh vegetables and bamboo-shoot soup. When she has nothing to do, she must have oranges, biscuits and water-lilies. She drinks a lot of rice wine; every evening, she eats fried sparrows and salted crayfish; she drinks three litres of wine made from a hundred flowers.' All of which, clearly, is debauchery, the caprice of the rich.

Chen Pan K'ia (1693–1765), poet, painter, calligrapher, and a very generous man, wanted all the people in his house to share in feast days. He wrote in his *Family Letters*: 'Every time there is fish, boiled rice, fruits and cakes, they should be shared out fairly.' The food mentioned in his letters include buckwheat girdle-cakes and thick, warm rice soups. Such was the norm. Even a very rich moneylender, the owner of a pawnshop, who is described in a medieval tale, although he pounces with delight on any *sapeke* coin he finds on the ground, lunches on 'a plate of cold rice with boiling water poured over it'.

Little, in fact, has changed in the twentieth century. In 1959, a journalist wrote: 'I know very well that Chinese cooking has always been the art of making something out of nothing; that a nation of too many people, forbidden to raise beef cattle – which is a gross waste of calories – tries to use everything that we let slip away.'

The Chinese remain vegetarians: 98 per cent of the calories they consume come from vegetable sources; they use no butter, cheese or milk, and very little meat or fish. Their carbohydrates come in part from wheat, and in the North from millet, while rice predominates in the South. Their protein comes from soya, mustard seed and various vegetable oils.

The one country that is changing its food habits, vastly increasing its fish consumption and above all turning to meat, is Japan.

The ubiquity of rice in the South-East and its export to the North are the reasons why this vegetarian diet is so widespread. The West, consuming wheat and other similar cereals, was obliged thereby to adopt, very early in its history, first the practice of leaving fields fallow and then the rotation of crops. Otherwise, the soil was rapidly exhausted and wheat produced no yield. Part of the land, therefore, automatically became grassland or pasture – all the more so because wheat growing required considerable help from animals. Rice, by contrast, can be grown in the same area every year, indefinitely. Most of the work is manual, and buffaloes are used only for light work in the mud of the paddy-fields. Everywhere, indeed, crops are tended meticulously by hand. In these circumstances, to feed on meat would be a fantastic waste. The animals would have to be fed on grain, which human beings themselves prefer to eat.

The prime result is to make possible a greater increase in population than would be possible on any carnivorous diet. Six or eight peasants can be fed from a single hectare (2.47 acres) if their diet is purely vegetarian. The food productivity of a given area used in this way is undeniably greater than if it is employed otherwise. This is what has made possible the 'teeming Asian millions'.

As in India, the population increase in China is relatively recent. It effectively began in Southern China in the eleventh and twelfth centuries, with the spread of early rice strains, making possible two harvests a year. In the thirteenth century, the population was probably 100 million. From the end of the seventeenth century it grew very rapidly. Today, it is so large that it could not adopt a different diet, even if it wished. 'The Chinese are thus shackled by determinism: their civilization has no option but to continue along the course which it has charted itself.' In the eighteenth century, the population of India also passed the 100-million mark.

Wittfogel holds that: a civilization based on rice implies a system of artificial irrigation, which in turn requires strict civic, social and political discipline. Rice links the peoples of the Far East to water: in Southern India, to tanks or reservoirs; in the Indo-Gangetic Plain, to wells or irrigation canals fed by watercourses. In China, likewise, irrigation takes many forms: in the South it relies on gentle rivers (and on the regular flooding of the Poyang and Tung Ting lakes on the edge of the Yangtze), on wells, on canals (of which the Imperial Canal, now the Grand Canal, was the model, as a means of both communication and irrigation), and on the wild rivers of the North, such as the Pei-ho or the Hoang-ho (the Yellow River), which had to be dammed and tamed – and which still frequently break their banks. Irrigation is practised everywhere, on the terraces of the Philippines or Java, in Cantonese China, in Japan; with its bamboo aqueducts and its primitive or modern pumps it entails strict working discipline and obedience – like ancient Egypt, the classical example of the constraints imposed by irrigation.

Rice-growing almost certainly began in about 2000 BC on levelled-out low-lying ground. It gradually spread to all land that could be watered; and at the same time it was improved by selecting seed which made possible early varieties of rice. From then on, K. A. Wittfogel has argued, rice-growing led to the establishment of authoritarian, bureaucratic regimes in the Far East, with hordes of state functionaries.

This thesis has been challenged, with some justice, on various points of detail. Above all, it is far too simplistic. Water supplies needed for rice, and rice itself, certainly determined many features of life in the Far East: but these constraints were only part of a far more complex structure. That should not be forgotten. Yet, at the same time, those very constraints must be remembered: they mattered, and they matter still.

Huge areas of the Far East remain wild or primitive. Here above all the civilizations of the plain predominate, based on irrigation. True, there are paddy-fields in the mountains too: but they are confined to narrow terraces, in over-populated regions where there are enough people for the immense labour involved, as for instance in Java. Regularly, where intensive cultivation succeeds, civilized people in the Far East occupy only small areas. The rest – especially mountains, isolated regions and certain islands – becomes the refuge of primitive peoples and cultures.

A book published by Georges Condominas in 1957, entitled *We Have Eaten the Forest*, takes us up-country from Saigon to the region beyond the summer resort of Dalat, and chronicles the daily life of a primitive tribe. Its members live in a forest, and every year they take more of it to grow crops. The trees are 'girdled', cut down or burnt. On the land thus cleared, 'planting is done with a dibber: a quick hole in the earth, a few seeds, and a toe to brush the earth back again'. Most of the crop is dry-grown rice. Part of the forest is eaten every year. After twenty years, the tribe returns to its starting-point, if all has gone well – i.e. if the forest, left to lie fallow, has grown again in the meantime.

This itinerant agriculture (known as *ladang* in Malay, and by various other names in the many other places where it is practised) is a primeval affair, practically without domesticated animals. It sustains a thousand different peoples, all extremely primitive. They are ill-adapted, obviously, to the present day: but they survive in isolated areas.

The West, by contrast, assimilated its own primitive peoples very early on. It had no lack of isolated, backward regions: they can still be recognized today. But it managed to reach them, convert them, link them to its cities, and exploit their resources.

No such process took place in the Far East. This immense difference explains the presence in China of so many peoples who have not been 'made into Chinese', and in India that of so many tribes outside the caste system and its taboos (and in effect outside Indian civilization).

It also explains many details of the present and the past. In 1565, at the battle of Talikoti, the 'Hindu' Kingdom of Vijayanagar in the Deccan, despite its million soldiers, was mortally defeated by the cavalry and especially the artillery of the Muslim sultans. The great and splendid city was left defenceless: its inhabitants could not even flee, for all vehicles and all draught animals had left with the army. But it was not the victors who pillaged the city: instead of invading it, they were diverted into pursuing the vanquished and cutting their throats. It was the primitive tribes around the city, hordes of Brinjaris, Lambadis and Kurumbas, who descended on the capital and sacked it.

A German doctor *en route* for Siam in the seventeenth century met a Japanese merchant who a few years before, in 1682, had been shipwrecked with others on a desert island near the coast of Luzon in the Philippines. There had been about ten of them: they had lived well on the abundant eggs of wild birds and the thick banks of shellfish along the coast. After eight years of this luxurious life they built a boat, bent sail, and finally arrived, exhausted, on the island of Hainan in the Gulf of Tonkin. There they learned that they had barely escaped certain death. Hainan was half Chinese and half primitive; and they had been lucky enough to land in the Chinese half. In the other half of the island, the savages would have shown them no quarter. Formosa (Taiwan) likewise, although conquered by the Chinese in 1683, long remained divided into Chinese and non-Chinese areas, like many islands and 'virtually watertight compartments of the continent'.

Present-day figures for the non-Chinese peoples of China remain impressive. While such peoples make up only 6 per cent of the total population, they occupy 60 per cent of China's territory (including, admittedly, such inhospitable areas as the Gobi Desert, Turkestan and Tibet). In terms of space, in other words, they are in the majority.

They include the Chuangs of Kwang-si, the Miaotse, the Lis, the Thais and the Yis (largely dispersed from Yünnan to Kansu); the Hui of Kansu, and the Yaos. *Vis-à-vis* all or most of them, the policy of Imperial China in the past, and of Chiang Kai-shek's China later, was strict segregation. The gates of Yi towns bore notices: 'Yis are forbidden to meet or to walk in the streets in groups of more than three' – 'Yis are forbidden to ride on horseback.' China today has improved their conditions and given them a certain autonomy, but not the semi-independence that the Soviets granted to their ethnic minorities. At the same time, all these backward societies (which practised slavery, as among the Yis of Liangsiang, or serfdom, *ula*, among the Tibetans) have been shaken to their foundations. Determined efforts have been made to give the most primitive among them written languages. Thus today only China concerns itself with its backward peoples (for their own good but certainly against their will).

Between the civilized areas, those occupied by primitive peoples are also the domain of wild animals. There are lions in the Punjab, wild boars on the coasts of Sumatra, crocodiles in the rivers of the Philippines and, everywhere, king of the great cats, the sabre-toothed and sometimes man-eating tiger.

Innumerable past accounts give a more colourful version of this fact. Father de las Cortes, a Spanish Jesuit shipwrecked in 1626 near Canton, spoke of the many tigers who roamed the Chinese countryside and often came into towns and villages to seize human prey.

A French doctor, François Bernier, visited the Ganges Delta in about 1600. Bengal, he reported, was certainly by far the richest and most populous part of India, 'a gift from the Ganges' as Egypt was a gift from the Nile, a great sugar- and rice-producing region. In the midst of this prosperity, however, there were uninhabited islands in the bends of the river, and they were frequented by pirates. 'These islands,' wrote Bernier, 'are peopled only by tigers, who sometimes swim from one island to another, or by gazelles, pigs, and once-domestic poultry returned to the wild. And it is because of these tigers that, when travelling between the islands in small rowing boats, as is the custom, it is dangerous in many places to set foot on land. At night, when mooring the boat to trees, one must take care to keep it some distance offshore, for some always drift in; and it is said that some tigers have been bold

enough to jump into the boats and carry off the people sleeping
there, even choosing (if local boatmen are to be believed) the
biggest and fattest.'

Barbarism against civilization: the evidence of history

The vast civilizations of the Far East – above all, those of India and
China – would have lived in peace if they had been disturbed only
from primitive areas within their borders, the domain of poor
'forest-eating' farmers. But the real scourge, comparable to the
biblical plagues of Egypt, came from the great deserts and steppes
(to the West and North of China, to the North and West of
India), which are torrid under the summer sun, and in winter
buried under enormous drifts of snow.

These inhospitable lands were peopled by pastoral tribes – Turks,
Turcomans, Kirghiz and Mongols. As soon as they appeared in
history, they were what they would remain until their decline in
the mid-seventeenth century: hordes of violent, cruel, pillaging
horsemen full of daredevil courage. Only in the seventeenth
century, in fact, with the aid of gunpowder, did the settled peoples
defeat these savage nomads. Thereafter, they kept them at a
distance: confined and cowed, they were reduced to merely surviving, as they have done to this day. Neither Inner and Outer
Mongolia (Chinese and Soviet), nor Chinese and Soviet Turkestan,
are now in themselves key countries on the chequerboard of the
world. All that matter are their extent and their airfields – which
are not their property.

What is the relevance of these nomads to the study of present-day
civilizations? Their fantastic onslaughts undoubtedly delayed the
development of the great civilizations that were their neighbours.
Hermann Goetz said that of India in his classic compilation *The
Epochs of Indian Civilization*, published from 1929 onwards: but his
remark applies equally to China. For India was open to the world of
the nomads only through the narrow Khyber Pass through the
Afghan mountains, whereas China had the misfortune to be bordered

by the vast Gobi Desert. The Great Wall of China, built from the third century BC onwards, was an important military barrier; but it was more symbolic than effective, and it was breached many times.

According to the Sinologist Owen Lattimore, the nomads were former peasants. The development of more advanced agriculture had forced out those less able to master it, towards the mountain country of the 'forest-eaters', and above all to the edges of the deserts and the steppes. Driven out from richer regions, all they now had were these vast but very sparse pastures. In this way, civilization had been 'the mother of barbarism': it had turned farmers into nomadic shepherds. But these barbarians kept returning from their places of refuge, because of internal crises, social revolutions and great increases of population. They came back to the farmlands – and rarely in peace. They came as raiders, triumphant conquerors: they defied and despised the settled peasants they defeated. Take as an example the *Memoirs of Zehir-Eddin Mohammed Baber* (1495–1530), the first Great Mogul of India, who in 1526 seized most of its provinces in the North:

Although Hindustan is a country full of natural charm, its inhabitants are ungracious, and dealings with them yield no pleasure, no response and no lasting relationship. Without ability, intelligence or cordiality; they know nothing of generosity or manly feeling. In their ideas as in their work they lack method, staying-power, order and principle. They have neither good horses nor tasty meat: they have no grapes, no melons, and no succulent fruit. There is no ice here, and no fresh water. In the markets one can obtain neither sophisticated food nor even good bread. Baths, candles, torches, chandeliers, schools – none of these is known . . .

Apart from the rivers and streams that flow in the ravines and valleys, they have no kind of running water in their gardens or their palaces. Their buildings lack charm, air, regularity and elegance. Country-dwellers and poor people mostly go naked. The only garment they wear is what they call a *langota*, which is nothing but a short piece of cloth hanging down some eighteen inches below their navel. Underneath this there is another piece of cloth fixed between the legs with the cord of the *langota*, which it passes through, and which serves to attach it behind. The women drape round their bodies a *lang*, one half of which they use to cover their loins, and the other half their heads.

The great advantage of Hindustan, apart from the huge size of its territory, is the great quantity of gold to be found there, either in ingots or in coin.

Thus this Muslim from Turkestan, flushed with victory, proud of his nomadic desert life, and looking down from the heights of Islam, passed judgement on the ancient civilization of India, its art, and its architecture. His disdain, although not that of a Westerner, is no more pleasant.

The details of great Mongol conquests need not concern us here, except in so far as they affected China and India, in each case striking a blow to the heart. As in the two last great waves of invasion, in the thirteenth to fourteenth and the sixteenth to seventeenth centuries. The sketch-maps on pp. 86, 192, 227 and 229 show the chronological limits and varying shape of these incursions, both towards the West and distant Europe, and towards the East, with a further drive towards the South and India, and some rebounds in the direction of China. This no doubt was because, from the beginning of the fifteenth century onwards, China was the 'sick man of Asia', attracting the raiders' greed. When Tamerlane (Timur Beg) died in 1405 he was preparing an attack on China.

Each time, in fact, that nomad aggression exploded, China and India were the victims. Nor were their capitals spared. Two pairs of dates by themselves tell the story. In 1215, the year of Philip Augustus's victory over Otto IV at Bouvines, Genghis Khan captured Peking; in 1644 it was captured again by the Manchu, with the help of the Mongols. In 1398 Tamerlane took Delhi; it was taken again by Baber in 1526.

These events were unsung catastrophes. Each time, millions of lives were lost. Until the twentieth century and its technological wars, the West produced nothing like such wholesale massacres. India, where these wars were further complicated by the clash of civilizations (the invading barbarians being converts to Islam), had an appalling history. Like China, it finally triumphed over these multiple invasions only because of its extraordinary hold on life. Moreover, it had never been completely subjugated as far as the tip of Cape Comorin; and the Deccan's economy had always been linked (sometimes by emigration) to the countries of the Indian Ocean.

For India as for China, these tidal waves of invasion meant repeated destruction and setbacks. In the long run, both absorbed their invaders, but at very great cost. Were the barbarians, then, largely responsible for the widening gap between the Far East and Europe? Is that the key element in the region's fate?

For India, this is arguably so. In the beginning (in the second millennium BC) the Aryans of the Punjab were comparable with the ancestors of the Hellenes, the Celts, the Italiots and the Germanic peoples. The counterpart of the *Iliad* and the *Odyssey* was the knightly culture of the *Mahabharatra*, recounting the wars to conquer the upper Gangetic plain. In the fifth century BC, at the time of the Buddha, Northern India was covered with aristocratic republics and small kingdoms not unlike those of Hellas, with the beginnings of commerce as in Greece. In the third century, Chandragupta and Ashoka founded the first Empire, which united Afghanistan and all of India except the southern tip of the Deccan, always beyond the conqueror's grasp. This was the period when Alexander's Graeco-Macedonian Empire was being built. From the time of Christ there began the invasion of the Scythians from the North. It culminated, from the third to eighth centuries, in the vast Gupta Empire, renewing India's endless struggle between fair- and dark-skinned peoples. Soon afterwards, as in the Western Middle Ages, there were masses of peasant serfs, and great feudal States. The parallels between India and Europe were not of course absolute, especially as regards the forms of their respective societies; but there was no overwhelming difference of degree between them until the thirteenth century and the great Mongol assault.

From then on, the gap progressively widened. And the same question arises for China: how far was its development slowed down by the Mongol conquest, completed in 1279, and by that of the Manchu between 1644 and 1683? Until at least the thirteenth century, China was ahead of the West in science and technology. From then, it was outdistanced.

It is clear, all the same, that the invaders from the steppes cannot be held completely responsible for the chequered fate of the Far East. The destruction they wrought was immense. But in time everything was repaired and healed. One might almost say: healed too well. The invasions, which in the West involved breaks with the past and the birth of new civilizations, were material disasters for China and India, but changed neither their way of thinking nor their social structures and way of life. There was never a great leap forward like that which took ancient civilization from Greece to Rome, or converted Rome to Christianity – or like that which led the Middle East to Islam.

The immobility of the Far East, its extraordinary fidelity to its own ways, was partly the result of internal factors. These in turn partly explain its lagging behind the West – which, incidentally, was entirely relative. The Far East did not really drop back: it remained where it was, but at the time when the rest of the world was visibly progressing, leaving it further and further behind.

Distant origins: the reasons for cultural immobility

It was in prehistoric times, undoubtedly, in the dawn of the first civilizations, that the die was cast. The civilizations of the Far East were entities which very early achieved remarkable maturity, but in a setting that made some of their essential structures almost impervious to change. This gave them astonishing unity and cohesion. But they also found it extremely difficult to adapt themselves, to want to evolve and to be able to. It was as if they had systematically rejected the idea of growth and progress.

What we must try to understand, forgetting our Westerners' experiences, is that the two great civilizations of the Far East are thousands of years old. In the Far East, monuments deteriorate and decay all too quickly, in so far as they are often made of fragile materials, as in China and Japan. Human society and culture, by contrast, seem indestructible. They date back, not a few centuries, but to a far more distant past. Imagine the Egypt of the Pharaohs, miraculously preserved, adapted more or less to modern life, but having kept its beliefs and some of its customs.

Hinduism, still very much alive, has been the almost unaltered basis of Indian civilization for more than a thousand years; and it in its turn has borrowed and passed on some religious ideas which date from a further thousand years back. In China, the cult of ancestors and of the gods of nature, which dates from at least the first millennium BC, has continued in Taoism, Confucianism and Buddhism, which have by no means suppressed it. It remains alive.

These ancient and tenacious religious systems are linked with social structures which are no less hardy – castes in India, family and social hierarchies in China. In both cases, perennial religion and perennial society seem to support each other. This is characteristic of primitive cultures, in which all ways of life and thought are totally and directly rooted in the supernatural. This is more disconcerting to find in civilizations like those of India and China, so highly developed in their different domains: but that only makes it all the more remarkable.

Unlike the West, which clearly separates the human from the sacred, the Far East makes no such distinction. Religion is involved with all aspects of human life: the State, philosophy, ethics and social relations. All fully partake of the sacred; and this is what gives them their perennial resistance to change.

By a curious but understandable contradiction, this involvement of the sacred in all aspects of life, including the most trivial, often disconcerts Westerners. Accustomed to place religion on a spiritual pedestal, they get the erroneous impression that in the Far East there is an absence of religious feeling, accompanied but not adequately replaced by formal rituals. What is difficult for Westerners to grasp is the importance and real meaning of these religious rites.

To perform them is to conform to the divine order which governs all human affairs. It is to live a religious life. Thus Hinduism essentially consists much more in the recognition of the values represented by the caste hierarchy than in 'belief in spiritual beings or the cult of the gods, both of which are only a fragment of the whole'.

The Chinese, likewise, are little concerned to distinguish among an infinity of gods. What matters is to perform *vis-à-vis* all of them all the obligatory rites, to do all the duties required by the cult of ancestors, and finally to meet, in family and social life, all the obligations imposed by a complicated hierarchy.

True, the spiritual contexts in India and China are very different: their religious and social systems bear no resemblance at all. If one simply contrasts the West with the Far East *en bloc*, one risks overlooking the latter's deep divisions. India is not China, needless to say. And if China, by contrast with the West, appears to be deeply imbued with religion, compared with India it seems like a rationalist country. In the distant past, in the fifth to third centuries BC, it underwent the major intellectual crisis of the Contending States, which has been likened to the vital philosophical crisis in ancient Greece that saw the birth of the scientific spirit. Confucianism, as we shall see, took up the legacy of this agnostic and rationalist upheaval, adapting it to political circumstances and enabling it to survive the great religious disputes of the third to the tenth century AD, and remodelling it into the neo-Confucianism which prevailed from the thirteenth century onwards.

In China, therefore, two strands of thought coexisted, and the immobility of society was due to political, economic and social factors as much as to religious influence; whereas in India religion played the dominant role. How, there, could one reform human society or even question it, when its organization reflected spiritual truth?

11. The China of the Past

The China of the past, with which we must begin because it has by no means entirely disappeared, took a very long time to acquire and develop its characteristic features. It then became a single entity, difficult to divide into the 'periods' beloved of historians. Over many centuries, through an interminable series of disasters and conquests, it seemed to remain unchanged and unchangeable.

Yet, however slowly this great leviathan evolved, it was never immobile. Like all civilizations, it accumulated experience, and made continual choices among its resources and possibilities. Nor, despite appearances, was it closed to the outside world. External influences reached it and made themselves felt.

Religion

Its first aspects – the most important and the hardest to understand fully – are those of its religious life. This is not easy to define. It included a number of different systems, as did Western religion; but they were not mutually exclusive. A believer might move from one form of piety to another, embracing mysticism and rationalism at the same time. Imagine a European passing from Protestantism to Catholicism, and even to atheism, without meeting the slightest intellectual or religious obstacle, and taking from each of them what he needed. 'In the most agnostic or the most conformist of the Chinese there is a latent anarchist and mystic,' wrote Marcel Granet. 'The Chinese are either superstitious or practical, or rather they are both at once.' It is this 'both at once' that a Westerner often finds hard to grasp.

These remarks, which apply even to the recent past, are worth remembering at the outset. They explain in advance one fundamental fact: that when Confucianism and Taoism took shape in China, at roughly the same time, followed much later by Buddhism, none of the three displaced the others, despite their arguments and struggles. Indeed, they were not always mutually distinct. They grafted themselves, in fact, on to a much older, more primitive and powerful religious life. It has been said that these 'Big Three' sailed on ancient religious waters. In reality, they foundered there.

The roots of China's religious life are far older than the three great spiritual disciplines that were grafted on to it. Many lively strains were present in that hybrid, and they permeated all religious practices. China's religious heritage dates back to before the first millennium BC, when the country itself was first taking shape. Nothing thereafter fundamentally changed it.

The introduction of the plough made possible much greater density of population, concentrated in villages and manors. China at that time practised both ancestor-worship and the cult of the gods of the manorial land. The obvious comparison is either with the earliest days of Greece or with the distant beginnings of Rome, each with its typical ancient cities.

Ancestor-worship placed exceptional importance on patrilinear family groupings, in which the name passed from father to son. Beyond these families, the larger group of the clan (*sing* in Chinese) consisted of all the people descended from the same ancestor and hence bearing the same tribal name. Thus for the Ki, the first ancestor was the sovereign Millet, while for the Sseu it was Yu the Great, the legendary hero who drained away the waters of the Flood.

Originally, ancestor-worship and its attendant family structure were confined to the patrician class. Later, plebeian families imitated this ancient model and began to worship their ancestors as if they were gods.

Alongside the ancestors, and little different from them, were the local gods of the manor, ranging from the gods of each house, of the hills, of the watercourses, and of the various forces of nature in different parts of the territory, right up to the gods of the manorial land, *chö*, who dominated all the others. 'A Chen prince defeated in 548 BC surrendered to his conqueror in mourning clothes, carrying in his arms the god of the Land, and preceded by his General, who bore the vases of his ancestors' temple. What he was thus offering was the manor itself' (H. Maspéro).

When China was politically united and the individual manors became subject to monarchical authority, a great god of the Royal Land – the Sovereign Land – took precedence over all the local gods. Not unnaturally, he was the god of the Dead: he 'kept them under guard in his sunless prisons, at the heart of the Nine Darknesses, near to the Yellow Springs'. There was also the god of the Heavens (the god of On High); there were gods of the mountains, of the Four Seas and of the Rivers (the Count of the River was the god of the terrible Yellow River, the Hoang Ho). In fact, there were as many gods as the thousands of characters in the classical Chinese alphabet.

This burgeoning polytheism embraced the immortality of the soul – either at the Yellow Springs or Hades, in the celestial realm of the God of On High, or on earth in the temple of the ancestors. The destination of the soul beyond the grave was often determined by the social position of its owner on earth. Princes, ministers and other important persons were destined for the good afterlife in Heaven, the greatest of them still attended by their servants. Ordinary mortals went to the Yellow Springs, the Nine Darknesses, i.e. to Hell. Those of intermediate status lived on in the tomb of their ancestors. All this was somewhat blurred at the edges, partly because everyone had several souls, and partly because the afterlife was possible only as a result of offerings and sacrifices made by the living, similar to those reserved for the gods. The dead and the gods all eat: 'We fill with offerings the cups of wood and cups of earthenware,' ran the ritual chant accompanying the sacrifice of the victims. 'When their aroma has risen the Lord of On High begins to eat.' Between the gods and the living, bargains were regularly struck: protection was given in exchange for offerings. A god declared: 'If you make sacrifices to me, I will give you happiness.' A prince pleaded: 'My offerings are abundant and pure. Surely the Spirits will support me.' Another complained: 'What crime have people committed today, that Heaven sends us trouble and affliction, a dearth of vegetables and grain! There are no gods that I have not honoured; I have not been sparing with victims!'

Between the fifth and third centuries BC, feudal China disintegrated in the troubled period known as that of the 'Contending States'. Then it was, amid continual wars, that the manors were swallowed up by more or less sizeable, more or less stable, principalities. At length the Han Empire arose and imposed a unifying peace. This long and violent crisis was accompanied by intense anxiety and ideological debate among Chinese thinkers, reacting against the formalized religion of the past. The whole intellectual future of China was affected by this time of upheaval, which recalls either the Greece of the fifth and fourth centuries BC or the Italy of the Renaissance with its political and social dramas, during which the main problem – for both the tyrants and their subjects – was simply to live, or to survive.

Thus China in the sixth to third centuries BC had its politicians (jurists), calculating what chance (*che*) circumstances might offer the Prince or the State. It also had its rhetors or 'sophists', concerned for public welfare. These sophists often belonged to the ancient school of Mo-Ti (or Mö-Tseu), whose doctrine was known as *mohism*.

Were the disciples of Mö-Tseu a kind of order of chivalry in the service of the oppressed, or a sort of congregation of Preaching Friars? These comparisons more or less indicate their activities and their 'commitment'. And the name that later historians have given them – 'sophists' – also reflects their passion for talking, for persuading by argument, for endlessly debating, each following a different line of thought. A whole relativist, rationalist philosophy, quite distinct from the precepts of religion, took shape in the background of these lively discussions.

Only a part of these philosophical novelties survived into the Han period. That, broadly speaking, was what became Confucianism. It was clearly rationalist, in reaction against ancient religion; but it was also a reaction against the rhetorical excesses of the sophists, the multiplicity of their doctrines and the political and social consequences they might involve. Confucianism, in fact, was a return to order in three respects – intellectual, political and social.

At the same time, it perpetuated in China a form of pseudo-rationalism which survived the religious pressures of Taoism and above all of Buddhism, which were very strong until the tenth century. In the thirteenth century, it consolidated itself as neo-Confucianism.

Confucianism was not only an attempt to explain the world in rational terms: it was also a system of political and social ethics. If it was not, as has been argued, a true religion, it was at least a philosophical attitude which could adapt itself as much to a religious frame of mind as to scepticism or even sheer agnosticism.

It owed its name to Confucius (551–479 BC according to tradition). Although he left no writings of his own, his doctrine being handed down by his disciples, he was indeed the founder of the system that became the badge of the Chinese intelligentsia of which he was a part.

Confucianism was above all, in fact, the expression of a particular caste, the educated class known as mandarins. They were the representatives of the new social and political order which gradually arose after China's feudal disintegration. In brief, they were the administrators and civil servants of this new China. Embodying as they did the authority of the State, these lettered functionaries grew more and more numerous as the first great principalities were formed and as writing became the necessary medium of discipline and government. For a long time they were allowed only subordinate posts, while the great aristocratic families monopolized senior positions; but the formation of the first great Empire, that of the Han dynasty (206 BC to AD 220), ensured the mandarins' ultimate triumph.

The development of Confucianism was closely linked with the teaching of the educated classes. The Great School founded in 124 BC by the Emperor Wu taught an already complex body of doctrine, based on reading and glossing the five classic books (Mutations, Odes, Documents, Springs and Autumns, and Rites) which were regarded as representing the Confucian tradition. In fact, they dated from both before and after his time, and their text was properly reconstituted and intelligibly commented upon by scholars only in the fourth and third centuries BC.

Each master taught only one book, always the same, and according to only one interpretation. In the Great School, therefore, there were as many teachers for each book as there were possible interpretations (fifteen, in the first century AD). Every master directly addressed only some ten or so assistants, who in turn taught the pupils. In the year AD 130, the School had 1,800 active students and 30,000 who merely attended lectures. Their studies were tested by stiff examinations. The questions were written on slips of wood, at which the candidates aimed with bow and arrow. Each had to answer whatever question the arrow struck.

In its broad outlines, this system survived until the early twentieth century. Naturally, however, the passage of time brought with it modifications, new commentaries and *summae*, virtually constituting new books. The most important of these revisions was undertaken between the eighth and the twelfth centuries by the Five Masters, founders of what became known as neo-Confucianism. The most famous of the five, Chu Hi (d. 1200), was responsible for the doctrine which until the fall of the Chinese Empire in 1912 remained the unchanging rule and official framework of Chinese philosophy.

As a doctrine for sophisticated people, Confucianism was an attempt to explain the world, respecting the general sense of tradition but rejecting popular primitive beliefs. Hence its rather lordly detachment, its contempt for superstition, and its obvious scepticism. Confucius never spoke of the gods; and although he respected the spirits, the ancestors, he preferred to keep them at a distance. 'If you cannot serve people,' he said once, 'how can you serve spirits? How can those who do not know the living expect to know the dead?'

The followers of Confucius gave a general explanation of the forces of nature, and of human relations with the supernatural world, which might be seen as a first attempt at a scientific theory of the universe. The life of the world, and its vicissitudes, they thought, were not determined by the caprices of the gods, gratified or angry, but by the interaction of impersonal forces. So they spoke of the heavens, not of the god of on high. Yet for these novel explanations, the followers of Confucius often used extremely old words and notions, of popular or even peasant origin, to which they gave new philosophical meanings. One example was *yin* and *yang*.

In popular language and literature, these two words simply implied contrast. *Yin* could be the shadow, *yang* the sun; *yin* the cold, wet season – winter, *yang* the hot, dry season – summer; *yin* feminine and passive, *yang* masculine and active. The Confucians took over these two words and used them to mean 'two concrete and complementary aspects of the universe which oppose each other in space and alternate in time'. Their mutual opposition was the source of all the energy in the universe. Their alternation was incessant. 'A time of rest called *yin* and a time of activity called *yang* never coexist: they succeed each other, endlessly, and their alternation determines everything.' This was most notable with the seasons: the *yin* of autumn and winter followed the *yang* of spring and summer; and the same went for day and night, cold and heat. In human beings, this same 'duel' produced love and hatred, anger and joy.

What produced the alternating phenomena of *yin* and *yang* was *tao*, which was the principle of alternation itself – and hence of every entity's unity and of all evolution. The proverb declared: 'One *yin* and one *yang* make the whole, *tao*.'

Unfortunately, if in nature all things follow their *tao*, their prescribed path, and if the *yang* of the heavens and the *yin* of the earth infallibly alternate to solve all the problems of nature and humanity, human beings are an exception to the rule. They are a special disturbing factor in the universe, uniquely endowed with the freedom not to follow their *tao*, and to deviate from their proper path. When they do so, their evil actions destroy the original harmony of the world.

The Confucians believed that in this way human beings precipitated all the disturbances from which they suffered, whether natural (eclipses, earthquakes, floods) or human (revolutions, public disasters, famines). The neo-Confucians, by contrast, limited the scope of human destructive power to humanity itself. Lacking virtue, human beings condemned themselves to abasement. This, as we shall see, was the principle of imperial power: sovereigns were automatically raised up or deposed according to whether or not they followed the path decreed by heaven.

Confucianism thereby established an ethic and a rule of life which tended to maintain order and hierarchy in society and the State, reacting sharply against the intellectual and social anarchy of the sophists and the jurists.

Starting from ancient religious practices, the Confucians relied, for moral serenity and control of the feelings, on a series of rites and family and social attitudes. These procedures determined everyone's lives, their rank, their rights and their duties. Following their *tao* meant above all remaining forever in the right place – or rather the place allotted to them – in the social hierarchy. 'That is the real meaning of Confucius's celebrated definition of good government: "May the prince be a prince, the subject a subject, the father a father, the son a son."'

Naturally, the obedience and respect that were due to the prince or the mandarin stemmed from their superiority. 'The prince's nature is like the wind, that of humble people is like the grass. When the wind blows, the grass always bends.' The cardinal virtue of the prince's subjects was absolute obedience, on which the community's harmony depended. Hence the importance that Confucianism continued to attach to 'ancestor-worship, purged of all religious feeling, but demanded as a cement of hierarchy', as Etienne Balazs puts it – because ancestor-worship maintained hierarchy and absolute obedience within the family itself.

Obviously, 'the virtues inculcated by the Confucians – respect, humility . . . submission and subordination to elders and betters' – powerfully reinforced the social and political authority of the educated class, i.e. their own. This formal and traditional ethic played a large part in China's continuity and social immobility.

Roughly contemporary with Confucianism, and born of the same prolonged crisis, Taoism was a mystical quest and a religion of individual salvation. In its popular form, it was bound up with the secret societies that were so important in China. Theoretically, it originated with the teaching of Lao-Tse, 'the Master', a mythical figure of the seventh century BC. But the book attributed to him, setting out his doctrine, dates only from the fourth or the third century BC.

Taoism is a mystic quest for the absolute and for immortality. Like the Confucians, the Taoists reinterpreted for their own use the general notions of *yin*, *yang*, and *tao*. For them, the *tao* was a mystical absolute, the primary life force 'from which everything derives'. To define it was hardly possible. Here is one attempt, from a text attributed to Lao-Tse:

The *tao* that people seek to express is not the *tao* itself; the name people wish to give it is not an adequate name. Without a name, it represents the origin of the universe; with a name, it is the Mother of all beings. By Non-Being, let us seize its secret; by Being, let us approach it. Non-Being and Being, issuing from a single source, differ only in their name. This single source is called Darkness. To darken that Darkness – that is the gateway to all wonders.

The perfection or holiness sought by the Taoists was mystic union with the eternal *tao*: it was 'to efface oneself alive in this original and sovereign presence which envelopes everything without itself ever being enveloped' – in the 'formlessness which engenders all forms, in the *tao* which possesses eternal life'. To do so was at the same time to achieve immortality.

That was a mystic experience, barely understandable in itself, and attainable only by asceticism and meditation. 'Listen not with the ear but with the Heart [which for the Chinese meant the Spirit]; listen not with the Heart but with the Breath . . . It is the Breath which, when empty, attains reality. Union with the *tao* can be reached only by Emptiness; this Emptiness is the fasting of the Heart.'

The aim was to achieve, by long years of meditation and purification, and by repeated good works, what an adept was said to achieve in a few days. 'After three days, he could detach himself from the outside world; after seven days, from the things around him; after nine days, from his own existence. Then . . . he attained clear insight and saw what was Unique. Having seen what was unique, he could reach the state in which there was neither present nor past, and finally that in which there was neither life nor death.'

Here, Taoism joins company with all the great mystical experiences, whether Christian, Islamic or Buddhist.

But the immortality sought by the Taoists was not only the salvation of the soul: it was also physical immortality, thanks to a series of recipes for long life, purifying and unburdening the body. These involved countless practices: breathing exercises to help the free circulation of the breath and the blood, and avoid 'obstruction, coagulation and clotting'; careful dieting, to avoid ordinary foodstuffs (especially cereals) and replace them with vegetable or mineral nostrums; finally, alchemy. This last included the gold vessel which purified all food, liquid gold (gold liquor) and above all cinnabar (red mercuric sulphide) when it had nine times been transformed into mercury and back again so as to make 'the red pill of immortality'.

After these various treatments, 'the bones turn to gold, the flesh to jade, and the body becomes incorruptible'; as light as a stalk of straw, it can rise to an apotheosis which carries the adept, now immortal, to the abode of the gods. To avoid troubling the world of the living, he pretends to die as others do, leaving behind him a stick or a sword which he has made look exactly like a corpse.

Alchemy, and the quest for elixirs of longevity, give point to the story of Chang-Chuen ('Eternal Spring'), a Taoist monk who was seventy-three (though thought to be 200) when Genghis Khan made him leave his monastery and come to him in Mongolia to bring him the recipe for a long life. When the old monk arrived, on 9 December 1221, the Emperor asked him: 'What remedy have you brought me?' The monk replied: 'None. I have with me only one *tao* to guarantee life.' He and the Emperor died within days of each other, in 1227.

There was finally a popular Taoist religion which ignored the holiness of the Masters and the complicated practices involved in the quest for a long life. The Chinese language itself distinguishes between 'the Taoist people', *tao-min*, and the true adepts, *tao-che*. The mass of the *tao-min* were content to take part in numerous services, to make abundant offerings and to perform acts of penance. They themselves could not claim immortality, but those who lived a pure life were assured of a better existence in the next world. They would not escape the Yellow Springs, but would serve as assistants to the god Earth, and would rule over the miserable throng of the dead. These details show how the people's version of Taoism had had to come to terms, as it did on other matters, with ancient beliefs.

Popular Taoism repeatedly formed extremely hierarchical churches, and a series of more or less secret sects with anarchistic and mystical tendencies. In the face of Confucianism, the traditionalist partisan of social order, Taoism was always the symbol of individualism, personal freedom and rebellion.

Buddhism, the latest arrival among the 'Big Three', was a religion imported into China by missionaries from India and Central Asia. But it too borrowed from the common pool of traditional Chinese thought and was profoundly altered in the process.

Buddhism arose in India in the sixth and fifth centuries BC. It flourished there under the Emperor Ashoka (273–236 BC). Gradually rejected, and assimilated by Hinduism, it kept some following in the North and North-West of India, among the Greek rulers surviving from Alexander's conquests, then it reached Central Asia, including Bactria (in the North of present-day Afghanistan) and the Tarim Basin (in Chinese Turkestan).

It was there, in about the second century BC, that the Chinese conquerors encountered it. Three centuries later, in the first century AD, it began to invade the Han Empire, partly along the central Asian trade-routes, but also by sea and across Yunnan in the South-West of China. Not until much later, in the third century AD, did it really spread through the whole of Chinese society, including both the élite and the masses. Its influence remained preponderant until the tenth century.

Buddhism teaches that after their death people are reborn in other bodies, for a new life which is more or less happy according to what they did in their previous lives, but which always involves suffering. The only issue out of this suffering is the way preached by Buddha: this makes it possible to attain Nirvana, that is, to melt into unconditional eternal life and to be delivered from the cycle of reincarnation. That way is difficult, because what causes people to be born again after their death is their eagerness to live. This has to be quenched by detachment and renunciation. To that end, it has to be understood that neither the Self nor what surrounds it has any real existence: they are only an illusion. Such understanding is not a reasoned conclusion, but an intuitive realization which the sage can reach only by contemplation and by spiritual exercises carried out in one lifetime or several.

The initial success of this religion, which was very alien to the Chinese spirit, was the result of a lengthy misunderstanding. It was not presented to the Chinese under its true colours. The first Buddhist adepts all came from Taoist circles; and they assumed that Buddhism was only a slight variant of their own religion. Both indeed were religions based on salvation, and their contemplative practices looked similar from the outside, although those of Buddhism were physically less painful and may have seemed more attractive. The debate might have been clarified by study of the relevant Sanskrit texts: but these came to light only slowly. They were very difficult to turn into Chinese; and when translations were eventually made, they were usually the joint work of Indian missionaries and the first Taoist converts, who naturally used the vocabulary of Taoism, thereby compounding the confusion. Thus it was that Buddhist illumination became union with the *tao*, Nirvana was translated by the Chinese word for the abode of the Immortals, and so on. This distorted form of Buddhism spread rapidly thanks to a vast network of male and female monastic communities.

As in the case of Taoism, a popular version of the religion united those of the faithful who were content to take part in its simplest rites, say prayers, give alms, avoid the five deadly sins and attend dramatic sessions in which the priest saved the souls of the ancestors by recalling them from their infernal dwelling-place. By the same means, the faithful themselves could hope to reach the Western Heaven after their death, if interceded for by the saints, saviours of the souls of the damned.

The misunderstanding was dispelled only when many translations of the Sanskrit texts became available – i.e. very late in the day, not before the sixth and seventh centuries.

In fact, Taoism and Buddhism were mutually contradictory. The one sought 'the drug of immortality', the survival of the body; the other considered the body to be a set of shackles imposed on people by their imperfections, and something which did not even really exist. For the Buddhist, the very Self was non-existent: in Nirvana all personality was dissolved. For the Taoist, in the Paradise of the Immortals, every saint would keep his own personality forever.

Only a few great Chinese thinkers were troubled by the belated discovery of these differences, and by the impossibility of 'using the Buddhist system to attain the sense of the *tao*', as one of them wrote in the seventh century. By then, Buddhism had become 'Chinese'. Favoured and persecuted by turns – and thus severely affected by the wave of repression in 845 which closed all the monasteries, Buddhism none the less perpetuated a certain number of 'duly selected beliefs, which China had admitted to its heritage without adapting them to its own usage' (Demiéville). In this way, faith in the transmigration of souls spread throughout China, even among educated Taoists, while Buddhist metaphysics deeply affected neo-Confucianism from the thirteenth century onwards.

It cannot be said, therefore, that Buddhism was destroyed by Chinese civilization. Instead, it added to it, setting its permanent seal upon it (as in countless works of art), while at the same time being indelibly steeped in its influence. This, however, has been the fate of all religions in China.

What then did religion mean to the majority of the Chinese, beyond the great neo-Confucian upheavals of the thirteenth century and later? In other words, what did that majority see in the brightly painted brick temples rising above the brown or grey of the ordinary houses with their walls of wood or clay? No particular religion, and all of them at the same time.

Each member of the faithful turned sometimes to the Buddhist priests and sometimes to the Taoists. Both officiated in the same temple; the statue of Buddha stood there, as well as the altar of the local god or the statue of Confucius, himself almost deified. Offerings were made to all of them. During the Second World War, a joint prayer was said in one Chinese temple, addressed to a list of 687 divinities – including Christ. What is interesting to note is that this pantheon of gods included some from the earliest times, and that none of the ancient religious disputes gave one form of belief any precedence over another.

At the time of Marco Polo, at the court of the Great Khan who then held in his grip both China and the Mongol Empire, a religious storm broke out which looked like destroying everything. The Khan had dismissed the Confucians (save for those he kept on as civil servants); he had persecuted the Taoists, in many cases to death; and he had encouraged the Mongol shamanists (animists), as well as, still more, the Buddhists of the Tibetan rite, welcoming at his court its lamas, miracle-workers and magicians. One Christian sect, the Nestorians, also enjoyed his favour. Shortly after Marco Polo's departure, a Western monk, Fra Giovanni di Montecorvino, even succeeded in building the first Catholic church at Cambaluc (Peking), so close to the Khan's palace that he could not fail to hear its bells. 'This extraordinary fact,' wrote Fra Giovanni, 'was known to people everywhere.' Yet neither his ambitions nor those of the Jesuits later came to fruition. Was it ever possible to convert the Chinese to one single religion? And especially to one from abroad?

Politics

Under this heading we must follow a long and complex process of evolution. Nor will it suffice simply to survey the mass of habits and rituals involved in the monumental institution of the Empire. We shall need to explain how it owed its strength to a corps of educated civil servants, the mandarins, who until the quite recent past were one of the most salient original features of Chinese society and civilization. We shall see, finally, that these institutions were justified by their achievements: the maintenance of stability in a huge society, and of political unity in an enormous domain. That unity was the *raison d'être* of the imperial monarchy.

The imperial monarchy illustrated 'Chinese continuity'. Following the lead of Chinese chroniclers and historians, one could trace the monarchy back through 4,000 years of history, with twenty-two dynasties which official chronology places end to end without indicating the slightest interval or interruption. But this neat arrangement should not be taken at face value. First of all, its

steady succession was interrupted by disturbances and impostures.
Secondly, there was no imperial institution until China was united
by the 'First Emperor' of the Ch'in, Ch'in Shi Hwang-ti (221–206
BC), and consolidated and stabilized by the Han dynasty (206 BC
to AD 220).

If one accepts this reasonable starting-point, the Chinese empire
lasted from 221 BC to AD 1911–12, which saw the fall of the
Manchu dynasty (also known as the Ch'ing dynasty), dating from
1644. So the Empire was long-lasting, an axis around which the
history of China turned, slowly, century after century. It is easy,
therefore, to understand what preoccupied Chinese philosophers
and historians: they sought to emphasize the longevity and
legitimacy of the monarchy, and if necessary to restore order,
retrospectively, to epochs where history had neglected to supply
it. All the more so in that China's imperial order was not merely
human but also religious, founded on supernatural values.

Social and supernatural order, in fact, were two sides of the
same coin. So the Emperor was both a temporal and a spiritual
ruler: none of his actions was purely that of a layman; and in fact
he supervised both natural and supernatural order in the world. As
sovereign in both domains, he not only appointed civil servants,
but also decided on the hierarchy in the temples, gave a name to
'this or that canonized sage' and presided over the ritual beginning
of farm work, by ploughing the first furrow at the Feast of
Spring.

Sinologists often stress that the Emperors of China did not rule
by divine right. This is no doubt true by comparison with the
Divine Right of Kings as propounded in the West in the Middle
Ages and early modern times. But there is more than one similarity
between the Chinese imperial monarchy and, for example, that of
ancient Rome. 'Chinese political philosophy never taught anything
resembling the Western doctrine of the Divine Right of Kings':
but was there any need to, if the Emperor was 'truly the son of
Heaven', if he ruled by virtue of a mandate from Heaven, a
contract which, according to one Chinese philosopher, 'rewarded

only virtue'? The role of virtue is important in explaining the disasters, to the Empire and to himself, which the Emperor could not always prevent. Floods, calamitous droughts, refusal to pay taxes, defeats by the barbarians at the frontier, peasant revolts (which were very frequent): all these troubles arose from a breach of the fundamental contract, a lack of virtue on the part of the Emperor, who thereby ceased to enjoy the mandate of Heaven. Such portents were unmistakable: they betokened a change of dynasty, failing which generations of people risked following an unworthy Emperor into sudden oblivion. Popular uprisings, at least in ancient China, were regarded as advance warnings that an Emperor was about to fall. An old proverb claimed (a little like the Western *vox populi, vox Dei*): 'Heaven sees with the eyes of the people.'

So the mandate of Heaven would legitimately pass from a family that had fallen from grace to a new dynasty which necessarily possessed virtue because it received the mandate. 'The Chinese expression *Koming*, which translates our word "revolution", and which Republican China has adopted, means literally "the withdrawal of the mandate". A ruler who has lost this indispensable protection is obliged to step down.' It was essential therefore, for the sake of imperial continuity and the unity of China, to adjust the chronology of successive dynasties so as to eliminate interregna (*jouen*) when, as we should say, usurpers ruled. As one dynasty ended, so another necessarily received the mandate of Heaven. Embarrassment begins, for the historian, when in a troubled period several rivals contest or even share power. The Chinese historian then finds it hard to say which were the true inheritors of the mandate, or of the 'continuity' (*chang-tong*) – the legitimacy, as we in the West should call it. For want of a better solution, he will then choose those who seem 'the most worthy', and give them in retrospect 'all the consideration that is owing to the Son of Heaven'.

The fact that legitimacy was accorded, by right, to whomever was strong enough to seize power (since his strength must have come from Heaven) explains the continuity of China's history despite the dramatic upheavals that punctuated it.

The public pomp of this unchanging monarchy was extraordinary and full of splendour: the court, the palace teeming with ministers, officials, eunuchs, courtesans and concubines, and the ceremonies brilliantly staged. When the Sung Emperor went to the southern outskirts of his capital Hang-chow to sacrifice in the temple there to his ancestors and to Heaven, the great avenue leading to the temple was levelled and sanded in advance. Soldiers lined the route, richly bedecked elephants walked before the imperial carriage; and when the procession began, the torches which had been lit at nightfall beside the road were all put out at once. It was a grandiose spectacle, and one that stirred popular emotion. True, every ruler in the world no doubt calculates the effect of a complex, well-drilled ceremony: the 'entries' of the Kings of France into their loyal cities, for example, were equally well-attended. The displays mounted by the Chinese monarchy had similar motives, but were still more splendid and more authentically religious. To gauge their effect, imagine the impact in Europe of a series of imperial dynasties maintaining the self-same style and significance from Augustus until the First World War.

This monarchy, in essence rather primitive, coexisted with a 'modern' corps of educated officials, the mandarins. The West was puzzled by them, misunderstanding their true position, and vainly seeking in the China of the Ming or the Manchu a close or distant social parallel with Europe, where alongside the monarchy stood the clergy, the nobility and the third estate. The importance of the mandarins made them look to Western eyes rather like aristocrats.

In fact, they were senior officials, few in number and recruited through complex competitive examinations. Their education, like their profession (but not their birth), made them an exclusive caste: in the thirteenth century they totalled perhaps ten thousand families. Although it was not a closed social caste, it was difficult to enter, since it was reserved for intellectuals, whose knowledge, language, concerns, ideas, and habits of mind united them in a kind of complicity and at the same time cut them off from the rest of the world.

Emphatically, they were not described as nobles, or lords, or plutocrats (which some of them were). Their closest counterparts, according to Etienne Balazs, are the 'technocrats' of our present-day industrial societies. These, representing a powerful State, are highly interventionist, concerned with efficiency and productivity, and rationalists to the core.

The mandarins resembled them: like them, they enjoyed social advantages and exceptional prestige as a result of their intellectual qualifications and examination success; like them, they were 'a tiny minority in number, but omnipotent in power, influence, position, and prestige'; like them, 'they knew only one profession – administration and government'.

A well-known passage from Mencius (Meng-tseu, d. 314 BC), on the difference between those who think and those who labour, neatly expressed the mandarins' ideal: 'The pursuits of men of quality are not those of the poor. The former work with their brains, the latter with their bodies. Those who work with their brains *govern the others*; those who work with their physical strength are governed by them. Those who are governed support the others; those who govern are supported by the rest.' Horror of manual labour was a mark of honour: the hand of an educated man, who let his nails grow to an extravagant length, could perform only one task – using the brush with which he wrote.

But what did governing imply in ancient China? Broadly speaking, as in a State today, performing all the tasks of administration and justice. The mandarins raised taxes, sat in judgement, policed society, if need be conducted military operations, drew up work schedules and built and maintained roads, canals, dams and irrigation systems. Their role, as K. A. Wittfogel has put it, was 'to correct the cruelty of Nature' – forestalling droughts and floods, laying in stocks of foodstuffs, and in brief overseeing the proper workings of a complex farming society which demanded strict discipline, especially to deal with the river system and ensure that irrigation was effective.

The mandarins represented this discipline, this stability in society, the economy, the State and civilization. They stood for order against disorder. Order, no doubt, was not an unmixed blessing. But it was 'the price to be paid for the homogeneity, longevity and vitality of Chinese civilization'. Only the iron hand of the mandarins was able to maintain the unity of a vast Empire, facing on the one hand feudal lords and on the other a peasant society which invariably lapsed into anarchy whenever it was left to fend for itself. So in the face of Taoism, which opposed all collective constraints and called for a return to nature, the mandarins preached the virtues of hierarchy, public order and Confucian ethics.

In this sense, they were largely responsible for China's social immobility. They maintained a balance between the great propertied landlords, held to their duties, and the poverty-stricken peasants, who nevertheless retained their own poverty-stricken land. The mandarins also kept an eye on any emerging capitalists, merchants, moneylenders and *nouveaux riches*. They in turn were restrained as much by the mandarins' prestige as by their surveillance: regularly, some day or another, the descendants of merchants who had made their fortune would let themselves be tempted by the life of letters and the attractions of power, and would take the famous examinations. This is at least one of the reasons why Chinese society did not evolve, as in the West, towards a capitalist system. It remained at the stage of paternalism and tradition.

Chinese unity meant the North plus the South. The territory of China was not really unified until the thirteenth century, when all of it suffered from disasters. The Mongol conquest (1211–79) culminated in the defeat of the Sung dynasty in the South and the capture of its capital Hang-chow, which Marco Polo visited shortly afterwards and saw in all its prosperity and beauty. The new masters of China not only pushed Chinese rule to its furthest geographical limits: they gave life and strength to this amalgam of different territories. The latter had often been joined together under the Han, the T'ang and the Sung dynasties, but it was now that the progress already accomplished reached its peak, confirming the wealth and supremacy of Southern China, and spreading prosperity throughout the Empire.

For centuries, the South had been a 'Far West', a 'semi-barbaric Mezzogiorno', with few inhabitants except occasional aboriginal tribes whom it was difficult to hold in check. From the eleventh century at the latest, however, the South awoke from its semi-colonial sleep, thanks to early varieties of rice which made possible two harvests a year. From then onwards it became the granary of China. If the first two millennia (before the eleventh century) had been dominated by the people of the Yellow River, the third (from the eleventh century to the twentieth) became more or less the preserve of the people from the Yangtze-kiang and further South as far as Canton. Hang-chow and Nanking, however, the capitals of the Blue River country, were both superseded by Peking, the capital established in the North for obvious geopolitical reasons, to act as a shield against the Northern barbarians and nomads.

The primacy of the South was soon reflected in the size of its population. By the thirteenth century, there were ten Southern Chinese for every one in the North. It also enjoyed primacy in quality and efficiency, as it still does. Over the last three centuries, the vast majority of Chinese intellectuals have been natives of Kiang-si and Che-kiang provinces, and most of the leaders of the twentieth-century revolution came from Hunan. Such is the result, today, of the shift in China's centre of gravity some ten centuries ago. Between the eleventh and the thirteenth centuries, the great Chinese hour-glass was turned upside-down, to the permanent advantage of the land of rice and to the detriment of the land of millet and wheat. But the new China was still the China of the past, which it continued and enriched. The South, so to speak, was China's America – as Manchuria became much later, in the twentieth century.

★

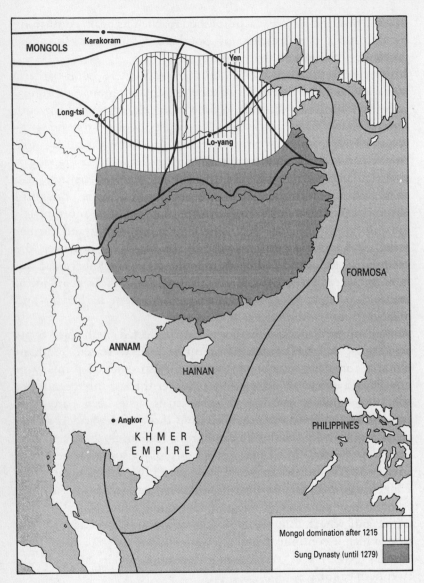

MONGOLS

Karakoram

Yen

Long-tsi

Lo-yang

FORMOSA

ANNAM

HAINAN

Angkor

KHMER
EMPIRE

PHILIPPINES

Mongol domination after 1215	
Sung Dynasty (until 1279)	

10. Roads and rivers in ancient China

Roads are shown with thick lines, rivers with thin.

Social and economic affairs

Underlying classical China's semi-immobility, her economic and social structures were semi-immobile too. They, indeed, were the foundations of that enormous house.

Like all global societies, China was a complex of different societies, all interlocked. Some were conservative, others more progressive. Any change came through slow imperceptible evolution.

The basis of Chinese society was largely agricultural and proletarian, with an enormous mass of needy peasants and impoverished city-dwellers. The world of the poor scarcely saw its masters – very rarely, the Emperor or the princes of the blood, few in numbers but extremely rich; rarely too the great landowners, but more often their hated bailiffs, at work at close quarters; and just as rarely the great and much feared State officials, who governed the country at a distance but 'with a rod of bamboo', as Father de las Cortes said. Everyone, however, sympathized with junior officials; and everyone constantly wished a violent death on usurers and moneylenders.

Such, at least, was the tenor of popular folk-tales from the Sung dynasty onwards. They described a society both patriarchal and based on slavery, both modern and peasant – very different, certainly, from the 'model' of Western societies. It was patriarchal on account of its powerful family links, the long unbreakable ligatures of ancestor-worship.

Family solidarity extended to the most distant cousins and even to childhood friends. This was not a matter of charity, but of justice. A privileged person who made his fortune was exploiting the advantages of the family unit, drawing upon the blessings of its ancestors. It was only fair that a man who had thus used up the luck of the family should share with all his relations the prosperity that he owed them.

This same society was based on slavery – or at least, if slavery was never its major feature, it was nevertheless a frequent practice. In general, slavery was the spontaneous outcome of unrelenting poverty and irremediable over-population. Its unhappy victims sold themselves when times were hard; and, throughout the Far East, parents sold their children. The practice continued in China until the law of 1908 which, almost at the end of the Manchu dynasty, forbade both slavery and the sale of children. However, it authorized parents 'in times of famine, to sign long-term work contracts which committed their children up to the age of twenty-five'.

Chinese society, with a vast majority of peasants, was not in the true sense feudal. It had no fiefs to be the subject of investiture, no peasant tenure, no peasant serfs. Many peasants owned their tiny patches of soil. But above them there were 'rural notabilities' (*chen che*), who rented out their land, sometimes acted as moneylenders, and required peasants to work for them and to pay to use an oven or a mill, usually in kind, in bushels of grain or pots of fat. At the same time, these notabilities had links with the mandarins (many of them large landowners), who as we have said represented the interests of the State, and thus tended to curb any excessive power of one class over another, and especially that of any feudal class which might be able to challenge central authority.

This complex social network kept order among the four groups of the old hierarchy: at the top, the mandarins (*che*); the peasants (*nong*); the artisans (*kong*); and the merchants (*chang*). The last two, who might have played a determining role, were held in check, like the others, by a watchful government. In any case, their influence would have depended on spurts of economic growth; and these were no more than intermittent.

Despite what many Sinophile specialists and historians maintain, China's economic achievements were modest and, to be frank, backward compared with those of the West. Not for one second, of course, could one accuse China of global inferiority *vis-à-vis* Europe. Her inferiority lay in her economic structure, her market outlets and her merchant middle class, less well developed than that of Islam or the West. First, and most crucially, there were no free cities. Nor were there entrepreneurs eager to make profits – a passion which may or may not be regrettable, but which in the West was certainly a spur to progress. As early as the thirteenth century, Chinese traders were willing to spend money on the pride and vanity of public ostentation: in this they resembled merchants in the West. But, rather more than their Western counterparts, they had a taste and a love for literature. One merchant's son could write poems of every kind. 'All the descriptions of merchants' lives that we find in folk tales from the Sung dynasty show that their aim was to make enough money to lead a comfortable life, fulfil their moral and social duties, and above all to discharge their obligations to their parents and their whole family.' And, in the case of the very rich, to enable some of their relatives to join the privileged mandarin caste.

In other words, they only half-heartedly shared the capitalist mentality of the West. Furthermore, many Chinese merchants, like the artisans, were itinerants, travelling from place to place; and this alone is a sign that the Chinese economy was not yet mature. Europe in the thirteenth century was already emerging from that phase. In the early Middle Ages, itinerant trade had been the norm, but now there were more and more business houses in place. Only poor traders had to travel with their own merchandise because they had no agents or branches and could not do business by letter. Only poor artisans, likewise, carried all their gear on their backs and wandered through towns and countryside looking for work. But in China, even in the eighteenth century, sugar craftsmen still came to the sugar-cane fields with their equipment, breaking the canes with their bare hands and making syrup and brown sugar. Industrial development, likewise, was sparse: a few rather primitive coal-mines in the North, and in the South the famous ovens for making porcelain.

Nor was there any credit system, at least until the eighteenth and (in some places) the nineteenth century. Hence the importance of the moneylender, long embedded like a painful splinter in Chinese society, and the sure sign of a backward, suffocating economy.

Finally, despite its rivers, its junks, its sampans, its rafts of logs, its free trade between provinces, its porters and its Northern camel-trains, China suffered from poor internal communications and still more limited links with the rest of the world. It was also very much over-populated.

Isolated as it was, China tended to live on its own resources. It had only two major outlets – the sea and the desert. Even these could be used only in favourable circumstances and when there was a potential trading partner at the end of the journey.

During the Mongol period (1215–1368), for about a century (1240–1340), both outlets were operative at the same time. Kublai Khan (1260–94), the friend and protector of Marco Polo and his family, made great efforts to build a fleet, so as to be free of Muslim ships and protect himself against Japanese competitors and pirates. At the same time, he kept open and free of obstacles the great Mongol road which led beyond the Caspian to the Black Sea and the prosperous colonies of the Genoese and Venetians in Kaffa and the Tana region.

Thus opened up, China was undoubtedly prosperous, supplied with silver money by Western merchants. Wonder of wonders, it also developed paper money. But that lasted only for a time.

In any case, the great national revolution, in which the Ming drove the Mongols back to the desert (1368) and purged China of these unassimilated aliens, virtually coincided with the closing of both her trading outlets. The desert was once more a barrier which the new China could not cross: the sea, in the end, proved equally disappointing. From 1405 to 1431–2, Admiral Cheng-ho mounted no fewer than seven successive sea-going expeditions, one of which consisted of sixty-two large junks with 17,800 soldiers on board.

All of these fleets left Nanking to re-establish China's protectorate on the Sunda Isles, which supplied her with gold dust, pepper and spices. They reached Ceylon and left a garrison there, then pushed on to the Persian Gulf, the Red Sea, and finally the coast of Africa, whence they brought back some marvellous giraffes which astonished the crowds.

This episode has seemed strange to Sinologists, and all the more interesting for that. A little more wind, and the Chinese ships might have rounded the Cape of Good Hope half a century before the Portuguese: they might have discovered Europe, and even America. But in 1431–2 the adventure came to an end, and it was not repeated. China, huge as it was, had to regroup its resources to face its eternal enemies in the North. In 1421 it transferred its capital from Nanking to Peking.

Later, in the seventeenth and eighteenth centuries, the Manchu emperors re-opened the desert road, taking over vast areas as far as Tibet and the Caspian, resisting the nomads and driving them off to the West. These conquests gave China peace in the North, and enabled her to go beyond Manchuria and seize part of Siberia as far as the Amur (Treaty of Nerchinsk with Russia, 1689). A further result, from the second half of the eighteenth century onwards, was the opening of the great trading fairs of Kiakhta to the South-East of Irkutsk, where furs from the Far North were exchanged for cotton, silk and tea from China. As for the seaway, the Europeans tried to open it in the sixteenth, seventeenth and eighteenth centuries. They succeeded in the nineteenth, but to their own advantage.

China expanded. By the thirteenth century there were probably 100 million Chinese (90 million in the South, 10 million in the North). The figure fell with the end of Mongol domination and the national revolution of the Ming dynasty in 1368. By 1384 the population had dropped to 60 million (a reliable estimate); but with the return of peace it seems soon to have risen to its previous level. There was a further fall, probably, at the time of the Manchu conquest (1644–83) – followed, when peace was restored, by an enormous expansion in the eighteenth century. Thereafter, the growth of the population reached dizzy heights.

This excessive wealth of manpower necessarily had drawbacks. It probably prevented technological progress. Teeming humanity made machines unnecessary, as slavery had in classical Greece and Rome. For human power could be used for anything. In 1793, a

British traveller marvelled at the sight of a ship being transferred from one level of water to another without going through a lock, but simply being lifted by human strength. Father de la Cortes in 1626 had already admired – and drawn – Chinese porters in the act of lifting an enormous tree-trunk. No task, in other words, was too heavy for human beings. And in China they came so cheap.

This over-population weighed on the life of China, immobilizing it in the iron grip of a conservative administration, and above all blocking the development of technology. There was such a thing as Chinese science, whose wealth, precociousness, ingenuity and even modernity are coming to light more and more every day. Joseph Needham, who carefully chronicled its development, remarked that its 'organic' conception of the world was precisely that to which present-day science is turning, in contrast to the Newtonian mechanistic view which prevailed until the end of the nineteenth century. Curiously, however, in China technology did not keep up with science: it marked time. The main reason, without a doubt, was the over-abundance of manpower. China had no need to devise machines to spare human labour. It was the permanent victim of the poverty resulting from endemic over-population.

12. China Yesterday and Today

The China of the past did not disappear overnight. It receded little by little, and not before the nineteenth century. Then, events moved rapidly. Ancient China was opened up by force, and suffered lengthy humiliation. It took a long time to realize how far it had fallen, and longer still to find remedies. It succeeded in the twentieth century, but only at the cost of a fabulous effort, for which history affords not the remotest precedent.

The time of imposed treaties: China as humiliated victim (1839–1949)

China was not occupied, like India, or reduced like her to the status of a colony. But Chinese territory was invaded, pillaged and regularly exploited. All the great powers took their share. And China emerged from the ordeal only when the People's Republic was established in 1949.

From the sixteenth century onwards, China was in touch with European trade. Important as that fact was, it had little effect on China – until later, when one-sided treaties began to be imposed.

In 1557 the Portuguese settled in Macao, opposite Canton; and from there they played an important role, especially between China and Japan. In the seventeenth century, the Dutch and the British seized the best pickings. Then, in the second half of the eighteenth century, the golden age of 'the China trade' began, although limited at that time to the single port of Canton.

For China, the trade was important; but it had little effect on the country as a whole. European merchants, the majority of them British, dealt with a privileged circle of Chinese traders, the *Co-hong*, who had a monopoly of buying and selling. In so far as this trade benefited both parties, it grew by leaps and bounds. It covered gold (which was cheap in China owing to the rarity and high price of silver: the ratio was 8 to 1 in China, as against 15 or more to 1 in Europe); tea, in ever greater demand in the West; and cotton and cotton goods, imported from India. This trade was financed by a belated credit system. European merchants advanced money to Chinese traders, who divided and re-loaned it in exchange for produce from the furthest corners of the Empire, forming thereby an already modern financial network. This was Europe's normal practice in overseas trade – to lend to a local merchant, in the course of each voyage, the money he needed to collect a cargo for the following visit, and thus enjoy priority in the market.

Undoubtedly, 'the China trade' dazzled Europe. Often, if not always, it made enormous profits. China benefited too, and did not resent the intrusion of foreign methods and merchandise: their economic impact was limited to a small circle and had little effect on the country as a whole.

But with the nineteenth century everything changed. Europe grew overbearing and greedy. It was strengthened, moreover, by the British conquest of India, which gave it a firm foothold in the East. As a result, Western intervention became brutal and destructive.

The Opium War of 1840 to 1842 opened five treaty ports to Westerners, including Canton and Shanghai (by the Treaty of Nanking). The T'ai-p'ing rebellion enabled the Westerners to intrude further, in 1860, and secure the opening of seven more treaty ports. The Russians then obliged China to cede them the Maritime Province, where they built Vladivostok. China's troubles, in fact, were only beginning. The first Sino-Japanese War lost her Korea; and the great powers profited from her weakness to make further inroads. The Russians settled in Manchuria. The Boxer rising in 1900, aimed against foreigners, precipitated further intervention by all the European powers, backed by the United States and Japan. The Russo-Japanese War of 1904–5 gave the Japanese some of what the Russians had already seized from China. The First World War gave Japan further advantages, this time via the Germans, notably in Shantung.

By 1919, therefore, China had lost important parts of its territory. Even within its frontiers, the West and Japan enjoyed liberties, privileges and 'concessions', the best known of which was the international concession of Shanghai. They controlled part of the railways and the customs – guarantees for the payment of interest on foreign loans; here and there they had established their own post offices, their own consular jurisdiction, their own banks, their own trading houses, their own industries and mines. In 1914 their total investments in China had amounted to $1,610 million, of which $219 million came from Japan.

Following the expedition of the eight powers after the Boxer rising, and the capture of the Imperial capital in 1901, the Legations' quarter of Peking was militarily occupied 'and surrounded by a glacis, where the Chinese were forbidden to build'. 'The Peking diplomatic corps strictly supervised, *de facto* if not *de jure*, all Chinese affairs, or at least all those controlled by the Peking Government.'

Dismantled economically, China was also subjected to a large-scale invasion by foreign culture and religion. It was submerged, physically and spiritually, at the time of the treaties imposed on it, which it rightly called 'the one-sided treaties'.

To shake off the yoke of the West, China needed first to modernize – i.e. in some degree Westernize itself. Reform and liberation were two tasks that were often mutually contradictory: yet both had to be performed. It took a lot of time and trouble, much hesitation and experiment, before the shape of the struggle ahead became clear. China was unable to learn Western ways overnight, as Japan did in the Meiji era of modernization. She had, in fact, a difficult double apprenticeship.

Thus the powerful, complex and 'traditional' (because peasant) T'ai-p'ing rebellion of 1850 to 1864, which briefly set up a separatist government in Nanking, was nationalist and xenophobic: but at the same time it sought to overthrow some of China's ancient social and political customs. During their short-lived triumph, the T'ai-p'ing rebels abolished slavery, emancipated women, suppressed polygamy and the binding of feet and admitted women to public examinations and official posts. They also hoped to achieve technological and industrial modernization, although their efforts did not go deep. Essentially, theirs was one more of the many agrarian revolts that had taken place in the past, usually on the eve of a change of dynasty. In that respect, the T'ai-p'ing uprising was an attempt to oust landowners and collectivize their estates. It finally failed, mainly because of the help that the West gave to the Manchu dynasty, so as to maintain Western trading advantages. A further reason was that T'ai-p'ing plans for modernization remained too vague, while China was in no state as yet to accept them.

The Boxer rebellion of 1900, led by a secret society with mysterious and terrifying rituals, was motivated solely by xenophobia. But that xenophobia was shared at the time by the whole of China, beginning with the fearful Dowager Empress Tz'e-hsi, who by giving the signal for action against the foreigner (probably in complicity with the Boxers) in fact ensured that both they and China were crushed in 1901. Tz'e-hsi, incidentally, was also a fierce opponent of reform. She had cleverly and skilfully foiled the enlightened attempt at modernization that had been made in 1898, known as the 'Hundred Days'. On paper, at least, this would have laid the foundations for a genuine revolution in China's institutions and economy.

At the beginning of the twentieth century, in other words, the hour of reform had not yet struck. Those seeking change had to confront 'the organic deafness of the mandarins, whose ears were harder to open than the Chinese ports', as Etienne Balazs put it. They also faced indifference on the part of the people, who were tempted only by 'the blind alley of xenophobia'. At the most, all they wanted was to learn the foreigners' 'tricks' – the secrets of their efficiency.

The double problem remained difficult to solve. The Western 'Barbarians' had to be driven out; but to achieve this China had to learn the science and technology of the West. Its very slow apprenticeship was the work of young middle-class intellectuals who met Westerners and travelled abroad, and still more that of the many poverty-stricken students attending the modern schools and universities set up by the Government in the final years of the Manchu dynasty. They helped form a series of secret societies, some frankly republican, others still monarchist, but all eager for the 'recovery' of China and for radical reform.

Thus there came into being China's first really revolutionary movement, closely linked with the name of Sun Yat-sen. Sun Yat-sen (1866–1925) was a doctor from a village in Kwang-Tung. He had been involved in a number of revolutionary movements, on account of which he had spent several years in exile outside China. In 1905, in Tokyo, he became president of a republican league which soon acquired great importance throughout China and produced a well-thought-out political programme. This movement was directly involved in the revolution of 1911 which overthrew the Manchu dynasty and installed Sun Yat-sen at the head of China's first republican government. This revolution, however, was thwarted almost at once. After fourteen days, Sun Yat-sen resigned in favour of General Yuan Shih-kai (d. 1916), who tried to re-establish the old regime with himself as its beneficiary.

So the liberal constitution of 1912 was suspended, and China sank into anarchy. The military governors of the provinces, soon to be called the Warlords, allied themselves with the rural notabilities to extort as much as possible from taxes and rents. They soon became the pitiless masters of China. Sun Yat-sen, who had once more gone into exile, founded a new party which he called the Komintang ('the party of the Revolution'). This was a play on words. The Kuomintang, founded in 1912 in the first euphoric months of the Republic, had meant 'the great party of the Nation'. The substitution of '*Koming*' (Revolution) for '*Kuomin*' (Nation) signified that the original party had not finished its work, and that the revolution had still to be pursued.

In the process, China had yet to suffer repeated misfortunes and crises, which came to an end only in 1949 with the victory of the Communists and the establishment of the People's Republic. The date has some significance: from the Opium War of 1840–42 it took China a century of effort and hardship to recover her independence and her pride. 'From now on,' declared a professor in 1951, 'we can again be proud that we are Chinese.'

During that century of expectation and struggle, the old regime began to decay, especially in its most traditional and conservative respects. It abandoned 'the hierarchy of mandarins with crystal or mother-of-pearl buttons, the ritual of Reports to the imperial throne annotated with a vermilion brush by the Son of Heaven, the audiences in brocade robes', and also the exorbitant privileges granted to the Westerners and the Japanese.

After much suffering, then, China reached one of those rare moments when a civilization renews itself by breaking apart, sacrificing some of those structural features which hitherto had been essential to it. For China, the crisis was all the more extraordinary in that it challenged what had been in place for thousands of years. Still, the destruction was not total: nor could it have been. In building afresh, China remained faithful to her own forms of thought and sensibility. It will certainly take a number of decades for the new Chinese civilization to assume its distinctive shape.

For the moment, all we can do is try to understand the experiments now in progress, which in fact have barely begun.

China renewed

This is not the place to praise or condemn the People's Republic of China, although one could do both. Our purpose is to note what it has done or tried to do, and then to see – or try to see – how this affects Chinese civilization, which is undergoing the greatest and most violent human experiment in all its very long history. What is being undertaken is an effort to establish order in many fields: social, economic, political, intellectual and moral.

This has meant placing things, people and classes – and if possible the outside world – in a new situation, created by Chinese will-power. Pride has its part in the process – pride as at least one link with the ancient past, when China was confident of its role at the centre of the universe.

The People's Republic of China has an enormous mass of people and resources – some real, some potential and needing to be exploited. Its economic development will depend on both.

China's population continues to grow. In 1952, it was 572 million; in 1953, 582; in 1954, 594; in 1955, 605; in 1956, 620; in 1957, 635; in 1958, 650; in 1959, 665; in 1960, 680; in 1961, 695. By 1984, it had passed one thousand million. These are not precise census figures, except for 1953 (and even there some reservations must be made): they are estimates, reasonably well founded. As in all less developed countries (and China in 1949 was the biggest such country in the world), the growth of the population, owing to a high birth-rate (in the region of 40 per 1,000) and a falling death-rate, poses appalling problems. Demographic growth on this scale limits in advance – and indeed seriously threatens – any real hope of higher living standards.

And yet China's economic growth-rate, from 1949 to 1962, was truly prodigious, unparalleled in the present or the past. Even Russia's first Five-Year Plan did not surpass China's, from 1953 to 1957 inclusive. Of course, the economy was more or less starting from scratch; and those who have lagged behind in the past have the chance to grow at relatively impressive speed. Poor to begin with, they can double their wealth without becoming rich. Later, when they have reached a certain level, they are likely to succumb to the law of diminishing returns, which spares neither capitalist nor socialist economies.

In measuring China's extraordinary development, one also has to remember that it is the fruit of inexorable will-power and effort on the part of the most populous country in the world. One might add that planning an economy is an art already demonstrated not only by earlier Soviet experience, but also by contemporary capitalism itself.

This is not the place to draw up a detailed balance-sheet. Relying on official figures for total revenue from 1952 onwards, without trying to scrutinize too closely statistics that are hard to check, one can note the following serial progression: 1952, 100; 1953, 114; 1954, 128; 1955, 128; 1956, 145; 1957, 153; 1958, 206; 1959, 249. The growth-rates in 1958 and 1959 respectively were 34 per cent and 22 per cent which is simply fabulous. Even allowing for the difficulty of working out the total revenue of so vast and various a country, economists cannot disguise either their astonishment or their admiration. This was indeed a 'Great Leap Forward'.

Non-economists may find it easier to judge the progress made by looking at figures for particular products. Steel (millions of tons): 1949, 0.16; 1952, 1.3; 1960, 18.4. Coal (millions of tons): 1949, 32; 1960, 425. Pig-iron (millions of tons): 1949, 0.25; 1960, 27.5. Electricity (milliards of kilowatt-hours): 1949, 4.2; 1960, 58. Cotton (millions of metres): 1949, 1.9; 1960, 7,600. Cereals, plus sweet potatoes and ordinary potatoes, counting their weight at a quarter of their fresh weight (tons): 1957, 185 million; 1958, 250 million; 1959, 270 million. Further data are supplied by the (triple) map of the Chinese railways, showing those that existed in 1949, those built by 1960 and those then planned. A further triple map could be drawn up for hydro-electric power-stations (old, new and planned), as also for ordinary power-stations. Nor should one forget the huge project for harnessing the Yangtze-Kiang, from the lower part of the Szechuan basin to the stretches of rapids and gorges, of which the longest is the Xiling. These great public works will provide an enormous reserve of energy, make possible major irrigation to the North, improve the course of the river, make thousands of kilometres of it navigable to deep-water ships, and in the gorges themselves encourage the establishment of ultra-modern factories.

These achievements were the result of superhuman efforts, made possible by the mobilization of China's huge society, which had not only to be pressed into political support and forced labour, but also to be remodelled.

This was not just a very effective means to an end: it was an end in itself – and a gamble. The regime deliberately staked its existence on its relentless modernization plans. And while it did not hesitate to apply draconian measures, it also began with some support from the Chinese masses, because it put an end to the dreadful corruption that had marred the previous regime in the last years of Chiang Kai-shek.

The whole of society was taken in hand: peasants, industrial workers, intellectuals and members of the Party. As for the wealthiest of the middle classes – the middlemen who had been intermediaries between Chinese and European merchants – they had fled in 1949 with the fall of Chiang Kai-shek. The industrial middle classes were reabsorbed into the system when private firms were turned into mixed enterprises (private and public) in 1956; and there remained, more or less untouched, only a limited number of middle-class businessmen, dealing with some aspects of trade but clearly in a precarious position.

Among the peasant population, reform was gradual but rapid. It began with the Agrarian Law of 30 June 1950, which ruthlessly ousted landed proprietors and rich peasants. Less well-off peasants lost part of their property; finally, each peasant was allotted a minute piece of land (just over one-third of an acre) – which in itself shows how vast a number of takers there were: of 600 million Chinese in 1954–5, more than 500 million were on the land. These innumerable scraps of land were the beginning of egalitarian ownership on a Lilliputian scale.

In October 1956 collectivization began, with the establishment of collective farms. A further step was the creation in 1958 of rural communes, each grouping together as many as 20,000 peasants, whereas a collective farm had only a few hundred. The communes were a new form of organization, and perhaps too ambitious: their role was at once political, agricultural, industrial and military. The peasant was also a soldier, and some peasants bore arms: this gave the regime the extra security of having an army on hand, ready to intervene at any time. However, on 20 November 1960, the communes seem to have been stripped of their prerogatives and responsibilities, in favour of production brigades, whose prospects looked uncertain. All that could be said was that the authorities were hesitating, not about their objective but about how to achieve it, given that food production was the only part of the economy whose growth remained slow.

The authorities similarly mobilized the industrial workers, whose numbers went on growing, and who were controlled by the trade unions in conjunction with the Party. The government asked them, like the peasants, to make superhuman efforts. After the second Five-Year Plan, it ran an active propaganda campaign to obtain further 'Great Leaps Forward' which the Plan had not envisaged. Hence spectacular feats of competition to reach productivity targets, and a host of slogans: 'More, better, quicker, cheaper'; 'One day is worth twenty years and a year is worth a millennium'; '1958 will be the first of three years of hard struggle for a thousand years ahead'.

It would be easy to quote thousands of examples of heroic effort – despite poor working conditions, low wages, insufficient food and lack of housing. One model working woman – and the title meant extra duties as well as prestige – was celebrated for rinsing her face in cold water to keep herself awake during her night shifts at the factory.

As for the intellectuals, the students and the members of the Party – was their heroism less in evidence, or were the targets assigned to them much less clear? What is certain is that the discipline imposed on them was more complex, more capricious and more cruel.

Members of the Party were never exempt from purges and

forced confessions. They had to endure such things as the campaigns against 'the three evils' and 'the five evils'. The first, in January and February 1952, attacked 'corruption, waste and bureaucracy' on the part of civil servants: it revealed a number of scandals, later deliberately exaggerated, which gave some former country-dwellers, who had become 'Party officials' in the towns the unpleasant surprise of losing jobs to which they had become all too comfortably accustomed. In the same year, the campaign against 'the five evils' (corruption, tax evasion, fraud, sale of State property and theft of economic secrets) caused enormous upheavals, including suicides and severe mass punishments. Other purges, other forced confessions and other suicides followed.

For students, whose numbers were constantly growing, there was barely a moment when the heavy hand of the authorities was not coming down on them, humiliating and disciplining them, and forcing them to do manual labour in the factories or the fields.

Teachers and other intellectuals by no means escaped persecution. They were very briefly allowed to speak their minds after the Soviet invasion of Hungary in 1956. This was the time of the so-called 'Hundred Flowers', when it was said that thoughts, like flowers, could blossom in a hundred different forms. Called upon to explain their own ideas, but hesitant to do so, the intellectuals found themselves in a strange situation – especially since what they said was at once published in the press. 'Marxism–Leninism,' declared one of them, 'is an old, outdated theory, unsuitable for China. It needs to be revised.' One teacher declined to give any opinion: 'I am afraid,' he said, 'of the present freedom. Its essential feature is that one has to talk. The pressure is painful. Let us relax for the moment. Later, we shall see what happens.' Another teacher noted: 'The people have not enough to eat, and yet some say that the standard of living has risen.' Mere heckling, one might think: a little recreation for old intellectuals who had disliked their Marxist re-education courses. But, on the contrary, it was a very serious affair. The Hundred Flowers did not last out a single springtime: they flourished 'vigorously for one short month', from 8 May to

8 June 1957. Then came repression. Many unwary people were summarily dismissed for what they had said.

All this is a reminder that China was engaged, not in an open debate, but in a life-and-death struggle. Its problem was to remodel society, to change its psychology, to purge its errors, its heritage and its possible regrets: to try to enthuse it with pride, with work and with self-satisfaction; and above all to impose obedience.

'If one constrains 650 million Chinese to think correctly, they will be brought to act correctly, according to the norms which the Chinese Communist Party judges essential to its march towards a Socialist China.' To this end the radio, the press and countless speeches engaged in incessant propaganda, unparalleled by any other 'socialist' or 'totalitarian' experiment. Its main weapon was criticism, organized daily through compulsory debates in every workplace. This was the way to find out those among the group whose attitude was satisfactory, those who could be persuaded and those implacably opposed. Everyone was called upon to attack these dissenters. 'Oral attack' (*tou-cheng*) was 'a humiliating mixture of violent criticism, combined with sarcasm, reproaches and – very rarely – mild physical chastisement.'

This ideological action was conceived as a 'long-term, complex and large-scale' campaign (Mao Tse-tung). Its rigour was adjusted to different social groups – moderate for the peasants, but very intense in factories, offices, universities, schools and units of the army. There was some resistance to indoctrination, and punishment was used to enforce it. At the beginning of the revolution, penalties were severe and brutal. Later, they grew milder but they remained extremely harsh.

In literature and art the Party had a 'cultural' commissar, in charge of discipline and the struggle against insidious bourgeois and reactionary infiltration in these fields. Every writer had to set an example, and not only in words. One author who lived in the country was praised for writing every morning in the 'collective literature' vein, and also growing a field of sweet potatoes and breeding pigs . . . Writers convicted of 'Right-wing deviationism' were liable to sanctions, like the well-known novelist Ting Ling, who was sent for 're-education by work' to a desolate region in Northern Manchuria, where she had to remain for two years.

Clearly, these punishments were mild by comparison with the terrible summary executions that took place in the first few months of the Revolution – and later. Clearly, too, the resistance and sabotage mentioned in official documents were the exception, not the rule. Sincere and enthusiastic conversions were far more numerous, and many were expressed in moving ways. To embrace the ideology that now triumphed was to embrace a fatherland and a nation: it was to believe in the future and to believe in China.

The agricultural experiment was the only major failure of Communist China. A few record harvests, some exaggerated statistics and a strong dose of official optimism managed to conceal the real facts until 1958. In the West, enthusiastic books and articles helped to sustain the illusion. But the catastrophic harvests of 1959, 1960 and 1961 severely punctured that optimism – in part unfairly. The unfairness lay in the fact that these very poor harvests were mainly the result of natural causes. China has always been subject to the equal and opposite misfortunes of droughts and floods, sometimes alternating, sometimes even simultaneous. They especially affect the great provinces in the North. In 1961, they destroyed more than half of the crops. Tornadoes and floods claimed millions of victims – whereas from March to June of that same year, below Jouan, one could cross the Yellow River on foot, since drought had reduced it to a ridiculous trickle. Droughts, typhoons, floods and venomous insects – none of these ancient enemies has surrendered to the new China.

One might add that China, like all the Communist States, has paid dearly for its industrial success. It has perhaps staked too much on industrialization at the expense of agriculture. The official press, as well as blaming 'natural calamities unparalleled for a hundred years', also accuses people, speaking of sabotage. 'Some of the officials and auxiliary workers who in August 1960 were sent to the country, to help the people's communes save the harvest, failed in their duty and disobeyed the orders of the Government and the Party', often with the connivance of 'retrograde elements in the population'. We should take this 'explanation by scapegoat' with a pinch of salt. It seems likely that collectivization, in China as elsewhere, met resistance from the peasantry, usually more traditionalist than the rest of the population. Some subsequent measures on the part of the authorities may have been concessions, like the emphasis placed on small rather than large production brigades.

China's poor harvests brought much in their train. They slowed down economic growth, and made it necessary to cut back the food exports to Russia, which had helped pay for imports of Russian goods and services. They obliged China to ask the capitalist countries for deliveries of grain: 9–10 million tons from Canada, Australia, the United States, France, Burma and even Taiwan. In London, where the sea transport for this enormous cargo was organized, it was reckoned that it would cost China £80 million a year for three years. How would she pay? Probably in mercury, gold and silver.

Without a doubt, this was a heavy blow for a growing economy, and it left a question-mark hanging over China's future. This, indeed, was the dark side of an economic success which in other respects was undeniably energetic and spectacular.

Chinese civilization in the modern world

None of this great progress would have been possible without the help of what in the immensity of China does duty for nationalism – a very individual sentiment which some have called, hideously, 'culturalism'. This is in fact a form of pride which is not national, but cultural, attached not to a nation but to a civilization. It is an ancient but enduring phenomenon, and it needs to be explored. For China today, which at first sight seems so novel and revolutionary, is linked thereby to a long and proud tradition which had been deeply wounded by the sad century (1840–1949) before the Communist Revolution.

China regards herself as a great power and a great civilization. She has always believed in her superiority over the rest of the world and in the supremacy of her civilization, outside of which, in her view, there was only barbarism. In the past, her pride was very like that felt by the West. For this reason, the century of one-sided treaties had been doubly cruel. The first humiliation was for China to find herself reduced to being one nation among many: the second was to be dominated by the Barbarians with their science and their arms. Chinese nationalism today, fierce and virulent as it is, can be seen as revenge – the firm decision to become a great nation, *the* great nation, whatever the cost. Hence the eagerness to redouble revolutionary efforts, to press on unstintingly, to seize on new resources like translations of Russian Marxist–Leninist manuals. Just as in the past China lapped up the sacred texts of Buddhism and sought acquaintance with Mr De (democracy) and Miss Sai (science), so now she pursues history, sociology and ethnography.

There is no doubt that Communist China feels that she has the vocation of leading the proletarian peoples against the over-fed and over-rich nations of the world, demonstrating how to achieve a swift revolution whose lessons she will gladly and generously teach. Despite her own difficulties, China has never stopped exporting supplies and capital: between 1953 and 1959, she distributed $1,191 million to Albania, Burma, Cambodia, Ceylon, Cuba, Egypt, Guinea, Hungary, Indonesia, Mongolia, Nepal, North Korea, North Vietnam and Yemen. This list does not include the aid given to the Algerian rebels, or an agreement made with Ghana in 1961. These and other facts (for instance that 40 per cent of the credits went to non-Communist countries) show that the People's Republic intends to play an international role, perhaps beyond its present resources, but certainly below the height of its ambitions.

The occupation of Tibet in 1950, followed by the latent conflict with India; claims on the island of Formosa (Taiwan) where Chiang Kai-shek's army had taken refuge; the desire to resume normal relations with Japan and with the West, whose economy would suit China's needs far better than would that of the Soviet Union – as witness the semi-clandestine import of machine-tools via Macao and Hong Kong; finally, the wish to enter the United Nations, where her place was at that time occupied by the nationalists in Formosa: all that reflected a desire for power and influence, as did the clash and near-breach between Chinese and Soviet Marxism which broke out at the 1961 Moscow Conference. China is determined to be a great power. In 1945, she was 'unable to make a motor-scooter'; by 1962 she was on the brink of producing an atomic bomb. Through this astounding revolution, she rediscovered her original pride and her dignity as a great civilization.

This is the point made by a leading Sinologist, Etienne Balazs, whose views of the Chinese revolution in its long historical context are summarized below.

If the Chinese experiment is a convincing success, all the less developed countries are likely to try to copy it. This is what makes so crucial and so agonizing, for China's friends and enemies alike, the fundamental question: will the experiment succeed, or is it already beginning to fail?

Let us admit, frankly, that there is no point in studying figures and statistics – partly because they are manipulated for the good of the cause, and more especially because Chinese statisticians are groping and floundering in trial and error. What is surprising is not that their estimates are shaky, but rather that they are good enough for planning to go forward without too many mistakes and for the results to be calculated accurately enough to register the general trend. All in all, that trend is positive.

One can of course point to some notorious failures in the five-year plans, such as the 'pocket' blast-furnaces, inadequate grain production or the difficulties of the people's communes. But the basic and stable features of the Chinese experiment are worth considering rather than criticizing, since they seem to have been well devised:

● the most determined industrialization, with a growth-rate far higher (and long likely to remain far higher) than that of either the Soviet Union and Eastern Europe or the less developed countries (on average, 20 per cent against 7 to 10 per cent);

● clear determination to 'walk on both legs' as long as necessary – i.e. to use the industrial income for investment so as to maintain the growth-rate, and to continue in other sectors to use the resources at hand, with rural artisans supplying agricultural tools and other consumption goods for the peasant masses;

● a general austerity programme, not confined to the masses and so making it possible to impose sacrifices on them;

● great flexibility on the part of the authorities, who can acknowledge their mistakes and immediately change tack.

All this is possible only because of certain essential facts of Chinese civilization.

First, numbers. The hardships involved in the experiment, even if they include the sacrifice of certain people, or even many people, cannot compromise the success of the experiment itself. There are too many people in China, and there always have been.

But, above all, the unprecedented mobilization of more than 600 million people by 10 million officials, disciplined and devoted members of the Party. And at the head of the Party, with a few exceptions, there remains the old guard, leaders hardened by thirty years of persecution, civil war, armed resistance against Japan, patient advances and retreats in military strategy and political tactics, with unequalled experience in governing things and people.

One cannot help thinking that they are the heirs of the great bureaucratic tradition in the ancient Empire, successor of the mandarins, those educated officials accustomed to governing a great State with a very firm hand. A new intelligentsia, bold and active, has eliminated the old one, bookish and conservative; and it masters. This powerful organization, seamless from top to bottom, and able to make everyone work unceasingly, is perhaps the secret of China's unique experiment. In a very short time, the most ancient living civilization has become the youngest and most active force in all the less developed countries. But this in turn is perhaps because it has been able to rely on one of the longest-lived and most solid features of its age-old civilization: its bureaucratic tradition.

A further question is posed by China's development: the Sino-Soviet conflict. Was a real conflict expressed by the demonstrations at the 22nd Congress in 1961 and the sly digs printed by the opposing official newspapers, Moscow's *Pravda* and Peking's *The People's Daily*? Or were these superficial appearances, against which Socialist solidarity would always prevail?

To tell the truth, divorce was almost impossible: it would have had international consequences which would be very dangerous for both sides. But the antagonism was real and deep; and here too there are historical reasons.

True, the conflict had modern origins. Here were two great people who have both tried the experiment of Communism in the hope of modernization. And while one was sighing with some relief after forty years of penury and suffering, the other was gasping in a super-human effort and bowed under miserable austerity. While the *nouveau riche* was flamboyantly taking his place in the councils of nations, the poor relation had no voice there, and was banished like a leper from the international scene. One was obliged to go forward at all costs, under pain of falling back: the other had grown wary and prudent. These were certainly reasons for friction.

But the rivalry surely lay deeper, in China's prickly nationalism and her desire for revenge on the West. For Russia, Socialist or not, was still Western, still Barbarian. China claims nothing less, in her effort to efface the past, than to become the capital of the Third World. Then, once more, she will indeed be 'The Middle Kingdom'.

13. India Yesterday and Today

India is an amalgam of areas, and also of disparate experiences, which never quite succeed in forming a single whole. It is too vast for that (4 million square kilometres including Pakistan, i.e. between three and four times the size of the six founder-members of the European Community). It is also too densely populated: without Pakistan, its inhabitants in 1963 numbered more than 438 million. Twenty years later, that figure had risen to more than 730 million. It is furthermore very diverse. In the South is Deccan, a region of conservative peoples and civilizations, obstinately resisting change. In the North-West, the arid lands of the Indus are linked with Iran and, beyond the Khyber Pass, with Turkestan and all of turbulent Central Asia. This North-West frontier, vulnerable to invasion, is India's dangerous and often tragic zone. Finally (except under the British Raj), no single political power has ever succeeded in dominating the whole subcontinent, either in the past or in the present, following its violent and sanguinary partition between India and Pakistan in 1947.

Ancient India (before the British Raj)

Without going back as far as the mysterious culture of the Indus (3000 to 1400 BC), one can distinguish three Indian civilizations which emerged gradually, slowly succeeded each other, and also overlapped:

- an Indo-Aryan or Vedic civilization, from 1400 BC to the seventh century AD;
- a medieval Hindu civilization (Hinduism), which replaced its predecessor until the thirteenth century;
- an Islamic-Hindu civilization, imposed like a straitjacket by the conquering Muslims in the thirteenth to eighteenth centuries, and whose vigorous and sustained colonialism was replaced by Britain's from the eighteenth century onwards.

None of these three civilizations, it should again be stressed, united the whole subcontinent: nor did any of the great 'universal' Empires they successively supported. Until the eighteenth century, India never experienced the imposition of a single regime such as marked – and greatly simplified – China's past.

Vedic India passed through three or four main stages between 1400 BC and the seventh century AD. These two millennia were dominated by invasion and settlement by Aryan peoples from Turkestan, who entered India from the North-West and slowly spread across the plains of the Central Indus, then the Central Ganges. Their civilization affected only a part of the Indo-Gangetic Plain; but this, very early on, was the living heart of India.

This first, 'Vedic' civilization (from *Veda*, sacred knowledge) drew partly on what the newcomers brought with them and partly on innumerable borrowings from those already there. It developed extremely slowly, clashing at times with the very varied brown or black indigenous population – pygmies who were early arrivals from Africa; Proto-Mediterraneans who had come later, no doubt from Mesopotamia, and whose physical type is preserved among the Dravidians in the South; and peoples from Central Asia with Mongoloid characteristics (especially in Bengal).

These pre-Aryans were for the most part already settled on the land, as farmers and stationary stockbreeders, grouped in villages and even in towns, on the banks of the Indus, the focus of an already ancient civilization of citizens and merchants. These pre-Aryans were numerous, and remained so; even today, they make up the majority of the Indian population.

The Indo-Aryans, by contrast, mostly but not invariably had pale skins and fair hair. They were nomadic herdsmen related to the many peoples who in the second millennium invaded the plains of Iran or Asia Minor and the distant countries of Europe. These invaders of India were kin to the Hellenes, the Italiots, the Celts, the Germanic peoples and the Slavs.

Stage one, before 1000 BC: invasion

The first Aryan invasion came from Turkestan towards Iran and India. It thus came to grips, from Mesopotamia to the Indus, with an already homogeneous and flourishing civilization of towns, tall houses and settled peasants. This civilization may have become decadent by the time the invaders reached the countries of the Indus; but those countries fought for a long time to preserve their independence from the newcomers, and much delayed their advance towards the East.

The Aryans' sacred texts, written in Sanskrit, describe these interminable struggles which took place before 1000 BC in the Punjab and the Kabul River area, involving men, gods and anti-gods (the *asoura* or divine protectors of the enemy). This long phase is reflected in the oldest of the sacred books, the *Rig Veda* or *Hymnal*, embodying the mythology and beliefs of a first Vedic religion. This included at least thirty-three gods, divided among earthly gods, gods of heaven and gods of the 'intermediate space' (the atmosphere). In the midst of these 'somewhat pale' deities, two gods stood out: Varuna, upholder 'of the cosmic and moral laws and observer of the guilty, whom he catches in his snares'; and, still more important, Indra, the fair-haired victorious hero of a thousand conflicts, who having defeated the demon Vita freed the waters of the sky, which ever since have flooded and fertilized the earth. All these gods mixed with human beings, like the divinities of Olympus who mixed with the warriors confronting each other beneath the walls of Troy. All demanded sacrifices: milk, wheat, meat and a fermented drink (*soma*) obtained from a mysterious plant.

In short, then, this was a formal and pluralist religion, consisting purely of rites. The Aryans had not yet completely given up their nomadic habits in favour of a settled life which would have involved more order, even in the religious domain.

Stage two, from 1000 to 600 BC: conquest and settlement.

The invaders gradually adopted a settled life in an area slightly further or slightly extended to the East, and of which the essential crossroads was what is now Delhi. This Eastward thrust went as far as what is now Varanasi (Benares), involving gigantic battles – or battles reported as such. By about 800, the invaders had reached Bengal and perhaps Central India.

The huge geographical, social, economic and political changes that resulted explain the enormous religious innovations recorded in new sacred books, then in the *Commentaries* (*Brahmanas*) and the *Upanishads* – that *Treatise on Approaches* which opened the secret doors of religious speculation. Although retaining its original basis, religion was gradually becoming more complex. It began to show monotheistic tendencies, although the intermingling of victors and vanquished flooded it with an enormous mass of non-Aryan beliefs. These included yoga ('self-mastery'), whose practices became an important part of Vedic religion alongside the ritual sacrifices.

More and more, religious beliefs and attitudes grew gloomier. Soon it began to be thought that people's souls were subject to incessant reincarnation, constantly returning to a new earthly existence, full of endless pain. At the same time, the first social divisions (*varna*) appeared in a society that was at once 'magic', 'pseudo-feudal' and 'colonial' – a mixture in which not everything could be explained (as used to be thought) in terms of victors and vanquished. In the highest rank, the brahmins were the priests, masters of spiritual matters. Then came the warriors, kings, princes and great lords (*kshatryas*). In the third rank were smallholding peasants, stockbreeders, artisans, and merchants (*vaisyas*); and in the fourth and last rank were the *sûdras*, who originally at least were native slaves. Later, this caste system slowly solidified, with its taboos, its exclusions, its multiple bans on inter-marriage and its strict divisions between *pure* and *impure*.

Temporal and spiritual power was divided between the two highest castes. Primitive royalty soon found itself deprived of any religious monopoly – in contrast to what was the rule elsewhere, in China as much as in, for example, ancient Egypt.

The relationship between the spiritual and the political principles of the *imperium* was made fully evident in a peculiar institution . . . It was not enough for the king, the model or essence of the *kshatryas* caste, to employ brahmins for the public ritual: he had to have a permanent personal relationship with *one* brahmin, his *purohita* (literally, 'one placed forward'). We might translate this as 'chaplain'; but one must bear in mind the idea of a spiritual avant-garde or delegated authority – a 'greater self'. Not only would the gods not eat the king's offerings without a *purohita*, but the king depended on him for his own actions, which would not succeed without the *purohita*'s help. His relationship with the king was like that of thought with willpower: it was as close as marriage. The *Rig Veda* had said it already: 'He lives, he prospers in his dwelling; the earth showers him with its gifts; the people obey him of their own accord. This is the king, in whose domain the brahmin walks in front.

(Louis Dumont)

Such, at least, is what the brahminical texts declare and repeat.

This religious primacy, associated but not identified with political power, was in Louis Dumont's view the main reason why Indian society was fragmented. Since the first two castes were associated with each other, they stood in contradistinction to the rest of society; and the first three castes, likewise, shunned the mass of the *sûdras*.

The brahmins based their pre-eminence on the inordinate fear that they inspired. The complexity of the ritual made them indispensable as organizers of sacrifices: if one single detail were omitted, the god being invoked would at once slip away, and the terrible Varuna would exact his pitiless revenge. As custodians of the ritual's secrets, the priests could act as they thought fit: they could attack the old, naïve anthropomorphism of the Aryans, or disparage Indra and all the divine heroes of the old hymns. For their own use they created a supreme god, Brahma, who presided over their sacrifices. To tell the truth, he was never very popular.

Two other leading gods, however, had an enthusiastic following – Siva Rudra among the peasants, and Vishnu, identified with the hero Krishna Vasudeva, among the aristocrats. What was more, 'warriors' and 'peasants' (the second and third of the castes) readily turned towards yoga, which the brahmins adopted too, and towards other indigenous ritual practices – or, in some cases, towards free philosophical speculation, which in the sixth and fifth centuries BC gave birth to two new religions, Jainism and Buddhism.

Stage three: the early success of Jainism and Buddhism in the sixth and fifth centuries BC.

Little by little there emerged minute royal principalities, then aristocratic towns, linked together by trade. The towns, which soon became densely populated, thrived on the luxury of their princely courts and on their rich middle-class citizens. Bankers and merchants made large profits from the sea and caravan routes, which brought among other things fine textiles in cotton, linen or silk. From 600 BC onwards, iron-working was practised, as shown by the weapons found in contemporary tombs. Distant Aden was the great market city which re-exported Indian iron towards the Mediterranean.

In this busy environment, somewhat comparable to that of Greece in the same two centuries, two great religions developed, each promising salvation: Jainism and Buddhism. The latter is better known and more important than the former, because it spread outside India; but within India both had equal support. Both, equally, were 'unofficial' and 'secular', adopted by the ruling classes independently of the brahmins, and disseminated by merchants. Both founded monasteries, and both propounded rules for individual salvation. Buddhism, as we have seen, preached a form of renunciation, negating the desire to live and the sense of life, and trying to break the vicious circle of reincarnation so as to attain Nirvana. Jainism, by contrast, saw in personal suffering, and the quest for suffering, an effective route to salvation. Both religions were founded by aristocrats: Buddhism by Siddhartha Gautama, perhaps a king's son (563?–483?), known also as Sakya Muni (the sage of the Sakyas) or the Buddha (the Enlightened); and Jainism by Vardhamana Mahavira (540?–468), the 'Conqueror' of the world (Jina).

The Buddha, who came from Nepal, had his 'revelation' in about 525; and after that he spent the rest of his life preaching in the Ganges Valley. His religion, which began to be modified soon after his death, was based on his sayings, as collected and transmitted by his disciples. They contain no statement about God; but this silence is not a denial: it remains characteristic of his doctrine, like its rejection of any kind of divine 'monism' – the belief that there is only one substantial thing or kind of thing in the universe. In agreement with the dominant ideas of his time (those of the *Upanishads*), he rejected also the idea that the world and the Universal Being were real. For him, nothing was real outside our consciousness. 'You have returned to me like a lookout-bird which had left the ship and flown to all points of the compass in search of land, but found it nowhere. For the elements (Earth, Fire, Water and Air) have their basis in the consciousness. They lose it when consciousness is lost. When consciousness no longer exists, all the elements in the universe will be totally destroyed.'

In fact, the Buddha was a 'renouncer', an abstinent (*sannyasi*). The 'renouncer' was a man who left society and wandered, living on alms, in search of a spiritual absolute capable of setting him free. He was concerned not with reforming society but with securing his personal salvation. So Buddhism was a religion for the individual, the 'desocialized' person. In this respect it resembled the many heresies which regularly arose in India and which were essentially ways of withdrawing, by personal asceticism and the quest for sainthood, from the religion of the brahmins and the constraints of society with which it was so closely linked. The Buddhist abstinent, in contrast to the Christian (whose aim was to escape death), tried to escape from life and its cycle of reincarnations. 'Here, my brother monks, is the holy truth about the suppression of pain: it is the hunger for existence and pleasure that leads from reincarnation to reincarnation ... Here, my brother monks, is the holy truth about the suppression of pain: the extinction of this hunger by destroying desire, by banishing desire, by renouncing it, by leaving it no room.' Such was the price of breaking the cycle of reincarnations and attaining Nirvana.

To reach it, the righteous must follow 'the road with eight branches' (including science, which dispelled all vanity); must respect the five prohibitions (of murder, theft, adultery, drunkenness and lying); must abstain from the ten sins (including insults, gossip, envy, hatred and dogmatic error); and must practise the six transcendent virtues (loving one's neighbour, patience, moral purity, energy, alms-giving and kindness). But to achieve perfection meant going further still. It meant becoming a *bodhisattva* or saint, and then a Buddha (receiving mystical enlightenment). Only Buddhas could dissolve in Nirvana.

Stage four: during the so-called 'Empire' period, from 321 BC to AD 535, Jainism and Buddhism spread very widely, dominating philosophy and the arts, but without for one moment displacing current ritual practices, whether or not derived from Vedism.

To defend their positions, the brahmins relied more and more on the popular cults which they gathered together as if to make a rampart. This slow process led in the direction of Hinduism, a vast eclectic synthesis to which we shall return shortly.

Thus it was that a hierarchical society took shape and hardened, notably into the caste system so peculiar to India, which grew up between 300 BC and AD 700. This, then, was a relatively late phenomenon, and not to be confused with the former *varnas*, which bore more resemblance to the social classes in pre-Islamic Iran. The castes, which still exist in India today, took about a thousand years to emerge, partly from the chance mixture of races and cultures, and partly as a result of the growing multiplicity of different trades. The result was several thousand castes (of which there were still 2,400 or so in 1960). At the bottom of the heap, the victims of every prohibition, were the pariahs, the 'untouchables'.

This composite civilization profited from the establishment of universal Empires (the Mauryas dynasty, 321–181 BC, and especially the Gupta dynasty, AD 320–525) to spread beyond the strict limits of Northern India, towards Nepal, the Himalayas, Tibet, Siam and Indonesia (notably after the fall of the Gupta), and to infiltrate not only the island of Ceylon, which it 'colonized', but also the Dravidian stronghold of the Deccan. Everywhere, it imposed 'classical and sophisticated' Sanskrit, which became throughout India the vehicle of a princely civilization in contrast to the culture of the masses.

With the Mauryas Empire and the justly famous reign of Ashoka (264–226 BC), Buddhism won the day. Centuries later, however, when a new classical India took shape, it did so under the victorious insignia of Hinduism, or what is known as the Hindu 'Renaissance', since this was the time of its artistic greatness, when India mastered all that it had learned from elsewhere. This included in particular the art of Greece, brought through Alexander the Great's conquests in the Indus area, 327–325 BC. But Indian art also affirmed its own character of purity and strength; and it invented, so to speak, the Hindu temple (the *sikhara* – literally its dominant spire), which for centuries was as typical of India as the cathedrals were of the West. Built on a huge platform with broad staircases leading up to it, the temple was surrounded by chapels or by an ambulatory. The sheer size of the sanctuary represented Mount Meru, the mythical Olympus on which the gods were believed to live.

The Hindu Renaissance was also a great literary period. It was at the court of Chandragupta I I (AD 386–414) that the 'nine precious stones' – the outstanding poets and thinkers of the time – lived and worked. There too, in particular, Kalidasa wrote *Sakuntala*, the drama which, when translated into English in 1789 and German in 1791, made such a lively impression on Herder and Goethe.

Because Hinduism inherited some very ancient traditions, one cannot precisely date its origin, whether at the end of the Gupta dynasty or at the dissolution of the rather ephemeral Harsha empire (606–47). But it certainly established itself as a whole during these Indian Middle Ages – roughly between the death of Harsha and the foundation of the Delhi sultanate in 1206. Hinduism is more than a religion or a social system: it is the core of Indian civilization, and while its origins were very ancient, it remains a living reality even in the India of Pandit Nehru and his successors.

In exploring this phenomenon, we may find that some useful light is shed by expressions drawn from the history of Europe – 'Middle Ages', 'feudal fragmentation' and so on. But if we use them, we should not take them literally. While Hinduism was as important to medieval India as Christianity was in the European Middle Ages, India bore scarcely any resemblance to Merovingian, Carolingian or even feudal Europe.

The historical context counts. Even before the end of the Gupta dynasty, trade was probably slowing down. This recession affected the merchants, the adherents and supporters of Jainism and Buddhism. Soon, both religions suffered persecution, with their devotees impaled and executed, their monasteries destroyed, and so on.

Throughout India's history, whenever its richest regions – from the Ganges to Gujarat and the edge of the Arabian Sea – were no longer flourishing under the stimulus of large-scale trade, the great

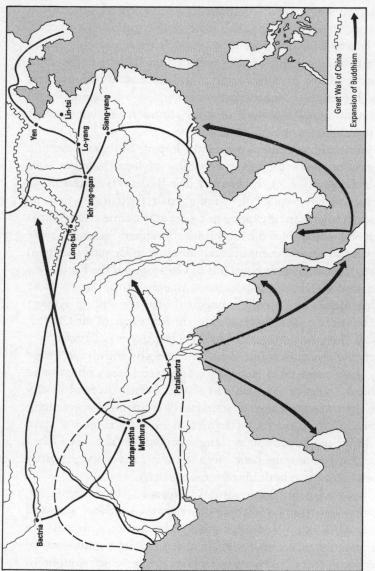

11. *China and India after Buddha (500 BC to AD 500)*

During this troubled period, Buddhism spread by sea to Indo-China and Indonesia, and by land towards the heart of Asia and China. In India, on the other hand, it declined Pataliputra was Ashoka's capital. The Greek Empire of Bactria (ringed by a broken black line, with the towns of Mathura ard Indraprastha) for a time stretched as far as Pataliputra. These hellenized regions acted as a relay for Buddhism.

Great Wal of China
Expansion of Buddhism

unifying Empires crumbled. Not that the mass of the Indian population was too much troubled by their collapse: the king and the ruling classes were always of a different caste from almost all their subjects. It was fairly natural, then, that on these occasions India split up into independent States, each of which then fragmented again, into a series of warlike principalities and lordships. The history of the Hindu 'Middle Ages', dominated by regional 'warriors', is made up of hundreds of local chronicles in which even learned specialists can easily lose their way.

What is interesting is not to pursue the history of these States one by one, nor to dwell on this burgeoning of local loyalties – in Bengal, in Gujarat, or in the Deccan (the 'Indian Byzantium', as some historians have called it, thinking of its particular fate, its powerful resistance and its expansion by sea at the time of the Chola Empire in 888–1267). No: the most important phenomenon for our purpose was the development of local literature in Bengali (Bengal), in Gujarati in the area round the Gulf of Cambay and the Kathiawar Peninsula, and in Dravidian languages, mainly in the South. (The word 'Dravidian', awkwardly coined in 1856 by Bishop Robert Caldwell but now unavoidable, denotes the languages of the Deccan, not its races. The most important of these languages is Tamil.)

In brief, the Hindu 'Middle Ages' and the slowing-down of the economy gave renewed strength and vigour to India's human and geographical diversity – which had always been powerful in any case. This diversity flourished as abundantly as 'tropical vegetation'; it was one of the basic characteristics of Hinduism, and it gave modern India the profusion of languages which it finds such a handicap. But at the same time, despite India's diversity, religious and cultural unity was undoubtedly taking shape.

Unity resulted from the brahmins' efforts to synthesize belief. Hinduism, in Northern India, was a religious synthesis achieved by the brahmins, using Vedic and post-Vedic elements, non-Aryan elements assimilated centuries ago, and finally the multiplicity of particular local cults, taken over by a religion which sought to embrace everything.

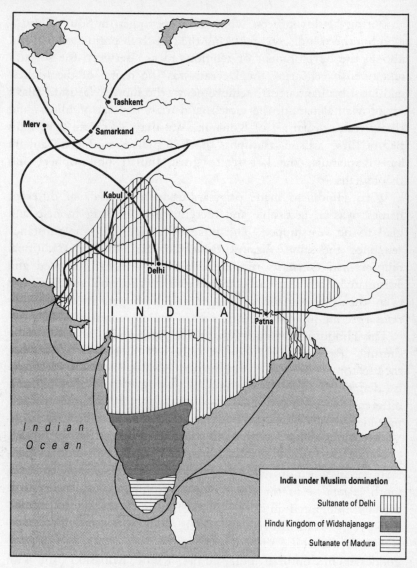

12.India in the fourteenth century

This map shows the main roads (thick black line) and the political divisions, with (in the far South) the short-lived Sultanate of Madura, set up in 1335.

During this slow process, what was happening in the South? Gradually, Southern India was replacing the North in politics, in art, and also in the development of religious ideas. Between the seventh and twelfth centuries, the Deccan was the home of the highest and most brilliant artistic achievements: the subtle, classical Pallava art of Mamalaparam, the violent and masterful art of Ellora, and the lyrical, sensual art of Konarak. We may also note that, long before these artistic triumphs, the South had produced Sankara and Ramanuja, the last really great Indian philosophers and theologians.

What Hinduism made popular, under thousands of different names, was an accessible and merciful god, willing to help and glad to be worshipped. The imagery varied, but the substance remained the same. Against Buddhism and Jainism, traditional religion had taken its revenge – although it had adopted and assimilated both sects' teaching of purity and non-violence, and even their vegetarianism. In general, however, it was simply reinterpreting in new language a set of ancient popular beliefs.

This Hinduism concluded that three great gods coexisted 'at the summit'. Brahma (who above all received 'literary homage') was the creator of the world; Vishnu was its preserver; and Shiva was its destroyer. Separate yet inseparable, they expressed in their different ways the supreme Being whose role it was to act as providence for humanity. This explained the occasions when they 'descended' to earth, as in the *avataras* of Vishnu – his numerous incarnations to preserve world peace. He might appear as a fish, a tortoise, an enormous wild boar, a man-lion or even – this was the ninth *avatara* – in the form of the Buddha, whose work was thereby integrated into the whole religious system. Shiva, the destroyer, was identified 'with death, with time: he was Hara, he who removes'. Like Vishnu, Shiva delegated his powers, often to goddesses. In Southern India, he had a wife, Minashki ('she with the eyes of a fish'), who was the daughter of a king.

It is impossible here to explore fully this rich and exuberant mythology, of which H. Zimmer's intelligent and agreeable book,

Myths and Symbols in the Art and Mythology of India (1951), gives a useful idea. Nor can we dwell further on the meticulous rituals of prayers and sacrifices, on the cult of the dead, on the cremation ceremony which remains general for the majority of Hindus (only ascetics and children being buried), or on the long and complex procedures for marriage. India was and remains extremely conservative as regards such rites.

For believers, the essential problem was personal salvation. If, favourably judged, they entered Paradise 'on the sun's rays', or if they were condemned and went to Hell, in either case the decision, whether reward or punishment, would not be long maintained. The soul would be reincarnated to continue its unhappy fate. However, by means of prayers, rituals and pilgrimages, or with the aid of talismans, people could sometimes escape from the *kharman*, the act which always has repercussions – and notably causes reincarnation. In this way, they would be 'saved': but their salvation would be negative, very different from the Buddhist progress towards spiritual freedom, which required individual purification and asceticism, and saintly renunciation.

The turbid waters of Hinduism – of Indian civilization itself – submerged Buddhism as they did Jainism. Some of its formal aspects were assimilated, but its spirit was rejected, even in Bengal, where it had put down deep roots. India felt the lack of it; the saint or 'renouncer' would always attract a following. Bowed down by the weight of a close-knit, inescapable society, the dominant religion allowed individual liberty only in the form of abnegation, of 'non-action'. In these circumstances, 'sects' naturally multiplied. They were a means of intellectual and moral liberation.

It was perhaps the void left by Buddhism which led to the massive conversions to Islam which took place in Bengal after the last persecutions the Buddhists suffered, in the twelfth century. Something similar happened in the Balkans in the fifteenth century, when Bogomil Christian heretics, so often persecuted, became converts to Islam after the arrival of the Turks.

Muslim India (1206–1757) was pioneered in the seventh century by the foundation of trading colonies on the Malabar coast, and confirmed in 711–12 by an invasion from Sind and the establishment of various inland colonies, Muslim India spread very slowly across the lands that led to the Indus and the Ganges. Later, it tried in vain to conquer the whole of the subcontinent. The Muslims fought for a long time to gain possession of the semi-desert area of Northern India. Even by the early eleventh century, in AD 1030, only the Punjab was in their hands. It took them two centuries more to found the Sultanate of Delhi (1206) and extend it to Northern India – a key stronghold which gave them everything, or almost everything.

This conquest, successful after countless setbacks, ended in wholesale military occupation. The Muslims, who were few in number and based solely in the larger towns, could not rule the country except by systematic terror. Cruelty was the norm – burnings, summary executions, crucifixions or impalements, inventive tortures. Hindu temples were destroyed to make way for mosques. On occasion there were forced conversions. If ever there were an uprising, it was instantly and savagely repressed: houses were burned, the countryside was laid waste, men were slaughtered and women were taken as slaves.

Usually, the plains were left to be run by native princes or village communities. These intermediate authorities were responsible for paying the heavy taxes which were sometimes the counterpart of a certain autonomy, as in the case of the rajahs of Rajputana.

India survived only by virtue of its patience, its superhuman power and its immense size. The levies it had to pay were so crushing that one catastrophic harvest was enough to unleash famines and epidemics capable of killing a million people at a time. Appalling poverty was the constant counterpart of the conquerors' opulence, including the splendour of the palaces and feasts in Delhi, which the sultans had made their capital, and which was a source of wonder to Muslim travellers such as the famous Ibn Batûta.

The sultans in Delhi had the good fortune to be largely spared the shock of the first Mongol invasions under Genghis Khan and his immediate successors, in the thirteenth century. They even profited from these troubles to extend their own conquests towards the South, which had hitherto resisted the establishment of Muslim rulers. The tide turned when Tamerlane invaded their territory and in 1398 successfully raided Delhi, and sacked it without mercy. Having conquered it, however, he at once withdrew with his booty and his files of prisoners – so that the Muslims were more or less able to re-establish their hold on India, although they never regained their former splendour.

It was an ailing and divided Empire that was overthrown some 130 years later, in 1526, at the Battle of Panipat, by an army of adventurers led by Baber, who claimed to be a descendant of Genghis Khan. His army was very small, but it was equipped with harquebuses and field guns, whose carriage wheels, on the field of battle, were secured with chains to resist possible mounted charges. After Baber's victory, moreover, he enlarged the army with mercenaries from Iran, from Kashmir, from Islamic countries, and later from the West.

Baber was a Sunni Muslim. His victory was therefore a victory for orthodox Islam, for those with pale skins and for gunpowder. With it was established the Empire of the Great Mogul, which in principle endured for more than three centuries, until 1857, when it was belatedly suppressed by the British after the Indian Mutiny. In reality, its lustre had died with the last of its great rulers, Aurangzeb (1658–1707), long before the British occupied Bengal in 1757.

From 1526 to the death of Aurangzeb, Muslim India attained renewed splendour, recalling the great years of the Delhi sultanate – with the same violence, the same forced coexistence, the same impositions, and the same successes.

The same violence: Islam ruled by fear, and founded its luxury on India's general poverty. Perhaps it had no alternative. On the one side were the fabulous riches admired by travellers from the West;

on the other, a series of famines, a fabulous death-rate and innumerable children abandoned or sold by their families.

The same forced coexistence: As time went by, there were more and more mutual links. Akbar (1555–1606), the greatest of the Mogul rulers, even tried to set up a less arbitrary administration and establish a new religion which would have brought Islam and Hinduism into a single system (the Din Ilahi or Divine Religion). This, however, had few converts outside the Emperor's immediate circle, and it died with him. Still, the attempt was a significant move.

In fact, the conquerors could not do without their Hindu subjects. Immense regions of India remained independent, whether they paid their taxes or not. François Bernier, a French doctor who worked for the Great Mogul, noted in 1670: 'In this same expanse of country, there are a number of nations of which the Mogul is not very much the master, since most of them have their own particular rulers and leaders, who obey him and pay tribute to him only when they are forced to, some paying very little, and others nothing at all.'

The necessities of war and of continual lesser conflicts tended to limit the Great Mogul's authority, although in principle it was absolute. His court was a vast army of 50,000 to 200,000 men gathered in Delhi: cavalry, musketeers, gunners; light field guns (the so-called 'stirrup artillery') and heavy cannon; reserves of horses and elephants – a whole crowd of soldiers, grooms and servants. Their leaders, the *omerahs*, enjoyed pensions and profits (land was granted them for life); they were adventurers, often of very humble origins, which by no means prevented their parading in the streets 'superbly dressed, sometimes on an elephant or a horse, sometimes in a palanquin or sedan chair, usually followed by a large number of horsemen and bodyguards, with a quantity of footmen marching in front and alongside to clear the way, dispel the flies and the dust with peacocks' tails, and carry toothpicks, spittoons, or drinking-water'. 'For one Muslim,' Bernier goes on, 'there are hundreds of infidels.' The whole army could not be recruited from among so-called Moguls with pale skins (who, for fear that their children might lose this privilege, preferred to marry white women from Kashmir). So soldiers had to be found among the infidels and the men with darker complexions.

The Delhi contingent always included Rajputs (natives of Rajputana), who were often led by their own rajahs. Some of the latter could if need be raise huge armies of native soldiers. They were required, sometimes, to fight against even Muslim mercenaries, or against such dangerous neighbours as the Shi'ite Persians, or against the Pathans, Muslims from Bengal, or against Hindu or Muslim princes from the Deccan, who were traditionally hostile.

All this was paid for by the Great Mogul's abundant treasury, supplied more by the trade of his vast States than by the income from his land. The treasury, in fact, was a centre for the collection and dissemination of wealth. Every time a silver coin was deposited there, it had a small hole punched in it: many coins bore several such marks.

A considerable part of non-Muslim India took part in this distribution system – or, as we might say, was in on it. Over time, coexistence was inevitable, involving compromise and limited mutual tolerance. We have already mentioned the mixed Islamic and Hindu art which developed in Delhi and other Mogul capitals. One thing is certain: it was a true hybrid, as much Indian as Muslim. On the cultural and religious plane, however, India remained itself. Despite everything, Islam did not affect it deeply. It was significant that Tulsi Das, the Brahman who became the greatest poet in the Hindi language, lived under the Mogul empire, from 1532 to 1623.

Indeed, Islam's authoritarian domination, whatever its other innumerable results, made less impact on Hindu society and the Indian economy than did the contact with the West which began at the end of the fifteenth century, increased in the sixteenth and seventeenth, and multiplied again in the general expansion of the eighteenth. Apart from gunpowder, which accounted not only for the Muslim victory in 1526 but also for the destruction of

Vizianagaram in 1565, Islam had no great advantage over the India it had conquered.

With the death of Aurangzeb in 1707, as we have seen, the Empire began to vacillate in the face of dangers from the West and the South. In 1738, the Afghans seized Delhi; and already in 1659 the Hindu Mahrattas of Central India had begun the very powerful attacks which had only briefly halted and which in the eighteenth century became triumphant.

That said, however, we should not be over-hasty in condemning the Muslim record in India. It would be unfair to isolate this colonial experiment, extremely violent and prolonged as it was, from the countless similar exploits then taking place in the world. Whatever else it did, this centuries-long occupation implanted into the teeming mass of India an enormous number of faithful Muslims, 24 per cent of the population according to the 1931 census (77 million, compared with 239 million Hindus), or roughly one Muslim for every three Hindus. Thirty years later, since the 1947 partition was very approximate, the percentage of Muslims in India was between 20 and 25 per cent, and closer to the second figure: 44 million Muslims out of a total population of 438 million, while the population of Pakistan was some 85 million, including a number of non-Muslims. So Muslim India, too, has miraculously survived, and it remains hard to isolate from the shared Indo-Muslim civilization of which it is a part.

British India (1757–1947): an ancient economy at grips with the modern West

In the sixteenth century, the Portuguese had a number of warehouses in the Far East. Vasco da Gama had reached Calicut on 17 May 1498, and Goa was occupied in 1510. But Portuguese India flourished for less than a century. In the seventeenth century, British, Dutch and French factories dominated the scene.

Even before the defeat of the French in 1763, Robert Clive's victory at Plassey (Palassi, to the North of present-day Calcutta) on 23 June 1757, in effect inaugurated British India. It lasted almost two centuries, until Indian independence in 1947; and thus virtually matched the longevity of the Great Mogul's Empire. Like that Empire, it grew gradually, and was not complete until it conquered the Punjab in 1849; equally, it left outside its direct control a number of autonomous States, the Native States and Agencies, although under British rule their independence was much more theoretical than real. In fact, the whole subcontinent felt the shock of Britain's aggressive domination, backed by immense economic superiority. Until the First World War, distant Britain was about the greatest industrial, trading and banking power in the world. The British Raj profoundly affected every structural aspect of Indian life.

India became an exporter of raw materials. Exploitation, gradually spreading as more of the country was conquered, was in the hands of the East India Company, which was not dissolved until 1858; and from the earliest, highly corrupt times of Lord Clive (who was attacked in the House of Commons and committed suicide in 1774), it took the triple form of exploiting local potentates, merchants and peasants. Exploitation was pursued without shame in the rich and soon conquered provinces of Bengal, Behar and Orissa. A modicum of order and justice was not imposed until 1784, after which a more honest regime was established.

In those early years, pillage and embezzlement had already led to fearful disasters. On 18 September 1789, Lord Cornwallis, the Governor-General of India, wrote: 'I can state without hesitation that a third of the Company's lands in Hindustan are now a jungle, inhabited only by wild beasts.' It was hardly an exaggeration. True, the new rulers, who bore their share of responsibility, were also the playthings and victims of a process over which they had scant control. Many of the evils in question were the result of developing a money economy in a country like India, which despite its very long exposure to world trade, had never known such a system before. British law, and Western concepts regarding land ownership, also led to unintended catastrophes. All in all, an ancient stability, achieved with difficulty and based on India's very remote past, was now severely shaken and at risk.

As the eighteenth century drew to a close, India was a rural world of countless villages, often very poor: groups of huts such as could still be seen, in 1962, near to Madras among other places. 'Wall of dried mud, a roof of interlaced palm leaves and the only entrance a low door ... The smoke from the fire, burning dried cow-dung, escaped as best it could through the slits in the roof.' But these villages formed close-knit, stable and self-sufficient communities, ruled by a chief or a council of elders, who in some regions even organized a regular redistribution of land. In the village there would also be artisans – blacksmiths, woodworkers, sawyers, goldsmiths – plying the same craft from father to son for centuries, and paid in kind for their services with a portion of the village crop. Some of these villages included slaves in the service of the wealthier peasants, who were responsible for feeding, housing and clothing them. The community as a whole was responsible for the taxes or forced labour demanded by the State or by the nearest lord. Part of its crops and its efforts were thus earmarked for elsewhere, for the minority India of the distant Government towns, from which nothing came back. Taxes were the sole link the town maintained with its villages, which were unable to buy from it any of the goods it imported or manufactured. Its industries' products remained luxuries, reserved for a small circle of town-dwellers, or for export. But if the pressure from these privileged persons became intolerably heavy, the villagers could decamp, looking for somewhere else to settle and hoping for a better fate.

The ancient subsistence economy of the villages lasted a long time. Since it comprised both farmers and artisans, it had little need of the outside world, except for salt and iron, and so remained almost a closed system. Its social organization was based on the castes, keeping all the villagers in their place, from the brahmin (who was at once a teacher, a priest and an astrologer), to the elders, or to the wealthier peasants who belonged to the higher castes. At the bottom of the scale, the majority were untouchables, labouring on the land.

This whole system deteriorated more and more in the eighteenth and nineteenth centuries. To raise revenue, the British used the existing tax-collectors, but they gave them ownership of the villages – which they had never had before. Thus there came into being, starting in Bengal, a number of spurious landlords, the *zamindars*. Their task was to supply the British authorities with the due amount of tax; but to secure their own commission they required more from the peasants. Soon, they ceased to live on the spot, and employed agents to do their work. The unhappy peasantry of Bengal found itself saddled with an impressive panoply of middlemen and parasites.

In places where they had not appointed *zamindars*, the British themselves collected the taxes, which were payable in cash. Any peasant short of ready money now had to resort to a usurer. Such moneylenders began to flourish all over India. In the past, they had had to be wary of peasant resistance and anger: now, they had the law and the judges on their side. If a debt was not repaid, they would seize the peasant's livestock, and then his land. Poor peasant, poor *ryot*! Since the price of land continually rose, the moneylender was well placed to become a landowner; moreover, speculative price-rises attracted investors to buy land as a guaranteed source of revenue. The result was a growing number of large-scale land-owners, normally little concerned to improve their soil, and simply living on their profits. By the end of the nineteenth century, out of 100 million peasants perhaps a third were still smallholders, and the average size of their holdings was less than ten acres, the minimum needed for survival. In the process, nine out of ten of the councils of elders (which are being revived today) had ceased to exist.

The situation was further worsened by:
● the squeezing-out of the village artisans by competition from

British and even Indian industry, and their relegation to work
on the land, where the pressure was already so great; and

● the dual policy systematically pursued by British capitalists, who
regarded India as (a) a market for their industrial products (they
were quick to destroy the very ancient Indian cotton industry,
which had developed rapidly in the eighteenth century, at a
time when Indian painted or printed textiles were becoming
fashionable in Europe); and (b) a market on which to buy
certain raw materials, such as jute from Bengal or cotton from
the dark, rich *regur* soil near Bombay, to be shipped to Britain's
cotton mills in Lancashire.

Raw materials earmarked for export were carried to the ports
by railways. These had been built quite early on, and during the
second half of the nineteenth century they revolutionized the interior of the country. Towns arose with no other purpose than to
collect and dispatch merchandise. More and more, too, Indian
peasants grew cash crops – products which were not intended to
feed their families or their villages. Growing crops for industry
overtook the growing of food, except in the grain-fields of the
Punjab, which however exported its wheat. The result, with a
growing population, was a series of catastrophic famines in the last
thirty years of the nineteenth century, and a general lowering of
food consumption, perceptible even in the imperfect statistics
which are all we have.

The world economic crisis of 1929, and the collapse of raw
material prices, led to a further concentration of property in the
hands of landlords and moneylenders. The size of free peasants'
holdings shrank even more, and their debts grew unreasonably
large. Crippled by that burden, the peasants' position *vis-à-vis* their
creditors was worse than that of former serfs *vis-à-vis* their masters.
Economically, the *ryots* had less and less freedom, however great
their theoretical freedom under the law.

The beginnings of modern industry appeared late in the day,
around the 1920s, at the same time as the first protective tariffs.
The growth of local industry at that time was helped by a number

of factors: an abundance of cheap labour, the emergence of modern towns with a large proletariat, easy access to raw materials and finally the activities of capitalists.

These came from three main groups. There were the Parsis, descendants of disciples of Zoroaster who had fled Persia more than a thousand years ago; they lived chiefly in the region of Bombay. There were the Marwaris, who came from a high caste in the interior of Rajputana, and who had been shielded from British competition because their regions had been so backward. Finally, there were the Jains from Gujarat.

Three industrial cities predominated: Calcutta with (150 miles to the East) the metal-working industries of the Tata group (a family of Parsis) and the mass-production of jute; Bombay, centre of the cotton industry and of automobile assembly; and Ahmadabad, 500 kilometres to the North, purely a cotton centre. These and other industries – above all, the food industries – developed chaotically during the Second World War, especially after 1942, with shortages of food and textiles which led to such fantastic price rises on the black market that for a time, given the threat from Japan, there were fears that India might be totally undermined.

In 1944, the industrialists adopted the Bombay Plan. Semi-official and over-optimistic, this foresaw large-scale investments made possible by Britain's repayment of the debts she had run up in India during the Second World War. The plan encouraged agreements with British firms and businessmen, like the Birla-Nuffield arrangements for automobile production. Even today, long after Indian independence, British capital is still invested in the many businesses controlled by the banks in Cliver Street, Calcutta.

This industrial boom only intensified the drift from the land towards the towns. 'If you are ruined,' says a Tamil proverb, 'run to town.' There was employment there, in workshops, factories and domestic service (where money wages 'were little better than nothing'). Unexpected links were forged between certain castes in

the Kathiawar Peninsula and the recruitment of cooks for well-to-
do households in Bombay, or between the poor on the South-
West coast of the Deccan and craftsmen making hand-rolled
cigarettes in Bombay factories. All this added to the general upheavals in the Hindu population, increasing its social mobility.

So, even before independence, India already had bustling
modern cities, with their sordid slum quarters, the *bustees* of
Calcutta, the all too famous *chawls* of Bombay or the *cheris* of
Madras, with mud walls like those of the villages.

Britain rethought her policy in India after the Indian Mutiny by
the sepoys or native soldiers in 1857–8. This, indeed, was an
opportunity to revise Britain's whole attitude and, on 1 September
1858, to end the rule of the East India Company, replacing it in
London with a large and powerful ministry, the India Office,
while in Calcutta a viceroy took the place of the Company's
former Governor-General.

Had the British not been too hasty, for instance, in annexing
princely territory in India? From now on, they determined to
respect local autonomy; and in 1881, when they restored the
independence of the sultanate of Mysore, which they had previously taken over, this was a symbol of the new approach. And if,
in this motley Indian world, they were no longer to rule directly,
the best course was carefully to maintain the country's existing
divisions, and use them – especially along the great divide between
Muslims and Hindus. First and foremost, these divisions must be
maintained in the army. On this subject, in 1858, Lord Elphinstone
used a significant metaphor. The safeguards for British power, he
said, were those steamers whose safety was ensured by the division
of the hull into water-tight compartments. 'I should like to ensure
the safety of our Indian Empire by building our Indian Army on
the same lines.' Hindus, Muslims and Himalayan Sikhs, that is,
would henceforth be kept in separate compartments, and would
never again serve in the same units.

These plans were soon overtaken by events. By the 1870s, a
long economic crisis in the world was affecting India, causing

famine, epidemics and peasant revolts. Well-meaning people thought that the regime should be liberalized, to bring some Hindus into the administration, and perhaps even the government. In 1885, with 'the Viceroy's blessing', the National Congress Party was formed. It became, as we might say now, the loudspeaker of nationalism – although at that time the nationalists were still only a very small but active minority.

Its adherents came – and came in growing numbers – from the busy middle class that was emerging in the towns and the universities. This was not the aristocratic or princely class, nor that of the big landlords, who were deeply attached to the traditional past, and whose social conservatism very well suited the masters of India. Instead, it was a real middle class, of diverse origins, pushed to the fore by changing conditions. It included capitalists like the Parsis, the Marwaris and the Jains, but also Ishmaelite Muslims or people whose castes had a political vocation, such as the Pandits of Kashmir, who were linked to the brahmins, and who had supplied a number of statesmen in the days of the Moguls (and continued to do with the family of Jawaharlal Nehru). Mahatma Gandhi likewise came of a family which for generations had produced ministers for the princes ruling in the Kathiawar Peninsula, in Gujarat.

Drawn by Western civilization, these men had enjoyed its benefits and seen both its advantages and its dangers. Gandhi's philosophy, for example, drew on the non-violent traditions of India, the vehement pacifism of Tolstoy and Jesus Christ's Sermon on the Mount. Members of this Indian intelligentsia sailed on troubled waters, dreaming of some religious synthesis whereby Hinduism might be purged. Consciously or not, many of them were inspired by some of India's innumerable heresies. One could cite ten or twenty names, beginning with Dayanand Sarasvati (1824–83), who founded a new Hindu sect, rejected both Christianity and Islam, but admitted that he was attracted by the West, and tried to find in the *Vedas* some elements of scientific modernity, including electricity and the steam-engine. The list might end with the names of Gandhi's master spirit, Gopal Krishna Gokhale (1866–1915) and Rabindranath Tagore (1861–1941), known the world over for his poems, for which in 1913 he received the Nobel Prize, and one of which, 'Jana Gana Mana', became the modern Indian national anthem.

A long period of unrest and propaganda, with much procedural wrangling, led at last to the independence and partition of India on 15 August 1947. With the demands of one side and the caution, backsliding and hypocrisy of the other, the negotiation was unedifying (but less so than any other decolonization process!). What was reasonable one day became unreasonable the next, and concessions were always made too late. Moreover, what satisfied the Muslims (the separation of Bengal into two provinces, that in the East being joined to Assam to form an ethnic whole in 1905) annoyed the Hindus; while the Muslims were annoyed, in their turn, when in 1911 the decision was postponed. For the nationalists, uniting Hindus and Muslims (grouped in the Muslim League in 1906) remained an insoluble problem.

Another major difficulty was to make contact with the masses. This was the extraordinary achievement of Mahatma Gandhi (1869–1948). After studying law in Bombay and London, Gandhi had practised in Natal from 1893 to 1914, defending Indian immigrants in South Africa. Returning to India in 1914, he quickly made an impression on the nationalists, dominated them, and mobilized their strength. His programme was 'to make religious use of political forces'. His title, Mahatma, meant 'Noble', 'Very Reverend'. The only force, he taught, with which one could constrain another's will was the force of truth, non-violence to all living creatures and purity. The religious emphasis in his work increased its effectiveness a hundredfold. Gandhi aroused the masses. This became clear with the first boycott (on 20 September 1920) of the 1919 Constitution which Britain had just conceded, and again in December 1921, when Gandhi called for a campaign of disobedience. When such powerful silent demonstrations were followed by serious disturbances and murders, Gandhi remained true to his doctrine and stopped the protest. His second campaign eight years later, on 26 January 1930, ended in a boycott of salt (sold by the Government), followed by agreements, a new and very long protest campaign (1932–4), and at length a new Constitution, the India Act of 1937.

Indian independence was therefore ripe before the outbreak of the Second World War, which precipitated it. On 8 August 1942, Congress adopted Gandhi's motion calling on the British to quit India. In 1942 and 1943, with the Japanese advancing in Burma and threatening Assam, the situation became very serious: stations and public buildings were destroyed.

When peace returned, tension increased. On 11 June 1947, the British Parliament at last accorded Indian independence. The ties were broken. But free India was internally divided: on 15 August, it split into two 'dominions' – the Indian union and Pakistan (the latter in two separate parts). The partition was imperfect: it left in India a minority of 44 million Muslims; while the political frontier in the East gave the jute-producing areas to Pakistan and the textile works along the Hooghly River to India. Refugees flowed in both directions, in appalling conditions, and there were innumerable killings. In vain, Gandhi tried to reach some agreement with Islam; but on 30 January 1948, a Hindu fanatic, believing that any agreement would be a betrayal of Hinduism, assassinated the Mahatma. Partition took place amid civil war and untold violence. The cost was 2 or 3 million dead.

It is often said that British policy was responsible for partition. Is that fair? The allegation lends too much importance to political gestures and transparently obvious tricks. Once again, India's past determined its present and took its revenge. That past was the real culprit.

So, as soon as it became independent, India split in two. In three, if one counts the independence and secession of Burma in 1947, and in four, if one adds the secession of East Pakistan as Bangladesh in 1971. Meanwhile on 4 February 1948, Ceylon too had become an independent dominion: with its own particular civilization it had always been a world apart and had never been attached to British India.

Will India be spared a Chinese-style revolution?

Since 1947, India has made considerable industrial progress, greater than in the preceding century and a half. In doing so, she adjusted to partition more successfully than Pakistan. She established order at home; she reached agreement with France, which gave up her Indian warehouses; she occupied and liquidated the States held by princes and maharajahs, and notably Hyderabad (September 1948); she seized Goa, Damao and Diu from the Portuguese in 1961. She established her rights in Kashmir, and resisted Chinese pressure along the uncertain Himalayan frontier. The brutality with which she occupied Goa certainly disappointed India's sincere friends throughout the world, in so far as she seemed to them one of the rare countries capable of political wisdom. Yet the prestige of Pandit Nehru survived the shock: while he lived, he remained the most eminent global spokesman for the Third World.

If one adds that India's parliamentary regime works reasonably well, as has been shown by elections to the central Lok Sabha and to the fourteen state assemblies, and that the country has been divided in a reasonable fashion into those fourteen linguistic States, it becomes clear that independent India has a number of valuable successes to its credit. But this is not the really original feature that India presents to the world and to her own teeming human universe. What is truly striking is her Government's patient effort, redoubled in the third and subsequent five-year plans, to lead her people out of their appalling difficulties. The Indian population in the early 1960s was already on the way to numbering 500 million; twenty years later it was nearly three-quarters of a billion. The Government's task was to assist their economic development without violence, without bombast, relying on nature, circumstances and people, and forcing the pace of events only where this was feasible and success seemed likely.

President Nehru explained his policy very well to a French journalist on 18 April 1962. 'We are not Socialist doctrinaires,' he said.

In the long term, we simply want to lead this country to prosperity; in the short term, we want to raise the standard of living and reduce social inequality. To that end, we are acting on the economy, but leaving plenty of room for private enterprise: part of heavy industry, all small and medium-sized industry, and the whole of agriculture, are outside the public sector. In the countryside, we are encouraging cooperatives, but we have no intention of imposing collective farming. Once again, we are not Socialist doctrinaires. We are going forward step by step, and trying to solve problems peacefully. Don't forget, for example, that while we dethroned the Maharajahs we left them their palaces, their immunities and their privileges, and we gave them a lifetime civil pension which was often very generous. You see: we always try to follow a democratic path.

The proper word would perhaps be *liberal*, with all its virtues, drawbacks and ambiguities. In any case, the problem is clearly stated: India adopted the methods and points of view of the 'free world'. It needed and wanted to bring about a revolution. Will it be able to do so without adopting the Chinese model?

Its task is to put an end to, and at least alleviate, India's evident and atrocious poverty. This, distressing but all too real, is the dominant problem, the starting-point from which we have to begin.

India, unlike so many other States, has the virtue of not concealing her wounds, either from herself or from others. She has always suffered from poverty. We know this from the very earliest witnesses, who remarked on apocalyptic famines in pre-Christian times. Today, poverty is still obvious to the naked eye. India's large cities – monstrous Calcutta, enormous Bombay, even the capital New Delhi outside its very attractive districts – offer pitiful spectacles of ragged clothing, diseased bodies, hovels for dwellings and mere scraps for food.

The most obvious index of India's poverty is her appalling

surplus of labour. In the days of the Great Mogul, so many children were sold into slavery by their parents that to buy them was an act of charity. In 1923, André Chevrillon noted:

The division of labour here is pushed to the nth degree. A coachman has to drive, a groom has to open the door, a peon has to shout warnings. The European has to put up with this fuss. It would be monstrous if he went on foot or carried a parcel. A British officer cannot move without dragging in his wake a procession of people and baggage. Last year, in London, a mere corporal remarked in my presence that in India he rang for his servant to have him pick up a handkerchief . . . Just as in Rome, where the patrician had his army of servants, clients and freedmen.

A picture from the past, some of whose details date. But also applicable today. What is one to make of those ordinary middle-class homes with ten or a dozen servants? Or of those miserable men, women and children by the river in Calcutta (in 1962), 'who squat in the filth, harassed by flies but too indifferent to brush them off or even stretch out a hand to beg from passers-by'? What is one to think, following the same witness, of those roadmenders' workshops that look like scenes out of hell: 'Naked men, women in saris and children in rags, spreading almost by hand the tar which is heated in enormous pots on wood fires'? If the workshops were modernized, the number of unemployed would immediately rise. At Bangalore, in the Deccan, an ultra-modern factory makes wagons, 'but human ants reappear at the end of the production line, where the painting is done by a multitude of workmen'.

These sad pictures are among the first to be included in the dossier of modern India: they come from an India that has always existed. A few figures summarize the situation: 438 million inhabitants in 1962; a very high death-rate of 25 to 30 per 1,000; a 'natural' birth-rate of some 45 per 1,000; hence an increase of about 20 per 1,000, i.e. 8 million more people every year. These figures are discouraging. They curb in advance almost any growth of income per head, even if the gross national product is increasing, as it clearly is. In 1962, income per head stood at 280 rupees a year, when the rupee was worth one French franc, so the daily income per head was less than 100 old francs or one new franc, i.e. approximately ten new pence. In the roadmending workshops, the wage was one rupee per day.

Can the growth of population be slowed down? Only by higher living standards – but that would mean that the problem was already solved. Propaganda for birth-control, publicly advocated, and sterilization (1,500,000 voluntary sterilizations) are not enough to stem this human tide. India is not as disciplined as Japan, where the same battle – although much more effective – is still not easy.

Besides, these are not the only problems.

There is no need to be an economist to understand what was proposed by the third five-year plan (1961–5). Like the previous plans, this concentrated on a number of tangible points: fertilizers for agriculture, transport, heavy industry, mechanical industry, etc. – everything that was fairly easy to change, and quickly, in the justified hope that the results would have wider repercussions. Intervention took every possible form; and the Government turned a deaf ear to the recommendations made in April 1959 by a group of experts from the Ford Foundation, who proposed that the whole thrust of the new plan then being prepared should be confined to agriculture. They proposed to raise India's grain production, in 1959 estimated at 73 million tons, to 100 million or even 110 million. Was it wiser, as other experts thought and the Government decided, not to give up the industrial effort and the investments required for it, in the belief that the food situation was not likely to become catastrophic by 1965? Food would certainly remain a very difficult problem; but India had survived other such ordeals.

Once priorities had been decided, the usual and almost invariable conditions were laid down. An important part of the national income was set aside for the necessary investments: 5 per cent for the first plan, 11 per cent for the second, 14 per cent for the third. These huge sums unavoidably worsened the budget deficit, all the more so since there had to be massive foreign purchases, usually on unfavourable terms. So the country was obliged to invoke foreign aid, some of it private and by no means free of charge, some of it in grants or soft loans. These brought into play once more the spectacular rivalry between the United States and the USSR. Each was to supply 5 per cent of the foreign aid envisaged in India's third five-year plan. The Soviet Union concentrated its funds on large-scale projects such as the Bhilai steel-works; the United States, which in the past had given twenty times as much as its rival, spread its aid over a number of areas. But the monotonous competition between the two superpowers need not detain us here. Nor need we dwell on the detail of the industrial investments – the race to build steel-works, or the establishment of a factory making cinematograph film, built by a French firm, and making India the second biggest producer of film in the world, after the United States.

What is interesting is that the economy is taking off. After Japan, and not far behind China, India is becoming one of Asia's great industrial powers. There is reason to believe that she enjoyed some advantage from having started early, by 1920 at the latest, and been ahead of the game. Today, at last, the economy looks as if it may win the race against soaring population figures. In 1963, it was impossible to believe that by 1970 the income per head might have doubled. By 1983 it had risen from 280 rupees to 2,400 rupees. This did not mean that India had reached the promised land: but she had started on her way.

The stony road ahead is littered with obstacles – political, social and cultural. The political difficulties included the moral dictatorship of Pandit Nehru and his family, which posed formidable succession problems. The pre-eminence of the Congress Party is not in itself an institutional system, and it makes difficult the interplay of fruitful, reasonable and constructive rivals for power. In the early 1960s, the reactionary right-wing accused the Communist and Communist-leaning left of eating beef – a disappointing polemic. In 1962, the Communist-inspired left won only 10 per cent of the votes, but in the local government of Kerala, before it was somewhat arbitrarily ousted, it showed rare qualities of probity and efficiency. The Socialists for their part accused Nehru, as they did his successors, of defending 'a corrupted regime'. But these opposition parties remained marginal, and Congress remained dominant.

As regards social problems, it is always easier to talk about a fair distribution of wealth than to impose it. On the crucial issue of land ownership, the many agrarian laws passed in various States have been ineffective in practice. Legally dispossessed, the big landowners have almost everywhere recovered their advantage over the small peasants. The latter are free, which is a great step forward; but they remain very poor and ill-equipped. Part of the arable soil still lies fallow. Even the large-scale irrigation projects favour the big landowners, who keep the water for themselves when it has to be paid for or is in great demand. The peasants enjoy little of these benefits. To make matters worse, the big landowners are conservative and reluctant to accept technological progress. There, indeed, is a 'corrupted regime' and a pre-revolutionary situation.

Finally, traditional civilization still holds the mass of Indians in its tight and manifold grip. For Hindus to step out of the caste system and join the social revolution of modern life is like making the necessary transition to a wholly different universe. Hinduism, in fact, is the major obstacle and the essential difficulty standing in the way of any serious move towards modernization. Its power can be measured by the incredible amount of offerings of food which an undernourished and near-starving population will in certain circumstances bring to the temples – as, for example, in 1962, when the conjunction of the stars was held to predict the imminent end of the world. The strings of wandering cows, taking their meagre fodder where they can, the flocks of crows stealing grain and the swarms of insects that are never attacked, even if they ruin the harvest – all these are concomitants of Hinduism. The cows are sacred, and all living beings must be respected.

The worst aspect of Hinduism is undoubtedly the caste system,

which kept the population cooped up in so many separate compartments. True, there is some social mobility; and in the long term
the system will no doubt disappear. But it persists. The
untouchables — the *harijans*, who number at least 50 million, and
whom Gandhi championed — have become as other people under
the law. The Indian constitution has abolished all legal distinction
between citizens. Furthermore, it is non-religious. But there
remains a vast distance between theory and practice. In this area,
change is very slow, and is confined almost entirely to the intellectual élite. Even there it remains hesitant: is it not significant that
many political battles are still as much a matter of caste differences
as of personal rivalry? However, a middle class is growing. Its
members seek their fortune by passing through one or other of
India's forty-six or more universities. Not all succeed: there is so-
called 'educated unemployment'. But most move on to become
officials in the administration, lawyers, doctors or politicians.

This many-faceted middle class is, at least in appearance, open
to all castes. Publicly, it models its dress and behaviour on the
British. Yet, for these very same people, family life is often a
refuge where they rediscover traditional dress and diet, and can
return to former ways. And modern life, in almost all its aspects,
represents a break with religious tradition. It is against tradition,
for example, to regard the public water supply as pure and not
polluted, because it has passed through so many 'impure' places. It
is against tradition to take cod-liver oil as prescribed by the doctor,
because fish is forbidden; to agree to inter-marriage, or to announce
a wedding in the press with a note saying 'caste immaterial'; or to
house engineers, managers and workpeople in the same building,
near some new factory, without regard for the taboos that are
broken when they are lodged together.

The fact that such cases occur shows that some progress has
been made in the reform of Hinduism, and that its formalism is on
the wane. Ever since the Buddha, indeed, the liveliest religious
thinkers in India have fought against its excesses. In 1800, Ram
Mohan Roy, the founder of a new sect known as the Brahmo

Samaj, tried to reform Hinduism in this way, and to move it towards monotheism. Other reformers followed, and others still will no doubt emerge.

For India is now conscious of the obstacle that her cultural tradition puts in her way. This awareness already existed at the time of Mahatma Gandhi, who was certainly responsible, more than anyone, for 'revealing' modern India, both by the enthusiasm and by the opposition he aroused. Gandhi in fact sought to harness all the spiritual traditions of India to the cause of progress as he saw it, and to enhance national pride. This was how, with unerring instinct, he awakened the Indian masses and formed a passionate popular movement. But, at the same time, the tradition that he sought to revive meant in a number of areas preventing India's adopting certain modern ways.

This was the basic conflict which in the end divided Gandhi from his Socialist fellow-militant, Pandit Nehru. Nehru himself summed it up: 'An abyss separates those whose psychology is turned towards the future from those who lean towards the past.' Gandhi's principles fatally distanced him from any kind of social revolution. For him, the revolution should take place in people's hearts. It was not a matter of changing the existing order of things, but of persuading people, whatever their wealth or influence, to devote themselves to the service of their fellow human beings and agree, in Gandhi's words,

to be filled with the art and beauty of abnegation and voluntary poverty . . . to embrace those activities which are the basis of the nation . . . by spinning and weaving with their own hands . . . to banish from their hearts all caste prejudice, in all its forms, to campaign for total abstinence from intoxicating drinks and from drugs . . . and, in general, to cultivate the purity of one's being. These are the means of serving which enable one to live at the level of the poor

– preferably in the traditional framework of village life.

In short, Nehru concluded, discussing Gandhi's views in his book *My Life and My Prisons*: 'For him, those who wished to serve the masses should not concern themselves so much with raising the standard of living as with lowering themselves, levelling themselves, so to speak, with the masses and mixing with them on an equal footing. That, for him, was true democracy.' Despite the admiration that Nehru and his friends felt for some aspects of this individual ethic and for Gandhi himself, they thought that to use it as a collective ideal was against the logical conceptions of 'every modern democrat, socialist, and even capitalist: it would mean returning to an outdated spirit of paternalism, which was unwittingly reactionary'. Above all, they thought, it would mean failing to face the break that India must make with certain aspects of her past if she wanted to emerge from under-development and mass poverty.

That India has in fact followed Nehru rather than Gandhi can be seen from the failure of Gandhi's disciple Vinoba Bhave, who in 1947, before the death of the *bapu* or 'father', founded the Bhoodan movement. Its aim was to solve the agonizing agrarian problem by persuading landowners to make voluntary gifts of land. These gifts would then be redistributed to the poor, either individually or collectively.

To understand the meaning of this idealistic movement, it has to be remembered that Vinoba Bhave, who came from a good family, and was highly cultivated and an excellent mathematician, had in 1916 burned all his diplomas, in the presence of his mother, to commit himself to the way of life of the 'renunciators' or Hindu ascetics. He had shared, prominently (i.e. often in prison), in all Gandhi's campaigns. When starting the Bhoodan movement, he had worked out that some 62 million acres of arable land would be needed to solve the peasant problem. Ten years later, he had secured only about 5 million. In quantitative terms, his failure was clear.

It was on foot, going from village to village, covering thousands of miles, barely eating, and every day spinning cotton as preached by Gandhi, that the saintly Vinoba Bhave had conducted his campaign. But what was possible in Gandhi's day, because of

Gandhi and because times had been different, had become anachronistic in modern India. Vinoba Bhave aroused some enthusiasm; but the boos that greeted him in some peasant villages in Gujarat were the sign of a new era, a new awareness. His failure, saddening though it might seem in an edifying storybook, perhaps marked the awakening of India in search of real, reasonable, modern solutions as against a mouldering *ancien régime*.

'Today,' Nehru concluded,

India's ancient culture has outlived itself. Silently, desperately, it is struggling against a new and all-powerful adversary, the civilization of the capitalist West. It will be defeated, because the West brings with it science; and science means bread for millions of hungry people. But the West also brings an antidote for the poisons of a civilization of cut-throat snatch-as-snatch-can; and that antidote is the principle of socialism, the idea of cooperation in the service of the community and for the good of all. Which is not so far away from the old brahmanic ideal of 'service'; but which also implies the 'brahmanization' (in a lay sense, of course) of all classes and all groups, and the abolition of class distinctions. And perhaps India, when it changes costume, as is inevitable, since the old one is in rags, will have the new one cut on this pattern, so that it fits both present conditions and old habits of mind. The principles which India will espouse must be in contact with its roots in the soil.

14. The Maritime Far East

At first sight, it seems arbitrary to group together Indo-China, Indonesia, the Philippines, Korea and Japan. But these places, distant as they are from each other, are all close, historically, to those two great human oceans, China and India, which have never ceased to wield very far-ranging influence. That closeness has been all the greater because of the sea-routes that have made for easy access. The seas of Eastern and South-East Asia – the Sea of Japan, the Yellow Sea, the East China Sea, the Banda Sea and the Sulu Sea, for example – are many of them small and shallow, epicontinental seas, hemmed in by the nearby land. Except in the neighbourhood of the Philippines and Japan, great ocean depths are only to be found to the East and the South, beyond the strings of volcanic islands that separate these narrow seas from the Indian and Pacific Oceans. The seas, in fact, are so many 'Mediterraneans', surrounded by land and dotted with islands: they are already on a human scale.

Another feature they share is that they are swept by periodic winds – the monsoons, which regularly reverse their direction at the beginning of summer and the beginning of winter. Everywhere, too, there are typhoons, sometimes of hurricane force. But these, though often tragic, do not last for ever. Normally, ships can sail peacefully, between islands or along the coasts, with a steady wind. Navigation here means island-hopping, sheltering from any sudden storms, and not losing sight of the shore, lined with mangroves. If the sea threatens to be too rough, the anchor is dropped to a seabed which is often very near the surface. Thus secured, the Arab dhow, the Chinese junk or the Dutch cargo ship could, as a hundred accounts testify, easily ride out heavy weather. When it passed, they went on.

Such were the advantages and possibilities of these familiar, domestic seas. They teemed with sailors who felt at home there, trading and privateering in a well-established routine. If necessary, they ventured further: some Malays sailed as far as Madagascar, while Polynesians in outrigger canoes went to Hawaii, Easter Island and New Zealand. Much more often, they stayed in home waters, whose ways they knew. Both the Japanese and the Chinese were cases in point. 'The Chinese,' declared Father de las Cortes in 1626, 'do not sail on the high seas.' Ocean navigation, however, took the Arabs to distant islands, followed later by the Portuguese, the Dutch and the British.

Busy traffic very soon humanized these inland seas, linking their coasts, their civilizations and their history. Each such entity kept its own permanent characteristics; but the sea performed miracles of culture-contact, encouraging interchange and leading to mutual resemblances.

Indo-China

Indo-China is not the best example of these maritime communities. It is a large part of South-East Asia, given its name by the Danish–French geographer Conrad Malte-Brun (1755–1826). A broad peninsula, divided by high mountains, it is also crossed by very broad valleys running roughly from North to South and looking a little like the spread fingers of a hand. To the South, it shrinks into the long, narrow Malay Peninsula; to the East and West, it is flanked by the sea. Even in its broader, Northern area it has been continually traversed since prehistoric times – so much so that all the races identified by prehistorians have left traces there: aboriginal Australians, Melanesians and Mongoloids from prehistoric China.

These races are the basis of the present population, the Melanesian type being found among the still primitive mountain people.

In historic times, four main movements of population have affected Indo-China. The first, coming from China, entered by force; the second, coming by sea from India, was peaceful. The other two both came by sea: the Islamic influx which reached and occupied the Malay Peninsula, and the European (French and British) invasion, powerfully reinforced in the nineteenth century. This submerged everything, until in recent times it was in turn submerged in the bitter and prolonged conflicts of decolonization.

The ancient civilization of Indo-China is flanked, and in large part explained, by the two vast areas of China and India.

Chinese civilization arrived by force in Tonkin and Annam (Northern and Central Vietnam) some ten centuries ago. This was a long-lasting colonial conquest, at once military, administrative and religious (Confucian, Taoist and Buddhist), carried out as a Southern extension of the occupation of South China, a major event in Chinese history. The native population was either driven back or dominated. Thus there came into being that lively culture of the Annamite people, which eventually spread further in the South of Indo-China.

The Hindu influence was that of merchants, who founded ports of call and warehouses out of which they traded, often in alliance with local chieftains. Some of the latter made their fortunes through these contacts: their technical and cultural advantages enabled them to spread their influence, impose themselves, and then set up kingdoms from which arose new, partly Hindu but very mixed civilizations. They included the kingdom of Chiampa on the coast of Central Vietnam; the kingdom of the Mons at the Western extremity of South-East Asia; and, in the Mekong Delta, the kingdom of Funan, later absorbed by Chel-La, which gave birth to the Khmer empire, the dominant power in South-East Asia from the ninth to the fourteenth century. The ruined city of Angkor attests to its magnificence.

Between the eleventh and the fourteenth century, invasions and conquests by Burmese and Thai ('free') peoples led to the emergence of more indigenous kingdoms, to the detriment of the Khmers and the Mons. These kingdoms eventually gave birth to the Burmese State of Lan-Xang, whose Eastern part survives as present-day Laos, and Siam (now Thailand, 'land of the free').

The Europeans, who arrived in the nineteenth century and left in the twentieth, only provisionally occupied these countries. Nevertheless, South-East Asia was deeply marked by this forceful colonial conquest, French in the East, British in the West, with between them the independent buffer state of Siam, whose status as such was recognized in 1896. The French in 1887 formed the Indo-Chinese Union out of Tonkin, Annam, Cochin-China, Cambodia and Laos. The British added Burma to their Indian Empire, and at the far end of the Malay Peninsula imposed their rule on the Malay States, making Singapore one of the biggest ports in the Far East.

The Second World War, which saw Japanese domination spread rapidly throughout South-East Asia, destroyed at one blow these short-lived colonial structures. The Malay States, Singapore and Burma secured their independence without a struggle, thanks to a wise British policy; but the Vietnamese fought a long battle with the French. The States of Eastern Indo-China did not become fully independent until the Treaty of Geneva, on 21 July 1954.

This left the former French Indo-China divided into four. The Geneva Treaty partitioned Annam at the 17th parallel, the Northern part, with Tonkin, forming the Democratic Republic of Vietnam, the Southern part, with Cochin-China, becoming the Republic of Vietnam. The independent kingdom of Laos had already been recognized by France on 19 July 1949, and that of Cambodia on 8 November 1949. Broadly speaking, Laos and Cambodia were neutral between the two blocs, the USA and the USSR. North Vietnam belonged to the Communist world and had ties with China, which weighed heavily upon it, with the Soviet Union, and with Czechoslovakia. South Vietnam came under the control of the United States.

At the start of this qualified independence, these States had to face the fearful problems that beset all less-developed countries: modernizing industry and agriculture, improving the balance of payments, keeping pace with – and, if possible, overtaking – the ever-pressing growth of the population. Would the Socialist methods of North Vietnam succeed better than the liberal measures taken elsewhere? It was impossible to say: politics and possible conflict prevented free choice and honest comparisons. There was nothing to be deduced, for example, from the fact that North Vietnam possessed armaments – old, traditional Russian armaments – or that Cambodia's assembly plants were exporting Citroën two-horsepower cars.

None of these young States faced a simple situation. North Vietnam, energetic as it was, was the only Communist experiment in South-East Asia; and while it gained certain advantages from its exceptional position, it was somewhat uneasy at the power of absorption enjoyed by its large and very near neighbour, China. South Vietnam profited from its alliance with the United States; but it had to put up with a war on its territory as a result: the maintenance of American-style semi-colonialism was opposed by part of the population, who preferred to ally with the Communist North. The end of the Vietnam War, of course, turned this alliance into the union of North and South under Communist rule.

Equilibrium in this area was and remains precarious, like the neutral status of Laos and Cambodia, now Kampuchea. The different interests involved are so numerous and so contradictory that no one could reasonably predict how present conflicts will turn out.

Beyond these immediate issues, the old cultural problems remain. Over-population in the plains still contrasts with the half-emptiness of the mountain regions. Two historical ages confront each other. The plains, growing rice, made possible the high density of population in the deltas of the Red River (the Hong), the Mekong, the Menam (the Chao Phraya) and the Irrawaddy. It was on this form of agriculture and this mass of people that the dominant civilizations were based. The Annamites, heirs to Chinese civilization, have always occupied the low-lying areas of the Red River Delta. In the seventeenth century, they destroyed the Hindu-influenced kingdom of Champa, and in the eighteenth they seized the Mekong Delta from the Cambodians. In historical terms, these were relatively recent triumphs.

To the East, the close-knit civilizations of the plains, in Cambodia, Siam and Burma, were strongly influenced by Hinduism, and Buddhism also maintained its hold on them. Higher up, however, in the mountains of all these countries, small, primitive, semi-independent peoples, with animist religions, grew crops in burned clearings. They still survive.

In the motley world of Indo-China, Christian missionaries had some notable successes, almost always outside Buddhist and Islamic territory (the main Islamic area being, as we have seen, the Malay Peninsula). After 1954, Christian peasants from North Vietnam staged a mass exodus of 300,000 people towards the South, where the Catholics were in power in Saigon. Not unnaturally, it was among the animists that Christian propaganda was most successful. Thus, in the Union of Burma, the conversion to Protestantism of a large number of the Karens enhanced their unity and strengthened them against the central power, essentially in the hands of Burmese Buddhists.

These details are not the dominant feature of South-East Asia's complex and uncertain future; but they shed light on it − as does the existence there still of British and French schools. South-East Asia remains a crossroads: it welcomes many influences, absorbing or rejecting them in different ways according to its own different ethnic and cultural composition.

Indonesia

Beyond the Malay Peninsula, 'Asia drowns in the Pacific'. Indonesia is its prolongation Eastwards: its thousands of islands form 'the biggest archipelago in the world'. It too has always been, and still is, a meeting-point of many colours. But this diversity has not robbed it of a certain unity, which has to be constantly safeguarded and often re-established, now as in the past.

The Indonesian archipelago has always been, as it were, the centre of a vast compass rose: it has constantly felt the shock of even very distant events. This was so as early as prehistoric times. In the first centuries of the Christian era, when seamen and merchants from India came to found colonies here, as they also did in Burma, Siam or Cambodia, they brought with them Hinduism and Buddhism, which flourished side-by-side, adapting to local insular 'cultures' and acting as a support to the new kingdoms.

The first of these new kingdoms was established in Sumatra; but the most important and powerful flourished in Java. Their influence, however, was more or less limited – as was that of the civilization they brought with them. Java had high mountains, huge virgin forests and a peasant population organized in villages, with very lively traditions which were sufficient unto themselves. As a result, Indo-Javanese civilization remained a thin veneer on the surface, whether represented by its script, derived from the pali script of India, by its poems, by its fables, based in Hindu models, or by its tombs and temples, such as make up the eighth-century architectural group that covers the Borobudur Hill – 'an image of the world according to the Buddhism of the Mahayana (the Great Vehicle)'.

Between the 'kings' of the *Kraton* fortresses there were continual wars, culminating in the emergence, at the end of the thirteenth century, of a 'universal' Hindu Empire, the Empire of the Majapahit. From Java, this ruled the other islands in a vast network of vassals and dependents, with the aid of a powerful and active fleet. It dominated Singapore, the 'city of lions', on its island off the Southern coast of the Malay Peninsula; in the East it reached New Guinea, and in the North the Philippines. In 1293, it disarmed a seaborne expedition sent against it by Mongol China.

But its greatness did not last. In 1420, the Muslims took Malacca;

and from 1450 onwards their victorious invasion finished off the Empire, or what remained of it. Political self-interest and holy war combined to demolish for good the huge structure of empire. When the Portuguese arrived at the beginning of the sixteenth century, nothing remained of it but ruins and memories. Only the island of Bali preserved, alongside its own traditions, the Brahman heritage of those ancient times.

The Portuguese occupied Malacca in 1511, and the Moluccas or Spice Islands (the source of cloves) in 1512. In 1521 they landed on the vast island of Sumatra. Their invasion was assisted by the political quarrels which divided the archipelago; but their occupation of the islands was a summary affair, with no great effort to put down roots. It left more or less untouched the traditional life of the archipelago, with all its comings and goings. These included the trade by Arab boats out of Achin, the Western tip of Sumatra, where they took on spices and gold dust bound for the Red Sea; and the regular trips by junks from Southern China which, from Marco Polo's time and before (indeed, from the seventh century as regards North-East Borneo), visited the Indonesian islands to bring knick-knacks, porcelain, silk, and their heavy copper and lead coins or *sapekes*, and to take in exchange rare woods, pepper, spices and the gold dust panned by the gold-washers of Borneo and Celebes.

The Portuguese invasion was the exploitation by force of ancient trading links which extended from Java to Macao, near Canton, and beyond as far as Japan. In the seventeenth century came a much more serious incursion, that of the Dutch. By 1605 they reached Amboina in the Moluccas; by 1607 they were in Celebes. In 1619 they founded Batavia and had subjugated Java, where they practised a policy of divide-and-rule by encouraging rivalry among the sultans of the island, medieval princes whose *Kratons* – (part-court, part-castle) – dominated the heights. By 1604, when they drove the Portuguese out of Malacca, the Dutch had become the rulers of the whole Indonesian archipelago.

From then on, they dominated the two great sea-routes: the

Malacca Straits between Sumatra and the Malay coast, on the way
to the West, to Siam and India; and the Strait of Sunda between
Java and Sumatra, the channel for the powerful sailing-ships which
came straight from the Cape of Good Hope without touching
India, and sailed back to Europe on the same route with their rich
cargoes from the East. Exploitation by one set of traders had been
replaced by another which, despite some early competition from
the British, culminated in the formation of the Dutch East India
Company. Founded in 1602, this remained for a long time the
flagship of Western capitalism – until its belated failure in 1798,
which was due to its own mistakes and muddles, but also to
exceptional political circumstances. For a brief time, the Dutch
East Indies were occupied by the British; but in 1816 they were
returned to Holland, and it once again settled there methodically
and comfortably – until the Japanese invasion on 28 February
1942.

At that point, the model structure collapsed. After Japan's defeat
in 1945, Indonesian nationalists (who had both collaborated with
the wartime invaders and fought fiercely against them), proclaimed
Indonesia independent under President Ahmed Sukarno, on 17
August 1945, in the midst of wild popular enthusiasm. 'When a
month later, on 28 September, the allied Commander-in-Chief
General Christison landed at Batavia with British and Indian troops,
he found the walls of the city covered with anti-Dutch slogans.'

The obstinate reaction of the Dutch Government, and its efforts
to re-establish the old order or at least save some of it, sparked off
a classical decolonization crisis similar to several in France's recent
history. While the 'colonialists' succeeded easily enough in the
sparsely populated islands such as Celebes and Borneo, where
Indonesia was more or less empty, they encountered fierce opposition in Sumatra, and still more in Java. Guerrilla warfare soon
immobilized the Dutch troops and nullified their victories around
the big towns. Their vast 'policing operation', begun on 21 July
1947, raised insurmountable difficulties. They had more success
with their blockade of the rebel regions in Java, which caused

unspeakable suffering. Intervention by India, Australia, the United States and the United Nations finally produced an imperfect agreement, on 17 February 1948; but this was followed by a second 'policing operation' as ineffective as the first. On 27 December 1949, in The Hague, the Queen of the Netherlands signed away her sovereignty over the former Dutch East Indies, save for the 'Dutch' part of New Guinea. At Batavia, renamed Jakarta, the red-and-white flag of Indonesia replaced the Dutch red, white and blue.

These details, which inadequately summarize a long and dramatic conflict, are essential for understanding Indonesia today. At heart, it has not yet emerged from its recent struggles: it is still reliving them; and hostility to The Netherlands is often used as an excuse for, and a counter-irritant to, its own difficulties. That hostility was a necessary unifying force for the new Republic. The tussle for West Irian (Netherlands New Guinea until 1 May 1963, when it became part of Indonesia) had no other *raison d'être*.

Had that last piece of Indonesia been arbitrarily kept by the country's former rulers? It was a primitive island: it possessed natural resources, but to exploit them was beyond the power of either Indonesia or The Netherlands. As for its inhabitants – the Papuans – they had nothing in common with either the Indonesians or the Dutch. But who cared about that?

Indonesian civilization is an extreme mixture of races, religions, standards of living, geographical features and cultures. All the islands, including even Java, harbour primitive peoples, often still living in stone-age conditions. They also include many different races. In Java, there are three Malay groups: the Sudanese, the Madurans and the Javanese themselves. In Sumatra, there are the Malays, the strange Minangkabaus, the Bataks and the Atchinese. And this is without counting the Chinese merchants in the towns. Detested but indispensable, they act as wholesalers, retailers, lenders and usurers; and although everyone regards them as parasites, no one can do without them. Since 1948, moreover, they have enjoyed the support of mighty Communist China.

All these peoples have their own languages or dialects. But they need a common language, a lingua franca, to link their closed worlds; and since the sixteenth century (and no doubt earlier) this has been Malayo-polynesian, or more familiarly Malay. It is the basis of the Indonesian language, Bahasa Indonesia, which was the official language of the nationalists even before it became that of the new Republic. Even so, it had to be adapted to new uses, notably in the scientific field. On one occasion, a commission on terminology adopted 37,795 new expressions in a single decree.

To all intents and purposes, in fact, it is a new language. Its role in Indonesia cannot really be compared with that of Hindi in India. There, Hindi is certainly a common language, but alongside English, which has remained very much alive. Dutch has not survived in the same way in Indonesia, for a number of reasons but essentially because the Dutch (with the exception of a few belated and inadequate efforts) did not develop modern technical education or the teaching of their own language. They wanted, claims one economist, 'to establish their superiority on the basis of the natives' ignorance. The use of Dutch would have narrowed the gap between the rulers and the ruled – and that had to be avoided at all costs.'

Indonesia's linguistic diversity is mirrored by cultural diversity, and even cultural confusion. In the archipelago, the great religions had curious adventures. They never triumphed by themselves: they coexisted with popular beliefs which beleaguered or overlaid them, and they sometimes merged with one of their major rivals.

Here, for instance, is the testimony of some villagers about twenty-five kilometres out of Jogjakarta, which briefly became the capital of Java when the Dutch reoccupied Batavia. They were talking with a traveller from Europe. '"In Java we are all Muslims," declared Karjodikromo, a peasant, without the slightest hesitation. "Then why do you speak of your gods? Muslims believe in only one God." Karjodikromo seemed embarrassed, and his father came to his rescue. "It's difficult," he said calmly. "We can't neglect the other gods. They can help us or harm us. Our rice depends on

Devi Shri, the wife of Vishnu." ' [Devi was in fact held to be the wife of Shiva.] (Tibor Mende)

In the whole country, moreover, there was not a mosque to be seen. The Muslim villagers offered fruit and refreshments on the altars of Devi Shri; and, to drive off evil spirits, put up bamboo flutes in the fields through which the wind could whistle. Equally, they were urged to cut the rice stalks silently, with the *ani-ani*, 'the little blade that the reaper hides in his hand'. Silently and quickly, so that the good spirits may not fly away.

A similar picture could be painted of Bali, that wonderful island, where the heritage of the great Indo-Javanese Empire and its Hindu beliefs has been preserved – but for how long? Here, the dead were cremated to enable their souls to ascend to the light. Yet, at the same time, a whole series of animist beliefs and practices survived, linked with the still prevalent cult of ancestor-worship.

It is not easy to maintain the unity of these diverse peoples. Hostility to the Dutch was not a panacea. Unification is difficult when the problem is to modernize a primitive, poverty-stricken economy or at the very least to instil patience into a population mostly made up of over-worked peasants. The greatest help that Dutch colonization gave the new government was that it exploited the rural population so completely that only small landowners were allowed to keep their holdings. So the young Indonesian Republic faced no large estates to redistribute, and had no need to fear agrarian unrest. All the peasants were equally poor.

They were prisoners, for the most part, of a subsistence economy. Rice was their basic food and their most important food crop, far ahead of maize, taro or sago. Buffaloes were bred solely as draught or pack animals. Little or no meat was eaten, and only small amounts of fish. Barely anything went to market: a little rice, some cloth, a homemade toy – a few such things sold in town would make just enough money for small purchases, including cheap cigarettes, 'perfumed with cloves and shaped like small elongated cones'.

Industry remained in its infancy, apart from oil installations, rubber plantations and their associated plant, and coal and tin mines, both in Sumatra (or on the islands of Bangka and Beliton in the case of tin), which were run by Anglo-American companies before Dr Sukarno nationalized them. But whether European, Chinese or national, Indonesia's industrial activities are scarcely in a position to hasten its economic growth. At the same time, since the break with The Netherlands, there have been fewer outlets for the major export products – rubber, coffee, tobacco, copra and sugar – that the Dutch developed at the expense of traditional food crops.

Even so, 75 per cent of Indonesian exports are still made up of raw materials such as rubber, oil and tin.

Although independent, therefore, the country remains in a typically colonial economic situation, dangerously dependent on fluctuations in world markets. Thus, in 1951, the end of the Korean War and the halt in the rise of raw material prices had a catastrophic effect on Indonesia's budget.

With galloping inflation and a population increasing by about a million a year, the situation in the early 1960s was continuing to get worse. Java would have starved without massive imports of rice from abroad. To which should be added the lack of qualified managers, a top-heavy administration, endemic lack of security and an ill-organized army. It is hard not to agree with a member of Indonesia's political opposition that too much time had been spent on slogans, propaganda and spectacular campaigns like that for West Irian, and not enough on systematic plans.

Plans, in fact, had become an urgent necessity. The recovery of freedom and the euphoria that it caused were certainly unlikely to encourage a huge effort on the part of the population: but that effort had to be made. Indonesia itself had to be united. What kind of unity could exist among so many scattered islands without a national navy and air force?

Java's large population gives it a central place in Indonesia's 'solar system'. In 1815 it had 5 million inhabitants, in 1945, 50 million, in 1962, 60 million – two-thirds of Indonesia's total population: it also had three-quarters of her total resources. But its population density (400 per square kilometre) was close to the practicable limit. There was no question of taking further land from the forest, which had already been reduced to the minimum: to go further would 'enter the danger zone'. A possible safety-valve was the island of Sumatra, with only thirty inhabitants per square kilometre, and with abundant land and mineral resources. But the Sumatran soil, less rich than that of Java, would need special treatment such as ordinary peasants could not provide.

Javanese centralism angers many Indonesians, encouraging active separatism and a number of movements calling for effective federation. In the late 1950s and the early 1960s, separatist insurrections multiplied, with the Republic of the Moluccas at Amboina, Dar ul Islam in Western Sumatra, Pansunda in Java, Dr Hatte's movement in the Padang region of Sumatra, and the secession of the 'Colonels' in Celebes. The last of these Colonels, Colonel Simbolon, surrendered on 27 July 1961.

There were further difficulties. The Government felt obliged to curtail the freedom of the Communist, Socialist and liberal Muslim parties. 'Sukarnism' then became the only party, with a programme of 'guided democracy'.

With freedom curbed and opponents, though pardoned, pushed aside, the 'strong man' – 'Bang Karno' (Brother Sukarno) – felt he could and should pursue spectacular policies. Hence the great conference of neutral Third World countries held in Bandung in 1955. Hence also the efforts to secure West Irian. Appeasing nationalism gave some support to a Government which in all fields and for many years to come faced only difficult and ungrateful tasks. In 1967, in fact, President Sukarno was deposed and succeeded by T. N. J. Suharto.

The Philippines

The case of the Philippines, which is not on the official French curriculum, is no exception to the general rule in South-East Asia.

These islands too have been a remarkable crossroads and meeting-point for different peoples.

Human beings were present there from at least Neolithic times; and ironworking took place a number of centuries before the Christian era. From the fifth century AD onwards, the archipelago was caught up in the Indo-Malay civilization whose main source was Java: under the opulent Majapahit Empire, that civilization pervaded the islands. Chinese traders, too, soon made their presence felt, forming an élite of merchants and mariners who imposed their authority on the peasants, serfs bound to the soil.

In the fifteenth century, Islam made its appearance on the large island of Mindanao. In the sixteenth, the archipelago was discovered by the Spaniards under Ferdinand Magellan, who died there in 1521: in 1565 they settled on Luzon, the other large island, in the North. With them, Christianity resumed its traditional battle with the infidels, the *Moros*, this time in the Far East.

Often in revolt, and in any case ill-governed by the authorities in Manila, the islands remained under Spanish rule until 1898, when an internal rebellion broke out and the United States fleet intervened. The upshot was not immediate independence, because at the end of the Spanish-American War, when the Treaty of Paris was signed on 10 December 1898, the Philippines were placed under United States tutelage, to the great indignation of the local nationalists. To calm his bad conscience, the US President William McKinley made it his task 'to teach and civilize the Filipinos as people for whom Christ died on the cross'.

Not until 1946 did the islands become independent, at least in theory.

By the early 1960s, after a fairly turbulent past, they had a very large population of 25 million inhabitants, increasing annually by 700,000, on some 300,000 square kilometres or 116,000 square miles – just over half the area of France. It was mixed population: 95 per cent of it Malay, but blended with other elements; 400,000-500,000 primitive peoples difficult to classify; 200,000 immigrant Chinese; and 70,000 Negritos.

There were then some 20 million Catholics – the only such large and close-knit Christian group in the Far East. The next biggest Christian grouping comprised 2 million Catholic dissidents or Aglypayans, so called after the founder of their sect, a former priest named Aglypya, who helped organize the 1898 rebellion; then came 500,000 Protestants. Muslims numbered some 2 million, and there were 500,000 pagans. Since 1898, English has largely replaced Spanish in the Philippines, except in a few old families; while Tagal, a Malay dialect, has come back into its own. Finally, a large number of other dialects are spoken. At least half the population, in the early 1960s, remained illiterate.

The country is poor, if not destitute, and essentially rural; and large estates continue to grow at the expense of the small peasant. What one American observer has called a 'parasito-feudal' society hinders reform and tends to thwart foreign aid. Only in Manila is there a money economy: the rest of the country relies on barter. Peasant poverty accounts for the huge Communist revolt of the *buks*, which was welcome when Japan was dominant in the Second World War, but savagely repressed by the Philippine authorities after the end of the war and the occupation. But fire continued to smoulder under the ashes: the Chinese example, and that of Fidel Castro in Cuba, still haunted people's imaginations. Even with American aid (and supervision), the country's progress was infinitely slow – so much so that the growth of the population absorbed any improvement in advance.

Korea

Between 1950 and 1953, Korea played a dramatic role, of which it was and remains the victim. The Korean War of those years was essentially a conflict between the world's major powers, an armed struggle between East and West.

During the Second World War, at Yalta in February 1945, and after it in December of the same year, the independence of Korea seemed to be taken for granted. The country had been liberated in the North by Soviet troops and in the South by American forces brought in from Japan. Their two occupation zones were separated only by the conventional dividing-line of the 38th parallel. But in spite of intervention by the United Nations, this line continued to divide Korea. In the South, an independent Republic of Korea was established on 15 August 1948; in the North, a Democratic or People's Republic on Communist lines. In 1950, Communist troops from North Korea invaded the South. There followed an armed riposte by the United States and its allies. On the North Korean side, Chinese volunteers intervened to redress the balance. In July 1953, an armistice re-established the dividing-line along the 38th parallel. But this arbitrary division of the country has not made life easier for either the North or the South.

Korea has been the victim of its peculiar strategic position, surrounded by the Japanese archipelago, Manchuria, Siberia and China. It is a prime example of the dangers that threaten small States in the neighbourhood of large ones, which think themselves justified in doing anything, in the present as in the past.

A huge peninsula of 220,000 square kilometres (85,000 square miles) stretching roughly from North to South, Korea is divided from Manchuria only by the narrow valleys of the Yalu and Tumen Rivers, which run parallel to the tall White Mountains – the barrier that maintains and perhaps originally established Korean independence. From the 43rd to the 34th parallel, the country is a stretch of land some 800 to 900 kilometres (500 to 560 miles) long, at a rough glance not unlike the Italian peninsula.

Like Italy, Korea has the misfortune to be a natural highway. China regards it as a gateway, and thinks that it must be watched over like Turkestan or North Vietnam. Japan feels at sea if it cannot by fair means or foul secure access to this peninsula to which geography has, as it were, moored its islands – on slightly too long a warp. So if ever Japan feels especially strong or especially threatened, Korea suffers in consequence. It did so more than once between Hideyoshi's abortive attempts to seize the peninsula, from

1592 to 1598, and the successful Japanese occupation of Korea from 1910 to 1945.

To cap it all, Korea was also 'the Soviet outlet when Vladivostok is blocked by ice'. The Sea of Japan freezes as far South as the 38th parallel; and as early as the beginning of the twentieth century Tsarist Russia had an interest in this key route. In the past, when the Japanese threatened the King–Emperor of Korea, he took refuge in the Russian Embassy.

A poor country, cold despite the presence of rice-fields and bamboo at least as far North as Seoul, and covered in the North with vast conifer forests, Korea has busy coasts and extensive plains only towards the West and the South. The plains supply none too adequate food for a large population of 31 million (more than 140 people per square kilometre). The Southern part of the peninsula stretches a long way seawards and is prolonged by a series of islands. The best known of them is Tsushima, in the middle of the Korea Strait. The distance between Korea and Japan is little more than 100 kilometres as the crow flies; that between Korea and the mouth of the Yangtze-Kiang is 500 kilometres.

So Korea is much affected by the sea: it is not only a nation of peasants living off the land, the forests and the mines, but also a nation of fishermen, sailors and merchants. Very early in its history it organized fruitful contacts between China and Japan; and from the Middle Ages onwards it served in particular as a link between Southern China, in touch with Arab and Persian trade, and the regions in the North. As a highway and a crossroads, it was a country of traders and emigrants.

Korea is almost an island, deliberately reclusive but also, willy-nilly, open to the outside world, by which it has been culturally enriched.

The remote history of the Three Kingdoms (from the first century BC to the seventh century AD) is that of China's cultural conquest in Korea. These three kingdoms appeared one after another in less than fifty years: that of Silla in 57 BC, that of Kokuryô in 37 BC, and the precarious kingdom of Paekche, backed by Japan, in 18 BC. They all belonged, therefore, to roughly the same epoch, but Chinese civilization came to them in turn. Buddhism was first established in Kokuryô, then in Paekche in AD 384, and finally in Silla in 527.

Silla, the most primitive of the three, bested the other two and from AD 668 to 935 held all of Korea in its grip. Thus enlarged, the kingdom enjoyed great and prosperous trade so long as the T'ang Empire continued to rule China (618–907): it lived in that reflected splendour.

After the breakdown of Silla's extended authority, Korean unity was restored by a new Unitary State, Koryô (913–1392), from which the country derived its name. Its civilization flourished, aided by the development of printing. This was a gift from China, which had invented it in the ninth century: but it was the Koreans who in 1234 invented metal type. Buddhism spread among both the educated class and the mass of the people, in the simplified form of Segn (in Chinese *Tch'an*, in Japanese *Zen*). At the same time, and more firmly, Confucianism took root and prospered. Cast-iron sculptures appeared, then dry-lacquer statues and dazzling ceramics 'in which can be detected the taste of the traditional Korean goldsmiths'.

This efflorescence was undoubtedly linked to general progress throughout the Far East. But Korea had the good fortune to be shielded from the onslaughts of the Barbarians who dominated China and who for a long time did no more than touch upon the peninsula. In the end, however, Mongol China, which had tried to burst open all the gates of Middle Kingdom and had failed against Japan, succeeded in Korea, dominating the country for more than a century, from 1259 to 1368.

When Korea recovered its independence, it came under the rule of its last dynasty, that of the Yi, which remained in power until the Japanese occupation in 1910. With the exception of some troubled years, as for instance between 1592 and 1635, when Korea was caught between Ming China and aggression from Japan, the Yi dynasty was a fruitful period of peace and independence.

The main feature of those centuries, without a doubt, was the emergence of a middle class, and the consequent rise of a civilization which drew part of its inspiration from the inexhaustible imagination of ordinary people. A change in handwriting helped this assimilation of popular culture. 'Until then, Chinese handwriting had enabled only lettered people to think and write in the spoken language. Novels previously written in Chinese now began to be written in Korean, and a whole new class of society acquired access to culture. In the eighteenth century, this enrichment resulted in an effervescence comparable to the Enlightenment in Europe' (Vadime Elisseeff).

At the summit of Korean society, however, there still remained an aristocratic, sophisticated civilization, characterized by the success of neo-Confucianism, with a rationalistic and stoic bent. It was then that there took root those family cults and that ethic on which neo-Confucianism is based. Even today, despite all their troubles, Koreans are still 'its most faithful representatives'.

Nothing can be said with confidence about the situation today. A country which nature has designed for unity, and which history has solidly united for centuries past, has been split apart by current events, turning it into two countries, eyeing each other like rivals from the same womb. The old capital of Han-Yang, commonly known as Seoul (i.e. 'the capital'), which belongs to South Korea, no longer commands the Seoul–Gen-san road. Imagine Italy cut in two and Rome deprived of the road to Ancona. The North has industry, steel, iron and electricity. The South, in the early 1960s, had only rice, large estates and the open sea.

At that time, they looked like two immobile puppets, abandoned because since 1953 no one has any longer worked or even held their strings.

15. Japan

Japan lies at the far extremity of the human world. Its Northern island, Hokkaidō (Yezo), lies in the remote, cold latitudes of the Sea of Okhost. To the East, where its best ports are found, it faces the vast and wondrous emptiness of the Pacific. To the West and South, less forbidding seas, often thick with mist, narrow a little between Korea and the Southern island of Kyushu.

As an archipelago, Japan has often been likened to the British Isles. They, however, are much closer to the nearby continent. Japan is more isolated, insular and alone. To break out of its solitude, it has had to make frequent and conscious efforts. If not, it would be naturally inward-looking. Yet a Japanese historian has pointed out that 'Everything that seems essentially Japanese in our civilization is actually derived from abroad'.

As early as the sixth century, in fact, there was what might be called 'a Chinese Japan'; and since 1868 there has been a highly successful 'Western Japan'. Nevertheless, both these key influences have merged into a 'Japanese' Japan whose insular origin is clear beyond all doubt. In this country of miniature gardens, tea ceremonies and flowering cherries, even the Buddhist religion, brought in through China, has been remodelled to suit the Japanese. And this Japanese version of Buddhism is even further removed from the original than the Chinese variant was and is.

Although apparently so malleable, Japan has turned its many borrowings into a very particular civilization of its own. It remains faithful to its old traditions: they coexist with the far-reaching

Westernization which it began to accept almost a century ago, without reservations, and indeed eagerly, as a key to greater power. This strange duality explains the remark made by a journalist in 1961: 'What is the most extraordinary thing about Japan? The Japanese.'

Japan before Chinese influence

From its earliest origins in the fifth millennium BC until the sixth century AD, when Chinese civilization made its first notable impact on the country, Japan was in the grip of a primitive but vigorous culture which developed only slowly. This early Japan is so little known that specialists freely declare there to have been no Japanese history before the arrival of Buddhism in AD 552. In fact, that distant past seems to have foreshadowed what happened later: under the impact of invasions and foreign innovations, Japan made and remade itself on lines copied from abroad.

From the fifth millennium BC until the beginning of the Christian era, little of Japan can be discerned except one favoured area, the central plain between what is now Kyôto and, to the South-East, Yamoto. Ancient documents call this region Kinki. It forms the heartland of the great island of Hondo, not far from Japan's narrow and beautiful Mediterranean, the Seto Naikai or Island Sea which links it with the Southern islands of Shikoku and Kyushu.

This central area was the scene of three great changes, one after another.

- It is almost certain that the first inhabitants of the archipelago were the primitive Aïnos, whose traces are still to be found in the Ryukyu Islands, but who today are confined to Hokkaidô and Sakhalin. The first culture that archaeologists have discovered includes elements from Korea, Manchuria, and from the far-off Lake Baïkal in Siberia; and prominent among them are primitive ceramics decorated with rope patterns impressed

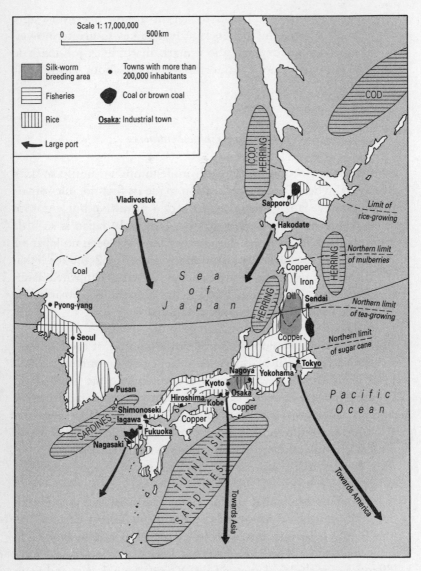

13. Japan, land of the sun and the sea

Japan is China's orient. That is the origin of its name, 'the land of the rising sun' – in Chinese 'Je-pen'.

on the clay when still wet – hence the name given to the culture, Jômon (meaning 'rope pattern'). From this mixed heritage one can deduce that people from the continent reached Japan very early on, and that at that time there began the struggle which so long pitted the Japanese against the Aïnos.

● In about the third and second centuries BC, a new invasion seems to have taken place, coming from China (especially South China) and distant Indonesia. A variety of new objects date from this epoch: the potter's wheel, bronze and bronze mirrors, bells, iron, Han Chinese coins and finally rice and the Southern type of house, open and well-aired. This is the so-called 'Yayoi Street' civilization, named after the Tokyo street in which such characteristic finds have been excavated. Among the innovations discovered, rice – replacing millet – was a revolution in itself. The idea of the King as a living god, which pervades the whole of Japanese history, may have been imported at the time by Proto-Malays coming from the South; but there can be no certainty either way.

● The second and third centuries AD were marked by the building of a number of nobles' tombs, which have been preserved to the present day. At this time, a series of clans emerged, with knightly leaders, more or less free peasants and artisans and an already large mass of serfs. The leaders claimed that they were the children of local gods. Under Korean influence, the artisans' guilds adopted the title *be* (meaning group or section), preceded by the name of their trade. The scribes became known as *fuma-be*; the weavers, *ori-be*; the saddlers, *kuratsukuri-be*; and the story-tellers, *katari-be*, who handed on the legends of heroic deeds.

There was already by now a political and religious system, whose primitive beliefs deified the various forces of nature. Profoundly conservative, Japan never abandoned this religion, which long afterwards, in the nineteenth century, came to be called Shinto (the way of the Gods). The West often calls it shintoism.

It was at this time, setting its face against the Aïnos' countries, and beginning in the Yamoto region, that Japan made its first attempt to form an Empire. The Empire traced its origins to the legendary imperial Japanese dynasty, born of the Sun-God Amaterasu: this tenacious religious tradition was still being celebrated in Shinto temples when Japan was defeated in 1945. Under the pressure of the US occupiers, the Emperor of Japan finally renounced his claim to divine descent.

The Empire took time to establish. In the eighth century, when the first Japanese chronicles were written, the country was still not completely united. It was a very slow process to link with the imperial dynasty the various regional clans (*uji*), each with its leader, its land, its peasants and its artisans – like the imperial dynasty itself. It was all the more difficult in that the clan leaders were often of foreign origin (Korean or Chinese). But the process of organization was made easier by the need to join forces against the Aïnos, the Barbarians 'from beyond the Eastern barrier'.

This system, royal and vigorously feudal, became fully formed in the sixth century, when the Koreans introduced into Japan Chinese writing, Confucianism and Buddhism. The influence of Confucian ideas was evident in the ordinances issued in 604 by Prince Shotoku, who proclaimed the rights of undivided central authority: 'The country does not have two rulers; the people do not have two masters.'

This was the beginning of the Japan known to history, with its hierarchy, its scribes, its chronicles and its embassies to the Emperors of China, the first being accredited in 607. A court aristocracy, the *kuge*, formed around the prince, the distributor of lands and 'benefices' (*shoen*), which everyone tried to transform into what the West would call 'fiefs'.

This imperial Japan soon developed under a new influence – the growing and finally all-powerful ascendancy of Chinese civilization. China even baptized the archipelago, calling it 'the land of the rising sun', in Chinese *Je-pen* (origin of our 'Japan'), and in Japanese *Nippon* (the Japanese pronunciation of the same ideograms).

Japan learns from Chinese civilization

For centuries, Chinese civilization dominated Japan. It flourished there in unexpected ways. Sometimes, what it brought was so altered as to become unrecognizable – as in the case of Buddhism, which in its Zen form became by a singular turn of fate, from the twelfth century onwards, the doctrine of the 'bloodthirsty samurai'. In other areas, Japan preserved its borrowings from China in archaic forms long forgotten by China itself. Such was the case with ancient Chinese music, lost in China but still played in Japan. In every instance, however, Chinese civilization was modified under the influence of a people, a society and a set of traditions radically different from those of China. This was all the more so in that Chinese ways often reached Japan through Korea, which did not always faithfully copy the original model.

The first Sino-Japanese civilization flourished in the golden age of ancient Japan. During this long transplanting process, Japan refused nothing from China: the classics, calligraphy, painting, architecture, institutions and law (that of the T'ang dynasty).

So Japan, like China, was divided into provinces – although far smaller than China's vast domains. When the capital, Nara ('the capital' in Korean), was built in 710, it was laid out on the Chinese model, copying the town of Lo Yang in Korea, with a chequerboard pattern and the Imperial palace at its Northern end. In 994, when the capital was transferred to Heïankyo ('capital of peace') or Kyôto ('the capital' in Japanese), it was again built on this same plan. From then on, incidentally, it ceased to move from place to place as it had in the past, when every emperor had built his own. By the time Nara was built, the court and its offices had become too sizeable to be transferred elsewhere so frequently, shifting anew with every reign. Once it had moved to Kyôto, the capital stayed there for centuries.

Chinese influence was everywhere, and the scribes' chronicles, which recounted the history of these times, were written in

mandarin style and in Chinese ideograms, although in the Japanese
language. Still, Japan's many borrowings from China should not
mislead us: the court at Kyôto, which soaked up Chinese culture,
was only the small centre of a much larger country; and the spread
of that culture in the rest of Japan was patchy and slow. Kyôto
was bathed in bright light: around it there were still many
shadows.

On its narrow stage, however, the late tenth to the early twelfth
century saw many splendours, linked it would seem with an
economic boom. When this early prosperity faded, Kyôto's
cultural golden age faded too, and sombre centuries followed.

What survives from that golden age includes the brilliant,
precious, poetic literature of the *monogatari*, part novels, part fairy
stories: one, entitled *Ochikubo monogatari*, or *The Cellar Story*, is
very like *Cinderella*. More striking still were the *nikki*, poetic
diaries which the ladies of the court wrote in Japanese, while the
men wrote in Chinese. This very lively feminine literature re-creates
for us the festivities of the court – concerts, dances, poetry contests,
imperial excursions into the surrounding countryside, 'pleasures
ruled by strict etiquette which made life in the palace a perpetual
display, as well-drilled as a ballet'. It also reveals, unsurprisingly, a
series of political and amorous intrigues, with 'the inevitable
promiscuity which occurs in these insufficiently segregated
quarters'.

It seems to have been an idle, futile world, 'corrupted by
literature'. A lady of the court whom we know only by her
nickname of Sei-Shônagon, and who lived around the year
1000, left occasional writings which are sometimes merciless and
always amusing. Their tone can be gathered from the distinction
Shônagon makes between agreeable and disagreeable things:
the latter, she says, are of course more numerous than the former.
They include 'a hair on one's writing-desk or a grain of sand in
the ink-rod, which grates when rubbed; an insignificant person
who talks a lot and laughs loudly; or, just when one wants to
listen to something, a baby crying; a dog which starts to bark

when it sees a man who is coming to meet one secretly at night; a man whom one has hidden, more or less, and who begins to snore. Or again, someone coming to see one in secret, puts on a tall, conspicuous hat, then when the time comes to leave, takes every precaution not to be seen, but bumps into something which falls with a loud crash' (based on R. Sieffert).

While the privileged classes lived and played in these ways, Buddhism slowly pervaded Japan in a new and democratic form. A freshly inspired clergy made contact with the 'middle classes' – artisans and small landowners. A highly simplified form of worship devoted itself exclusively to the saviour Buddha, Buddha Amida, who guaranteed to believers their access to the Heaven of the West. Rather as in China, knowledge of the ideas and beliefs of true Buddhism soon became confined to a few rare theologians and members of the élite, while popular Buddhism took everything on board, including the old beliefs of Shinto: so much so that the two religions were virtually fused into one. This was *Shingon*, in which the local gods became particular and temporary manifestations of the Buddhist gods.

Shinto sanctuaries came under the control of this new sect, known also as Dualist Shintoism. With the worship of Amida, a new Buddhist iconography arose. The magnificent 'rolls' that date from this period also show the Japanese landscape, and picture the activities of various social classes in scenes which are often full of humour.

At the same time, writing became more widespread, mainly using a simplified alphabet of only forty-seven syllables.

From the twelfth century onwards, this imperial system collapsed. It had long shown signs of weakness. While it had copied the institutions of the brilliant T'ang dynasty in China, it had not managed to establish a corps of educated civil servants which would have enabled it to break the power and ambition of the old aristocracy. Soon, the Empire gave way to the Shoguns, who ruled Japan from 1191 to 1863 – the seemingly interminable counterpart of the Middle Ages in Europe.

From the end of the eighth century until 1186 – almost four centuries – feudal clans threatened the imperial authorities. The Emperors still reigned, but they barely ruled. They were the prisoners and playthings of the all-powerful Fujiwara family, which controlled the key posts and supplied the Emperor with wives and concubines selected exclusively from among Fujiwara relatives. The family even deposed Emperors and chose their successors. As one historian has said, 'The power of the Mikado was an empty box whose key the Fujiwara jealously kept to themselves.'

The end of the Fujiwara's long reign ushered in the interminable period known as the Shogunate. This unexpected turn of events more or less institutionalized, in the person of the Shogun, the Emperor's domination by the seignorial clans, huge families that were often descended from the Emperors' numerous children, forming a kind of privileged nobility. Their reign, the Shogunate, saw different clans jockeying for power and replacing each other, but within a framework of underlying agreement. If nothing else, they were united in seeking to dominate the rest of the population. Of its castes – nobles, peasants, artisans and merchants – only the nobles were left in peace. At the bottom of the scale, the very poorest – notably the leather-workers – were untouchables, although far fewer than in India.

With the economy less prosperous, the Shogunate represented a feudal and military reaction in leaner times. It was marked also by a belligerent aristocracy. This, far away from the court, carved out for itself very extensive domains in newly colonized and still rebellious areas in the North and East of Hondo, 'beyond the barrier', where they practised large-scale horse-breeding. As against Kyôto, with its effeminate, and much hated upstart courtiers, the new regime put itself forward as an egalitarian government of soldiers, the *bakofu* or 'bivouac government', headed by a general or Shogun. It has been compared to the rule of the Mayors of the Palace in the later, decadent days of the Merovingian kings in Europe. There was, however, one difference: in Japan, the ineffectual titular ruler was never deposed. The Mikado continued to reign, but not to rule, alongside the Shogun whose investiture he performed by virtue of his divine authority, as in Europe was done for the Emperor by the Pope.

The first shoguns established themselves near the end of the Tokaido (the road from Kyôto, to Yedo, now Tokyo) at Kamakura, which became in effect the capital of Japan. It remained there until 1332; then it was moved back to a district of Kyôto, Muromachi, from 1393 to 1576. In 1598 it was finally settled in Yedo, until then a fishing port, where it stayed until 1868. Historians commonly refer to the Kamakura, Muromachi and Yedo periods, which together virtually extend throughout the long centuries of the Shogunate (1192–1868).

In all these periods, the dominant figures were the warriors, the knights, the *bushi*. As the dominant caste, they easily imposed their views, their tastes and their brutality, as well as – at the beginning especially – a certain simplicity in government, as in dress and domestic life. The *suikan* and the *hitatara*, rather plain clothes, replaced the swollen and cumbrous garments, the *noshi* or the *sokutai*, which were formally required by ancient etiquette. Hunting, jousting and horse-racing, too, replaced the stuffy pleasures of the past.

The habitual violence of the time was tamed somewhat when the Shoguns settled in Kyôto, from 1393 to 1576. The ancient city then recovered its rights and its role, with the result that the classical golden age was not wholly tarnished in the age of the knights and the soldiers.

The last years of the sixteenth century and the first years of the seventeenth marked a violent break in the midst of the Shogunate's lengthy rule. For more than two centuries, in fact, the Tokugawa revolution isolated Japan from the rest of the world, and tightened the grip of feudal habits and institutions.

In the late sixteenth century, a son of peasant stock named Hideyoshi established a dictatorship in the archipelago. Although he did not take the title of Shogun, he restored order and undertook a long and perhaps ill-justified war against Korea

(1592–8) which ended only with his death. Soon afterwards, the Tokugawa clan obtained supremacy under the patient and skilful Hideyori or Iyeyasu. Made Shogun by the emperor, he decided to establish himself at Yedo, in the sensible belief that it was from that turbulent region, and not from Kyôto, that Japan could and should be governed. By abdicating in favour of his son, Hideyori succeeded in making the Shogunate hereditary in his family, which thus 'reigned' until 1868.

In 1639, the Yedo government took the fateful decision to close Japan to foreigners. From then on, only Chinese and Dutch ships with special permits were allowed in; and the Dutch were permitted to bring only munitions, arms, spectacles and tobacco. For the rest, the archipelago could and did live off its own resources. The ban covered Japanese as well as other vessels: it had even begun with them, in 1633. It had lasting results. Can it be explained?

It would appear that the rulers of Japan had become afraid of Westerners. The first arrivals, the Portuguese, had reached Kyūshū in 1534. Their cannons, harquebuses and enormous ships impressed the islanders; so, still more, did the numerous conversions to Christianity which the newcomers very quickly secured. Might this religion not encourage revolt on the part of the nobles and peasants, as it rather did in 1638?

At the same time, a very deep and widespread economic recession was starting, led by China but also affecting distant India. Was Japan feeling the pinch, needing to protect itself and in particular to halt the outflow of precious metals? Since the heroic days of Hideyoshi, Japan's aggression against Korea and China, whose ships it subjected to countless piratical raids, seemed to show that the country was more and more fending for itself. The brilliance of Ming China touched it not at all. Finally, its rulers were anxious to immobilize an unstable society and a peasantry too eager for freedom, though often reduced to despair. The self-imposed blockade thus 'froze' Japan's institutions until the arrival of Admiral Perry's 'black ships' in 1853.

Until then, Japan lived on its own, preserving its clans and its archaic aristocracy, to which essential class everything was subordinate – as witness the sustained success of *dhyâna* or *Zen*, that strange variant of Buddhism.

Yet this isolationist Japan, triple-locked as it were, was perhaps less unfortunate and deprived than might at first be thought. It was obliged to exploit its own resources, spiritual as well as material. One sign of such health and wealth was the emergence of vernacular literature in the sixteenth century, and its development during the 'Osaka century' from 1650 to 1750. Thus there arose, alongside the traditional Nôh plays, the lively part-dancing, part-singing kabuki theatre. During the Shogunate, darkness was never quite complete.

The rule of the Shoguns was feasible, of course, only under strict discipline and what amounted to a police state. The great nobles or *daimyos*, the heads of clans and districts, numbered about 270. They had at their beck and call a multitude of 'faithful servants', the samurai, who were rewarded with money or benefits in kind but never, as in the West, with grants of land in perpetuity, which would have given them a certain independence. The *ronin*, a samurai who had lost or (if it were conceivable) left his lord, was condemned either to starve or to become a brigand.

All accounts state, repeat, and proclaim that the samurai was devoted body and soul to his master, in accordance with his religious code of honour, the oral code of *Bushido*. The story of the forty-seven *ronins* whose master had killed himself by committing hara-kiri, who avenged him and then committed suicide themselves on his grave, in the winter of 1703, has been told many times. This rough code of honour was developed in the pitiless school of continual civil wars.

For it was among themselves and against each other that the Japanese mostly fought. Nothing more was heard of the Aïnos. Mongol China tried twice, in 1274 and 1281, to hurl an armada against Japan, but a 'divine wind', the *Kamize*, blew into a storm which destroyed the invading fleet. Against Korea, as we have seen, Japan's war lasted only six years. So it was among themselves that the Japanese used the lance and the sword; and continual fighting trained them to respect a hierarchy that was fixed once and for all. So much so that in the Japanese language, as late as 1868, verbs 'indicated the status of both subject and object'. For example, the use of the auxiliary *ageru* showed 'that the action expressed by the main verb was performed by an inferior for the benefit of a superior'.

The result was a country extraordinarily disciplined, divided into castes, firmly ruled, and at one and the same time ostentatious and desperately poor. This double image of wealth and splendour for some and destitution for others is vividly described in the traveller's tale of a Westphalian doctor, Herr Kämpfer, who was working for the Dutch East India Company, and whose book, published in 1690, is a masterpiece of observation. No one who has read it is likely to forget its accounts of gruelling journeys, of rivers that have to be forded under the protection of a cordon of ferrymen from bank to bank, holding hands to moderate the current and make the crossing a little less dangerous. Equally telling are Kämpfer's memories of villages with miserable hovels, and of peasants kneeling in the fields by the side of the road when sumptuous processions of great nobles go by. The roads between Kyôto and Yedo, headquarters of the Shogun, were busy with the passage of *daimyos*, whose duty it was to pay him regular visits. Their entourages were veritable armies of halberdiers, gunners and servants accompanying their master on his journey to the capital.

These rich feudal lords were required to spend six months a year in their palaces at Yedo. The façades of the buildings were adorned with rich armorial bearings, which Rodrigo Vivero had described with admiration in 1609. Set apart from the rest of the town, the palaces were grouped near that of the Shogun. Yet, beautiful as they were, in reality they were prisons. When in residence, their occupants were under surveillance; when absent, they left their families as hostages. They could hardly ever escape – no one could escape – the swarms of judges, informers and watchdogs on the roads, in the towns and in the taverns. In town, every street was isolated, as in China, by gates at each end which were shut as soon as any incident took place, such as theft, pilfering or some other crime. The culprit – real or suspected – would immediately be seized, and punishment would swiftly follow, usually involving death.

Similarly severe and detailed supervision was applied to the only trade allowed, with restrictions, after 1639 – i.e. that of the Chinese and the Dutch. (The latter had shamelessly lent their ships and their cannons to help crush uprisings by Japanese Christians in 1638.) Whenever the ships of the Dutch East India Company arrived, they were put in quarantine at the island of Deshima within the harbour of Nagasaki, and all goods, sailors, merchants, agents and officials of the Company were carefully checked. Contemporary accounts give the impression of a watchful, mistrustful regime, of a country bristling with fortresses and teeming with soldiers. Justice was harsh in the West; but here it was harsher. Every traveller was struck by the sight of gibbets and tortured bodies. One of the hills near Kyôto was called 'the mount of severed ears'.

In matters of culture and religion, feudal Japan certainly evolved. As in Korea and China, Buddhism here took various forms (one of them being Zen, another the fanatical cult of the Lotus of Good Faith, which held that Japan was the only country of the true Buddha). Zen, which also came from China, was identified from the twelfth century onwards with the samurai. Whereas rationalist neo-Confucianism was a convenient doctrine for the Shogunate, Zen became a soldier's faith, far removed from its original role as a religion of love and non-violence. But this transformation, of course, was characteristic of that time and that society.

The teachings of Zen were encapsulated in very short anecdotes, *koans*, intentionally absurd, with unexpected moral lessons. They sought at all costs to liberate the unconscious, instinctive self which was normally half asleep. 'Let go of your wits and become like a ball in a mountain torrent.' It was a strange kind of self-discipline, to set free and awaken one's instincts and then trust oneself to their impetus. In retrospect, it sounds like a psychoanalytic cure, calling for no more complexes: 'When you walk, walk; when you sit, sit. Above all, never hesitate!' Hesitate at nothing, in fact: that is the most frequent advice, obviously apt for a soldier. 'Clear all obstacles out of your path. If the Buddha is in your way, kill the Buddha. If it is your ancestor, kill your ancestor. If it is your father and mother, kill your father and mother. If it is a relation, kill your relation. Only in this way will you succeed in liberating yourself. Only in this way will you escape from your fetters and be free.'

This language, of course, is not to be taken literally. The Buddha, the ancestors and the relations merely symbolized all the constraints of a society obsessed with etiquette, where from the earliest years every girl and boy was enclosed in the straitjacket of an education that was all iron rules. Everyone was drilled to obey a code dictating how one should eat, speak and sit: it even laid down the position in which one should sleep, motionless, with one's head on a small wooden cross-piece. One must 'never lose control of one's mind or one's body', as a result of conditioning aimed at quelling the most natural reflexes, rather as the miniature garden curbed the natural growth of plants and trees. All the teachings of Zen, earmarked for soldiers, seem to have been directed against the inhibitions and constraints of what is called Japan's 'code of politeness'. As in every society, real life modified and reconciled opposites. Japan was both rigorous and flexible at the same time. Zen was its indispensable counterweight.

Modern Japan

Japan's break with the outside world lasted more than two centuries, until the Revolution which began the Meiji era in 1868, soon followed by the intense industrialization of the country. Japan's industrialization was a unique phenomenon, an 'economic miracle' that shed new light on Japanese civilization. Its speed, and above all its extraordinary success, cannot be explained only by the arguments normally advanced by economists, relevant though they are. Something more was involved.

The isolationist centuries contributed. From 1639 to 1868, despite being almost wholly cut off from the rest of the world, Japan made very great progress. By the eighteenth century, this had become obvious. The population increased: so did rice production: so did the growing of new crops. Towns grew bigger. In the eighteenth century, Yedo had at least a million inhabitants. This general quickening of the economy would not have been possible without a surplus of agricultural produce, especially rice, to put on the urban markets. It also benefited from the ease with which grain could be stored and transported, and from the possibility of supplying the towns with enough fuel in the form of charcoal.

Society itself encouraged economic development. The *daimyos*, whom a suspicious Government uprooted and forced to live in Yedo, were systematically ruined by their continual and costly journeys. When a money economy really began, in the seventeenth century, it was more vigorous than in China, though on a smaller scale; and urban luxury implied – indeed required – the expenditure of cash. This obliged the great nobles to sell part of their vast rice harvests, as well as to borrow money – made easier because the credit system, which had been known for a long time, now began to be general in Japan, in the form of various notes and bills of exchange. Nobles, like samurai, were forbidden to trade: they therefore employed nominees. So a merchant class arose and prospered, lending money to the *daimyos*, joining their entourage and, in a country where, more than elsewhere, fine feathers made fine birds, copying their dress. The merchants soon managed to place their sons and daughters in aristocratic families, infiltrating them by marriage and adoption. However, warned off by a few spectacular executions which the Government used as pretexts for confiscating sizeable fortunes, the merchants mostly kept out of sight.

They were particularly important in Osaka, then the economic hub of Japan. It was here that all the wealthy, both nobles and businessmen, met in the 'Flower Quarter', a city of pleasure within the town itself, where geishas, 'expensively educated' courtesans, played 'the role that had been fulfilled by the noble ladies of the court at Eïan' (Kyôto). Mocking, caustic stories about the Flower Quarter and its scandals, suicides and murders delighted the uncultivated public. True lovers of literature supposedly spurned these popular entertainments, preferring 'the delights of Confucian scholasticism'.

All this shows that even before 1868 Japanese life was in rapid flux. By the eighteenth century, an economic boom had resulted in an active type of pre-capitalism, ready to take off. In the nineteenth century, things began to move faster still. The Meiji era would be incomprehensible were it not for the transfers and positionings that had gone before, the preliminary accumulation of economic resources and capital, with all the social tensions that they implied.

Too many *daimyos* had been ruined by politics or luxury. Gradually, Japan began to see more and more samurai without masters, *ronins*, poverty-stricken knights. It was a little like Germany in the fifteenth century, where might was right. At all events, it was this group of the dispossessed that gave the first successful impetus to the Revolution. The arrival of the American fleet in 1853 had been 'the spark that lit the powder'. And when the Emperor Mutsu Hito seized power in 1868, he had no difficulty in overthrowing the old feudal regime and its traditional castes. All he overthrew, in fact, was a façade.

Industrialization is not simply an economic phenomenon: it always involves social changes, and these may assist or hinder the economic process itself. In the case of Japan, society was no hindrance. That fact is all the more remarkable in that, generally speaking, industrialization dislocates society. In the West, as Karl Marx observed, it produced the mass proletariat, class conflict and the Socialist movement.

Japan was a case apart. In a way that at first seems

incomprehensible, it achieved its Industrial Revolution, with all its attendant changes of activity, without any revolutionary breaks in the structure of society. 'This immense transformation was digested by a culture already changing, and it followed a path which, on reflection, may well be revealed as entirely new.'

There were perhaps several reasons. Japanese society was highly disciplined, and it maintained its traditional discipline during the new experience it underwent after 1868. Obedient, respectful of hierarchy, it had always accepted uncomplainingly that luxury was reserved for the few; it equally accepted, without always realizing the fact, that modern capitalism in Japan should be built in the midst of relationships that remained feudal. If one thinks of Russian industrialists in the eighteenth century, settled in the Urals in the midst of their serfs, a similar picture – *mutatis mutandis* – could be painted of Japan's great industrial firms. They it was who in the nineteenth century ensured the success of the operation and drew the profits, without provoking any reaction from the labouring masses.

Before the outbreak of war in 1942, fifteen families at most accounted for more than 80 per cent of Japan's capital. Colloquially, they were known as *zaïbatsu* – a term which has become classic. There were the famous Mitsui, Mitsubishi, Sumitovo and Yasuda, plus the imperial House, which according to experts was by far the richest of these very rich families. In the social hierarchy, these lords of big business were the equivalent of the *daimyos* of the past with their clans. The workpeople were their serfs, and the foremen, managers and engineers were the modern samurai. The firms remained family businesses, a mixture of feudalism and paternalism in this world where 'free enterprise and communism were both regarded as strange, foreign ideas, likely to destroy the Kodo, the imperial path of Japan'. The authorities could and still can impose their wishes on this docile, patiently frugal people, content to work for only small reward.

This explains the miraculous volte-face that took place in 1868. The Shogun handed over power to the Emperor, who in theory embodied the most traditional authority in the country: imagine, in the West, the Pope assuming lay power over people and property. And the Emperor who exerted this traditional authority decided to opt for revolution: he abolished the feudal system, ordered industries to be established, found the necessary investment and himself set up factories. After which, he quite often ceded the firms to selected private individuals, much as he might have ceded vast fiefs of a kind hitherto unknown. At the same time, he imposed on Japan an immense programme of work. It was carried out. The son of the Sun, venerated in the temples on account of his divine origin, had ordered the country to industrialize. For that, Japan had no need of some new ideology or faith: they existed already, enabling the whole country to be manoeuvred as one.

In these circumstances, it is hardly surprising that Japan could be both very modern and very traditional. 'The mystical character of the Emperor's authority served both the status quo and the revolution' – both social immobility and a completely new economy.

This is not a misleading explanation: it is confirmed by the conscious revival, in the eighteenth and still more in the nineteenth century, of the very ancient national beliefs that were organized under the name of Shinto. Shinto was the way of God, *kami*; but the meaning of *kami* in this context was closer to that of *mana*, which in the distant South Seas signified the impersonal supernatural power that resided in beings and things. Supreme *kami* belonged to Ameratsu, the goddess of the sun, who transmitted it to the long line of her sons.

The surrender of Japan after the atomic bombs were dropped on Hiroshima (6 August 1945) and Nagasaki (8 August) was followed by an unprecedented collapse. The country had only recently conquered much of South-East Asia: now it lost it all. Worse still, it lost all that had been built up since the Meiji era (1868), which had made Japan such an extraordinary anomaly in the Far East in the first part of the twentieth century.

Japan's post-1945 miracle (the second in its history), like those of Germany, France and Italy, relaid the foundations of its prosperity and gave it a level of development never attained before. It was a dizzying achievement. Japan was no longer, now, the military power it had been before 1942. But it was a great economic power.

The 1961–70 plan called for Japan's national income to be doubled by the final year, with spectacular growth in several sectors of the economy. Taking 100 as the base in 1955, industrial and mining output was intended to be 648 by the 'target year', steel production 296, machine tools 448 and chemicals 344. These calculations were not certain, of course; but they were not irresponsible: the recent past proved that.

Between the end of the nineteenth century and the Second World War, Japan's average growth rate had been 4 per cent per year; from 1946 to 1956 it was 10.6 per cent (compared with 4.3 per cent in France); from 1957 to 1959, 9.2 per cent; and from 1959 to 1962 it remained extremely high. These were record figures which only the German Federal Republic and the Soviet Union could rival, if that. The 1961–70 plan assumed an annual growth rate of 8.3 per cent.

The reasons for this progress are not far to seek. The most important, no doubt, was the fact that the US occupation authorities eventually allowed the trusts to be re-established more or less as before. The old patriarchal *zaibatsu* they dissolved for good, although a few reappeared: but very large new firms emerged, to become some of the biggest in the world. Japanese capitalism, which triumphantly achieved this unprecedented progress, was like American capitalism based on enormous units, able to use labour and capital more efficiently than the small artisan firms which – with some difficulty – survived only on account of family work or very low-paid labour.

At the same time, since the big Japanese firms were no longer self-financing, as they had been before 1941, industrial success involved the establishment, under the protection of the Bank of Japan, of a whole system of large banks and investment trusts, with much greater freedom than in France. These attracted small savers' capital with every resource of American-style publicity and propaganda. The result was a delirium of buying on the stock market, even on the part of naturally cautious peasants, which was encouraged by the fabulous profits made on the Tokyo stock exchange during the booms: it did 400 times as much business as before the war. From June 1961, however, a fall in prices curbed this excess of gambling and helped shift personal investments back to deposit accounts and savings banks.

The abundance of small savers explains the very high level of investment in Japan (in 1962, more than 20 per cent of national expenditure) and the interest which foreign and especially American capitalists have shown in Japanese firms. Their interest has so far been rather platonic, since in 1960 Japan had not yet fully liberalized its exchange controls, and profit on capital invested there was hard to get out of the country. A Swiss newspaper of 12 April 1961, envisaging the possibility of complete liberalization, declared: 'All in all, we prefer Japan to South Africa, where a great deal of European capital is stagnating. There is no doubt that the country is in full expansion, that its abundant labour force has exceptional skill, and that its leaders have not only unshakeable faith in their success, but also astonishing ability.' If foreign capital were to become seriously involved, Japan's growth rate could become even more impressive.

Can anyone identify the driving forces behind such progress? It is always difficult to analyse an economy in rapid flux. Statistics quickly grow stale and out of touch with reality. But it is certain that until recently a powerful stimulus was the superabundance of labour. Japan's economic plan estimated its population at 94 million in 1961 and 104 million in 1970 – an annual increase of a million, year in year out. By 1984, it had reached 120 million.

These increases have not hindered economic growth: the plan looked forward to a doubling of national income by 1970; and birth control was expected to slow down the rate at which the population grew. In 1962, moreover, the smaller numbers born during the war came on to the labour market, with the result that vacancies (especially for skilled workers) exceeded supply. Hence a subsequent increase in the salaries paid to engineers and teachers.

Undoubtedly, both wages and the standard of living remained at that time much lower than in the West or the United States. Given Japan's different habits and needs, however, the situation was far from catastrophic. There were certainly slums around Osaka and Tokyo (where the population was increasing by 400,000 per year, 300,000 of them immigrants). But the average food consumption was 2,100 calories a day, and the annual income in dollars between $200 and $300 – four times that in India. By 1984 it had reached $8,810. The enormous increase in fishing, where Japan was ahead of every other nation with an annual catch of 6 million tons, drawn from as far away as the Atlantic and the Caribbean; improved productivity on the land, where the US authorities had insisted on all holdings of more than six acres being sold, and where growing under glass, in winter, had made possible a second harvest and an earlier rice crop, avoiding the summer typhoons; and finally the slow attempt to exploit the resources of Yezo (Hokkaido), the cold island in the North: all contributed to great and stable growth.

The domestic market likewise supported the expansion of industry. A higher standard of living meant new purchases: washing machines, transistors, television sets, and cameras (Japan's huge factories flood the home market first). New tastes brought changes in demand – for more meat and fish, for Western-type pastries, canned and frozen goods, pharmaceutical remedies (especially tranquillizers), beer (more and more replacing rice wine) and Ceylon tea (replacing green tea, of which Japan produced 77,000 tons a year). Dress and interior decoration began to follow Western models. Admittedly, the average Japanese remained what the journalist Robert Guillain called 'bi-civilized', wearing Western clothes in the street but in the evening reverting to traditional Japanese costumes and habits. But the Japanese are clearly more and more affected and attracted by Western ways, and are succumbing to them.

Obstacles nevertheless remain. Not everything augurs well for the Japanese economy. Although it is a miracle of effort, of patient and intelligent work, it has its limits, its frailties and its dangers. Nor should one forget that the agrarian reform has produced a myriad smallholders, the poorest of them dependent upon those slightly better off, and all incapable of grouping together or yielding to truly modern and scientific methods. 'Only Socialism,' claimed one reporter, 'would succeed in that.' A likely story: agriculture has been the stumbling-block of almost all socialist experiments. Besides, all attempts at agrarian reform, at all times and in all countries, have led to great disappointments when they have tried to be rapid and radical. Agricultural habits are the most ingrained of all.

What is more, Japan has a population almost twice that of France in an area only half as large (300,000 against 550,000 square kilometres); while its arable land is only 15 per cent of the total compared with 84 per cent in France. It also has meagre natural resources. Wool, cotton, coal, iron ore and oil all have to be imported for its industries; and Japan's growth rate is such that it also requires large purchases of foreign machinery and equipment. Hence, in 1961, disturbing signs of a weakening trade balance, despite official optimism. On a reasonable estimate, it seemed that a favourable balance would not have been possible without the US occupation army's opportune expenditure in Japan. This shows how vulnerable its success still was.

The problem, for a country very much attached to its industrial prosperity, was not so much to produce as to sell. Here, Japan remained dependent on the prosperity and goodwill of its trading partners in the 'free world'. And this goodwill could not be taken for granted. The West, and especially France (which is always too hesitant in these matters) remembered the commercial dumping that Japan had practised relentlessly before 1939, and feared the powerful price competition that its industries now practised as a result of low wages. The West's reservations were made clear by its slowness to conclude even imperfect trade agreements, and its constantly calling them in question.

All this was disquieting enough to tempt Japan to become 'neutralist like Nehru', and involve itself to the hilt with the economy of China and South-East Asia. At the same time, Japanese Socialists and Communists could not help fearing that when the US presence was removed, a number of social gains would be at risk, notably the parliamentary constitution of 1951 and, still more, the trade unions, which had been slow to develop in so docile a country, all the more so since large-scale capitalism accepted them very reluctantly. These conflicting concerns explained the results in the 1961 election, which gave only a 'routine victory' to the 'moderate liberals' – i.e. big business, which according to informed observers spent more than 5,000 million yen (100 yen = roughly 1 French franc) to 'save this last chance' and defeat the Socialists.

But the problem cannot be put off for ever, if only because Japan's prosperity imposes superhuman tasks involving continual tension. Tokyo (which with its suburbs had a population of 10 million in the early 1960s) is the most populous city in the world, and is growing so fast that it is already suffocating and thinking of filling in part of its bay to build on. Osaka has already set the example, to provide space for the heavy industries attracted there by the huge reservoir of labour. These details indicate how the grandiose and the precarious coexist in Japan's fabulous growth.

But it is in politics and in the broader field of civilization that the greatest uncertainties arise. Japan did not become a parliamentary democracy overnight, by American decree. It could not have been expected to; and a number of small, significant details confirm the fact. Japan's industrialists are still paternalistic, and wary. The nationalist aggressiveness of the past is by no means extinct. Japan has its violent and fanatical right-wing political parties, invoking the country's always fervent traditionalism. The Imperial family, humiliated by the victors in the Second World War, remains in place; and anyone rising against it would still risk being lynched. The eternal Japan of the past is far from dead or forgotten.

On 12 November 1960, the Socialist leader Inegiro Asanuma, 'the Mirabeau of Japan', spoke on television. He denounced 'the felony of the so-called Japan-American security pact, the aggressive tool of Yankee imperialism.' Millions of Japanese could hear and see him on the screen. Then they saw a student, still not seventeen years old, rush forward and stab him, his hands crossed on the dagger in the hold recommended by *judoka* to keep the blow straight. Three weeks later, the student committed suicide in his cell. The crime and the suicide produced a huge wave of emotion. Japan could not help admiring someone who was willing to die for his ideas, even if his crime was unworthy and repellent. It would be a mistake to see this attitude, and others, as a reflection of religious beliefs. By comparison with other countries, Japan is not particularly religious, not particularly concerned with the after-life. In this, it is the opposite of India. What dominates Japan is a certain code – in society, in education: a code of honour and civilization: *its* civilization.

III. European
Civilizations

We began our survey with non-European civilizations: Islam, Black Africa, China, India, Japan, Korea, Indo-China and Indonesia. There was an advantage in beginning at some distance from Europe, going abroad to realize more fully that Europe is not, or is no longer, the centre of the universe. Yet the contrast between Europe and non-Europe is fundamental to any serious attempt to explain the world as it is.

So we now return to ourselves, to Europe and its own impressive civilizations. We shall see them more objectively for having studied the others. And by Europe we mean not only the West and the Old World, but also the New: the Americas which derive directly from Europe, and the complex phenomenon of the Soviet Union, now the CIS, which despite what is often said has always remained European, even in its ideology.

PART I: EUROPE

To begin with, it may be useful to recall a few basic notions, obvious as they may seem:

That Europe is an Asian peninsula — 'a little cape': hence its double role. First, it is linked with the East by a broadening continental land mass. Once, this was difficult to cross; then, railways spanned it; now, air travel virtually ignores it. Secondly, Europe is linked, in all directions, with the seven seas. An essential part of its history is that of ships, convoys and the conquest of distant oceans. Peter the Great acted shrewdly when, on his first visit to Europe in 1697, he went to work in the shipyards of the extraordinary village of Zaandam, near Amsterdam. Already by the end of the fifteenth century, the expansion of Western Europe through the voyages of discovery decisively confirmed its double role.

That there are contrasts between East and West and between North and South: between the warm Mediterranean, the *Mare Internum* or internal sea of the South, and the cold 'Mediterraneans' of the North — the Channel, the North Sea and the Baltic. The contrasts are of every kind: in people, in diet, in tastes and in the age of the respective civilizations. Various 'isthmuses' link North and South — the Russian, the German and the French — and grow shorter as one travels Westward. To a geographer, Western Europe looks like the narrow end of a funnel whose broad end lies to the East.

That these East–West and North–South contrasts are as much

the result of history as of geography. Historically, the West looked to Rome and the East to Constantinople. The major separation, in the ninth century AD, was the decisive success of Sts Cyril and Methodius in preaching the Gospel and shaping the future of the East along Greek Orthodox lines. A later division occurred, this time between North and South, with the Protestant Reformation which, rather curiously, 'split' Christendom roughly along the ancient *limes* of the Roman Empire.

16. Geography and Freedom

===

The history of Europe has everywhere been marked by the stubborn growth of private 'liberties', franchises or privileges limited to certain groups, big or small. Often, these liberties conflicted with each other or were mutually exclusive.

Clearly, these liberties could exist only when Western Europe as such had taken shape and become relatively stable. Undefended, or strife-torn, it could afford no such luxury. Liberty and stability were inseparable.

Europe takes shape: fifth to thirteenth centuries

The accompanying maps, showing the major invasions of Europe, make it unnecessary to recount at length the accidents and catastrophes in the course of which the Western end of the European Peninsula gradually became a coherent whole. Europe's geographical area was defined in the course of a series of wars and invasions. It all began with the division of the Roman Empire, confirmed but not caused when it was partitioned on the death of Theodosius in 395 AD.

The Eastern Mediterranean has almost always been populated, endowed with a very old civilization, and engaged in a number of economic pursuits. From the very beginning of the Roman conquest, there was also a Western Mediterranean – a Far West, so to speak, which was primitive if not barbaric. There, by founding cities, Rome partially established a civilization which, if not always exactly Roman, was at least an imitation of the original.

Once the 395 partition had occurred, the *pars Occidentalis* underwent a series of disasters on the three frontiers surrounding it: in the North-East along the Rhine and the Danube; in the South on the Mediterranean; and in the West on the extensive 'ocean frontier' from Denmark to Gibraltar, which for a long time had been peaceful and secure. The new threats, and the reaction to them, defined and settled Europe's geographical area.

In the North-East, the double *limes* of the Rhine and the Danube could not resist the pressure of the Barbarians, fleeing from the Huns. In 405, Radagaisus led a Barbarian army into Italy as far as Tuscany. Soon afterwards, on 31 December 406, a horde of Barbarian peoples crossed the frozen Rhine near Mainz and overcame the Gallic provinces.

Once broken through, the door was not closed again until the defeat of the Huns at Châlons-sur-Marne in 451. After that, reconstruction was fairly rapid. Merovingian Gaul re-established the Rhine frontier, and it was soon shifted well to the East: the Carolingians maintained it far beyond the river, imposing their authority over the whole of Germany and pressing as far as 'Hungary', then under the Avars. Conversion to Christianity, in which the great St Boniface played a leading role, consolidated this huge Eastward advance. The West succeeded, in fact, where the caution of Augustus and Tiberius had failed.

From then onwards, Germany protected the Western world against the Asiatic East. It halted the Hungarian cavalry at Merseburg in 933, then crushed it at Augsburg in 955. The Germanic Holy Roman Empire derived its *raison d'être* from this protective role when in 962 it replaced the Carolingian Empire, which had been founded by Charlemagne on Christmas Day in the year 800.

No longer threatened, the Eastern frontier became a growth point, and was pushed Eastwards with the birth of Christian States

in Poland, Hungary and Bohemia, as a result of Germanic colonization in the eleventh to thirteenth centuries. Here, indeed, there
was relative peace until the huge Mongol invasion in about 1240,
miraculously halted on the edge of Poland and the Adriatic. Its
only victim was South-Western Russia.

In the South, a dangerous frontier was created by the first successes
of the Muslim conquest – all the more so because of successive
'defections', by North Africa (hitherto Christian), by Spain and
then by Sicily. In the West, the Mediterranean became a 'Muslim
lake'. The first effective reaction against this was the establishment
of heavy cavalry, which gave Charles Martel his victory at Poitiers
in 732. The result of that victory was the immense but short-lived
triumph of the Carolingians, whose influence was felt beyond the
Rhine, and as far as Saxony and Hungary.

But Islam was a powerful neighbour, and Christianity had to
undertake a difficult and dramatic campaign against it, inventing
its own Holy War, the Crusade. Crusading became interminable.
The First Crusade – not, obviously, the first war against Islam, but
the first that was collective, self-conscious and spectacular – was
launched in 1095. The last, which was by no means the end of the
struggle, was St Louis's expedition to Tunisia in 1270.

Although the Egyptian recapture of Acre in 1291 put an end to
these great Eastern adventures, the appeal of crusading continued
to trouble and excite emotions in the West, leading to unexpected
upsurges in the fifteenth and sixteenth centuries. In the seventeenth
century, again, there were 'the lonely Crusaders', as they were
called by Alphonse Dupront, an historian who has traced as far as
the nineteenth century this obsessive mystique. It can even be
detected as an element in the last days of colonialism.

Recent and very doubtful calculations have estimated that
between 1095 and 1291 the Crusades cost the West 4 or 5 million
men out of its small population of barely 50 million. No one can
say whether these figures are accurate. But in any case the Crusades
were a dramatic experience for Europe in the making, and its first

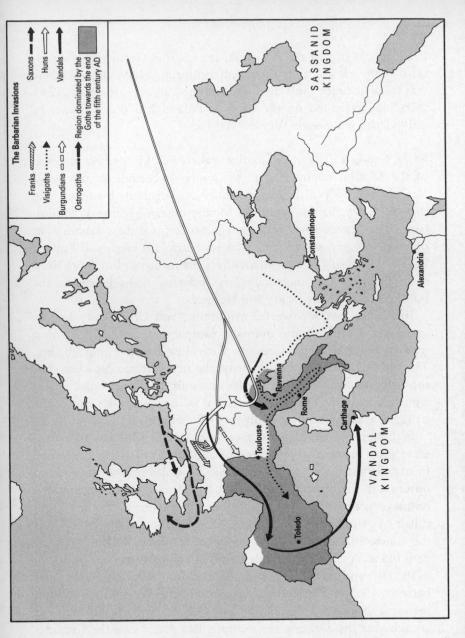

The Barbarian Invasions

Franks
Visigoths
Burgundians
Ostrogoths

Saxons
Huns
Vandals

Region dominated by the
Goths towards the end
of the fifth century AD

SASSANID KINGDOM

Constantinople

Alexandria

Ravenna

Rome

Carthage

Toulouse

Toledo

VANDAL KINGDOM

14. The great invasions (1)

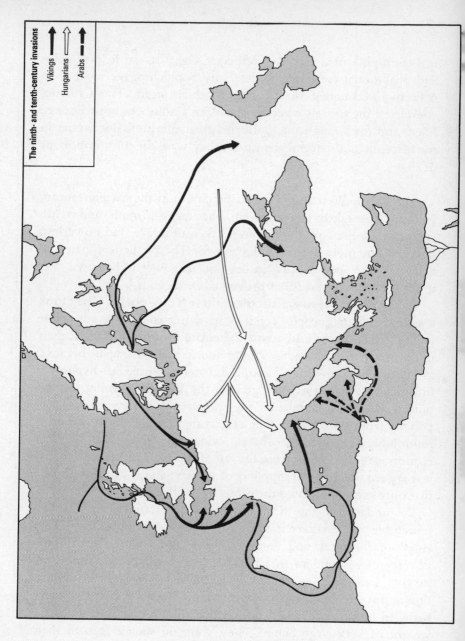

15. *The great invasions (2)*

real triumph – in at least two respects. The first was its precarious and provisional recapture of the Holy Sepulchre; the second, its definitive reconquest of the rich Mediterranean. The Crusades completed the process whereby the West's Southern borders were fixed; and for a long time, until the great maritime discoveries in the fifteenth and sixteenth centuries, they were the most important of all.

To the North-West and West, as far South as the Mediterranean, Europe was taken unawares, in the eighth, ninth and tenth centuries, by the Norse invasions – taken unawares and powerless, hence all the more distressed. Except for The Netherlands, Ireland and Italy, Europe was slow to develop seapower of her own. Yet in the long run the invasions proved advantageous.

To say this is not to defend the pitiless Norse pirates. They took a savage toll of Europe. Yet it is hard not to admire admirable exploits: their excursions across the entire breadth of Russia, their discovery of America – no sooner found than lost again because, as Henri Pirenne wrote, 'Europe did not yet need it.' Economic historians are still more indulgent to the Vikings, arguing that by putting back into circulation the treasures that they pillaged, especially from the Church, they reactivated capital which had been immobilized as precious metal, lying idle since the Western economic recession following the fall of Rome. The Vikings' thefts, it is argued, made them suppliers of money; and it was this money that once more stimulated the economy of the West.

To understand the first European civilization, one has to remember the disasters it suffered, imagine the appalling 'Dark Ages' of the ninth and tenth centuries and realize the primary poverty of a continent that had to struggle every day simply to survive. Lacking broad outlets, reduced to a subsistence economy, this impoverished Europe was in Marc Bloch's words 'a citadel besieged or rather invaded'; and at that time it could not bear the weight of very large States. They were no sooner formed than they collapsed or crumbled. Charlemagne's Empire, rapidly built, disintegrated not long after the death of the great Emperor in 814. The Germanic Holy Roman Empire fairly soon became a huge dilapidated mansion, and Western Europe split into countless tiny domains. The feudal system (based on the fief or, in Latin, the *feodum*) maintained units that were more theoretical than real within the various kingdoms of the West, some of which were very slowly modernized, like France, while others remained wilfully archaic, like the German Empire.

Yet this troubled world, oppressed from within and attacked from without, was already quite clearly a homogeneous civilization. Despite its diversity, it has to be called, in Lucien Febvre's words, a 'feudal civilization', which everywhere tackled the same major problems, in conditions and with solutions that were often alike. This civilization was born of many ethnic and economic strains, with repeated struggles, common beliefs, and above all the same difficulties which it tried to remedy.

Feudalism built Europe. In the eleventh and twelfth centuries, Europe achieved its first youthful vigour under a lively feudal regime – a particular and very original political, social and economic order, based on a civilization that was already at its second or third fermentation.

But how should this multi-coloured civilization be defined?

There could be no feudalism, in Europe or elsewhere, without the previous fragmentation of a larger political entity. In the present case, the entity in question was the huge Carolingian Empire – the first 'Europe', its name affirmed as such (*Europa, vel regnum Caroli*), which disappeared soon after the death of its great Emperor, whom a court poet hailed as '*pater Europae*', the Father of Europe.

Feudalism was the natural consequence of the Empire's fragmentation. In June 1940, when France was falling to the Nazis, a French officer had a dream: he wished that every unit of the army could by some miracle recover for a moment its autonomy, the right to act as it saw fit, without obeying the general orders which bound it to a High Command that was growing less and less effective and, without wishing to, was dragging everyone into the drift towards defeat. The feudal system was born of a similar reaction – but with the essential difference, among others, that the disaster which prompted it was less rapid than that of June 1940. It took several centuries for feudalism to be formed. Yet its very nature was both defensive and local. The castle on its mount, with the village or villages it protected huddled close to it: this was not an accidental or optional arrangement but a defensive weapon.

Nevertheless, feudalism was something else as well. It was a society based on relations between man and man, a chain of dependencies; it was an economy in which land was not the only but the most frequent recompense for services rendered. The lord received from the king, his suzerain, or from a lord of higher rank than himself, a fief (*feodum*) or lordship. In return, he had to supply a series of services, including assistance in four cases. 1. He had to pay his lord's ransom. 2. He had to pay when his eldest son was dubbed a knight. 3. He had to pay when his eldest daughter was married. 4. He had to pay when his suzerain went on a Crusade. In turn, the lord ceded parts or elements of his own lordship to those subordinate to him, whether minor lords or peasants. To the latter he granted land (we still refer to 'tenure' and 'tenement'), which the peasant tilled, paying a rent as money (quit-rent), as a portion of the crops (a tithe, or share-cropping), or as labour. The lord in return defended and protected the peasant.

This social pyramid, with its obligations, its rules and its allegiances, mobilizing economic, political and military strength, enabled the West to survive and to safeguard its old Christian and Roman heritage, to which it added the ideas, virtues and ideologies of the seigneurial regime (its own civilization).

Europe by then had forgotten the name of Europe. In practice, it had become a compartmentalized world, where all that mattered was the small region, the narrow, limited mother country.

Certainly, in these early days of Europe's life, there were very great advantages in each region's being able to grow at leisure in its own way, like a plant in the wild. Each was thus able to become a robust and self-aware entity, ready to defend its territory and its independence.

What is interesting is that nevertheless, despite this political compartmentalization, there was a convergence in Europe's civilization and culture. A traveller on a pilgrimage (to St James of Compostela, for instance) or going about his business, felt as much at home in Lübeck as in Paris, in London as in Bruges, in Cologne as in Burgos, Milan or Venice. Moral, religious and cultural values, and the rules of war, love, life and death were the same everywhere, from one fief to another, whatever their quarrels, their revolts or their conflicts. That is why there was indeed one single Christendom, as Marc Bloch said: there was what might be called a civilization of chivalry, of the minstrel and the troubadour, of courtly love.

The Crusades expressed that unity, because they were mass movements, collective adventures and passions, common to all the innumerable small-scale mother countries.

Liberty and rights: eleventh to eighteenth centuries

Imagine that it might be possible to assemble the sum total of our knowledge of European history from the fifth century to the present, or perhaps to the eighteenth century, and to record it (if such a recording were conceivable) in an electronic memory. Imagine that the computer was then asked to indicate the one problem which recurred most frequently, in time and space, throughout this lengthy history. Without a doubt, that problem is liberty, or rather liberties. The word liberty is the operative word.

The very fact that, in the twentieth-century conflict of ideologies, the Western world has chosen to call itself 'the free world', however mixed its motives, is both fair and appropriate in view of Europe's history during these many centuries.

The word liberty has to be understood in all its connotations, including such pejorative senses as in 'taking liberties'. All liberties, in fact, threaten each other: one limits another, and later succumbs to a further rival. This process has never been peaceful; yet it is one of the secrets that explain Europe's progress.

But the word 'liberty' has to be defined. Here, it means not so much individual liberty, the normal criterion in the 'free world' of today, but rather the liberty of groups. It is no accident that the Middle Ages spoke much more of *libertates* (liberties) than of *libertas* (liberty). In the plural, the word meant very much the same as *privilegia* (privileges) or *jura* (rights). Liberties, in fact, were the franchises or privileges protecting this or that group of people or interests, which used such protection to exploit others, often without shame.

These collective liberties were slow to develop to their full extent. Later, they were also slow to be brought within reasonable limits, or abolished. In general, they were stubbornly long-lived.

The peasants were among the first to begin to be liberated, but certainly the last to be fully free. It could even be argued that their liberation is still incomplete today. The peasant is free, in our sense of the term, only if no outside interest – seigneurial, urban or capitalist – comes between him and the land; if he is subject to no bond-service; and, finally, if his work is productive enough to feed him and leave a surplus, and if this surplus, should it reach the nearby market, does not simply make the fortune of some intermediary, but enables the peasant to buy, at the very least, what he needs.

That amounts to quite a few conditions. While European peasants in the past can be said to have enjoyed some advantages and even certain liberties, this is only by comparison with other peasants who were certainly much more downtrodden. Broadly speaking, European peasants benefited from every economic boom.

Thus it was at Europe's economic awakening, which began no earlier than the tenth century. At that time, agricultural production increased everywhere: not only in the 'new' countries of the North, where three-year crop rotation spread from the Germanic lands and from Poland, but also in the regions of the South (Italy and Southern France), where two-year rotation (one year of cereals, one year lying fallow) remained the rule.

This rise in production was linked to the increase in population and to the growth of towns. The latter was an essential precondition for greater output; but the towns benefited from it too.

From the eleventh century onwards, and as long as economic growth continued, the lot of the peasants rapidly improved. Hitherto, they had been bound to the soil as serfs. 'After having belonged to the man of the sword and to his rival the man of the Church, the land fell into the possession of the man of the plough ... It was abandoned to any workers who sought to take it over, in exchange for a very small annual interest paid to the former owners.' This quit-rent system applied 'at a time when land was abundant and people were scarce, so that human labour was more sought after than land' (d'Avenel). There can be no doubt that over large areas (but not all) the peasants enjoyed a certain degree of freedom. 'We were free by the twelfth century,' the historian Henri Pirenne liked to say, referring to peasants in the West.

But this liberation was neither complete nor universal; nor, above all, was it definitive. A certain equilibrium existed, it is true, and was widespread. In practice, it left the land with the peasants, who were lords and masters in their own domains, and who could pass on or sell their holdings. Their money rent, moreover, was fixed quite early on, which in the long term was to their advantage, since over the centuries coinage went on losing its value, so that rents established once and for all eventually became derisory in real terms.

These advantages, however, had no very firm legal basis. The lord continued to enjoy superior rights over the land, and could recover his oppressive powers if the time, the place and the circumstances were right. The history of peasant revolts is the proof of that: the *jacquerie* in France in 1358, Wat Tyler's rebellion of workers and peasants in 1381, the sudden vast rebellion of the German peasants in 1524–5, or – in France again – the repeated peasant uprisings in the first half of the seventeenth century. Every time, these risings, these 'general strikes', were put down. Only the ever-present threat of them helped the peasants to retain part of the liberties and advantages that they had earlier acquired.

These privileges were called into question again, throughout Europe, with the capitalist economic development of the modern world. Beginning in the sixteenth century, and still more in the seventeenth, capital faced economic recession: finding no easy outlets elsewhere, it turned back to the land. A large-scale 'seigneurial' reaction – as much middle-class as aristocratic – spread outwards from the towns, large and small, into the surrounding countryside. Properties of a new type (farms, 'granges', 'metairies' – the words vary from region to region, and do not always bear their modern meanings) were established, preferably with a single tenant and at the expense, above all, of peasant smallholdings. Their owners were usually imbued with a genuine capitalist spirit: they looked for productivity and profit as moneylenders. The peasants became indebted to them, so much so that one fine day their holdings might be seized, or the land would become subject to one of the innumerable registered rents paid to the rich, contracts for which abounded in notaries' files. Everything at that time was to the peasant's disadvantage – even the tenancy contracts which called for payment in kind, in wheat, and not always in cash.

Although this reaction was detectable all over Europe, it was particularly tragic in Central and Eastern Europe – in Germany beyond the Elbe, in Poland, Bohemia and Austria, and even in the Balkans and in Muscovy. As the sixteenth century ended, there was established throughout these regions (some of them 'still barbarian') what historians more and more tend to call 'the second serfdom'. The peasants were enmeshed once more in a seigneurial regime, this time worse than that of the past. The lord was the head of the farm, the entrepreneur, the wheat merchant. To meet the growing demand for grain, he forced his peasants to increase the amount of bond-service they owed him – five days a week in

Bohemia, where peasants could till their own land only on Saturdays, while in Slovenia, where it had been ten days a year in the fifteenth century, it was six months a year by the end of the sixteenth. Bond-service was performed on the land held directly by the lord (the home farm or 'reserve'). This system, which in the East continued until the nineteenth century, was no doubt largely responsible for the extra backwardness of these areas by comparison with the West.

In the West, in fact, under a relatively liberal regime, changes favourable to the peasants began in the eighteenth century – in France, with John Law's banking system, which sparked off everything (including rural drunkenness). The French Revolution completed these developments, by freeing peasant holdings, at a stroke, from the feudal dues they laboured under. This example was copied elsewhere during the revolutionary and Napoleonic Wars.

The towns were motors that never stopped. They bore the brunt of Europe's first advance, and were rewarded by their 'liberties'.

The long decline of the West resulted, in the tenth century, in the near-ruin of the towns, which barely survived.

But when the economic tide turned, with the boom of the eleventh to thirteenth centuries, the towns enjoyed a remarkable renaissance. It was as if, in this great recovery, the towns prospered more rapidly than the lumbering territorial States. These hardly began to show any modern characteristics until the fifteenth century at the earliest: but the towns broke through the fabric of the feudal States they grew in, as early as the eleventh and twelfth centuries. Modern, and ahead of their time, they signalled the future. Indeed, they were the future already.

Of course they were not always, nor had they at first been, strictly independent. But great free cities emerged early in Italy, which was then the most advanced country in Western Europe. The same was true of The Netherlands, 'that second Italy'. Venice, Genoa, Florence, Milan, Ghent and Bruges were already 'modern' cities at a time when the kingdom of Louis IX was still typically 'medieval'.

Following these cities, governed by Dukes, Doges or Consuls, countless lesser towns fought for and won the right (by virtue of their charters) to govern themselves and look after their finances, their legal system and the land they possessed.

In general, complete liberty could be achieved only through material prosperity sufficient to enable certain specially favoured towns not merely to guarantee their economic survival but also to provide for their external defence. These were city–states. Only a few towns attained that status; but all of them relied on their trade and the work of their craft guilds to give them a certain independence and a right to private liberties.

The guilds worked both for the local market and for distant trade. There can be no doubt that the urban economy was able to prosper as it did only because it largely overflowed its local confines. In the fifteenth century the town of Lübeck – the most important of that huge trading group of cities between the Baltic and the Rhine known as the Hanseatic League – had links with the whole of the known world. The same could be said of Venice, Genoa, Florence or Barcelona.

In these privileged centres, primary capitalism triumphed as a result of distant trade. It was the beginning of the age of the Merchant Adventurers. They supplied raw materials and labour, and ensured the sale of industrial products, while the guild masters became more and more wage-earning employees, like their 'companions' in this *Verlagsystem* – an untranslatable word used by German historians to denote, very roughly, production to order. The merchants were the leading lights of the *popolo grasso* or rich bourgeoisie. Their underlings, the 'thin people', often staged rather unsuccessful revolts – in Ghent, for example, or in Florence, where the violent revolution of the Ciompi broke out in 1381.

These internal conflicts in the manufacturing towns betokened social tensions which were already class struggles: '*taquebans*' was the word used by Beaumanoir when speaking of the Flanders artisans, who staged what we should now call strikes for higher wages. Gradually, a further gulf appeared between the guild masters and the 'companions'. The latter, held back by the need to make costly and difficult 'masterpieces' in order to secure promotion, formed groupings, associations and 'lodges', and frequently travelled from one town to another. They were in fact the first working-class proletariat.

Such proletarians, however, if they were citizens, were privileged by virtue of their citizenship – at least as long as the great days of the independent or semi-independent cities lasted.

Was there, as Max Weber thought, a special typology applicable to medieval European towns – 'closed towns', as he called them? It is true that they were exclusive, refusing to give any consideration to those outside their walls. Nothing was superior to them: there was no equivalent of the efficient despotism exerted by the Chinese mandarins as agents of the State. The countryside around them was often under their control: the peasants, who could not be citizens, were obliged to sell their grain exclusively to the town markets, and were often forbidden to own looms – unless, that is, the town required their services. The system was certainly very different from that of the city–states in the ancient world, which had been politically open to the country around them: the Athenian peasant, at that time, had been a citizen with the same status as an inhabitant of the town.

No wonder the rights of citizenship were granted only grudgingly, except when the town urgently needed to increase its population. In 1345, for example, shortly after the Black Death, Venice promised citizenship to anyone who would settle there. Normally, the 'Signoria' was less generous. It recognized two types of citizenship. One, known as *de intus*, created only second-class citizens; the other, known as *de intus et de extra*, conferred full rights, and was jealously scrutinized by an aristocracy anxious to safeguard its own privileges. It took fifteen years' residence in Venice to acquire *de intus* citizenship, and twenty years for the other. Distinction was also made, on occasion, between 'new' and 'old' citizens. A decree of 1386 laid down that only 'old' Venetians had the right to trade with the German merchants based in the city.

Egoistic, vigilant and ferocious, towns were ready to defend their liberties against the rest of the world, often with very great courage and sometimes without any concern for the liberties of others. Bloodthirsty wars between cities were the forerunner of the national wars to come.

The liberty of the cities was soon threatened, however, when modern States, which had been slower to develop, grew more powerful in the fifteenth century. Then, the towns were often brought to heel by the State, which could both confer privileges and impose sanctions. Hence some serious crises, such as that of the Castile *comunidades* in 1521, or the crushing of Ghent by Charles V in 1540. There were also, inevitably, compromises, since modern monarchy needed the towns' support. They had to submit to authority, renouncing some of their privileges in order to safeguard others. In compensation for giving up certain liberties, they gained access to the new world of the modern State – greater trade, profitable loans, and also in certain countries such as France the purchase of public office. A territorial economy grew up, replacing the urban economy which had preceded it. But this territorial economy was still controlled by the towns. Alongside the State, they continued to rule the roost.

So-called 'territorial States' (i.e. modern States) were latecomers to Europe. The ancient form of kingship, based on blood links and on relations between suzerain and vassal, took a long time to disappear – or at least to be transformed. The turning-point came in the fifteenth century, and at first almost exclusively in areas where the urban revolution had been least marked. Neither Italy nor The Netherlands, and not even Germany, which had had so many free, rich and active towns, was the chosen terrain for this new type of government. Modern monarchy developed above all in Spain, France and Britain, with rulers of a new kind: John II of Aragon (the father of Ferdinand the Catholic), Louis XI and the Lancastrian Henry VII.

These territorial States were served by 'functionaries' – or, to avoid anachronism, let us say 'officers': all of them servants of the State, like the 'jurists' trained in Roman Law, and the great Secretaries of State, the 'Ministers'.

The States were aided also by the loyalty of the masses, who saw the Monarch as their natural protector against the Church and the nobles. In France, the monarchy was able to rely on popular devotion until the eighteenth century: the historian Jules Michelet called it 'a religion of love'.

The modern State arose from the new and imperious needs of war: artillery, battle fleets and larger armies, made combat ever more costly. War, the mother of all things – *bellum omnium mater* – also gave birth to the modern world.

The modern State soon recognized no authority higher than its own – neither the Holy Roman Empire, increasingly ignored by its own Princes, nor the Papacy, whose moral and political authority had once been immense. Every State wanted to be isolated, uncontrolled and *free*: reasons of State became the ultimate law. (The expression *'raison d'Etat'*, now amounting to the *ultima ratio*, first appeared in a speech that Cardinal della Casa made to Charles V on the subject of an ignoble incident during the capture of Mantua in 1552.) This was a stage in the evolution of Western political systems away from traditional kingship, with its paternalist and mystical overtones, and towards the modern monarchy of the jurists.

Several writers were quick to note the emergence of States which acknowledged no higher authority – *'superiorem non recognoscentes'*, in the words of the fourteenth-century jurist Bartolo de Sassofarrato. But they were well in advance of political events. In France, it was not until 1577 that Jean Bodin advanced the theory of the State's undivided sovereignty, in his *Traité de la république* – 'republic' in this case meaning nothing more specific than the Latin *res publica*, the body politic. For Bodin, the sovereign State was above all laws except Natural and Divine Law: there was nothing superior to it on the human scene.

Just as the Pope never ties his hands, as canon lawyers say, so the sovereign Prince cannot tie his own hands, even if he wishes. Hence we see, at the end of edicts and ordinances, these words: For such is our pleasure. They are there to make it clear that the laws of the sovereign Prince, while they are based on good and sufficient reasons, nevertheless depend solely on his pure and simple will.

The will of the sovereign invaded the State. '*Das Ich wird der Staat*' – 'The I becomes the State' – wrote a German historian. This is the famous dictum '*L'Etat, c'est moi*' generally attributed to Louis XIV, but also ascribed at least once to Elizabeth I of England. Although Spanish monarchs called themselves 'Catholic Kings' and the French 'Very Christian Kings', they on occasion opposed the Papacy, defending the liberties of the Gallican Church or the temporal and spiritual interests of Spain. These were signs of changing times. There had of course been precedents for such action: but now it was becoming systematic, natural, and a matter of course.

As the modern State tightened its grip, so European civilization became 'territorial' and national. Hitherto, it had been urban, maturing in many small, diverse and privileged cities. Now the Golden Century in Spain (which really extended from 1492 to 1660) and the Great Century in France were both coterminous with entire States.

At the heart of these larger civilized entities, an important role was played by the capital cities, sustained by the presence and the expenditure of the Government, and hence raised to the previously unknown rank of super-cities. Paris and Madrid acquired their lasting reputations; London virtually became England. The weight and the life of the whole State began to centre on these urban monstrosities, henceforward unrivalled instruments of luxury, machines for creating both civilization and misery.

One can easily picture the immense movement of people, capital and wealth that these great States engendered – and the redistribution of liberties that was involved, some being abolished or maintained on sufferance, others encouraged or invented afresh.

Specially privileged towns included Marseille, the *de facto*
headquarters of trade with the Levant; Lorient, founded in 1666
and soon accorded the monopoly of trade with India; and Seville,
which in 1503 had obtained the far greater privilege of exclusive
rights to trade with America, 'the India of Castile'. In 1685, however, Seville's monopoly was transferred to Cadiz.

Certain liberties were secured because the State could not do
everything or retain all its rights. In France, for example, from the
death of Colbert in 1683 until the Revolution in 1789, the absolut-
ist State gradually grew less effective; and the bourgeoisie, which
bought 'offices' of state, acquired a sizeable share of political
authority. It was against the King that provincial liberties were
asserted. The social privileges of the clergy, the nobility and the
Third Estate were encrusted in the structure of the French State. It
could not get rid of them, and hence it missed the 'enlightened'
reforms of the eighteenth century elsewhere.

Even those countries which at that time won political freedom
did no more than hand responsibility for the State to a powerful
group of privileged persons. This was the case in the United
Provinces, with their middle-class businessmen; it was also the case
in Britain after the Glorious Revolution of 1688. The British
Parliament represented a double aristocracy, Whig and Tory,
bourgeoisie and nobility – certainly not the country as a whole.

While 'liberties' and privileges were accumulating, what became
of individual liberty? This question makes no sense if 'the freedom
of the individual' means what it does today – everyone's freedom
as a person, simply by virtue of being a person. It took a long time
for the concept of that kind of freedom to become clear. At the
most, therefore, one can only inquire whether individual liberty
was increasing *in fact*, or not. The answer has to be both contradictory and pessimistic.

The intellectual ferment of the Renaissance, and that of the
Reformation in so far as it raised the principle of individual
interpretation of revealed truth, laid the bases for freedom
of conscience. Renaissance humanism preached respect for the

greatness of the human being as an individual: it stressed personal intelligence and ability. *Virtù*, in fifteenth-century Italy, meant not virtue but glory, effectiveness, and power. Intellectually, the ideal was *l'uomo universale* as described by Leon Battista Alberti – an all-rounder himself. In the seventeenth century, with Descartes, a whole philosophical system stemmed from *Cogito, ergo sum* (I think, therefore I exist) – *individual* thought.

The philosophical importance thus attached to the individual coincided with abandonment of traditional values. This was encouraged by the progressive establishment, in the sixteenth and seventeenth centuries, of an effective market economy, hastened by the arrival of precious metals from America and by the growth of credit facilities. Money upset and weakened the old rules governing such economic and social groups as town authorities and craft or merchant guilds, all of which at the same time lost some of their usefulness as well as their former rigidity. In daily life, therefore, the individual rediscovered a certain freedom of choice. But, at the same time, the apparatus of the modern State imposed a new order which strictly limited such freedom. The individual owed a duty to society, and had to respect privileges and those who enjoyed them.

One of Descartes's letters states the problem clearly. If, in theory, everyone is free, a self-sufficient individual, how then will society survive, and what rules will it follow? It was Princess Elizabeth, Princess Palatine, daughter of James I, who put the question; and on 15 September 1645 Descartes replied as follows.

Although every one of us is a person separate from the others, and hence endowed with interests that are in some ways distinct from those of the rest of the world, one must always reflect that one could not survive alone, and that one is in effect one of the parts of the universe, and more particularly still one of the parts of this earth and one of the parts of this State, this Society, this family to which one is linked by residence, by oath and by birth. One must always serve the interests of the whole of which one is a part, in preference to those of one's own person in particular.

In the name of these 'interests of the whole', the seventeenth century undertook a strict 'training programme', not only for the poor, but for all 'useless' elements in society – all those who did not work. True, there was a worrying rise in the numbers of the poor, owing partly to the increase in the population throughout the sixteenth century and to the economic crisis which began at the end of that century and grew worse in the seventeenth. The growing numbers of the poor were reflected in begging, vagrancy and theft, all of which led to repressive reactions. In 1532, the Paris Parlement had the capital's beggars arrested 'to force them to work in the sewers, chained together in pairs'. Compare also how the town of Troyes treated its indigent population, in 1573.

But these were transitory measures. Throughout the Middle Ages, the poor, the vagrants and the mad had been protected by the right to hospitality and alms to which they were entitled in the name of God, because Christ had sanctified poverty by one day wearing the garments of the poor – and the poor might always turn out to be God's emissaries. The whole spiritual movement personified by St Francis had exalted the mystical value of Lady Poverty, holy poverty. And in any case the unfortunate, the mad, the derelicts of society tended to wander from one town to another: most people were eager to send them on their way rather than keeping them within the city walls.

Hence a certain form of liberty, at least in the physical sense, was open to a peasant who fled from his lord to find another who was less oppressive, or to take refuge in the town. The same was true of a soldier in search of a recruiting officer, or of an immigrant leaving for better wages or for the New World and the illusion of a better life. There were also the unemployed, the inveterate vagrants, the beggars, the mental defectives, the handicapped and the thieves – kept alive without work by charity or crime, and therefore in some senses free.

All these people, protected hitherto under the shadow of the Almighty, became in the seventeenth century the enemies of a society that was urban, already capitalist, attached to order and efficiency, and shaping the State in the same spirit to the same ends. Throughout Europe (in Protestant as well as Catholic areas), the poor, the sick, the unemployed and the insane were pitilessly locked up (sometimes with their families) alongside delinquents of every kind. It was what Michel Foucault (who studied the phenomenon in connection with madness in early modern times) called 'the great imprisonment' of the poor − legalized detention organized by a painstaking administration. This also made it possible not only to put away a debauched or prodigal son or a spendthrift father, at the request of their families, but also, with a *lettre de cachet* from the king, to incarcerate a political rival.

A very large number of establishments were founded for these purposes: hospitals, charitable workshops, workhouses, *Zuchthäuser*. Whatever they might be called, they were simply draconian barracks, with forced labour as well. In France, after the decree establishing the Hôpital Général in 1656, which at the same time set in motion this whole new social policy, almost 1 per cent of the Paris population found itself locked up! The severity of this repression was not moderated until the eighteenth century.

In a world where liberty already existed only for those with privileges, the seventeenth century thus helped to impose real restraints on the elementary freedom to abscond or become a vagrant − the only freedom which until then had been allowed to the poor. At the same time, as we have seen, peasant privileges were curbed. Shortly before the 'Enlightenment', Europe plumbed the depths of misery.

There was one solitary corrective to this gloomy picture. Liberty, which so few could attain, remained in Europe that ideal towards which people's thoughts, and also their history, slowly progressed. It was a major trend in the history of Europe, as was shown by the many peasant revolts in the seventeenth century, by the no less frequent popular uprisings (in Paris in 1633, in Rouen from 1634 to 1639, in Lyon in 1623, 1629, 1633 and 1642), and by political and philosophical developments in the eighteenth century.

The French Revolution itself did not succeed in establishing complete liberty, any more than we can boast of having established it today. True, the Revolution abolished feudal privileges on the night of 4 August 1789; but peasants still had to face creditors and landlords. In 1791, by the Le Chapelier law, it equally abolished corporations; but that left workers at the mercy of their employers. It took a century before trade unions became legal in France, in 1884. Nevertheless, the 1789 Declaration of the Rights of Man and of the Citizen remains a landmark in the history of freedom, a fundamental fact in the development of European civilization.

Liberty, or the quest for equality? Napoleon believed that the French did not want liberty, but sought equality – equality before the law, the abolition of feudal rights – in a word the end of private liberties and privileges. From liberties to liberty: that phrase encapsulates one of the fundamental thrusts in the history of Europe. The still abstract, theoretical notion of liberty, which developed from the Renaissance and Reformation until the French Revolution, grew more powerful when it was spelled out in the Declaration of the Rights of Man and of the Citizen. With the advent of liberalism, it became a doctrine.

Thenceforward liberty – in the singular – became an explicit factor in world affairs and in history. It was invoked – legitimately or not – by almost all the ideologies and claims advanced in the nineteenth century by the very varied movements covered by the artificial term 'liberalism', which is highly equivocal because it has so many meanings.

In one of its definitions it denotes a political doctrine, seeking to increase the power of the legislative and the judiciary and limit that of the executive. In this sense it is opposed to authoritarianism. In another definition, liberalism is an economic doctrine with the triumphant slogan *'laissez faire, laissez passer'*, seeking to prevent the State's intervening in economic relations between individuals, classes and nations. Finally, liberalism is a philosophical doctrine, calling for freedom of thought and maintaining that religious unity is not a *sine qua non* for social or national unity. This necessarily implies the idea of tolerance and of respect for others and for the human individual, as expressed in the ancient tag *Homo homini res sacra*.

So liberalism is more than 'the doctrine of a party . . . a climate of opinion'. Grappling with the many varied problems of the nineteenth century, it tackled innumerable tasks and faced innumerable obstacles. In Germany and Italy, it identified with nationalism: was not the primary liberty that had to be won that of Nation itself? In Spain and Portugal, it clashed with the monstrous power of a solidly entrenched *ancien régime*, supported by the Church. In Britain and France, by contrast, it virtually achieved its political objectives. Slowly and imperfectly, the liberal, constitutional State took shape, embodying fundamental freedom: freedom of opinion, of the press and of parliament; individual liberty; and the gradual extension of the right to vote.

At the same time, throughout the first half of the nineteenth century, liberalism served as a screen for the political emergence of a new propertied class, the business aristocracy and bourgeoisie. 'Outside a small circle, the individual whose rights liberalism defended with so much zeal was still only an abstraction, unable to benefit fully from these advantages.' This was as true in Britain, with its Conservatives and Liberals, its old and its new money, as in France at the time of the Restoration and the July Monarchy. The propertied class which called itself liberal was immediately opposed to universal suffrage and to the masses in general. Yet how could such political egoism be sustained in the face of industrial society, whose appalling realities so soon appeared? Economic liberalism, which presupposed equal competition among individuals, was no more than a pious fiction. The more time went by, the more the enormity of that fiction became obvious.

In fact, this first, 'bourgeois' form of liberalism was above all a defensive action, by no means disinterested, against the aristocratic *ancien régime* – 'a challenge to the vested interests that the traditions of half a millennium had made sacred'. In this way it came between the aristocratic society of the *ancien régime* which it had destroyed and an industrial society in which the proletariat was beginning to demand its rights. In other words, the bourgeoisie's espousal of liberty was not all that it seemed to be: it was much more like the old struggles for liberties pursued by groups that were really seeking privileges.

The revolutions of 1848 were a crucial landmark for liberty. In France, it was then that universal suffrage was established, whereas in Britain the key electoral reform took place in 1832. Henceforward, with or without the franchise, the only form of liberalism that could survive was political liberalism, in principle open to all classes of people. Alexis de Tocqueville and Herbert Spencer, each in a different way, noted this development and foretold the triumph of the masses, which both feared. But although liberalism thus gathered new strength, it soon clashed with the ever more direct and powerful thrust of Socialism, as well as with such prophets of authoritarianism – some nowadays even call it 'fascism' – as Carlyle or Napoleon III.

The political scene was flanked, therefore, on the one side by the up-and-coming revolution of Socialism in all its many varieties, and on the other by a counter-revolution which knew neither its own name nor how far it might go. Between the two, liberalism continued its life, formed its many governments, and practised its bourgeois wisdom and egotism. It recovered its fire a little, in France, only in its battles with the Church. The Liberals were henceforth aware of their limitations, and even began to doubt their own cause. In 1902–1903, the sensible *Revue de métaphysique et de morale* published a series of articles on 'The Crisis of Liberalism', concerned particularly with the monopoly of education. But the real and final crisis came a little later, between the two World Wars.

But who would dare to argue that liberalism, virtually banished now from active politics, and intellectually devalued, is really dead today? It was more than a political epoch and more than the contrivance or camouflage of a particular class. For Western civilization it was a high ideal; and, however much it may have been tarnished or betrayed, it remains part of our heritage and our language: it has become second nature. Any breach of individual liberties affronts and incenses us. Politically, too, in the face of authoritarian or technocratic States, and societies which are always coercive, a certain defiant and anarchic liberalism, invoking the individual and his rights, continues its leavening work in the West and in the world.

17. Christianity, Humanism and Scientific Thought

═══

The spiritual and intellectual life of Europe was always subject to violent change. It favoured and created divisions and discontinuities, and indeed dramas, always with the aim of building a better world.

Yet these *coups de théâtre* should not distract attention from the tenacious continuity of Europe's thought and civilization, evident throughout all its successive phases, from the *Summa* of St Thomas Aquinas to the *Discours de la Méthode* of René Descartes, and uninterrupted by the Renaissance, the Reformation and the French Revolution itself. Even the Industrial Revolution, a decisive break with the past, did not affect all aspects of Europe's life and thought.

Christianity

All religions evolve. All in their different ways, however, are separate worlds, with their own loyalties, their own permanence, and their own frames of reference.

Western Christianity was and remains the main constituent element in European thought – including rationalist thought, which although it attacked Christianity was also derivative from it. Throughout the history of the West, Christianity has been at the heart of the civilization it inspires, even when it has allowed itself to be captured or deformed by it, and which it contains, even when efforts are made to escape. To direct one's thoughts against someone is to remain in his orbit. A European, even if he is an atheist, is still the prisoner of an ethic and a mentality which are deeply rooted in the Christian tradition. He remains, one might say, 'of Christian descent', in the same way that Montherlant used to say that he was 'of Catholic descent' although he had lost his faith.

Already widespread in the Roman Empire, Christianity became the official religion as a result of the Edict of Constantine in 313, three centuries after the birth of Christ. The Roman Empire comprised all the Mediterranean countries and, in Europe, several outside the lands of the olive and the vine. This was the region inherited at the outset by the new triumphant religion – the 'Christian vineyard', to adapt a phrase of Paul Valéry's, using a play on words ('*aire*' meaning both 'area' and 'threshing-floor') to mark Christianity's links with the land, with bread, wine, wheat, the vine and even holy oil – all characteristic of the Mediterranean starting-point from which Christian belief was later to spread so widely.

In this way, before the ordeal of the fifth-century invasions and the disasters following Islam's victories between the seventh and the eleventh centuries, Christianity had time to adapt itself in some degree to the Roman world. It established its hierarchy there; it learned to distinguish clearly between the temporal – 'the things which are Caesar's' – and the spiritual; and it overcame the ferocious dogmatic disputes which arose not only from the subtleties and the agility of the Greek language and the Greek mind, but also from the need to define the theological bases of Christianity, to give it shape, and to decide where it led.

This slow and difficult task fell to the first Councils (of Nicaea in 325, Constantinople in 381, Ephesus in 431, Chalcedon in 451 and so on), and to the Fathers of the Church. These included the Apologists, who before Constantine were embattled against paganism, and then the Dogmatics, who defined Christian doctrine as distinct from the teachings of dissident sects. St Augustine was not the last in this succession (which some believe to have continued into the eighth and even the twelfth century); but he was by far the most important to the West. A Berber, born in 354 at Thagaste (now Souk-Ahras) in Africa, he died as Bishop of Hippo (later Bône, now Annaba) in 430, while the Vandals were besieging the town. The exceptional brilliance of his works (*The City of God, The Confessions*), his contradictory nature, his desire to bring together faith and intelligence, classical and Christian civilization, the old wine and the new — these deliberate efforts made him in some ways a rationalist. For him, faith came first: but he nevertheless declared '*Credo ut intelligam*' — 'I believe in order to understand.' He also said '*Si fallor, sum*' — 'If I am mistaken, I exist' — and '*Si dubitat, vivit*' — 'If he doubts, he is alive.' It would be misleading to see in these remarks a very distant anticipation of Descartes's '*Cogito ergo sum*': but they clearly have affinities with it. Posterity undoubtedly concentrated its attention on St Augustine as a theologian, and on what he wrote about predestination. But Augustinianism gave Western Christianity some of its colour and its ability to adapt and debate — if only by insisting on the vital need to embrace the faith in full awareness, after deep personal reflection, and with the will to act accordingly.

It was not a hesitant or infant Church that was overtaken by the apocalyptic disasters of the barbarian invasions. In that dark fifth century, it had already taken shape like the Empire itself, as the civilization of the ancient world which it had taken over, and which it was to save, in some respects, by saving itself.

The Church saved itself in an imperilled world, but only by dint of countless heroic feats. It had to convert the new arrivals; convert those peasants who were still barely Christian or who too readily neglected the teaching of the Church; convert the inhabitants of the new regions occupied by the West. It had to maintain a hierarchy linked to Rome and to the Bishop of Rome, the Pope — at a time when feudalism was splitting the West into tiny districts and many bishoprics. It had to fight hard battles, of which the most famous was that between the Empire and the Papacy, ended but not settled by the Concordat of Worms on Investitures in 1122. Altogether, this was an immense and laborious task, a repetitive and tedious campaign of persuasion, marked by defeats and new beginnings in which everything was called in question, over and over again. But the development of monastic life, with the Benedictines and the Cistercians, led to the material and spiritual colonization of the countryside in the eleventh and twelfth centuries, while the preaching of the friars, Dominican and Franciscan, in the thirteenth century, made a powerful impact on the towns.

Every century had its challenges and battles. In the thirteenth century, there was the struggle against the Cathari; in the violent fifteenth century, the great debate between the Councils and the Papacy at the Councils of Constance and Basle. In the sixteenth century came the explosion of the Reformation, then the Counter-Reformation led by the Jesuits, the conversion of the New World and the authoritative pronouncements of the Council of Trent (1545–63). The seventeenth century saw the Jansenist challenge. The eighteenth produced a more determined struggle against adherents of a new kind of atheism, less discreet than that of the seventeenth-century 'libertines'. That battle had not been won when the century ended: it had barely been started when the French Revolution broke out.

Finally, apart from the hostility of adversaries with conscious and articulate ideologies, the Church had constantly to deal with a regular, monotonous process of de-Christianization, which was often no more than a crude lapse from civilization back to barbarism. Wherever communications were difficult, off the beaten track (for instance in the Alps or on the edges of Europe, in Mecklenburg as late as the thirteenth century, or in Lithuania and Corsica in the fifteenth and sixteenth centuries), old pagan cults sprang up again at every opportunity. In one place it might be the cult of the snake, in another that of the dead and the stars. So numerous were the superstitions, and so tenaciously rooted in folklore, that the Church often had to content itself with clothing them in light ecclesiastical garb.

In these battles, Christianity used every kind of weapon: education, preaching, temporal power, art, religious drama, miracles and the popular cult of the saints, which was sometimes so intrusive that the Church's servants themselves took fright and reacted against it. In 1633, in Lisbon, two Capuchins felt obliged to admit that 'St Anthony of Padua seems to be the God of Lisbon . . . The poor ask for alms only in his name and . . . invoke only him when they are in danger. For them, their St Anthony is everything: he is their magnetic North and, as the preacher says, the Saint of needles; if ever a woman looks for her needle, she finds it with the help of St Anthony.' The fashion for St Anthony even crossed the sea. A century later, a French traveller in Brazil reported 'prodigious devotion' to him.

Popular superstition, in fact, was always liable to undermine or compromise religious life from within, distorting the very bases of the faith. When it did so, everything had to be started again.

When St John of the Cross settled with two companions at Duruelo in Castile, where St Teresa had located the first monastery of the Reformed Carmelites, it was to lead the most frugal monastic life amid the snows of winter, but not in any cloistered sense. 'They often went out barefoot along the worst of paths to preach the Gospel to the peasants as if to savages . . .' This proves, if proof were needed, that conversion still remained necessary, even in a Christian country.

The work of Christianity thus had to be done on two different levels. One was that of intellectual life, where it had to defend itself against adversaries who were sometimes well-intentioned but never lacking in numbers. The other was that of the masses, whose hard life and isolation too easily cut them off from religious feelings and simple faith.

Christianity ebbed and flowed: it had successes and setbacks and long periods of stagnation. We can trace these only crudely, from outside, in so far as the daily experience of religion, and its reality for the average person, too often remains unknown. Very broadly, however, its general evolution is unmistakable.

From the tenth to the thirteenth century, Christianity was advancing vigorously everywhere. Churches and monasteries still stand, in many cases, as witnesses: the whole Church was carried along by a powerful movement that was also economic and social: Europe was active, full of life, and expanding rapidly. Then came the Black Death and a brutal, catastrophic decline. Everything suffered, even the progress of Christianity, during the long series of disturbances and strife that historians call the Hundred Years' War (1337–1453). Its repercussions went far beyond the main belligerents, France and Britain: they extended, in fact, to the whole of the West.

In the second half of the fifteenth century, a new religious resurgence occurred, affecting the whole of Europe, which was returning to peace but also to serious disquiet. From about 1450 to about 1500, there was what Lucien Febvre has called 'a time of trouble'. Some historians have simply labelled it 'the pre-Reformation'; but this is a misnomer, since the anxiety that was then general was in no way bound to lead to the 'Protestant', protesting attitude of the Reformation. In those countries that remained faithful to Rome, the same religious anxiety led to another kind of reform, a Catholic reform, which most historians call 'the Counter-Reformation'. Here again, the word is not particularly apt.

However that may be, the sixteenth and seventeenth centuries were a time of keen religious passions, of fierce spiritual disputes whose vehemence should not surprise us. Such for instance was the sharp quarrel between the rigour of the Jansenists and the simpler, laxer, but very human ethic of the Jesuits at the time of Saint-Cyran, of the Gentlemen of Port-Royal, of Mme de Sévigné, of Racine, and of Pascal.

With the eighteenth century, there was a great reverse. This time, material progress did not serve the cause of the Church. It went with a scientific and philosophic movement which on the contrary opposed the Church in the name of progress and reason.

★

Humanism and humanists

European thought is inconceivable except in the context of a dialogue with Christianity, even when the dialogue is sharp and the dispute violent. This context is essential to the understanding of humanism, one of the fundamental aspects of Western thought.

To begin with, a question of vocabulary: the word humanism is ambiguous, and can be hazardous unless we at once define its usage and its civic status. It is a learned expression, coined by German historians in the nineteenth century (and, to be precise, in 1808). Pierre de Nolhac, the author of *Petrarch and Humanism* 'has claimed the honour of having introduced it into the official language of the French University in 1886, in his course of lectures at the *Ecole des Hautes Etudes*'. So the word is a relative neologism, and therefore lends itself easily to personal interpretations, for good or ill. Until then, only the word 'humanists' had been used, referring to a precise group of men in the fifteenth and sixteenth centuries who had taken that name themselves.

But the word humanism did not remain restricted to these 'humanists' and to the 'spirit of the Italian and European Renaissance' that they embodied. It meant that, but also many other things – so many that it brought to present-day usage a huge wealth of connotations. An inquiry in 1930 turned up expressions such as '*new* humanism', '*Christian* humanism', '*pure* humanism' and even '*technical*' and '*scientific* humanism'. A survey today would produce similar results, proving that if the word was once a learned or technical expression, it has tended to become popular and take on new meanings, and therefore corresponds to living questions and concerns.

In historical studies, we find references to the humanism of the twelfth century (underlying scholasticism), to that of the Renaissance or the Reformation, to the humanism of the French Revolution (by which is often meant its originality and many-sidedness) and even to 'the humanism of Karl Marx or Maxim Gorky'. One can only wonder what this series of 'humanisms' has in common, apart from the need and the obvious eagerness to treat them all as a family of problems.

Perhaps we may reasonably borrow from Augustin Renaudet, the historian of Tuscan and European humanism, a broad definition which seems to cover this very general sense.

The name of humanism can be applied to an ethic based on human nobility. Turned towards both study and action, it recognizes and exalts the greatness of human genius and the power of its creations, opposing its strength to the brute force of inanimate nature. What is essential remains the individual's effort to develop in himself or herself, through strict and methodical discipline, all human faculties, so as to lose nothing of what enlarges and enhances the human being. 'Reach towards the highest form of existence,' said Goethe at the beginning of Part Two of *Faust*, 'by dint of uninterrupted effort.' Similarly, Stendhal said to Eugène Delacroix on 31 January 1850: 'Neglect nothing that can make you great.' Such an ethic based on human nobility requires of society a constant effort to embody the most highly perfected form of human relations: an immense feat, an immense cultural achievement, an ever greater knowledge of humanity and of the world. It lays the foundations of individual and collective morality; it establishes law and creates an economy; it produces a political system; it nourishes art and literature.

This eloquent definition ought to be adequate. But it does not stress powerfully enough that sense of the movement which is exaggerated, on the other hand, by Etienne Gilson's curt definition: Renaissance humanism, he declared in substance, was the Middle Ages 'not plus humanity but minus God'. The phrase is unfair and too extreme; but it does indicate the natural inclination, conscious or unconscious, of all humanist thought. Humanism frees and magnifies humanity, diminishing the role of God even if not completely forgetting it.

In a certain sense, too, humanism is always against something: against exclusive submission to God; against a wholly materialist conception of the world; against any doctrine neglecting or seeming to neglect humanity; against any system that would reduce human responsibility . . . It is a perpetual series of demands – a manifestation of pride.

Calvin had no illusions. 'When we are told to rely on our own strength and ability, are we not being raised to the uppermost end of a reed which cannot bear our weight and immediately breaks, so that we fall down?' Calvin was not one of those who placed their first faith in humanity.

For the humanist, it was quite otherwise. His faith, if he had a faith, had to accommodate his confidence in humanity. And it is in the light of this inveterate tradition of European humanism that one can understand the remarks of the sociologist Edgar Morin when he left the Communist Party: 'Marxism, my friend, has studied economics and the social classes. That's marvellous, my friend. But it forgot to study humanity.'

Humanism is all drive, an embattled march towards the progressive emancipation of humanity, with constant attention to the ways in which it can modify and improve human destiny. Its history has been complex and fitful, marked by checks and reverses and by those obvious contradictions which pervade all of Europe's past.

Europe seems always to have been anxiously seeking some solution to its problems and difficulties other than those already to hand. Hence an almost morbid quest for what was new, difficult, forbidden and very often scandalous – something on which the West is a very rich source of information. For want of space, we shall limit our account to three exceptional but significant cases: Renaissance humanism, its near contemporary Reformation humanism and, much later, in the eighteenth century, the passionate humanism of the French Revolution.

Renaissance humanism was a dialogue of Rome with Rome, between pagan Rome and Christian Rome, between classical and Christian civilization. It was certainly one of the most fruitful and continuous debates that the West has ever known.

It was a matter of living, or living once more, with the classical past. The short, decisive final sentence of Machiavelli's *Dell'arte della Guerra* has often been quoted: 'This country [Italy] seems born to revive dead things.' But if these *cose morte* were so eagerly brought back to life, it was a proof that life had need of them, and that they were within reach, and not dead at all.

To tell the truth, pagan Rome never died out in the West. Ernst Curtius, in a technically meticulous study, has shown how amazingly tenacious the civilization of the Lower Empire proved to be, and how the West relied on it to an unheard-of degree for its literary themes, its ways of thought, its metaphors, and even its clichés.

It was natural for Christian Europe to accept this day-to-day contact with ancient Rome, because there was no alternative, no rival civilization to tap. Equally, Christianity had acquiesced in such coexistence before the Roman Empire fell. In the second century, St Justin had declared that any noble thought, 'wherever it comes from, is the property of Christians'. St Ambrose said: 'All truth, whoever its interpreter may be, comes from the Holy Spirit.' Only Tertullian asked: 'What have Athens and Jerusalem in common?' But his voice raised barely an echo.

Yet, while the classical heritage had entered into the life, language and habits of thought of the Western Middle Ages, classical literature and its poets, philosophers or historians had often ceased to arouse the passions or even the interest of intellectuals. While Latin remained a living language, Greek was now almost unknown. In the finest libraries, manuscripts of classical works lay forgotten in the dust. The humanists sought these texts everywhere, to re-read them, edit them and add their impassioned commentaries, so as to restore to public honour the works and the languages of classical antiquity – Greek and Latin – with which they henceforth lived.

No one, perhaps, expressed it better than Machiavelli, during his second period of exile, in 1513, in the evening of his life. He was then living among peasants and woodcutters . . .

Night falls, and I return to my dwelling. I go into the library, and as I cross the threshold I cast off my everyday clothing, covered with filth and mud, and put on the costume of the royal court . . . Thus honourably clad, I enter the classical court of the Ancients. They welcome me warmly, and I feast on the nourishment for which I was born and which is mine *par excellence*. There I have no qualms at speaking with them, and inquiring about the motives for their actions. And they, by virtue of their humanity, duly reply.

Renaissance humanism was marked by such reading, such continual conversation. Rabelais and Montaigne were humanists of this sort: their books, full of memories of their reading, are the living proof. Beside every humanist, one can recognize – with a smile of complicity or malice – the Ancient who leads him by the hand, and thereby explains or exposes him. Erasmus of Rotterdam, now known as the Prince of humanists, was called by his detractors 'Lucian'. Other 'Lucianists' included Rabelais and Bonaventure des Périers; while Machiavelli 'was' Polybius.

It is not easy to assign dates to this broad current of thought. Our artificial word 'humanism' and the term 'Renaissance' (invented, almost as artificially, by Jules Michelet and Jacob Burckhardt) tread on each other's toes. The two phenomena overlap in both time and space.

Avignon was undoubtedly the starting-point of humanism and, with it, the Renaissance. The town came to life with the return of Petrarch in 1337; and thanks to the presence of the Popes it was for a long time the most 'European' and the most luxurious city in the West. Even after the Papacy had returned to Rome in 1376, the Anti-Popes enabled it to retain its luxury and lustre. However, it was in Florence that the Renaissance fully established, later, its 'cultural hegemony', which lasted at least until the death of Lorenzo the Magnificent in 1492, and even until the city's capture by Clement VII and the Imperial forces of Charles V, in 1530. These chronological limits, 1337 and 1530, are certainly applicable to the bulk of the phenomenon which affected not only Italy, but the West as a whole. The last great humanist, Erasmus, born in Rotterdam in 1437, died in Basle in 1536. But these two long centuries cannot be fully understood unless the historical net is cast more widely, backwards beyond 1337 (an indeterminate date in any case) and forwards beyond 1530.

Backwards into the past, because the transition from the Middle Ages to the Renaissance was not the total break that used to be imagined. The Renaissance was not at the opposite pole from medieval philosophy, despite the gibes that humanists hurled at scholasticism. 'Fifty years ago,' wrote one historian, in 1942, 'the Middle Ages and the Renaissance looked as strikingly different as black and white or night and day. Then, one argument compounding another, the frontier between the two has become so confused that to distinguish between them one begins to need a compass.'

Forwards beyond 1530 or 1536, because it is not at all obvious that after the death of Erasmus (the hero of all liberal-minded people today) the civilization of the Renaissance lost its freedom and died under the cold blast of the religious wars that dominated the next century and more.

They certainly interrupted the triumphant advance of the Renaissance. But where the realities of civilization are concerned, what has lasted two centuries cannot be destroyed overnight. In the long term, the humanists won some important points. They won in the realm of education, where classical antiquity has remained an essential element almost to the present day: we are only now beginning to move away from it. But above all, since the humanists, Europe has never lost the confidence in human ability and intelligence which they proclaimed and which has remained the greatest inspiration in the life and thought of the West.

Humanism was the work of 'a few élite spirits' in relatively narrow circles – passionate Latinists, less numerous but no less passionate Hellenists, and Hebraists like Thomas Platter, the rope-maker, or Pico della Mirandola. But their influence was by no means confined to a few cities or brilliant princely courts like that of Francis I. The humanists were scattered all over Europe, and linked by copious correspondence: the marvellous Latin letters of Erasmus fill a dozen octavo volumes in the edition by P. S. and H. M. Allen and H. W. Garrod. All Europe was affected by the humanist phenomenon: Italy to begin with, but also France, Germany (without forgetting the special role of Bohemia), Hungary, Poland, The Netherlands, Britain ... Lists of names could be quoted to prove the point (as could, in France, the establishment of 'Royal Lectors') in fact, supernumerary professors – commissioned by Francis I to teach subjects banned by the University; later, they became the nucleus of the Collège de France.

Was Renaissance humanism an attack on Christianity or not? Must the movement be seen as heading straight towards atheism and irreligion? Or should Machiavelli, Rabelais or Montaigne at least be hailed as authentic precursors of free thought?

To do so is perhaps to judge the Renaissance too much by present-day criteria. That it turned aside from the traditional teaching of scholasticism and theology is certain. Equally certainly, it relished classical literature that was wholly pagan, and the thrust of its thinking was the exaltation of humanity. But this does not necessarily mean that humanism opposed either God or the Church.

The conclusion of Lucien Febvre's detailed and closely argued study of Rabelais's work is that it was impossible, or at the very least extremely difficult, for anyone in Rabelais's day to embrace with confidence philosophic atheism. The mental equipment of the period scarcely allowed such thoughts: it lacked the key words, the conclusive arguments, and the indispensable scientific support. The Renaissance did not neglect scientific research, but it by no means gave it top priority.

In truth, no valid conclusion can be reached unless one is prepared to weigh and weigh again the thoughts and feelings of the time, rediscover the atmosphere of those distant days, and re-examine one by one the over-hasty accusations of atheism made by the polemics of contemporaries or the passion of historians. In almost every case, the judge will encounter insoluble errors and ambiguities.

The dialogue by Lorenzo Valla, *De Voluptate* (1431), which caused a scandal at the time, is a dispute in Ciceronian Latin between Epicureans and Stoics. Since the latter had been in vogue hitherto (with Petrarch, Salutato and Poggio), the dialogue sought to redress the balance a little by favouring the Epicureans. But at the end of what was a purely literary debate, the author reappeared, to reaffirm the supernatural order of Christianity.

Hypocrisy, one might imagine today. But it would be a facile rewriting of history if we refused to recognize that atheism was forged much later, on the anvil of solid materialistic science. In the sixteenth century, as a general rule, the denial of God scarcely entered into people's concerns, desires or needs.

Nor should Machiavelli be too hastily accused of being a pagan because he criticized the priests and the Church 'who have made us irreligious and evil', or because he reproached Christianity for 'having sanctified the humble and the contemplative, and having made humility the supreme virtue . . . whereas the religion of classical antiquity exalted greatness of soul'. It might be fairer to blame him for having learned too well the lesson of the terrible times he lived through, and removed ethics from politics – an operation that has yet to be reversed . . .

In the same way, let us be clear about the Academy founded by Lorenzo de' Medici. Its basis was Neo-Platonist, and it sided with Plato's idealism against Aristotelian philosophy – perhaps seeking a compromise between classical antiquity and Christianity. But the fact that Pico della Mirandola, who attended it, made a speech about the dignity of humanity – *De dignitate hominis* – in no way prevented him, at the end of his too short life, from hoping to go and preach the Gospel, 'crucifix in hand, barefoot, in the cities, towns and countryside', or from having himself buried in his robes as a Dominican of the Third Order. His was one example, among a hundred others, of what has been called 'religious humanism'. Even the case of the Paduan Pompanazzi, who for some was an obvious atheist, remains for others undecided. That of Bonaventure des Périers, the strange author of the no less strange *Cymbalum Mundi* (1537–8), was studied in a brilliant book by Lucien Febvre, published in 1942. He concluded that if the character of Mercury in these dialogues represents Christ, as seems certain, then this time Christ is under attack, and atheism has to be suspected. We should neither ignore nor exaggerate the importance of Bonaventure's book, which is a very unusual instance in the literature of its time.

Philippe Monnier, a devoted historian of the Florentine *quattrocento*, claims that the humanists, fascinated by the prestige of the Ancients, 'copied them, imitated them, repeated them, adopted their models, their examples, their gods, their spirit and their language' and that 'such a movement, pushed to its logical extreme, would tend towards nothing less than the elimination of the Christian phenomenon'. According to our logic, perhaps. Perhaps not according to that of the fifteenth and sixteenth centuries. 'It would be . . . senseless,' wrote the sociologist Alexander Rustow,

to look for such antagonism, given that the triumph of classical antiquity over the Church . . . was almost complete and was taking place within the Church itself. Did Rome not develop as a flourishing centre of the Renaissance, and were the Popes not initiators of the movement? It was Alexander VI who executed the humanists' enemy in Florence, Savonarola, burned on 20 May 1498. What was more, the classical antiquity now revived in people's minds was tolerant. Greek philosophers had attended the feasts and services of the gods, whether they believed in them or not. Why should their disciples attack a Church which showed so little hostility to them? It was Erasmus who exclaimed: 'St Socrates, pray for us!'

The Renaissance distanced itself from medieval Christianity much less in the realm of ideas than in that of life itself. It could perhaps be called a cultural, not a philosophic betrayal. Its atmosphere was one of lively enjoyment, relishing the many pleasures of the eye, the mind and the body, as if the West were emerging from a centuries-long period of Lent.

The Renaissance bears witness to a sociology, a psychology of joy. Rarely in history did people feel so powerfully that they were living in fortunate times. 'The *Memento mori* of the Middle Ages was replaced by a *Memento vivere*.' The contemplation of death and the *danses macabres* of the late fifteenth century disappeared as if by magic, as if the West had 'parted' (in Michel Foucault's sense) or separated itself in spirit from meditation about death. The change can be traced in the many successive *Artes moriendi*, tracts on how to die a good death. In them, death gradually ceased to be a calm, celestial journey to a better life: it became earthly, with all the fearful signs of bodily corruption – a human death, the supreme ordeal that humans have to face. No one any longer willingly said with St Augustine: 'We here below are travellers longing for death'; but at the same time no one any longer believed that 'this life is rather death than life, a kind of hell'. Life recovered its value and importance.

It was on earth that people had to build their kingdom; and this new conviction coloured the emergence of all 'the positive forces in modern culture: freedom of thought, mistrust of authority, the victory of intellectual education over the privilege of birth (i.e., in terms of the *quattrocento*, the victory of the concept of *humanitas* over that of *nobilitas*), enthusiasm for science, and the deliverance of the individual . . .' (Nietzsche).

The humanists were well aware of this new ferment of ideas. 'Without doubt, this is the golden age,' declared Marsilio Ficino (1433–99). In 1517, Erasmus said almost the same thing: 'We must wish the century good luck: it will be the golden age.' In his famous letter of 28 October 1518, to the Nuremburg humanist Willibad Pirkheimer, Ulrich von Hütten wrote: 'What a century! What literature! How good it is to be alive!' One dare not add the example of Rabelais's fictitious Abbaye de Thélème, because it is so very well known . . . And yet!

No one would deny that this acute awareness of humanity's vast and varied potential prepared the way, in the fullness of time, for all the revolutions of modern times, including atheism. But the humanists were much too busy organizing their own kingdom to think of contesting that of God.

From the first third of the sixteenth century, the impetus and exhilaration of the Renaissance began to be curbed. 'Sombre people' gradually filled the Western stage. Like all periods of joy, of bright sunshine, like all great periods of good fortune, real or supposed, like the century of Alexandria's brilliance, like the century of Augustus, like that of the Enlightenment, the perfection of the Renaissance was only short-lived.

Protestant humanism was the source from which the great flood of the Reformation flowed between the fifteenth and the sixteenth centuries. A key date was 31 October 1517, when Luther's Ninety-five Propositions were displayed on the doors of the Schlosskirche in Wittenburg.

The Reformation was accompanied by the appalling excesses of the Wars of Religion. These began in Germany in 1546, the year when Luther died, and ended more than a century later, in 1648. Meanwhile, they spread to other countries; and everywhere they left behind them widespread ruin. Tardy and more or less enduring compromise agreements were signed: the Peace of Augsburg in 1555, the Edict of Nantes in 1598, the Letter of Majesty in Bohemia in 1609. But the Reformation, unlike Renaissance humanism, quickly became a mass phenomenon, and thousands of men and women, to defend their faith, had to face civil war and violent repression (as in the Netherlands at the time of Philip II, or in France after the Revocation of the Edict of Nantes in 1685, and at the time of the Cévennes insurrection). The alternative was exile, either in the New World or in a country that upheld their faith, following the random principle of *Cujus regio, ejus religio*.

All this violence died down in the eighteenth century, and sometimes earlier. Protestantism survived it; and today it colours a large part of the Western world, notably Anglo-Saxon, Germanic

16. Europe's three Christianities

and Nordic countries, with its own particular variety of humanism.
It is not easy, however, to identify the precise nature of Protestant
humanism, since there is not one Protestant Church, but many,
each expressing the different views of different people. Nevertheless,
they all belong to the same family, especially when they are contrasted
with their neighbour, the Catholic West.

What interests us here is not the Reformation in itself, but the legacy it left to modern Europe. So we shall not linger over the traditional history of Reformation Protestantism. That can be studied, if necessary in the useful summary supplied by Emile Léonard.

Within a matter of twenty years, two types of Protestantism – two long 'waves' – followed each other. One was dominated by the passionate activity of Martin Luther (1483–1546); the other was led by the thoughtful and authoritarian John Calvin (1509–64). The two men were almost totally different. Luther was a peasant from the frontier regions of Eastern Germany. There was something direct, strong and natural in his rustic spiritual rebellion – what Nietzsche called a 'peasantry of the spirit', *ein Bauerstand des Geistes*. To denounce the abuses, absurdities and complications of the Church; to dispel uncertainty by staking everything on redemption by faith ('just people are saved by their faith'); to be content with spontaneous, emotional views without seeking to reduce them to meticulous order – that was the clear and simple message of the young Luther. It was romantic and revolutionary. 'God will not put up with this for long!' he cried: 'We are not living in yesterday's world, where people were hunted and herded like game!' True, Luther could not for ever sustain this attitude, which antagonized the rich and powerful. In 1525, he had to distance himself from the German peasants between the Elbe, the Rhine and the Alps, who had mounted a revolt which was partly inspired by his teachings.

Yet he remained at the opposite pole from Calvin, the city-dweller, the cool intellectual, the patient, tireless organizer, the lawyer who must always follow his logic to the end. Luther met Predestination as revealed truth: Calvin treated it as a mathematical formula and deduced the results. If the elect had always been predestined for salvation, was it not their vocation to rule the others? This was the logical conclusion that Calvin applied in Geneva in 1536–8 and 1541–64, with a firm hand but invoking the spirit of humility. It was what Oliver Cromwell did in the British Isles in the harsh days of the Puritan Revolution.

Such were the two major strands in Protestantism. They prevailed in different places, but they had points in common: the break with Rome and with the cult of the Saints, the abolition of the regular clergy, the reduction of the sacraments from seven to two (Eucharist and baptism), although with lingering disagreement about the Eucharist. Nor should one forget what for simplicity's sake (for a complete list would be long) one can call eccentric or marginal forms of Protestantism, such as the early humanist varieties (Zwingli in Zurich, Oecolampadius in Basle, Henry VIII in Britain) or the 'pietistic' Protestantism of the much persecuted Anabaptists.

The frontier between the Catholic and Protestant worlds is still a tangible feature of European civilization. Was it fixed only by the fortunes of war?

Like the rings of a tree-trunk, Europe grew in successive layers. Its oldest wood – the heart of the tree – was what had been conquered (and civilized) by the Roman Empire, when it stretched West and North as far as the Rhine and the Danube in one direction and the British Isles in the other (although here it held, insecurely, only part of the whole, mainly in the South-East). Beyond these frontiers, European civilization was a late arrival, after the fall of the Roman Empire: here, the sapwood was young and thin. Medieval Europe colonized the surrounding territory (in the best sense of the term), sending missionaries and building churches. The abbeys and bishoprics established there by distant Rome laid sturdy foundations.

Is it coincidental that this old frontier of the Roman Empire, the frontier between ancient Europe and the new, recently 'colonized' Europe is broadly speaking the same as that which divided the Catholic from the Protestant world? Of course, the Reformation had its purely religious aspects: it was one outcome of the rising tide of religion that was evident throughout Europe, making the faithful ever more aware of the abuses and disorders in the Church, and the limitations of worship that was too matter-of-fact, too much a matter of gestures rather than true devotion.

These feelings were common to Christendom as a whole. But the old Europe, no doubt more attached to the religious traditions linking it so closely with Rome, maintained that connection, while the new Europe, younger and more mixed, less firmly tied to the religious hierarchy, broke completely away. Already one can sense here something of a national reaction.

The later development of the two worlds has often lent itself to what might be called sectarian pride. The virtues of Protestantism have been credited with the rise of capitalism and of scientific thought, i.e. with that of the modern world. But the respective positions of Protestantism and Catholicism can be explained more reasonably against the background of economic and general history. In fact, it is hard to see anything in Protestantism that would make it intellectually superior – or inferior – to the Catholic world. On the other hand, it has certainly affected European culture, bringing to it a new and original contribution of its own.

To make clear what that contribution was, we must distinguish between the early, militant Protestantism of the sixteenth century and the victorious, established Protestantism of the eighteenth.

Inaugurated under the banner of liberty and revolt, the Reformation soon lapsed into the same degree of intransigence of which it accused its enemy. It built a structure as rigid as medieval Catholicism, 'in which everything was subordinated to the scale of spiritual values derived from revelation: the State, Society, education, science, economics and Law'. At the top of the scale was 'the Book', the Bible, and – as its interpreters – the Protestant Church and State. The latter (it might be a Prince or a city) enjoyed the *jus episcopale* of old.

Needless to say, this system by no means produced the religious liberty for which people had originally fought. Order, strictness and the iron hand: these were the watchwords of the early Protestant Churches, whether at Basle or at Zurich. The Reformers might be followers of Erasmus; but they had no hesitation in drowning the dreadful Anabaptists. There were similar massacres in The Netherlands. It was paradoxical. That the 'Papists' should have hunted down, hanged, butchered or drowned the unfortunates who denied the Holy Trinity or the divinity of the Son, and simultaneously attacked the Church, the State and the wealthy – that, if by no means charitable, at least had a certain logic. But on what grounds did the Reformation inflict the same persecution? One example was the *tragoedia serveta*. Michel Servet, a Spanish Protestant physician, was arrested one day in Geneva on his way out of church. Accused of pantheism and of denying the Trinity, he was tortured and burned at the behest of Calvin, who had long had him under surveillance. In 1554, Sebastian Castellio (1515–63), a 'Savoyard' humanist and apostle of liberal Reform, protested against this in a moving and indignant pamphlet ad-dressed to the ruler of Geneva, whom he had earlier served and liked. He was indignant because no one felt more keenly the errors and crimes of the triumphalist Reformation. 'There is almost no sect,' he wrote, 'which does not regard others as heretics; with the result that, if you are thought to be right in one city or region, in the next you will be thought a heretic. So much so that if anyone today wants to live, he must have as many religions as there are cities or sects – just as anyone travelling from one country to another has to change his money from day to day, because what is valid here becomes valueless elsewhere.' Himself, Castellio determined to remain faithful to the free interpretation of Scripture. 'As for the Anabaptists,' he said, 'it is up to them to decide what they do with what they sense, think or write about the word of God.'

Castellio's remained an isolated voice. He died in poverty, sur-rounded by a few loyal followers. But in the seventeenth century, at the time of the disputes between the strict Calvinists and the Arminian or Socinian dissidents, his works were republished in Amsterdam, one of them bearing the significant title *The Candle of Savoy*. Indeed, Castellio the Savoyard became one of the harbingers of the new course that Protestantism finally took.

Later Protestantism favoured liberty of conscience. Dogmatic rigour gradually lessened, especially in the eighteenth century, perhaps with the waning of active pressure from Catholicism and the energetic Counter-Reformation. But Protestantism also evolved of its own accord towards greater freedom of conscience, in the same spirit as the Enlightenment, and mainly under the influence of scientific progress. As always, it is very difficult to disentangle cause and effect. Did Protestantism, by returning to its spiritual origins and to the free study of the Scriptures, help Europe towards greater independence of mind? Or was the evolution of Protestantism itself part of the general evolution of philosophical and scientific thought in Europe? Both possibilities may have been combined, each influencing the other.

It cannot be denied that Protestantism, unlike its Catholic rival, fitted into the evolution of the great liberal century. But it has to be admitted, too, that countries of Catholic tradition and training such as France were also leading spirits in that evolution.

At all events, Protestantism now inclined towards the free study of Scripture, historical criticism of sacred texts and a kind of deist rationalism. In so doing, it put an end to its internal squabbles; and that was what mattered. All the marginal sects, hitherto spurned as suspect – the Puritans in Britain, the Anabaptists in Germany and The Netherlands – now flourished and even multiplied. The Anabaptists, under the name of Mennonites, prospered in Britain, went to America, founding a colony in Providence, Rhode Island, and became a powerful Protestant sect in the United States. At the end of the seventeenth century there reappeared – descendants of the 'Inspired' of the sixteenth century – the group that called itself the Society of Friends, known more generally as the Quakers. In 1681 the Quaker William Penn founded the colony of Pennsylvania. There was a similar upsurge in Germany, with the pietism of the pastor Philip Jakob Spener, a protégé of the Elector of Brandenburg (who later, in 1701, became the first King of Prussia, Frederick I). Spener was also involved in the foundation of the influential University of Halle in 1681. In the middle of the eighteenth century, the whole of Lutheran Germany was stirred up by his disciples. But none of these movements was as powerful as, in Britain, the Methodism of John and Charles Wesley and George Whitefield.

There would be little point here in enumerating these successful sects, other than to show how freely Protestant thought flourished in a religious movement no longer subject to any strict theology. 'Theology is no longer identified with religion,' wrote a Protestant university teacher, Ferdinand Buisson, in 1914; 'one must pass so that the other may endure.' This, fundamentally, is what now distinguishes Protestant from Catholic society. The Protestant is always alone with God. He can, so to speak, work out his own religion, live it, and remain in keeping – conform – with the religious world. More than that, he can choose from among the many sects that which solves, without pain, his own personal problem. One might almost say that each of the different sects corresponds to a different social group or class.

As a result, Protestant society is untouched by the schism between lay and confessional matters that marks modern Catholic societies, where everyone has to choose between a certain mental obedience or a break with the Church – a community to which one either belongs or not. With Catholicism, spiritual conflicts are in that sense public: one is obliged to state one's position. In Protestant society such conflicts certainly exist, but they take place in private. Hence the series of differences in behaviour and attitudes which draw an imperceptible but indelible line between the Anglo-Saxons and Catholic Europe.

Europe has always been, and still is, revolutionary. All its history confirms that fact. But at the same time it has always been, and still is, endlessly counter-revolutionary. Here again, what matters is not the series of revolutionary movements in themselves, but rather their effect on the future – which we shall call 'revolutionary humanism'. By this unfamiliar phrase we mean the human content and the intellectual 'legacy' of the Revolution. Others refer to 'the revolutionary mystique' or 'the revolutionary spirit'. We refer, of course, to the French Revolution, the only one with European and world significance before the Russian Revolution of 1917.

Revolutionary movements and the Revolution

Until the Russian Revolution, the French Revolution of 1789 was always referred to – in France, at least – as 'the Revolution', implying that it was the first and only one. In fact, however, a number of revolutionary movements had occurred earlier, in a Europe that was tense, restive and unwilling to put up with the worst. But historians have been reluctant to call them 'revolutions'.

They would scarcely give that name, for example, to the numerous peasant revolts that we have already noted in various parts of Europe between the fourteenth and seventeenth centuries. And it is often in a particular sense that the word 'revolution' is used, for instance about struggles for national liberation: by the Swiss cantons, definitively freed in 1412; by the United Provinces, finally victorious in 1648; by the American colonies of Britain, the future United States, in 1774–82; by Spanish America between 1810 and 1824. It can also be applied to the emergence of the Scandinavian countries – Sweden, Norway and Denmark – securing their independence either peacefully or by brute force. All these were no doubt reactions against the modern State: but they were still more against foreigners – an important nuance.

A 'real' revolution is always against a modern State: that is essential. And it always comes from within, with a view to the State's reforming itself. Before 1789 in Europe (if we ignore the failures of the Catholic League and the Fronde), only the two English revolutions had been worthy of the name – the first involving a violent Civil War (1640–58), the second peaceful (the 'Glorious Revolution' of 1688). But the French Revolution, which overthrew from within one of the strongest States in the West, had quite different repercussions. Between 1789 and 1815 it spread throughout Europe; and the memory of it acquired, for the world as a whole, the value of a powerful symbol, seen afresh by every generation and always able to arouse new passions.

The power of that symbol is still great. Travelling in the USSR in 1958, a French historian was surprised to find that when his Soviet colleagues said 'the Revolution', they were referring to the French Revolution, and not their own. The same historian, teaching at the University of São Paulo, Brazil, in 1935, echoed Albert Mathiez by pointing out that most of the so-called 'giants' of the 1792 Convention were simply mortal men and in some cases rather ordinary. His Brazilian students reacted at once, as if at sacrilege, and one of them declared: 'We, you know, are waiting for the French Revolution.'

So the 1789 revolution lives on throughout the world, even when it might have been supplanted, as a myth, by the October Revolution in Russia. In France, the Russian Revolution tends totally to dominate the trade-union and revolutionary press, in so far as it relates to the practical realities of the day. But the fervour still aroused, even fairly recently, by 1789 can only really be appreciated by those who remember the monstrous uproar and excitement that greeted the Sorbonne lectures by Alphonse Aulard (who died in 1928) and the eagerness of those who went there to hear Albert Mathiez (d. 1932) or Georges Lefebvre (d. 1960). The survival of the Revolution in the political and ethical thinking of Europeans affects their arguments and attitudes, even when their attitudes are hostile to it.

There were two, three or four French Revolutions. Like a multi-stage rocket today, the Revolution involved several successive explosions and propellant thrusts

It seemed at first to be a moderate, 'liberal revolution', although involving some dramatic episodes like the Fall of the Bastille and the Terror. This first Revolution developed rapidly, in four successive stages: an aristocratic revolt (the Assembly of the Notabilities in 1788), a bourgeois revolt 'by lawyers', as has been said (the meeting of the States General), then an urban and a peasant revolution, both of which were decisive.

A second and brutal Revolution followed, after the declaration of war against Austria on 20 April 1792. 'It was the war of 1792 that led the French revolution astray,' wrote Alphonse Aulard. It is true; and the occupation of The Netherlands after Jemappes made the conflict inevitable. We should recognize also that by turning France into a modern nation (and before the song and dance of the Federations that dramatized the fact), the Revolution affirmed and revealed its strength and prepared the subsequent explosion. This second phase, which was as violent within as without, ended with the fall of Robespierre on 27–28 July 1794 (9–10 Thermidor in the Year II).

The third Revolution (if the word is still appropriate) took place between Thermidor and Brumaire (from 28 July 1794 to 9–10 November 1799) and covered the last months of the Convention and the whole of the Directoire. The fourth Revolution included the Consulate, the Empire and the Hundred Days (1799–1815).

Napoleon certainly continued the Revolution, stabilizing and mastering it, but adding to the uncertainties of its broad future the dramatic insecurity of his own career and the fragility of an illegitimate regime which had to justify itself, come what may, by uninterrupted successes. After his defeat at Austerlitz, the Emperor Francis II, applauded by his loyal subjects, remarked to the French ambassador: 'Do you think, Sir, that your Master would be welcomed thus in Paris if he had lost a battle such as I have lost?' This sally bears comparison with the exclamation of a French royalist who was fascinated by Napoleon's glory. 'What a pity,' he said, 'that he was not a Bourbon!'

If the French Revolution had maintained its original intentions, it would have resembled 'enlightened despotism'

In this eventful history, only the second Revolution involved dramatic violence: it was an unexpected deviation from the norm. It has often been argued that, if the revolution had not drowned in blood in the spring of 1792, there could have been an almost

peaceful, moderate revolution on the British model, as so many
French thinkers had hoped. One such was Montesquieu, who
wrote in his *Lettres persanes* in 1721: 'Existing laws should be
touched only with a gingerly hand.' Another was Rousseau, who
believed that an ancient nation could not survive revolutionary
upsets. 'As soon as its fetters are broken,' he declared, 'it falls
asunder and no longer exists.'

The beginnings of the Revolution seemed to reflect this spirit,
not so much revolutionary as seeking reform. A firm king should
have been able to maintain or restore that state of affairs. But
neither the advice of Mirabeau nor that of Barnave could wean
Louis XVI away from the privileged persons who surrounded him
and made him a prisoner in his own Court. Need this ancient
debate really be revived?

It was not the first time that sensible political solutions had been
rejected. The plans of the enlightened reformers in France had
always been blocked, since the beginning of Louis XVI's reign:
hence the dismissal of Turgot in 1776. And the same stubborn
reaction occurred everywhere in the Europe of enlightened despotism, in which so many worthy people had believed that all they
need do was persuade the prince or the king, and that once he had
become a 'philosopher' all would be well. But the sovereigns of
the Enlightenment preferred half-measures. Even when Frederick
II brought the Prussian aristocracy to heel, he did so with such
moderation that on his death in 1787 Prussia witnessed a
widespread aristocratic revival.

How could Louis XVI be expected to succeed where Frederick
II had failed? When, finally, Louis invoked foreign assistance, he
unleashed the adroit manoeuvres of counter-revolution and European conservatism. Overtaken by events, the Revolution
developed in ways that its sponsors had not expected.

They admitted as much. 'Revolutionary is not what one is, but
what one becomes,' said Carnot. 'The pressure of events may lead
us to results we had not thought of,' said Saint-Just. The revolution
continued for only a few months along this unexpected path, to its

own cruel detriment and that of others; then the fall of Robespierre opened the way to reaction and to the pleasures of life renewed. 'Paris became sparkling again,' wrote Michelet.

A few days after Thermidor, a man who is still alive and who then was ten years old, was taken by his parents to the theatre. On the way out, he admired the long line of brilliant carriages which he had never seen before. People in servants' livery, hat in hand, said to the people coming out: 'Do you need a carriage, *Sir*?' The child hardly understood this new locution. He had it explained to him, and was told only that the death of Robespierre had brought a considerable change.

But was Michelet right to end his *History of the French Revolution* (1853) at 10 Thermidor? Logically, no: once the Thermidor reaction had ended, France returned to the moderate 'first' Revolution, whose essential achievements the Directoire and the Consulate maintained. What was rejected was the work of the terrorist Convention.

Abroad, in any case, no one believed that the Revolution was over. On 12 September 1797, the Russian ambassador in Britain wrote to his Government (in French): 'What was likely . . . has happened in Paris: the dictatorial triumvirate has arrested two directors and sixty-four members of the two Councils, without any kind of legal proceeding. They are to be sent to Madagascar. So much for France's fine constitution and her wonderful liberty! I would rather live in Morocco than in that land of alleged equality and freedom.' Why the rancour? Not everyone outside France spoke ironically of 'her wonderful liberty'. It was in the name of the Revolution that Napoleon pursued his conquests; and, everywhere that his regime was established, laws, customs and feelings were permanently affected, despite the resentment or hatred that the occupation aroused. Goethe and Hegel supported Napoleon. In the face of a reactionary Europe far behind the political and social stage that France had reached, they saw him as what Hegel called 'the soul of the world on horseback'.

The Napoleonic Wars extended to Europe what had been a

civil war in France. For a quarter of a century, to all those countries menaced by Napoleon, the Revolution was both a reality and a threat. Thus perceived, as an imminent possibility, the message of the Revolution, whether admired or abhorred, made powerful headway in the West, stirring passions and dividing opinion. And finally, with its drama, its vivid colours, its saints and martyrs, its lessons, and its aspirations – often disappointed but always revived – the Revolution looks to the twentieth century almost like Holy Writ.

The message of the French Revolution

True, to all appearances, the Revolution seems reduced to silence after 1815. It lived on, however, in people's hearts and minds, and its essential achievements were maintained.

The Restoration did not restore all the social privileges that the Revolution had abolished (and certainly not the old feudal rights). National property was not returned to its previous owners; and even if its distribution was unfair, too much having gone to the rich, the Revolution's achievements in this area were safeguarded – as was the principle of individual rights guaranteed by the Charter of 1814. When the Government of Charles X seemed to be preparing reactionary measures, there was an instant outcry, followed by the July Monarchy and the return to the tricolour flag. Revolutionary language and ideology had largely reappeared.

Already in 1828, a companion of Gracchus or François Babeuf, Philippe Buonarotti, had described in his _History of the Conspiracy for Equality, known as the Babeuf Conspiracy_, how the 'Equals' had planned a sort of 'plebeian Vendée', how they had failed and been executed – though Babeuf stabbed himself on 26 March 1797 to escape execution. It had been a 'Communist' or communal movement, faithful to Rousseau's dictum: 'You are lost if you forget that land belongs to no one and its fruits belong to everyone.' The example and the book both had immense success. Auguste Blanqui, that impenitent revolutionary whom no one, in retrospect, can fail to like, was a passionate reader of Buonarotti.

This example may help to show how it was that the Revolution could always, even now, speak more or less the language that every generation wanted to hear. After its apparent eclipse in the Second Empire, from 1875 onwards, its symbols continued to form the ideological basis of the Third Republic and of the whole revolutionary Socialist movement.

What revolutionary humanism essentially believed was that violence could be legitimate if it was used to defend law, equality, social justice or the much loved mother country. The revolutionary might be its author – or its victim, for 'to take to the streets' could as easily involve dying there, making a final protest, as emerging victorious. But to dare embrace violence – to dare to die or to kill – was acceptable only if it were the sole means of deflecting destiny, making it more human and fraternal. In a word, the Revolution meant violence in the service of an ideal. The Counter-Revolution sprang from similar roots. Its failing, in historical terms, was that it looked backward and tried to move backward. And to return to the past is possible only by wrenching things out of true – momentarily, at that. In the long term, no action can last and bear the weight of history unless it goes in history's direction and at history's pace, instead of trying in vain to slow it down.

However that may be, it remains remarkable that 1789 should have still inspired mass workers' movements even as late as the twentieth century. First, because in its earliest intentions as in its results, the French Revolution was always a prudent affair. Then, its heroic legend, full of miracles performed by demigods or 'giants', has been partly destroyed, tarnished by the demythologizing efforts of objective historians. None have done so more effectively than those on the Left, anxious to substantiate their revolutionary fervour by reference to the documents. In this way, the Revolution has lost many of its saints. But, at the same time, its message has become clearer.

Historical revisionism, in fact, has rehabilitated the 'red' period of the Terror, identified the significance of the suffering it underwent as well as that it inflicted, and brought to light, in plea of justification, the tragic aspect of its situation. Henceforward it is the 'Incorruptible' Robespierre and then that tardy hero Gracchus Babeuf who take precedence over Danton or Carnot, 'the organizer of victory'. And it is their language that reaches out to us, a powerful language, because it anticipates what was to come. Universal suffrage, the separation of Church and State, the Ventôse decree providing for some redistribution of wealth – all these ephemeral victories won by the 'second' Revolution, and repudiated after Thermidor, were instances of anticipation. It took a long time, in some cases, for them to be revived in our time and for our benefit.

At all events, it is thanks to them that the revolutionary humanism of 1789 still lives on. The hesitations and reservations that European Socialism felt, especially recently, in the face of Communism (with its different ideal and its different form of revolution) – these are signs that a certain left-wing ideology, fed on memories and on some key words, refused to identify its revolution with that of Marx or, later, the Soviets. One example is the criticism that Jean Jaurès made of Marxist ideas after the signature of the pact with Jules Guesde in 1905 which established Socialist unity 'under the auspices of the Communist Manifesto'. At the beginning of his *Socialist History of the French Revolution*, Jaurès announced that it would be 'at once materialist with Marx and mystical with Michelet' – i.e. faithful to Michelet's 'revolutionary mystique', the Revolution's living heritage. Only late in the day, and incompletely, did Western civilization in France and elsewhere manage to distance itself from that heritage and the ideals of 1789.

Scientific thought before the nineteenth century

The growth of scientific thought in Europe before the eighteenth century raises the question of the infancy of modern science – indeed, of pre-science (in the same sense as one may speak of 'pre-industry' before the Industrial Revolution). This is not the place to summarize the evolution of science, or even to try to identify the dividing line between pre-science and modern science. The problem is to discover not how, but why science developed, and only in the context of Western civilization. As Joseph Needham, the chemist and Sinologue, unambiguously put it, 'Europe did not create just any science, but world science.' And it did so almost alone. Why then did science not develop in much earlier civilizations – in China, for example, or out of Islam?

All scientific proceedings are undertaken in the context of a certain view of the world. There can be no progress, no reasoning and no fruitful hypothesis if there is no general set of references with which to locate one's position and then choose one's direction. The way in which different views of the world have succeeded one another provides the best background for studying the development of science.

The history of the sciences (and of science), if seen from a certain distance, looks like the very slow transition from one general rational explanation to another general explanation, each being treated as a theory that took account of all the scientific data currently available, until the moment when that all-embracing theory was exploded because new data violently contradicted it. So another hypothesis had to be put together as best it might; and that in its turn became the point of departure for further advance.

Since the thirteenth century, Western science has lived with only three general explanations or world systems: that of Aristotle, which although of ancient lineage entered the interpretations and speculations of the West in the thirteenth century; that of Descartes and Newton, which founded classical science and which is an original Western creation except for its decisive borrowings from the work of Archimedes; and finally the relativity theory of Albert Einstein, announced in 1905, which inaugurated contemporary science.

These vast interpretations of the world dominate science, but never of course fully encapsulate it. Their establishment poses complex problems; and so does their eventual deterioration. The moment when they no longer fit the facts usually heralds real progress, a turning-point in the general history of science.

Aristotle's system was a very ancient inheritance, from the Peripatetic School of the fourth century BC. The essentials of its teaching reached the West much later via Arabic translation, in Toledo, and the commentaries of Averroës. In Paris, this meant a veritable revolution. In 1215, the University's syllabus was changed from top to bottom; formal logic replaced the study of Latin literature, and especially of the poets. 'Philosophy is invading and abolishing everything.' Translations of Aristotle abounded, leading to an enormous mass of commentaries. There followed a very fierce dispute between the Ancients and the Moderns. In a contemporary poem, written in about 1250, the Philosopher says to the Poet: 'I have devoted myself to knowledge, while you prefer puerile things like prose, rhythm and metre. What good are they? You know grammar, but you know nothing of Science and Logic. Why do you puff yourself up so, if you are only an ignoramus?'

The world system worked out by Aristotle dominated Europe until the seventeenth and even the eighteenth century, because it did not immediately yield under the attacks of Copernicus, Kepler and Galileo.

Aristotle's theory of the cosmos is of course completely out of date. But it is a theory, elaborately although not mathematically worked out. It is neither a crude verbal extension of common sense, nor a childish fantasy: it is a doctrine which, although naturally based on the findings of common sense, nevertheless elaborates them systematically, in an extremely strict and coherent manner.

Alexandre Koyre

Undoubtedly, Aristotle stated as an axiom that there was a 'cosmos' – a single *uni*verse. But was Einstein any different? When Paul Valéry asked him: 'But what proof is there that there is unity in nature?' he answered: 'It's an act of faith' (Paul Valéry, *L'Idée* *fixe*). And Einstein said elsewhere: 'I cannot think that God plays dice with the cosmos.'

This Aristotelian unity of the world was an 'order': every being had its natural place there, and so should remain permanently at rest. Such was the settled position of the Earth at the centre of the Cosmos and its successive spheres. However, the Cosmos was disturbed by a variety of movements. Some were natural, like that of a body that falls to the ground, or a light body – flame or smoke – that rises in the sky, or like the circular movement of the stars, or rather of the celestial spheres. Some movements, on the other hand, were violent and abnormal, being imparted to a body by pushing or pulling it: they stopped when the impulsion stopped. There was one sizeable exception: that of a body thrown, a projectile. Its movement was not natural; but it was not any longer bound up with the impulsion – it was neither pushed nor pulled. The projectile must therefore be propelled by the whirling of the air it passed through. This solution came to the rescue of the system; but it was the weak point that all its critics attacked.

Unfailingly, they asked: *a quo moveantur projecta?* It was a question that raised a number of problems, including the inertia or acceleration of the fall of heavy objects; and these were matters that were already tackled by the Parisian 'nominalists' of the fourteenth century, including William of Ockham, Jean Buridan and Nicholas Oresme. Oresme, who was a mathematical genius, discovered the principle of the law of inertia, the fact that the speed of falling was proportional to the time taken to fall, etc. But his thought was not immediately followed up.

The history of the experiments and disputes which resulted in Aristotle's system being dethroned by classical Newtonian physics and science generally would be fascinating to recount, and very long. That 'great leap forward' was brought about by exceptional people all over Europe who were in touch with each other. Science, by now, was international: it transcended political or linguistic barriers and occupied the whole of the West. Progress was undoubtedly aided by the sixteenth century's economic boom, and equally by the widespread distribution of ancient Greek scientific works, made possible by printing. The works of Archimedes, for example, became known only late in the day, in the last years of the sixteenth century. And his thought was very fruitful: foreshadowing differential and integral calculus, he put forward the useful idea of a limit. To appreciate the value of that, think of calculating π.

But progress was slow. In mathematics, the five great steps forward, as listed by an historian of science, were made with long intervals between them: the analytic geometry of Pierre de Fermat (1629) and René Descartes (1637); Fermat's higher arithmetic (around 1630–65); combinative analysis (1654); Galileo's dynamics (1591–1612) and those of Newton (1666–84); Newton's universal gravitation (1666 and 1684–7).

Nor was this true only of mathematics. In the vast subject of astronomy, although the Greeks themselves had briefly entertained the notion of an heliocentric universe, the geocentric system inherited from Ptolemy strenuously resisted change, and it took a long time for Copernicus (1473–1543) and Kepler (1571–1630) to be vindicated.

The major event, transcending all these efforts, was the establishment of a new model of the world: the abstract, geometrized universe of Descartes and, still more, of Newton, in which everything depended on one principle, that of universal gravitation, whereby bodies attract each other in proportion to their mass and in inverse ratio to the square of the distance between them (1687).

This picture of the world was also tenacious. It survived all the scientific revolutions of the nineteenth century, until a new magic explanation of the world appeared – Einstein's special (1905) and general (1916) theories of relativity. Anyone who completed his studies before 1939 will still have lived, in spirit, in the clarity and definiteness of the Newtonian universe.

Descartes was 'a free man'. That geometrized or mechanized universe was not the sole creation of any of the scholars we have cited or could have cited. Still, without yielding to misplaced nationalism, let us give René Descartes (1596–1650) the mention he deserves.

We must begin with a parenthesis. Descartes eludes biographers because he was discreet, deliberately shy and of restrained sensibility. After 1628, apart from a few visits, he lived outside France and mainly in Holland. He died in Stockholm, the guest of Queen Christina of Sweden. In Amsterdam, where he spent much of his time, he was delighted to be able to lose himself in the crowd, 'never recognized by anyone'. To reconstruct his thought and rediscover its movement is as difficult as investigating his secretive life.

His *Discours de la Méthode* (1637) has tended to simplify our picture of him. We have been tempted to notice only its peremptory rules – whereas it is in fact the preface to three works: *La Dioptrique*, *Les Météores*, and the very well-known *Géométrie*; and they should not be isolated from each other. Moreover, the *Discours* is in some ways a simplified, shortened version of the *Regulae*, which were not published until after Descartes's death. Were the *Regulae* written, as it would appear, around 1629 and taken up again in 1637, to be distilled into the *Discours de la Méthode*? Or, alternatively, do the four precepts of the Method date from the famous winter of 1619–20, as the *Discours* explicitly says? In that case, the *Regulae* would be a later, longer and more complicated version of them. The fact is that the style of thinking differs as between the books. The strict and austere *Géométrie* contrasts with the richer, more inventive mathematics offered us in Descartes's *Letters*, where he is as it were stimulated, heated by 'the challenges of his critics'. Hence a number of doubts must remain: but they in no way alter the significance of the whole. From Descartes we have the first systematic and modern critical appraisal of knowledge, a first heroic struggle against all intellectual or metaphysical illusions, all errors arising 'from poetic intuition'.

On the scientific plane, more than a few words are needed, even if we limit our study of his work to those aspects of it that concerned the future and have survived to our day, leaving aside his physics and optics, which were clearly not revolutionary, and concentrating on his geometry – the discipline in which, in his own view, he had best applied his Method.

Descartes rid himself, not without difficulty, of the 'geometrical realism' of the Greeks. His mathematics introduced pure abstraction. 'The scope of thinking, instead of being imposed in a realist way, is then determined by a network of relationships.' By this means, going further than his predecessors – notably François Vieta, whom he knew, and Buonaventura Cavalieri, whom he should have known – he advanced 'with giant strides the theory of equations. For any further progress, mathematics had to wait for Evariste Galois (1811–32)'.

The fact that Cartesian mathematics can be understood today by a student just beginning the subject should not disguise the magnitude of Descartes's achievement. Thus he evoked, alongside the 'true' (positive) and 'false' (negative) roots of an equation, its 'purely imaginary' roots. Thus his demonstration implied, although without fixing them precisely, the axes of coordinates (orthogonal or not). Thus he decomposed, or rather composed in advance, a function made up of a certain number of binomials in the form of simple equations multiplying each other, as $(x-1)$ $(x+4)$ $(x-7)$, etc.

The historian Lucien Febvre was right to see Descartes as living his reason as he lived his faith, erecting a barrier against all that the sixteenth century, in its naturalism, had brought with it by way of fables, approximations, pre-logical thought, qualitative physics, and also resisting all those Renaissance 'rationalists' who had seen in Nature only 'a box of miracles or an incentive to dream'.

The key years 1780–1820 raised a final problem: crossing the threshold that led to truly modern science. Magnificent as the eighteenth century was, it was not yet on equal terms with modern science, conversant with its attitudes, its language and its methods.

This was demonstrated by one of Gaston Bachelard's finest

books, *The Formation of the Scientific Spirit* (1935). It sought to enumerate the trouble and awkwardness experienced by scientists who were trying to free themselves, not without difficulty, from common prejudice and from a certain pre-logical mentality whose power and weight seem astonishing today. This psychoanalysis of the Enlightenment obviously concentrated only on its darker side, its errors, aberrations and absurdities. But are absurdities not the eternal accompaniment of the advancing scientific spirit? May we not suffer from them in connection with the science of tomorrow?

In the eighteenth century, the biggest obstacle to progress was perhaps the compartmentalization of science into different sectors, each independent of the others. Some were advancing rapidly: mathematics, chemistry, thermodynamics, geology and economics (if that is a science). Others were lagging behind, and sometimes stationary, as were medicine and biology. At that time, the various disciplines remained separate. The language of mathematics was not commonly used; and – no less serious a failing – links with technology were spasmodic.

These difficulties were gradually resolved. In France, new ground was not fully broken until about 1820–26, when the Academy of Sciences became 'the most brilliant meeting of scholars there had ever been: Ampère, Laplace, Legendre, Biot, Poinsot, Cauchy . . .' (Louis de Broglie). There was similar brilliance all over Europe.

Why, precisely, was the threshold crossed, forging the scientific future of a civilization that then, and then only, was definitively carried away by its impetus? There is an obvious materialist explanation. The unprecedented economic growth that occurred in the eighteenth century affected the whole world, and Europe became its reigning power. Material and technological conditions increased their demands and their constraints. Little by little, a collaborative response appeared. Industrialization, the subject of the next chapter, was thus the decisive element, the *motor* of change. Which amounts to explaining one obviously Western phenomenon – science – by another, industrialization. These two seem to echo each other and they certainly go side by side. This is what Joseph Needham, already quoted, likes to affirm. Much earlier than the West, China possessed the rudiments of science, in an elegant and advanced form. But she failed to reach the decisive stage, because she never experienced the economic impetus that spurred Europe on – that 'capitalist' tension which at the end of the race, or during it, enabled Europeans to cross the decisive threshold. The beginnings of that creative tension had been felt long before, with the rise of the great medieval trading cities, and above all from the sixteenth century onwards.

All Europe's strength, material and spiritual, combined to produce this development, the fruit of a civilization plucked when it was fully ripe and with full awareness of the responsibility it entailed.

18. The Industrialization of Europe

One of Europe's key responsibilities was that of bringing about the Industrial Revolution which spread, and is still spreading, throughout the world. This formidable technological advance was Europe's own achievement, and one that was relatively recent in the history of civilizations, since it took place only two centuries ago. Until then, Europe – for all its brilliance – was in material terms underdeveloped, not by comparison with the world around it, but by contrast with what Europe itself was to become. How then did Europe succeed in crossing this industrial threshold? How did its civilization react to the results of its own achievement?

These are the questions that arise immediately. And they concern our immediate interests.

They require a preliminary look at the state of Europe before industrialization. And that economic *ancien régime* still prevails in many parts of the world that are trying to go beyond it.

The Industrial Revolution is a complex phenomenon. Nowhere did it take place in one single process. Certain sectors lagged behind for a long time, as the wool industry in Yorkshire or ironmongery around Birmingham did until the middle of the nineteenth century – to take examples only from Britain, which was the first in the field. The contrasts that are visible in South America today, for example, are normal in all countries in the process of industrialization.

Europe's example proves that, from its very beginnings, industrialization raises serious problems. Any country that undertakes to industrialize itself must envisage at the same time a change in its social structure, if it wishes to avoid the long gestation of a revolutionary ideology such as those which so much affected and afflicted Europe.

The origins of the first Industrial Revolution

There were four successive Industrial Revolutions, each of the last three building on its predecessor's achievements: that of steam, that of electricity, that of the internal combustion engine and that of nuclear energy.

The problem for us is to examine as closely as possible how this series of revolutions began. That means looking at the leading position of Britain between 1780 and 1890. Why was she the first to industrialize? How? And before 1780, what was the general situation of Europe in industrial matters?

The word 'industry', before the eighteenth century – or rather, before the nineteenth – risks evoking a false picture. At the very most, then, there was what may be called 'pre-industry'. The very first 'industrial revolution', may be said to have occurred in the twelfth century, when wind- and water-mills spread throughout Europe. But after that, for some seven centuries, there was no major technological innovation. Pre-industry, even in the eighteenth century, had only medieval sources and forms of energy. The power of a water-mill was normally in the region of 5 horsepower; that of a windmill, in windswept regions such as Holland, sometimes exceeded 10 horsepower, but its output was intermittent. Without abundant energy resources and powerful machines, industrial life was condemned to semi-immobility, despite a multiplicity of small and often very ingenious technical inventions. Such industry as there was found itself hemmed in by an archaic economic system: derisory agricultural productivity, costly and primitive transportation, and inadequate markets. Only labour was super-abundant.

And industry in any modern sense was virtually non-existent. Local artisans, working close to home, often met the essential needs of the nearby population. In a few sectors only were there firms which worked for much wider markets, or which specialized in luxury products. Such, in France, were certain 'royal' manufactures dating from the seventeenth century. Examples of this kind were fairly common in the up-to-date textile industries. It was here, indeed, that the British Industrial Revolution began.

In fact, the textile industry more than any other made possible relatively large-scale production in a still traditional artisan world. In the sixteenth and seventeenth centuries, and even in the thirteenth century in the textile cities of Italy and Flanders, rich merchants *'qui faciunt laborare'* (who commissioned work) encouraged the establishment of quite large organizations in town – a few big workshops and some retail outlets. 'Masters' (often ordinary wage-earners with two or three assistants) worked at home, as very frequently did peasant men and women outside the town involved in the same enterprise.

A sixteenth-century document describes the Segovia merchants, enriched by cloth-making, as 'real fathers of families who, in their own houses and outside, support a large number of people, in many cases up to 200 or 300, and thereby employ other hands to produce a huge diversity of the finest cloths'.

In Laval in about 1700 the linen industry employed some 5,000 workers in and around the town. With their families, they numbered 20,000, 'the richest of whom had not 100 francs in the world'. There were a further 500 master weavers who bought their thread from the tow-sellers, 'known as *cancers* because they devoured the unfortunate weavers'. Above them there were thirty wholesale merchants, the real organizers of the industry: they bleached the raw linens and sent them to distant markets. These merchant entrepreneurs represented what a typological historian calls 'commercial or merchant capitalism': they supplied the raw materials, paid the wages, stored the goods and sold them, often exporting them over long distances and usually buying, in return, other profitable products.

Since travel was so slow, these commercial transactions took a long time to complete. In the fifteenth century wool washed in Spain and sent to Florence to be worked, was then sold as fine cloth in Alexandria, Egypt, in return for oriental goods which were sold in Florence or elsewhere in Europe – all of which took three years and often more. So the operation, although usually profitable, was a long-term affair. It immobilized a lot of capital for a lengthy period, and was not without dangers. The merchant entrepreneur dominated the system, since he alone had the capital to finance it – usually in association with others, so as to spread the risk. He took both the responsibility and the profits.

Manufacturing: the word, for a long time ill-defined, in retrospect seems to fit fairly well the concentration of workmen in the same building (or in buildings close to each other), supervised by foremen. In the eighteenth century, this practice grew more widespread; and at the same time there was some division of labour in the workshops. An article in the *Encylopédie* in 1761 ascribed the superiority of the Lyon silk factories to the fact that they employed a large number of people (there were 30,000 silk workers in the town) in such a way that 'one worker does only one single thing, which he will do all his life, while another does something else; hence everyone performs his given task promptly and well'.

This organization, however, was singled out as an exception. Ordinary artisan work, with no division of labour, remained the rule, even when the first signs of the Industrial Revolution were about to appear.

Pre-industrial Europe, then, lacked neither entrepreneurs nor capital; it was not deaf to the demands of the market, including the international market; in places, it had a labour force already partly mobilized in large numbers and ready to serve the entrepreneurs. It suffered, however, like today's less developed countries, from a badly organized economy. The agricultural sector, in particular, was too weak to enable any economic boom to develop fully. The market outlets were inadequate; the competition was cut-throat; the slightest crisis ruined everything. There were frequent bankruptcies among industrialists and merchants. A trading guide dating from the mid-eighteenth century drew attention to the dangers of 'fashion' in manufacturing: 'In the provinces we find vestiges of defunct manufacturing firms; every year we see one of them collapse, while others arise, soon to fall again in their turn.'

In fact, pre-industry survived only as a result of very low wages. Did the conditions of workers improve in some regions where prosperity finally allowed wages to rise? Paradoxically, no: where that happened, industry died, or was at least in a very bad way, under the onslaught of foreign competition. This was the case with Venice in the seventeenth century and Holland in the eighteenth. In 1777, the Administrator of Picardy noted: at present, day labourers need twice as much money to live on, yet they earn no more than they did fifty years ago, when food was half as cheap; so they have no more than half of what they need.

Nothing can change, or will change, without technological innovations. But we should acknowledge at once that such innovations cannot themselves determine everything. This can be seen by looking at the special case of Britain. There, the technological innovations occurred in two key industries – textiles (above all) and the mines. Their repercussions were not always rapid; but they reached a long way into other sectors of the economy.

The British mines, and especially the Cornish tin mines, which had been worked for a long time and at ever deeper levels, were constantly plagued by the infiltration of water. It was an old problem: it had been raised in the sixteenth century by Georg Agricola in his treatise *De re metallica*. But were the large hydraulic wheels then in use capable of working powerful enough pumps, or relays of pumps? To create a vacuum, they used air pressure and could not exceed its power: each time, they raised a theoretical column of water only some ten metres tall.

The search for powerful pumps finally produced the large, heavy and very costly steam-engine invented by Thomas

Newcomen, from 1712 to 1718. When repairing one of these, the Scotsman James Watt, from the University of Edinburgh, made the discovery that led him to devise his own much simpler and more efficient machine, first conceived in 1776. So steam was in use before Watt: from the beginning of the eighteenth century it was working machines which were used much more than was once thought, as recent studies have proved. Some were even in use in France around 1750, in the Anzin coal mines near Valenciennes. More spectacular achievements – the first automobile, the first steamboat made by Beugnot and Jouffroy – came in and around 1770.

The textile industry, however, was the main driving-force, as it continued to be until the mid-nineteenth century and the advent of the railways. It led all the others, being both a producer of basic necessities and a provider of luxuries.

According to Max Weber, the textile industry's ups and downs dominate all the material past of the West. First came the age of linen (Charlemagne was dressed in something like canvas); then the age of wool; then the age of cotton – or rather a craze for cotton – in the eighteenth century. And it was for cotton that the first real factories came into being. Bound up with the Indian, African and American trade, and with the traffic in black slaves, cotton was established in or around the great colonial ports such as Liverpool and Glasgow. It profited from their energy and their accumulated capital. No wonder then that these popular industries demanded and even initiated technological improvements.

New machines appeared, each with its nickname: John Kay's flying shuttle in 1733; James Hargreaves's improved spinning-jenny in 1767; Sir Richard Arkwright's water-powered spinning mill in 1769; Samuel Crompton's spinning mule in 1773. The summit of these achievements, although in France, was undoubtedly the improved loom invented by Joseph Marie Jacquard in 1800 and first exhibited in 1801.

Here, then, is one explanation. Economic growth favours some particular sector of industry, and technology responds to the demand. Everything happens spontaneously and empirically. Technology made demands on science, which naturally and promptly responded. *Homo sapiens* joined forces with *homo faber*; from now on, they moved forward together.

Science had made obvious progress during the eighteenth century. But in general it was a deliberately theoretical affair, unaccustomed to working with technology, which was still at the artisan stage and which scarcely asked it any questions. At the end of the eighteenth century everything changed. From then on, industry itself began to make requests of pure science rather than merely of technology, that science of the hand and the craft.

The admirable James Watt (1736–1819), for instance, was not just a self-taught artisan: he had a scientific mind, and was well versed in both engineering and chemistry. A professional scientist, John Black, born in Bordeaux in 1728 of Scottish parents, was Professor of Chemistry at Edinburgh, where he did notable work on alkalis, and died in 1799. It was he who may have suggested the principle of latent heat on which Watt based his steam-engine: by keeping the cylinder warm with a jacket, he used the expansive force of the steam, which hitherto had been condensed on entering the cooled cylinder and thereby wasted.

Science made hundreds of similar contributions to the growth of industry. One such concerned the bleaching of linen. The traditional process had involved spreading the cloth in the fields and watering it, soaking it in various solutions, first alkaline and then slightly acid. This had required large spaces and much time, sometimes as long as six months. For an industry rapidly expanding, this was a bottleneck, especially since the weak acid that was used for what was called 'souring' was buttermilk, and that was not produced on an industrial scale. One improvement was to use very dilute sulphuric acid, which worked more quickly; but that had to be produced in large quantities. It was here that a real scientist, a doctor called John White, a former pupil of the University of Leyden, made his contribution. The discovery of chlorine in 1774 by the Swede Carl Scheele, its use by the Frenchman

Claude Louis Berthollet for bleaching textiles and the development in Britain of a practical method of doing so – all brought the process close to perfection. And that, clearly, was the result of international scientific efforts.

Nothing, perhaps, is a better illustration of the collaboration between science and technology than the career of Matthew Boulton (1728–1809). Of modest origin (a 'new man'), he was a practical and creative industrialist: he financed the work of James Watt. But he was also a scientist, passionately devoted to chemistry. His circle included not only Watt, but a doctor and mathematician, William Small, the doctor and poet Erasmus Darwin (grandfather of Charles Darwin and Francis Galton), and many others. Industrial Britain was becoming scientific Britain, with its capitals, significantly, in Birmingham and Manchester. London, the headquarters of merchant capitalism, remained for a long time outside the scope of these novelties, and only recovered its place in British scientific life in about 1820. That fact alone is noteworthy. It was the growth of industry that obliged science to act.

But is that a sufficient explanation? In France, applied science was undoubtedly ahead of Britain: we have only to think of chemists like P. J. Macquer (1718–84) or Claude Louis Berthollet (1748–1822). So why was the progress of French industry so much less rapid? The fact is, clearly, that the Industrial Revolution arose from other causes too. Some (the most important) were economic; others were social. The broader explanation – economic and social – is indeed the best.

Long before, owing to its 'Glorious' or 'bourgeois' Revolution in 1688, Britain had acquired political stability. Its society was open to capitalism: the Bank of England had been founded in 1694. Its economy had benefited from many investments in projects of general utility, such as roads and canals: in the eighteenth century there was even a 'canal craze'.

The Industrial Revolution in Britain began, too, as part of a general economic boom in the eighteenth century which then affected the whole world.

But would it have been possible without the rapid increase in Britain's population that took place in the eighteenth century – of the order of 64 per cent? Similar increases occurred elsewhere in the world, in China as in Europe; but it was more marked in some countries than in others. In France, for example, it was only about 35 per cent. For Britain, the result was a superabundance of inexpensive labour.

Finally, a very important role was played by the changes in British agriculture – the enclosures and new scientific methods – which loosened the perennial straitjacket of inadequate food production.

The Industrial Revolution in Britain came in two phases: the first in the cotton industry, between 1780 and 1830, and the second in metal production. The latter, involving heavy industry, was made possible by the building of the railways. This second phase had an enormous impact; but it was financed by the profits made from the first. Cotton had led the way, and it is to cotton that we must return to form any judgement of how the Industrial Revolution began.

The fashion for cotton was then widespread in Europe, including Britain. The British had for a long time imported, for themselves and for other markets in Europe and elsewhere, the printed or painted cotton goods that came from their Indian trading-stations, known in France as *indiennes* and in Britain as chintz, from the Hindi word *chint*. The success of these fabrics led British manufacturers to imitate them. Stimulated by technological progress, the cotton industry expanded more and more. There was great demand for its products on the coasts of Africa (where a slave was known as a 'piece', *'uma peça d'India'* in the old Portuguese expression, meaning the item of printed cotton for which he was exchanged). The next big market was in Brazil, opened up and monopolized by the British in 1808, before they repeated the same procedure two years later in the whole of Spanish America. Later, British cotton goods competed directly with Indian products in Britain itself, completely wiping out their

Indian rivals. The British also exported to the Mediterranean. And between 1820 and 1860 the sale of British cotton textiles to the rest of the world continually grew. The amount of raw cotton used by British mills rose from 2 million pounds in 1760 to no less than 366 million pounds in 1850.

This immense success had many repercussions. Buttressed by the prodigious boom in cotton, Britain flooded the world market with all kinds of goods; and from it she excluded others. Her aggressive Government, willing to wage war whenever necessary, reserved for British industry this vast domain where expansion seemed to know no limits. No one could wrest this world market from Britain's stranglehold, because the rise in output was accompanied (as became the rule in the future) by an astounding decrease in costs. Between 1800 and 1850, the price of cotton goods went down more than 81 per cent, while that of wheat and most other foodstuffs fell by barely a third. Wages remained more or less stable, but because machinery had greatly reduced the human element, their incidence on costs was very much less. Not surprisingly, this first instance of mass production greatly improved the lot of the people. Michelet observed a similar phenomenon in France when discussing the cotton crisis of 1842.

The expansion of the metallurgical industry came very much later. Here, until the nineteenth century, production had depended exclusively on war. 'Cast iron in the eighteenth century meant the casting of cannons,' wrote an Englishman in 1831; but the British had scarcely any except on board ship: land warfare concerned them relatively little. In the eighteenth century, in fact, they produced less iron than Russia or France, and often imported it from Russia or Sweden. The decisive technological discovery was that of coke smelting, made in the seventeenth century; but it was not widely used, and smelting by charcoal continued for a long time.

The coming of the railways, between 1830 and 1840, altered everything. They were heavy consumers of iron, cast iron and steel. Both at home and abroad, Britain set about building them.

At the same time, the arrival of metal-hulled steamships turned British shipbuilding into an enormous heavy industry. With that, cotton ceased to be the key sector in Britain's economic life.

The spread of industrialism in Europe and beyond

In other countries, in Europe and elsewhere, industrialization came at different times and in somewhat different contexts. Nevertheless, history seems on the whole to have repeated itself every time, although it was concerned with different societies, different economies and different civilizations. Reduced to its economic essentials, in fact, every industrial revolution followed roughly the same fairly simple 'model', as economists would say.

Three stages: this was the hypothesis put forward in 1952 by the American economist Walt W. Rostow. Although debatable, it certainly clarified the discussion.

At the beginning, the key moment is take-off. As an aircraft accelerates along the runway, then lifts off, so an economy about to expand rises quite steeply from the industrial *ancien régime* that held it down. Normally, take-off occurs in a single sector, or at most in two. It was cotton in Britain and in New England (the special case of an 'American' take-off); in France, Germany, Canada, Russia and the United States it was the railways; in Sweden it was building timber and iron-ore mines. In each case, the key sector darts forward, modernizing rapidly: the speed of its growth and the modernity of its technology are precisely what distinguish this phenomenon from previous industrial expansion, which lacked both explosive force and long-term staying power. The industry that has thus shot ahead increases its output, improves its technology, organizes its marketing and then stimulates the rest of the economy.

After that the key industry, having served as a motor, settles at its cruising altitude: it has performed its task. The reserves it has helped to accumulate then move to another sector, often related to the first; and that in its turn takes off, modernizes and reaches its ideal height.

As this process extends from one sector to another, the economy as a whole attains industrial maturity. In Western Europe, after the take-off of the railways (i.e. of iron, coal and heavy industry), it was the turn of steel, modern shipbuilding, chemicals, electricity and machine tools. Much later, Russia followed the same path. In Sweden, the essential roles were played by wood pulp (for paper-making), timber and iron. Generally speaking, it was in the first years of the twentieth century that the Western world as a whole reached the threshold of maturity. Britain, which had crossed it in about 1850, now found herself more or less on a level with her partners.

At that point, these experienced and fairly well-balanced economies, which had secured adequate incomes and achieved a certain abundance, no longer saw industrial expansion as their primordial goal. Where now were they to direct their power and their possible investment? Faced with the choice – for choice had become possible – not all the industrial societies reacted in the same way. Their different responses reflected the nature of the history they had so far lived through, and partly determined their future. It will be no surprise to learn that they based their choices, consciously or not, on the nature of their different civilizations.

Time to choose: what has to be chosen is a style of life to suit a whole society. There are a number of options. One might concentrate on careful social legislation, taking as its priorities the security, well-being and leisure of the whole population. One might decide that well-being depended on widespread mass consumption, with enough goods and services of a high standard produced to supply the vast majority. Or one might, finally, use the greater power of the society or the nation in the often vain and always dangerous quest for dominance in world politics.

The turn of the century, around 1900, saw the maturity of the United States. Briefly but significantly, it then tried power politics, in the form of the 1898 war against Spain for Cuba and the Philippines. This would seem to have been a conscious gesture, in view of Theodore Roosevelt's writing at the time that 'the United States needed a war', or that it had to be given 'something to think about other than material gain'. A few years later, it made timid and ephemeral attempts to pursue a progressive social policy. But after the interruption caused by the First World War, the United States committed itself fully to the option of mass consumption, with the boom in automobiles, in building and in household gadgets.

In Western Europe, the moment of decision was delayed by two World Wars and by the need for postwar reconstruction. Broadly speaking, mass consumption made its appearance after 1950, but with the restrictions and modifications imposed by government policy and by the pressure of a powerful Socialist tradition. In France, for example, these included the series of social laws ranging from free education to the medical organization of 'social security'. Some sectors, moreover, lagged behind completely, by force of circumstances or on account of reluctance to abandon traditional ways. To take one example, the agricultural revolution, American-style, ran into countless obstacles in continental Europe. The constant problems faced in this field by the Soviet Union are well known; and the situation is also complicated in France and Italy, neither of which has yet full modernized its agriculture.

Finally, not all regions were equally involved in the process. Just as the South of the United States remained backward long after 1900, so large parts of Europe lagged behind. They included the South-West and West of France, the *mezzogiorno* in Italy, the whole Iberian Peninsula outside the industrial centres of Barcelona and Bilbao, all the Communist republics (except the USSR itself, Czechoslovakia and the German Democratic Republic), the rest of the Balkans and Turkey.

In short, there have always been these two Europes, described by a journalist in 1929 as the Europe of the car and the Europe of the cart. To take one symbol out of thousands, we need only go near Cracow, on a road where narrow four-wheeled wagons laden with wood, and flocks of geese with their drovers, are more numerous than the automobiles. Yet suddenly we see the huge installations of Nova Huta, that town of metallurgical industries founded from nothing by Socialist Poland. Such contrasts are still an integral part of life in Europe today.

Credit, financial capitalism, and State capitalism: a credit revolution accompanied the Industrial Revolution, and fully profited from its success.

Capitalism of a kind has always existed, as witness ancient Babylon, which had bankers, merchants engaged in distant trade, and all the instruments of credit, such as bills of exchange, promissory notes, cheques, etc. In this sense, the history of capitalism extends 'from the Hammurabi to Rockefeller'. But credit in Europe in the sixteenth and seventeenth centuries still had a very restricted role. It developed considerably in the eighteenth century. By then, if only on account of trade with India and the East India Companies, or trade with China, which helped develop Canton, there was already a form of international capitalism, covering most of the commercial centres in Europe. At that time, however, financiers as such hardly concerned themselves with trade or industry: they managed public funds in the service of the State.

With the success of industrialization, banking and finance developed very rapidly. So much so that, alongside industrial capitalism, financial capitalism gained the upper hand and sooner or later controlled all the levers governing economic life. In France and Britain, its ascendancy became clear in the 1860s. Old and new banks extended their networks, and specialized as deposit banks, credit banks, merchant banks, etc. To follow the modernization of banking, it would be useful to trace in France, for example, the history of Crédit Lyonnais, founded in 1863, that of Pierpont Morgan in the United States, or the international network of the Rothschilds. Everywhere, banks succeeded in attracting a huge clientele, 'all the savings-minded public'; they sought and captured 'all dormant or sterile deposits', no matter how small. And the craze for 'shares' began. Industries, railways, shipping companies were gradually caught up in this complex banking network; and the operations of financial capitalism at once became international. French banks allowed themselves to be tempted more and more by the attractions of foreign loans. Thus it was that French savers took the perilous path of loans to Russia. Yet these foreign loans were at one time an important source of income for the French economy: a favourable balance of payments offset a deficit in the balance of trade. After 1850, they also contributed to basic investments in much of Europe and elsewhere.

Today, the heyday of financial capitalism in Europe seems to have passed, despite the theoretical debates that the subject can always arouse, and despite a certain number of exceptions that prove the rule. Thus, a merchant bank like the Banque de Paris et des Pays-Bas is still a very major power, and London, Paris, Frankfurt, Amsterdam, Brussels, Zurich and Milan remain vital financial centres. But – despite disillusionment with State Socialism, and despite efforts to limit public spending, partly by privatization – State capitalism has become a leading feature of the scene.

In the 'nationalized' sectors of those economies where State control has increased, the State itself has become an industrialist and a banker. Even elsewhere, its role has grown enormously since the nineteenth century. Extensive taxation, coupled with investment in public funds such as (in France) *comptes-chèques postaux*, *caisses d'épargnes* and *bons du Trésor*, or (in Britain) National Savings, Government loans or Treasury Bonds, has put at Governments' disposal enormous sums of money. The State is the grand master of investment in the infrastructure of industry, without which there can be no policies of growth, no effective social programmes and in a word no future.

Every year, even to ensure progress as modest as ours appears to be, a large slice of the national income has to be invested. Investment multiplies its own initial impact by stimulating a whole series of economic transactions. More and more, it looks as if

States need to plan their economic development, if only in the sense of setting targets and predicting the results of concerted action. The Soviet Union's famous five-year plans have been imitated all over the world. In January 1962, President J. F. Kennedy actually announced a five-year plan for US trade! France's own indicative five-year plans have in the past provoked lively controversy. They are, in their way, a national heart-searching as well as an economic balance-sheet. One of their aims is to assist take-off in backward regions by what they call 'a policy of training'.

Looking back on the Industrial Revolution and its repercussions, we should neither omit nor exaggerate the driving force of colonialism. It did not give Europe her central, predominant place in the world; but it may well have helped her to retain it. By 'colonialism' – another debatable word – we mean all European expansion, at least since 1492.

Undeniably, expansion favoured Europe. It gave her access to new areas in which to settle her surplus population and, nearby, rich and exploitable civilizations which she did not fail to exploit. The major landmarks in this process of exploitation were: in the sixteenth century, the arrival of 'treasures' (gold and silver ingots) from America; the brutal opening-up of India after the battle of Plassey (23 June 1757), at which the British defeated the nawab of Bengal; the forced exploitation of the Chinese market after the First Opium War in 1839–42; and the partition of Africa at Berlin in 1885.

The result, in Europe, was to establish huge trading concerns in the Iberian Peninsula, the Low Countries and then the British Isles, altogether greatly strengthening some of those capitalist networks which assisted the progress of industrialization. Europe gained a large surplus from these distant lands overseas.

And that surplus played its part. It was no coincidence that Britain, so successful overseas, was the first to enjoy 'take-off'. It still remains to be established whether, as we believe, the Industrial

Revolution later consolidated colonialism, to Europe's benefit, by confirming European primacy and prestige. There is no doubt, however, that France's industrial growth was independent of her presence in Senegal, or her establishment in Algeria (1830), Cochin-China (1858–67) and Tonkin and Annam (1883).

Equally debatable is the human and moral record of colonialism as such. It is a complex question, in which guilt and responsibility are not all on one side. Colonialism had both positive and negative aspects. Only one thing is certain: the history of that type of colonialism is over: the page is turned.

Socialism and industrialism

To the credit of the West, it tried very hard to find a valid and effective social, humanitarian response to the many hardships involved in industrialization. It worked out what we might call a social form of humanism, if we had not already overworked that convenient word.

The search for decent solutions went on throughout the nineteenth century – an age at once sad, dramatic and marked by genius. It was sad, because of the ugliness of daily life; it was dramatic, on account of continual upheavals and wars; and it was marked by genius, as shown by its progress in science and technology, as well as, to a lesser degree, in social affairs.

At all events, the upshot is clear. Today, long after the nineteenth century, a sober collection of social provisions, which could still be improved, is enshrined in laws which aim to give the mass of people a better life and to disarm revolutionary demands.

This complex and imperfect achievement did not result automatically or easily from dispassionate moral or factual analysis. It arose from a very determined struggle, which in the West involved at least three phases. (We shall return to the particular case of Russia and the Soviet Union.)

The revolutionary and ideological phase was that of social

reformers or 'prophets' (as their many enemies called them). It lasted from 1815 to 1871 – i.e. from the fall of Napoléon Bonaparte until the Commune. Its true turning-point was perhaps 1848, the year of successive revolutions.

The phase of militant organized labour (trade unions and political parties) actually began before the siege of Paris, but was essentially concentrated between 1871 and 1914.

The political or governmental phase largely began after the First World War. The State began to undertake social measures after 1919 and 1929; it intensified them, with the help of greater affluence, from 1945–50 until the present day.

This chronological framework suggests that in the face of industrialization the protests and demands of working people often changed both their direction and their tone, in line with variations in material prosperity. They were vehement in times of economic hardship (1817–51; 1873–96; 1929–39), and less so in periods of economic growth (such as 1851–73, or from 1945 onwards). One historian, discussing such fluctuations in Germany, has declared: 'In 1830, the word proletariat was not yet known; by 1955 it had almost passed out of use.'

Of the three phases in question, the first (which concerned only social ideas) was perhaps the most important, because it marked a turning-point for an entire civilization. From 1815 to 1848 and 1871, this great movement of ideas, acute analyses and prophecies broadly shifted ideological interest from politics to society. From then on, the State was no longer the target of people's demands: now, it was society that had to be understood, healed and improved.

With a new programme came a new language. With words like *industrial* and *industrialist*, *industrial society* and *industrial firm*, *proletariat*, *mass*, *Socialism*, *Socialist*, *capitalist*, *capitalism*, *Communist* and *Communism*, revolutionary ideology found a new vocabulary.

It was the Count de Saint-Simon who invented the noun and adjective *industriel* (derived from the old word industry) and probably the phrase *société industrielle*, seized upon by Auguste Comte,

Herbert Spencer and many others. For Comte, the expression denoted that form of society which had supplanted military society, hitherto (in his view) the dominant mode. While military society had been warlike, industrial society, he thought, would have to be peaceful – a claim that Herbert Spencer rightly refused to make.

The word *proletariat* was included in the French Academy's Dictionary in 1828. *Mass*, in the singular and especially in the plural, became the key word, 'the terminological symptom of the changes that became explosive in the reign of Louis-Philippe'. 'I have an instinct for the masses: that is my sole political asset,' said Alphonse Lamartine in 1828. And Louis-Napoléon Bonaparte in his *Extinction of Poverty* (1844) declared: 'Today, the reign of castes is over: one can govern only with the masses.'

These 'masses' were above all the poor, exploited, urban working-class masses. Hence the idea that the present time was dominated by conflict between social classes – what Karl Marx called 'the class struggle'. This, of course, was an age-old phenomenon, present in all materially advanced societies in the past. But there is no denying that in the nineteenth century it greatly intensified, causing a good deal of heart-searching.

Socialist and *Socialism* came into general use in the 1830s. So too did *Communism*, in the vague sense of economic and social equality. Thus Auguste Blanqui, 'General of the revolutionary masses', felt able to write that 'Communism is the safeguard of the individual'. The word *capitalism* was used by Louis Blanc in his *Organization of Work* (1848–50) and by Proudhon in 1857; it appeared in the Larousse dictionary in 1867, but it was not overwhelmingly popular until the beginning of the twentieth century. The word *capitalist* was more vigorous. In 1843, Lamartine exclaimed: 'Who would recognize the Revolution as it is now? Instead of enjoying independent work and industry, we see France sold to the capitalists!' Less successful new words included 'bourgeoisism' and 'collectism'.

Nevertheless, memories of 1789 had not lost their power. The

Jacobins, the Terror, the Committees of Public Safety — all these were words and ideas that continued to haunt people's minds, either as models or as monsters. For most reformers, 'the Revolution' remained a talisman and a source of strength. At the time of the Commune, in 1871, Raoul Rigault declared: 'We are not seeking legality: we are making Revolution.'

From the Count de Saint-Simon to Karl Marx, the working-out of 'massive philosophies' (to use Maxime Leroy's expression for philosophies inspired by the problems of the masses) was largely completed by 1848. February of that year saw the publication of the *Communist Manifesto* by Karl Marx and Friedrich Engels, which still remains the Bible of the movement.

A detailed list of the many reformers who were active in this first part of the nineteenth century would show fairly clearly the leading role of the three countries then facing industrialization — Britain, France and Germany. It would also show how important French thinking on the subject was: a question to which we shall return shortly. Finally, it would emphasize the part played by the Count de Saint-Simon. This unusual man, slightly mad but also a genius, was in a sense the ancestor of all social, Socialist, and non-Socialist ideologies, and indeed of French sociology itself (as Georges Gurvitch has said). He certainly influenced another and much greater giant, Karl Marx, who as a young man in Trier read Saint-Simon's writings and drew from them many of his own arguments and ideas.

With the exception of Saint-Simon, the social reformers can be divided into three age-groups: those born in the last three decades of the eighteenth century (Robert Owen, 1771; Charles Fourier, 1772; Etienne Cabet, 1788; and Auguste Comte, 1798); those born in the first decade of the nineteenth century (Pierre Joseph Proudhon, 1809; Victor Considérant, 1808; Louis Blanc, 1811); and the more homogeneous generation of Karl Marx (1818), Friedrich Engels (1820), and Ferdinand Lassalle (1825). This German group brought up the rear. It has been said that the death of Lassalle, killed in a duel in 1864, removed the only colleague who could rival Marx, and so ensured the success of Marxism. But it would be more accurate to ascribe its success to the authoritative power of *Das Kapital* (1867).

This is not the place to study these 'massive philosophies' one by one. All are in effect analyses of 'developing society' – *'la société en devenir'*, in Saint-Simon's elegant phrase. They are, so to speak, medications or courses of treatment. For Saint-Simon and his disciples (Barthélémy Enfantin and Michel Chevalier, who made business fortunes under the Second Empire), effort was to be concentrated on the organization of production. The French Revolution, which they disliked, had failed, they thought, because it had not organized the economy. Fourier, who also detested the Revolution, thought that the priority should be to organize consumption.

Armand Barbès and Auguste Blanqui, Louis Blanc and Pierre Joseph Proudhon, all remained faithful to the principles of 1789, the two former as men of action, the two latter in order to 'fulfil and perfect' those principles. Victor Considérant, on the other hand, rejected them, though less violently than his master Charles Fourier.

Apart from Marx, of whom more later, the most original of these thinkers was Proudhon, so attached to liberty as to be almost an anarchist, as much *vis-à-vis* the Church as against the State. What he sought was a social dialectic which could illuminate scientifically a society on the move, in all its contradictions. It was necessary to resolve them, he thought, in order to grasp the social machinery that they implied. This was scientific speculation, very far from the passions of religion or action. It was at the opposite pole from the spirit of those like Owen, Cabet and Fourier who founded the phalansteries, and was equally opposed to that of the revolutionaries and of Karl Marx, determined to build with their own hands the better world of which they were the prophets.

The primacy of French thinking in these fields, very evident in the early years of the nineteenth century, requires explanation. France was undoubtedly the country of the Revolution – the great Revolution. She was certainly on hand for the revolutions of 1830 and 1848; and in 1871, alone and under foreign conquest, she none the less fed the proud revolutionary flame of the Paris Commune.

Yet, these characteristics apart, the Socialist tradition in France was one of the results of the country's industrialization. As elsewhere, reforming or revolutionary thought in France was the work of intellectuals, the vast majority of whom were socially privileged. And, again as elsewhere, these ideas acquired life and strength only when they were taken up and acted upon by working people. But, more than elsewhere, intellectual reactions in France were both early and extreme – whereas industrialization there came later than in Britain, France's take-off occurring around 1830 – 60.

This is so: but the take-off theory over-simplifies the real process. It names an H-hour when the great industrial rocket is supposed to lift off in one go. Is there ever so clear an economic H-hour? To imagine so is to ignore the whole incubation period that precedes any such sudden spurt. Recent studies have found that France's industrial growth-rate, between 1815 and 1851, was fairly high – about 2.5 per cent a year. Such growth was enough to increase the move to the towns in the eighteenth century, to change existing society and to give France, already shaken by the Revolution and the Napoleonic Wars, that 'demolition-and-building-site' look which so much struck contemporary witnesses.

The growth of towns alone produced a rapid worsening of their human and material condition. From Balzac to Victor Hugo, all observers found this worrying. Poverty, begging, robbery, delinquency, truancy, epidemics and crime: all were increased by the rapid crowding of working people into the unspeakable promiscuity of the slums. And the newcomers never stopped coming. As late as 1847, Michelet noted that the peasant 'admires everything in the town; he wants everything; he will stay there if he can ... Once he has left the land, he hardly ever returns.' Yet in 1830, a troubled year, Orléans had to support 12,500 needy people out of a total of 40,000 inhabitants – i.e. nearly one in three. In Lille in the same year, the proportion was one in 2.21.

It would seem as if town life at that time was especially bedevilled by industry. Industry affected the town and drew people towards it, but it could not raise local standards or even provide for those it attracted. It may be that urban poverty then was no worse than poverty in the country. But in the towns, in view of everyone, there was the alarming spectacle of a population of workers who were victims of the industry that gave them work but cared little about how they lived.

So, when the beginnings of industrialization began to transform the towns, the first 'ideologists' were confronted with a society not unlike that of less developed countries today. Later, from 1851 onwards, with the economic boom and growth that accompanied the Second Empire (1852–70) the condition of working people began to improve.

From organized labour to social security: this question is too large and complex to be treated in depth here. Would it be possible, in any case? It would mean collating, on the one hand, Socialist thinking (a family of ideas evolving, complementing and contradicting each other), and on the other the demands of organized labour, in the real context of work and daily life. How were Socialist ideas treated by the tough and turbulent mass of working people?

The question is hard to answer, especially since organized labour often pursued its own policies, as in Britain, in a realistic, cautious and practical way, ignoring ideology and extremist militant politics. Then again, if the first phase had been that of social theorists, the second that of trade unions and the third that of workers' political parties, the final phase was that of the States. In some cases, they refused workers' demands (or made reluctant concessions for prudential reasons, which amounted to almost the same thing). In other cases, they met or even anticipated the claims, drawing their sting in advance.

In this process, therefore, at least four groups were involved: theorists of every kind, trade unionists with many different attitudes, politicians from among (or sympathizing with) the workers, and representatives of the State. All were very different from one another. Yet there was a general evolution in Europe, in roughly the same stages, at least in the three key countries – Britain, France and Germany – and in their neighbours – The Netherlands, Belgium, the Scandinavian countries and Switzerland. Outside these privileged areas, progress was slower, and has not always been completed, even today. Here are some of the landmarks in that progress, where it has occurred:

Before 1871:

In Britain, large numbers of trade unions were established from 1858–67 onwards. From the beginning, they campaigned for the abolition of the old laws on relations between master and servant. The first Congress of the trade unions was held in 1866. At that time, the unions included only skilled workers.

In France at this time there were few positive steps. In 1864 there was a Combination Law which allowed legitimate strikes; in 1865, the French Section of the International opened an office in Paris, following the opening of the first, in London, in the previous year; in 1868 it opened another in Lyon. The Second Empire was at once 'progressive and compressive': it improved workers' conditions, but was careful to limit their liberties.

In Germany, the situation evolved just as slowly. In 1862, Lassalle founded the Allgemeiner Deutscher Arbeiter Verein. Seven years later, the Congress of Eisenbach saw the establishment of the Workers' Social-Democrat Party, with Marxist leanings.

Before 1914:

Up to that date, immense progress was made.

In Britain, in 1881, Henry Mayers Hyndman founded the Social Democratic Federation to spread 'Socialist' ideas among the workers, who had hitherto been impervious to politics as such. At about the same time, in 1884, the trade union movement began to reach poorer, unskilled workers. Not till ten years later, however, did the London dockers stage their great historic strike. In 1893, the Independent Labour Party was established, and five years later the General Federation of Trade Unions. The electoral successes of the Labour Party were followed by an almost revolutionary development, the 'radical' Government of 1906. A series of welfare laws followed, promising a gradual transformation of Britain.

In France there were similar developments. In 1877 Jules Guesde founded the first Socialist newspaper, *L'Egalité*, and two years later the French Workers' Party, the Parti ouvrier français or POF. In 1884 the trade unions were legally recognized; from 1887 onwards, labour exchanges began to be set up. The year 1890 saw the first celebration of 1 May, Labour Day; and 1893 the first election of Jean Jaurès, Socialist deputy for Carmaux. In 1895, the Confédération Générale du Travail was established. In 1901 came the foundation of two Socialist parties – the Parti socialiste de France, led by Jules Guesde, and the Parti socialiste français, led by Jean Jaurès. In 1904 the newspaper *L'Humanité* was founded; and in 1906 the two Socialist parties were merged as the Parti socialiste unifié.

In Germany, the Socialists were harassed by Bismarck's emergency laws of 1878; but from 1883 onwards the State passed a number of welfare measures. After Bismarck's resignation in 1890, the trade unions reorganized, and soon had more than a million members. They also had great political success, with 3 million left-wing votes in the 1907 election, and 4,245,000 in 1912.

All this being so, and without exaggerating the strength of the Second International, it could be argued that in 1914 the West was not only on the brink of war, but also on the brink of Socialism. The Socialists were close to seizing power and building a Europe as modern as it is today – and perhaps more so. In a few days, a few hours, war destroyed their hopes.

It was a very great failing on the part of European Socialists that they were unable to prevent the First World War. This is freely

admitted by those historians who are most sympathetic to Socialism, and who are anxious to know who in particular should bear
the blame for this reverse. On 27 July 1914, Léon Jouhaux and his
colleague Dumoulin, Secretaries of the French CGT, met K.
Legien, Secretary of the German Trade Unions, in Brussels. Did
they meet by chance, in a café, or with no purpose other than to
admit their despair? We do not know. Nor do we know what to
make of Jean Jaurès's last actions, on the very day he was assassinated (31 July 1914). He had gone to Brussels to try, in vain, to
persuade the German Socialists to strike rather than accept mobilization for war.

Western Europe today, in so far as it has adopted Socialist ideals,
has done so slowly and incompletely, by the ballot box, by laws
and by the establishment in France in 1945–6, and in Britain a
little later, of a social security system. Already, the European
Community, by declaring the principle that all States should bear
equal burdens in this field, has in effect opted for the eventual
adoption of similar rules throughout its member countries.

19. Unity in Europe

An historian of humanism, Franco Simone, has warned us to be wary of the supposed unity of Europe: a romantic illusion, he says. To reply that he is both right and wrong is simply to affirm that Europe simultaneously enjoys both unity and diversity – which on reflection seems to be the obvious truth.

The preceding chapters have described a number of things shared by the whole of Europe: its religion, its rationalist philosophy, its development of science and technology, its taste for revolution and social justice, its imperial adventures. At any moment, however, it is easy to go beyond this apparent 'harmony' and find the national diversity that underlies it. Such differences are abundant, vigorous and necessary. But they exist just as much between Brittany and Alsace, between the North and the South of France, between Piedmont and the Italian *mezzogiorno*; between Bavaria and Prussia; between Scotland and England; between Flemings and Walloons in Belgium; or among Catalonia, Castille and Andalusia. And they are not used as arguments to deny the national unity of each of the countries concerned.

Nor are these national instances of unity a contradiction of Europe's own. Every State has always tended to form its own cultural world; and the study of 'national character' has enjoyed analysing these various limited civilizations. The brilliantly clever books of Elie Faure or Count Hermann Alexander Keyserling are not in this respect completely misleading: but let us simply say that they peer too closely at the individual tiles in a mosaic which, seen from a greater distance, reveals clear overall patterns. Why must one be forced to choose, once and for all, between the detail and the whole? Neither need exclude the other: both are real.

Outstanding art and culture

Some of Europe's shared characteristics can justly be called 'brilliant'. It is they that give European civilization, on the highest plane of culture, taste and intellect, a fraternal and almost monolithic air, as if bathed in a single, unvarying light.

Does that mean that all the nations of Europe have exactly the same culture? Certainly not. But any movement that begins in one part of Europe tends to spread throughout it. Tends only: a cultural phenomenon may very well face resistance or rejection in one part of Europe or another – or, conversely, it may be so successful that, as often happens, it goes beyond Europe's frontiers, ceases to be 'European', and begins to belong to humanity in general. Nevertheless, broadly speaking, Europe is a fairly coherent cultural whole, and has long acted as such *vis-à-vis* the rest of the world.

Art enjoys multiple resonance. Artistic phenomena in Europe spill over the borders of their native countries, whether Catalonia (probably the source from which early Romanesque spread), the Ile de France, Lombardy, fifteenth-century Florence, Titian's Venice or the Paris of the Impressionists.

Regularly, every centre where princely houses, palaces or churches have been built has attracted artists from the four corners of Europe. This was shown in the fifteenth century, to take one example among a thousand, by the Dijon of the Dukes of Burgundy and of the sculptor Claus Sluter. The wanderings of Italian Renaissance artists readily explain how the style of one city was so easily contaminated by that of another. A particular fresco, begun by one artist, might be completed by a second; a particular church might have called for work by a succession of architects.

Santa Maria del Fiore, in Florence, for instance, had to wait for the bold Filippo Brunelleschi before it was crowned by its cupola.

A prince's or a rich merchant's caprice or love of luxury had a role to play: without such stimulus, it would be hard to understand how styles spread so rapidly at a time when communications were slow and less numerous than now. In the fifteenth and sixteenth centuries the Italians, like those whom Francis I of France summoned to his court, were in effect the teachers of all Europe. In the eighteenth century it was the French who carried classical art far afield: they were to be found even in Russia. And how many Versailles Europe possesses – how many gardens *à la française*.

So Europe has been swept by great waves, if not tides, which have been slow to cover all the area, but slow also to recede. One has only to think of those great successes when all Europe seemed to march in step: Romanesque, Gothic, Baroque and Classicism.

Each time, the phenomenon was surprisingly long-lived. Gothic art held sway, in general, for three centuries. To the South, it reached little further than Burgos and Milan: the true Mediterranean spirit rejected it. Yet Venice, at the beginning of the sixteenth century, was entirely Gothic – in its own unique way. Paris was still Gothic in the mid-sixteenth century. Renaissance architecture was confined to a few places: to the Louvre, which was under construction; to the Palais de Madrid, now demolished; and to Fontainebleau, where Francesco Primaticcio ('Le Primatice') had worked and where Leonardo da Vinci returned before he died. From the sixteenth century onwards, Baroque enjoyed immense success: an offshoot of both Rome and Spain, it was the art of the Counter-Reformation (so much so that at one time it was known as 'Jesuit art'). But it also spread to Protestant Europe; and it made great inroads toward the East, in Vienna, Prague and Poland.

In the eighteenth century, French architecture took much less time to establish itself. To understand how so many French towns, like Tours and Bordeaux, were remodelled, the most illuminating sight is that of the former Leningrad. St Petersburg, built in an empty space with no buildings to restrain the freedom of the architects, certainly was and still is the most beautiful of eighteenth-century cities, and the one that best expresses that century's sense of grouping, proportion and vistas.

Painting and music spread no less freely. Musical techniques or pictorial preoccupations were easily taken up into general circulation, and went the rounds of Europe.

It would be impossible to deal adequately in a few lines with the fascinating story of the rapid changes in musical instruments and techniques which accompanied successive stages in Europe's history. The instruments used in classical antiquity, from the flute to the harp, were handed down from generation to generation; next came the organ, the harpsichord, the violin (made popular especially by Italian virtuosi, although the present-day bow, which dates from the eighteenth century, was invented by a Frenchman), and then the various types of piano.

The history of musical form is obviously bound up with the development of musical instruments. In the Middle Ages, singing predominated, whether accompanied or not. Polyphony, which developed in the ninth century, used the organ as bass accompaniment to liturgical song. In the fourteenth and fifteenth centuries, the *Ars nova* of the Florentines was a vocal polyphony in which a number of instruments were introduced as if they were voices. This 'new art' reached its zenith in the *a capella* music of Palestrina (1525–94).

But vocal music gave way to instrumental music, especially with the development of bow instruments. It was the beginning of the concert, of so-called 'chamber music', written for a small number of instruments (for example, a quartet). Originally, chamber music meant secular music, or that of the court as distinct from that of the Church. In 1605, Enrico Radesca was *'musico di camera'* to Amadeus of Savoy; in 1627, Carlo Farina was *'suonatore di violino di camera'*. Chamber music was above all a form of dialogue: it was the art of conversation. Italy was its birthplace, with the concerto in which groups of instruments conferred together, followed by a solo instrument responding to the whole orchestra. Arcangelo Corelli (1653–1713) was the first to play as a soloist; Antonio Vivaldi (1678–1743) was the master of the art. Germany preferred the sonata, with two instruments or sometimes one alone. In France, the suite very freely brought together a number of dance movements.

With the symphony, finally, came large-scale orchestral music – large-scale in the number of instruments and in the number of listeners. In the eighteenth century, with the Stamitz family, the sonata form was already treated symphonically. In the next century, in the Romantic period, the tendency was to enlarge the orchestra, but also to give a more prominent role to the soloists, of whom Niccolò Paganini and Franz Liszt were characteristic examples.

Special mention must be made of Italian opera, which seems to have originated in Florence at the end of the sixteenth century. It went on to conquer Italy, Germany and Europe: Mozart, Handel and Gluck all at first wrote operas 'in the Italian manner'. Then, of course, came German opera.

Revolutions in painting – and they were virtual revolutions – also affected the whole of Europe. Even when ideas about painting seemed contradictory, the same contradictions appeared everywhere. There were perhaps two major revolutions. One was Italian, that of the Renaissance, when the pictorial space became geometric, with the laws of perspective, long before the science of Galileo and Descartes had 'geometrized' the world. The second revolution took place in France towards the end of the nineteenth century, and affected the very nature of painting itself, leading to cubism and abstract art. We have mentioned Italy and France only to identify the places where these revolutions began: in fact, if one takes the great names or the great innovators, they clearly belong to European painting as a whole. Today, indeed, we should have to say 'Western painting', since it has travelled far beyond Europe's own shores.

Philosophies, too, carry unique messages. Europe has had a

single philosophy, or something very like it, at every stage of its development. At the very least there has always been what Jean-Paul Sartre liked to call 'a dominant philosophy', reflecting the needs of society at the time – no doubt because the whole of the West, at any given moment, has had a single dominant economic and social structure. Whether or not the philosophy of Descartes was that of a rising bourgeoisie and a slowly growing capitalist world, it certainly dominated and pervaded the Europe of its day. Whether or not Marxist philosophy is that of the rising working classes and of Socialist society, or industrial society, it has clearly played a dominant role in the West and in the world, which it divided as, until only very recently, it divided Europe.

For philosophies to spread so readily, there had to be innumerable international links. Take two important periods in German philosophy: from the publication of Immanuel Kant's *Critique of Pure Reason* in 1781 to the death of Hegel in 1831; and from Edmund Husserl (1859–1938) to Martin Heidegger (1889–1976). The influence of these German thinkers cannot be understood unless one bears in mind the many translations – French, English, Italian, Spanish, Russian, etc. – that were made of each of their works. Translation is one measure of the degree to which two major movements in German philosophy were integrated into the intellectual life of Europe.

It may be noted that, in the case of existentialism, it was its reinterpretation by Jean-Paul Sartre and Maurice Merleau-Ponty that retransmitted it to the rest of the world, and especially to Latin America.

As regards the natural sciences, there can be no question: they were strictly pan-European from the time of their first success. It is difficult to give any one nation in Europe the credit for this discovery or that, because so many of them were the result of work that was going on everywhere at once, in a series of stages that successively involved all the scientists in Europe. Any example will serve to prove the point. That of the Keplerian revolution, so well described in Alexandre Koyre's 1962 study, is ideal for the purpose. Johann Kepler (1571–1630) belonged to a virtual family of kindred spirits – his predecessors (above all, Copernicus), his contemporaries (above all, Galileo) and his disciples. If we were to mark on a map their birthplaces and the centres where they worked, the whole of Europe would be covered with black dots.

Medicine, biology and chemistry showed a similar pattern. None of the sciences can be described as having been German, British, French, Italian or Polish, even for a short time. They were always European.

Developments in the social sciences, by contrast, resembled those in philosophy, in the sense that they tended to originate in particular countries and then spread rapidly to the rest of Europe. Sociology began as a predominantly French speciality; economics, especially in the twentieth century, has been mainly a British or Anglo-American achievement; geography has been both German and French (as witness Friedrich Ratzel and Vidal de la Blache). In the nineteenth century, history was dominated by Germany and by the great name of Leopold von Ranke (1795–1886): German historiography impressed all Europe with its erudition and its meticulous reconstruction of the past. Today, the situation is less simple; but European historiography – now in fact world historiography – forms a coherent whole. Within it, a French school is important, dating from the days of Henri Berr, Henri Pirenne, Lucien Febvre, Marc Bloch, Henri Hauser and Georges Lefebvre, supported by economists like François Simiand or sociologists like Maurice Halbwachs. This school seeks to synthesize all the social sciences, and it has revitalized the methods and prospects of historiography in France.

Literature in Europe shows the fewest signs of unity. Rather than European literature, there is national literature, and while there are cross-frontier links, there are also considerable contrasts. The lack of unity in this field is by no means regrettable, and indeed is natural. Literature, whether essays, novels or plays, is based on what most differentiates national civilizations: their language, their daily life, their way of reacting to sorrow, pleasure, the idea of love, or death, or war; their way of entertaining themselves, their food, their drink, their work, their beliefs. Through their literature, nations once more become characters, individuals whom one can try to analyse – even to psychoanalyse – with the help of this essential evidence.

There are, of course, clear and lasting cases of convergence: literature has its fashions. In the nineteenth century, for instance, the Romantic Movement that followed the rationalist Enlightenment affected the whole of Europe; and in its turn it was followed by social realism. There has been ceaseless interplay of 'influences' – between individuals and among groups of writers or 'schools'. Clearly, however, every literary work has its roots in a particular social and emotional milieu, and in unique personal experience. One can scarcely speak of unity in national literature. How then, *a fortiori*, can one seek unity on a European basis?

Is there not, furthermore, a major obstacle in the question of language? No translation can fully convey a literary experience. Each of the great languages of Europe, it is true, owes some of its riches to others, even if only one of them could become the lingua franca, like Latin in former times and French in the eighteenth century. The royal treatment that Voltaire received, in St Petersburg or in Paris, can be explained only by the royal status of the French language. Today, however, resort to a single language is possible for science (which has almost created a universal artificial language with its international technical terms): but it is not possible for literature – the more so in that literature is all the time growing more demotic. The 'international' French of the eighteenth century was after all the language of an élite minority.

Should the cultural unity of Europe be safeguarded, or does it need to be completed? With Europe bent on abolishing its internal frontiers, is this chequered cultural unity enough? Evidently not, because those who seek a politically united Europe are much concerned with the unifying effects that could be achieved by a well-thought-out reform of education. If qualifications were harmonized it would be possible to pursue one's studies from one university to another; and this, more than the establishment of one or more European universities (such as that now set up outside Florence), would create a European arena for study and research.

And would that not promote, of necessity, a modern form of humanism embracing all the living languages of Europe?

Economic interdependence

For centuries, Europe has been enmeshed in what has amounted to a single economy. At any given moment, its material life has been dominated by particular centres of privilege and influence.

During the later Middle Ages, Venice was the channel where everything gathered, to pass in or out. With the beginning of modern times, the centre of gravity for a time was Lisbon, then Seville – or rather, it alternated between Seville and Antwerp until the last quarter of the sixteenth century. Then, at the beginning of the seventeenth century, Amsterdam became the great trading centre until the early years of the eighteenth century, followed by London, which maintained its supremacy until 1914 and even 1939. There has always been an orchestra and a conductor.

Each time, the centre of gravity has been all the more influential, at its best, because not only European economic life has been attracted there, but also the economic life of the wider world. For Europe, on the eve of war in 1914, London was not only the great market for credit, for maritime insurance and reinsurance, but also for American wheat, Egyptian cotton, Malayan rubber, Banca and Billiton tin, South African gold, Australian wool and American and Middle Eastern oil.

Very early on, Europe became a coherent material and geographical whole, with an adaptable monetary economy and busy communications along its coasts and rivers and then via the carriageways and roads for pack animals that complemented its natural thoroughfares.

Early in Europe's history, pack animals conquered the great barrier of the Alps, through the Brenner Pass (on the way to Venice), the Gothard and the Simplon (on the way to Milan) and by the Mont-Cenis. At the time, the curious term 'great carriages' was used to describe the mule trains that carried this trade across the mountains, enabling the Italian economy to expand towards the North and North-West of Europe, eager for its luxury textiles and for the products of the Levant. In Lyon, in the sixteenth century, trade and trade fairs flourished owing to the confluence of carriage roads, river traffic, and these 'great carriages' from the Alps.

From the mid-nineteenth century the railways rid continental Europe of its rigidity and inertia, and spread a civilization of material well-being and rapid communications, boosted by busy industrial and commercial cities.

Two examples out of this long history may illustrate Europe's economic interdependence, although they do not explain it. One is that of the *mude*, the fleets of Venetian merchant galleys. In the fifteenth century they mostly plied the Mediterranean, but some went as far as London and Bruges, while well-frequented land routes, especially through the Brenner Pass, led from the North to Venice, where the German merchants shared a huge warehouse, the Fondego dei Tedeschi, near the Rialto Bridge.

The second example, in the sixteenth century, is that of the circulation of money and bills of exchange, starting from Seville and going the rounds of Europe. In fact, approximately the same sums passed from hand to hand and place to place in the process of trade and payments.

It is easy to understand, then, why the different regions of Europe were affected almost simultaneously by the same cycles of economic change. In the sixteenth century, a huge price rise began in Spain as a result of the sudden influx of precious metals from America. The same price inflation affected the whole of Western Europe, and penetrated even as far as Moscow, then the centre of a still primitive economy.

This does not mean that all of Europe has always developed at the same rate or attained the same level. A line could be drawn from Lübeck or Hamburg, through Prague and Vienna as far as the Adriatic, to divide the economically advanced Western part of Europe from the backward area to the East – a fact already attested by the difference in the respective situation of peasants on either side of the line. The contrast is beginning to fade; but it still exists.

Furthermore, even in prosperous Western Europe, there are richer centres – 'growth areas' – interspersed among less developed regions, some of them backward or 'under-developed'. Even today, in almost all European countries, some places are still poor by comparison with the nation as a whole, the more so since new investments tend to be attracted to the most thriving areas.

Indeed, there can be no commercial relations, and hence no economic interdependence, unless there are differences of voltage or of development, in which some regions lead the way and others follow. Development and under-development complement and depend upon each other. By way of brief illustration, take the history of banking in France. In the second half of the nineteenth century it expanded rapidly owing to the belated mobilization of savings and dormant or semi-dormant capital in parts of the French provinces and countryside. The immediate beneficiaries were banks like the Crédit Lyonnais, established in 1863, and destined to grow very powerful; but the once backward areas that had supplied the capital soon felt the recoil, as it were, stimulating their economy and linking it to the general life of the nation.

The logic of the Common Market: despite the differences between regional and national economies, economic links have long bound Europe together. Can they be organized to form a coherent and fully interdependent whole? That is the question facing the series of ventures launched since the end of the Second World War, of which the Common Market or European Community is the most successful, although it was not the first and is not the only such endeavour.

Everything began, undoubtedly, on account of Europe's miserable situation after 1945: its total collapse threatened the
equilibrium of the world. Hence the first constructive steps: the
United Europe Movement publicly launched in London in May
1947; the Marshall Plan (3 July 1947), conceived for a variety of
reasons, some political and military, others economic, cultural and
social. Europe – a certain kind of Europe – was groping forward.

For the moment, let us consider only economic problems. From
this point of view, the relative failure of EFTA, the Europe of the
Seven ('the shipwrecked', as one journalist called them), cleared
the way and the future for what was then the 'Europe of the Six',
commonly known as the Common Market but in fact grouping
in the European Community three legal entities: the ECSC, set up
by the Treaty of Paris in 1951, and the EEC and Euratom,
established by the Treaty of Rome on 25 March 1957. Even now,
the European Community does not include all Western Europe,
let alone Europe as a whole. But if Europe is really to be built, the
Community will grow both broader and deeper.

At the time of writing, in February 1962, a number of requests
for entry were under negotiation. Since then, the Community has
grown to number twelve; and further applications for membership
or association are pending. So the Community may well grow to
cover the whole of what is traditionally known as Europe – even
if it is forbidden to stretch 'as far as the Urals'.

Through the Common Market, then, it should be possible to
gauge the chances of achieving European economic union.

The formation of the EEC or Common Market resulted from
the laborious negotiation of the Treaty of Rome, whose complex
provisions began to come into effect from 1 January 1958. This
experiment is still relatively recent, and must therefore, be judged
with caution.

The undeniably rapid economic growth enjoyed by the Six
during the early years of the Common Market was the double
result of a favourable world climate and the beneficial effects of
the first measures taken by the Community itself. The gradual

opening of frontiers was clearly a stimulus, as was shown by the increase of trade among the countries concerned.

All the same, the vital part of the experiment still lies ahead. The Treaty of Rome and the subsequent decisions of the member Governments provide for a series of further steps. The question is: do the steps taken so far promise well for a future which, on paper, should involve total economic integration?

Contrary to some pessimistic forecasts, the Community's industries (including those of France which it was once feared might prove more vulnerable than their German competitors) have adapted well to the Common Market. There have been structural changes, including a tendency towards mergers which has favoured large-scale firms such as the Régie Renault or Pechiney and St-Gobain in France. There have had to be industrial shake-ups: for instance, certain less productive coal mines have had to be closed – although these painful decisions would have been necessary in any case.

Certainly, if only industry were concerned, agreements and compromises would be easy. Given modern technology, firms can be flexible *vis-à-vis* the market and *vis-à-vis* government plans. Equally, there are few difficulties with credit, which depends on the stability and mutual support of Europe's currencies. These enjoyed a long period of relative calm, so much so that the dollar gradually and fitfully ceased to be the only standard currency held in reserve alongside gold. Plans for closer monetary integration in Europe, moreover, made great strides in those years.

Such, then, is the rosy, reassuring side of the Common Market. But that is not the whole story, as recent events have shown. And there are further shadows. Some are political, and to these we shall return in a moment. Others are economic.

These economic problems concern: the geographical limits of the Common Market within Europe; its relations with the rest of the world; and the internal difficulties of agriculture.

The Common Market is clearly incomplete. It has important lacunae in the West. In the East, there was for a long time the

'Iron Curtain', behind which Comecon tried to develop its own counterpart to the Common Market in the West. At the time of writing the major problem was whether or not Britain would join the Community: negotiations had begun in 1961, and they were still in progress. Since then, Britain, Denmark and Ireland have joined, followed by Greece, Spain and Portugal. But Britain's entry, in particular, posed a number of problems. She had greatly to loosen some of the ties that bound her to the Commonwealth, in particular the preferential economic regime which was a relic of Empire. This was difficult from an economic point of view, and required Commonwealth agreement. Psychologically, it also meant as it were turning the last page in the most successful imperial history ever known.

No less important is the problem of the Common Market's relations with the rest of the world, and in particular with Africa south of the Sahara. (The North African countries, with the exceptions of Libya and Egypt, remained for a long time within the economic orbit of France.) This problem of the Community's external relations also included that of relations with the Commonwealth – solved for the most part, with the exception of the former Dominions, by the Lomé Convention linking African, Caribbean and Pacific countries with the Community. Last but not least, there was the question of the Community's relations with the United States. In 1962, some feared that a 'colossal' Atlantic market might swallow up the European Common Market. Others saw Europe as the first step, the Atlantic as the second and the world as the third. They, however, were unrealistically optimistic. All these problems, moreover, were also political; and that in no way made them easier to solve.

The problems of European agriculture, on the other hand, are primarily economic, and of great importance for the Common Market. They are also extremely complicated.

Change was inevitable for the old peasant world of Europe – an admirable world, deeply rooted in the past, but with a fairly modest level of productivity, as the statistics show. The six founder-member States of the European Community had 25 million country-dwellers (families included) out of a total population of 160 million. In the early 1960s, Sicco Mansholt, the former Dutch Minister of Agriculture who was then Vice-President of the Common Market Commission responsible for agricultural policy, estimated that 8 million of these farmers would have to find other employment if farming was to be modernized.

Modernizing agriculture meant increasing the output per person and reducing the number employed in it, not only because greater productivity implied more mechanization, but also because the total agricultural income lagged behind the general growth-rate of the European economy. In an expanding economy, growth tends to concentrate on industrial goods and services. In developed countries, an increase in income no longer leads to greater demand for food. If I have more money, I buy a car, a television set, books or clothes; I travel; I go to the theatre. But I do not eat more bread and meat or, let us hope, drink more wine or spirits.

Broadly speaking, then, if farm incomes were to increase at the same rate as those in other sectors of the economy, it was calculated in the early 1960s that by 1975 one farmer in three should leave the land so that more could be produced by a smaller number of people. The annual reduction, it was thought, should be about 4 per cent, whereas the actual rate was 2 per cent in Britain and 1.5 per cent in France. At that pace, it would take Britain twenty-two years and France twenty-seven to reach the target figure. What was more, there could be surprises. The tapering-off of Europe's boom years meant that there were fewer jobs in industry for former farmworkers; and in Italy, for example, with a peasant population originally numbering 4.5 million, those who left the land were mostly unemployed farmworkers; so, despite the drift to the towns, the structure of agriculture remained almost unchanged.

For all these reasons, European farm prices remain uncompetitive on the international market, where American and Canadian surpluses are sold at very low prices – lower sometimes than on the home market, owing to government subsidies. So the high prices of European agricultural products remain possible only as a result of protection, which isolates them from the world market.

The other serious agricultural problem for the Common Market lies in the disparities in production and prices as between different member States. Before the Community adopted its Common Agricultural Policy, France (which was more than self-sufficient, especially in cereals) could sell its surpluses abroad only at world prices. This obliged the French Government to buy them at home-market prices and sell them at a loss outside France. Thus in 1961, French wheat and barley were sold to Communist China, and chilled meat to Russia. Italy had the same problem with fruit and vegetables, and The Netherlands for dairy products. Germany, by contrast, imported many of the agricultural products it needed, but it bought them outside the Common Market, and was reluctant to lose the export opportunities that were the counterpart of these imports.

Farm prices were also different from country to country, depending both on relative productivity and on the degree of protection that governments were willing or obliged to supply. Thus, grain prices were lowest in France and highest in Germany, while milk was cheapest in The Netherlands. At what level, in a Common Agricultural Policy, were prices to be levelled out?

Finally, since agriculture had to be modernized, and since this was costly, who was to foot the sizeable bill? The solution adopted in Brussels, when the Common Agricultural Policy began to be established on 14 January 1962, was that the Community as a whole should bear the expense. This solution was unfavourable to Germany, whose economy was predominantly industrial. But the predominantly agricultural countries – France, Italy and The Netherlands – refused to move to the second stage of the Common Market's transition period unless at least the outlines of the Common Agricultural Policy were in place. The agreement took so long to reach, after 200 hours of discussion, that for a time the fate of the Community seemed to be in the balance. Which led one journalist to remark that 'Europe happily swallowed coal and steel and the atom, but it baulked at fruit and vegetables.'

The agreement provided for progress by stages: the first steps were to be taken in July 1962. But the Governments and the farmers' unions knew that the days of the old national systems were numbered and that adaptation was now unavoidable.

The movement of farm products throughout the Community was to be unrestricted, if necessary with compensatory taxes to offset remaining differences in price. This principle alone required institutional arrangements, regulation and supervision. Means already existed for the settlement of disputes. At the same time, there had to be a variable levy at the Community's external frontiers to prevent its prices being undercut by imports from abroad.

In later years, the Common Agricultural Policy was subject to countless arguments, criticisms, adjustments and compensatory arrangements: it seemed always to be undergoing reform. But it made possible a Common Market in farm produce, however much it might be flawed. With a single market in industrial products due to be perfected by the end of 1992, the Community was on the way to becoming an economic union. Will it stop at that stage? No. There remains the problem of political unity.

Political delay

Invited to build European unity, culture responds readily; the economy is more or less willing; only politics drags its feet. It has its reasons. Some are good, some less good, some false. Some are based on outdated, nineteenth-century concerns. Others are of the present; others still result from looking ahead.

The truth is that all of Europe has long been involved in the same political system, from which no State could escape without grave risks to itself. But that system did not encourage unity in

Europe: on the contrary, it divided European countries into groups of varying membership, whose basic rule was to prevent any hegemony being imposed on the whole family of nations. This was not out of pious respect for the liberty of others. Each State, in fact, pursued its own selfish ends. However, if it was too successful, it sooner or later found the others lined up against it.

Such, very broadly, was the principle of the 'European balance of power'. Has the Europe of today really given up this age-old policy?

The nineteenth century did not invent 'the balance of power' or 'the concert of Europe', although it practised them assiduously. In reality, similar constraints had been accepted for centuries. They were not the result of careful calculation by diplomatists or even by their masters, but rather, on the contrary, the outcome of a spontaneous, instinctive sense of equilibrium, of which statesmen were only partly aware.

The basic rule was always the same. When a State seemed to be too powerful (even if the impression was false, as in the case of France under Francis I, in 1519–22), its neighbours would jointly tilt the scales in the opposite direction so as to make it more moderate and better behaved. Francis I's defeat and capture at Pavia in 1525 showed that a mistake had been made: the too powerful monarch was the victor, Charles V. So the scales were tilted in the opposite direction: even the Turks were invited to add their weight.

The growing power of the States made this imperfect balancing-act ever more dangerous. Only Britain, from the safety of its island, could pursue the balance of power with impunity: not being on the seesaw, she was happy to weigh down one end or the other with money or troops, but preferably money. For a long time, she pitted her weight against the French, automatically ally-ing with France's rivals. But when Germany became far too power-ful, defeating France in 1871 because Britain and a divided Europe had failed to intervene, there came the Entente Cordiale and the Franco-Russian alliance. After 1890, above all, economic growth

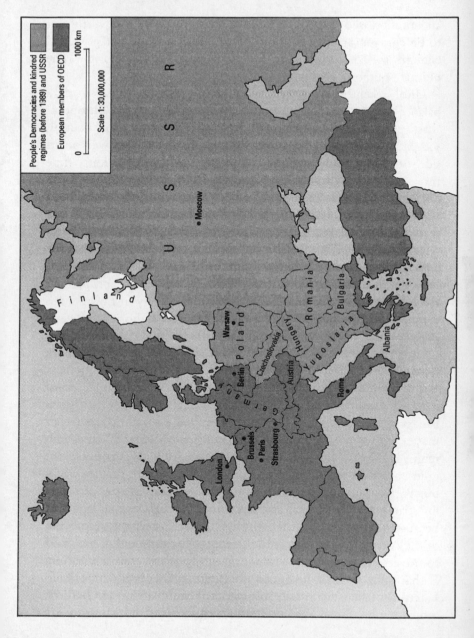

17. *The two Europes*

and an increased population had made Germany too powerful not
to be enraged at being isolated by her enemies, yet not powerful
enough to convince them of her inexorable superiority. The
ultimate outcome was war.

Until recently, the world as a whole was the prisoner of a
balance of power which had become global rather than European.
'East' and 'West' were two camps between which the neutrals
sought a third role which was valid only if it had power on its
side. It was an old system, certainly, which for a long time
threatened the world with the results of its breakdown, as its
failures had so often caused suffering in Europe.

Unity by force always failed. The only moral of this monotonous
story is that violence has never been enough to enable anyone to
seize the whole of Europe.

Without going back as far as Charlemagne, let us look for a
moment at Charles V (1500–58), the least unpleasant and perhaps
the most attractive of those who sought hegemony in Europe. His
dream was to conquer Christendom and use his authority to defend
it against the infidel Muslims and the Protestant Reformation. For
Charles V, the 'Imperial idea' had its roots in the historic Spanish
crusade.

The Emperor lacked nothing: he had troops, admirable com-
manders, passionately loyal followers; he had the support of great
bankers like the Fuggers; he had incomparable diplomatists,
mastery of the sea and finally 'treasure' from America. Under his
reign, indeed, Spain became the warehouse which distributed the
gold and silver from the American mines, partly to finance trade,
but partly also to meet political necessities. Did Charles V fail in
his struggle with France, as has been claimed? Yes and no. Yes,
because none of his victories enabled him to master the vast extent
of the country, which lay at the 'heart' of his Empire but was hard
to traverse at the speed (or rather the slowness) of communications
at that time. In 1529, he signed the Peace of Cambrai with France.
Later, he failed against Protestant Germany (1546, 1552–5); he
wore out his forces against Turkish Islam, and the Muslims not

only threatened Vienna but also raided the coast of Spain as far as Gibraltar and beyond.

In other words, it was a 'concert of Europe' that defeated Charles V, using every method including even the scandalous stratagem of alliance with the Sultan.

Louis XIV imposed his will on Europe only during the lean years of the seventeenth century, when everyone fell back, as it were, on traditional strengths, which profited France with its peasant economy and its very primitive capitalism, well controlled by a strong Government, until the death of Jean Baptiste Colbert in 1683. When the world economy picked up again, probably from about 1680, France soon lost her supremacy. Already in 1672 the flooding of Holland had prevented the French army from reaching Amsterdam; in 1688 William of Orange came to the throne in Britain; and in 1692 Admiral de Tourville's fleet was utterly defeated at the battle of La Hogue off the Eastern coast of the Cherbourg peninsula. In the great War of Spanish Succession, France was unable to match all her enemies, nor to seize the Iberian Peninsula and, beyond it, the wealth of Spanish America.

Napoleon's adventures surely followed the same pattern. On the one hand, so many victories; on the other, resounding defeat at Trafalgar in 1805. While France's conquests were confined to the continent, vast as it was, Britain could deploy her strength on the open sea. It took only 100 or 150 wooden hulks to defend the Straits of Dover, which some had thought to 'stride across' in 1805; and the same applied to the Straits of Messina. So while Naples belonged to the French or to Murat, Sicily remained the refuge of the Bourbons.

Hitler's Germany, likewise, united against itself a coalition that matched the threat it represented – a coalition including the greater part of the world.

The Common Market seeks political unity. Can the political unity of Europe be achieved today, not by violence, but by the common will of the countries concerned? A plan is taking shape, and it arouses obvious enthusiasm in some quarters. But it also raises serious difficulties.

Some of these difficulties we have already noted. In particular, only Western Europe is so far uniting: the building of Europe had to begin 'with what remained of it'. Then again, unity in Europe poses problems elsewhere, in so far as it affects the economic and political equilibrium of the world. Already on 14 November 1958, a banker declared: 'In certain parts of the world there are fears that the European Union may adopt a discriminatory policy *vis-à-vis* non-member countries' – i.e. that it might follow certain options, for example preferring the tropical products of Black Africa to those of Latin America. Similar fears of 'fortress Europe' have been expressed, however unjustifiably, about the Single Market to be achieved by the end of 1992.

But the primary difficulties are internal and institutional: they are not of a kind that can be easily solved by a treaty or by compromise.

Is it possible that the Governments of 'Europe of the States', in General de Gaulle's phrase, will make concessions and sacrifice part of their sovereign rights?

As long ago as 8 August 1950, André Philip told the Council of Europe: 'For a whole year, to avoid disagreements, our Assembly has accepted every kind of compromise. The result? Nothing has been done. Public opinion will be disgusted with us very soon unless we prove that we really came here to build Europe.' On 17 August Philip threatened 'to go and build Europe elsewhere'.

Eleven years later, in Brussels, Paul-Henri Spaak, the Belgian Foreign Minister, declared, on 10 January 1962, four days before the agreement on the Common Agricultural Policy (which he could by no means predict):

Everything leads me to believe that there cannot be a united and effective Europe without supranationality. The so-called 'Europe of the States' is a narrow, inadequate idea. The longer I live, the harder I shall fight against the rule of unanimity and the veto. A few weeks ago, I was at the United Nations and saw the Soviet veto at work. More recently still, I had a similar experience at Nato: on the German question and Berlin, the opposition of one Government prevented Nato from taking a firm and constructive position. What is happening now at the Palais des Congrès on the subject of Europe's Common Agricultural Policy is very far from making me change my mind. In these discussions I look in vain for the spirit of Community. Everyone is defending the interests of his own farmers ... If the accursed rule of unanimity were abolished, the negotiations in the Council would go much faster ... We are offered a Europe of the States in the field of foreign policy. What would that do except create chaos? All the member States bar one might discuss the question of Communist China, and the one might block all decisions ... So I wonder if it would be at all a good idea to give up the spirit of supranationality in these matters.

All these arguments are good. But in a very divided group, majority voting is not necessarily a panacea that can solve all problems. A majority may be formed by wheeler-dealing, by private compromise, by what in some Assemblies are called 'conversations in the corridors'; and these may no more produce a coherent or disinterested policy than bargaining about the veto. The essential question is how far the political views of the present States in Europe can be reconciled, at least on certain deep and basic principles. If not, it will mean a return to the hazards of the 'European balance of power', but this time inside the new Community edifice.

The advocates of political unity affirm, and go on affirming, that the unity they seek will be a matter of free decisions.

No predominance, declared one German businessman in 1958: no Napoleonic or Hitlerian Europe. 'Unity thus based on force can only provoke an explosion, once the grip of the dominant nation is relaxed. Let it be said in passing that today we have an example of that before our eyes: i.e. the States grouped round the power of Russia [*sic*] in the Warsaw Pact are controlled, economically as well as politically, only in the interests of Russia [*sic*].'

That quotation, selected from hundreds of others, helps to

elucidate the problem. For many people at that time, the aim was to regroup Europe, or 'what remained of it', against the Soviet danger. This was clearly the American policy, that of a 'buckler' against the USSR. When the Schuman Plan for the European Coal and Steel Community was being debated on 15 December 1951, the French Premier Paul Reynaud was categorical: 'Let us remember that Pentagon's abandonment of its plan to defend Europe only at the Pyrenees is thanks to General Eisenhower, who has never ceased repeating that the European countries, with France in the lead, want to build Europe. Draw your own conclusions about what would happen if the Schuman Plan were rejected.'

Against this spirit of political and even military calculation, one can imagine another, which is more reasonable because it is more realistic. This is how Senator André Armengaud, a Member of the European Parliament, put the problem in a remarkable lecture he gave in February 1960. In his eyes, Europe was flanked on the one side by the growth of a Communist economy, born in 1917 in 'Petrograd', 'which all traditional economists had said would have no future', and on the other by the great liberation, throughout the world, of the peoples once colonized by Europeans. So Europe too must organize itself in a wholly new way, not simply for capitalist profit, which creates regimes in which the advantages are 'reserved for minorities', but in order to make the optimum use of the labour force. In other words, start from the opposite end.

It would seem wise to see Europe not as a matter of profit for profit's sake, but as a question of the benefits for people; and equally to see East–West competition in terms of the best solution for the human problems of twentieth-century society. Will such wisdom have the chance to be heard?

It is not only a question of knowing whether European union will be achieved and whether it is viable: we have also to ask whether it will be accepted by the other major powers in the world. One or another might be made uneasy by the Union's economic claims or its possible political orientation. Will it lead one day to a peaceful Europe, including in its prosperity a Germany reconciled to the changes in some of its former frontiers? Or will it create an aggressive Europe? Will the new Europe agree to make its contribution to the solution of the world's development problems – on which everyone's lives depend in today's interdependent world? Or will it be unable to catch up with the future, and continue to believe that nationalistic self-interest still makes sense, and that 'European nationalism' can carry on where the nation-States of Europe were forced to leave off? In a word, will it be an inventive Europe, making for peace, or a routine Europe, still creating the kind of tensions that we know only too well?

To ask that is virtually to pose the fundamental question: what can European civilization still do for the world of tomorrow?

Need one point out that this seems to be the least of the concerns of those who are currently building Europe? Their rational debates about customs duties, prices and production levels, like the most generous of their mutual concessions, address only the spirit of calculation. They never seem to go beyond the purely and highly technical level of specialists who are experts in the remarkable projections of economic planning. No one would deny, of course, that these are indispensable.

But we misunderstand people if we give them only these sensible addition and multiplication sums, which look so wan alongside the waves of enthusiasm – and the not unintelligent 'crazes' – that have enlivened Europe in the past, and even the recent past. Can a European consciousness be achieved solely through statistics? Might it not, on the contrary, escape them and overflow them in unpredictable ways?

It is disturbing to note that Europe as a cultural ideal and objective is the last item on the current agenda. No one is concerned with a mystique or an ideology; no one pays attention to the misleadingly calm waters of Revolution or of Socialism, that still run deep; no one seems concerned by the living waters of religious faith. But Europe will not be built unless it draws upon those old forces that first formed it and still move within it: in a word, unless it calls forth the many forms of humanism that it contains.

In fact, it has no choice. It will either work with them or, inevitably, sooner or later, they will overturn it and cast it away. 'Europe of the peoples' is a fine slogan; but it remains to be achieved.

PART II: AMERICA

20. Latin America, the Other New World

═══

America consists of two great cultural entities. The word 'America' by itself is loosely used to denote the United States (plus, sometimes, Canada, so much within the US orbit). That is the New World *par excellence*, the land of amazing futuristic achievements. The other America, the bigger of the two, seems to have accepted its relatively recent name of 'Latin America', first used in about 1865 by France, partly for her own reasons, and later adopted by Europe as a whole. This America is both one and many, highly coloured, dramatic, divided, and full of rivalry.

To begin with Latin America helps to avoid the immediate comparison with North America, which otherwise might overwhelm it in advance with the habitual weight of its immense material wealth. In this way, we can better observe Latin America as it deserves to be seen, with its deep humanism, its own particular problems and its own very evident progress. In the past, it was far ahead of the other America: it was the first rich America, and for that reason envied and coveted. In the past. Then the wheel of fortune turned. The present state of Latin America is very far from happy: it is overcast with heavy clouds. Here, the day has not yet fully dawned.

★

Geography, Nature and society: literature bears witness

More than any other region in the world, Latin America is constantly and rapidly changing. Today's pictures of it are likely to be worthless tomorrow, or at least to look false.

If we cannot see it for ourselves, we should at least read its admirable literature – direct, unsophisticated, naïvely and frankly political. It offers a myriad journeys for the spirit, and its testimony is sharper than anything to be found in reports or in sociological, economic, geographical and historical studies (although many historical works are nevertheless excellent). Literature also reveals – and this is invaluable – the essence of countries and societies which are always private and often secretive, despite the warmth and apparent openness of their welcome.

Geographically, Latin America is vast. Its still sparse population seems shrunk, as it were, in such outsize garments. There is an immense amount of space, an intoxicating amount.

Flying, of course, has reduced and humanized this vastness, making distances almost disappear. So the foreign traveller is more and more likely to overlook the fundamental fact of Latin America's size. Already a few years ago it took no longer than six hours to cross the Amazon basin – or, rather, to fly over it, because travelling through it is still extremely difficult: *isto é matto*, 'that is forest', say the Brazilians. Flights over the Andes, between Argentina and Chile, were then made by twin-engined light aircraft which flew along the La Cumbre pass just over its little rack-rail train, buffeted from one side to the other of the broad valley, but *between* the mountains – beneath them, in fact. Now, four-engined aircraft fly right over the Andes every day, and the mountains are no more than ten or fifteen minutes of glaciers sparkling in the sun before the plane descends towards the Chilean coast or the empty Argentine plain. Above all, flying has become universal: its buoyant song is now heard everywhere in Latin America.

Km²   12 millions   8 millions
Inhabitants   125 millions   62 millions

18. Spanish America and Portuguese America

In grey, Spanish-speaking regions; vertical lines, Portuguese-speaking regions. The two bar charts show the respective areas (above) and populations (below) of these two regions of Latin America. Spanish America has an even higher proportion of people than territory, and so is relatively more densely populated than Portuguese America.

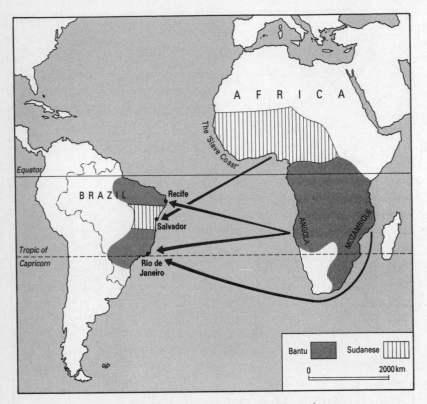

19. The origins of Latin America's black population

But in fact only privileged travellers experience these prodigious
leaps, these luxury excursions which take them from Mexico City,
where the Nortes (the North winds) are still freezing the plants in
the gardens, to deposit them a little while later in the heat of
Yucatán or Vera Cruz, or transport them to the flower-strewn
paradise of the Pacific Coast at Acapulco. Likewise only profitable
or luxury goods are carried by air: seafood from Chile bound for
Buenos Aires; animals on the hoof, or choice cuts of meat, from
Mendoza across the Cordilleras to Santiago or to the Chilean
miners in the Northern desert.

So the shrinking of distances remains an exception, despite appearances. On the airfields of Rio de Janeiro an aircraft lands or takes off every minute. But the passengers are only a tiny fraction of the population, basically its middle class. In Latin America, the airways are not a mass transportation system like the trains, buses and private cars that have given Europe so tightly knit a communications network.

Latin America lived and still lives, as it was shaped, in an area measured by the steps of people and animals. Its pace was not set by the railways, which are few, or by the roads. Some of these latter are superb, as in the case of the Mexican *carreteras*; but they too are not numerous and are continually under construction or repair. Latin America still bears the mark of these leisurely ways.

One must realize and accept the immensity of distances in Latin America if one is to ride or travel with Martin Fierro, the gaucho of the heroic past, invented by José Hernández in 1872, or with Segundo Sombra, the last free, wandering gaucho on the Argentine pampas, invented in his turn by the brilliant Ricardo Guiraldes in 1939. Similar awareness helps one to see 'the backlands' of North-Eastern Brazil, the up-country area of drought and hunger described by Euclydes da Cunha in *Os Sertões* (1902). It also helps understanding of Lucio Mansilla's account of his negotiations with the Indians, written in instalments for *La Tribuna* in Buenos Aires, and published in 1870 as *Una excursión a los Indios ranqueles*, a marvellous picture of the vast Argentine interior and its indigenous peoples. A still better example is the work of the naturalist and novelist William Henry Hudson (1841–1922), which includes an account of Patagonia, then almost virgin territory.

Nor should we forget the magnificent travel writings of the German Alexander von Humboldt (1769–1859) and the Frenchman Auguste de Saint-Hilaire (1799–1835), who although foreigners were so much captivated by the countries they described that South American literature virtually annexed them from the start.

One of the most vivid images from these classical accounts is that of the mule trains, with their fixed routes, their almost fixed timetables, and their regular 'halts', the *ranchos* where people, animals and goods stayed overnight before continuing the trail next day. Such mule-trains have been called the first trucking service, the first railways. They were certainly the first means of crossing wide open spaces that are still vast and untamed, even today. For, as we know, if people do not settle firmly in one place, as in the West, if they uproot themselves so readily, it can only be because they see wider horizons a little further on. So even now, streams of animals still pour across the heart of the continent as they did in the sixteenth and seventeenth centuries, to wind up at traditional cattle markets like those in up-country Bahia. It is a primitive, inexpensive way of exploiting resources, a kind of cut-price capitalism, so long as the land is available at little or no cost.

So people were isolated – lost or drowned in these vast areas; the towns were far, far apart, and far from the mother countries or the colonial capitals; and some of the provinces were larger than Italy or France. What more natural, then, if all of them, especially in the past, ran their own affairs as they thought best: there was no alternative, and the first priority was survival. In both North and South America, 'American democracy' with its principle of self-government is partly a result of there being so much space. Space moderates everything and conserves everything – until it is conquered.

Until recently, the great objective was to free the peasants from the barbaric constraints of Nature. In South America, Nature produced and still produces admirable people, poor, tough and hard-working: the gauchos of the pampas, the Brazilian *caboclos*, the Mexican peasants or peons. These last were naturally rebellious, provided they had a real leader like Emilio Zapata, who fought for their cause between 1911 and 1919.

Was not the real problem, then, to free these people from the poverty which was the really barbaric constraint on their lives? All the idealistic intellectuals of the nineteenth and twentieth centuries dreamed of doing just that. Not to train people (unless it was vital) in the way that one breaks in a wild horse: but to teach them to live better, to care for their health, to read. It was an urgent task, and one as yet unfinished: there are still 'illiteracy crusades' led jointly and enthusiastically by travelling groups of teachers, doctors and health experts.

The peasants, those 'barbarian' heroes, naturally figure in many novels of the nineteenth and twentieth centuries. In the past, they were often portrayed as at grips with civilization in a sort of duel of love. This sentimental symbolism often produced sob-stories – but they too had evidential value: adjust them a little, and they could be *romans noirs*.

Martin Fierro (1872), in the Argentine pampas, is a primitive creature, but a Christian and a minstrel who sings his own songs. He gives up his outlaw life to join the Indians in the desert; but he had always had his *pundonor*, his point of honour – although it often involved a knife-blow in some *pulperia*, a fortified inn selling liquor in the middle of the desert. *Doña Bárbara* had a woman as central character. It was written in 1929 by Rómulo Gallegos, who in 1947 became a democratic President of Venezuela until he was exiled by a military coup in the following year. Bárbara's name was chosen to make its symbolism clear: dazzlingly beautiful but savage and ruthlessly unscrupulous, she has the qualities and faults that enable her to take whatever she wants, shamelessly. But have no fear: she cannot finally defeat the gentle, naïve and likeable 'doctor of laws' whom an inheritance brings to the *llanos*, those pastoral plains at the head of the rivers, up which the boats travel at a snail's pace – which at least gives the passengers time to shoot at sleeping alligators. And of course the doctor is a crack shot . . . The heroine of *La Negra Angustias* (which in 1944 won its author, Francisco Rojas Gonzales, the Mexican national literature prize) is also beautiful and naïve. But she is also – and disbelief has to be suspended to make the novel work – a cruel and pitiless bandit leader. One fine day, this innocent tigress is suddenly tamed by a modest teacher who teaches her to read. The miracle takes place. Angustias marries her teacher and espouses civilization.

Not all the novels in this vein are quite so sentimental. *La*

Vorágine, written in 1925 by the Colombian José Eustasio Rivera, is the sad story of a couple swallowed up by the Amazon jungle. But whether the books be optimistic or otherwise, it is *Nature* they blame — Nature which turns people into savages, and which is all that needs to be conquered if they are to be civilized and freed. According to the Chilean novelist Benjamin Subercaseaux, Chile's misfortune is its 'crazy geography' (*Chile o una loca geografía*, 1940).

That vision and that literature belong to the past. Today, their world is gradually slipping below the horizon — which in some respects is a matter for regret.

A literature of peasant and social protest is coming into being. Today, the literary hero *par excellence* is still the pauper, cut off from the world by Nature, distance or poverty itself, but now taken up by a new kind of literature — combative, violent, direct and highly coloured. This presents the poor as above all the victims of society, of civilization, which seems as indifferent to their suffering as untamed Nature itself. This literature marks a turning-point, the beginning of a new era. Its tone is certainly revolutionary: it bears witness to an acute awareness of South America's specific problems, and a lack of confidence in the benefits to be expected from 'civilization' by itself. Hence its sombre realism and its despair.

Los de abajo (1916), by the Mexican novelist Mariano Azuela (1873–1952), is one long cry of defiance. It hurls us into that complex mass revolution which after 1910 made modern Mexico without completing it, costing perhaps a million poverty-stricken lives. It tells the story of a handful of revolutionary soldiers who were killed (and whom the author saw die, since he was an army doctor with a group of revolutionaries): the disenchanted story of poor devils ill-equipped to fight an implacable society whose rich members were too rich and too ferocious, while its poor were too numerous and too naïve.

The very long novels of the great Brazilian writer Jorge Amado, most of them set in the Bahia region, a country of hunger, emigration and perpetual poverty, combine violence and beauty to an exceptional degree. However great their political commitment and polemical tone, they form an extraordinary and truthful reportage on an incredibly primitive peasantry and its battle with hunger, in an almost feudal countryside where people have not even the beauties of nature to console them.

Everywhere in this literature the same painful testimony recurs. The novelist Jorge Icaza takes us to his native Ecuador. On the map, it looks small. In fact, it is bigger than Italy: with the Galapagos Islands, it covers some 123,000 square miles. In 1962, it had only 2 million inhabitants, and had offered to take a further million immigrants; twenty years later, its population was over 9 million. Alfonso Pereira, the hero of Icaza's 1934 novel *Huasipungo* (translated into English in 1962), takes his family to his estate high in the mountains, far from Quito and reached by a rough mule track. He cannot stay in town, because his daughter is pregnant by an Indian she was foolish enough to trust, and only in the mountains will the illegitimate birth pass unnoticed. The journey is strange and eventful. When the mules reach the edge of the upland marshes, they get bogged down. Everyone dismounts. Then:

The three Indians wiped the frost off their faces with the back of their sleeves and prepared to take their employers on their backs. They took off their ponchos, rolled their rough, baggy trousers up to their thighs, removed their hats, and rolled their ponchos round their necks like bandits' scarves, exposing their bodies to the biting cold that came in through the holes and tears in their cotton clothes . . . Then they offered their shoulders so that the family (father, mother, and daughter) could exchange the backs of the mules for the backs of the men.

And the procession pressed on through the frosty mud . . .

A little strained as literature, but always moving. Perhaps, simply because the life it described was so hard, it dwelt on what amounted to a violent agrarian dispute and so was content to see only the poverty of the countryside. That of workers in the industrial suburbs or in remote mining regions was beyond its scope and experience. One of the rare accounts of urban poverty to be published (apart from sociological studies for specialists) is the disturbing diary of an almost illiterate black Brazilian, Carolina María de Jésus, living in a São Paolo shack-town. This daily record of her life is not a work of literature, and still less a sociological treatise, but a piece of evidence in the raw. (A French translation was published by Stock in 1962 under the title *Le Dépotoir*.)

With rare exceptions like this, what monopolizes the literature is rural poverty, which seems cut off from any kind of hope or remedy other than revolt, violence and revolution. That is no doubt one of the reasons why Fidel Castro's revolution in Cuba, so much a peasant revolution, has made such an impact throughout Latin America. Whatever its failings or its fate, it marked a moment in history. At the very least, it underlined the absolute necessity for a serious examination of Latin America's political and social problems and the solutions they require. This is something of which all Latin American intellectuals are aware, whatever their personal opinions.

Racial problems: quasi-fraternity

Nevertheless, whatever hesitancy, delays and mental reservations there may have been, Latin America has solved or at least is solving one of its most serious problems: that of race. The first and not the only difference between North and South America is surely the latter's spontaneous and growing freedom from ethnic prejudice. All is not perfect, of course, in this domain. But where in the world have people done better, or even as well? There has already been immense success.

Yet history had stacked the cards against it, by placing side by side in Latin America the three great 'races' of the world with their contrasting skin-colours: yellow (in the case of the Indians, wrongly called 'Red' Indians), black and white. All three were very vigorous: none was prepared to let the others eclipse it.

Ethnic problems would not have arisen, obviously, if pre-Columbian America had remained untouched, with its own coherent civilizations: the Aztecs (plus the Mayas), i.e. broadly speaking, the Mexicans; the brilliant series of Andean civilizations in the high mountains which the Inca Empire had more or less united under its pseudo-'Socialist' authority; and the primitive cultures that occupied the remaining vast areas of the New World.

Nor would ethnic problems have arisen if Europe at the end of the fifteenth century had been overpopulated, able to impose its law by force everywhere, instead of a small world of only some 50 million inhabitants, busily (and of necessity) producing their daily bread, and only sparingly sending a few individuals on American adventures. In *all* of the sixteenth century, only some 100,000 people left Seville for the New World. They might be able to conquer, but could they really grasp the America they invaded?

Finally, the ethnic problem would have lacked its third constituent if the coasts of the Gulf of Guinea to begin with, and then the whole African littoral, had not supplied the manpower that was missing: the black slaves without whom there would have been no sugar, no coffee and no gold dust.

Thus it is that the three races now face each other. None was powerful enough to eliminate the others, or even to try to. Obliged to live together, they have managed – despite a little inevitable friction – to accept the fact, to mix and to achieve a certain degree of mutual tolerance and esteem.

Ethnic regions remain: nothing is clearer, in any case, than the geographical demarcation of the different races, which in fact is a relic of the past.

It was the Indian civilizations that the first white conquerors encountered. The newcomers treated the Indians savagely; they might have swept them away. The effects of conquest were followed by the still greater catastrophes of exploitation and forced labour. The indigenous population decreased in alarming proportions. Everywhere that the Indians had remained primitive – nomadic, tribal, living on cassava – they were driven out, almost as soon as the Europeans arrived; they survived only in a few very remote regions where a few whites arrived late and with great difficulty, as in Amazonas.

Yet the really tightly knit Indian civilizations all managed finally to survive. Unarmed, lacking in tools (they had neither iron nor the wheel, neither gunpowder nor any domestic animals save the llama), and attacked immediately in their heartlands of Cuzco and Mexico, then Tenochtitlan, they were certainly an easy prey. They were saved only by their tenacious solidarity. Today, Mexico is proud to call itself 'Indian territory'; and on the Andean plains the old native life continues – miserably poor, but lively and deeply rooted, irreplaceable.

The blacks, on the other hand, remained where chance, the climate, the plantations, gold seams or gold dust, and urban life took them from the sixteenth century onwards and kept them when slavery was abolished. Later, they often moved to active industrial centres. Logically, therefore, they were to be found on the Atlantic coast, and where Indian labour was lacking. So they were preponderant in Northern Brazil – the heart of the country in colonial times – and they abounded in all its large modern cities. In the West Indies, they were at home everywhere.

The whites, finally, took possession of the American continent in at least two main stages. Each time, different peoples were involved.

In the course of the first conquest, they settled wherever they could live, preferably in those areas where the great Indian civilizations already existed. There they found 'subjects' to rule, and supplies ready to hand. This was the case of the Spaniards, whose great colonial cities were Mexico, Lima (which they founded) and, in the high Andes of present-day Bolivia, Potosi, also founded by them, on account of its silver mines: in 1600, it already had 150,000 inhabitants, living at an altitude of more than 13,000 feet. Spanish colonial art, mainly baroque in style, is still there, bearing witness to the splendour enjoyed by the newly rich in these colonial cities. But most of their inhabitants, remember, were Indian.

The Portuguese in Brazil, by contrast, encountered only a weak scattering of Indians. Hence the decisive importance of the blacks. The great Brazilian cities of the colonial era were in substance African: Bahia, the old capital, with its 365 churches (one for every day of the year); Recife, the great Northern sugar centre, established by the Dutch during their brief occupation (1630–53); Ouro Preto ('Black Gold'), founded in the interior owing to the gold rush; Rio de Janeiro, which became the capital in 1763. São Paulo at that time was no more than a small town with a population of adventurers; there were a few whites and many Indians, as well as those of mixed race who at the time were called 'burnt wood', or (in Portuguese) *mamelucos*.

Memories of the colonial epoch call to mind the achievements of Creole America; and to the British and the French they evoke in particular the West Indies – Santo Domingo and Jamaica, the islands of sugar and then coffee. But the picture was the same everywhere: a strange mixture of primitive, medieval, slave existence and capitalist life. Only the owner of the land, the sugar-cane mills, the silver mines or the gold fields was involved in a money economy, not his slaves or his servants. The result was strange families like those of classical antiquity, whose *paterfamilias* for a long time had the power of life or death over all members of his family or household, with the master's grand house towering above the rows of huts for the slaves. Then the towns sprang up with their luxury houses (the *sobrados*, as houses with several storeys were called in colonial Brazil), their merchants' shops, and also the slums of the poor, known in the past as *mucambos* and now as *favelas* – the equivalent of the shack-towns or oildrum cities in so many conurbations today.

After 1822 and 1823, Latin America was freed from the Spanish and Portuguese mother countries – and from the Cadiz and Lisbon merchants. But then it was exploited systematically and shamelessly by capitalists from all over Europe, and especially from London. The newly independent States were far too naïve as clients of

European industrialists and bankers. Thus, for example, London sold to Mexico in 1821 the rather outdated war supplies that had helped Britain to win the battle of Waterloo.

At the same time, however, Latin America now accepted, more than in the past, immigration from Europe, and no longer solely Spanish or Portuguese. On a small scale at first, with artists, intellectuals, engineers and businessmen, it grew rapidly from 1880 onwards, when steamships began to ply the South Atlantic. They brought huge numbers of Italians, Portuguese and Spaniards, as well as thousands and thousands of other Europeans.

Not all of South America took them in equal numbers. They brought new wealth to Southern Brazil, South of the latitude on which São Paulo stands, Brazil in the past having been centred on the North. They did the same for Argentina and Chile. Over vast areas, this immigration acted like a human bombardment, destroying the old social order – not overnight, but rapidly all the same. It began to fill the countryside. What the 'doctor of laws' in *Doña Bárbara* could not achieve, the immigrants made possible. They created modern Brazil, modern Argentina, modern Chile. Before 1939, a European visitor could in the course of his travels in Latin America find an admirably hard-working Italy in one place, and in another – in the Rio Grande do Sul, in Santa Catalina, or in Chile – a Germany still faithful to its civilization, its distant mother country and its eventful history.

It was these immigrants who did so much for the pioneer areas and young industries. It is they, again, who are to be found on the edges of the populous regions: on the Chilean 'frontier' South of Bio-Bio; in Patagonia, so recently a desert; or in the depths of the State of São Paulo, with their new coffee plantations (*cafezais*). Since these quickly exhaust the soil, the *fazendas* have to move on in search of new land, often burning the forests to provide it. All that is a familiar and fateful story, which could be retold. But it is not what essentially concerns us here. The essential point is the fraternity that exists among the races: all of them have worked together, in their different ways, to make Latin America.

They have also clashed, many times, and for social reasons. Difference of colour was and remains a social difference. True, anyone who grows rich or wields authority crosses or will cross the dividing-line, whatever the exact shade of his skin. But in Peru, for example, Indians and those of mixed race call those who rule them '*blancos*'. In other words, wealth and power have been, and usually still are, in the hands of genuine whites.

In so far, that is, as 'genuine' whites exist. For the most part – and this is important – the races are very extensively mixed. The Recife sociologist Gilberto Freyre, writing about his own North-Eastern area of Brazil, *O Nordeste*, (although the 'Nordeste' has spread over much of Brazil), has smilingly declared: 'We all have a pint of black blood in our veins.' Where mixed blood is most frequent, in Mexico (whites and Indians) and in North-East Brazil (whites and blacks), tolerance and inter-ethnic fraternity are also more noticeable than elsewhere.

Even in these areas, however, there have been problems. Mixed-race Latin America long had an inferiority complex *vis-à-vis* faraway Europe, which in turn tended far too much to encourage it. North America, too, set a notoriously bad example. Travelling to the United States, on the other hand, has been a kind of cautionary experience for many South American intellectuals with white but not pure white skins: it has taught them tolerance and given them the precious gift of self-respect at the same time as respect for their countries.

Latin America's inferiority complex and its attendant prejudices have not disappeared as if by magic. But a great wind of change has been blowing since 1919, or 1930, and even more since 1945. One might still feel drawn to Europe, but could one still owe it so much respect after the follies of the first World War, the economic disasters that followed 1929 and the horrors of the Second World War? Largely free, and largely welcoming immigrants, the Latin American countries have gradually been acquiring greater self-esteem. The change is slow, and is not yet complete, but it has been under way for a long time. In 1933, the early works of

Gilberto Freyre were published in Brazil. They no longer spoke
the traditional literary language of the novel or the essay, but
adopted the crisp tone of the new social sciences. This was a
decisive turning point in the biggest, most human and perhaps
most humanistic country in the New World. Likewise, the pro-
Indian revolution that began in Mexico in 1910 not only
inaugurated a series of political and agrarian revolutions. It also
opened the way to hope.

The degree to which the races enjoy equality and fraternity
obviously differs from place to place. Too often, past social
stratification forms an obstacle. There are some countries in Latin
America where almost the whole population is white, as in
Argentina (with only a few remnants of the Indian peoples in the
far North or the far South). There are also countries where, according to anthropologists, the mixture of races has already produced
new, uniform and stable ethnic types. One example is Costa Rica.

But even if fraternity among the races is not always complete or
not always possible, it is a general phenomenon, and one of the
special features of this 'other America' – its distinguishing
characteristic, its most attractive aspect, and something recogniz-
ably unique. Landing in Panama on the way back to his own
country, a South American traveller feels a sudden thrill: all the
different skin colours, the ringing voices, the cries, the songs – no
doubt about it: this is already home.

The economy: civilizations on trial

Despite its carefree air, its love of pleasure, its exuberance and its
noisy popular festivities, Latin America today is as full of deep
suffering as it was in the past. Keyserling called it 'the continent of
sadness'. Like all countries or continents that embark on genuine
industrialization, it has to face a total transformation of its structure
and its behaviour; and the shock, for Latin America, is especially
hard.

Why? Because this is a world which is unstable, changing, uncertain and lacking economic and social order – owing to the fact that for centuries it has been continually destroyed and rebuilt. It is a world that has been buffeted, a contradictory world where the most primitive kind of human existence continues right alongside the enclaves of an ultra-modern life. Altogether, it is a world full of vitality, and therefore all the harder to define, organize and steer.

Economic fluctuations are unpredictable tidal waves. Latin America is speeding towards material wealth. This is a race it has been committed to for centuries, willy-nilly, and more often as a loser than as a winner. In doing so, it was no doubt following a world trend. But in any race it is one thing to be among the leaders, setting the pace, and quite another to be the last, making desperate strides to catch up. South America was certainly the last in this race, leaping and stumbling in ways that looked almost comic – to everyone else. It had to hurry; and if it wanted to sell it must at all costs produce sugar, or coffee, or rubber, or *charque* (dried meat), or nitrates, or cocoa, and always sell them cheap. And so, each time, it was caught off balance by successive 'cycles' in the world economy, with their sudden unexpected downturns.

This process explains South America's present economic situation as well as its past. It adapted itself to all the requirements of the world's demand for raw materials in an economy that to begin with was of a strictly colonialist type, and then after the colonial period became an economy based on dependence.

Foreign capitalists (or rather, large international firms), in alliance with the big landowners and local politicians, encouraged the production of exportable raw materials, leading the productive areas to concentrate all their efforts, manpower and resources on one single activity, to the exclusion and the detriment of everything else. The resultant growth might in the long run have borne fruit for the whole of the country, if frequent shifts in demand had not regularly wiped out these investments. When that happened, efforts had to be switched to another sector of production – and at the same time, very often, to another region.

The variety of its climates and the vastness of its territory enable South America to survive these extraordinary changes of direction which in fact, on a national basis, were an unheard-of waste of space and people: everywhere, they prevented the establishment of lasting, stable and healthy economic structures and the formation of a settled peasant society.

The first of these economic cycles was that connected with precious metals; and it began with the European conquest itself. The 'gold' cycle lasted barely longer than the middle of the sixteenth century; the 'silver' cycle, affecting above all the mines in Mexico and Potosi, ended around 1630–40. Their cost was heavy sacrifice. If the Indians had not been ruthlessly conscripted for the task, who would have accepted work in the Potosi mines and foundries, at the exhausting altitude of 13,000 feet in bitterly cold mountains lacking wood and food and even, sometimes, water? The silver ingots were taken to the Pacific, then to Callao, Lima's port, and finally to Panama; from there, by mule-train and then by boat on the Chagres River, they reached the Caribbean sea coast. After that, Spanish fleets carried them to Spain.

Who profited from this great system? Spanish merchants and 'civil servants', and (already) international businessmen such as the Genoese men of affairs or *hombres de negocios* who were accredited lenders to the King of Spain. The beneficiary was certainly not America itself, constantly losing its ingots and silver coins, its very currency, in exchange for a few fabrics, some wheat flour, jars of oil, barrels of wine and black slaves.

The Potosi silver mines began to be less productive in the seventeenth century; and with that Spanish America was almost left to its own unhappy fate.

In 1680, it was the turn of Portuguese America to experience a gold rush, based this time on the work of black slaves. This slowed down in about 1730 – at the same time as the silver mines of New Spain (present-day Mexico) began to revive. The Brazilian province of Minas Gerais ('General Mines') then lost much of its role and its population, and converted as best it could to the production of cotton.

One could trace in the same way the cycle of stockbreeding with its many variations, down to its present-day practice in Argentina; the cycle of sugar production begun on a large scale in Brazil and shifting at the end of the eighteenth century towards the Caribbean (Jamaica, Santo Domingo, Martinique); the cycle of coffee-growing, which became especially important in Brazil from the nineteenth century onwards, taking up an immense amount of space, and encroaching more and more on the interior. The Argentine Chaco, formerly known for its *quebracho*, a tannin-producing shrub, has since 1945 seen a rapid increase in cotton production.

A whole book could not do justice to the vast subject of these 'cycles' in specialized products and single cash crops. At present, rightly denounced as catastrophic, the system may well be in its final phase, to be replaced by the beginnings of real industrial production and coherent national economies. But the whole economic structure of South America has been marked by this old, unstable, irrational practice, with its abrupt changes and incessant moves from place to place: every time, provinces and towns were first animated and then deserted, or at best obliged to undertake formidable and costly reconversions.

Major crises followed these cyclical changes. Their destructive power was enough to upset the whole economy of a strong and healthy country. A single example will suffice. It has the advantage of being, sadly, up to date. It concerns Argentina in this century.

In about 1880, Argentina began to be really prosperous. In a few years, by completely transforming the old structure of its economy, it became a major exporter of grain and meat to the European market. Until then, the Argentine pampas, the enormous plain around Buenos Aires, had been a desert roamed by wild cattle, which the gauchos hunted almost exclusively for the export of leather. From that time onwards, rather like the prairie in the United States, the pampas was turned over to wheat-growing and to grazing for selected cattle stock, carefully fed and fattened.

Until 1930 (and leaving out the difficult decade from 1890 to

1900) Argentina enjoyed incredibly rapid growth: in population first of all, thanks to a large number of Italian immigrants; in production, thanks to regular exports; then in capital investment, with silos, mills and freezing plants. Out of this there soon came the normal development of light industry. Wage-earners' purchasing power, the return on capital and even the number of cars per thousand of population all reached a peak.

From 1930 onwards, the crisis began, imperceptibly at first on account of the general euphoria. Then the war, which favoured all exporters of raw materials, delayed any realization that things were going wrong. But after 1945, with the steep fall in farm prices on the world market, the whole Argentine economy declined, and this time rapidly. Official figures admit that the national income per head went down by an average of 0.4 per cent per year after 1948; but US economists believe that this figure should be at least 2 per cent – a fact made still more serious by an average fall of 3 per cent a year in the investment rate per head. Argentina's trade balance was in deficit; wages and the general standard of living had fallen considerably; so, as a result, had the possibility of sustaining fairly well developed national industries like textiles, food, leather, etc. Unemployment was increasing; the countryside was losing its population to the towns, which swelled beyond measure even when they had no work to offer. Five per cent of the country's total population – i.e. about a million people – were living in shack-towns, called in Argentina *villas miseria*. Industrialization, the sole hope of rescue, had come to a halt. Above all, there seemed no way out: the State budget was on the brink of bankruptcy.

In other words, Argentina, which before the Second World War was the richest country in South America, favoured by its climate and the quality of its soil and its people, had become not the poorest – it was too far ahead for that – but the country that was regressing the fastest. Euphoric confidence had given way to confusion. This explains the series of political crises in Buenos Aires that marked the following decades.

Argentine economists believe with some reason that the agrarian system, built from scratch by the boom in wheat and meat, was in reality harmful. On the one hand it involved a myriad tiny holdings, far too small to be economic, covering 34 per cent of the land farmed; on the other, a handful of big landowners had 42 per cent of the territory and 64 per cent of the cattle. That is undoubtedly the main obstacle in the way of national recovery, which needs agrarian reform able to ensure rational production and to rebuild a national market, without which industry can obviously not survive.

Economic incoherence is a hindrance to modern industrialization: the development of South America has generally produced unbalanced and rather incoherent economies.

What is obvious everywhere is the inadequacy of existing means of communication. They were not built rationally to serve the national economy, but arbitrarily to link production areas with seaports for the export trade, leaving between them enormous stretches of territory without the smallest road. The airways, although they exist everywhere, serve only as a partial remedy. The hero of *Huasipungo*, Alfonso Pereira, failed to appreciate the privilege of keeping his feet dry when his Indian carried him through the marshland. 'Ah,' he sighed, 'if only my father had been cleverer he would have forced all his *péones* to build roads, and then we should not have been in this plight today!'

Another anomaly is the violent contrast between underdeveloped areas, or those abandoned after a period of development, and those which are relatively overdeveloped. There are still a few poetic little towns in the Brazilian interior, places like Minas Velhas, living as primitive a life as a very modest medieval city, far from anywhere, with only a few patrician houses recalling better days; while the 'civilized' zone is too often confined to a strip of land along the coast, linked to the great export routes of old.

Finally, there is something missing. Nowhere in Latin America is there the equivalent of Europe's farmers, a strong and solid basis for the economy, the heirs of traditions going back for thousands of years.

Sucked into the mad mercenary world of the single cash crop, herded into vast holdings hastily funded by foreign importers, then suddenly abandoned with these domains themselves, owing to some unexpected change in demand, much of the farming population is made up of nomadic agricultural labourers. Sooner or later, many of them are drawn by unemployment towards the nearest town, either in the hope of a problematical job or in order to emigrate to another province, still in search of work. Hence the apparent paradox that in some countries where there is more than plenty of land, and where the farm population makes up 60 or 70 per cent of the total, there is a lack or at least a shortage of food crops. Why? Because on the one hand there is no breed of settled peasants, who really know how to get the best from the soil, while on the other hand ownership of the countryside is so unequally divided that this alone prevents any true settlement on the part of the peasants and any normal production. All too often, one is reminded of feudal Russia.

Alongside this archaic rural world, industry has developed in those areas – generally along the coasts – which were favoured by the recent past. Here, an accumulation of domestic or foreign capital, the presence of people who have come into fruitful contact with Europe or the United States, a certain number of scientific and technical personnel and a further contribution by immigrants, have made it possible to switch from agricultural exports to industrial production. The results are sometimes surprising: ultra-modern cities with large numbers of skyscrapers have grown like mushrooms. São Paulo, in Brazil, is a dazzling example.

As a result, Latin America has a double economy: one sector, developed and even relatively overdeveloped and over-industrialized, lives a modern life; but it coexists with huge sectors of agricultural life that are still very primitive and absolutely archaic. The dichotomy is worsening, too, in so far as all new developments are concentrated in the sector that is already developed.

One example of this is Brazil. Its development, unlike that of Argentina, began late: it was already notable, however, by 1930 or so, and after the war it expanded vigorously. In the fifteen years up to 1962, its production doubled in real terms. Even per head of population, its gross national product increased, from 1948 to 1958, by an average of 3 per cent a year. During that time, São Paulo and Rio de Janeiro mushroomed even more rapidly than the most famous fast-growing cities in the United States. Light industries and textiles led on to the establishment of some heavy industries. Statistics showed impressive economic growth.

No doubt: but that growth was mainly in the industrial field. During the same period, agricultural production grew only as fast as the population – i.e. by about 1.5 per cent a year. Cultivated land made up only 2 per cent of the total area! Almost 70 per cent of the population was living, or rather vegetating, in this meagre farm sector, covering some 50 million acres, with very low productivity. The North-East, with a third of Brazil's population, was purely agricultural, and so was exposed to real hunger, and to all the diseases associated with malnutrition.

This situation could not change quickly, because the already developed part of the country attracted so much of the available private investment, State aid and credit, and even the currency earned by exports from the North, such as cocoa, sugar, cotton and vegetable oils.

Discussing Brazil or Mexico, several observers have suggested that these countries' developed sectors are in the same position *vis-à-vis* their undeveloped sectors as the mother countries once were *vis-à-vis* their former colonies. A very great part of the country can attain neither production nor income, and hence cannot meet its minimum consumer needs: one is sacrificed to the other.

The Brazilian Government, at grips with the urgent problem of industrialization, clearly went for the solution that was most economic and most likely to produce quick results. But were these results the most lasting?

For a number of years, Brazil's industrial expansion rate showed signs of slowing down: there was a danger of over-production, for want of a big enough domestic market. Unemployment, inflation and a considerable rise in the cost of living, which squeezed the national market still more, were all signs that industrial development could no longer continue without a policy which explicitly sought to improve the agricultural sector of the economy so as to achieve a growth in consumption and a decent standard of living for the mass of the people, without which modern industry would have no firm foundations to build on.

There is a grave social problem. The need to solve it faces all the Latin American countries undergoing industrialization, and in much the same terms: it is all the more pressing because their social problem is so acute. There is an ever-growing gap between that section of society which shares in development and profits from it, and that which remains on the outside. This is an explosive situation.

Another explosive factor is the growth-rate of the population, which at about 2.5 per cent is the highest in the world, compared with 2 per cent or so in Africa and 1.3–2 per cent in Asia. A mass of rural proletarians descends on the towns to become an urban proletariat, often unemployed, the more depressed because alongside it is the luxury of an industrialized society to which almost all ways of entry are barred.

All sociologists in recent years concur in their judgement of the immense efforts made by Latin America today. Its industries could not have failed to be impressive, since they have benefited from the latest advances of modern technology. Architects and engineers in South America, whether native or foreign, have nothing for which to envy their colleagues elsewhere. But the human side of the story is appalling: destitution and chaos stare in at the gates of order and luxury.

Take for example the Huachipato blast furnaces, in the far South of Santiago, Chile. The 6,000 middle-grade employees who work there are technically outstanding and in good trim. What a contrast with the condition of some of the workmen's families, who are crowded ten deep in little huts on the edge of the works, which the Company lets us visit so as to reveal openly (to the inquiry team) the difficulties it faces. And the situation there is far better than in the nearby mining town of Lota. I have rarely seen a sadder sight than that of miners there spending what could be their leisure hours on the threshold of their houses, squatting in the coal-dust, while here, there and everywhere the children are swarming in the filth of the streets or around the market stalls of Lota Baja, where evil-smelling meat lies open to the flies and the dust. More children still swarm in the slums and the squalid quaysides of nearby Talcahuano . . . I was told in Lota that barely a quarter of the poor children there would manage to escape from that sad community: three-quarters of them would live and die there.

(Georges Friedmann)

A similar report on the coalmines of San Geronimo, at Rio Grande do Sul (Brazil), or on the Bolivian tin mines, would be scarcely more optimistic. On the edges of the most luxurious towns in Latin America, even around São Paulo, the same proletarian poverty is to be seen. It spreads into the heart of Buenos Aires, of whose 6 million inhabitants (in 1962) 55 per cent were working-class, 60 per cent of them ex-farmworkers who had left the land. As was once the case in Europe, these rustics are unsatisfactory as factory hands: they clock in one day, but fail to reappear the next. Many firms replace 75 per cent of their workforce every year. The workers' ignorance compounds their poverty: everywhere, failure to follow the most elementary rules of diet makes undernourishment worse. There are few skilled workers in the European sense; and the few there are tend to be overpaid, forming a kind of urban middle class outside the world of ordinary workpeople, and little inclined to show solidarity with them.

Everything conspires, therefore, to isolate and ignore that poverty-stricken world and leave it to its own devices. Official labour laws are often the most liberal imaginable: but there is an enormous gap between the letter of the law and what happens in

practice. Trade unions exist, but they have nothing in common
with those in the industrialized countries, except for the name;
they are not even organized on a national basis. In a word, the
working class is poor, uneducated, disorganized, often illiterate
and often a prey to an emotional and romantic form of politics (of
which Peronism was an example). It finds no solid support
anywhere, either materially or intellectually. All this presages a
difficult future, for a long time ahead.

An intellectual élite of writers, good teachers, some rare politicians,
a few cultivated doctors and some lawyers have courageously
faced these new and daunting problems. Unhappily, however, the
weakness of the ruling classes and the political and economic élite
is another of South America's serious and permanent handicaps.
The crisis of industrial growth pitilessly eroded an old, fastidious
and cultivated society, which might have proved unable to cope
with the modern world but was none the less extremely attractive.
The misfortune is that nothing as yet has appeared which could
fully take its place.

Before 1939, when Latin America was still semi-colonial, only a
few actors seemed to occupy the small stage of political life and
culture, at the same time as they dominated the peaceful world of
business. Charming, likeable and cultivated, they owned hundreds,
thousands of acres, as well as the richest of libraries. Some of them
were veritable Renaissance princes, just the type to captivate a
journalist, traveller or intellectual from Europe. On the eve of the
Second World War, however, they already gave the impression of
being a social anachronism. They bore immense responsibilities –
one in charge of almost all the British capital in Brazil, another the
representative of something like the Dearborn Chemical Society,
another running public finance, governing a State or hoping to
become President of the Republic, and yet another a General risen
from the ranks. But they all seemed to rule, as it were, from the
inner sanctum of their thoughts and their libraries, as if in an
unreal universe. They believed in the virtues of culture, civilization

and reason. They seemed to belong to the liberal and aristocratic mode of nineteenth-century Europe, in an atmosphere of benevolent despotism, or perhaps enlightened paternalism.

And at the same time, outside their charmed and firmly closed circle, there were new men, industrialists and immigrants who had made their fortune. They were beginning to achieve astonishing economic success; and only their children would acquire a certain polish.

Today, society has evolved and the wheel has come full circle. Broadly speaking, power has passed from the landlords to the industrialists and bankers; vast family properties have given way to sumptuous mansions – in Brazil on the beaches of Rio or behind Petropolis; in Mexico at Vera Cruz, Acapulco or Cuernavaca below the capital, or in the rich suburbs of Mexico City itself. The towns, meanwhile, have taken on the appearance of major cities, with luxury hotels, skyscrapers and restaurants perched at the top of their thirty storeys in the American style. Not to mention that last wonder of the world which eclipsed all the others: Brasilia, the artificial capital city in the heart of up-country Brazil. This whole new world is taking its revenge on the old.

What South America continues to lack are consistent political parties and, still more, élites, a stable middle class or *medio pelo*, as it is called in Chile (where the term ordinarily applies to cross-breed cattle). A few intellectuals are by no means enough. It needs time, calm and an economy less sharply split between very poor and very rich, before such a middle class can emerge. But it will be indispensable for social equilibrium in a world which so far remains fundamentally capitalist.

The relative lack of a middle class on which serious political parties could rely explains why governments in South America have traditionally been so unstable. Competition among the parties has been usurped by competition among men. The army has played a very important role, following the still surviving tradition of the *libertadores*, the romantic Generals who successfully championed independence at the beginning of the nineteenth century.

However, the rapidly growing political awareness that urbanization is creating, even among very ordinary people, may force Latin America to undertake the immensely difficult task of extensively reforming its present social and economic system. Without such reform, a Mexican author has argued, it will remain for ever in the ante-room of truly modern capitalism, the power-house of wealth and well-being, without being fully admitted. That in turn would lead willy-nilly to violence – which would not necessarily, by any means, open the doors to genuine Social-ism.

A Brazilian, Josué de Castro, perceptively wrote in 1962: 'There is no doubt that Brazil' – and he could have written 'Latin America' – 'needs to achieve a giant leap in social history. What we have to ensure is that the leap does not end in the abyss: so we must muster our strength to reach the other side.'

South Americans' sense of insecurity, instability and uncertainty is undoubtedly justified. Less justified, perhaps, is their pessimism. The instability they feel is more than anything that of a civilization trying to find itself and define its own nature, under the pressure of painful but powerful realities.

For a long time, the only civilization that modern Latin America knew was alien to it: a faithful copy, made by a small group of highly privileged people, of the civilization of Europe, with all its refinements. There, too, literature bears witness. How many books there are by nineteenth-century South American authors which contain no clue to suggest that they were written outside Europe! Culture, for many people at that time, was an ivory tower in which they took refuge from time to time from the life which surrounded them and which had no place in the higher realms of the spirit.

That intelligentsia closely followed European thought, with both satisfaction and passion. That is why one still encounters, throughout South America, a very lively form of revolutionary humanism, and some traces of Auguste Comte's positivism which at first sight seem strangely out of place. (The slogan *Ordem e Progresso* on the Brazilian flag was in fact a homage to Comte.)

Those times are past. South American civilization now involves the mass of an increasingly urban population: it is feeling the impact of a powerful indigenous way of life, and can no longer simply accept its inheritance from Europe without adapting it very substantially. Latin America is building a new civilization – its own.

The emergence of a mass culture throughout the world, spread and imposed by the press, radio, television and the cinema, would sooner or later have made change inevitable. What is important for Latin America is that its intellectuals have anticipated the inevitable and already given it a shape. The eclipse of Europe's prestige owing to the First World War and above all the Second World War, and a certain defiance *vis-à-vis* the might of the United States, have coincided for them with the discovery of their own riches and their own tasks. The sense of guilt about the injustices of society, of which we spoke at the beginning of this chapter, has done the rest: the people, the *caboclo*, the *peón*, the Indian and the black have at last taken their places at the common table. They have ceased to be savages whose only interest was as passive recipients of the blessings of white civilization. Now, the interest lies in their own life, their thought, their proverbs and their religion; they have become the subject of sympathy and study by sociologists, and at the same time part and parcel of the national culture which is beginning to evolve.

That is what explains the publication, unthinkable fifty years ago, and the success (120,000 copies sold in Brazil, equalled only by some of Jorge Amado's novels) of the humble diary we mentioned earlier. As one Brazilian critic remarked, this book by Carolina María de Jésus is anything but a work of art. 'It is a document written by a woman of the people, an unequivocal message of fraternity, understanding and social justice.' Nor has it only made its author relatively wealthy: the slums that it describes (which can be seen in the film *Orfeu Negro*) have partly been demolished with a view to reconstruction.

The same change is evident in the growing interest in South America's popular folklore, which if understood aright is not only picturesque but sturdy. Sometimes, admittedly, it is already a little adulterated, like the loud and charming music of the Mexican *mariachis*, fiddlers who play in mixed groups in the bars of Mexico and elsewhere, and whom tourists' attentions have already somewhat spoiled. Their name is said to derive from the 'marriage' feasts at the time of the French occupation. If the etymology is perhaps dubious, it at least indicates, surprisingly, that the French presence did not leave too bitter an after-taste in popular memory.

Of course, one must leave the tourist routes behind if one wants to find true folklore and hear those old sentimental or lugubrious Brazilian songs which as always invoke the sorrowful moon or, still more, enjoy the dances and songs that are improvised to the music of primitive instruments. Thus in a market deep in the interior of Bahia, alongside the cattle pens, humble stalls offer a choice of, say, steaming rice, a live piglet, a scraggy quarter-chicken, or for a few *tostoẽs* every kind of tropical fruit – and a blind beggar will improvise his entreaty, his thanks and even a song. Any foreigner who is thought generous – and who has had himself described for the purpose – has a right to a long piece of improvisation in which personal compliments are mixed with the traditional blessings.

In fact, all the events of daily life are grist to the mill of these popular singers. Ubatuba, a small remote port on the Atlantic coast near São Paulo, was linked to the rest of the world, in 1947, only by one old car which twice a week came down from the Serra do Mar along an absurd mule track. Then it was decided at least to give it an electricity supply; and pylons advanced on the town through the forest, one by one. This *chegada da luz* – the arrival of light – was the theme of a song improvised one night by a musician with a *violão* (a primitive instrument) – an interminable hymn to the glory of civilization.

Each country in Latin America has its own folklore, its own music, its own stories, deriving from Indian, Spanish or black traditions. Folklore also deeply colours religious life. Despite the work of Protestant missionaries, which has often been more spectacular than effective, Catholicism predominates: but it is a primitive, medieval form of Catholicism, firmly believing in miracles; the Christian story mingles with Indian myths, and magic rites from the African past are confused or combined (*candomblés*) with Roman ritual. The fact that there are few priests encourages this free interpretation, which dilutes not only the Christian faith but also the native traditions. One day, Latin America will have to put its religious house in order. One historian of Protestantism, Emile G. Léonard, who is a Protestant himself, believes that the spiritual situation is reminiscent of Europe at the time of the Reformation or shortly before it: there are keen spiritual needs on the one hand which are poorly met on the other. However, signs of change abound.

Modern literature and all of life and culture in Latin America are in fact engaged in a return to their native sources. From this point of view, the best example is Mexico, where there is a broad and powerful movement towards 'Indianity', seeking the living springs of the nation. Mexico is remaking itself. It has taken much suffering; it has involved revolution and catastrophe. But out of them has sprung a popular, populist literature, as well as a revolutionary art, prefigured by José Orozco in the vaults of Guadalajarra Cathedral, and taken up by a whole new school of painting. One might add, finally, the emergence of an indigenous cinema, one of whose early fruits was the admirable *Maria Candelaria*.

21. America *par excellence*: the United States

====

This America has always insisted that it is unique. As a civilization, it was for a long time a traveller without baggage, convinced that the future would forever grow brighter and that seizing it was simply a matter of willpower. Thomas Jefferson, one of the authors of the 1787 Constitution, declared: 'America is new in its forms and principles.' Since then it has never ceased to consider itself new every morning, and to think with Jefferson that 'the land belongs to the living'. It was certainly able to stride confidently through economic, social and political crises: its reserves and its stock of optimism never seemed on the point of running out.

That has been so, at least, until relatively recent times. A first shock was the unexpectedly severe crisis of 1929, which began in Wall Street and was all the more painful because it struck at the heart of a thriving economy, rapidly expanding and, as it were, off its guard. America then found itself facing its first material catastrophe. To recover, psychologically, it was not enough to become more prosperous than ever. For the first time, America took a long look at its past – not so much to understand itself, since the average American has no spontaneous belief in the explanatory powers of history, but rather to seek some sort of consolation.

The growth of a taste for retrospective nostalgia accompanied the slow decline of traditional faith. When competition and enterprise were rapidly growing, Americans thought about the future; when they were flourishing, they thought about the present. Now, in the age of mergers, of giant corporations and monopolies, which reduce the scope for competition and the opportunities to be seized, they turn with regret to the golden age behind them.

Thus one percipient observer, Richard Hofstadter, in 1955.

America, still so young, has grown a little older. The Vietnam War has aged it still more. It has become conscious of its history, and is approaching the moment of truth. It has realized that its former refusal to be interested in the past, its fierce individualism, its isolationism and its rejection of any restraint on individual or national freedom, were all reflections of the 'unity of cultural and political traditions on which American civilization was based'.

Could it be that the situation of the United States today has made those implicit traditions redundant? Certainly, the past is beginning to weigh on its shoulders.

A reassuring past:
opportunities and setbacks

For a long time, America believed that it was forging a new future, unshadowed by what had gone before, because the past was effaced automatically and at once. The golden rule was to avoid any ties or attachments to one's roots, and to gamble on the unexpected. The operative word was 'opportunity'. Any man worthy of the name must seize his opportunity when it came and exploit it to the hilt. In the ensuing 'competition' with others he proved himself and showed his worth.

As an entity, the United States behaved in the same way. Its past is a series of opportunities offered, seized almost at once and fully exploited – a series of 'coups' to be brought off, usually with success. Let us begin with a balance-sheet of these opportunities, from both the distant and the more recent past.

*

Colonization and independence

The first opportunity was the rather belated conquest and occupation of part of the American seaboard. To be settled is to begin to exist. The race for the whole of America was begun by the epoch-making voyage of Christopher Columbus in 1492. Spain (Castile) was the winner. Eight years later, in 1500, the Portuguese under Alvarez Cabral seized the land of the Holy Cross (Santa Cruz), in the present-day country that owes its name of Brazil to the wood used for red dye, the *pao brasil*. Then came the French. Their merchantmen and pirate ships (sometimes indistinguishable) roamed all the Atlantic coast of the New World, from Newfoundland (discovered by the beginning of the century) to the Caribbean, Florida and Brazil (held by the Portuguese, but more in theory than in practice). In 1534–5 the French reconnoitred Canada, and settled there in 1603. The British were the last to arrive. In the last years of the sixteenth century, Walter Ralegh landed on the shore of what at once became Virginia, but the settlement he founded there was short-lived; and the *Mayflower* pilgrims reached Cape Cod, in what was to be Massachusetts, in 1620.

At first sight, these parts of the New World were not a very attractive geographical package: a cheerless coast, broken up by estuaries, gulfs and inland seas like Chesapeake Bay, and also wooded and marshy, cut off in the West by the Allegheny Mountains. Altogether, it was a vast area whose different parts were cut off from each other except by slow coastal navigation. There were also later rivals from Holland and Sweden to cope with, as well as surprise attacks by the native Indians. The French, nevertheless, starting from the St Lawrence River, had seized or at least explored and then occupied the Great Lakes and the huge Mississippi Basin as far as the delta, where New Orleans was built. They had thus executed a vast pincer movement, and won the first round.

From then on, the British bridgehead was squeezed between Florida, where the Spaniards had established their outposts, and this over-mighty French Empire, with its trappers in search of furs and its active Jesuit missionaries. When the British seriously began expanding Westwards in the eighteenth century, they came up against the forts of the French garrison towns.

Where in all that lay the 'American' opportunity? Probably in the fact that the British colonies, although fairly small in relative terms, were solidly occupied, especially in the North, where Boston, Massachusetts, was springing up, and in the centre, with New York (formerly New Amsterdam) and Philadelphia, the Quakers' city.

Linked with the mother country and its trade, these cities, founded in the wilderness, had the advantage of self-government: they enjoyed a quasi-liberty like that of typical medieval cities in Europe. Unrest in Britain served their interests: it exiled across 'the herring pond' not only unruly members of Protestant sects, but also 'cavaliers' who were frowned upon by Cromwell. There were so many such newcomers that by the time the real struggle ended, in 1762, the British numbered a million, against only 63,000 French. The British or 'American' opportunity was to have achieved this overwhelming numerical superiority in the teeth of both France and Spain.

Alfred Sauvy made the point well.

Once there were a million English on this continent, against some 70,000 French, the issue was decided, even if the fortunes of war had smiled on Montcalm at Quebec in 1759. Long before Voltaire, colonization and, above all, peopling the colonies did not essentially interest the French authorities. Mistakenly, they feared that France might be depopulated; and they also faced other domestic difficulties and concerns. So much so, that (bearing in mind the countries' respective sizes) thirty people from Britain left Europe for every single person from France. What a strange discrepancy between cause and effect: if the English language and its accompanying culture dominate the world today, that is because only a few French ships every year carried to the New World a minute number of people, most of whom were illiterate.

It can be a mistake for historians to play at 'what might have been'. An American, a passionate and single-minded Francophile, amused himself one day — not without admitted regrets — by imagining what North America would have been like if it had inherited French clarity, *douceur de vivre* and gastronomy. But that dream is well beyond the bounds of what history would have made possible.

America's first great economic advance took place against a background that was mainly agricultural. But its success (much greater than that of Canada) derived also from its connection with the sea. In North and South alike, water and waterways played an important role. Barques, fishing and merchant ships, and later the magnificent racing clippers swarmed on the seas, some reaching the Caribbean and South America, some going to Europe and the Mediterranean, others penetrating as far as the Pacific. During the War of Independence from 1776 to 1782, the American 'Insurgents' came as far as the English Channel, threatening Britain's shipping and commerce; and British frigates were repeatedly defeated during America's victorious war against Britain from 1812 to 1815 — an episode eclipsed, in many general histories, by the better-known struggle against Napoleon.

These maritime ventures helped make the fortune of a number of American cities, from the seventeenth century onwards. Admittedly, Britain's mercantile laws required on the one hand that the American colonies buy from the mother country all the manufactures they needed, even if they were imported from other European countries, and on the other that they sell to Britain and her colonies almost all their agricultural produce (except for a few products like grain and fish whose import into Britain was banned). Yet in 1766 Pennsylvania bought £500,000 worth of goods from Britain while selling her only £40,000 worth. It was a paradox often noted.

'Well then, how do you settle the difference?' Benjamin Franklin was asked when he was summoned before a House of Commons committee to explain this anomaly. 'The difference,' he explained,

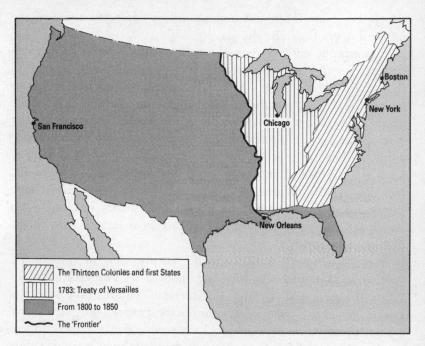

San Francisco

Chicago

Boston

New York

New Orleans

The Thirteen Colonies and first States

1783: Treaty of Versailles

From 1800 to 1850

The 'Frontier'

20. The expanding United States

is paid for by the goods we send to the West Indies, and which are sold in our own islands or to the French, Spaniards, Danish and Dutch; or by those which we send to other North American colonies – New England, Nova Scotia, Carolina and Georgia; or again, by those we send to the various countries of Europe . . . Everywhere we receive money, or bills of exchange, or goods, all of which enable us to pay Great Britain. Everything, added to the profits from the activity of our merchants and sailors on these round voyages, and to the transport offered by their ships, finally comes to Great Britain to right the balance.

This large-scale triangular trading system added the profits of freight service and trade among foreign countries to the commerce legally permitted by Britain – not forgetting some very active smuggling and some privateering that occasionally bore fruit. Nor should we omit fishing. America's sailors neglected none of the opportunities offered by the sea.

Towards the end of the eighteenth century, indeed, there was no question: the tonnage of American shipping was greater than that of any other country except Britain. In proportion to population, the United States was the biggest maritime nation in the world. This involved it willy-nilly in the world economy, forcing it to accept the ensuing constraints and pressures, but enabling it to enjoy the benefits too. All the precocious and ingenious devices of a society built on credit, as no other had been, derived from the fact that it was obliged to compensate for its own subordinate position and seek out the precious metal which it lacked, but which for that very reason it had to pass on as soon as possible, so as to pay its debts.

Every history of maritime good fortune tells of distant and surprising adventures. In this case there is an embarrassment of riches: the arrival of convoys of 'American' wheat in the Mediterranean or in the ports of revolutionary France; the Americans' success at the same time in blockade-running in the direction of the Spanish and Portuguese New World; the way in which they reached the Pacific via Cape Horn, and then, much later, from San Francisco. Scarcely had the former colonies won their freedom from Britain, in 1782, than they were trying to sail to China. And it was the desire for a port of call on the way to China, and for a safe haven for Pacific whalers, that led America in 1853 to send Admiral Perry's 'black ships' into the Bay of Tokyo, with the fateful consequences that everyone knows.

Nothing is more revealing than chance encounters with American ships in those days, travelling the seven seas. The *Lion*, the three-master carrying Lord McCartney to China as British Ambassador, put in at the island of St Paul in the South Atlantic in February 1793. There they found five seal-hunters (three French and two British) who were preparing to send 25,000 sealskins to sell in Canton, on board a Boston ship that was half-French and half-American and was also carrying to China a cargo of Canadian beaver furs. A few months later, the Ambassador had the pleasure of seizing this imprudent ship, in the waters off Canton, as a prize of war – because she was vaguely French, because war had been declared between France and Britain in January 1793, and because he had just heard the news.

Another tiny example: on his second journey round the world in the service of the Tsar, Otto von Kotzebue, son of the German poet and dramatist, was in a Southern Alaskan port on 26 April 1825. He met there an American two-master which had come straight from Boston to this small Russian outpost via Cape Horn, laden with foodstuffs which it was exchanging for 21,000 skins of 'sea cats', which were inferior to the precious furs of sea-otters, but which their purchaser hoped to take via the Sandwich Islands to sell in Canton. 'When the ship arrived in port in Alaska, the whole crew was drunk, including the captain; only by luck did they avoid the reefs and the shoals; but the Americans are so skilful that even when drunk they can always manage.'

This was also the heyday of whaling, the speciality of New England and the State of New York. The novelist Herman Melville (1819–91) described this rough world, where he had lived himself, its tough and dangerous life, and the prosperous little towns that depended on this one occupation – towns like New Bedford and Nantucket. Whaling declined after 1850, when mineral oil and gas replaced spermaceti oil as a source of light.

At about the same time, United States shipping found itself facing stiff competition from British iron-clad steamers. Its relative failure to recover from this blow was partly due to the fact that its attention was now turning inwards, to the frontier in the West. Conquering the continent – its own continent – pressing on Westwards, building railroads, encouraging coastal and inland navigation to provide further links: this huge task drew it away from the ocean. It was the new opportunity.

As so often in American life, when one activity is no longer essential, another presents itself. The latter becomes urgent: the former is left behind. In this case, it could be said that America exchanged the ocean, in which it now had less than a 50 per cent share, for a huge area of land which it seized in its entirety, and for itself alone.

No historical event is better known than the American colonies' seizure of their independence from Britain (1776–82). Even so, it has to be placed in context.

With the end of France's Empire in America in 1762, Britain's aid to the colonies at once became less vital and her demands upon them became more onerous. However, neither they nor Britain intended to bring about a break. The breach between them grew by itself, a result of misunderstandings, inadequate concessions and ineffectual violence. Every subsequent instance of decolonization, even today, has involved a similar succession of largely irrational events.

Was Britain wrong in not making swifter and bigger concessions? In imposing taxes to pay the huge costs of the war against France, then removing them, but leaving in place the tax on tea, with the result that the tea-chests on board two East India Company ships were thrown into Boston harbour on 16 December 1773? No taxation without representation is part of Britain's political tradition; and the British in America were not represented in Parliament at Westminster. So it was a major error.

A British historian writing in 1933, moreover, was surely right to point out that from the mid-eighteenth century onwards the centre of gravity of the British Empire began to shift from America and the Atlantic to India and the Indian Ocean. Bengal was occupied in 1757; and the rush for 'the China trade' began at about the same time. Was Britain being drawn away from the New World and towards the Far East by the eagerness of capitalism in search of still greater profit margins?

However that may be, some such series of reasons led to a spectacular war with the American colonies, and finally to Britain's humiliating defeat. The intervention of France and Spain hastened the success of the 'Insurgents'; but in 1782 the latter signed a secret peace with Britain, abandoning their allies. The result was that at the Treaty of Versailles in the following year Britain lost less than she might have feared. She also quickly realized that economic prosperity would more than make up for her political defeat. Historians may wonder, however vainly, what might have happened if the Industrial Revolution had not supervened to give Britain the makings of lasting power.

If, moreover, what interests us is the future of the United States, we should go beyond the international aspects of the story – beyond La Fayette, beyond the distant exploits of Admiral de Suffren de Saint Tropez, beyond even the plain and realistic intelligence of Benjamin Franklin. What mattered was independence itself, spelled out in the Declaration of Independence on 4 July 1776, and in the slowly matured Constitution of 1787. In those crucial years, young America found itself.

By 'young America' we mean a particular America, the first to take shape. Geographically, it was limited to the Atlantic coast and its hinterland; economically, it was above all agricultural; socially, it was dominated by the land-owning class of the Founding Fathers themselves, those 'founders of American democracy' idealized in picture-book history.

It is not disrespectful, and it may be useful, to see them for a moment as they were, from George Washington to Thomas Jefferson – men who had the will-power to draw up what they were convinced would be the best constitution in the world. It has long been said that the founding fathers based their constitution 'on the philosophy of Hobbes and the religion of Calvin'. For them too, man was 'a wolf to man' and his 'carnal spirit' was far removed from God. After the Shays Rebellion in 1787, General Knox wrote to Washington: 'The Americans after all are men – men with the turbulent passions which belong to that animal.'

The Declaration of Independence proclaimed both the right to rebel and equality before the law. But the great idea which preoccupied and motivated these landowners, businessmen, lawyers, planters, speculators and bankers – these 'aristocrats' – was to safeguard property, wealth and social privilege. America was new-born, but it already contained wealthy people, whose wealth (however modest) qualified them to lead the others. As proof, one has only to listen to the founding fathers, gathered in the Philadelphia Convention to draw up the Constitution, or to read their letters and those of their like. Their basic assumptions are very clear. Charles Pinckney, a young planter, proposed that only someone who possessed at least $100,000 should be able to be President. Alexander Hamilton called for 'the impudence of democracy' to be curbed. All of them, like Peggy Hutchinson, a Governor's daughter, regarded the masses as 'the dirty mob'. A young diplomat and statesman, Gouverneur Morris, declared: 'The crowd is beginning to think and reason. Poor reptiles! They warm themselves in the sun, and the next moment they will bite . . . The gentry is beginning to fear them.' And the lawyer and politician James Murray Mason acknowledged: 'We have been too democratic . . . Let us beware of going too far to the opposite extreme.' No one, finally, was more imbued with the sacrosanct principles of democracy than Jeremy Belknap, a New England clergyman; yet he wrote to one of his friends: 'We should uphold as a principle the fact that the Government derives from the people, but oblige the people to realize that they are not fit to govern themselves.'

That indicates the general line of thought. The order to be imposed in the name of liberty and equality was already a capitalist order, modest as the capital involved might be. Power and responsibility belonged to the rich. The others were granted the great concession of being protected against the rich, as the rich were, conversely, against them. Thereafter, it mattered little that the American Constitution was thought to be revolutionary, new, egalitarian and fair, in so far as it sought to balance against each other the impulses of the human animal, always selfish and fierce.

The 1787 Constitution is in effect a machine full of ingenious counterweights. Powers, Jefferson said, 'have to be so divided and balanced among the different bodies . . . that none of them can overstep the legal limits without being effectively countered by the others'. As for society, there was no question of abolishing privileges, and certainly not those of property, which was sacrosanct; but care would be taken to ensure that the road to privilege – i.e. wealth – was open to all. That, surely, would be easy in a vast and still 'new' country like America.

Richard Hofstadter summarized this ideal with good-humoured irony. 'The Founding Fathers believed,' he said, 'that a well-thought-out State would check interest by interest, class by class, faction by faction, and one branch of government by another, in a harmonious system of mutual frustration.'

It has to be admitted, however, that while nineteenth-century American history turned 'healthy competition' into a huge and ferocious struggle among private interests, the struggle there was more genuine and therefore fairer than in the capitalist countries of Europe. In America, profit was not reserved to a narrow, closed social class; everyone had a chance to seize opportunities in a society with more openings and advantages than elsewhere, and so one day to cross the great divide. The 'self-made man' is the classical symbol of that early America, which today may be on the way out.

Conquering the West

From the beginning, the United States saw itself as a pioneering nation. The same can be said, in fact, of all nations with a huge territory to take, to tame and to humanize – whether Russia, Brazil or Argentina. Geographical expansion is the first form of growth, and the key to all the others. This is true of an economy, a nation, a State, and indeed of a civilization.

History arranged things well. It enabled the United States to expand from the Atlantic to the Pacific, almost without hindrance. Imagine France spreading, virtually unmolested, from the Atlantic to the Urals! In 1803 the United States purchased Louisiana; in 1821 it acquired Spanish Florida; in 1846, to the possible detriment of Canada, it received Oregon from Britain; at about the same time, at the cost only of a too one-sided war, it took Texas, New Mexico and California from Mexico, enlarging its territory even further in 1853. If one thinks of the terrible invasions and catastrophes that attended the expansion of Russia, for instance, or of Europe itself, America's pioneering history – although at the expense of the Indians – looks relatively easy. In reality, the task was immense. Alone, young America would not have been able to master it.

From the beginning, a 1787 law had wisely stipulated that the territories so far unoccupied in the West should become the common property of the Union. Subsequently, as they were peopled, these lands became new States, eventually numbering forty-eight (with Alaska becoming the forty-ninth, and Hawaii the fiftieth). Colonization took many forms. It began in 1776 at the latest, and can be regarded as having ended with the distribution of the last portions of Oklahoma in 1907. Historical narratives, novels and films have made it familiar, from the covered wagons of the first emigrants and their battles with the Indians armed with bows and arrows, to the slow journeys of the last colonists, on the railroads built from coast to coast. Is there any point in returning to these hackneyed images of the heroic Far West?

What needs to be stressed, in fact, is how much the 'frontier', the territory conquered by the whites, represented a great adventure, both material and psychological. Material, in that credit, i.e. capitalism, played a key role in it, from the beginning. Psychological, in that it revealed new dimensions in Protestantism and, beyond that, in American civilization at its second and decisive stage.

Capitalism organized this great move Westward. Picture a settler who has just received his 160-acre homestead, who builds his house by fitting together its pre-cut wooden sections. At first, he tills the light soil on the hills, then gradually moves down to heavier land, and even into the valleys, sometimes clearing them of brushwood, sometimes of timber. He is a farmer, but not a peasant. Until now, he may well have followed a quite different trade. To survive, the only skill he needs is to be able to drive a team of horses; the crops, usually wheat, can be grown without elaborate preparation, and the ground need not be manured. Especially if he is the first to arrive, he will almost certainly have only one idea: to resell his property. He will have lived there for a few years, and will have spent scarcely anything, since all he needs will have been advanced to him in his remote outpost. He will have lived off canned food (already), and used coal for heating if the railroad has reached the neighbourhood. Once two or three good harvests have provided him with capital, he no longer hesitates; he sells his homestead, he takes the profits that will have accrued with the arrival of new settlers, and he moves on – further West, that is, to start over again. To go back East would be a confession of failure. (Based on Louis Girard.) So the settler was not a peasant or farmer, rooted in the soil: he was a speculator. He brought off a coup, as one historian has rightly said. He gambled; and of course he did not always win. But he went on.

A very similar case would be that of a town being built in the Middle West in about 1860. Picture it reduced to its essentials: a rudimentary railroad depot, an equally rudimentary hotel, a general store, a church, a school, a bank. The town has only just been founded, but already everyone is speculating on its growth, and hence buying good land around it and recruiting newcomers. Soon, it has electricity and a tramway; not long afterwards, the telephone. To cite Louis Girard once more, 'Travellers very often notice that electric light and trams are brought into streets which as yet have no houses. Precisely, they are told: this is so that houses will be built, so that the land will sell faster.' In Bismarck, the capital of North Dakota, founded in 1878, and dominated by German settlers, they inaugurated the capitol in 1883.

The inhabitants of Bismarck organized a grand ceremony. They invited not only the up-and-coming James Bryce (who five years later wrote *The American Commonwealth*), but also General Ulysses S. Grant, a distinguished soldier and former President. There was also Sitting Bull, a great Sioux chief who had fought valiantly against the white man: he came to enhance the prestige of the ceremony, and said a few gracious words in his native tongue. What amazed Bryce, a commonsense Scotsman, was that the future capitol was a mile away from the town. His astonishment surprised the inhabitants of Bismarck. They said: but since the city is going to grow, the Capitol has to be a long way from the present town.

The point is clear: that town, like the others, could not live only in the present. It also lived in the future – the secret of all economic success. It counted not on the money it had but on the money that was coming, whether it came or not. What was admirable was that, except during reverses like the recession of 1873, the money always came. The gambles very often paid off.

The America that conquered the West and the Far West was essentially Protestant. Protestantism was alone in facing the settlers' difficult human situation when they were so quickly scattered over such an expanse of land. There they were, without pastors, reduced simply to reading the Bible – if that. True, many of the settlers lived in a kind of medieval simplicity, and their spontaneous religious life was lively: it was sometimes fertile in inventing new beliefs, like those of the Mormons, the founders of Utah. It is to the credit of American Protestantism that it kept alive and quickened the flame of faith: that was one of its finest achievements.

To succeed, it had to adapt to its task, grow simpler, and to distance itself somewhat from the sects already in being (like the Congregationalists or the Episcopalians). It had to curtail its theological teaching and its liturgy, to rely on feelings and on the impact of spectacular meetings. The itinerant ministers of the Baptists, the Methodists and the Disciples of Christ did so remarkably well. They were not the inventors of such emotional forms of worship: Protestant reawakenings and revivals had supplied the model for them. But at least they were able to adapt Protestantism and to simplify it. The Baptists, for instance, abandoned their sectarianism, and the Methodists their Anglican heritage. The new preachers always stressed 'individual study of divinity', 'individual sovereignty' and 'works rather than faith'. The language of Christ was reduced to direct and simple communion.

Beyond their strictly religious aims, these Western preachers fashioned – without knowing it – the American way of life. This was the ideal, the model, the pattern of civilization to which immigrants in the second half of the nineteenth century, Protestant or not, found themselves obliged to adapt.

These spontaneous developments, on the part of the congregations as on that of their pastors, were the work of ordinary people, 'the only makers of churches'. They shared out the vast domain of the frontier like the conquerors they were: the Disciples founded their little churches in the West and Middle-West, the Methodists went to the North-West, the Baptists to the South-West. Altogether, what they did was comparable to the work of the Spanish missionaries who, from the sixteenth century onwards, had to spread the word of God among the immigrants who had come to the New World from Spain at the same time as they sought to convert to Christianity the mass of the Indians, thereby laying the foundations of what is now Latin America.

Industrialization and the growth of towns

The word 'industrialization' by itself is inadequate to describe the way in which the material life in the United States has been transformed between 1880 and the present day. During this century or so, a mainly agricultural country became mainly industrial, as the following figures show. This change would not have been possible without the enormous growth of towns.

There would be no point, here, in tracing the detail of this enormous change, with a mass of statistics and economic indicators. Books on economics and geography give all the necessary facts. Historically, however, it is worth noting that in New England, as in Britain, industrialization began with the expansion of textiles,

A. *Value of agricultural and industrial production*
(in billions of dollars)

	1880	1899	1909	1919
Agricultural	2.4	4.7	8.5	23.7
Industrial	9.3	11.4	20.6	60.4

B. *Rural population (in millions and percentages)*

	1880	1899	1909	1919	1950
Population	32.9	39.3	41.6	44.6	—
Percentage	65.0	51.7	45.3	36.4	15.6

and that – as in many European countries – it became firmly entrenched at the time of the railway boom, from 1865 to the crisis of 1873.

It would be more relevant to show: (a) the huge scale of America's success, which still deeply affects its human geography, as has been shown by the twentieth-century boom in the 'Deep South', on the edge of the Gulf of Mexico; (b) the advanced nature of certain achievements, harbingers of 'the life of the future'; (c) the way in which capitalism has continually revolutionized itself (a subject to be pursued in our next chapter); (d) the arrival of European labour, as vital to the building of industry and giant cities as it was to the opening-up of the West; and (e) the way in which this huge human and material development was moulded, more or less effectively, into the existing civilization that is known, for want of a better term, as 'the American way of life'. But for the moment we shall look only at the last two of these vast subjects.

Until about 1880, the United States had taken on English and Scottish immigrants, the first layer of its European population. Then came an influx of German and Irish people – the latter making America a little less British and even a little less Protestant. Yet the country was still dominated by British culture, and by Protestantism, until between 1880 and 1914, when it took on 25 million Slavs and Mediterraneans, most of them Catholic.

They were absorbed, not so much by the agricultural West as by the urban and industrial East. They changed the East, but not out of all recognition, as for example Argentina was changed, at about the same time, by a wave of Italian immigration which flooded both countryside and towns. There was nothing surprising in the contrast. The United States had towns and industries that were already flourishing; it also had immense powers of persuasion and assimilation. The absorption of the new immigrants was rapid and highly effective. 'Consider a group of Americans taken at random,' wrote André Siegfried in 1956. 'The Nordic types are far from dominant among them. One could as well believe that they come from Naples or Vienna as from London or Hamburg. Yet they are certainly Americans, and they behave and react as Americans. From this point of view, assimilation has worked.'

What had succeeded was a combination of factors: the language, the American way of life and the enormous power of attraction that the New World held for its immigrants. This last was the most important of all. Furthermore, by the quota laws of 1921–4 and the McCarran Act of 1952, the United States virtually closed the door. Since then, the arrival of new immigrants has been a mere drop in the human ocean, despite the sensational scientific achievements of a distinguished few.

Today, there is very little immigration in the South except from Mexico and Puerto Rico, and in the North except from French Canada, some of whose strays are to be found in Detroit, Boston or even New York. All such immigration, now, is a mere trickle. True, New York is the biggest 'Puerto Rican' city in the world; but then Paris is a great 'North African' city in the same sense and for the same reason: every large city looks for unskilled, low-paid, menial labour, and if it fails to find it at home it looks elsewhere.

America's new arrivals supplied its industry with the cheap labour that helped it to start up and then to expand. They also supplied their poor and their proletariat to the great cities, of which New York is the unrivalled prototype. The growth of towns was exceptional and never-ending: the whole of the Eastern seaboard, in fact, from Boston as far South as Washington, has now become a single built-up area – a megalopolis, in geographers' terminology: only here and there are there trees, a few cultivated fields, or suburbs which meet and intermingle. Princeton University stands in the centre of one of these reserves of grass and trees, between Philadelphia and New York City. A moment's inattention, and it would be submerged by these familiar nearby monsters.

And yet, despite this vast transformation and this massive influx of immigrants, American civilization has held its own. It has assimilated everything – machines, factories, the amazing growth of the 'tertiary sector' (services), the swarms of automobiles (of which Europe offers only a distant foretaste), and finally the arrival of non-Protestant immigrants.

American civilization took shape in three stages: on the Atlantic seaboard; from the Atlantic to the Pacific; and then 'vertically', by industrialization. It was the second stage, that of the Far West and the new forms of Protestantism, which settled, perhaps, the essential elements in the American way of life: respect for the individual, extremely simplified religious faith, heavily concentrated on works (mutual aid, singing together, social duties, etc.), and the supremacy of the English language, eclipsing all the rest.

Can such a society be called religious? Yes, the opinion polls answer: almost 100 per cent. Benjamin Franklin said as much in 1782, when America was in its infancy: 'In the United States, atheism is unknown; unbelief is rare and secret.' Today, official language still invokes religion. Any move in foreign policy can readily be called a 'crusade', whether by Woodrow Wilson or by General Eisenhower. Equally, social differences find religious expression. At the bottom of the scale there are the Baptist communities, made up of modest people who until recently were very poor. More 'chic' is the world of the Methodists; and finally, most distinguished of all, there are the Episcopalians (i.e. those with Bishops), whose liturgical ceremonies derive from the Anglican Church. Episcopalianism, one historian has written, is also the Church of the newly rich – those who have 'kicked away the social ladder' they have climbed.

Indeed, in their own eyes, it matters little how Americans organize their beliefs. Their religious life is tolerant, pluralist, divided into different sects or denominations. There is only one Church in the old, exclusive sense of the term; and that is the Catholic Church. Members of the same family find it natural to belong to different sects, since everyone is free to believe in his or her own way, provided they believe: that is the only obligation. In Boston there is a small 'church' built in ultra-modern style. At the entrance, a plaque announces that no particular cult is celebrated on the premises, which are devoted to prayer by all believers in the world, whatever their faith. The only part of the interior which is not in shadow is a great slab like an altar, which is lit from an opening in the roof by a beam of light, reflected down by a large curtain made of pieces of mirror, reminiscent of a Calder mobile.

Wonderful tolerance, a European might think – if he were unaware that atheism and secularity on the Western model, and in particular governmental and educational secularity as in France, are rare in the United States, if not actually inconceivable. On the other hand, a certain kind of non-religion or rationalism is prevalent in some quarters, as it has been in Europe since Charles Darwin's *Origin of Species* and Ernest Renan's *Life of Jesus*. Rationalism of this kind has encouraged the growth of more and more nebulous deism.

The important fact for America's cultural cohesion is that what might have been a divisive factor, that is the Catholicism of certain immigrants, beginning with the Irish, then the Germans, Italians, Slavs and Mexicans, finally adapted – and adapted well, to American life, finding a place for everyone. On this point, the role of the first Catholic immigrants – the Irish – was decisive.

In any case, while the Catholic Church has safeguarded its world unity and its hierarchy, in America it has fully accepted the separation between Church and State, in contrast to its attitude in countries where it enjoys a majority. It has also fully accepted American nationalism. Finally, it has agreed deliberately to emphasize works as distinct from faith, thereby moving with the main current of American life. One statement among many may be quoted as an illustration: it comes from an American Archbishop: 'An honest vote and good behaviour in relation to others will do more for the glory of God and the salvation of souls than flagellation in the middle of the night or pilgrimages to Compostela.'

Like the Protestant sects, the Catholic Church (which now has 30 million American adherents) has organized its own associations, schools and universities. What is more, while the Protestant Churches have had little success in converting the poor in the cities, the Catholic Church has made notable headway in this area.

The relative failure of the Protestant Churches in the towns may be due to its rural success in the nineteenth century, as well as to the growing wealth which has made it more middle-class and lessened its fervour (despite recent signs of revival). For religion in America – and more generally American culture as a whole – is continually threatened by the drift of its adepts towards bourgeois wealth.

Religion, however, is only one of the reasons why American civilization is so coherent. Others include its rapid growth, the attraction of a society in which social differences are marked only by money, and in which – at least until very recently – the road to wealth was anyone's to take. For a European immigrant, to accept these social rules was to step out of the old European social categories and open the way to hope.

Such is the liberal side of a civilization which in other ways imposes constraints, barely allowing the individual to escape from the tacit rules of the American way of life. If the immigrants themselves have some difficulty in adjusting, if they sometimes suffer from nostalgia, their children are eager to melt into the American mass. All sociologists have noted this desire, on the part of immigrants' children, to lose the traces of their origin.

Finally, what has played the biggest role in this process has been the abundance of 'opportunities' in America: the frontier, industrialization and the growth of the great cities have all been wealth creators, and wealth assists assimilation. There is a great distance between the quarrelsome Irish immigrant of the first generation in the 1830s, living in a shack or a slum, and the 'lace-curtain Irish' of the second or third generation. The rising tide of America's prosperity has borne up its first civilization over the new waves of humanity that have swept on to its shores.

While this first civilization soon marked itself off, decisively, from its British origins, it none the less remains more Anglo-Saxon than truly European. Continental Europe has always blended Mediterranean and Nordic traditions. To quote André Siegfried once more: 'This interpenetration of the two civilizations is lacking in the United States, where the Anglo-Saxon side has absorbed everything.' This is no doubt regrettable, in that the hazards of history have made the rest of the American continent, save for Canada, a strictly Latin world, first Portuguese and Spanish, then deeply marked by Italian immigration. It is a fact that the two Americas find it hard to understand each other: they are ill-equipped to do so. And that, at the present time, could be dangerous.

22. Failures and Difficulties: From Yesterday to the Present

===

So far, we have noted opportunities and successes. There have also been difficulties and mishaps. They seem to have accumulated in more recent times, growing with each successive historical 'watershed' – in 1880, 1929 and perhaps 1953. Yet they may mislead us, and in two ways. Looked at closely, is there any human grouping that is immune from the difficulties inherent in life itself? And in so vast a civilization as that of America the distinction between good fortune and bad cannot be either clear or decisive. Every difficulty demands effort, stimulates a response and (as in mathematics) 'changes its sign'. A mishap is a warning, a test. It only rarely spells universal disaster. Heinrich Heine's well-known words, 'A new Spring will restore to you what Winter has taken', are often true for individuals, and more often still for nations. The United States has problems, and may face crises; but it remains in the best of health – more so, perhaps, than it imagines.

An old nightmare: Black America, an ineradicable colony

In the midst of America's opportunities, a major difficulty arose in its very early days, and one that could not be wished away. This was the presence of black Africans, brought to its shores from the seventeenth century onwards as the Southern plantations developed: tobacco in Virginia from 1615 onwards; rice in

Carolina from 1695, and then in Georgia; cotton in the nineteenth century in all the area to the South-West of Virginia.

History and geography bear the responsibility. The Atlantic seaboard, where the United States began, has a series of climatic zones, all close together. New York, despite its being on the same latitude as Naples, is affected by a cold current from Labrador, and has the same climate as Moscow. Only an overnight train journey, however, divides it from tropical areas and their exotic products. In the South, slavery was established almost as a matter of course, a kind of extension of the Caribbean economy that was so prosperous in the eighteenth century. The Spanish maintained it in Florida, and the French in New Orleans (from 1795 onwards, for sugar cane), as did George Washington and Thomas Jefferson in their Virginia properties.

Thus was introduced into Anglo-Saxon America a lively and wayward Africa, unstoppable by force, by prejudice or by concessions. The 1787 Constitution, however liberal in tone, did not actually abolish slavery. All it did was to provide for the elimination of the slave-trade after a delay of twenty years – which indeed it was, in 1807.

From that date, blacks were no longer brought into America legally, although clandestine shipments continued for many years, and they were being reared like cattle. In the nineteenth century, the cotton boom paradoxically worsened their condition. Hitherto, they had lived in their employers' houses: but now they were herded into great work-gangs, as on the estates of Ancient Rome. Ruling over these penniless black workpeople was a society of cultivated, well-mannered whites, a powerful colonial aristocracy. In 1852, Harriet Beecher Stowe's novel *Uncle Tom's Cabin*, revealing the plight of the blacks, unleashed a wave of sympathy in the North. Another more recent novel, Margaret Mitchell's *Gone With the Wind* (1936), spoke of the charm and the pleasures of life in the old South: but the life in question was mainly that of the privileged white owners. The tense and complex stories of William Faulkner are set in a later phase of this same Southern life, full of nostalgia for the civilized past, telling of hunting parties and conversations over the corn liquor or the moonshine. All these books reveal a dual truth, black and white – and probably contain dual lies.

In short, whereas the Indians, the first victims of colonization, virtually disappeared after their struggle against the Europeans, surviving hardly at all outside the reservations where they live as representatives of a vanished race, the blacks, without wholly meaning to, put up a stiff resistance. So the United States contains within it a colony which has not been truly liberated, despite all the official measures taken – an ethnic minority whose weight and presence nothing can remove.

In the mid-nineteenth century, the question of whether slavery should be abolished or maintained sparked off the explosion of the Civil War (1861–5); but it was only one of many issues in the fratricidal dispute between the States of the North and those of the South.

● The North was industrial, and in favour of high customs tariffs; the South, which sold cotton, preferred to buy its manufactures from Europe, where the quality was higher. It therefore called for the policy of the open door.

● The dispute had a political aspect too. Of the two parties jockeying for power, the Democrats were strongest in the South and the Republicans in the North.

● The dispute was all the more bitter because a prize was at stake. Which of the two blocs, North or South, would win the allegiance of the new States emerging in the West?

● On a practical point, finally, the crisis raised a serious problem. Could individual States that were part of the Union oppose measures adopted by its central Government? Did they have the right, if necessary, to secede?

All these reasons for rivalry crystallized round the two sides' violent disagreement on the abolition of slavery. The South began the War by attacking Fort Sumter on 12 April 1861; it ended it by capitulating on 9 April 1865, after an appalling, exhausting struggle. On 18 December 1865, the 13th Amendment to the

Constitution abolished slavery. It freed almost 5 million blacks (4,800,000 in 1870, compared with 33 million whites), or 12.7 per cent of the total population. This proportion later increased: it reached 13.1 per cent in 1880, then declined regularly as European immigrants arrived. By 1920 it was 10 per cent, and it seems to have settled at about this figure.

Countless details of daily life could easily be cited to show how hollow the political concessions made to the blacks have turned out to be. Political rights have been by-passed to keep blacks in 'their inferior position'. All the more so because many of them, before 1914, remained in the South, where habit and tradition automatically tended to keep them down. In the industrialization that began there around 1880 they found only a subordinate role, mainly as manual labourers, while better-paid posts went to 'poor whites'. It was only with the First World War that there was large-scale black migration Northwards, to Harlem in New York, to the 'black belt' in Chicago, to Detroit and elsewhere.

The black minority has followed and shared in America's economic expansion. Today it has its wealthy members, even its 'new rich'; it has universities, churches, musicians, writers and poets. But always, as it advances, true equality still retreats out of reach. 'As often happens,' wrote André Siegfried in 1956,

a systematic desire to look on the bright side could lead one to believe that the problem is now solved. A number of European visitors have made this mistake. The truth is that social discrimination continues, somewhat attenuated in the North, but hardly at all attenuated in the South. In the East and the Middle West, we shall no doubt see blacks effectively involved more and more in the life of the whites. A distinguished black may now and then be invited to a dinner or a social gathering; more and more representatives of the once persecuted race will be elected without discrimination to administrative posts. This is a long way from supposing that the barrier will soon fall or be substantially lowered. Most blacks in the United States simply feel and want to be American, without mention of race; but for the whites they remain

'American blacks' — a considerable nuance. Colour, in fact, seems to be an insurmountable obstacle to complete assimilation.

It seems, indeed, to be caught up in the hopelessly slow process whereby cultural changes take place, when they do. The prejudices involved, the antagonism, and the attitudes struck (see Faulkner's novels) are much more in tune with yesterday than with today. Segregation, lynching (now very rare), open or hidden hostility: all lag behind the movements that are making them obsolete. But those movements have at last begun. The incidents at Little Rock, Arkansas, where white schools, backed by the State Governor, had refused to accept blacks, as the new federal law required, was an early landmark. When the federal Government finally won, it was a sign of the times and the future, however great the problem and the segregationist passions it aroused. Even so, things are changing very slowly; and only the astonishing patience and political loyalty of black Americans holds out any hope that the problem will be solved peacefully.

In conclusion, should we see this problem as a misfortune, both for America in general and for black America, so put-upon and so patient? No: because in addressing the problem American human-ism finds itself facing a difficulty whereby it will be judged and enhanced. No again: because the United States has been offered from Africa a very special and original cultural contribution, already being incorporated into American civilization (and es-pecially into its music). What is more, this Africa-in-America is materially and intellectually by far the most advanced of all black communities in the world, industrious on its own account and also enjoying the momentum of American culture and civilization. Time is on its side; but if time does not remove this serious contradiction in American life, lasting intellectual and moral unease will remain. That is something that no one in his heart of hearts can desire. It is vital for America to find and to apply a satisfactory solution.

Capitalism: from the trusts to State intervention and oligopoly

Fortune or misfortune: once more one hesitates to make a judgement, this time about the history of capitalism in the United States. It too has helped as well as harmed the civilization on which it has left its indelible imprint – and by which it has been no less deeply marked in its turn. Money has been and still is king in the free democracy that America seeks to be. The reign of business is an obvious fact: it makes itself visible, if only in the giant buildings of Lower Manhattan. But American capitalism, with its free and sometimes too free interplay of supply and demand, has brought material prosperity unequalled anywhere else in the world. All other countries, whatever their political regimes, try to copy and equal it. And American idealism, whose vigour and often total unselfishness no one can deny, is in part a response to the pervasive materialism of big business, an escape from it and also a reproof. Capitalism, in the United States, has often had a guilty conscience.

More than that, it can be argued that American capitalism has gradually been made more humane, under the pressure of a society which is pragmatic rather than revolutionary, and too wealthy no doubt to nurture subversion as in Europe before 1848 or 1914.

As we have seen, America was a farming nation until about 1880. Then, all at once, it underwent the most amazing transformation, and seemed caught unawares by its sudden access of industry, wealth and power. The European Community, in the early days of the Common Market, found what it was like to enjoy rapid material progress. Everything was affected by the rising tide – including the growth of moderate, pragmatic Socialism. In America, likewise, capitalism developed only by adapting, by making more and more concessions, by offering shares in progress, so to speak. It has undergone considerable evolution, from the trusts of the late nineteenth century to the huge oligopolies which in twos or threes dominate the vast domestic market.

It is clear that capitalism, growing, checked or diverted, but always evolving, is the driving force of material life and, beyond that, of politics and civilization in the United States. In transforming itself, it has transformed America. That, in part, is the origin of the present and permanent crisis of American civilization.

To see how American capitalism has evolved, we must return for a moment to the time of the trusts (bearing in mind that 'trust' also means 'confidence' and that a trustee is an agent or proxy). Legally speaking, a trust is a union of stockholders with shares in different companies, the shareholders delegating to trustees the task of representing them. As a result, a group of trustees may bring together *de facto* a number of companies whose articles forbid them to merge. So this can be a way of evading the law. Some trusts may bring together companies active in kindred or complementary industries; and when they are powerful enough they naturally aim at establishing a monopoly – although the immense size of the United States has always made that difficult. An operation of this kind was successfully mounted by John D. Rockefeller (1839–1937) between 1870, when Standard Oil of Ohio was formed, and 1879, when the Standard Trust was effectively established. The trust went well beyond the strict limits of the original business, since it involved a series of firms extracting, transporting, refining and selling oil (especially abroad) – the sales soon being linked with the enormous spread of automobiles.

The United States Steel Corporation, founded in 1897, was also certainly a trust, and more certainly still a giant enterprise. Rockefeller, retired from Standard but not from speculation, had profited from the virtual absence of fiscal controls to amass an enormous fortune: he used it later to finance an immense amount of charitable work. Meanwhile, Rockefeller had bought some iron ore deposits near Lake Superior – he had received them, in fact, as payment by insolvent clients. Shortly afterwards, he secretly arranged for the building of a cargo fleet to carry the ore via the Great Lakes. Then, more by necessity than from choice, he made an agreement with the steel king Andrew Carnegie (1835–1919), owner of the great Pittsburg steelworks. With the help of the banker John Pierpont Morgan (1837–1913), the giant US Steel Corporation came into being, covering 60 per cent of American production. A last touch was added when the shares were floated on the stock exchange: Morgan doubled the capital, successfully doubling the value. He had speculated, with good reason, on the rapid rise of the shares.

These operations, and others that could be cited, notably in discussing the rivalry between railroad firms, illustrate a technique and a climate – that of fierce, remorseless capitalism, analogous to Machiavellian politics. Nor were Rockefeller, Carnegie and Morgan so very different, in some respects, from the determined princes of the Renaissance.

The heyday of that business boom was between the California gold rush of 1849 (or 1865, after the surrender of the South at Appomatox) and the beginning of the twentieth century. Its plutocrat princes, some hard-faced, some debonair, ruthlessly pursued their vision of America. They broke or brushed aside the obstacles that stood in their way, and made no secret of paying any necessary bribes. One of them wrote: 'If you have to pay to get a fair solution, it is simply right and proper to do so. When a man has the power to do great harm, and will only act straight if he is paid an inducement, since it saves time, then it's one's duty to go ahead and pay the judge.' The end justifies the means; whatever suits us is right . . .

This was the age of the great economic achievements, the railways, the gold rush, the settlement of the West and the new men, the new rich who exemplified the reassuring and not always accurate myth of the 'self-made man'. It was the age of unwittingly cynical capitalism. Its leaders, in the midst of their struggles and connivances, could not be expected to see themselves through our squeamish eyes. They were fighters who cared little what methods they used and thought only of their objective: size, efficiency or even the public good – all of which would certainly enhance their own wealth and status, but since 'the best man won' did they not, in all fairness, deserve their reward?

But it would be a mistake to think that these activities, or the later propaganda which made out all successful businessmen to be 'self-made men' were always greeted with approval and credulity. Far from it: the public, and even some businessmen, were acutely uneasy about monopolies and the measures that seemed to encourage them. Spontaneous and 'natural' mergers between firms, together with the long-lasting boom that followed the turn of the century, made for more and more trusts and monopolies. They seemed to spring up like mushrooms: 86 of them between 1887 and 1897; 149 between 1898 and 1900; 127 between 1901 and 1903. But very soon they began to fight each other; and the Presidential campaign of 1896 was partly a struggle between the opponents of the trusts, led by William Jennings Bryan, and their supporters, led by the successful candidate William McKinley. Then some of the trusts fell victim to their own excess of ambition, like that in the merchant marine which Pierpont Morgan had planned.

The short, sharp economic crises of 1903 and 1907 made public opinion very sensitive on the subject; and there was widespread approval when President Theodore Roosevelt broke up a railway trust in 1904. Measures such as this, and much campaigning, led to the Clayton Anti-Trust Act of 1914, named after a Democrat friend of President Woodrow Wilson.

Many observers have argued that this was merely beating the air – that it was vain to imagine that the trend towards ever bigger economic concentrations could be stopped by a law. An American Socialist leader, Daniel de Leon, actually allied himself with that movement. 'The ladder,' he wrote, 'that humanity has climbed towards civilization is progress in working methods, more and more powerful means of production. The trust is at the top of the ladder, and around it modern social storms are raging. The middle class is trying to break it, and turn back the march of civilization. The proletariat is trying to preserve it, improve it, and open it to everyone.'

That attitude is clear: leave untouched the technological progress that is America's triumph and pride, but humanize the process, and if possible share in the progress. To pursue such a policy, the only arbiter with enough size and power was the Federal State, because the trusts spanned individual States' frontiers and operated in a number of States at once. Only the Federal State was really in their league. Even so, it had to grow, to strengthen itself and impose itself as a power in the land. The trusts, or big business, had for their part to realize that there was an advantage in facing only one authority whose support they could secure, whose opposition they respected and whose decisions they accepted, willingly or not. One example, in 1962, was President John F. Kennedy's opposition to a rise in the price of steel.

Today, it has been said, with the oligopolies, the labour unions and the 'countervailing power' of the State, 'something like neo-capitalism is being established in the United States, adaptable in its developed form to twentieth century conditions, and already very different from traditional capitalism'.

This neo-capitalism is difficult to define: it has many aspects, and all of American civilization is expressed in its complex but orderly system. Could anyone ever list all its elements? Efficiency, including automation and its offshoots; mass production for an enormous homogeneous market with standardized tastes, encouraged by all-pervasive, all-powerful advertising; and in the bigger firms, a major role for public relations and human relations departments – acting as foreign ministries and ministries of the interior, whose respective duties are to justify the firms *vis-à-vis* the public and the consumers on the one hand and the workers on the other. A thousand details are important in this scheme of things: but the key to them all is economics. It is worthwhile, therefore, to look at the rules, the limits, and the success of that great motive force. To this end, let us consider a number of elements one by one: the role of the market in nineteenth-century liberal economies; the oligopolies; the labour unions; and the Federal Government.

The market (supposedly free, of course) was for liberal economists the regulator and arbiter of all economic life. Through the sacrosanct medium of competition, it put everyone and everything in the right place. The ideal economy, according to capitalist tradition, was one in which competition had full rein (and hence without monopolies), where there was no State intervention, where equilibrium was achieved automatically through the interplay of supply and demand, and where crises, unemployment and inflation were abnormal phenomena which had to be resisted. Unemployment, which had to be explained because it was present, even before the twentieth century, was even blamed on abnormal pressure by the labour unions.

To complete this traditional picture, it has to be repeated that production was always held to be beneficial. All goods produced, in fact, stimulated trade, according to the law of outlets formulated by Jean-Baptiste Say in 1803. 'Products,' he declared, 'are traded for products'; so to make a product was to give oneself a supplementary medium of exchange. This had been the doctrine of liberal economists from Adam Smith to Jeremy Bentham, David Ricardo, Jean-Baptiste Say and the great Alfred Marshall. In other words, in this competitive 'model' of economic life, everything was self-regulating, including the propensity to save or invest. And if by some mischance that propensity required regulation, it was enough to adjust the interest rate, raising or lowering it by the right amount.

However, at a certain stage in the development of capitalism, all these old rules, taught and repeated *ad nauseam*, were belied by the facts. In the twentieth century, monopolies, crypto-monopolies and oligopolies came to dominate large sectors of the economy, and the most advanced sectors at that. They distorted the sacrosanct free play of competition. The State intervened, as in the New Deal or, outside the United States, in so many five-year plans. Finally, long crises began to appear from 1929 onwards: unemployment and inflation played a large part in them, and came to be seen, after all, as regrettable but normal phenomena in economic and social life. Hence the importance of *The General Theory of Employment, Interest and Money*, published in 1936 by the British economist

John Maynard Keynes (1883–1946). This marked a break with liberal economics and its traditional competitive model. America accepted it as the law of the prophets in twentieth-century economics and often used it as a basis for political action.

The oligopolies: there is oligopoly, or imperfect competition, or incomplete monopoly, when a few large suppliers 'try to satisfy the needs of a multitude of purchasers'. In fact, as we have seen, the battle against the trusts did not put an end to natural, organic mergers between firms. In many industries, and not only in the United States, mergers resulted in the formation of giant companies. Thus, before 1939, a single enormous company, the Aluminum Company of America, dominated the aluminium market. Normally, a few giant firms shared this branch or that; there were three or four, for instance, in tobacco and cigarette manufacture.

Alongside the giants, small firms continued, living as best they could, and likely sooner or later to disappear. They were no more than survivals from the past. While it may be easy to enter an infant industry which attracts risk capital, as with oil when Rockefeller was young, or cars when Henry Ford was starting out, it is much more difficult when the industry is well-established, and when experience, economies of scale, technological progress and self-financing are the vital areas in which privileged firms hold all the cards.

Studies and statistics underline the fact: 200 large-scale enterprises control about half the fabulous material wealth of the United States. Often, they are impersonal corporations, sometimes owned by their employees. In these conglomerate empires, wages and salaries are enormous by comparison with Europe; but they are usually fixed rather than profit-related. 'Profits as such,' explained Henry Ford, 'belong to the firm itself: they protect it and allow it to grow.'

Thus were established this exceptional form of capitalism and the reign of the 'giants', against which anti-trust laws can now do so little – as was seen, for example, in the attempted Government action against the makers of Chesterfield, Lucky Strike and Camel cigarettes in 1948. Perhaps if there were only one monopoly ... but 200! It would take radical reform, a revolution, to change matters; but no one dreams of such a thing. The oligopolies will not be divided into small-scale firms.

So the leading roles are filled and well filled. 'In the aristocracy of business, the Dukes are the Presidents of General Motors, Standard Oil of New Jersey, the Du Pont de Nemours Chemical Society and the United States Steel Corporation. The Counts, Barons, Knights and Squires follow on, in strict proportion to the assets of their different firms.' Those who enjoy such vested interests intend to keep them. 'The present generation of Americans, if it survives, will buy its steel, its copper, its brass, its automobiles, its tyres, its soap, its switches, its breakfasts, its bacon, its cigarettes, its whisky, its cash-registers and its coffins from one or other of the few firms which currently supply them' (J. K. Galbraith).

True, as has often been said, these giant firms have their advantages. They follow and brilliantly exploit technological progress, and supply high-quality goods at low prices. This is clear if one compares those industries which, when modernized, merged into large corporations and those which continued on nineteenth-century lines. For the United States was built on at least two basic structures, the old capitalism and the new. Agriculture in general, dressmaking, and the mines are examples of the old, in the sense that the firms involved are of very moderate size. In agriculture, they are often minuscule. In Missouri, a 'big' producer may market 9,000 bales of cotton. In absolute terms, that is an enormous amount; but as a proportion of total production it is very small – so small that its producer can have no influence on prices. In fact, he is at their mercy – and so are all his fellow-producers of cotton. Similarly, there is a huge difference between the 'petropoly' organized by the American oil majors, whose growth has been sensational, and the archaic situation of the 6,000 coal-mining firms, which have gone on relying on the work of ill-paid miners, and whose technological progress, such as it is, has depended on relatively recent intervention by the State.

But the market is recovering its role. Clearly, prices never take the big firms by surprise. They control them in advance; and, true to the principle of 'fair and honest' competition, they intervene in them only after having worked out what effect a decision to raise or lower them is likely to have on rival firms which could do the same to them. The result is that prices are fixed fairly high to ensure the security and the profits of the giants, which is why smaller firms still manage to live, to exist, to survive in the shadow of the big corporations, thanks to prices which they can match. This being so, and a price war being avoided, all that really remains is an advertising war, which is clearly a luxury confined to 'affluent societies'. One can hardly imagine advertising at all in a really poor society.

Nevertheless, the 200 giants (no longer controlled, it seems, by the banks, whose power suffered from the 1929 crash) do not reign undisputed or alone. The natural tendency that has concentrated sales in a few hands, at least in certain advanced sectors, has also concentrated purchases, this time in a few other hands.

So the 'economic power' of the producers comes up against the 'countervailing power' of the purchasers. In this balancing act, the advantages of monopoly can be on either side: a big supplier may face many purchasers, a big purchaser may face many suppliers, or – as is often the case – one giant may face another. In this case there has to be compromise. If the steel producers tried to fix 'arbitrary prices' in Detroit, they would have difficulty in imposing them on a clientele as important and powerful as the local automobile manufacturers.

Clearly, an oligopoly can play both roles, buying and selling, and so exert both economic power and countervailing power, either in turn or simultaneously. But for the most part there will be conflict and tension between the two.

The labour market is where countervailing power has most obviously grown. Industrial giants have seen the rise, in their own sectors, of giant unions. These too have tried to profit from the giant firms' monopoly influence on the market. Since the firms can raise their prices, they only have to be squeezed enough and they will raise wages, enabling their workforce to share their privileges. That word is no exaggeration, in view of the fact that some American labour unions are themselves rich companies, with enormous buildings, large and well-managed capital and a president and staff who are royally paid.

At the other extreme, where capitalism is still backward, the unions can hardly exert such effective pressure. Is this why so much of American agriculture remains outside the scope of active union organization?

At all events, the traditional rivalry between producers and labour unions is tending to take a very different shape in the United States today. It often looks more like a form of association – for which the consumer risks having to pay. The giants of industry have made possible the emergence of giants of labour, whose countervailing power acts as a control on wages and prices.

Nevertheless, since this control can be erratic, mistaken or rigid, and since any errors on such a scale can have appalling consequences, the role of the State has grown more and more, making it the supreme regulator, pledged to ensure the proper working of the whole machine. Since the trauma of 1929, few people contest this need, although it flatly contradicts the tradition of economic liberalism.

Obviously, the economic evolution of the United States has compelled the Federal State to intervene, with care, as a 'countervailing power'. It was no longer a question of intervening blindly, as in the anti-trust measures that followed the Clayton Act of 1914. What it now had to do was to analyse in depth the various elements in the economic situation, to predict its likely development, using all the tools of modern economic science, and to be ready at any time to act in this sector or that, whether to mop up unemployment, stimulate production, curb inflation or whatever was needed.

It is easy to see why the size of the Federal Administration has grown since the New Deal. Whereas Herbert Hoover had a staff of only thirty-seven, Harry S. Truman had 325 officials and 1,500 other employees. In the past, the White House alone was big enough for the work of the Presidency. Today, there is also an Executive Office Building – and that is already overcrowded. Little by little, power is being concentrated in the White House, and the whole country is feeling the effects. A large bureaucracy is backed by an army of expert technicians, immune from the uncertainties of the old spoils system, which often led to officials being replaced according to the results of elections. This new permanence in the bureaucracy is a revolution in itself. These days, the President is in charge of well-qualified executive personnel.

The whole great system of the Federal Administration, organized to deal with the decisive matters which can and should guide the economy, finds itself confronted at the same time by America's social problems. Can even a limited degree of economic intervention take place without intervention on social policy too?

As soon as the State takes some responsibility for economic organization, it becomes responsible for social injustice. It can no longer ignore those Americans who are not organized, who are on the fringes of the labour unions or completely outside them, like the 2 million farmworkers who have no rights and who form a rural proletariat of outcasts. Should there be a minimum wage? Should America move towards a system of social security on European lines?

If it did, there would be a social policy, in an affluent society which has solved many old problems but also created new difficulties, some of them needing urgent attention. It would certainly be a further break with the traditions of American civilization, which is ferociously individualist and which above all believes in the ability of people to 'make it' on their own. Almost all citizens of the United States dislike the idea of the State's intruding into the way society works. The question is whether, today, that can be avoided.

To illustrate the problem, and the need to make a choice, consider the reactions of Soviet citizens who took refuge in the United States after the Second World War, and whom a sociologist asked for their impressions. Generally speaking, they recognized that their material life was better; but they very much missed the free medical treatment and, still more, the equality among all patients that they had enjoyed in the Soviet Union. Even a visitor from France realizes, once in the United States, how valuable the French social security system is. For all America's wealth, it has nothing equivalent to offer. A young teacher in a big American university suddenly finds that he has an incurable disease. He can no longer work. What will become of him? He failed to take out insurance, you are told. So he and his wife and children lose house and home . . .

Many authorities believe that America should and eventually will adopt a social welfare policy. Public opinion is becoming aware of the problem. Despite special pleading by certain newspapers, Federal taxes are no longer seen as an unfair punishment imposed on the strong and able producers of wealth to benefit the lazy and incapable. Ever since the New Deal, the Federal Administration has been regarded 'as essentially beneficent', and in any case necessary.

This immense change is altering and diminishing, more and more, the role of the individual States, which used to be virtually autonomous republics. It may also profoundly transform the structure of American society and civilization – and all the more so because the United States has begun to revise its view of its role, its tasks and its responsibilities in the world.

The United States in the world

In this century, after a long tradition of general isolationism, the United States has rediscovered the world. This has presented it with a series of new and often painful problems. Instinctively, it would be glad to ignore them. But the very might of the United States inevitably involves it with the rest of the world: in foreign policy, as in domestic affairs, it has no choice. The world has become too small; and anything that America does, intentionally or not, has repercussions on a global scale.

It is very hard to realize to what degree isolationism has been a basic feature of the United States. It arose in part from a feeling that emerged very clearly as soon as America was independent – the sense of having founded a new world, entirely different from the Europe of the past, and very much better. Psychoanalysts have called this a 'revolt against the parents'. But it was encouraged also by Americans' awareness of having made their own history, independently, in the broad new expanse of the American continent and the security that distance gave them.

America, in fact, was free to concern itself only with what happened within its borders and to maintain prosperity there; free to erect protective tariffs that cut it off like a Great Wall of China with no fear of threats from any neighbour; free to expand without shame or remorse. Its own conquests by land simply enlarged its territory; others' conquests by sea were appalling colonial adventures. In the nineteenth century, the only inescapable ties it felt were with the rest of the American continent: in 1823, that solidarity was expressed in the Monroe Doctrine of 'America for the Americans'. The message – for it was indeed a message, and from James Monroe, the President of the United States – also in effect affirmed the United States' lack of involvement in European affairs. Both the positive and the negative aspects of the Monroe Doctrine were often repeated and reaffirmed in later years.

But the rest of the world could not be ignored: it was linked to America by trade, imports and exports, and by diplomatic relations. In 1898, a wave of belligerence even took the Americans to Puerto Rico, where they remain, to Cuba, which is no longer theirs, and to the distant Philippines, which they have never really left, even after Philippine independence. The world has also flocked to America, with its hordes of European, Japanese, Chinese and other immigrants. In a natural reaction which experience proved to be dangerous, the United States closed its doors to immigration from 1921 to 1924. It was perhaps the most disastrous decision that could have been made from the point of view of Europe and the world in the unhappy, crisis-filled years after the First World War: in effect, it removed a safety-valve.

In 1917 and 1918, the United States had played a decisive part in the First World War. But after the Treaty of Versailles, which it had instigated, it withdrew from active international politics, and did not join the League of Nations. It abandoned the world to Britain's false and fragile domination – an ancient achievement relying on lengthy sea-routes and left in place, as we have seen, by the war. One of America's more important reasons for intervening in the war in 1917 had no doubt been to safeguard Britain's world position, which suited the United States, if only because it helped guarantee the future of Anglo-Saxon civilization – *their* civilization.

The well-meaning Woodrow Wilson had not wanted America to turn in on itself, but he had failed to prevent it. By contrast with that failure, can Franklin Delano Roosevelt be judged to have succeeded in the various 'summit' meetings at Casablanca, Teheran and Yalta which preceded his own death and the end of the Second World War? He certainly helped to reshape a world whose future was admittedly hard to predict. But did he not concede too much to the needs of the moment and to principles that were even less valid than those of Woodrow Wilson, and often morally debatable? It was certainly in line with American tradition to encourage the liberation of the colonial empires; but it also meant weakening the West and, sooner or later, calling into question the status of Latin America, which in economic matters could be regarded as a 'colonial' dependency of the United States. Then, at the same time, to let half of Europe fall under Soviet domination was a very far cry from the sacrosanct principle of self-determination. But Roosevelt believed that world peace required small countries to cease their trouble-making. He wanted to disarm the whole world, with the exception of the then Big Four – China, the USSR, Britain and the United States. Perhaps he was still nostalgic for isolationism: if we are obliged to concern ourselves with the rest of the world, let us at least make sure that it keeps quiet . . .

This is a view of Roosevelt and his policies that has been expressed in the United States itself. It is certainly open to question. But is fairly widely shared among non-Americans, especially in the West. These observers from outside the New World believe that the United States, without having wished it or realized it in advance, has assumed the leadership of the world. They also believe that America has often thought problems to be simple, a matter of common sense and good will, and any difficulties the outcome of prejudice or selfishness on the part of the Old World. In fact, quite a few of its policy decisions have been unfortunate, and have got out of control. They have proved that loans and good intentions are not enough as means of world leadership, and that domination by trade and money, however legitimate from America's traditional viewpoint, today arouses almost as much mistrust as the old colonial domination that it resembles. The Americans, meanwhile, have tended to believe that their failures were a proof of ingratitude or envy on the part of the peoples they had helped or sought to help.

In fact, like everyone else, they have had to serve their apprenticeship, and take the precise measure of a world they had so long ignored or tried to ignore, a world which now, for their own safety's sake, they must watch over and if possible lead. They have taken this task seriously and recognized some of their own errors. That too is an American tradition, both likeable and fruitful: to believe in what one is doing, but be ready to admit one's mistakes. The sooner one corrects one's aim, the sooner one is likely to hit the target.

An example of this was President Kennedy's initiative in gathering round him the leading intellectuals and economic and political experts of the day, to make a serious study of the problems he faced. Reporting on their discussions, a journalist wrote on 21 May 1962: 'After getting the "talents" and "brains" around him to work at full pressure, he made a synthesis of their conclusions as a guide for future policy. Uncertainties remain, here and there. Some options are still open. But the essential line he has chosen is clear. For the first time in many years, we know quite a lot about the intentions of the US President.' That should not be attributed only to the President's own efforts, or to those of the intellectuals and Harvard professors he summoned to clarify the political agenda. In reality, during the tense and dramatic years between the Marshall Plan and the Korean War, and through later dramas – Berlin, Cuba, Laos, Vietnam, the Middle East, China, Eastern Europe and the USSR – the United States and its public opinion have realized both the huge extent and the necessary limits of their world role and responsibilities. The days of isolationism are long gone.

Power entails responsibility. The emergence of the United States as a world leader – a role which it has had to assume for fear of dangerous instability – is one result of the prodigious growth in its power. To describe that power, we need quite a number of adjectives: economic, political, scientific, military and global.

The power of the United States became obvious with the end of the Second World War and the dropping of the atomic bomb on Hiroshima in 1945. It immediately posed the problem of European and world leadership in the terms of a duel between East and West. In the past, Europe had almost always been divided into two rival camps, whose membership varied according to which leading nation was the source of the danger or the threat. In the years after the Second World War, the whole world lived according to this ancient pattern, which Raymond Aron aptly called 'bi-polar'. It was not only ideology that divided the free world from the Communist bloc: indeed, as the years went by, they began to share points of resemblance. The Communist world started to organize its industry in large units, and the free world started to enlarge the role of the State.

Leadership, in the postwar world, seemed to offer two alternative power centres: either Washington or Moscow. The neutrals in the Third World, and the allies or satellites of the superpowers, were little more than spectators at the drama that so much affected them: their only role was to add their own very modest weight to the balance. The superpowers might dominate them, but they equally had to woo them, attract them and keep their loyalty.

In 1945, the United States was the winner, and was lulled by its superiority, confirmed decisively and tragically by the bombs on Hiroshima and Nagasaki. On 12 July 1953, when the Soviet Union exploded its first hydrogen bomb, equilibrium was restored. In 1957, with the launching of the first Sputnik, the Soviets won an important point, all the more important because the conquest of space meant the construction of very long-range missiles, capable of striking targets more than 6,000 miles away. In the years that followed, achievements by one side or the other alternated, maintaining a precarious balance of power. The armaments built up on either side were more and more terrifying in scope and scale, and the Cold War was intensified by the mutual fear they aroused. No less afraid and angry were the other nations of the world, following the drama with open eyes and empty hands. For, while the balance-of-power policy pursued by Washington and Moscow was neither better nor worse than that of Europe in the past, the fearful weapons it involved posed a very different threat. Humanity was in danger of destroying itself.

That struggle obsessed the United States, affecting not only its policies but also its life and thought. The year of the Soviet hydrogen bomb was a turning-point like 1929, for very different reasons but with no less impact on people's minds. The tension of the Cold War frayed their emotions, their imaginations and their hearts. It distorted everything, replacing America's normal climate of freedom with the mistrustful psychology of war. The McCarthyite panic of the 1950s was one of the symptoms; and the fever took a very long time to disperse. It seemed as if the whole world might be dragged into the same destructive state of mind.

The golden rule for world peace is surely to think with, not against; and for a whole generation both the United States and the Soviet Union obstinately thought against each other.

From both sides, denouncing each other and piling up weapons of defence that neither dared use, the Cold War exacted a heavy price.

Let us close that sorry, bygone chapter and finally consider American novels. Their rich and complex evidence will suggest an appropriate verdict on the civilization they interpret. To be complete, we ought no doubt to call as witnesses the rest of literature, from poetry to theatre and cinema, as well as art, architecture and the natural and social sciences. The flowering of American culture and intelligence includes the economists of Harvard and Chicago just as much as the artists, the toolmakers, the functionalist designers and the industrial technologists.

But in this brief summary we have to choose; and we choose the testimony of the novel for two reasons. First, because for many years it has had a great influence on European and world literature; and secondly because its development since the beginning of the twentieth century sheds light on the development of American life.

American literature was 'discovered' by Europe around 1920–25; but its reputation in Europe grew particularly in the years that followed the Second World War.

Large numbers of translations, presented and annotated by writers like Jean-Paul Sartre, André Malraux or Cesare Pavese, were eagerly welcomed; and the influence of American novelists was so obvious, not only in Britain but also in France, Italy and Germany, that one critic called that period 'the age of the American novel'. It was also the age of 'Americanism', whose traces could be detected in jazz, in dance, in clothes, and even in the art of the cartoon, of which the *New Yorker* offered splendid examples whose style was sometimes copied abroad.

In the novel, what Europeans discovered was a new kind of

writing, a narrative technique very different from their own tradition of the psychological novel. It was what has been called 'an art of bare and objective reporting', 'a photographic art', whose aim was to show, not to comment. To plunge the reader into a character's mental world, the novel made him feel directly, brutally, the sensations and emotions the character experienced, without ever trying to make sense of them. It was the method of the cinema, whose influence here was very clear.

For Europeans, the American novel was marked not only by this technique, but also by a climate of violence and brutality. It was, wrote a French critic,

literature made by and for the cinema, coloured by the habit of 'hot news' and the detective story . . . brutal, passionate, feverish and frenetic, without an ounce of refinement, literature like a blow of the fist, enjoyed despite or because of that, according to taste. It is fast and hard: there is something healthy, lively, and strong about it which at present is found nowhere else.

In reality, these words describe a certain movement in the American novel, called by the Americans 'naturalism', which developed between the two wars: its leading representatives included Ernest Hemingway, William Faulkner, John Steinbeck and John Dos Passos. These writers were all born between 1890 and 1905. By their age and their work, they belonged to an earlier generation, more and more remote from the way the American novel developed after the Second World War. This was away from naturalism and towards an older tradition – no less brilliant and original, but less familiar to the continental European public: the nineteenth-century tradition of Herman Melville (1819–91), Nathaniel Hawthorne (1804–64) and Henry James (1843–1916).

What is pertinent to our purpose is the general movement, and what it reveals about American civilization. One constant fact is worth noting: writers do not enjoy in the United States the natural, respected role that 'men of letters' tend to have in Europe. The American writer is always an isolated individual. He lives on the margin of society, and very often comes to a tragic end after a more or less brief success. 'There are no second acts in American lives,' said one of them, F. Scott Fitzgerald (1896–1940); and his remark applied to him and a number of his colleagues, few of whom lived to a successful old age. Characteristically, then, the American writer is an asocial being who is not content merely to express his revulsion or his unease at the world around him, but lives out his rebellion and constantly pays the price in pain and solitude. So the evolution of the American novel faithfully reflects that of America's social tensions.

In the nineteenth century, the spectre haunting the background of Melville's and Hawthorne's sombre works was America's Calvinist Puritanism. It gave them their obsessive theme of the tragic struggle between good and evil – even if, at the same time, they rejected the weight of that obsession. Both Melville and Hawthorne in a certain sense denounced the society they lived in; and in both cases it exacted its price.

With the beginning of the twentieth century, there was a general movement against the intransigence of Puritanism. The Puritan tradition is still powerful, notably in the social taboos which have in some respects taken over from moral taboos in the United States. But already by the end of the nineteenth century Puritanism had ceased to be the symbol of society's misdeeds. It was then that naturalist novels in the manner of Emile Zola began to appear, often with Socialist leanings. They coincided with the huge expansion of America's power in the years after 1880.

From then onwards, until the Second World War, industrial and capitalist society – the 'futurist' side of American life – became the favourite target of literary non-conformists. One of them was Sinclair Lewis, whose well-known novel *Babbitt* (1922) was a vengeful caricature of the American businessman; but there were also the voluntary exiles who lived in Paris or elsewhere in Europe between the wars: Hemingway, Fitzgerald, Dos Passos, Henry Miller and Katherine Anne Porter – the 'lost generation' as they were called by Gertrude Stein, one of their number whose

Parisian salon was a rallying-point for such Americans abroad. Other rebels included James Farrell, Faulkner, Steinbeck, Erskine Caldwell and Richard Wright. There was a whole generation, in fact, of 'left-wing intellectuals'. They were scandalized by the trial and execution of Nicola Sacco and Bartolomeo Vanzetti in 1927 (Dos Passos himself was imprisoned on that occasion), by the Spanish Civil War (see Hemingway's novel, *For Whom the Bell Tolls*), by Mussolini's aggression and by attacks on Roosevelt's New Deal. Many of them saw Socialism as a hope of salvation for the society of their day.

The Second World War and its aftermath, the beginnings of the Cold War, overthrew that belief. American novelists first rediscovered a sense of solidarity with their own country, then realized the hollowness, for them, of the Marxist dream. The new American generation was far removed from social realism. It preferred novels in which symbols, poetry, and art for art's sake reclaimed their place. It looked back to Henry James, to Melville, and also to Fitzgerald, a very individual member of the 'lost generation', who was only forty-four when he died. Had rebellion ceased to be at the heart of American literature? For a time, it seemed so, with the sharp recrudescence of nationalism after the war, as well as the emergence of a generation of university writers who enjoyed some security and so more willingly identified themselves with their own civilization. But those same years also saw the appearance of the 'beatniks', young intellectuals who completely rejected the norms of the society around them, and in this sense resembled their elders in the 'lost generation', but were otherwise utterly different. The men and women of the 1920s and 1930s, who had believed in the future of the Left, were succeeded by a group whose only refuge was art, alcohol or drugs, and whose main theme was that of solitude and 'incommunicability' in a world now signifying nothing.

But let us not forget that America lives in advance of modernity. It is still the country of the future – and that, at least, is a sign of hope and a proof of vitality. Its huge resources will surely enable it to recover its old optimism and self-confidence. Claude Roy wrote in his *Clefs pour l'Amérique – Keys to America*:

America is one of those places in the world where, despite everything, humanity's *potential* continues to flourish ... Coming back from the United States, one is completely confident that a new kind of people can be born, more certain of their ability, more imbued with wise, down-to-earth, practical contentment. We may make fun of the refrigerators and vitamins, the accumulation of gadgets ... But I do not believe that we have the right to make fun of a certain type of American who has already mastered the art of living and asserted the power of humanity over what once seemed ineluctable fate.

23. An English-speaking Universe

═══

From the eighteenth century until at least 1914, London was the centre of the world. Even a brief visit still reminds one of its greatness: Buckingham Palace, St James's Palace, Downing Street, the Stock Exchange, dockland on the lower reaches of the Thames – all these continue to evoke the past. More than anywhere else in the West, the British Isles have established outposts over distant seas. Who can fail to admire such immense success? Rudyard Kipling divided his life between India, a house in South Africa, a North American ranch, Egypt, and many other places. He was right in thinking that Britain could best be understood from afar, from its warlike imperial frontiers, and especially from India. That may be why one of his French friends, arriving in Algiers one day in 1930, cabled him: 'Now that I am in Algiers, I shall at last understand France.'

Little remains of either the British or the French Empire. But to the British the idea of Empire still has special importance. Much more than in France, it accounts for a number of institutions and political reflexes. Hence the agonizing choice that Britain seemed to face when contemplating joining the European Community: should she opt for the Commonwealth or the Common Market? To choose the latter meant joining forces with continental Europe, from which she had hitherto preserved 'splendid isolation'; it appeared to imply abandoning the world dimensions of which she was justly proud, and renouncing one of her most powerful traditions.

★

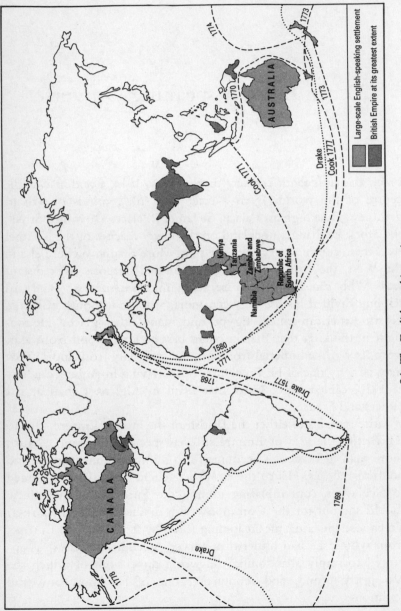

21. *The English-speaking universe*

In Canada: France and Britain

Britain lost 'America', but she kept Canada: she even helped it to extend from the Atlantic to the Pacific (*a mari usque ad mare* – from sea to sea). The essential dates in this process were: 1759, when Montcalm was defeated outside Quebec; 1782, when the British and American 'loyalists', still loyal to the King after the revolt of the American colonies, reached Ontario and the Maritime Provinces; 1855–85, when the Maritime Provinces and their British inhabitants grew more and more prosperous, their ships and sailors on the Atlantic more than rivalling those of the United States; 1867, when after many mishaps the Dominion of Canada was founded, consisting of Ontario, Quebec, Nova Scotia and New Brunswick. In 1870, Manitoba joined the Dominion; in 1871 British Columbia; and in 1873 Prince Edward Island, the seventh province. Between 1882 and 1886, the Canadian Pacific Railway was built, 'virtually along the frontier with the United States'; it made possible the colonization of the prairies, from which the 'half-breeds' (born of French Canadians and Indian women) were driven out. Even so, the Canadian pioneers were of fairly mixed stock. They advanced Westwards much like their United States counterparts, founding two further provinces – Alberta and Saskatchewan (1905). Newfoundland, finally, became the tenth province after a plebiscite in 1948.

French Canadians today make up a third of Canada's population: they number some 6 million people. Confined (so to speak) in the immense province of Quebec, they broadly occupy the Eastern outskirts of Canada, the estuary of the St Lawrence River and its lower and middle reaches. Although encircled, they are none the less deeply entrenched.

Today's French-speaking Americans are the descendants of some 60,000 peasants from Western France, divided between the Mississippi and the St Lawrence. When they were abandoned by the Treaty of Paris in 1763, they managed to hold the province of

Quebec and strike deep roots there. French Canadians are peasants,
not farmers like their English-speaking compatriots. They were
not tempted by the call of the West: they only slowly moved to
the towns, and took a long time to be attracted away by the
factories of New York or Detroit. As a people, they are lively,
straightforward and cheerful.

British Canada, which established itself to the West, cut off the
French Canadians from the great expeditions to the heart of the
continent, and in a sense encircled them: the Maritime Provinces,
the United States and Ontario actually surround Quebec and make
it a kind of insular territory. French Canada accepted that fact. It
clung to its land; it remained strictly faithful to its clergy – which
was its salvation after 1763; and it retained its language, which
essentially is eighteenth-century French. Today, it has every appearance of a closed, introverted society and civilization – peasant,
conservative and with an active clergy which has defended and
maintained tradition and spread a classical form of culture.

The break with France in 1763 was a wound that has still not
healed: the French Canadians felt shamelessly abandoned.
Thereafter, Canada lost touch with 'the old country' – past and
present France. What contacts there are do not always bear fruit.
For France has changed since the eighteenth century: it has
experienced the Revolution, a Republican regime and secularism;
it has also kindled the flame of an avant-garde, socially concerned
Catholicism, which is revolutionary in its own way.

French Canada, as has been said perhaps too often, finds these
innovations hard to understand: it is surprised by them, and shies
away. But it too is evolving. Its Catholic, peasant civilization is
changing, accepting the needs of progress; its universities are
making a huge effort to modernize themselves and to come to
terms with the various social sciences. And this whole movement
is undoubtedly motivated by stubborn resistance to the other
Canada – British Canada – and to 'Americanization'.

British Canadians make up about half (48 per cent) of Canada's
population. They have virtually adopted the American way of life

(which also affects French Canada). They in fact inhabit a second America. Toronto is its characteristic city, looking firmly Southwards to the United States. Its Americanization is obvious and all-pervasive: in the houses and apartments, in furniture, in cooking and in education, where children are left to their own devices at an early age, and are free to start having girlfriends and boyfriends just like their American contemporaries across the border. Still more, the world of business is organized on the active and powerful American model. In other words, Anglo-Saxon Canada would find it easy to draw even closer to its powerful neighbour after cutting its ties with distant Britain. The most recent immigrants, moreover, mainly located beyond Ontario, come from various countries outside the Anglo-Saxon world, and feel the same attraction. In the end, what preserves Canada's independence is the fact of its internal divisions, and in particular the latent tension between British and French Canadians, which has by no means been removed by economic growth and well-being.

With a population of 18 million in 1962, growing at the rate of 28 per cent a year and reaching 25 million two decades later, and with a land area of nearly 3.5 million square miles (sixteen times the size of France), Canada is an 'international power'. Its economy is rapidly expanding, partly thanks to its many natural resources and its enormous reserves of hydro-electric energy. Everywhere, American-style industry is on the increase, although some older economic activities still flourish – including forestry, with its rafts of logs floating down the great rivers.

What is more, Canada is independent. Its allegiance to the British crown is no more than theoretical, and the Governor-General who represents the monarch has only a ceremonial role, and is actually a Canadian.

These political and economic facts, however, cannot remove the tensions which, whether deliberately or not, tend to isolate French Canada. After Paris, Montreal is the biggest French city in the world; but it is visibly dominated by 'British' banks, hotels and shops, and its business life is conducted in English.

British Canada may be richer than French Canada: but economic grievances are not the main problem. The really divisive factor is the rejection of one civilization by another. It may seem surprising that Canada, alongside the United States with its prodigious example of rapid and total cultural assimilation, should still after two centuries not have fully absorbed 60,000 French people – although by now they number 6 million. Perhaps it was because the British, not always intentionally, kept them out of the conquest of the prairies and the West. This may have helped to make them turn in on themselves, a closed peasant community, *ipso facto* traditionalist, and unreceptive to influences from outside. At all events, now as in the past, the division between the two groups is visible and profound.

Might it, at a time which seems to encourage all 'national' demands, eventually take a political form? That would be another matter. Some, it is true, are already talking of independence, and even proposing future dates. There is a 'Lawrentian Alliance' which is explicitly nationalist: but it also presents itself mainly as 'a national educational movement'; and one of its members declared in 1962: 'We are not a mass movement.' In fact, 'a Canadian France' exists, stubbornly determined to live and survive: but, in the world of giants that is America, would it be possible for a mere 6 million people to organize themselves in a political and economic unit that was viable yet truly independent? That is the essential question.

Southern Africa: Dutch, British and Blacks

In South Africa, an old port of call on the sea route to India, and formerly essential for sailing vessels, the British established themselves in 1815. They replaced and dominated the Dutch, who had been there for more than a century, since 1652, just as in 1763 they had taken over from, and imposed their will on, the French Canadians. The result was unrest and serious tension, which culminated in the Boer War of 1899–1902, but also dragged on after it.

White Africa, already rent by these violent internal quarrels, and facing the arrival on the East Coast of immigrants from India (including Gandhi, in 1907), was above all involved in a potential confrontation with the black Africans themselves. In the long run, this threatened to be violent and dramatic; but even now it is still in its early days. The storm – or the solution – is yet to come.

The development of the 'frontier', in the American sense of the word, is the dominant feature of South Africa's evolution. To be understood, it has to be seen alongside many other shifting frontiers – in the United States, in Brazil, in Argentina, in Chile, in Australia and in New Zealand. What is involved here is not so much local or African history, but the history of the world.

In South Africa, the frontier came into being when the first few cautious white colonists arrived (almost at once accompanied by coloured slaves) and came into contact with the indigenous tribes – either the Bushmen of the Kalahari Desert or, to the North and East, under various tribal names, the Bantu, cattle-breeders ready enough to trade their animals for iron, copper, tobacco, or bric-à-brac. Gradually, the frontier began to move inland from the Cape, further and further from the growing township, across a land that was dry and almost empty: because the native Africans, despite thefts of cattle and occasional violent raids, were never strong enough really to endanger the small white colony.

Not until the 'Great Trek' of 1836 did the colonists make a decisive move towards the Orange Free State, Natal and the Transvaal. The reasons help to explain the nature and the problems of this first Northward and Eastward thrust. The stimulus came, not so much from the city of Cape Town itself, which for a long time was modest in size and influence, but rather from the ships that put into port there or further to the North in Saldanha Bay. Disembarking their crews, and leaving in hospital those who were ill with scurvy, they were all anxious to buy food, and especially fresh food. Wheat production in South Africa was not very profitable: it could be bought more cheaply in India, at Surat or in Bengal. Nor was wine-growing: Cape wines at that time had a well-deserved poor reputation. So the local peasants opted for the far more remunerative production of meat. They began to sell carcasses and (despite prohibitions) cattle or sheep on the hoof. Cattle-breeding was not only a less costly investment than crop-growing: it was also far more profitable. What was more, distance was no object, as it was for wheat or wine, since the animals made their own way to the port.

So, from the eighteenth century onwards, the stockbreeders pushed back the frontier and pressed further into the interior. The same movement continued in the nineteenth century, sometimes more rapidly, sometimes less, depending on the number and needs of the ships. The Franco-British wars in the eighteenth century were a great opportunity for profitable trade.

But there were also political reasons for this expansion. In 1815, Britain occupied South Africa; and in 1828 the British government of the Cape Colony issued the famous Fifteenth Ordinance making whites and coloured people equal before the law. In 1834, more-over, slavery was abolished in the British Empire, former slave-owners receiving indemnities (which they complained were too small). In 1828, it had been reckoned that for 55,000 whites in South Africa and 32,000 free blacks, there were 32,000 slaves. Their liberation, and a black African raid on the Eastern frontier in the same year, 1834, helped to trigger off the Great Trek which two years later took the Boers (farmers) or Voortrekkers into the vast grassy plateaux of the Orange Free State and the Transvaal. These set themselves up as independent Republics and were eventu-ally recognized as such by Britain in 1852 and 1854. Ten years earlier, in 1843, she had purely and simply annexed neighbouring Natal.

The vast expansion that began with the Great Trek was the major event in the history of the Afrikaners, akin to the conquest of the West in that of the United States. It scattered the white population over a very broad area, greatly increasing the likelihood of contact and conflict with indigenous black Africans, and especially with the federated Zulu tribes, which were simultaneously expanding Southwards, and were not brought to a halt until 1879.

In 1884, after a war with the Boers, Britain formally recognized the independence of the Boer Republics; but she never fully accepted it. The result was the Second Boer War.

The discovery of gold and diamonds in Witwatersrand had already led to further conflict. Cecil Rhodes, Premier of the Cape Colony, in effect representing both British imperialism and the interests of the mining companies (he was a founder of De Beers), precipitated the major clash. He encircled the Orange and Transvaal Republics by establishing chartered companies in Bechuanaland (Botswana) and Rhodesia (Zimbabwe); he fomented incidents over the foreign labour brought in to work the mines; and in 1895 he connived at the Jameson Raid, a simple act of piracy on land, which obliged him to resign as Premier in the following year.

Open war did not break out, however, until October 1899. When it did, it at once proved disastrous for the British, turning to their advantage only late in the day, partly owing to their establishment of concentration camps during the long period of guerrilla warfare that followed the main engagements. The Treaty of Vereeniging, on 31 May 1902, incorporated the Transvaal and the Orange Free State in the British Empire, but promised them eventual self-government, which they finally received in 1907. Three years later, the Union of South Africa became a dominion under the British Crown.

South Africa's essential problem is that of race relations, usually referred to under the inadequate name of Apartheid.

Since the Second World War especially, South Africa has enjoyed rapid urban and industrial growth. But this has only worsened the human conflicts that threaten it. Today's descendants of the Dutch colonists and French Calvinist refugees, who came to the Cape from the seventeenth century onwards, are for the most part landowners. Their farms are very large, with an average size of some 1,800 acres; but their productivity is generally low on account of the climate and the poor quality of the soil. Only 4 per cent of the country, besides, is under cultivation. What was needed, after the war, was to shift from extensive to intensive farming, with greater mechanization to reduce the enormous numbers of seasonal workers crowded into compounds like those used for industry and the gold mines. There was scope for greater use of fertilizers, for establishing crop rotation in place of uninterrupted single-crop maize production over vast areas, for integrating cattle with arable production and for putting an end to the most backward forms of stockbreeding. All that required time, loans, investments, and also the maintenance of large holdings, big enough to bear the necessary costs.

Many of the big landowners are blunt and sometimes headstrong people who look back nostalgically to distant days before the arrival of the British, when life was simple and 'biblical', with docile black Africans around them, born to be servants or slaves. The great majority of the landowners are descendants of the Boers and speak Afrikaans, a derivative of Dutch. English-speaking South Africans, descendants of the British, are almost as numerous: but they for the most part live in the towns and have been responsible for the industrialization whose profits they have enjoyed.

Until 1939, the British and the Afrikaners tried to keep on good terms with each other, and to deal jointly with the formidable problems of relations between black Africans and whites. But this political understanding broke down when Dr Daniel François Malan's Nationalist Party won the 1948 election and Malan pursued a policy of intolerant nationalism which sought both the 'Afrikanerization' of the British elements in South Africa and, more particularly, absolute segregation (*apartheid*) of South African blacks.

In 1961, South Africa left the Commonwealth. Britain had refused to associate herself with its dangerous racial policy, which had aroused violent condemnation throughout the world. It was surely a policy of desperation. The growth of the population and of the economy threw the situation into sharp relief. The figures were there to show it: in 1962, out of 15 million inhabitants, 10 million were black, 3 million 'European', 1.5 million 'Cape coloured' of mixed race, and 0.5 million Asian. The whites, in other words, made up 20 per cent of the total; and that proportion was only very slightly declining with the passage of time.

The policy of *apartheid vis-à-vis* black Africans and Asians (found only in Natal) was deliberately and efficiently selfish. The succession of laws which put it into effect were like a sea wall continually under repair and reinforcement at any weak points. Their aim was to exclude black Africans (and even Asians) from certain areas, forbid them to own land and confine them to 'Native Reserves' where they were supposed to be protected. This raised two immediate problems. It was almost impossible for black Africans to live on the meagre soil of the Reserves, which not only were too small, but also became unproductive when over-exploited by primitive farming methods. At the same time, white agriculture needed labour – more so even than industry, which was rapidly expanding and which had been designed for mass production by an unskilled labour force. The combined result, against which *apartheid* fought its unceasing battle, was 'the invasion of the white man's territory'. Black Africans outnumbered whites in Durban and Johannesburg; and their incomes were 17 to 40 per cent lower.

To stem the flow from the Native Reserves, the South African Government at that time tried to improve the productivity of agriculture within them, by organizing specialist training; and to bring industry into them or near them. But the latter policy meant depriving white industries of cheap labour at the same time as exposing them to new competition from the Native Reserves.

There was also, at that time, the question of the British protectorates of Bechuanaland (now Botswana), Basutoland (now Lesotho) and Swaziland. Despite the provisions of the Act setting up the Union of 1910, they were never transferred to South Africa; and, although economically close to it, they eventually became self-governing and then politically independent. Similar aspirations were expressed by Namibia, the former South-West Africa, whose SWAPO guerrilla organization fought a long battle to attain that end.

'From many points of view,' it has been said, 'the Union of South Africa is at a crossroads: in the midst of an agrarian and industrial revolution, it is also having to face a social revolution' – which is mainly racial. Now, it is looking for new ways to break the stalemate and bring together its different civilizations, European and local. A viable solution still seems a long way off.

Australia and New Zealand, or Britain at last unchallenged

In three of her overseas settlements, Britain has managed to remain alone: in the United States, at least to begin with, and in Australia and New Zealand. Her solitude has been fruitful. In Australia as in New Zealand, what we see are lively, homogeneous versions of Britain: they are neither Canada, with its two peoples, nor South Africa, with its dramatic problems. These antipodean Dominions, 'the furthest away from the mother country, are the most British of all'.

Both Australia and New Zealand are relatively recent creations, or at least recent recruits to a European, international way of life. Australia dates in this sense from 1788, or just over two centuries ago; and for a long time its beginnings were modest, with 12,000 Europeans in 1819 and 37,000 in 1821. New Zealand dates from 1840, if one ignores the establishment of Protestant missionaries there in 1814 and Catholics in 1837. So it was only a century and a half ago that the British settled in the North Island in 1840, a few years ahead of the whalers, who arrived in 1843. At that time, there were only about a thousand colonists in New Zealand.

Australia and New Zealand owe their homogeneity to the virtual extinction of the indigenous population after the coming of the whites. In Australia, the aborigines almost vanished. In New Zealand, the Maoris were at first decimated, but later somewhat recovered and revived.

Geographically, Australia and New Zealand are very different. Australia is a massive continent; New Zealand consists of islands with high mountains, flanked by stormy seas along a jagged coastline. The history of the native populations offers similar contrasts.

In Australia, very ancient human migration, in the sixth millennium BC, brought the Australoids – apparently adventurous travellers who were soon trapped in a prison where the soil, the flora and the fauna were all extremely poor. The Australasian tribes stagnated and regressed there, always on the edge of famine. They became a living museum of archaic, primeval ways, from which sociologists and ethnographers have gleaned a wealth of knowledge about primitive societies. All discussions and interpretations of totemism are based on the study of these meagre lives.

It is a hard truth that these peoples, still living in the Stone Age, could not survive contact with the whites. Their fragile society fell apart. The last aboriginal Tasmanian died in 1876. In Australia itself, the aborigines were almost all driven back into Queensland and the Northern Territory: there were some 20,000 of them.

In New Zealand, the contact was more dramatic, but finally less disastrous for the native population, the Maoris. These were Polynesians who had settled mainly in the North Island; they belonged to the old and flourishing civilization of Polynesian seafarers. They had probably arrived in New Zealand between the ninth and the fourteenth centuries AD: it marked the Southernmost extent of their wanderings, far from their own tropical countries, lands of the banana, the elephant's ear plant and the yam. New Zealand was very different from that tropical world. What delighted its European colonists was its temperate climate, unlike that of Spain, to which it was diametrically opposite on the globe.

The Maoris therefore had to adapt as best they could to the North Island. They hunted its many birds – its only fauna; they bred dogs, the only domestic animals they had brought with them; they fished, not in the stormy sea, but in lakes and rivers; and they dug up roots. They coped with the cool climate by

building wooden houses and spinning linen garments. Hardened
by incessant wars among their tribes, they put up fierce resistance
to the Europeans.

The wars they fought were murderous for their opponents and
still more for themselves. They were finally defeated in 1868.
What was more, the new diseases that came in with the whites
decimated them. However, at the beginning of the twentieth
century the Maoris began to recover from the crisis that had
nearly exterminated them. In 1896, they numbered only 42,000.
By 1952, there were 120,000, by 1962, 142,000. A high birth-rate,
family allowances and employment in cities like Auckland, all had
helped to bring about the increase. But they were still only some 6
per cent of New Zealand's total population of 2,230,000, and
seemed no threat to the unity of its civilization.

The short history of Australia and New Zealand is marked by a
series of economic opportunities, regularly linked to the vicissitudes
of the world's economy or its history. These opportunities were
sudden, and had to be seized immediately, like a moving train that
could be caught or missed.

One opportunity for Australia was Britain's need, after the
American War of Independence, to find an alternative to Virginia
as a place to transport its convicts. So the first colony in Australia
began as a penal colony. The first shipment of prisoners reached
Port Jackson (where Sydney now stands) on 18 January 1788. The
transportation of criminals to New South Wales was not abolished
until 1840.

Almost at once, however, alongside the settlers or small landowners, 'squatters' began to breed merino sheep for their fine wool.
The undemanding tasks of sheep-breeding suited the convicts'
temperament; and, at the same time, capital from the big landowners and brisk demand from Britain and elsewhere made the
fortune of Australian wool, which even today is still supreme in the
world.

Soon afterwards, from 1851 to 1861, there was a gold rush
similar to that in California in 1849. It spread throughout New

South Wales undisciplined bands of 'diggers'; but it helped to people the country and encouraged economic growth. The newcomers had to be fed.

New Zealand, too, experienced successive booms – in wool, in wheat and also in gold, which was first discovered in the South Island, in 1861. The North Island was discountenanced for a time and put at a disadvantage by the gold rush: in 1865, the capital was even transferred from Auckland to Wellington (where it remains). But the New Zealand economy benefited greatly from the stimulus, since here too the gold prospectors had to be supplied and fed. From 1869 to 1879, both islands enjoyed enviable prosperity.

But this is not the place to record in detail these periods of growth and good fortune, often followed by stagnation or slump – as suffered by both New Zealand and Australia from 1929 to 1939. What matters here is to note the successful industrialization of Australia. So far, despite huge hydro-electric resources, New Zealand has not had comparable success.

What is clear in the case of both these distant European outposts is that their fortunes are linked with those of the rest of the world – and much more so than they are inclined to think. Perhaps they are misled by the ease and comfort of their lives, by a degree of well-being that seems all the more striking at a few hours' flying time the less developed countries of the Far East, where poverty and overpopulation prevail. Australia and New Zealand are 'European' countries in their own right, and not colonies: despite their allegiance and loyalty to the Commonwealth (their biggest supplier and a vital customer), they are both independent States (Australia since 1901, New Zealand since 1907).

The constant concern of Australia and New Zealand has been to keep for themselves the great advantages that their immense area offers, to control immigration, and to maintain at all costs a high standard of living and a pragmatic social policy which works well because it is backed by abundance.

By the beginning of the twentieth century, New Zealand was

already a true modern democracy. It had an eight-hour day in 1856; the separation of Church and State in 1877; votes for women in 1893, when land reform also broke up the biggest estates; compulsory conciliation procedures between unions and employers in 1894–5; and old-age pensions in 1898. There were similar developments in Australia, where the door to immigration, closed in 1891, opened for the new and final gold rush that in 1893 led to the foundation of Coolgardie, deep in the desert of Western Australia. A social policy on New Zealand lines was established without difficulty, and under the Australian Labour Party's rule the country became 'the workers' paradise'.

The vast sums spent on social security had obvious beneficial effects: on wages, on the standard of living, on infant mortality and on the expectation of life. But all this welfare had to be paid for; and it made great inroads on public finance and the national income. In Australia, with the growth of industry and of giant cities like Sydney and Melbourne, with nearly 2 million inhabitants, frequent strikes could be extremely expensive. For example, 'according to the *Chamber of Commerce Journal* for October 1949, they cost Australia 20,800,000 tons of coal between January 1942 and June 1949'. Such demands and difficulties explain why the Labour Parties of both Australia and New Zealand have had their reverses at the polls. But these have not led to excessive polemics, or to extreme changes in basic policy. The practitioners have changed, but the practice has remained broadly the same.

Is that practice, finally, reasonable? It consists broadly speaking, in reserving the wealth of a quasi-continent for 15 million Australians (0.75 to a square mile), and that of New Zealand, with more land than Britain, for 3.2 million inhabitants (4.5 to the square mile). But in today's world, the 'proletariat at the gate' is growing at threatening speed. The Second World War brought the Japanese to the very shores of Australia, which was saved only by the US naval victory in the Coral Sea, in May 1942. The lesson has not been lost on the Australian Government, which has tried, not very successfully, to welcome immigrants to increase its strength and supply its industry. But New Zealand has continued to go its own way; and affluence there has begun to produce its usual results – a slower birthrate (29 per 1,000 in 1962) and an ageing population, with a death rate of 9.3 per 1,000. New Zealand may be a new country and an early democracy: but in terms of population it is no longer young.

Part III: The Other Europe: Muscovy, Russia, the USSR, and the CIS

The other Europe developed late too, almost as late as America, but on the continent of Europe itself and therefore cemented to the West. This other Europe was Russia, the Muscovy of early days, which became the USSR and then the CIS. What we shall look at is: its origins and its long, long past; its adoption of Marxism after the Revolution of 1917; and its situation after years of Communism — its *entelechy*, as philosophers might say.

And all the time, of course, the subject is the same. A subject whose prestige derives in part from its political Revolution, but also from the speed with which it accomplished its admittedly imperfect industrial revolution. Barely industrialized in 1917, by 1962 it had become a counter-weight to the powerful United States. That spectacular success seemed to hold out hope to the less developed countries. Could they too make a similar Great Leap Forward? Did it depend, or not, on Communism to make it possible?

24. From the Beginning to the October Revolution of 1917

It is not at all easy to summarize in a few pages, in reasonable fashion, a past as long as that of Russia, marked as it is by violent disasters on a scale almost unmatched by the many vicissitudes suffered by Western Europe.

The first difficulty is the sheer immensity of the area in which this complex and many-sided history evolved. Its 'planetary' size also makes it very diverse. The second difficulty is that the Slav peoples came only late on a scene where they were never absolutely alone. The cradle of the Slavs, the ancestors of the Russians, was in the Carpathians and what is now Poland – the only country whose Slav inheritance is really unmixed. So the actor in question is not the first to enter: but when he does he dominates the stage.

Kiev

This vast area, so long virtually denuded of people, recalls the wide open, empty spaces of the American continent. In such immensity, human beings shrink to nothing. Endless plains, giant rivers, regions monotonously unchanging, mile after mile of crushing distance, interminable carrying of boats over land from one river to another: this is Nature on an Asian scale.

To the North of an imaginary line between Kiev and Perm, huge forests continue those of Northern Europe, linking them with the mainly coniferous Siberian taiga on the far side of the Urals. This ancient mountain chain, running from North to South, is a minor barrier rather like the Vosges, but it acts as the conventional Eastern limit of Europe, the frontier between Russia-in-Europe and Russia-in-Asia.

To the South stretches the treeless expanse of the steppes (the word is of Russian origin): the black steppes with their fertile *chernozem* or 'black soil'; the grey or chestnut-coloured steppes with their tall grasses, which in the dry season grow almost as high as a rider on horseback; the white steppes with their patches of saline soil, along the banks of the Caspian Sea.

Russia is made up of these great low-lying lands between the White Sea, the Arctic Ocean, and the Baltic in the North and the Black Sea and the Caspian in the South. The Baltic and the Black Sea are the busiest and most welcoming of these seaways, and essential to Russia, whose vocation, it would seem, is to link them, using them as doors and windows through which to communicate with the West and the Mediterranean, i.e. with European civilization.

But Russia also opens out on to the troubled Asia of the steppes – the Asia of those nomads whose quarrels, wars and incursions we have already traced, threatening invasion as late as the sixteenth century. If these nomads from the East overran Iran and headed for Baghdad, that was no problem: the storm was diverted, and Russia could only profit from the result. But because there was no room for everyone under the Middle Eastern sun, many of these Asian visitors had no alternative but to move on towards the Russian steppes, from the Volga to the Don, the Dnieper, the Dniester and even further. These invasions struck at Muscovy many times.

So Russian territory acted as an enormous frontier zone between Europe, which it protected, and Asia, whose violent blows it painfully absorbed.

Russia could not really exist unless it filled the whole isthmus between the Baltic and the southern seas, and controlled any links between them. For this reason among others, Russian history begins with the Kiev principality in the ninth to thirteenth centuries AD.

The Eastern Slavs, of Aryan origin like all Slavs, brought their tribes and clans, after many adventures, as far as the towns, fields and plains of the Dnieper Basin. This migration, begun in the early years of the Christian era, was completed in about the seventh century AD. In the East, these Slavs found a number of peoples already settled: Finns who had come down from the distant Urals; survivors of the Scythians, Sarmatians and Kama River Bulgarians, all of whom had come from Central Asia; Goths from the Vistula and Niemen Rivers; Alans and Khazars (the latter subsequent converts to Judaism) from the shores of the Caspian and the Don.

This early Russia, a mixture of peoples from Europe and Asia, was that of the so-called 'Little Russians'. The intermingling of races and the prosperity of the towns – that whole burgeoning of life between Great Novgorod in the North and Kiev in the South – depended on the flourishing trade routes that stretched from the Baltic to the Black Sea and beyond. They went as far as Byzantium, whose wealth and luxury dazzled the inhabitants of Kiev, tempting them into foolhardy expeditions against it, and even to Baghdad, then just entering its heyday. From North to South along these routes came amber, furs, wax and slaves; from South to North went fabrics, rich silks, and gold coins. These last have been unearthed by archaeologists all along the trade-routes – a line of golden dots to prove how prosperous they were. Prosperity, indeed, was the key. It supported cities far too big to live off the rudimentary farmland around them: cities which joined hands across great distances, from Novgorod to Kiev, exchanging their goods, their quarrels and their princes.

The Russia of Kiev constantly had to defend itself, especially against attacks from the South. But the far Scandinavian North was always willing to supply it with useful mercenaries – servants one day, masters the next, but always warriors. These 'Normans', or rather 'Varangians' came mostly from Sweden, still rustic and primitive, but sometimes also from Denmark. They were readily attracted by the Dnieper road that linked the Russian towns and led 'toward the Greeks' across this whole wealthy area which they significantly called the Gardarikki, 'the kingdom of cities'. One family of these soldier–adventurers founded the Rurik dynasty. Its origins are obscure, but in the tenth century it dominated Kiev and the other towns. The Russia of Kiev goes under various names: one is 'the Principality'. Another is Rurikovitchi – the dynasty of Rurik.

The splendours of this early Russia can be understood if one looks at their historical context. At that time, the Western Mediterranean had long been closed by the Islamic conquest of the seventh and eighth centuries: so the overland route between Novgorod and Kiev was an alternative link between the countries of the North and the rich lands of the South. When in the eleventh and twelfth centuries Muslim supremacy at sea came to an end and the Western Mediterranean was open again, there was less reason to take the interminable land route, which involved not only river travel but also portage, carrying the merchandise from one waterway to another. The Latin occupation of Constantinople in 1204 put an end to it altogether: the sea had conquered the land.

Even before that date, the Kiev princes found it more and more difficult to defend their frontiers and to reach the Balkans and the Black Sea. An old saying alleged: 'When it comes to eating and drinking, people go to Kiev, but when Kiev has to be defended, there is suddenly no one there.' This was certainly true. The nomads from the South continually hurled their mounted warriors against the lands and cities of the Principality: after the Pechenegs came the 'Turci', and later the Kipchaks or Kumans, whom Russian chroniclers called Polovtsians.

In the eleventh century, some of the people of Kiev moved – one might almost say fled – to the North-West, settling in clearings that the peasants made in the vast forests near Rostov (Rostovlaroslavski, a small Northern town, not to be confused with today's Rostov-on-Don). There, a new Russia took shape, and a new mixture of Slavs and Finns. The latter, of Mongoloid origin, made up the bulk of the population: together, they formed the group known as the Great Russians. This new Russia, barbaric but robust, had already emerged before the lights of Kiev were extinguished. In fact, the powerful Mongol attack which overcame Kiev on 6 December 1241, destroyed a State that had long been losing ground. Five years later, a traveller saw only 200 poverty-stricken houses where the great city had once stood.

The old Russian cities were Western cities. For centuries, the Russia of Kiev was renowned for its material success and the splendour of its cities. There was no trace then of any difference or time-lag between Eastern and West Europe.

Comparative historians have nevertheless noted that the cities of the Kiev Principality differed in some respects from their contemporaries in the West. The latter were surrounded by a sprinkling of small towns, often almost villages, which shared the tasks of their big neighbour. The Russian cities were not. Nor, more especially, were they sharply cut off from the surrounding countryside. Thus, the lords of the land round Great Novgorod sat in its assembly, the Veche, whose decisions were law in the city and in its vast hinterland. They were its masters, together with the Council (*Soviet*) of leading merchants. And in Kiev, pride of place went also to the lords or boyars who made up the *druzhina* or guard of the Prince. These, then, were 'open' towns like those of antiquity, such as Athens, open to the patrician eupatrids of Attica, and not at all like the towns of the West in the Middle Ages, closed in upon themselves, jealously guarding the privileges of their citizens.

The Russian Orthodox Church

Through its conversion to Orthodox Christianity, the Kiev Principality determined Russia's future for centuries to come.

Kiev's trade routes, in fact, carried not only merchandise but also the preaching of missionaries. The Principality's Christian conversion resulted from the policy of Vladimir I also known as St Vladimir or Sunny Vladimir. For a time he had thought of adopting Judaism for himself and his subjects, but he was dazzled by the beauty of Byzantine ritual. In about 988, he officially converted the whole population: the people of Kiev were Christened *en masse* in the waters of the Dnieper. But in fact the new religion had been spreading, especially in the South and in Kiev itself, for more than a hundred years. This had been part of the general movement that had followed St Basil's decisive mission to the Khazars in 861, the conversion of the Moravians in 862, the Bulgars in 864 and the Serbs in 879. The conversion of Russia, therefore, was only one event among several. It was a further proof of the exceptional influence enjoyed by the old Byzantine Church, after the iconoclast dispute had at last been settled at the Council of Nicaea in 787 – a sign of return to health in a Church whose preaching then reached out to the heart of distant Asia.

But it took some time before Christianity thoroughly penetrated first Little Russia and then Great Russia. Its great successes came later. The cathedral of Santa Sophia in Kiev was built between 1025 and 1037, and Santa Sophia in Novgorod between 1045 and 1052, while one of the first monasteries, the Monastery of Caves, was founded in Kiev in 1051.

The fact is that town and country dwellers in Russia were attached to their pagan cults, and that these were eradicated none too rapidly and none too well. Pre-Christian beliefs and habits of mind survived in some cases into the twentieth century, especially as regards marriage, death and healing. They permanently coloured Russian Christianity, whose special contribution to Orthodox liturgy, like its cult of icons and its emphasis on Easter celebrations, has often been underlined.

The fact that the world and civilization of Russia were sucked into the orbit of Byzantium from the tenth century onwards helped to distinguish Eastern from Western Europe.

The differences between Catholics and Greek Orthodox Christians, often explained in various different ways, pose a major problem which it is more important to formulate (if possible) than to resolve. From our viewpoint, those differences are mainly historical.

Western Christianity has been subjected to particular ordeals. It was in part the heir of the Roman Empire. It had conquered that Empire, but its victory had coincided with 'Christian imperialism'. This bore fruit in the West when, after the fall of the Empire in the fifth century, Christianity inherited its tasks and its 'universal structure'. The Western Church was oecumenical: it transcended nations and States; it used its language, Latin, which everyone shared, as a way of maintaining unity. Finally, it retained the Empire's hierarchies, its centralization, and its ancient, august capital, Rome. Even more, the Church in the West confronted all the political and social problems that were so numerous and pressing in the first Dark Ages of Western civilization. It was the great community that could meet all needs, spiritual or physical: it could preach to the heathen, educate the faithful, and even clear new arable land.

The Byzantine Church, in the tenth century, was part of a solid and still surviving Empire which gave it neither the duties nor the dangers of expansion into the temporal sphere. The Byzantine Empire dominated it and confined it to its spiritual tasks. The Orthodox Church which became that of Russia was less distinct from the laity than was the Roman Church, and half indifferent to political affairs. It was ready to accept whatever national framework it was offered, and little concerned with organization or hierarchy. Its only aim was to impart the spiritual tradition it had imbibed from tenth-century Greek thought.

As the language of the liturgy, the Greek Church jealously preserved Greek, 'regarding it as an élite language of which barbarians were not worthy'. In Slav countries, therefore, the liturgical language was Slavonic, into which Sts Cyril and Methodius (between 858 and 862) had translated the sacred texts, for use by the various Slav peoples they had undertaken to convert. They had had to invent an alphabet for it, since the Thessalonian Slavonic into which they were turning the Scriptures was only a spoken language. Hence the importance of liturgical Slavonic, that first written language, in the cultural history of the Slav peoples.

The difference between the spiritual traditions of the two Churches can be seen in several ways. Thus, for instance, the word for 'truth', in Greek and still more in Slavonic, means 'that which is eternal and constant, really existing, outside the created world' as our reason perceives it. So the word *pravda* means both 'truth' and 'justice', as distinguished from *istina* or 'earthly truth'. 'The Indo-European root *var* has given the Slav languages the word *vera*, meaning "faith"' – not truth. In Latin, on the other hand, the word *veritas* (*verité* in French, *verità* in Italian, *verdad* in Spanish), in its legal, philosophical or scientific sense always means 'a certainty, a reality for our reason'. Likewise the word *sacrament*, in the West, involves the religious hierarchy which alone can administer it; whereas in the East it means above all a 'mystery' – 'that which transcends our senses and comes from on high' directly from God.

Certain liturgical details also reveal profound differences. The Holy Week before Easter is marked in the West by mourning, concerned with the passion, suffering and death of Christ the man. In the East, it is full of joy, with songs that celebrate the resurrection of Christ as Son of God. Russian crucifixes, too, show Christ at peace in death rather than the suffering Saviour more familiar in the West.

This may well be because Christianity in the West was confronted from the start with human, collective, social and even legal problems, while religious thought in the East remained more circumscribed, more individual and purely spiritual, easily becoming mystical. Some see in this the origin of the general cultural differences that Alexis Khomiakov described in terms of 'mystical Orthodox and rationalist Westerners'. Is Western Christianity thus partly responsible for the characteristically European spirit of rationalism, which so quickly developed into free-thinking criticism, and against which Christianity defended itself before finally adapting to it?

Russian Orthodoxy, by contrast, has not faced such perilous battles, at least until recent years. But it had to choose, in the seventeenth century, between a purified official religion (purged, for instance, of the habit of making the sign of the cross with two fingers of the right hand, contrary to Greek Orthodox practice) and a popular, conventional, moralizing religion which soon became mutely rebellious. The popular reformers were excommunicated, and there was Schism, *Raskol*. From then on there was a continual campaign against the Raskolniki. And these, of course, were only internal struggles. Attacks from outside, by freethinkers, scarcely began before the last century of Tsarist Russia. Then after the Revolution of 1917, the Orthodox Church had to fight for its life, for its very existence, by surreptitious actions and the acceptance of compromise. Has it won from this all-out combat some hope of renewal? Is it willing to try new paths, parallel to Social Democracy, such as twentieth-century Catholicism has deliberately explored over the past fifty or more years?

Greater Russia

The second Russia, the Russia of the forests, reached maturity when it too spanned the isthmus between the Northern and Southern seas. This was when Ivan the Terrible (or rather 'Grozny', the Fearsome, 1530–84) managed to subdue Kazan (1551) and then Astrakhan (1556), and control the great Volga River, from its sources all the way to the Caspian Sea.

He secured this double success by use of the cannon and the harquebus. The invaders from Asia, whose horses had carried them 'into the flank of the West', finally fell back when faced with gunpowder. Ivan could not reach the Black Sea, which had been in the hands of the Turks since the fifteenth century, and

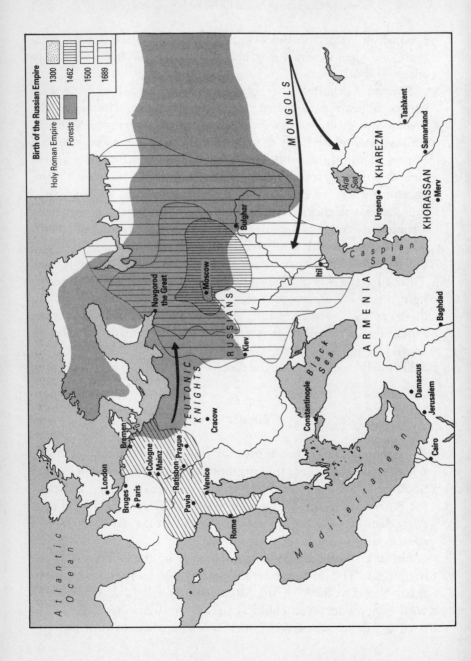

Birth of the Russian Empire

Holy Roman Empire
Forests

1300
1462
1500
1689

Atlantic Ocean

London
Bruges
Paris
Bremen
Cologne
Mainz
Ratisbon
Prague
Pavia
Venice
Rome

TEUTONIC KNIGHTS

Cracow

Mediterranean

Constantinople
Black Sea

RUSSIANS

Kiev
Novgorod the Great
Moscow
Bulghar

Itil

Caspian Sea

ARMENIA

Damascus
Jerusalem
Cairo
Baghdad

MONGOLS

Aral Sea

KHAREZM

Urgench
Merv

KHORASSAN

Tashkent
Samarkand

which they kept jealously and powerfully defended. But the Caspian, which he did reach, was on the way to Persia and India.

So a new Russia slowly took shape and triumphed, starting from another latitude and in difficult circumstances, very different from the favourable conditions in which the Russia of Kiev had begun life. Here, by contrast, there were poverty, serfdom and feudal fragmentation.

Even before the fall of Kiev in 1241, the whole of Southern Russia – the steppes – had been occupied by the Mongols – the Tatars, as the Russians called them. They had then formed a great independent Mongol State, adding to its vast homeland in the steppes those Northern Russian States and cities that recognized its authority. This State, the Khanate of the Golden Horde, had its capital at Sarai on the banks of the lower Volga.

The establishment and maintenance of the Khanate depended not only on its army, but also on its tax-gatherers and its wealth. This lasted a long time, at least as long as the 'Mongol route' to India and China remained open, until about 1340. It was used mainly by Italian merchants, chiefly from Venice and Genoa. After its closure, although the Golden Horde survived in the South, it gradually lost its hold on the forest country in the North.

It was there that the Principality of Moscow had grown up, in

22. The expansion of Russia

At the beginning of the eleventh century Kiev, on the Dnieper, dominated the Southern part of what is now Russia (some sixty principalities). Its princes became converts to the Greek Orthodox Church. Kiev was an important staging-post between the Slav countries and Byzantium, between the West and the Far East. At the end of the twelfth century, it lost its importance, and then was overrun by the Mongols. In the fourteenth century Moscow, sheltered by its forests, for a time escaped invasion. Daniel, a son of Alexander Nevsky (Prince of Novgorod the Great), guided the first steps of the Muscovite State. Ivan the Great (1462–1505) was the first great enlarger of Russian territory. Under his rule, Muscovite warriors crossed the Urals and established a foothold in Siberia. Peter the Great (1672–1725) was the legendary founder of Russian power, conqueror of the Swedes and the Turks, great reformer and the founder of St Petersburg (1703). The towns of Bulghar and Itil were destroyed by the Mongols in the thirteenth century.

the midst of obscure struggles among many small feudal domains. Founded in the thirteenth century, it gradually 'reassembled' Russian territory (rather as the Capetian kings had recovered French territory to add to the Ile-de-France), and finally threw off the Tatar yoke in 1480. With that, the 'Tsar' of Moscow replaced the Khan of the Golden Horde. The remains of the Horde, mainly the Tartars of the Crimea, between the Volga and the Black Sea, survived until the eighteenth century, owing to support from the Ottoman Turks, whose more or less docile vassals they were.

But this whole process had taken three centuries; and during this time, while Russians and Tatars had very often fought and opposed each other, they had even more frequently been at peace, trading with each other and sometimes helping each other too. The leaders of the Golden Horde had in general favoured and supported the rise of Moscow. Being late, lax converts to Islam, they were largely tolerant, letting the peoples they conquered believe and worship as they wished. At Sarai, there was actually an Orthodox church.

Between rulers and ruled, moreover, many marriages took place – so much so that there was talk in Muscovy of a 'semi-oriental' aristocracy. In the fifteenth century, too, when the decline of Tatar power was already evident, many Muslims settled in Russian States, became Christian converts, and entered the service of the princes, arousing jealousy on the part of native Russians. Several great families, such as the Godunovs and the Saburovs, are of Tatar origin.

The Mongols imposed their prestige on the Muscovite princes for a long time. They came from a more civilized society, a better organized State (on which the Muscovites modelled their own), and a money economy unrivalled in the North. The Russian language today still retains some characteristic words of Mongol origin: *kazna*, the fisc; *tamojna*, the customs; *iam*, a postal station; *dengui*, money; *kaznachei*, a treasurer. This more advanced civilization left a certain Asian imprint on manners and customs in Muscovy, which behaved a little like a barbarian society subjugated and enlightened by its betters. The situation was a little like the coexistence of Christians and their brilliant Muslim invaders in Spain, but with less violent mutual clashes. The Tsar of Moscow began to dominate the Muslim Khan, incidentally, in about 1480 – at the very time when the Spanish Reconquista was about to culminate in the taking of Granada in 1492.

Moscow's predominance was the outcome of countless minor struggles with its neighbouring principalities. It was not assured until the reign of Ivan III (1462–1505), whom some Russian historians have compared and even preferred to Peter the Great. In 1469, soon after coming to the throne, Ivan married Sophia, the heiress of the Palaeologi, the last Greek Emperors of Constantinople. So Moscow, shortly after the fall of Constantinople (Czarigrad), captured by the Turks in 1453, could have become the Third Rome, 'dominating and saving the world'. But this long-term and largely honorific success (the title of 'Tsar', perhaps a corruption of 'Caesar' being adopted by Moscow hereditary princes only in 1492) was less important than victory over the Lithuanians, the Golden Horde (whose tutelage was thrown off in 1480) and the great trading city of Novgorod.

The struggle with Novgorod was long, hard-fought and dramatic. In 1475, Moscow waged a 'cold war' and entered the city peacefully; in 1477–8, Ivan had the bell of the Veche removed; in 1480, he exiled a hundred noble families; in 1487, he drove 7,000 inhabitants out of the city. It was the end of what had been called Gospodin Velikyi Novgorod – My Lord Novgorod the Great.

As much as the idea of being a Third Rome, or the adoption of the new title 'Tsar', what made clear Moscow's ascendancy was the arrival there of Italian artists: Ridolfo Fioravanti, nicknamed 'Aristotle', from Bologna; Marco Ruffio and Pietro Solario, builders of palaces and churches. 'It was then that the Kremlin took its present shape.' The cannon-maker who gave Ivan III's army its powerful artillery was also an Italian, Paolo Debossis. So, almost a century before Ivan the Terrible and the decisive victories in Kazan and Astrakhan, Muscovite power was making its first forceful mark, and this already involved, undoubtedly, renewed contact with the West.

All these successes and innovations demanded an immense effort by the State. Ivan Peresvetov, an ideologue from the time of Ivan the Terrible, worked out a political theory based on terror. And we know that the *oprichina*, the police system set up by Ivan the Terrible, enabled him 'to crush the opposition of the princes and the boyars and strengthen the centralization of the Russian State'.

Russia turned more and more towards Europe. That was the crucial fact in its history in modern times, until 1917 and even beyond. By this policy, which it pursued with tenacity, Russia acquired modern technology, which itself was rapidly improving. The industrial age gave it an early revenge on Asia, which had threatened it for so many centuries. Later, it also stole a march on Europe.

Did Asia play some part in the rise of Russia? Two historians, the Kulischer brothers, believe that it did. In their view, the peoples of Asia, over the centuries, have tilted this way and that: sometimes towards Europe and the Mediterranean, sometimes towards the Far East and especially China. Russia's situation, they believe, has been partly determined by this process, which from the fifteenth century onwards led the nomads to move Eastward. This relieved the Asian pressure on Southern Russia. Tatar Islam lost some of its strength in its Far Eastern adventure; and when the balance tilted back again towards Europe in the eighteenth century, it was too late. The Westward advance of the Kirghiz and Bakshir nomads, caused by pressure from the Chinese in the seventeenth and eighteenth centuries, was halted by a solidly built barrier, which even the semi-Asiatic revolt by Pugachev in 1773–4 was unable to break.

This no doubt over-simple explanation needs to be corrected. Clearly, while there was less pressure from Asia, Russia was also better able to resist it, on account of the superior technology it had acquired from the West and begun to deploy. The Russian economy was improving too, if only because of contact with more and more active European trade in the Baltic outlets. Nothing is more typical, either, than the temporary Russian occupation of the Baltic port of Narva in the sixteenth century. That outlet was shut again almost immediately, but it was not long before Russia had its revenge.

The dialogue between Muscovy and the West, which as we have seen began at least as early as the reign of Ivan III, continued and intensified. A traveller from Germany, Baron von Herbestein, was held to have 'discovered' Moscow in 1517, rather as Christopher Columbus 'discovered' America. At all events, more and more people – merchants, adventurers of every kind, vendors of advice or plans, architects and painters – went to this other New World. This was long before Peter the Great, as a child, made friends with the foreigners in the suburb of Sloboda, whom he later appointed as counsellors. In 1571, the Duke of Alba, then Governor of the Spanish Low Countries, warned the German Reichstag that all Christendom was in danger from the smuggling of arms to Muscovy, which might well become its enemy. Twenty years earlier, in 1553, the English navigator Richard Chancellor, having lost his other ships in a storm, reached St-Nicholas-of-Archangel on the White Sea. From there the Muscovy Company, founded by London merchants, traded for a number of years across the breadth of the country as far as Persia.

Closer ties between Russia and the West, already adumbrated, multiplied and loomed larger, like a close-up in the cinema, with the bold, brutally hasty measures taken by Peter the Great (1689–1725) and the long, outwardly glorious reign of Catherine II, Catherine the Great (1762–96). As a result, the frontiers and the external shape of modern Russia *vis-à-vis* Europe were greatly changed. In the eighteenth century, in fact, it continually sought to dominate and extend its own territory, if necessary at others' expense. The main link with the West was organized from St Petersburg (later Leningrad), the new capital built from scratch on the Neva, starting in 1703. With more and more British and Dutch ships calling there, its trade continually grew. Russia was becoming more and more European. Most European countries assisted in the process, but especially the Balts and the Germans. Russia's neighbours had the front seats.

The definitive conquest of the South (begun but not completed by Peter the Great) and the colonization of the Crimea in 1792 took place in a relative vacuum. Hence the 'Potemkin villages' – collapsible façades – which Catherine the Great's favourite, General G. A. Potemkin, had erected and dismantled in the course of her famous journey to the South. Here, there was still no proper link with the Black Sea; it was not fully established until the beginning of the nineteenth century and the development of Odessa by the Duke de Richelieu. It was 1803 before the first wheat from the Ukraine reached the ports of the Western Mediterranean, to the alarm of landowners in Italy and later in France.

Altogether, then, both in general and in the detail of its many endeavours, the history of Russia in the eighteenth and nineteenth centuries is one of all-absorbing 'culture contact', with its illusions, its errors, its absurdities and snobbery, but also its positive results. 'Scratch a Russian and you will find a Muscovite': the saying may have come from Russia, but it was very popular in the West. But why should the Muscovite not remain a Muscovite, with his own tastes, his own peculiarities and his own qualms? In Moscow today, one can visit the Ostankino Palace (now also a museum), which Prince Sheremetyev had had built by his serfs in the eighteenth century in the purest classical style. Visitors are often surprised at the freshness of the internal painting, with its gilt, its decorations and *trompe-l'œil* ceilings, much of it scarcely retouched. The guide explains that the whole building, whose thick walls seem to be of masonry, is in fact made of wood, which resists humidity. The prince had declared, not without reason, that nothing equalled the comfort of Russia's wooden houses, to which he had always been accustomed. So he had kept to wood but dressed it *à la française*.

That was rather typical of eighteenth-century Russia, which called in countless Westerners to help it, even to build its industry

– or what industry there was at that time. Crowds of engineers, architects, painters, artisans, musicians, singing teachers and governesses descended on a country eager to learn and ready to tolerate anything in order to do so. The mass of buildings in a city like St Petersburg; or – a small symbolic detail – Voltaire's library, still intact; or, still more, the enormous numbers of documents in French in the public archives: all these bear eloquent witness to the great apprenticeship which the Russian intelligentsia underwent, and with rather good grace at that.

France, in fact, played a privileged part in this cultural process. In return, it was somewhat dazzled by 'the Russian mirage'. The autocratic Catherine was thought liberal in France because she had *The Marriage of Figaro* staged in Russia before it was authorized by Louis XVI. We should be less gullible, In reality, Catherine II's Government was socially retrograde: it consolidated the power of the nobility and worsened the condition of the serfs.

Only aristocratic culture was readily influenced by Paris and Versailles. It contained small seeds of revolution, and spread to intellectuals and students, who could hardly fail to watch with envy the events of 1789, which shook the old Europe even if they failed to transform it. But it was against the Russian colossus that the French Revolution (or Napoleon's Empire, which was its sequel) came to grief – a fact that deserves to be remembered.

In the background, out of sight but sometimes surfacing, revolution nevertheless ran like a thread throughout the history of modern Russia, from the sixteenth century to the explosion of October 1917.

After the brilliance of the Kiev Principality, which itself concealed many disturbances and social tensions, in the Middle Ages Russia remained backward. Feudalism took root there just when it was waning in the West. From the fifteenth century to the twentieth, Russia became more and more European: but only a small part of the population was involved in the process: a few great aristocrats, some landowners, intellectuals and politicians. What was more, the growth of trade with the West, in Russia as in Central Europe, turned the aristocracy into wheat producers and merchants. A 'second wave of serfdom' was the obvious result, from the Elbe to the Volga. Peasants' liberties lost their meaning. Until then, serfs had had the right, unless they were in debt, to change masters every year on St George's Day. Now they lost it. A ukase by Ivan IV (Ivan the Terrible) in 1581 forbade any further move. At the same time, rent and forced labour weighed ever more heavily on their shoulders.

Admittedly, they could and did still flee to Siberia or to the great rivers of the South. They could even cross the frontier and join the outlaw Cossacks. In this way, the Moscow region lost half its peasants, eager for liberty and adventure. But as soon as the Government established in these distant regions either its own control or that of a nominee, the liberty they had won in practice was contested in law. It was the old, old story of Russian liberties, perpetually won and perpetually lost again. Was it not always the lord's right to seize a fugitive? The Code of 1649 even abolished any time-limit on that right.

Undoubtedly there were huge, widespread and fearsome revolts. In 1669, for example, 200,000 rebels – Cossacks, peasants and natives of Asia – seized Astrakhan, Saratov and Samara; overrunning the lower Volga, they killed landowners and members of the prosperous middle class. Their leader Stenka Razin was not captured until 1671, when he was executed and quartered in Moscow, on Red Square. A century later, in the same regions, Pugachev's uprising had equally massive initial success. Cossacks from the Don and the Ural Rivers, Bakshirs, Khirgiz, serfs from seignorial domaines and from the great iron and copper foundries in the Ural Mountains, all joined the revolt, known as the Pugachevina. The rebels advanced as far as Nijni-Novgorod, hanging landowners as they went and promising everyone land and liberty. They took Kazan, but did not immediately march on Moscow. Pugachev was captured and beheaded in 1775. Order seemed to have been restored.

These facts are very well known. Soviet historians have been glad to make much of them, and with good reason. The more time passed, the worse the plight of Russian peasants became. For when the 'second wave of serfdom' began, there was also 'a second wave of aristocracy'. The boyars of the time of Ivan the Terrible were no longer the boyars of the Kiev Principality, similar to lords of the manor in the West, masters of their own land. Ivan had systematically crushed these independent noblemen: he had executed them by the thousand; he had confiscated their estates and given them to his own men, the *oprichniki* – noble officials who held their lands, or as we might say their 'benefices', only for their lifetime. This being so, the very retrograde reform carried out by Peter the Great was the Entailment Law of 1714, which gave these officials and their heirs, in perpetuity, full possession of the lands they held. So the 'second aristocracy' was confirmed in its privileges, with its ranks fixed for good by the imperial court. Menchikov, Peter the Great's favourite, thus received 100,000 serfs. This showed the double face of Russia in all its contradictions: modernity *vis-à-vis* Europe, medieval backwardness at home.

From that time onwards, a kind of pact united Tsarism with aristocracy that surrounded and served it, always submissive and fearful in face of the master's caprice. The peasants suffered in consequence: they were trapped in insoluble difficulties. Even mass emancipation, in 1858, 1861 and 1864, did little to help. Half the collective constraints imposed on the village, the *mir*, remained in place. Lands recovered from the lords could be bought back. What was more, the landowners still kept part of their domains. The question was not dealt with until 1917, when there was the greatest agrarian explosion in Russian history, a profound and practical reason for the Revolution. Even then, it found no permanent solution: for no sooner had the peasants thrown off their old fetters than collectivization began. Peasants in Russia had a very brief experience of owning their own land.

The explosive rural situation had created revolutionary tension throughout Russian life. It explained the immense and immediate response to the French Revolution of 1789, commented on day after day in all the newspapers, not only in St Petersburg and Moscow, but as far away as Tobolsk in Siberia. The Revolution in France was followed passionately by liberal aristocrats, by bourgeois merchants and by intellectuals and publicists, many of them of humble stock. (See the short study by Michael Strange, *The French Revolution and Russian Society*, which appeared in French translation in Moscow in 1960.) The Declaration of the Rights of Man, the news of riots in France, the spread of the Terror 'touched immediately on the most burning questions in a regime of autocracy and serfdom': they expressed the feelings which, according to one contemporary, could be read in Russia 'in the face of every peasant'.

Other tensions arose alongside this essential peasant problem as industrialization began in the mid-nineteenth century. It was a time when, in the reign of Nicholas I (1825–55), but certainly not at his bidding, Russian literature took giant strides, with Pushkin (1799–1837), Lermontov (1814–41), Gogol (1809–52), Turgenev (1818–83), Dostoyevsky (1821–81) and Tolstoy (1828–1910). All in all, this was an immense period of Russian self-discovery.

New types of revolution or revolutionary unrest soon began and proliferated. There was the limited movement of the 'Decabrists' or 'Decembrists' in 1825; there was the shooting in front of the Winter Palace in 1905; there were the Nihilists in the 1860s; there was the foundation in Minsk in 1898, of the Russian Social-Democratic Party, the first Marxist party; there were the Slavophiles (sometimes chauvinist revolutionaries); there were extreme 'Occidentalists'. Above all it was students, together with intellectuals, young people generally and exiles, who bore the torch of the revolution that was to come. All of Russian history had been kindling its flame.

25. The USSR after 1917

Since we have already glanced at the political, economic, and social antecedents of the Russian Revolution of 1917 and its aftermath, this chapter will be concerned with the more general problems of Soviet civilization: How was Marxism involved in the Russian Revolution? What influence does it have on the Soviet Union in a human sense, quite apart from the plans and statistics, important as they are? Amid all the vicissitudes, constraints and shocks, what are we to make of the present and future of Soviet, now CIS, civilization?

From Marx to Lenin

Karl Marx's thought fairly quickly caught the attention of intellectual and revolutionary circles in Russia, which were favourable to the West and therefore at odds with the Slavophile traditionalists. Thus Marxism very soon won converts among economists and historians at the University of St Petersburg – partly, it was said, in opposition to its conservative counterpart in Moscow.

Marxism was the fruit of collaboration between Marx (1818–83), the key figure, and Friedrich Engels (1820–95) who worked with him for forty years and survived him for twelve. With its elaborate doctrine, it marked an essential turning-point in revolutionary thought and action in the nineteenth and twentieth centuries, arguing that revolution was a natural and inevitable outcome of modern industrialized capitalist society. It seemed to offer an overall view of the world which closely linked social analysis and economic explanation.

Marx's dialectic (the search for truth through contradictions or statement and counter-statement) was inspired by Hegel, although it spurned his philosophy. For Hegel, things of the spirit dominated the material world ('mind over matter'), and consciousness was humanity's essential trait. For Marx, by contrast, the material world dominated things of the spirit. 'The Hegelian system,' he wrote, 'stood on its head; we have set it on its feet'. This did not prevent Marx's dialectic taking over the terms or successive stages of Hegel's: (1) the thesis or statement; (2) the antithesis or negation; (3) the synthesis or negation of the negation, i.e. the statement of an evolving truth taking account of both thesis and antithesis, and reconciling them.

This way of reasoning was always in the background of Marx's arguments. As the Russian revolutionary Alexander Herzen put it, 'Dialectic is the algebra of revolution.' It was certainly the language of Karl Marx, a device for identifying and defining contradictions, once they were 'scientifically' recognized, and then overcoming them. Marxism has been defined as dialectical materialism. The phrase is not inaccurate, although Marx himself never used it and, as Lenin remarked, he emphasized the dialectic far more than the materialism. Following Lenin, others made the same remark about historical materialism, a rather unhappy expression devised by Engels: Marx, it was said, had emphasized the history far more than the materialism. He undoubtedly drew the dialectical arguments for his revolutionary doctrine from an historical analysis of society. That was one of the major innovations in his work.

Western society in the mid-nineteenth century seemed to him to be suffering from a major contradiction, dialectical analysis of which was the basis of Marxist thought. To summarize it briefly: work, for humanity, was a way of being freed from Nature, of mastering it. By working, people became aware of their own nature, which was to be part of a society, as workers among other things. In society, which meant both work and freedom, there was both 'human naturalism' and 'natural humanism'. This was the thesis, the statement about the value and purpose of human work.

Then came the antithesis, the negation. In the society that Marx was studying, work did not free people: it enslaved them. They were not allowed to own the means of production (the land or the factory) and its profits. They were obliged to sell their work, to part with it while others enjoyed its fruits. Modern society had made work a means of enslavement.

So what was the synthesis, the negation of the negation, the way out of that contradiction? When capitalist society (which entailed the selling of people's labour) reached the stage of industrialization, with mass production and mass manpower, it led to the formation of a growing class of wage-slaves, the proletariat. This automatically sharpened the class struggle or class war, and therefore soon provoked revolution.

Industrial capitalism, Marx believed, was the last stage of a long historical process that had brought human society from slavery to feudalism and then to capitalism, first commercial and finally industrial. The world of the nineteenth century had thus simultaneously reached the stage of industrialization and that of revolution, which would abolish private property. The next step would be communism.

But communism would not replace capitalist society overnight. ('Capitalist', incidentally, was a word that Marx used, at least from 1846 onwards: 'capitalism', although very useful, he did not.) As he explained in 1875, there would be 'an inferior stage of communism' during which the new society would emerge as best it could from the old. This stage was known as Socialism: its slogan was 'To each according to his work'. The next and higher stage was Communism proper. It was rather like the promised land. With it, society could proclaim on its banners: 'From each according to his ability (at the production stage), to each (at the consumption stage) according to his needs.' Manifestly, Marx's dialectic was optimistic: it was an 'ascendant' philosophy, as Georges Gurvitch has written.

To Russian revolutionaries, however, Marx's message may well have seemed pessimistic. For the moment, after all, he had concluded that revolution in Russia was theoretically impossible, although he had second thoughts on the subject around 1880, when revolutionary unrest there was once more in the news. In Russia, he thought, the industrial proletariat had not yet fully developed: it would take years for the new conditions created by capitalism's productive power to operate to the full. Only then would there be 'a period of social revolution'. As yet, the time was not ripe.

Marx and Engels pondered, explored and debated this problem, using Britain as an example. When the first volume of *Das Kapital* was published in 1867, Britain was already in the midst of her Industrial Revolution – or, more precisely, in the midst of the difficulties it had caused without as yet providing ways of overcoming them. Marx and Engels also considered the examples of France and Germany, the latter by now only slightly behind the former and rapidly gaining ground. All such examples, of course, were very far removed from conditions in Tsarist Russia.

That being so, how could one expect a social revolution in the name of Marxist principles in Russia at the end of the nineteenth century, where industrialization had made very little headway and where the peasants made up 80 per cent of the population, and industrial workers only 5 per cent?

Lenin was well aware of this contradiction, from the time when he published *The Development of Capitalism in Russia* in 1899, and still more just before and after the Revolution of 1905. Admittedly, as a disciple of Marx, Lenin was the prisoner of doctrines he admired and in which he felt at home. He had very few ideas not already to be found in Marx's writings. On the other hand, although his real talent was for planning revolutionary action, he was far more original, even as a thinker, than is often said.

He came, in fact, from the minor Russian aristocracy, as his voice and accent showed. He was not, therefore, simply a 'representative of the Russian people', its simplicity and its 'practical intelligence'. Nor was he solely a man of action. In fact, when he was accorded 'the honour of cleaning the Second International's Augean Stable', it was because he had already produced original and concrete analyses of its problems and searching criticisms of its practice. When he went into action, it was always after passionate and lucid thought. Wherever he differed from Marx, therefore, it was where disagreement was to be expected: on revolutionary strategy and tactics, which he saw in a Russian context and in terms of relations between the 'proletariat' and the 'Revolutionary Party'.

In a word, Lenin gave politics systematic priority over economic and social matters, and the 'Party' priority over the proletarian mass. He was in favour, one might almost say, of 'politics first'. For Marx, revolution was the result of social explosions that were almost natural events, occurring in their own good time under the pressure of industrialization and the class struggle. The proletariat, herded into the towns as a result of industrialization, was explosive and revolutionary by its very nature. Alongside it, part of the bourgeoisie had been the forcing-house of the new ideologies; but now it had already fulfilled its revolutionary role. On occasion, perhaps, the help of the democratic and liberal middle classes might still be useful: but for a long time Marx and Engels were very hesitant to use it. And after 1848, not without reason, they especially mistrusted the reactionary potential of the French peasants, whom they saw as 'false proletarians' deeply attached to their parcels of land.

Debates about what form revolutionary action should take continued long after Marx's death in 1883. Rosa Luxemburg (1870–1919), from Germany, shared Marx's views. For her, only the industrial proletariat was to be trusted: it must be the sole driving force of revolution, since all the other classes were its enemies. The 'Party', therefore, must belong to the proletariat, which must watch it closely from within and control it. That, she believed, was the only way to prevent its being bureaucratized.

Lenin took a different tack. Like some reformists, he doubted whether the proletariat ('under imperialism') was naturally and spontaneously revolutionary: and in any case spontaneity horrified him. The time had come, he thought, to emphasize the Party and possible alliances which might rally to the proletariat's cause any other oppressed social groups, whoever they might be. In 1902, in *What is to be Done?*, he maintained that, without the leadership of a centralized party of professional revolutionaries, the proletariat would opt not for revolution, but for reformism and trade-unionism, dreaming perhaps of a utopian working-class aristocracy. Was it not the case that in Britain at that time, the up-and-coming Labour Party was having to oppose the Trade Unions' hesitant conservatism, as in France, where the unions were more anti-Socialist than is often thought. Contradicting Rosa Luxemburg and some others, Lenin added that the age of national wars was not yet over, and that there had to be alliances with the liberal bourgeoisie. Furthermore, and still in disagreement with Rosa Luxemburg and 'Luxemburgism', he called for a programme of agrarian reform, and refused in any case to regard the peasants as re-actionary. On that crucial point, he was surely influenced by Russia's revolutionary Socialists. Like them, he saw the enslaved peasantry as the essential driving-force of revolution, and did not intend to ignore its immense explosive power. In the event, it ensured success for the 1917 Revolution. As regards Russia, Lenin had been right.

This is not the place to examine in detail the ideological discussions and declarations that marked and in some cases influenced the development of the Soviet Union after 1917. Suffice it to say that there was a cultural shift, from Marxism to Leninism. The latter was a revised form of Marxism 'reinterpreted', as anthropologists might say, to adapt it to the under-industrialized, still mainly agrarian Russia of the Tsars at the beginning of the twentieth century – so near in time still, and yet so far. 'The proletariat,' declared Lucien Goldmann, 'was too small in numbers, and therefore too unimportant, economically, socially and politically, to spark off by itself a revolution which would at once have ranged the rest of society against it.'

The Russian Social-Democratic Party, later the Communist Party, was founded in 1898 by the second generation of Russian Marxists (Lenin, Julius Martov and Fyodor Ilich Dan) with the agreement of the first generation (Georgy Plekhanov, Pavel Axelrod, Vera Zassulich, Lev Deutsch), who while abroad had formed the Group for the Liberation of Work (Grouppa Osvobojdeniya Trouda).

During the Social-Democratic Party's second congress, in 1903 in London, a deep split occurred. On one side were the Bolsheviks (Russian for 'the majority', although in this case it was by one vote); on the other were the Mensheviks ('the minority'), including Plekhanov himself. Why the dispute? Because of Article 1 in the Party's statutes, into which Lenin had introduced measures that went by the name of 'democratic centralism'. They provided for:

- a preponderant role for 'professional revolutionaries', i.e. technicians;
- strict, indeed iron discipline by the Party;
- wider and dictatorial power for the Central Committee over the whole of the Party, and especially its grass-roots organizations;
- if need be, a small Bureau to take over all the Party's powers.

Was that clear enough? It made the Party an autonomous war machine, which the Mensheviks accused of dictatorship and disregard for democratic principles. (Trotsky predicted that Lenin's measures would end in the dictatorship of one man, the Chairman of the Central Committee.)

All the same, there is plenty of evidence that this tactical approach was made necessary by the state of social and industrial development in Russia at the time. In 1905, Lenin attacked the argument advanced by a small number of Socialists who believed, he said, 'that a Socialist (i.e. proletarian) revolution was possible, as if the productive forces of the country were sufficiently developed for such a revolution to take place'. More revealing still is the last-minute argument between Lenin and Georgy Plekhanov, the founder of Russian Marxism, on the eve of the seizure of power by the revolutionaries in 1917. Lenin denied planning to take power: if he took it, he said, it would simply be in the hope of support from the Socialist revolution that was about to break out in the advanced capitalist countries – a hope which the Russian Revolution would soon have to abandon, condemned as it quickly was to stand alone. Plekhanov, reverting to basic Marxist arguments – the weakness of the industrial proletariat, the backwardness of Russian capitalism, the huge majority of the peasant population – warned Lenin that if he seized power he would be forced, whether he liked it or not, to impose dictatorship and terrorist methods of government. Lenin retorted that to talk like that was to insult him. But he seized power, and he unleashed the agrarian revolution, just like Mao Tse-tung thirty years later.

Even so, these problems continued to worry him. When in 1921, with the New Economic Policy (NEP), he for a short time put the machine into reverse, his public statements characteristically echoed the same line of thought that had run through earlier polemics. 'We were mistaken,' he declared. 'We acted as if one could build Socialism in a country where capitalism scarcely existed. Before we can achieve a Socialist society, we must rebuild capitalism.' In the event, the New Economic Policy barely survived Lenin's death. From 1928–9 onwards, Stalin espoused industrialization, which was pursued with whatever means lay to hand. Its difficulties and its achievements are a matter of history.

But let us return to 1883, the date of Marx's death, to illustrate the debate more clearly. Georgy Plekhanov, imagining a case in which the revolutionaries seized power 'by accident' or 'by conspiracy', wrote that 'in those circumstances all they would be able to build would be a Socialism like the Empire of the Incas', i.e. with an authoritarian regime. In saying this, Plekhanov was echoing a remark of Marx's own. Discussing a similar eventuality, Marx had spoken of 'convent Socialism' or the 'Socialism of the barracks'.

To recall these words and these debates, as has often been done, is not to condemn the events of October 1917 and their consequences in the name of some 'pure Marxism' which history has somehow swept aside or scorned. The point is that, by chance, the Socialist revolution occurred in the least industrialized country in Europe at the time. So it was impossible for it to take place in accordance with the Marxist scenario of a seizure of power by the proletariat. Power was seized by the Communist Party (as the Social-Democratic Party became) – i.e. by a tiny minority of the vast Russian population, perhaps some 100,000 people all told. This highly organized minority took advantage of the appalling stampede of 10 or 12 million peasants, escaping from the army and flooding back to their villages. On the way, some of them fought and killed each other; when they arrived home, they began to commandeer the estates of aristocrats, the rich bourgeoisie, the Church, the convents, the Crown and the State.

Lenin is said to have asked: 'If Tsarism could last for centuries thanks to 130,000 aristocratic feudal landowners with police powers in their regions, why should I not be able to hold out for a few decades with a party of 130,000 devoted militants?' He is also said to have remarked, in Napoleonic fashion: 'We'll attack, and then we'll see.'

'To hold out for a few decades' until Russia had reached a degree of development and industrialization that might have allowed a 'reasonable' revolution: that, for years, seemed to be the crucial problem. It was also the motivation for an implacable dictatorship which was never the 'dictatorship of the proletariat' but that of the communist leaders – in the name of a proletariat that did not yet exist. 'Under Stalin, the dictatorship of the leaders even became that of one single man.' The historical example that those sombre and dramatic years in the life of Russia cannot fail to evoke is that of the Committee of Public Safety in 1793–4: but in this case dictatorship did not so quickly fail. The reason was undoubtedly the iron discipline of a single Party which prevented any lasting rebellion: quite the reverse of what happened in Paris in 1794.

*

Marxism and Soviet civilization

For many years the USSR had lived under a political dictatorship, without freedom of the press, freedom of speech, freedom of association or freedom to strike, with a single, disciplined, 'monolithic' Party in which underlying conflicts only came to the surface now and then as dramatic personal confrontations. After the death of Stalin in 1953 there was a certain liberalization – or rather, humanization, since 'liberalization' was then for Communists a dirty word. It was a slow process, but apparently irreversible. And was not the reason for this 'de-Stalinization', as some called it, the fact that the dramatic, emergency days of the Committee of Public Safety were long past? The USSR had not emerged from all its internal difficulties, by any means, but it had joined the ranks of the major industrialized countries, the privileged nations. It had won its place by the sweat of its brow, but it was there. At the same time it had built, whether knowingly or not, some of the structures necessary to a mass civilization. For the first time, perhaps, it had the chance to choose its own road, its own revolution, internally at least – since its role in world politics as a leader of the other Communist countries placed other constraints upon it, from the outside.

Even by then, Marxism had already changed. Fifty years of effort and conflict on all fronts had been a long ordeal. No wonder that during that time Marxism–Leninism, as a State doctrine, while maintaining its cherished themes and doctrines, evolved a great deal. It would have been a wonder had it not.

Official speeches went on repeating the sacrosanct clichés: the class struggle, *praxis*, slavery, feudalism, capitalism, relative pauperization, dialectical materialism, the material base or the coming of a wonderfully happy classless society. But that did not mean that the whole massive ideology of Marxism, like all ideologies and religions, had not by virtue of its own position been obliged to come to terms with real life. In any case, the

revolutionaries, like the Russian intelligentsia of the turn of the
century before them, had always held that an idea was valid only
if it took shape in practical life, in praxis. As a system of tightly
knit ideas, Marxism could therefore be valid only if it were
embodied in the actual experience of millions of people. And if it
'became concrete' in this way, bringing itself 'up-to-date', experience was bound to rub off on it. Its disciples claimed that 'Marxism
was a conception of the world that overtook itself'. Sympathetic
observers made the same point. 'Twentieth-century Communism,'
they said, 'underwent transformations comparable to those of
Christianity in the first to the fourth century.'

One would have to be a casuist to count all the changes, infi-
delities and heresies of which Marxism accused itself and Marxists
accused each other. To catalogue them would not be without
interest, so long as no particular detail were allowed to take
precedence, however significant it might seem. A catalogue of that
sort would make sense only against the practical background that
would explain it and be explained by it. Nor is it the clearest or
most important way of appraising the Soviet experiment.

In fact, if the years since 1917 seem a long time to those who
have lived through their vicissitudes, they are still not long enough
to reveal how deeply or otherwise that brutal break with the past,
and the ordeals and further revolutions that followed it, have
affected the nation's underlying ideological, social and cultural
evolution. We should need to distinguish what in all that experience was an aberration (especially but not exclusively in the early
transitional years before 1930) and what was not. Only then could
we hope to determine what relationship there has been between an
ideology imposed by force and a society sucked into an experiment
which it had not chosen and which it neither fully accepted nor
even fully understood.

How far, for example, was the re-establishment of widely differ-
ing wage-rates, already planned by Lenin, an accident, a decision
expressing Stalin's all-powerful will, a social necessity or an inevitable economic trend? The result, in any case, was a social hierarchy,

with obvious privileges for those in its higher ranks. A Soviet university teacher remarked with a laugh: 'We are the Soviet bourgeoisie.' Of course, such a hierarchy can re-establish a class system only if its privileges, which go with office, can be passed on to the next generation, so that the children gain advantages (education, money or jobs) from their parents' social position. This tendency is natural in every society with a strong family life, and Communism in the Soviet Union has in no way destroyed it. Stalin even strengthened it.

A further basic problem has been agriculture. Soviet attempts to organize it on collective lines were failures, and were resisted by the peasantry, with long memories of their maltreatment by Stalin. But this peasant discontent, so often echoed in muffled form by Russian novels, is surely also a normal and almost inevitable reaction on the part of any traditional culture suddenly torn from its ancient habits by rapid economic modernization. The problem would seem to arise in all countries seeking to modernize at speed, irrespective of the solutions adopted.

It is by no means clear, meanwhile, that the last word has been spoken in the more or less tense dialogue between Soviet ideology and the Orthodox Church – if, indeed, there is such a thing as a last word. In the face of 'religious alienation', the regime adopted militant materialism, aggressive rationalism – not denying God but vehemently affirming human concerns. The Second World War helped to revive orthodox belief, and led to a compromise between the Church and Stalin, who re-established the Patriarchate of Moscow, abolished by Peter the Great. Stalin even made reference, in a speech on 7 November 1951, to Alexander Nevsky, prince and saint of the Orthodox Church. No doubt the majority of the practising faithful are of the older generation. But what are the real attitudes of most people when it comes to baptism, marriage and funerals? The pomp and circumstance with which the State tried to surround civil weddings may be a proof that it had a fight on its hands, or at least had to fill a vacuum.

Finally, with successive generations, the dramas of the past have begun to recede in people's memories. Marxism–Leninism has now moved into the background, rather as Western Cartesian thinking, though still pervasive, has become less conscious as a philosophy. This need not imply that the ultimate ideals of Communism have been totally abandoned: but they are no longer burning issues, to be discussed every moment of the day. Even in the 1960s, out of 220 million Soviet citizens, only 9 million were members of the Party. Marxism–Leninism was their trademark, their watchword, their everyday language. But what about everybody else?

The biggest change that Communism brought to life in the USSR, however, was rapid industrialization, and the hope of successfully completing it by building on its successes, overcoming its difficulties and repairing its failures.

In human terms, the change cost Soviet citizens dear. The leaders of the Revolution in 1917 did not inherit an industrial infrastructure ready-made, 'supplied in advance by capitalism'. They had to build it; and this in part explains the particular nature of Stalinist dictatorship. It took on the basic task 'that elsewhere was performed by nineteenth-century capitalism'. The cruelties of Stalin's regime are not wholly to be explained either as the whims of a power-mad dictator or as the stern necessities of Socialism or Communism. They were also in part a response to underdevelopment, a ruthless State policy devised to invest human labour in the race to industrialize a backward and mainly agrarian country.

How far that goal was attained will be debated by specialists for a long time to come. Statistics are a fertile ground for controversy. Their language is international, so peoples compare themselves with each other like children comparing their height. It is important of course, to use the same units of measurement. Official figures, for example, show industrial production in France to have increased by 7.7 per cent a year between 1953 and 1959 (1953 = 100, 1959 = 156), by 8.3 per cent in Germany (1953 = 100, 1959 = 169), and by 11.3 per cent in the USSR (1953 = 100, 1959 = 190). But these official statistics are not directly comparable. The

West calculates its indices in net value, the Soviets in gross value. The Soviet economist Strulinin showed that industrial production in 1956, calculated in gross value, was 22.9 times that in 1928, but only 14.7 times that if calculated net. With discrepancies on that scale, it was easy to imagine how long the USSR's critics and its apologists could be locked in debate.

However, while the Soviet Union's economic goals remained beyond its grasp, in the 1960s they were not entirely out of sight. Immense progress had been made, with quite extraordinary achievements in a number of places, not excluding Siberia.

Great social changes followed the 1917 Revolution. In all the Soviet Republics, industrialization began to change people's lives; and this fact in its turn affected the life of the Union. Everywhere, new structures began to emerge.

A first major change was the influx of peasants into the towns. The USSR imposed the growth-rate of an American boom on a people traditionally stolid and in 1917 still essentially peasant. Everywhere, tension arose between pace and peace, between the ubiquitous pressure for change and the stolidity which often became stubborn resistance to it. In the Central Asian Republics, the coexistence of Americanism and orientalism was more extraordinary still.

The figures show the scale of the change. In 1917, 80 per cent of the Russian population were peasants, and only 5 per cent were industrial workers. By 1962, the peasants were barely in the majority, with 52 per cent, while the proportion of industrial workers and managers had risen to 35 per cent. Over the same period, the number of bureaucrats had been multiplied by 10, and the number of intellectuals by at least 100. Altogether, there had been a huge drift from the land and into the cities.

The results could be seen almost everywhere. With the exception of the former capital, Leningrad, which retained the metropolitan air it had always had, cities old and new, including Moscow (which had become a sort of gigantic Chicago), took on a peasant appearance. Their life became curiously rural. Intellectuals and students were no exception. 'A new race was created in Russia', invading every sphere of life, from the humblest job to heights of scientific research — the summit of the social scale. Stalin's double programme of industrialization in the cities and collectivization on the land created urban jobs and rural jobless, forcing peasants to seek work in the towns whether they liked it or not — all this in only a few years.

In 1947, peasants were still recognizable in the towns they had invaded: they wore rustic clothes; they moved slowly; they shouted as they scrambled on to buses and trams. Already by 1956 a change was visible. The peasants had become more urbanized, and with a higher standard of living they were better dressed. By 1958, one no longer saw women and children walking barefoot; behaviour in theatres and cinemas was exemplary; peasant boorishness was on the wane. And yet people's rural origins, still so recent, showed in a myriad tiny ways. That is perhaps why in Leningrad, by contrast, everything seemed more urbane, the women more elegant, the language spoken more correct. Thanks also to its physical appearance, admirably restored after 1945, the place gives the impression of an old European city, quick, attractive and cultivated, linked by its busy port to the wider world. It has not been swamped by the countryside. Yet perhaps, despite its industrial suburbs, it still remains a little cut off from the extraordinary bustle of life — that very feature that makes Moscow so clearly a capital.

The influx of labour from the countryside quickly outnumbered the skilled workers of the past. Peasants filled the factories, ignorant, ill-trained, clumsy and, like all peasants, suspicious of machinery. Turned overnight into factory-hands, they at first achieved only low productivity. So, to make up the lack of production, more of them were drafted in.

There was a similar influx of peasants, or at least of their children, into the schools and universities. In 1917, at least 75 per cent of the population was illiterate. By the 1960s, it was claimed, illiteracy had been totally eradicated. This would certainly explain the growing numbers of libraries, reading-rooms and popular editions of Russian classics (although not of Dostoyevsky or Sergey Yesenin until 1955). These, as well as selected foreign translations, were often printed in enormous numbers – on occasion, as many as 10 million. True, the price of books, on mediocre paper, was derisory. Was this why the classics were so popular? Or was it because contemporary authors seemed lame, and the press was dull and difficult? At all events, radio, television and records were also extensively devoted to further education.

What O. Rosenfeld has called 'this cultural revolution' in itself encouraged a genuine social revolution – an immense desire for emancipation, a hunger to learn and rise in the social scale. 'Crazy over-ambition', a harsh observer might say. Let us call it rather an eagerness for culture, the key to both money and prestige. Whatever their motive, there were more and more students at universities and technical schools, or taking correspondence courses and evening classes. Often, the children of peasants had the best results. In this way, the USSR was training the intellectual élite it needed – engineers, research workers, officers, professors – out of its inexhaustible human resources. What happened in France after Jules Ferry's educational reforms, and then with free education in secondary schools and universities, was organized by the Soviet authorities at vertiginous speed – and therefore not always without mishaps. It still seems astonishing, for instance, that from 1947 to 1956, secondary education in the Soviet Union was fee-paying, not free.

By the 1960s, however, the level of education was generally said to have fallen.

Once made, that statement calls for qualification. The Russian spoken today, it is true, is no longer the refined language of the past. The education so widely offered is utilitarian, mass-producing the specialists needed by modern society, from the school-teacher to the engineer or even the university professor. 'Semi-intellectuals', said one observer, not normally so unkind.

Unkind or not, was the remark fair? Was this mass semi-culture simply a normal feature in a new country, as is often suggested, or

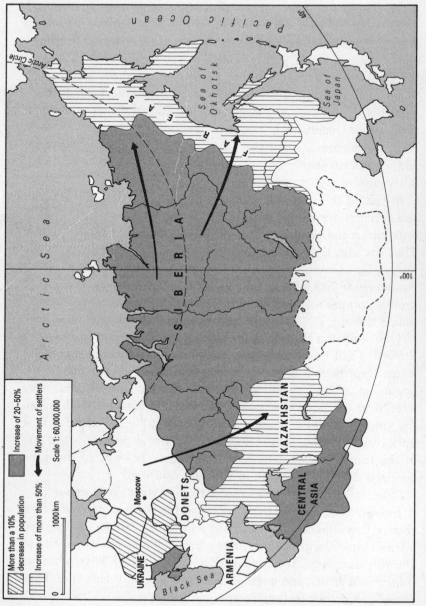

23. *Emigration within the USSR*

more simply still characteristic of an emerging mass civilization? In all the highly industrialized countries in the world, in Europe or America, universal education tends to produce more specialists, and a lower level of general culture. Yet the number of people forming a true intellectual élite has not diminished: at the very worst, it has remained the same. Instead of the very small intellectual élite and the very large mass of illiterates that traditional civilizations maintained, modern civilizations present a more complex picture: a small élite, a very small number of illiterates and a mass of people for whom education is mainly vocational, not a form of higher intellectual training.

In fact, at this higher level, Soviet or CIS intellectuals, scholars and teachers are in our view (and taking account of ideological differences) comparable with those in Europe or the United States. They are also the heirs of the same culture. For a Parisian intellectual, for example, to go from French universities to the Moscow Academy of Sciences is to feel at home, to enjoy immediate mutual comprehension in any discussion or jest. The first impression is that the USSR's total isolation since the Revolution – the physical isolation that cut it off from uninterrupted relations with Europe – had no effect at this academic level. At first sight, this seems surprising. But on second thoughts, one recalls that at the beginning of the twentieth century Europe and Russia were steeped in the same civilization. And in the life of a civilization, the time since then is relatively short. Despite all the fantastic upheavals that have shaken so many social and political structures in the former Soviet Union, it still largely belongs to the same civilization as that of Russia in 1917, i.e. our own.

True, literature and the arts seem to contradict this assertion.

Indeed, if we look in them, as usual, for the best portrait of the society that supports them, in the case of the Soviet Union that portrait looks decidedly pale. But were the pious official works, so absurdly unrealistic, to be regarded as truly representative of Soviet writers and artists, and even of Soviet society and daily life? They were of course the fruit of exceptional circumstance.

Their unconvincing tone was absent from the works of Marx, Engels and even Lenin. It emerged only at the beginning of Stalin's ascendancy, around 1930. Then, the authorities attacked any intellectuals who questioned or rejected Stalin's iron discipline and the mobilization of 'the artistic and literary front' in pursuit of the five-year plan. The first victim was the Association of Proletarian Writers, the RAPP: it was dissolved in 1932, together with similar organizations for music and the fine arts. In their place a single body was formed, under the direct control of the Communist Party.

At the same time, artists and writers were ordered to become 'engineers of human souls'. In 1934 Andrei Zhdanov, the Party Secretary, defined their dogma, 'the method of Socialist Realism'. What artists and writers must do was to describe with 'veracity' the 'historically concrete character' of Socialist reality, and in particular the conditions of production, thus contributing to 'the ideological transformation and the education of workers in the spirit of Socialism'. Their duty, as Zhdanov himself put it, was to be 'tendentious', to produce 'edifying' works, in which people were clearly divided into 'positive heroes', the true Communists, and 'negative characters' – all the rest. The avant-garde movements that had flourished in all the arts at the beginning of the Revolution, and which in the Soviet Union continued to be called 'left-wing art', were now condemned as 'formalist' and suppressed. A number of writers and theatre directors were arrested, and mysteriously disappeared. Most writers took refuge in silence or semi-silence. Mikhail Sholokhov, the author of *Quiet Flows the Don*, whose first three volumes were published between 1925 and 1933, and the fourth in 1940, wrote nothing more until the death of Stalin.

After the Second World War, to counteract the influence of 'the corrupt West', the 'Zhdanov line' was even more strongly enforced. Literature, theatre and the cinema were all kept under close surveillance; the slightest deviation was denounced and punished. In 1948, the great composers Sergei Prokofiev, Dmitri Shostakovich and Aram Khachaturian were violently attacked for writing 'hermetic' music and misusing dissonance.

In other words, throughout Stalin's dictatorship, artists were brought to heel like the rest of the Soviet population. All the products of that period were conformist and mediocre.

Did the death of Stalin change everything? Yes and no. There was certainly an immediate reaction, and a sudden slackening of tension: but the liberal explosion was thought dangerous, and at that time it was very soon damped down.

The end of 1953 and the following year saw a profusion of plays satirizing the faults of Soviet society; and an article by a young critic on 'sincerity in literature', published in the magazine *Novy Mir*, ridiculed the official distinction between 'positive' and 'negative' characters. Although the authors of these squibs were punished for their boldness, de-Stalinization and the attack on the 'cult of personality' encouraged further outspokenness. Hundreds of thousands of deportees returned, and assurance was given that severe sanctions would no longer be applied. This sparked off intense intellectual excitement, and what might be called a literary changing of the guard: those writers who had made their names under Stalin now fell silent, and those of his former victims who were still alive reappeared in print. So great was the effervescence that the authorities were worried. In 1957, they were advised and warned to avoid 'revisionism' and systematically blackening Soviet reality in the guise of a refusal to 'embellish and varnish it'. This reaction was a clear expression of the policy pursued by Nikita Khrushchev.

He certainly condemned Stalin's methods. Even defeated political opponents were no longer executed or subjected to physical violence; and there was some liberalization in cultural matters and relations with other countries. But to open the floodgates to a violently critical campaign, at the very moment when the revelation of Stalin's crimes had deeply shaken a generation of his young and faithful admirers, would have looked like endangering the regime and the USSR's position as leader of the world's Communist countries, as well as perhaps weakening its international power. So the Government reacted – forcefully.

Was the public, then, concerned by that struggle? Huge popular audiences enjoyed the classic plays of the Russian or foreign repertoire; they liked folklore, 'pure, stylized or adapted'; they flocked to classical operas that were a revelation to people until recently still peasants. Hence the success of *Faust, La Traviata* or *Carmen*, rivalling the Red Army dancers or Tchaikovsky's ballet *Swan Lake*. But it would still be a mistake to believe that in these matters there was a sharp distinction between 'lowbrows' and 'highbrows', the general public and the intellectual élite. The freedom of expression that Soviet writers and artists were seeking was in fact a crucial problem, then and in the future.

The problems that beset art and literature hardly affected mathematics and the natural sciences. These, for the most part, were in a very flourishing state. There were many reasons for this. The sciences, as an intellectual discipline, have usually been subject to little detailed control. Very often, they have no relevance to political or ideological debates, and can avoid them. At the same time, the Russians have always been exceptional mathematicians. Furthermore, the Government has not been sparing with either cash or encouragement; and there is something inspiring about building a new world or imagining others as yet undreamed of. Finally, it has to be admitted that in the field of research there is something to be said for authoritarianism. In the capitalist countries, research tends to be dispersed among the different branches of industry, and is partly determined by industry's needs. In the USSR, it has been concentrated on Government priorities. Industry has lost out; so, still more, have consumer comforts, for so long disdained. But research has benefited, as has the organization of scientific teams. And today, success in research depends more on teams than on brilliant individuals. So there may be homage due to the Academy of Sciences of the USSR.

What conclusion can we draw? That in the years after the Second World War, the Soviet Union was still emerging from immense difficulties; and that it had the potential for great material success. Some things it had already achieved. But the establishment of a new structure was far from completed. It was haunted by tragic memories, as well as, paradoxically, by its own world reputation. At a time when it could almost be free to choose its own future, it had to take account of what international repercussions its choice might have.

This somewhat limited its freedom – a limitation that continued long after de-Stalinization. It also limited its own 'superstructures' of art and literature, those means of 'escape' without which no civilization can fully explore itself or express itself. Let us hope that before long the arts will spring into sudden life, like the apple trees in Bolshoi Square in Moscow in the first warm sunshine in May.

The Congress of October 1961

The dramatic 22nd Congress of the Communist Party, in October 1961, threw a fantastic light on the then situation of the USSR. There is no point now, of course, in recalling the dramatic clash of personalities, the lists of condemnations, of excommunications, of the 'living dead' or the 'walking corpses'. Nor is there any need to analyse in detail a turmoil that so much recalls a Dostoyevsky novel – perhaps the tormented and tormenting characters of *The Brothers Karamazov*.

What mattered, and what was first clearly shown at that time, was Soviet civilization itself, confronted with its difficult tasks and choices, in both domestic and foreign affairs. The future depends on how they are tackled. There are three major problems. The first concerns the non-Russian nationalities, the people of other races and civilizations within the union of federated Republics. The second is the economic and material situation (but is it only material?) of ex-Soviet civilization as a whole. The third is the fate of international Communism, which already in 1961 was ceasing to be monolithic and becoming 'polycentric', a kind of 'Communism of the States'.

As regards the first problem, what is at stake is the Union itself. The USSR, as its name implied, regarded itself as a federation of Republics, or States that were in principle independent, but bound together. In the CIS, can their mutual relations be improved in such a way as to produce a powerful and unified civilization?

The Union was first formed by the Empire of the Tsars; and even before 1917 it had already suffered many misadventures. Divided, restored, consolidated, then called in question again, it continued to pose a difficult problem with no perfect solution. While clearly autonomous, none of the Republics was truly independent, since its defence, its policing and its communications were under control by the central authorities, represented by delegates on the Central Committee of each Republic. There was local nationalism – 'chauvinism' – and it was condemned. Clashes occurred. Georgia had to be brought back in the Union in 1921; forty years later, de-Stalinization offended its fidelity to its most famous son. The Baltic States, freed in 1918, annexed in 1940 and reoccupied in 1945, had had privileged status under the Tsars: but the Soviet Union long refused to renew it. There was a crisis in Kirgizia in 1949–51, when the Soviet authorities banned the national epic poem, *Ma as*. And in 1958 the Supreme Soviet announced its intention to recognize Azei as the only language of Azerbaijan.

Local interests and cultures, traditional languages and historical memories, fidelity or otherwise to Communism, and the immigration or intrusion of Russians or Ukrainians into other Republics: all these gave rise to problems, and sometimes to tensions, of a colonial type. To take one example, after the reclamation of virgin land in Kazakhstan, there were more Russians there than Kazakhs.

The only policy of which the USSR was capable came as no surprise: it sought to maintain and safeguard the life and 'harmony' of the Union. This it did by making reasonable and even very generous concessions to the non-Russian Republics – especially since they represented, all told, only a very small part of the USSR's strength. This was the policy that emerged at the 20th

Congress of the Party in 1956. The result was a series of measures to give them greater autonomy – an avowed return to Lenin's nationality policy. To a Westerner, all this was reminiscent of the traditional problems of colonization and decolonization – but with one importance difference. In the case of the USSR, the 'colonies' and the 'mother country' were geographically and physically in direct contact. On the agenda of the 21st Congress of the Communist Party there was explicit mention of the word 'assimilation' – a highly charged and evocative term. Was it possible? And would the USSR be able to achieve it, when the West had so often failed?

In 1959, the Secretary of the Kazakhstan Communist Party declared: 'Lenin's thesis that nations can merge by growing economically and doing more and more together has been confirmed by experience.' This is perfectly possible. There have been examples of successful assimilation in the past. A common policy, mutual concessions and the need to live together can be powerful influences; so can the building of new structures, political, economic and social, which both sides share as a result of so many years' experience of Communism. Nevertheless, civilizations are tenacious. This can be seen in the matter of language alone: the Republics of the USSR defended theirs with stubborn success. They were not prepared to renounce their local civilizations. At the time of writing, the debate was still going on – as it is today. It may well have been that the fight against illiteracy, and the spread of education, actually helped to intensify national awareness among the peoples of Central Asia.

Prosperity or 'bourgeois' civilization: the announcement of a twenty-year plan to lead the USSR to the delights of Communist society did not seem a vain project in 1962.

So long as such and such a condition was met, said the experts, the USSR should be able to make its 'Great Leap Forward' into prosperity. They never agreed on what the conditions were. But the Soviet public passionately wanted peace and longed for material progress, which it believed was possible. That is why in the

1960s so many younger people eagerly took part in the active running of the country. An immense change seemed to be imminent, whatever form it might take and whatever label it might later receive.

In 1962, Soviet life was dominated by the hope of rapidly advancing towards the final stages of the Industrial Revolution. The Khrushchev revolution seemed to open the way to such progress, since the seven-year plan of 1958 had stressed the new industries by a 'sophisticated' consumer society – electronics, electro-mechanics, nuclear energy, plastics, chemicals. All of these were industries which, even before they called forth a new generation of consumers, required and would have to train 'a new type of working class' – white-coated technicians, technologists, scientific and industrial research workers, and so on. The pressure of these new social forces would sooner or later make the democratization of the USSR inevitable and irreversible, concluded the sociologist from whom we gleaned these details.

But that pressure, of course, had to make its way through both the live and the inert counter-pressures of Communist society and the Party itself. It was logical, moreover, for the Party to try to control and apportion any new prosperity and comfort, so as to make the success its own.

That might have been possible, but only if the USSR could have proved that its years of Communism had radically changed it: that, if the Russia of 1917 was still part of Western civilization, the Soviet Union could achieve prosperity along lines different from the 'bourgeois' West, where it had been the best way of staving off revolution.

On this point, at the time of writing, it was impossible to make predictions. The future remained entirely open. It did, however, still seem possible that the former USSR might invent its own solution, copying neither the American nor the European model.

International Communism? There too, the future remained open, with few hints of what was to come. Western commentators on the October 1961 Congress tended to see it as marking the end of the monolithic International Communist Party. It seemed to them that the USSR was consciously abandoning its leadership and the sacrifices that implied, in order to concentrate on its own 'Great Leap Forward' and become the only Communist country to achieve Communist perfection, thanks to material prosperity. It seemed, in a word, as if the USSR was accepting 'bicentrism' for itself and China, or even polycentrism – 'Communism of the States', leaving everyone to their own problems and their own fate.

It seemed rash to be so categorical. Even in the great Communist family, politics follows its ordinary rules. Anger, quarrels, even threats, are often followed by reconciliation and compromise (which is not only an Anglo-American idea). Soviet mistrust of China is nothing new: it has roots in centuries of history, and also in the nineteenth-century conflicts in which Russia was one of the great powers that shared the spoils of China's wealth. But Soviet mistrust of the United States was no less deep-rooted at the time of the Cold War. The same reasons that obliged the United States to emerge from isolationism make it impossible for the USSR, like it or not, to concern itself only with its own economic problems. It has to see its internal policy in the context of international reality.

Nevertheless, in the 1960s, there seemed to be signs of differentiation among the various Communist parties in the world, gravitating round the USSR like planets around a sun, and many of them quite unlike each other.

In outer orbit were the national Communist parties. Some were in the hostile environment of prosperous Western countries like France or Italy, or even virtually non-existent, as in the Anglo-Saxon countries or West Germany. Others, at that time, were living underground lives in Western countries politically hostile to them but economically weak: this was the case in Spain, Portugal and Latin America. Others again were fighting their political battles in the open, in less developed countries still fascinated by the Soviet and Chinese experiments, and still living on hope.

Closer, but none the less distant, were the satellite Communist countries. Those of the 'glacis' facing the West had protected Soviet territory, like buffer states, since the Second World War: Eastern Germany, Poland, Hungary, Czechoslovakia, Romania and Bulgaria. In all of them, great economic and social changes were under way. All except Bulgaria, perhaps, were rapidly industrializing; both Eastern Germany and Czechoslovakia, moreover, had inherited viable industrial economies from pre-Communist days. Outside the 'glacis', finally, were Albania's eccentric Communist system and the equally individual Yugoslavia.

The position of these countries at that time was complex. On the one hand, they could not stray far from the Soviet Union; on the other, some of the structural reforms on which they staked their future (agrarian reform, the break-up of huge estates in Poland and Hungary, and industrialization) would not have been possible, or would certainly have been much harder, without the brutal intrusion of Communism. In fact, their relations with the USSR and with Communism itself differed from country to country, more or less confident, free and fruitful according to their various economics and the different civilizations from which they sprang.

Finally, in the far distance, weighed down by its difficulties but upheld by its pride, there was Communist China, the largest less-developed country in the world. It was certainly the least docile and the most dangerous of the USSR's partners.

This rapid sketch-map reflects not only political positions as they then were, but also economic situations which change less rapidly. These do not determine the future, but they influence it in advance. The former USSR, whose decades of effort put it in some ways in the lead, may well have to suffer the solitude its efforts have earned.

Index